Principles of
Organizational
Behaviour

Third Edition

Robin Fincham

Peter S. Rhodes

OXFORD
UNIVERSITY PRESS

OXFORD

UNIVERSITY PRESS

Great Clarendon Street, Oxford OX2 6DP

Oxford University Press is a department of the University of Oxford.
It furthers the University's objective of excellence in research, scholarship,
and education by publishing worldwide in

Oxford New York

Athens Auckland Bangkok Bogotá Buenos Aires Calcutta
Cape Town Chennai Dar es Salaam Delhi Florence Hong Kong Istanbul
Karachi Kuala Lumpur Madrid Melbourne Mexico City Mumbai
Nairobi Paris São Paulo Singapore Taipei Tokyo Toronto Warsaw

with associated companies in Berlin Ibadan

Oxford is a registered trade mark of Oxford University Press
in the UK and in certain other countries

Published in the United States
by Oxford University Press Inc., New York

© Robin Fincham and Peter S. Rhodes 1999

The moral rights of the author have been asserted

Database right Oxford University Press (maker)

First published 1999

British Library Cataloguing in Publication Data

Data available

Library of Congress Cataloging in Publication Data
Fincham, Robin
Principles of organizational behaviour / Robin Fincham
and Peter S. Rhodes. — 3rd ed.
p. cm.
Rev. ed. of: The individual, work, and organization. 2nd ed. 1994.
Includes bibliographical references.
1. Psychology, Industrial. 2. Industrial sociology.
3. Organizational behavior. I. Rhodes, Peter S. II. Fincham,
Robin. Individual, work, and organization. III. Title.
HF5548.8.F46 1999 158.7—dc21 98-50445

ISBN 0-19-877577-6

1 3 5 7 9 10 8 6 4 2

Printed and bound in Italy by
Giunti Industrie Grafiche, Florence

Brief Contents

Principles of Organizational Behaviour

.10

Contents

5 Motivation and Job Satisfaction   **131**

Section 2 Groups and Work   **161**

6 Social Interaction   **165**

7 Group and Intergroup Behaviour   **186**

8 Leadership   **212**

List of Boxes

Introduction

The nature of Organizational Behaviour

Our reasons for wanting to write this book arose initially from a common enough experience of academics, that of teaching in an area for which there seemed to be no adequate textbook. This impression has to be qualified, for there has long been an extensive coverage of the 'behavioural' disciplines—with organizational behaviour (OB) as the largest of these subject areas. In the past OB has tended to be based on psychology. Treatments of individual, group, and occupational psychology were informed by accounts of organization theory, again usually from a psychological perspective. As a discipline OB has grown in recent years, with topics being added to reflect developments in psychology, though OB has mainly changed by moving into the more 'critical' and structural aspects of organization theory and industrial society. Topics like the social and organizational effects of technology, organizational power and politics, and the future of work and management, have been added to the more traditional ones of organizational design and development.

In contrast our approach has been, from the beginning, to develop OB by drawing equally on the two major disciplines—psychology and sociology—or, to be more precise, on specific areas of these disciplines. The way in which these have been selected and integrated ought to become clearer as we go along.

The development of OB has been an integral part of the development of business and management studies as a whole. On vocationally oriented degrees a discipline-based approach is regarded as too narrow to encompass the many-faceted nature of business problems. Instead, an interdisciplinary approach is favoured where practical problems are tackled by bringing together the relevant parts of various disciplines. Early formulations of business studies degrees in the then polytechnics saw economics and accounting as major building blocks, with the central business topics of corporate policy and decision-making taking precedence in later years. Psychology and sociology formed a third major part of the foundation. Nowadays business and management are taught on a greatly expanded range of courses, at different levels and to many different audiences. These subjects are particularly important for university undergraduate degrees and fast developing post-graduate business education—the ubiquitous MBAs.

Not surprisingly, what is thought to constitute 'business education' has become very fluid, and along with that the social and behavioural sciences are also treated in a variety of ways. Related subjects, like organization theory and management theory, can be integrated with a behavioural or sociological perspective in many different, but still perfectly valid combinations. Nevertheless, a broad foundation in industrial psychology and sociology remains important for any business education. This includes an understanding of the methodology of the social and behavioural sciences as well as the 'human' problems of work. It also forms the basis of more advanced study in areas like organizations, strategy, and human resources.

Integration and application

It is important at the outset to have a clear idea of the basis on which the subjects of psychology and sociology are being brought together. Attempts to integrate different academic disciplines have sometimes been confused because of the terms themselves being defined rather loosely. Part of the problem is that a fully integrated, or interdisciplinary, approach involves a true synthesis between disciplines. And this would mean, in effect, a new discipline being created with its own distinctive methodology and theory. The great demands that such an approach would make on the teacher mean that in practice something more modest is usually attempted, and different disciplines are brought together in a co-ordinated fashion while retaining their distinctive identities. In this way, the developed theories and subject matter of the separate disciplines can still be drawn upon.

The model of integration that we have employed to some extent reflects both the above options. On the one hand, the individualist perspective of psychology and the structure and process perspective of sociology are quite distinctive, so it is appropriate that they should be developed as complementary but separate frameworks. In addition, though, something much closer to a true integration of the two subjects occurs in the subdiscipline of social psychology. The study of groups, with which social psychology is concerned, is an area of common ground on which the individual and social perspectives overlap.

This kind of subject integration follows from a clear commitment to an applied emphasis. The belief in the promotion of managerial effectiveness, and the study of business as an entity in its own right, have meant a shift from a strictly 'academic' approach. In this context, the topics covered in this book reflect an abiding concern with the practical problems of the workplace. Topics of central relevance to managerial efficiency and effectiveness—such as the development of occupational skills, the control of effort and motivation, and organizational goals—are all treated prominently. At the same time, there are other issues not reflecting quite so directly on human performance which are still of great practical interest. The basic processes of human behaviour, such as learning and group interaction, fall into this category, as do the more critical sociological topics, like the impact of technology on work and the role of women in employment.

Of course, these issues also constitute intellectual problems, the study of which supports broader education aims. In this book we have tried to do justice to the theoretical developments of organizational behaviour, for we believe strongly that there is a place for a critical behavioural science within a business and management context, and that students are not averse to such an approach so long as its relevance to real-world problems is clear. Nor are they averse to an analytical framework being developed if this can broadly be seen to support the understanding of practical issues.

These practical and education concerns affect each other in several ways. At one level, we have attempted to provide a rigorous and thorough introduction to a range of central topics in a behavioural science. However, for the students for whom the book is intended, a fully developed introduction to psychology and sociology would hardly be appropriate. These subjects are being studied not primarily for their own sake, but for their wider relevance. This does not mean that we have abandoned all concern with theory and method. Rather, the emphasis will be on treating them in the context of discussions about concrete issues and problems.

Treatment of topics

The original idea of organizational behaviour as a combination of established disciplines does give rise to constraints of space, and the upshot has been the adoption of a *selective* approach in formulating its contents. Not everything within the disciplines concerned can be covered, even in an introductory fashion; and there are good reasons for taking fewer topics in order to treat the ones selected in some depth. It is important to show how debates have taken shape, and how empirical evidence has been used to support or refute particular arguments, especially if knowledge is ever to be put to practical use.

Our own selection of materials inevitably contains some personal bias, and others no doubt would have chosen differently to some extent. The reasoning behind our choice of topics reflects a range of concerns. The desire to provide a foundation in organizational behaviour, and to pick out areas which have an applied emphasis, were obviously prime criteria. But the problem of translating a practical criterion into actual teaching materials is not always straightforward. We have tended to stick closely to the work setting, so that topics relating more broadly to industrial society have been played down, though not omitted entirely.

The selective emphasis and limitations of space can also give rise to problems to do with the *level* of materials in what is after all an introductory subject. Of course, a core of introductory materials remains the basis of the book. But there is less of an emphasis on building this up than there would be on a standard, discipline-based course. This tendency is reinforced from within the areas of business and management studies, where naturally there is a demand for the most up-to-date arguments that the social sciences have to offer.

These difficulties, which are common in business education, can be tackled in several ways. In some cases the topics being considered are not necessarily complex in themselves; rather, they relate to a particular context in some vocational area, and once their relevance has been established then no further problems arise. But for other topics which are perhaps rather difficult to grasp—the managerial uses of power, for example, can present these sorts of problems—then *presentation* becomes vitally important. Making issues as clear as possible, avoiding unnecessary jargon, is a prime responsibility, and the only way in which OB can have a broader relevance. The critical test is whether the most important findings and arguments of behavioural and social scientists can be made intelligible to the non-specialist, and their connection with real world problems spelled out.

Presentation and language are all the more important because one of the things we have also tried to do in the book is give a flavour of the *debates* and contemporary issues in OB. Presented in the wrong way debates can be hard work for students. The presentation of different sides of an argument, or a theory that has been demolished by a set of critics, can seem long-winded if not entirely pointless. Why not get to the point and simply give the currently accepted theory? Or better still why not just present the 'true version' of events? However, in reality the 'truth' is not always easy to ascertain. Organizational life is made up of many issues about which there may be differing or conflicting viewpoints. Rather like sailing against the wind, you cannot always get where you want to by the most direct route; you may have to tack from side to side. Debates in this sense are attempts to get at a complex reality by a series of manoeuvres, each one hopefully getting closer to the final destination. Of course, there is the added complication that in organizations, as in all social life, there is frequently no 'final' version of events. Technical problems may have solutions, but where beliefs and values play a part—as they do in organizational life—often there are no cut-and-dried answers. Many of the most important debates are open ended, with protagonists renewing their arguments, and established theories being challenged by new positions. If all this seems daunting, the simple fact is that many occupational, managerial, and organizational issues have to be tackled through different theories and perspectives; they are of a level of complexity that needs the 'rich picture' that comes from a variety of approaches.

OB disciplines and methods

Like all systems of rational enquiry OB provides a set of conceptual tools which help in classifying and explaining the phenomena in their area of study. Unlike most other disciplines, however, the subject matter of behavioural science—the structures and processes shaping the social world and human behaviour within it—makes up the everyday experience of the general population. This means there is a pre-existing 'baseline' of common-sense understanding of the social world with which the explanations of behavioural science have to compete.

The claim of being able to advance from common-sense understandings of human behaviour and society rests on the developed theoretical frameworks and research methods. Firstly, it can be argued that much common-sense knowledge is flawed by the limitations of everyday experience. People's knowledge of the social world necessarily reflects the set of experiences that have occurred during their lives. Thus, for example, it would be difficult for an individual to form abstract propositions about the functioning of the labour market—such as the level of job choice available—when his or her experience has been restricted to one occupational group, and knowledge of other parts of the market is based only on anecdotal evidence. There are also biases present in people's thinking which produce a great deal of selectivity in what is noticed, understood, and remembered. People tend to think in the form of attitudes and stereotypes which oversimplify complex patterns of social interaction. In contrast, the analytical frameworks and theories that behavioural scientists develop provide a sounder basis for understanding human social behaviour.

Secondly, behavioural scientists claim they can improve on the baseline of commonsense understandings by using research techniques to collect data more systematically than the layperson could. Research methods include laboratory experimentation, questionnaire and interview surveys, and participant observation. The value of the first of these three can be greatly enhanced by using statistical techniques that enable propositions about the social world to be tested. For example, if we are interested in the effects of certain *variables*, such as social class, intelligence and the type of school attended, on the qualifications that individuals leave school with, we can, by using statistics, isolate both the specific effect of each of these variables and their interaction—thus, being intelligent in one kind of school might have more effect on the level of examinations passed than it does in another institution.

Laboratory experimentation involves careful manipulation of aspects of the experimental setting, known as the *independent variables*, and seeing what effect these have on the *dependent variable*. Occupational psychologists have for some time been interested in the effect of the environment on people's work rate. Thus, independent variables have included levels of heat, lighting, noise, and humidity; and these have been related to dependent variables like workers' output per hour, their level of fatigue, and their job satisfaction. Laboratories have also been used to study complex social phenomena. For example, the emergence of a leader in a small group can be observed and perhaps related to the amount that the individual contributes to the group's discussion. Although critics claim that laboratories are an artificial situation which necessarily generates artificial knowledge, a lot of evidence suggests that individuals can quickly forget the setting and participate in the activity, virtually unaware of being observed. In fact, in one notable study in which subjects were given the tasks of playing the parts of prisoners and prison warders, the researchers had to stop the experiment because subjects were playing their parts too realistically—prison warders had become aggressive and prisoners had become withdrawn (Zimbardo *et al.*, 1973).

Questionnaire and interview surveys are also powerful techniques for the collection of data on a range of biographical and attitudinal variables. Questionnaire design and interviewing both require a high degree of skill and experience. A well-constructed questionnaire uses no ambiguous words and phrases, and is lengthy enough to obtain the information needed but not so long that it taxes the stamina and goodwill of the respondent. Surveys of this kind can be used extensively, covering hundreds or even thousands of respondents, and where the data collected is necessarily standardized and fairly superficial; or they can be used intensively to obtain much more detailed information, though usually from fewer respondents.

While laboratory experimentation and survey techniques mainly collect *quantitative* data, participant observation is especially useful for collecting *qualitative* data. Here, the experimenter actually becomes involved with the individuals who are being studied, often engaging in the same activities. The assumption is that whatever is lost in terms of not being able to control the experimental environment is made up by gains in the realism of the observations. The insights gained by attempting to experience the world in the same way as the people being studied, and to establish the 'rules' which structure their behaviour, can be particularly valuable. Some of the most notable studies of real-life organizations, such as factories, schools, and mental hospitals, have been carried out using this method.

All this is not to say, however, that social scientists are necessarily dispassionate or detached observers of the social world. They possess, as much as anyone else, values, beliefs and principles; and they often pursue particular social or political ends. But the important point is that such values should not be allowed to compromise the objectivity of research. Research groups within the social sciences manage, on the one hand, to make their values explicit, while on the other demonstrating integrity in their research. To do otherwise would be counterproductive. If researchers were to cut short proper research procedures they would reduce the chances of their conclusions standing up to critical scrutiny, and therefore ultimately damage their cause.

If social scientists' claims about being able to improve on the everyday understanding of the social world are correct, then their skills will be especially useful in the workplace—an area where competing interests and perceptions often generate misunderstandings and prejudice. This, however, can be challenging for business and management students, because research often opposes existing interpretations, or theories may make totally different assumptions about events from those that students are used to. But while the social sciences can and do produce critiques of existing workplace practices, this relationship between academics and practitioners is not the only one available. Very often the insights provided by social scientists can join with managerial thinking and practice. And social scientists themselves may become involved in the workplace as *change agents*—using diagnostic skills to enhance organizational effectiveness and employee well-being.

A strong claim can therefore be advanced for the practical contributions that each of the social science disciplines has made to positive change in the workplace. Occupational psychology has had a significant impact on selection, training and job design. Social psychology, with its group dynamics emphasis, has formed the basis of management development. And industrial and organizational sociology have helped in the wider policy study of issues such as the impact of technology on work and the role of women in employment. It is to brief accounts of the separate disciplines that we now turn.

The psychological perspective

Psychology is a highly diversified field of study which bridges the gap between biology and sociology, and has as its chief focus the individual and the individual's interaction with the environment. All psychologists try to respond to one key question: why did this person behave in this way? An adequate answer involves not only explaining why the particular behaviour occurred in the particular situation, but also, more importantly, producing a theory of the psychological processes which caused the behaviour, and cause it in similar situations. By developing such theories future behaviour can be predicted. This means that psychological theory can be of great value in the workplace, where effective decision-making requires accurate information about human psychological functioning.

The list of the basic processes investigated by psychologists includes perception (the functioning of the senses), human information-processing, memory, and learning. All of these have considerable practical implications. Human information-processing, for example, is concerned with the way people detect and respond to signals in the environment. The simplest question here is, how long does it take to perceive a signal, say a light or tone, and respond to it? More complex questions might ask, what are the boundaries to human information-processing capacity, and how do we cope with these limits? Psychologists have demonstrated that there are indeed limits to the amount of information that can be processed (about one bit of information per second) and that we are unable to perform other actions while the nervous system is occupied with this task. To compensate we develop various 'search strategies', so that what information-processing capacity we have is used economically. It has also been shown that our attention is highly selective—in general we cope by processing only a small fraction of the incoming signals.

Much of the research into information-processing has been funded by military sponsors who needed guidelines for the design of man-machine environments, such as aircraft cockpits and air-traffic control systems. However, information-processing is an example of a universal psychological process, and increasingly industrial jobs make considerable demands on human information-processing capacity. The limits of that capacity, and the search strategies we develop to cope, are psychological properties that all individuals bring to the workplace, and some of their implications for an understanding of workplace behaviour are described below, in Section One, when we consider skill acquisition and stress.

Some psychologists, however, are more concerned with the ways in which people differ, and the study of these differences represents a key area in the modern discipline of psychology. Much research effort has gone into discovering the fundamental dimensions along which people's personalities and intellects vary. Closely associated with this research is a branch of psychology known as psychometrics, the measurement of the various attributes that have been identified within the broader field of psychology.

Like the study of processes within individuals, research into individual differences also has important applications in the workplace. If psychologists have discovered the fundamental ways in which people's personalities and intellects differ from one another, to what extent do these differences predict variations in job performance between individuals? In Chapter 3 we will look at psychologists' success in answering this question. And in Chapter 4 we examine how these differences are assessed in the workplace

In sum, then, psychology has an important role to play in understanding workplace behaviour, and as we will see it has made a major contribution to the design of, for example, training programmes, employee selection procedures and physical working environments—and thus ultimately to the whole of the quality of working life.

The social-psychological perspective

Social psychology has as its basic unit of analysis the social group. Social psychologists assume that an individual's behaviour can be better understood if reference is made to the groups which he or she identifies with or is a member of. In this sense, social psychology represents the interface between psychology and sociology, since it describes and explains how social structures can become *internalized* by individuals and thus affect their psychological make-up—their attitudes, perceptions, and beliefs—which in turn affect behaviour. These structural forces, generated on the wider social stage or in specific groups, form the chief part of the subject matter of social psychology.

Within groups there emerge customary ways of behaving among members, the observance of special rituals, or even a shared style of dress. Similarly, specific patterns of behaviour will be enacted by individual members—the roles of leader and follower are two very common ones—and each member will enjoy a particular standing or status within the group. The point to bear in mind is that although we usually think of concepts like role and status as qualities which inhere in individuals—we frequently think of roles in terms of the behaviour of the people filling them, while the possession of status also seems to be an individual characteristic—in reality these are social factors generated in the process of interaction. The truth of this can readily be demonstrated if roles are regarded as rather like 'scripts' written for us by society; we may interpret them in individual and personal ways, but we are still expected to 'act out' the basic role according to the images that other people hold. Similarly, the example of changes in status—of enjoying high status in one social group but low status in another—is a common experience, and again it shows the social character of this process. In both cases the distinctive feature of group structure is evident, namely the existence of forces outside the individual and present in the social group as a whole.

What is also evident is that the behaviour and attitudes of individuals are being modified by their membership of groups—they are having to conform with ways of behaving already established. Much of this process does not take an oppressive or coercive form at all. It will seem natural to individuals, on entering new situations, to learn the accepted manner of interaction with other people. What social psychologists have observed, however, is the massive potential that groups seem to have for enforcing conformity, whether unconsciously or through more coercive means.

Over and over again it has been shown that groups have quite astonishing power to induce members who might otherwise want to express some non-conformist behaviour—an independent opinion, or resistance to some group norm—to fall into line. Even where group members do manage to resist having to conform, the very pressures they have to withstand in order to retain their independence demonstrate the forces of control that groups are bringing to bear. For instance in a famous series of experiments conducted by the American social psychologist Asch, subjects were persuaded to change their identification of various images and pictures presented to them—literally to deny the evidence of their own eyes—merely because the other group members had already given their answers and established a group consensus.

This is all the more remarkable when one is reminded that the controls in question may be purely social in nature. In real-life situations people's careers or other major rewards may depend upon their conforming, but these pressures can also be reproduced without any 'material controls' acting on the individual. Group conformity can be obtained simply via social rewards, like acceptance in the group, or through the threat of negative sanctions, such as ostracism or ridicule. These effects can readily be reproduced in the laboratory, and newly set-up experimental groups quickly generate such normative patterns of behaviour. Yet the dynamics of group interaction are often so subtle that it can be difficult for the outsider to detect what is taking place.

The practical uses of such research findings—which form the main topic of the chapters in Section Two—become apparent when we recognize that virtually all interaction in organizations can be tied down to groups of one form or another. In the work setting, for example, it is common nowadays to find group techniques being used to improve the environment for workers. Also, the recognition of the power of informal groups and friendship cliques to influence workers' behaviour has served, and still serves, as the impetus for an enormous research effort.

In addition, there is now increasing interest in decision-making situations. It can readily be seen that many, perhaps most, important decisions are taken not by individuals acting alone but by small groups of influential or technically qualified people. Think of the specific contexts where decisions are taken, like the flight deck of an aircraft or a hospital operating theatre, or large organizations where the corporate group which holds real power will number, say, five or six senior managers. In all these sorts of situations, processes of conformity and integration within groups may compete with technical expertise, and group pressures may even have the power to override the habits of training. It is all the more important, then, that the dynamics of groups are understood so that optimal use may be made of the skills possessed by decision-makers.

The sociological perspective

In the past the role of sociology in the teaching of business and management has been more problematic than that of psychology. The reason has been the prominence of radical or Marxist accounts, while consensus-based theories like functionalism and systems theory have seen their influence wane. This has caused some to worry about how sociology could be fitted into business programmes. It was never suggested that radical sociology should somehow be gagged. But Marxist accounts might be restricted to explanations of social conflict in organizations, while more 'conventional' sociological theories could be applied to the broader range of topics. Problems of this sort led to the concern that sociologists would either have to compromise their discipline or risk antagonizing students. As a result, the views of sociology's role have tended to polarize—one camp in effect saying that the discipline should not be taught as part of business and management, and the other stressing that sociology should select only theories from the body of the discipline that are sympathetic with a business ethic.

The view we have taken is neither of these—and indeed most of the above problems are ancient history. By now it is widely accepted that an approach drawn from sociology's full range can very usefully engage with management interests. Advances in the teaching of business and management studies have outflanked other views. The degree courses involved have 'come of age' and are fully able to benefit from a variety of alternative perspectives. And radical theories, for their part, are now inseparable from broader sociological analysis. Indeed the 'radicalization' of sociology was always something of a myth; the middle ground of the discipline has long been held by interpretive sociology, and this has hardly changed. Other strands of sociology that reflect conflict (and consensus still, for that matter) only add to and enrich our thinking. As Thompson (1989, p. 36) has asserted, we now have a 'new sociology of work' in which radical theories and an existing tradition are joined in an exciting and fruitful debate.

Explanations that sociology provides are based on the idea of social action as a *duality* comprising the structures of behaviour to which people conform, and the more creative and active role played by the human agent. As before, structure refers to the patterns of expectations and forms of behaviour which have become ordered and which persist over time. It suggests that society consists of a 'world out there' existing independently of any one of us. This is only part of the picture, though. Even at the social level behaviour obviously originates in the interaction between people—and the intervention of these interests and motives introduces the possibility of changes and developments. Together, structure and agency account for the opposing forces of stability and change present in all human affairs.

Social structure There are a number of dimensions of social structure, one of the most important of which is *social class*. The class structure has always been one of the chief interests of social science and explains much about the power relations in society and the control of wealth and authority. Our focus on work and organizations means that we will not be concerned with these broad patterns of inequality. We attempt to treat class not as an issue in its own right but as something that can throw light on the nature of work and occupations.

Class may firstly be thought of as a relationship, and in the work context this translates into the relation between the employer and employees. In Section Three, where we set out basic theories, the analysis of work as an *employment relationship* has been vital in understanding one of the major issues in industrial sociology, that of conflict in the workplace. Secondly, class may be thought of in *occupational* terms. An individual's class position is based on his or her occupation, and changes that affect occupations also affect the class structure. The power of occupations to attract material rewards and status represents a dynamic and changing aspect of social class. Likewise, when occupations are 'degraded', or lowered in social standing, this reflects on the class position of the incumbents.

Another key structural dimension, that of *gender*, rivals class as a means of understanding the industrial and organizational world. Sexual divisions define different but equally important patterns of inequality and expressions of social identity. Gender in employment is treated as a topic in its own right in Chapter 18, but in some senses attempting to separate off its effects is misleading, and in other chapters (in Sections Three and Four) the gendered aspect of work relations is integrated as a constant theme in the account.

Human agency and meaning Aside from structure, sociology's emphasis on the creative aspects of social action shares with psychology a concern with the individual. But unlike psychology this is not a question of individual processes or differences. Rather, the concern is with the subjective responses shared within particular groups of people—how a workforce experiences its employment, for example, or the manner in which a community perceives some event that impinges upon it. In other words, the concern is not simply with opinions or attitudes, but with the social character of the *meanings* that people assign to situations they find themselves in. Social situations turn out to be complex, many-sided events, giving ample scope for different groups affected to perceive them in quite different ways.

The meanings that people assign—how *they* understand and define situations—take on a concrete reality. Meanings become self-fulfilling 'social facts' because they form the basis on which people act. This viewpoint provides an answer to another criticism often levelled at sociology, that it is concerned only with subjective factors and not with objective events in the real world. The answer we can give is to point out that subjective meanings have an objective reality, because people's *understanding* is the basis of the response they make. In the discussion in Sections Three through to Six we will encounter several cases where knowledge of how particular groups define their work situation is the key to understanding behaviour.

Social conflict Another difference of emphasis between the psychological and sociological perspectives hinges on the question of conflict. On the whole, the individualist approach is not concerned with issues of conflict unless the resolution of personality conflicts is considered, or perhaps the conflict between external demands and human needs that causes stress. But as we move to the social level, structural conflict comes much more clearly into focus.

Concern with the conflictual aspects of social relationships lies behind another criticism of sociology, namely the complaint that the discipline is not 'scientific' and cannot provide 'solutions' to real-world problems. The response we might give is that social life itself involves conflicting interests, and that solutions to complex problems are rarely unambiguous technical answers, but options and choices which emerge from the inter-play of more than one set of interests. The mobilization of power in pursuit of interests is part of day-to-day reality—and nowhere is this more evident than in the work and organizational context. Our analysis recognizes this, stressing that conflict is not irra-tional, or always the result of misunderstandings; it is a form of social action that must be explained in its own right.

The readiness to take issues of conflict seriously reveals the critical nature of sociolo-gical analysis, for academic disciplines cannot divorce themselves from their own subject-matter. Most of the topics we cover in Sections Three through to Six attract some very different views and opinions, and our aim will be to explore these debates and alternative perspectives.

Structure of the book

The discipline-based approaches discussed above broadly correspond with the structure of this book, which divides into four distinctive levels of analysis: individual, group, organizational, and social. The IGOS framework represents the basic design of the book, and is a useful way of encompassing the approaches to explaining social action and behaviour. It helps both in separating the different levels and mapping out the linkages between them.

In Section One we look at the ways in which *individual differences* affect behaviour. As already indicated, the psychologist wishes to know how processes within individuals, such as learning and motivation, are manifest in behaviour—and also how the differ-ences between individuals in terms of their aptitudes, abilities, and personalities can be studied. The occupational psychologist is concerned with applying these explanations to the work setting.

In Section Two processes occurring in the context of the work group are explored. The emphasis here is on *social interaction* and the ways in which behaviour in organizations is generated and adapted in face-to-face situations. The main forms of group dynamics—including the emergence of basic rules of human interaction, the processes of group for-mation, the modification of behaviour, and the leader–follower relationship—are all of special interest here.

In Sections Three to Six the wider organizational and social aspects of IGOS are mapped out. Here, as already noted, we are not so much concerned with the properties of individuals, or the nature of group-based interaction, but with wider processes and relatively enduring social structures. Section Three provides the basic understanding of *patterns of work* that is the foundation for all that follows. This includes the classic theory of industrial society, modern theories of the labour process, and of the employment relationship that inform virtually all of modern debate—as well as fundamental con-cepts like conflict and consent in the workplace, work design, and the nature of indus-trial power and authority.

Sections Four and Five look at the structures and processes of the *organizational context*. Organization theorists have shown how modern, large-scale organizations function—both from a managerial perspective concerned with efficiency and production, and from a critical perspective concerned with the exploitation of human effort. There are also more dynamic processes that define organizational life (decision-making, culture, power) which have attracted much recent attention.

In Section Six the social and work context is explored further. This follows on from the organizational themes of the previous sections, but also from the understanding of the nature of the work covered in Section Three. Three crucial aspects of wider *divisions of labour* are discussed in these chapters: occupations, gender, and technology. These broader categories have all cropped up before, but here they are analysed in more depth and in their own right. The economic and occupational structures of work, and the role of gender, can both constrain and enhance the choices of individuals and their chances to control their fate. Similarly, technology in the workplace (particularly information technology) massively affects the modern experience of work, as well as helping to define new systems of work organization.

In the above sense the distinctive levels of analysis of the IGOS framework ought to provide a holistic view of the human issues of work. Complex, multi-dimensional problems like these depend for their resolution on a variety of approaches and perspectives being applied—one approach rarely has all the answers. As Gowler and Legge (1982) have noted, 'problems although surfacing at one level in the organization are likely to have antecedents and effects at different levels'. Similarly, according to Landy (1982), we need to be able to describe the relationships between levels of analysis and estimate their relative importance in explaining behaviour. Organizational behaviour as a discipline has shown an increasing willingness to consider this interaction between different levels of analysis, the assumption being that one level provides the context or environment for the next. This is the real basis of an integrated approach to understanding the human problems of the workplace.

Section 1

The Individual and Work

The Individual and Work

By the beginning of the First World War many psychologists in Europe and the United States had recognized that there were problems within the workplace which could be both analysed and remedied using the concepts and methods developed more broadly within their own discipline. As with many other areas of research with military or industrial applications, wartime conditions provided the impetus for a rapid development of industrial psychology. Firstly, the armed forces began to realize the value of a systematic psychological assessment of recruits as an aid to decisions about a soldier's rank and suitability for technical training. Secondly, the increased demand for output and the reduction in available manpower produced by wartime conditions prompted many managers to seek the assistance of psychologists to improve the productivity of the residual workforce.

After the First World War, interest in industrial psychology was consolidated by groups of psychologists who wanted to offer their skills to employers forming research and consultancy companies such as the National Institute of Industrial Psychology in Britain and the Psychological Corporation in the United States.

Industrial psychology in these formative years, therefore, was attempting to answer two broadly inter-related questions. Firstly, what factors increase a worker's productivity? And secondly, how can the match between the employee and the job be improved?

Early attempts to answer the first question involved the careful measurement and manipulation of environmental factors such as temperature, lighting, noise levels, humidity and aspects of work like the length and number of rest breaks, and establishing their effect on a worker's productivity. This approach produced some remarkable early successes. For example, a wartime study demonstrated that a drop in daily hours from twelve to ten actually increased productivity and brought about a large decrease (50 per cent) in the accident rate. At the time, industrialists had believed that output could be improved by increasing working hours.

It was gradually realized, however, that the relationships between objective work conditions and productivity were moderated by subjective phenomena, such as the employees' attitude to work and job satisfaction. Thus, seemingly straightforward concepts like fatigue were found to involve physiological processes such as the build-up of lactic acid in muscle tissue, as well as the psychological willingness of the individual to work.

The second question—how to improve the employee-job match—produced a variety of answers. Some psychologists believed the answer lay in more careful selection of employees. This involved preparing an inventory of the relevant skills, aptitudes and temperaments required for high job performance, and constructing psychological tests which identified individuals who possessed these qualities. Other psychologists developed the 'training solution', allowing individual deficiencies to be compensated for by training employees up to the required standard. Finally, a solution which emerged during the Second World War—the 'equipment solution'—proposed a radically different approach to the problem. It suggested that a better match could be achieved by applying psychological knowledge of human capabilities and particularly their limits to the design of man-machine systems. The body of knowledge these psychologists produced became known as ergonomics.

What answers to both questions—improving productivity and the employee-job match—had in common was the assumption that solutions could be sought based on the individual employee as the fundamental unit of analysis. In this first section, we will examine the main research findings based on this assumption and which underpinned the solutions to the initial questions psychologists were asked to provide answers for.

In Chapter 1 we look at the research on the training solution which seeks to explain how people acquire complex occupational skills. Humans, as we will see, have a remarkable capacity to learn; in fact virtually all of our behaviour is acquired through learning. The practical implications of this in the workplace are considerable, and an understanding of how learning occurs obviously enables better training programmes to be designed.

While Chapter 1 describes the remarkable adaptive capacities of humans, Chapter 2 explores one consequence of the limits of this capacity, stress. Trying to adapt to certain types of environment involves severe mental and physical health risks, but the problem of stress at work has been recognized only recently by psychologists and employers. We will examine some of the types of stress that have been identified in the workplace and discuss methods of reducing their damaging effects.

In Chapter 3 we look at the research on which the selection solution was based. We focus on personality and intelligence, perhaps the most important ways in which individuals differ from each other. We will also examine some of the implications differences in personality and intelligence have in the workplace.

In Chapter 4 we explore how assessments of individual differences occur in the workplace. We will examine a number of assessment techniques and discuss the relative merits of each.

Finally, in Chapter 5 we examine the two most significant contributions psychologists have made to the understanding of employees' productivity: the concept of motivation and job satisfaction. As we suggested above, although early successes were achieved by manipulating objective aspects of the workplace, it was soon realized that subjective factors, particularly the needs workers brought with them to the workplace and the way employees felt about their jobs, also affected their productivity. This realization, combined with the rising expectations of employees after the Second World War and relatively full employment, prompted an enormous amount of research and discussion on how employees' needs could be met and thus how a motivated and reasonably satisfied workforce could be created.

1 Learning

Summary points and learning objectives

By the end of this chapter you will be able to

- describe the basic components of classical conditioning;
- provide an example of how classical conditioning helps explain workplace behaviour;
- describe the basic components of operant conditioning;
- detail the schedules of reinforcement;
- provide some examples of how operant conditioning helps explain workplace behaviour;
- discuss the idea of a technology of behaviour;
- give examples of a technology of behaviour in the workplace;
- describe learning strategies;
- discuss what helps and hinders transfer of training back to the workplace.

Introduction

The effect of education and training policies on the health of national economies has long been the subject of disputes between economists. But the success of the German, Japanese, and Swedish economies—where investment in 'human capital' has been heavy—has encouraged governments to place education and training high on their list of spending priorities. In the UK, for example, Chancellor Gordon Brown's first budget was driven by the view that 'new products, new services, new opportunities challenge us to change; old skills, old jobs, old industries have gone and will never return.' For Brown the 'dynamic economies of the future will be those that unlock the talent of all their people'.

The current concern with learning manifested in fashionable expressions such as the 'learning society', 'lifelong learning', 'learning organizations', and jobs for 'learning managers' clearly represents not so much an upsurge of interest in the welfare of employees and development of individuals but a response to the new economic imperatives of responsiveness and adaptability.

In addition psychologists have recently realized that it is not only globalization of markets increasingly characterized by uncertainty which has emphasized requirements for responsiveness and adaptability but also recent changes in manufacturing processes. New manufacturing initiatives such as total quality management greatly intensify the problem-solving or cognitive demands on employees (e.g. Parker, 1996).

So how do we go from political rhetoric and economic and technological imperatives to workplace reality? How do people acquire the skills required to survive and prosper in an intensely competitive and increasingly cognitively demanding labour market?

It is in this context, answering these key questions, that in this chapter we examine *theories of learning*. We will see that learning forms the basis of our understanding of much human behaviour. The development, via evolution, of a relatively large brain has provided us with an enormous mental capacity which has meant that learning has displaced instinct as the basis of our behaviour. Instinctual behaviours seen in other animals appear only briefly in the first year of human life and then recede.

Theories of learning assist in achieving political and economic imperatives in a number of ways. First, training designed with an awareness of how people learn is clearly more likely to be effective. In addition, trainers need an understanding of what might facilitate learning: for example, which instructional media or modes of delivery are most effective. Crucially, in vocational settings trainers need to know what improves the *transfer of learning* back into the workplace.

If training is designed on solid psychological principles then it is better value for money. There is more impact on individuals' performance and potentially on an organization's 'bottom line'. And effective training is more likely to enable trainees to acquire more confidence in their learning skills and thus their ability to confront and cope with future learning demands.

Secondly, if learning theories can explain how people initially acquire competence they might help explain what differentiates excellent from merely competent individuals. In many jobs this difference can be accounted for by motivation, personality, intelligence, or aptitudes. However, there are often key differences between the way excellent and competent individuals perceive and comprehend their environments. If identified, these can become the basis of training and development aimed at bringing about the changes in perception and comprehension necessary for improved performance. An example of this is the use of what is termed 360-degree feedback in management development. This involves providing a manager with information about how he or she is perceived by colleagues, subordinates, and his or her own manager. By improving comprehension of how others perceive and react to him or her the manager is better placed to form more effective relationships in the future.

Finally, learning theories can also help when considering how work is described. Trainers need valid methods for describing what people at work do in order to identify what skills individuals need to do a job and what opportunities a job provides for the development of skills in individuals. Traditionally the main concern has been to develop ways of describing the tasks that people actually perform. Learning theories also suggest that it is often as important to describe *skills*, how people accomplish the tasks involved in their jobs, and the learning processes involved in acquiring these skills.

In this chapter we will examine the two main types of learning theory: stimulus response and skill theories. The former focuses on conditions *external* to individuals. A stimulus, is something perceived by an organism in the environment. A doorbell, a supervisor's request, and the smell of food are all examples of stimuli. A response is a unit of behaviour (usually observable) emitted by an organism. Answering the door, anxiety, and salivating are all responses which might be associated with the respective stimuli. Stimulus–response theorists explain how responses are acquired by examining what precedes the response and what happens in the environment after the response has occurred. Many researchers, however, have preferred to stress the part that *internal* cognitive processes play in learning. As we will see, both approaches have contributed a great deal to our understanding of how learning, perhaps the most important of human capacities, occurs.

Learning theories

Stimulus–response theories I: classical conditioning

The initial concern of the Russian physiologist Pavlov (1849–1936) was the innate reflex responses of animals. While studying one of these reflex responses, salivation, he noticed some dogs would sometimes salivate when the lights in the laboratory were switched on in the morning or when they were removed from their pens. At first he found these 'psychic secretions' a nuisance since they disrupted his experiments. He soon realized, however, that these responses were far more important than the simple physiological reflexes he had intended to study. He began a series of experiments to investigate them in more detail. In a typical experiment Pavlov would present a dog with a neutral stimulus such as a tone or a bell. This would be quickly followed by meat powder to which the dog would automatically salivate. If the pairing of a neutral stimulus with the meat powder occurred enough times, Pavlov found the salivation response could be elicited by the tone or bell alone. The dog had been *conditioned* to respond to the neutral stimulus.

Pavlov's contribution to the explanation of learning has proved to be of immense significance. It explains how a wide range of human responses are acquired. It has also helped in the treatment of a number of behavioural problems, from phobias to sexual difficulties such as impotence.

In order to generalize Pavlov's research methods to other situations, a specific vocabulary describing the components of conditioning has been devised. The original reflex is composed of an unconditioned stimulus (UCS) and an unconditioned response (UCR). In Pavlov's experiment the meat powder was the UCS and the dog's salivation was the UCR. The neutral stimulus—the bell, buzzer or tone—is known as the conditioned stimulus (CS). When salivation occurs after the presentation of the CS on its own it is termed the conditioned response (CR) (Figure 1.1). The CR is never quite as strong as the original UCR. In Pavlov's experiments the dogs salivated less for the CS than for the UCS. If the CS is presented on a number of occasions without the UCS, the CR will decline further in strength. This decline in the CR is known as *extinction*. Zero extinction is said to occur when the CS does not elicit a CR at all. However, even at zero extinction the association between CS and CR does not disappear altogether as relearning the CR requires fewer pairings than were necessary for the original conditioning.

Two important features of the conditioning process have been identified: *generalization* and *discrimination*. Generalization refers to the organism's capacity to respond in a similar way to stimuli that are similar in certain respects to the original CS. For example, young children sometimes refer to all adult males as 'daddy'. Generalization in evolutionary terms is highly useful: it reduces the complexity of the stimulus environment since the organism can apply the same response to a range of stimuli. However, as we shall see later, generalization can also be maladaptive if the learned response is generalized to situations in which it is inappropriate. Discrimination is the opposite tendency, allowing organisms to respond differently to similar stimuli. The young child eventually learns to apply the word 'daddy' to one adult male only.

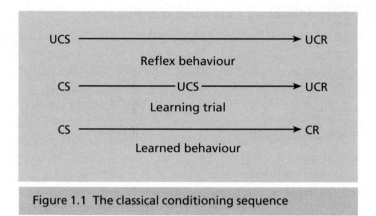

Figure 1.1 The classical conditioning sequence

Classical conditioning has been observed in a number of human and animal subjects and there seems little doubt that it is a basic learning process. However, when it came to more complex behaviours Pavlov believed that these could be acquired through *secondary conditioning*. This occurs when the CS–CR connection is so well established that a CS acts as a UCS in subsequent conditioning. For example, if a child automatically responds to an unpleasant stimulus (UCS) such as a smack from a parent by experiencing anxiety (UCR), words which precede the blow, such as 'no' or 'stop that', can become conditioned stimuli. Through conditioning, then, these words may be enough to control a child's behaviour without resorting to physical punishment. Through secondary conditioning the child may even learn that particular facial expressions precede these words so that they, in turn, become the conditioned stimuli which elicit the anxiety response. In this way the child learns to recognize increasingly subtle indications of parental disapproval.

Classical conditioning is particularly useful in explaining behaviour mediated by the autonomic nervous system. This is the part of the nervous system which controls reflex action and emotional states such as pleasure and anxiety. Extreme emotional reactions—phobias, like the fear of heights, crowds, or small places—can be acquired through classical conditioning. If phobias are acquired through classical conditioning they can also be cured by helping individuals to 'unlearn' the phobia by replacing the conditioned anxiety with a more neutral emotional response. In fact, treatment based on conditioning principles is now commonplace and has very high success rates. Weaker emotional responses, such as the emotions that inanimate objects like buildings, rooms, and food can elicit, are also often the result of classical conditioning. An aversion to a particular food, for example, can be the result of a single pairing of the food (CS) with a powerful aversive stimulus (UCS) such as food poisoning. The single pairing may be sufficient for the food to elicit anxiety or nausea (CR) on subsequent occasions and the food is therefore avoided.

Conditioning can provide us with what are termed *patterns*. These are conditioned thoughts, feelings, or behaviours which are fairly fixed and come to characterize the way we respond to certain events or people. These patterns are often formed during experiences which have caused an individual distress. In childhood, distress is particularly significant because it tends to be associated with situations which occur frequently. Being simpler than adults, children are also less likely to understand what the causes of distress are. Distress is then generalized so it can be elicited by a range of situations.

Once patterned, we can only pay attention to the characteristics of the situation which elicit distress. This means we are unlikely to acquire improved methods of dealing with these situations. One example might be the way we deal with authority figures in adult life. If we had particularly punitive parents we might find it difficult to shed the patterns we acquired in childhood. We could continue to experience distress in the presence of authority figures and perceive them as threatening even though in reality they no longer are. Our conditioned distress will prompt the same rapid unthinking response that it did in childhood. For example, we may find we automatically acquiesce to requests from our superiors since this quickly reduces the unpleasant feelings restimulated by these situations. This pattern becomes even more unhelpful (particularly to our careers) if we then demonstrate our oppositional feelings by not getting the job done, forgetting, or in other ways being inefficient.

Whilst some conditioned patterns are formed over a period of years they can also be the result of a single extremely traumatic event. These patterns can form the basis of what is now termed post-traumatic stress disorder (Scott and Stradling, 1992).

Training programmes often attempt to make participants aware of their own patterned feelings, thoughts, and behaviours. Participants can begin to explore and practise more effective methods of dealing with the situations which elicit their maladaptive responses. For example, one of the authors was involved in the design and delivery of a course for a national rescue service. This helped participants deal with powerful negative thoughts and feelings conditioned by working in disasters. Delegates were provided with methods of managing these thoughts and feelings more effectively. This learning was crucial if they were to function effectively and not put colleagues at risk in any subsequent disasters they were required to deal with (Rhodes and Joseph, 1997).

Classical conditioning also has implications for task performance and training in organizations. We have a fixed capacity to attend to a given task. The capacity available for any task depends on the number of other demands on our attention. Thus, pleasant or unpleasant feelings evoked at work (or elsewhere) demand part of an individual's attention and will interfere with his or her ability to attend to a task. This impairs an individual's performance and can increase the likelihood of accidents (Iverson and Erwin, 1997). Coercive or punitive supervisors can become the conditioned stimuli which elicit negative feelings. The conditioning may be generalized to the organization. Even physical locations—a headmaster's study, or a supervisor's office—can through conditioning acquire a negative emotional tone.

In training programmes some participants may already have conditioned negative feelings about being in instructional situations and being instructed. Trainers on government training schemes for young people who have recently left schools having achieved few formal qualifications are often faced with the problem of having to deal with individuals who have conditioned negative feelings elicited by learning environments. Individuals who experience these feelings are both unlikely to learn much and likely to prove disruptive to other trainees. A good deal of research has been undertaken recently to devise training programmes in which the anxiety that learning situations have normally evoked is unlearned and replaced with more positive feelings.

Another context in which conditioned negative feelings that are likely to impair task performance can be elicited is when taking an ability test as part of a selection procedure. Here the skill of the test administrator is crucial in turning a situation which can easily be perceived as a threat into one of challenge and opportunity.

Stimulus–response theories II: operant conditioning

Learning of stimulus–response associations also occurs through operant conditioning. An operant is a unit of behaviour emitted by an organism; eating a meal, placing a bet, and smoking a cigarette are all examples of operants. The most noted operant theorist, B. F. Skinner (1916–1997), believed that the environment *shapes* an individual's behaviour by maintaining certain responses and suppressing others.

Skinner's major contribution has been to outline how the shaping of an individual's responses by the environment occurs. He believes the most powerful shaping mechanism is *reinforcement*. If we return to the hypothetical example of the patterned behaviour elicited by authority figures, classical conditioning, as we saw, explained why anxiety was experienced. Situations in which authority figures make demands are perceived as threatening. This perception elicits the classically conditioned anxiety response, which in turn is followed by an operant: acquiescence. But in operant conditioning the key question is, what occurs after a response? In this example the response caused an immediate reduction in anxiety. In operant terms the response was reinforced. The reinforcement has been powerful enough to stamp the response into an individual's behaviour pattern.

Reinforcement operates either negatively or positively. *Positive reinforcement* occurs when a pleasant stimulus follows a response. Money, status, recognition, and praise can all act as positive reinforcers since they all increase the likelihood of the preceding response being emitted again.

Any response which reduces the intensity or removes an unpleasant stimulus is said to be *negatively reinforced*. Like positive reinforcement, negative reinforcement produces two types of learning: *escape* and *avoidance*. Acquiescing to the demands of authority figures in the example above falls into the first category since it allows individuals to escape from their conditioned distress. An individual could also learn to avoid supervisors and thereby reduce the threat of anxiety-loaded encounters.

Behaviour once initiated and reinforced acquires a 'behavioural momentum'—it is likely to persist even in the face of environmental challenges (Nevin, 1996). Skinner believed escape and avoidance behaviours were very common in human society. Aversive conditions are, wittingly or unwittingly, frequently created by other people. Unwittingly, other people can be boring, annoying, or unpleasant, and we quickly develop avoidance relationships with them. Aversive conditions are created intentionally as a method of social control. A supervisor, for example, may become more autocratic, coercive and punitive to increase output. To escape these aversive conditions, workers may increase their work rate, which in turn reinforces the supervisor's belief in the effectiveness of an autocratic style of supervision. However, other escape behaviours can be learned: striking, sabotage, or displacing the aggression their aversive environment has caused on to people outside the workplace are all possible consequences. Alternatively, workers may acquire avoidance behaviours which put them out of the aversive stimuli's range, for example, by staying at home or changing job. Proponents of operant conditioning believe a number of social phenomena are explained by avoidance or escape learning. Conformity, for example, may be the result not so much of the positive reinforcement of behaviour by others but of learning to perform in a way that avoids their contempt.

While positive and negative reinforcement serve to increase the strength of responses, *punishment* and *omission* have the opposite effect. Punishment involves an aversive stimulus following a response. Contact with aversive stimuli very quickly reduces the probability of a response reoccurring. A child who puts his or her hand on a hot oven ring is unlikely to do it again. In adult life we learn to withhold the responses that have attracted contempt, ridicule, or criticism. The term 'omission' is used to describe the removal of unpleasant stimuli after a response. Parents make use of this contingency when sending a child who misbehaves to bed. This removes pleasant stimuli such as television or the company of siblings. Table 1.1 provides a summary of these four response categories.

Operant theorists believe that reward is a more powerful method of shaping behaviour than punishment. Reward has the virtue of indicating what behaviour is required, while punishment only indicates what response an individual should withhold. Punishment can also cause anxiety, hostility, and resentment in an individual. Aversive stimuli, as we have already seen, can also lead to avoidance learning. The individual can

	Present	Remove
Pleasant stimuli	Positive reinforcement	Omission
Unpleasant stimuli	Punishment	Negative reinforcement

Table 1.1 The four types of reinforcement proposed by Skinner

learn to avoid the parent, teacher, or supervisor or to perform the undesired response out of their range. Skinner (1971) believed that society in general has gradually shifted from systems of control based on the use of aversive stimuli to ones which use reward. Teachers now try and make children want to learn through reward rather than through punishment. Parents increasingly offer rewards to their children in the form of approval rather than using punishment to shape their children's behaviour. And some organizations have replaced aversive autocratic managerial practices with the potentially more rewarding democratic supervisory styles.

Skinner was also interested in the effect of what he termed *schedules of reinforcement* on behaviour. The simplest schedule is one in which every response is followed by a reward. These are found in complex physical activities such as swimming, bicycling, or skiing where what is known as *continuous reinforcement* maintains the responses necessary to be successful. However, continuous reinforcement is highly unlikely in other areas of life. Teachers, parents, colleagues, or supervisors cannot reinforce every desired response. You are more likely to experience *intermittent reinforcement schedules* in which behaviour is not always reinforced. For example, you were not rewarded as a child each time you performed a desired response such as sharing a toy, but you may have been rewarded intermittently. Experiments have found intermittent schedules of reinforcement exert a more powerful influence on behaviour than a continuous schedule since we seem to learn not to expect reinforcement each time we make a particular response. This means behaviour persists in the absence of reinforcement whereas responses learned with a continuous schedule, where an organism expects reinforcement after every response, rapidly disappear when not reinforced. In fact, intermittent schedules can often have a major influence on behaviour in return for very little reward. For instance, a gambler does not need to win very often to sustain the habit.

Reinforcement schedules have been used to explain a number of workplace phenomena: motivation, absenteeism, and the effect of different payment systems. Ferster and Skinner (1957) argued there are two basic types of intermittent schedule. First, there are those schedules in which reinforcement occurs after a fixed number of the desired responses have been made or after a fixed period of time has elapsed. Secondly, there are those in which reinforcement occurs regularly or irregularly. By combining these two criteria, four intermittent schedules are created, which they believed had different effects on behaviour.

1. A *fixed-ratio schedule* is one in which reinforcement occurs after a given number of responses. The schedule can produce a great deal of the desired behaviour for very little in return. Piecework, where an employee is paid for producing a fixed number of units, is an example of a fixed-ratio schedule. In theory, piece-rate working ought to produce the response pattern normally associated with the fixed-ratio schedule: a high and constant response rate. In practice, however, many employers have found a pay structure which attempts to link specific rates with pay too cumbersome and have opted for a 'flat' weekly wage. In a car plant, for example, the rate of pay for each of the thousands of assembly tasks has to be negotiated and renegotiated every year. Employees also tend to learn a work rate which is not high enough to cause management to increase the response–earnings ratio and not so low as to reduce earnings below a desired level.

2. A *variable-ratio schedule* can be even more effective in terms of the effort–reward ratio in producing the desired behaviour than a fixed-ratio schedule. A gambling machine, for example, pays out on average once in fifteen bets. Since a variable ratio makes it difficult to know when a payment is likely, gamblers are prepared to place bets at a constant (often high) rate. Some payment systems are variable-ratio schedules. For example, selling double glazing is often based on 'cold calling', simply picking names from a telephone directory and calling. Payment for cold calling is based on the number of appointments booked. On average an appointment is made after thirty calls. However, this ratio, on any given evening can stretch to well above this level. But like a gambling machine it is impossible to know whether a call will be rewarded with an appointment and work rates are therefore high and constant. This explains why the salesperson persists even in the face of considerable hostility from individuals who resent having their evenings disrupted!

3. In *fixed-interval schedules*, reinforcement occurs at regular intervals, regardless of what response precedes it. Monthly or weekly payment systems are examples of this schedule. Fixed-interval reinforcement produces a distinctive pattern of responding. As the reward time approaches, the response rate increases, dropping immediately after reinforcement. This drop in response rate indicates that the organism has learned there is no relationship between response and reward in the period closely following reinforcement. The absence of any relationship between response and reward immediately following reinforcement in this schedule may help to explain higher rates of absenteeism found in organizations after a pay day.

4. The length of time between reinforcement in a *variable-interval schedule* varies around some average value. This schedule elicits moderate and constant response rates. For example, if the time between assessments of suitability for promotion varies in an organization employees learn their performance needs to be consistently good to ensure a favourable rating. Also behaviours which can seem 'anxious' such as constantly going to a window to see if someone—relative or friend—has arrived are the result of variable-interval schedules.

Stimulus–response theories: a technology of behaviour?

Skinner has argued that operant theory provides the framework for a '*technology of behaviour*'—enabling environments to be designed so that desired responses are systematically strengthened while less desirable responses are weakened. An example of this which you can attempt yourself is provided in Box 1.1.

An important instance of this application of operant principles is known as *behaviour modification*. This is often found in clinical settings although can be applied equally well in an organizational context (Bryant and Gurman, 1996). But operant principles are seldom applied in the workplace. First, staff may be unaware of what they have to do to gain rewards such as a rise in pay or status. Secondly, hard work is sometimes punished, rather than reinforced by loading more work onto conscientious staff. Attractive early retirement packages may sometimes be offered to employees who are seen as less effective. Thirdly, group or departmental productivity bonuses weaken the link between individual performance and reward. Finally, managers tend to think reinforcement can best be achieved via monetary reward. But while this may well be the case generally, for some staff recognition and praise can be more potent reinforcers.

However, there have been a number of attempts to apply operant principles to the workplace. Behaviour modification begins by identifying *critical behaviours*. These are the operants thought to be necessary for effective performance. For example, the initial approach to a customer may be a critical behaviour for effective retail selling. The second phase establishes the *base rates* for target behaviours. These are rates at which these critical behaviours normally occur. Identifying base rates enables the impact of the programme to be assessed at a later stage. The third stage, termed *functional analysis* involves careful observation of what normally precedes and follows various types of work behaviour. For example, a functional analysis may reveal that customers are normally greeted only if they approach a member of the sales staff. After the functional analysis has been completed an *intervention strategy* is devised. This makes reward contingent on critical behaviour. For example, sales staff may be rewarded with pay, free package holidays, or time off for demonstrating these behaviours. Finally, there is a *systematic evaluation* of the intervention strategy. Do the critical behaviours now occur at a level above the original base rate?

Interestingly, in behaviour modification programmes the intervention can *generalize* to non-targeted but functionally related behaviours. One programme tried to improve the occupational safety of pizza delivery drivers, who have an accident rate three times the national average. Whilst the targeted critical behaviour was complete stops at road junctions, rates for two non-targeted behaviours, safety-belt and indicator use, were also collected by observers. Rates for all three behaviours went up during the intervention phase (Ludwig and Geller, 1997).

Whilst widely used in clinical settings, as yet behaviour modification has not been widely used in European organizations. None the less, some insights provided by operant conditioning are clearly pertinent: motivation and performance can be low because contingencies are unclear, rewards insufficient or inappropriate, and desirable performance punished rather than rewarded.

Box 1.1 Shaping

Skinner's application of his learning theory produced impressive behavioural changes even in animals we would not normally consider to be trainable, such as pigeons. He was, for example even able to train two pigeons to play a modified version of table tennis. This is achieved by a process Skinner called shaping. The technique involves rewarding behaviour which in some way resembles the target behaviour but gradually restricting the reinforcement to behaviours which are closer and closer to the target behaviour. For example with a withdrawn child any form of interest in those around him or her, such as eye contact, could be rewarded. But reward would then be made increasingly contingent on uttering words and ultimately on interacting fully with his or her peers and carers. In reality the process is more complex than in this example. It also often involves considerable skill on the part of the trainer. Skinner would argue that in everyday life the environment shapes our behaviour. In some instances the shaping is more contrived and targeted such as in what are termed *token economies* found in some institutions such as children's homes or hospitals for the mentally ill. In token economies target behaviours or, if the behaviour is being shaped, approximations of it are rewarded with tokens which can be exchanged for rewards.

Whilst some of the most striking applications of shaping have been with animals there have been vivid illustrations of the power of reinforcement with humans. In fact, Skinner himself was once the unwitting recipient of a shaping experiment conducted by his students. One half of the lecture theatre frowned somewhat if he moved or turned towards them. The other half smiled slightly at him if he turned towards them. By the end of the lecture he was facing this group and unwittingly ignoring half of his students. Shaping has also been applied to verbal behaviour. Verplanck (1955), for example, simply engaged individuals in conversation. The experimenter responded positively whenever the individual expressed an opinion. But no such approval followed other kinds of remark. Expressions of opinion increased dramatically during the conversation. Other experiments have targeted types of words such as plural nouns. Try this yourself. Pick a type of verbal act such as expressing or requesting an opinion or even a type of word. Reward can consist of agreement, smiling, or even a positive 'mmhm'. See if you are able to increase the frequency of the target behaviour without your colleague being aware of the reinforcement.

A second example of Skinner's technology of behaviour is *programmed instruction*. Skinner was very critical of traditional teaching methods and believed teaching objectives needed to be specified in very precise operant terms with constant reinforcement provided to learners. If you had enrolled on a mathematics course which used this method in its original form you would have interacted not with a tutor but with a teaching machine. The machine would take you through the course by presenting you with a series of *frames*. These would contain a small amount of information, for instance, a worked example of multiplying fractions, followed by a question. If your response to a question was correct, the machine moved you to the next frame. Two views have developed about the place of *incorrect responses* in programmed instruction. Skinner believed an incorrect response was a wasted opportunity for providing reinforcement. He believed programmes should be designed to make the chances of a learner making a mistake as close to zero as possible. This means material has to be broken up into a large number of frames, each containing a small amount of information. With a mathematics programme a number of examples of the same procedure would be used, each frame presenting a question only slightly more difficult than the previous frame. The increase in complexity in the material between each frame is therefore kept to a minimum. The disadvantage of these *linear programmes* is that learners are all presented with the same order of frames whatever their previous knowledge may be. *Branching programmes*, in contrast, create more flexible instruction by using errors diagnostically. If your response is incorrect you are 'shunted' into a series of remedial frames until a response indicates you are able to rejoin the main programme. Since larger increases in the complexity of material between frames are possible with branching programmes, learners familiar with some of the programme's content can progress rapidly through mainstream frames until they reach a point where their responses indicate remedial frames are necessary.

The availability of relatively cheap and increasingly powerful small computers has meant that very sophisticated branching programmes can now be written and made widely available. The arrival of interactive videodiscs and CD rom have added further realism to this form of training. Programmed instruction, however, need not involve investing in personal computers, laser video or CD rom technology. A series of cards, each of which is a frame, and a piece of cardboard to mask answers can constitute a linear programme.

Programmed instruction has been utilized in commercial, industrial, military and educational settings and a number of advantages have been claimed for it.

Firstly, it enables organizations to specify what is called *terminal performance*, what trainees will need to do to pass the *criterion test* at the end of the programme, and *pre-entry behaviour*, the level of competence required before training commences.

Secondly, it enables employees to use free time available for training as and when it occurs. In many occupational settings, training may be possible only at irregular times of the day.

Thirdly, it allows the slow learner to learn at his or her own pace, thus experiencing less anxiety and embarrassment than when learning with a teacher and peers.

Finally, it is thought to be highly cost-effective, with savings in training time more than offsetting the capital cost of any equipment involved.

However, programmed instruction does have some disadvantages. Firstly, producing a good course based on programmed instruction is very difficult. Programme writing is a highly skilled task requiring a knowledge of both the subject and operant principles. In addition, there may not be a simple correspondence between a learner's responses and his or her comprehension of material. Learners do not always fully understand why their responses are correct or incorrect. Some studies also indicated learning achieved with programmed instruction is not necessarily superior in terms of retention of material over time, to what is possible in conventional methods.

However, the power and flexibility of modern computers has enabled increasingly sophisticated learning programmes to be written. Programmes can now decide on how strongly to praise or admonish a learner according to how close he or she was to the correct response. Learners can now engage in a lively dialogue with learning programmes. Records can be compiled of learning progress and, as a reinforcer, certificates of achievement can be printed for learners. Programmes such as those used to help children to learn to read can provide sophisticated diagnosis of the types of errors the learner is making. Thus Skinner's vision of the teaching machine and programmed instruction lives on in modified form as Computer Assisted Instruction.

Both these applications of operant theory produce changes in behaviour by establishing a link between certain responses and the environmental outcomes an individual experiences. In organizations the principles of operant conditioning suggest that work settings should encourage employees to perceive some relationship between their effort and some valued reward. And, in contrast, the condition that should be avoided in organizations is *learned helplessness*, where employees believe there is no link between the events they experience and their behaviour (Seligman, 1975). Organizations that create environments which foster a sense of helplessness in employees face the immense problem of managing staff whose motivation has been drastically lowered. Organizations, therefore, should always create conditions in which it is difficult for employees to learn helplessness.

As well as computer assisted learning the major residue of operant conditioning and Skinner's 'Technology of Behaviour' is the 'competence revolution' (discussed in Chapter 4). David McClelland, an influential and early advocate of competences, argues that what is important is to focus on clearly successful individuals in jobs and then identify the operant thoughts and behaviour causally related to this success (Spencer *et al.*, 1994). In other words, whereas historically personality or ability test scores might have been seen as the explanation of differences in performance, for McClelland and others in the competence movement the focus has to be on identifying *what people actually do*, the behaviours they generate. In the UK, for example, the persuasiveness of these arguments has resulted in the very clear specification of behavioural outcomes in vocational training under the guidance of the National Council for Vocational Qualifications. Their qualifications have clear standards of competence and performance criteria for assessment. Whilst numerous criticisms of the competency approach exist, for example, for reducing standards in some areas or for their potential as a control mechanism (Du Gay *et al.*, 1996) they have become a very attractive method of defining what individuals need to develop or bring to a job in order to function effectively.

The acquisition of skill

Many researchers have argued that stimulus–response theories are overly mechanistic and reductive. Mechanistic because by using only observable phenomena such as stimuli and reinforcement schedules and treating humans as passive recipients of them, they take no account of the mental activity which may occur in individuals during learning. Reductive because the theories have to break down complex behaviour into small stimulus–response units in order to explain how they are acquired. Critics of stimulus–response theories have claimed we need to develop more holistic units of analysis and accept that internal mental processes, though difficult to monitor, do play an important part in the learning process.

There is some empirical support for the claim that these mental or *cognitive* processes do need to be included in explanations of learning. For example, studies during the Second World War of air-gunners tracking simulated enemy aircraft found they often displayed negative response times. They were able to respond before the stimuli appeared. This indicated that gunners had developed mental models of the flight paths of enemy aircraft which enabled them to predict positions of aircraft and respond before they appeared. Similarly, in a classic experimental study of behaviour analogous to that of refinery process workers, Crossman and Cooke (1962) found the behaviour of their subjects could not be explained adequately within a stimulus–response framework. Their subjects were simply asked to control the temperature of boiling water by using a thermometer and adjusting a thermostat dial. If a subject's performance was shaped simply by feedback of response outcomes, the size of the adjustments should have correlated with the size of temperature error and its rate of change. These correlations appeared in inexperienced subjects only. Experienced subjects were able to predict the effect of adjustments on temperature, and this indicated that they had developed a mental *model* of the process. Experienced subjects' actions were therefore not simply controlled by information provided by the thermometer.

There is some evidence, then, that complex human activity does not fit easily into a stimulus–response framework. What seems to happen is that people actively develop models of the systems they are interacting with. In other words, individuals do not respond directly to the environment, as stimulus–response theories assume, but to the *models* they construct of it. A number of researchers have claimed that a concept which can accommodate these less observable aspects of learning is *skill*. The definition of 'skill' is complicated by its wide use in ordinary language. In industry it is used to mean 'time served', or a qualification to carry out a craft or trade. Work is often classified into skilled, semi-skilled, and unskilled. But in psychology the term is used in a much wider sense to refer to all the factors which go to make up a competent, expert, rapid, and accurate performance. Skills in this sense are seen as natural units of activity which cut across task boundaries. This means that although two jobs involve different tasks, they can require similar skills for effective performance. It is these *transferable skills* which are therefore particularly important, especially, for example, for people entering the labour market or for individuals made redundant who need to target their job search on jobs which have a similar skill content to the one they are leaving.

Cognitive theorists believe improvements in performance can be related to changes in the models people possess of the systems they are interacting with. Gibson (1968) provided an influential description of the changes that human perceptual systems progress through. He proposed a sequence of developmental stages, each representing an increase in the ability to process, store and cross-reference information from different perceptual systems. Gibson suggested that at first we learn the range of stimulus inputs. We can understand a specific input better if we are able to relate it to the entire range of inputs. A learner driver, for example, will learn to discriminate between engine noises by learning the range of possible engine noises. This is the basis of what Gibson termed *learning affordances*, understanding what meaning or value an input has and what its implications for action are. This involves individuals developing *categories* for processing information. A learner driver, for example, develops categories for processing ranges of engine noise which indicate whether he or she should accelerate, decelerate, change gear or take no action.

The concept of categorization has important practical implications. Techniques have been developed which enable differences in the categories used by the skilled individuals and beginners to be identified, thus providing important insights into the nature of the skill and a firm basis for the design of training programmes.

Gibson suggested individuals will then establish the covariation between inputs from different perceptual systems. We can make more sense of an input if we can associate it with inputs or cues from other senses. In many skilled activities it is essential to learn the auditory, tactile and balance inputs associated with a visual input. This also enables the skilled individual to make more use of sensory information derived from receptors in muscles and joints. These *kinaesthetic* cues are more immediate than visual cues and so make possible increases in the rapidity and accuracy of movement. Knowing what efficient performance 'feels like', gear-changing for example, is an important guide to skilled activity.

We also acquire what are termed *constancies*. These allow us to perceive certain characteristics of the visual world, shape, size, colour and brightness, as constant. Without constancies the visual world would be extremely confusing; objects would appear to change shape if viewed from different angles, they would very rapidly diminish in size as they moved away from us, and would vary in colour and brightness according to the specific lighting conditions in which they were viewed. A dinner plate, for example, appears circular if viewed directly from above; if seen at an angle the shape formed by the parcel of light rays reflected from it on to the retina is an ellipse. The plate does not, however, change its shape as we change our angle of view. Constancies appear to be learned early on in life but can break down and need to be reacquired. Colour constancy, for example, disappears with unfamiliar objects, and size constancy can fail in specific visual environments such as when travelling at very high speeds.

Next our perceptual system incorporates what Gibson termed the *invariants in events*; these are the unchanging characteristics of the systems we interact with. We first learn the laws which determine how objects fall, roll, collide, break and pour. We then move on to learn more abstract invariants such as inertia.

These developments in the perceptual systems of individuals increase the *selectivity* of attention, enabling more efficient monitoring of both performance and the environment: 'only the information required to identify a thing economically tends to be picked up from a complex of stimulus information' (Gibson, 1968, p. 286). This means skilled individuals need less information to select a response. The skilled driver, for example, requires less visual information than the learner driver to be able to perceive a shape in the distance as a child emerging from behind a parked car. Similarly, skilled process workers in refineries can assess the state of the system with quick and infrequent inspections of display panels (Bainbridge, 1978).

Constructing models of the environment which categorize and store inputs also reduces the demand on memory. Descriptions of human memory usually assume two stores, termed *primary or short-term memory* and *secondary or long-term memory*. This division implies that two processes are involved in the storage of information. Primary memory appears to be the conscious or working store in which information can be stored for a few seconds. If important, information is transferred to a secondary, long-term store. Primary memory is thought to be located in circuits in the frontal lobes of the brain, whereas secondary memory appears to involve irreversible changes in the molecular structure of the brain cells. Primary memory is a fragile store and is easily disrupted. For example, if you have to attend to another input while trying to memorize a telephone number, you are unlikely to be able to remember what the number is. Fatigue and stress also disrupt the primary memory.

As well as being a fragile store, primary memory also appears to have a limited capacity. Whereas secondary memory has an almost infinite storage capacity, primary memory seems to be able to hold a small amount of information. In fact its capacity seems to be between five and nine 'chunks' of information (Miller, 1956). These chunks need not represent individual items such as numbers. By subjectively grouping items more information can be contained in the primary store. A nine-figure number, for example, can be remembered as three chunks each containing three digits. Skilled workers seem to be able to deal with many more items of information by chunking them according to the action-relevant categories they have developed. By reducing the load on short-term memory, skilled individuals considerably increase their resistance to the effects of stress and fatigue.

It is useful to think of skill in terms of two dimensions: *horizontal* and *vertical*.

The horizontal dimension refers to the organization of activity over time. Unskilled performances are marked by a confused response order and imprecise timing. Learner drivers, for example, usually stall at the points where they are required to make a number of responses in a particular order with reasonably precise timing.

In the training context this implies that 'micro'-behavioural training, in which trainees acquire a specific response routine—for example, sales trainees being drilled with 'scripts'—may be inadequate. The correct sequencing and timing of responses may vary in specific contexts, and a trainee's ability to vary the order and timing of responses will depend on more macro-cognitive learning—for example, understanding how to provide information at a rate which corresponds to the client's ability to understand it.

The vertical dimension reflects the hierarchical organization of skills. It is believed skilled activity differs in the extent to which it involves conscious awareness. Some behaviours, termed *subroutines*, are so well learned that they can be retrieved from secondary memory and employed without passing through our conscious or primary memory. For highly skilled individuals so much of their activity consists of automatized subroutines that their conscious memory has little to do. This can give rise to the strange feeling they often report, of being able to 'step outside of themselves' during an activity which appears to observers to involve a great deal of conscious effort. Further up the hierarchy are *operating programmes*. These convert the contents of our models into behavioural outputs by triggering patterns of subroutines. The model is then updated to include outcomes of the action. Operating programmes can themselves be relegated to subroutine status if they are so well learned that they can be elicited without conscious awareness. At the apex of the hierarchy is the *executive programme*, which selects the skill most appropriate to a situation.

Improvements in performance occur when either the model or the operating programme develop. The model contains more powerful representations of the situation, the operating programme acquires new sequences of subroutines. These improvements need not happen in parallel; the operating programme and model can move out of phase with each other, one leapfrogging over the other. For example, when an individual's modelling of a new system, whether mechanical, human or administrative, improves, the model is able to include enhanced states of that system. However, for this new state to be achieved, the operating programme must acquire new responses. This process continues until the operating programme is unable to produce a sequence of subroutines which would result in outcomes not already contained in the model. Similarly, the model reaches a point where it both deals economically with all relevant inputs and cannot produce improvements in the state of the system that are not already included in it. What sets the upper limit on the refinement of model and operating programmes is the individual's level of *motivation*. Highly motivated individuals will always struggle to improve their modelling of a situation and the ways they are able to respond to their models. A racing-car driver, for example, requires a more highly developed model and operating programme for driving than an ordinary driver. A highly motivated student will try to comprehend how academic performance can be improved upon and attempt to acquire the information-gathering, analytical, and writing skills that enable the improvements to be realized. In general, the development of models and operating programmes slows down once we feel we have mastered the system we are interacting with.

Skill theory has considerably improved our understanding of the way in which people acquire complex behaviours. It is now possible to appreciate the crucial role that people's construction of the environment plays in their level of skill. We can see that skilled activity is in a sense an extension of their understanding of the systems they are interacting with into the external environment. These insights are important since they provide clues about the practical analysis and development of skills in training programmes.

Learning and work

The economic imperatives described at the beginning of this chapter, the need to unlock potential, create greater flexibility, and enable individuals to cope with increasingly complex work, has heightened interest in how people acquire skills. But the reality is, all too often, that the training an individual experiences is ineffective and fails to transfer back to the workplace.

Research into training effectiveness and transfer of learning has focused on the features of courses, trainees, and the wider work environment.

Features of courses

Courses need to be perceived as relevant and useful. In one analysis of the impact of a range of variables on the transfer of training the perception of relevance was one of the best predictors of transfer one month after the course (Axtell *et al.*, 1997). The implications for organizations of this are clear. First, wherever possible, organizations need to heighten the perception of relevance. Rather than being 'off the shelf', courses need to be *customized*. The organization I work for will, for this reason, only deliver courses after diagnostic interviews with managers which enable scenarios and examples used in course notes and activities to relate clearly to participants' experiences. Secondly, relevance can be increased through careful internal marketing of courses or learning programmes. This will highlight the relevance of the learning for participants.

Another important determinant of the effectiveness of a course is the extent to which it is based on a mixture of both cognitive and stimulus–response learning (Anderson, 1990). Both forms of learning are involved in acquiring complex behaviours. Stimulus–response theory has increased awareness of the need to identify key operants and provide opportunities for reinforcing them. Cognitive theories have emphasized the importance of facilitating the selection, encoding, and active organization of material. (Such a mixture can be found in Box 1.2, which provides a technique for learning the contents of this book.)

Features of individuals

Whilst the principal focus of research has been on the features of courses, more recently interest has shifted. There is now considerable interest in the characteristics of learners which might affect learning and its subsequent transfer. Whilst some of the differences might be accounted for by intelligence, a view we will discuss in more detail in Chapter 3, there are important differences over and above ability. Whilst many management consultants run courses on 'learning styles' which suggest that people fall into one of a

---

Box 1.2 Learning this book

An effective method, termed PQ4R, for learning complex material was devised by John Anderson (1990). You will see that it combined both stimulus–response and cognitive principles.

Preview. For each chapter survey the contents to get a general overview of the content. Identify the sections which need to be read as units. Now apply the next four steps to each of these sections.

Questions. Make up questions about the section. These can be as simple as transforming the section headings into questions. For example a section heading might be Correlates of Job Satisfaction. Questions might then be: what are the correlates of job satisfaction? We have also included a list of questions at the end of each chapter to assist the consolidation effect of questions.

Read. Carefully read the section trying to answer the questions you constructed or the ones we have provided.

Reflect. As you read the text reflect on it, for example by trying to relate the material to any prior knowledge you might have or thinking of examples. This encourages a deeper and more elaborate processing of the material.

Recite. After each section try to remember the information it contained. Try answering the questions you made up for the section. If you cannot remember enough to answer the questions, re-read the portion you had difficulty recalling.

Review. After you have finished the chapter go back through it mentally trying to recall the main points. Again try answering the questions you made up.

---

range of styles according to which typology is being used, there is actually very little empirical evidence for the existence of these differentiations. Warr and Gardner (1998) suggest instead that the key difference in learners is in the effectiveness of the learning strategy they adopt. The difference between strategies and styles is in the degree of fixedness they assume. Learning styles are assumed to represent a relatively enduring characteristic preference to learn in a certain way, whereas strategies are less fixed and can be adjusted.

Two basic primary strategies exist: *cognitive* and *behavioural*. Cognitive strategies involve rehearsal (repetition and copying), organization (identifying key issues and creating structures which group and inter-relate material), and elaboration (making mental connections and examining the implications of what is being learnt). Behavioural strategies involve interpersonal help seeking (getting others to check and reinforce learning), seeking help from written material (obtaining information from written documents), and practical application (testing learning through practical activities). Alongside these primary strategies other secondary strategies come into play which enable individuals to regulate their anxiety and motivation.

Learning strategies are strong predictors of transfer of training. In one study of the impact of an open learning programme on a group of junior managers, the adoption of a cognitive strategy significantly predicted transfer of training. This was somewhat unexpected since in open learning—with its mix of instructional media (video, audio tapes, and text), self-pacing, and less opportunity for interaction—a behavioural strategy was expected to be especially valuable (Warr and Bunce, 1995).

The practical implications of learning strategies research are immense. Learning how to choose the correct strategy for a particular activity can increase confidence in our learning abilities. What is termed 'learning self-efficacy'—fundamental and sometimes disabling feelings individuals have about their ability to learn—can be improved. Learning self-efficacy is in itself strongly predictive of learning success. Acquiring effective learning strategies is particularly important for older workers who have to learn against the backdrop of a slowdown of certain aspects of their cognitive functioning (Fisk and Warr, 1996; Birdi *et al.*, 1997).

Features of the environment

The amount of control and autonomy an individual has over the way he or she works is a very significant predictor of transfer of training (Axtell *et al.*, 1997). This is because the more control and autonomy an individual has the more he or she can create opportunities to reinforce new skills. Practising the new skill appears to be particularly important in the immediate period back at work. However, this is also precisely the time when mistakes are likely to occur. This means support from colleagues and management is particularly important. Management in particular can help create a transfer-of-training climate which helps reinforce and sustain new skills.

Conclusion

In this chapter we have reviewed two major approaches to understanding how people learn: stimulus–response and cognitive theories. Both have an important contribution to make to workplace learning programmes. We have seen how stimulus–response theories focus on environmental factors which reinforce learning. We have also seen how cognitive theories emphasize the active mental processes individuals use to learn skills.

In the last section of this chapter we looked at what encourages learning and transfer of learning at work. One of the implications of the last section was that individuals can become aware of their own learning strategy. Training can be designed to encourage the acquisition of effective learning strategies. This will help individuals tackle disabling personal myths such as 'I am not good at figures'. What is important ultimately is to improve individuals' confidence in their own learning abilities.

However, as you progress through this book, you will encounter other factors which interact with your ability to learn. In the next chapter we examine what happens when the environment begins to exceed our intellectual capacity. And work is increasingly, given the new manufacturing initiatives, raising the attentional and problem-solving demands on individuals. In Chapter 3 we will see that there are other sources of differences between individuals—such as conscientiousness—which can affect the outcome of a learning programme. But the importance of learning and learning to learn for individual success in the workplace is clear. And we will return to the notion of learning in Chapter 14, when we consider what capacity organizations have to learn.

Study questions for Chapter 1

1 Describe the differences between classical and operant conditioning.
2 What are schedules of reinforcement; which are more effective and why?
3 List some everyday examples of each of the reinforcement schedules.
4 What relevance do operant and classical conditioning have to the explanation of workplace behaviour?
5 To what extent can there be a 'technology of behaviour'?
6 Why is learning theory important to modern economies?
7 In reality, workplace learning is a mixture of both cognitive and behavioural learning—discuss.
8 How can the transfer of training be encouraged?
9 What are learning strategies and how might they help the design of training programmes?

Further reading

Booth, A. and Snower, D. (eds.) (1996) *Acquiring Skills, Market Failures, their Symptoms and Policy Responses*. Cambridge: Cambridge University Press.

Forrester, K., Payne, J., and Ward, K. (1995) *Workplace Learning: Perspectives on Education, Training and Work*. London: Avebury.

Harri-Augustein, S. and Thomas, L. (1991) *Learning Conversations*. London: Routledge.

Hartley, J. (1998) *Learning and Studying*. London: Routledge.

Hill, W. F. (1997) *Learning: A Survey of Psychological Interpretations*, 6th edn. Harlow: Longman.

Komaki, J. L. (1998) *The Operant Model of Effective Supervision*. London: Routledge.

Skinner, B. F. (1971) *Beyond Freedom and Dignity*. New York: Knopf.

2 Stress

Summary points and learning objectives

By the end of this chapter you will be able to

- define the concept of stress;
- describe the various ways in which roles can become stressful;
- understand the effect of stress on decision-making;
- understand the notions of over- and under-stimulation;
- describe the evidence for Type A and Type B personalities;
- describe individual methods of coping with stress;
- distinguish between individually focused and organizationally based worksite stress-management techniques.

Introduction

In Chapter 1 we examined theories of learning. These described the processes which enable people to adapt to their environments. These adaptive capacities, however, have limits and risks attached to them. For example, the person who constantly struggles to master a turbulent environment or a demanding task faces an increased risk of peptic ulcers, mental illness, hypertension, and coronary heart disease. Less dangerous but still serious symptoms, like headache, eyestrain, dizziness, loss of appetite, depression, and nervousness, may also occur. And these can result in responses, like the increased consumption of tranquillizers or alcohol, which only compound the problem.

These are all stress-related symptoms, and their prevalence in occupational and wider contexts has given rise to much interest in the causes and alleviation of stress. There is no doubt that stress has sometimes had rather 'elitist' overtones; it has traditionally been associated with executive and managerial occupations. But, in point of fact, stress has never been a 'middle-class disease'; incidents of stress-related symptoms are just as frequently caused by factors like shift working or excessive fatigue which are typical of manual jobs. In addition, the new manufacturing initiatives such as total quality management, just-in-time, and the advanced manufacturing technologies (discussed in Chapters 19 and 20), increase the attentional and problem-solving demands on blue-collar workers as well as their responsibility for any errors in production. For some time there has been considerable concern over the impact of word-processing on secretarial work and the incidence of stress-related symptoms among typists. Working with VDUs has been the subject of an EU directive since 1992. The costs and prevalence of stress and stress-related symptoms are enormous. For example, in one sample of 11,000 individuals working in the UK health service, 27 per cent reported significant levels of minor psychiatric disorder (Wall *et al.*, 1997).

But, as we will see, the concept of stress is by no means straightforward. In fact, some writers have suggested that the term is so over-used and misused that it has been stripped of all its meaning and should be abandoned. In this chapter we will critically examine the concept of stress, identifying common causes of stress at work, and assessing the extent to which stress can be 'managed' and alleviated in the workplace.

What is stress?

Whilst there is little disagreement about the prevalence of stress there is considerable debate about what the word actually refers to. In ordinary conversation we seem to be willing to apply the word to both cause and effect (Beehr, 1995). In other words, the common sense view of stress is that it is a combination of external *stressors* and our *response* or the physical and psychological *strain* we experience as a result. Stress was conceptualized as a response in the early and highly influential research of Selye (1936). He observed an identical series of biochemical changes in a number of organisms adapting to a variety of environmental conditions. He termed this series of changes the *general adaptation syndrome*. During the initial phase, termed the *stage of alarm*, the organism orients to the demand the environment is making on it and begins to experience it as threatening. This state cannot be maintained for very long. If the stimulus which has elicited the alarm response is too powerful (for example, a poison) the organism dies; if survival is possible the organism enters the *stage of resistance* in which the organism musters the resources to cope with the demand. If the demand continues for too long these adaptive resources are worn out and the organism reaches the *stage of exhaustion* in which serious damage can occur. Selye was not sure what it was that an organism lost in the stage of resistance that caused it to pass into the stage of exhaustion, although he was convinced it was more than simple calorific energy (Selye, 1983). The general adaptation syndrome can operate at different levels, from a subsystem to an entire organism. Certain kinds of athletes (footballers, for example) make severe demands on specific ligaments and joints in their training and performance. The general adaptation syndrome and the consequences of the stage of exhaustion will therefore tend to be localized.

Selye's discovery of the biochemical and physiological pathways of the stress response has been of immense significance. His concern to find the psychological mediators of the response to stress has, for example, created the field of psychoneuro immunology, an interdisciplinary area of research which explores the varied and complex way the immune system reacts to stressors (Evans *et al.*, 1997).

But a number of researchers, however, have not followed Selye in seeing stress as simply a response. One major group of writers has argued stress has to be seen as a function of an individual's *appraisal* of a situation. As we saw in our earlier discussion of skills, people do not respond directly to a stimulus but to the meaning a stimulus may have in relation to their model of the environment. This implies that events in the environment are not of themselves stressful; they must be *perceived* by the individuals as a threat before the stress concept can be applied. The stress experience, according to this view, is therefore determined by the *appraisal of what is at stake* and the analysis of the resources available to meet the demand.

A large body of evidence has developed demonstrating the importance of an appraisal in mediating the stress response. For example, Tomaka *et al.* (1997) asked two groups of individuals to perform an identical mental arithmetic task. Physiological responses associated with stress were recorded continuously during the task. In one group the task was presented as a threat by emphasizing the objective evaluation of their performance which would occur. The other group were encouraged to do their best and to see the exercise as a challenge. Although the instructions provided for the exercise varied only slightly between the groups, they experienced very different physiological consequences.

The notion of appraisal broadens the concept of stress to include psychological factors, particularly personality variables. There is, for example, considerable interest in the notion of the *hardy personality* (e.g. Kobosa, 1979). Hardiness incorporates the appraisal concept of stress by suggesting the specific cognitive mechanisms which attenuate responses to stressors. High hardy individuals see life as *meaningful*, *controllable*, and *challenging*. Seeing life as meaningful enables high hardy individuals to retain a basic sense of purpose. They believe in themselves and what they are doing. Their sense of control means they feel they make things happen rather than things happening to them. Their interest in challenge means, for example, seeing change as opportunity rather than threat. Some support for the notion of the hardy personality has come from studies which indicate different cardiovascular responses to laboratory-induced stress between high and low hardy groups (Wiebe and Williams, 1992). However, many psychologists have argued hardiness is little different to neuroticism and the value of the concept in explaining health differences cannot be fully evaluated until the notion is better defined.

Despite some misgivings about the value of the hardy personality as currently defined it is clear that appraisal mediates the effect of stressors on individuals. In other words, what one person sees as a threat another may see as a challenge. These different appraisals seem to produce specific physiological changes which, in turn, have different implications for the health of the individual. So the concept of stress which dominates current research is an extension of the appraisal hypothesis that stress represents a relationship between a stressor and an individual's reaction to it (Beehr, 1995). Current research is based on the assumption that stress, inferred from physiological, behavioural, psychological and somatic signs and symptoms, is the result of *a lack of fit between a person (in terms of their personality, aptitudes and abilities) and the environment*, and a consequent inability to cope effectively with the various demands that it makes of him or her. One study which tested this view found that, while neither a worker's report of the actual complexity of a job nor the level of complexity a worker wanted was related to a measure of depression, there was a strong relationship between measures of the person–environment fit and depression. The relationship the researcher found was curvilinear; when the person–environment fit was exact, depression was minimal, but when there was either too much or too little complexity present in the work, the depression score was increased (Harrison, 1976).

Types of stress at work

Role interaction

Though individuals' perceptions of the environment play an important part in determining the experience and consequences of stress, it is none the less possible to identify objective features of work which are likely to be perceived as threatening. An individual's activities within an organization are a function of what *role(s)* he or she occupies in it. A role can be defined as the set of expectations that others have of a role incumbent's behaviour. There are a number of ways in which roles can become stressful.

1. *Role ambiguity*. A person experiencing role ambiguity would answer not at all true or a little true to the following questions (Beehr, 1995).

> I can predict what others will expect from me tomorrow.
> I am clear what others expect of me in my job.
> In my job, whatever situation arises, there are procedures for handling it.
> I get enough facts and information to do my best.

As the questions suggest the essence of role ambiguity is information deficiency. Potential sources of information deficiency are peers, managers, subordinates, and even individuals outside the organization such as customers or suppliers. A number of studies have shown role ambiguity reduces organizational commitment, job involvement and job satisfaction. Role ambiguity increases reported tension, anxiety and the intention to leave an organization (Fisher and Gitelson, 1983; Jackson and Schuler, 1985). Role ambiguity is likely to become even more prevalent as roles become increasingly 'fuzzy' as the pressure on individuals for teamworking and flexibility grows. Role ambiguity can also be built into organizational structure. Matrix forms of organizational design, for example, may increase role ambiguity by overlaying product and project responsibilities to the point when it becomes unclear what responsibilities, duties or tasks take priority.

2. *Boundary-spanning roles*. These are roles which involve taking the activities of the organization to the outside world and seem to carry a higher than average level of stress. Jobs such as selling or negotiating carry boundary–spanning pressures. The most stressful boundary–spanning role would involve performing complex tasks in a changing environment with a variety of outside parties to whom there is a long-term

commitment and where there are clear performance ratings and independent sources of information on achievement available to the parent organization. Thus, the role incumbent is exposed to numerous novel and unanticipated problems, as he or she attempts to develop relationships with different types of client, while the availability of hard performance data means that employers can press the individual for results and ignore the delicate processes involved in building relationships with customers.

3. *Single role conflict*. This form of role stress is caused by the various components of a role becoming difficult to reconcile. Single role conflict is particularly prevalent in 'first-line supervisory' roles. The expectations of a supervisor's staff, particularly when the individual was promoted from the team, may include defending their interests, taking an interest in them, and affording them a significant degree of freedom in their work. The supervisor's managers, however, might have very different expectations. They may expect the supervisor to represent the interests of senior and middle management and to employ a much tougher style of supervision, for example by confronting lateness or absenteeism and pushing very hard for output. Many first-line supervisors resolve the conflict by returning to their former positions.

4. *Multiple role conflict*. If you can answer strongly, agree or not agree to these questions, you are experiencing multiple role conflict (Beehr, 1995).

> My work and family lives seem to get in the way of each other.
> What I should do in my work and what my family want of me are two different things.
> My family expects me to do things at work that conflict with my own judgment.

These questions are designed to elicit the extent to which the demands of one role clash with those of another. People invariably fill more than one role and multiple role conflict in some degree is inevitable. Whilst there has been much research on employed individuals trying to reconcile competing familial and occupational demands, multiple work conflict can occur within an organization. For example, a manager who is also the factory's safety officer, might find the demands of each role difficult to reconcile, resolving the conflict may mean taking short cuts such as removing safety guards.

5. *Work role transitions*. This refers to the stress experienced when an individual enters a new job and is faced with a novel, uncertain environment. This is a fairly common form of role stress since about 33 per cent of individuals are moving into newly created jobs where they are without predecessors (West *et al.*, 1987). Therefore, individuals entering these jobs have less help available, for example, feedback from others. And socialization into the role tends to be achieved informally and somewhat randomly. While some individuals find that these conditions provide an opportunity for personal growth and *role innovation* (changing the role) others may find them traumatic and stressful (Bunce and West, 1994).

6. *Burnout*. An increasingly common source of stress occurs when individuals feel locked into roles. Such stress is particularly common in large bureaucratic organizations where employees may believe they are unable to change their job, because very few job opportunities are available or they are not sufficiently able or qualified to move into another post. This can be caused by distortion in the promotion patterns in orga-

nizations. If an organization has recently been reorganized or created, new senior posts may be filled by relatively young people. Once these posts are filled there is little opportunity for promotion within the organization. The stagnation experienced when career paths are blocked leads to frustration, apathy, and eventually to the burnout, where the initial enthusiasm for the job is replaced with negative attitudes. Burnout was originally identified in the caring professions such as social work and nursing but is identifiable outside these occupations. The defining features of burnout are emotional exhaustion, depersonalization (feeling distant from others), and a sense of diminished personal accomplishment (Lee and Ashforth, 1996). The energy depletion involved in the first of these is regarded as the core of the syndrome. Personnel departments and senior managements in large organizations are increasingly recognizing the problems in terms of reduced physical and mental well-being of staff feeling locked into roles. Strategies for reducing burnout attempt to reduce the concern an individual has with the limitations of his or her current position within a hierarchy by negotiating career plans which may involve sideways as well as upward moves or secondments, or by setting up project teams which create new networks of responsibility and authority in addition to the existing ones. It may also be possible to provide realistic career changes for people by a general restructuring of career scales within an organization.

Decision-making stress

Uncertainty, economic and organizational, characterizes for many their experience of work. And uncertainty is currently seen as the underlying source of much occupational stress (e.g. Cooper, 1997). Uncertainty is a common thread, for example, in many of the role stressors discussed in the last section. Of course, there is something individuals can do to reduce some forms of uncertainty: make decisions. But the decision-making process is itself not stress-free. In fact, in the process individuals may experience an acute form of uncertainty. They may become aware of the limitations of their knowledge and abilities and the losses which may result from choosing any of the options available. This makes *decisional stress* a particularly potent form of stress which may result in a significant reduction in the quality of an individual's decision-making.

Decisional stress might be seen as essentially a managerial problem, but as Wall *et al.* (1996) point out, the new manufacturing initiatives of just-in-time, total quality management, and advanced manufacturing technologies increase the attentional and decision-making demands on operatives, making decisional stress as much a feature of blue-collar work as it is for managerial jobs.

Some manifestations of decisional stress include: categorical thinking—the tendency to assume erroneously there is one right choice—forgetting, misinterpreting information, and not thinking beyond the immediate decision (Butler and Hope, 1995). At its most extreme, decisional stress can cause people simply to withdraw from a situation and make a decision without seeking out or considering relevant information. More usually, as Janis (1982) suggested, individuals display one of five decision-making styles when attempting to deal with decisional stress:

1. Unconflicted adherence, where behaviour is unchanged, and information about the risks of continuing in the same way is ignored.
2. Unconflicted change, which involves uncritically adopting whichever course of action is most salient or most strongly recommended without making contingency plans and without psychologically preparing for setbacks.
3. Defensive avoidance, where the individual procrastinates but eventually chooses the least difficult alternative, ignoring any information that suggests this decision may be wrong.
4. Hypervigilance, which involves searching frantically for a way out of the conflict and seizing upon any plan which seems to offer an immediate solution.
5. Vigilance, which consists of a careful search for relevant information followed by a thorough appraisal of the alternatives.

Of these five strategies, Janis suggested vigilance was the only one which involves enough cognitive work to meet the criteria of true decision-making. Hypervigilance, where attention shifts on to a variety of sometimes quite trivial cues, introduces the most error into a decision. The individual's thinking in this condition tends to be based on simple stereotypes and can involve obsessional dwelling on the worst possible outcomes. Janis saw 'time pressure' as the main cause of hypervigilance. When individuals are constantly overloaded with urgent business, they are more likely to commit themselves impulsively to courses of action which soon after appear to have been inappropriate.

Decisional stress is of particular interest to those involved in the disaster and emergency services, when good decision-making can mean the difference between life and death. Psychologists, this author included, have developed courses which help individuals understand what might undermine their decision-making under pressure and how to cope with it. Courses are normally based on the early work of two psychologists—Cameron and Meichenbaum (1982)—and use the approach known as stress inoculation. Their programme, driven by the appraisal concept of stress, has three stages:

1. *Conceptualization*, in which individuals' understanding of decision-making situations and their own experiences in them are improved by explaining the appraisal model of stress. Cameron and Meichenbaum believed this model provided individuals with a highly effective conceptual framework within which they could organize their own experience of stress. To achieve accurate appraisal, they are encouraged to recognize that appraisals of situations are often inaccurate or incomplete and that allowances have to be made for the biases which creep into their perceptions. Individuals then consider the skills which enable pertinent evidence to be examined and reasonable propositions to be formulated.

2. *Skill acquisition and activation*. This part of the programme examines whether an individual lacks a particular skill for accurate diagnosis of a situation, or possesses it but does not apply it. A relevant skill might be efficient gathering of information about the likely outcomes of a decision. In a rescue service a crucial skill was handling effectively what are termed automatic negative thoughts which intrude on decision-making.

3. *Rehearsal and application.* For the course to be effective individuals have to be able to transfer their newly acquired coping skills back to the workplace. This final phase of a course provides opportunities for participants to practise and apply the newly acquired coping skills. This might involve role-play or one-to-one follow-up sessions.

The attitudinal, personality, and cognitive variables which provide the psychological context for coping with decisional stress are deeply embedded in individuals. Complex changes, particularly in an individual's sense of self-efficacy (how competent individuals feel) are necessary before improvement in coping with decisional stress can occur. Individuals and organizations have to be committed to encouraging the transfer of learning, for example, through opportunities for regrouping in individual follow-up sessions with tutors, for the improvements in coping with decisional stress, stemming from such brief interventions, to become permanent.

Over- and under-stimulation

Humans and many other organisms appear to have evolved to function under conditions of moderate stimulation. Such aspects of the environment as noise, temperature, light, humidity and barometric pressure are tolerable at moderate levels but cause stress if they are too high or too low.

In the work context, the level of stimulation a job provides is likewise associated with the amount of stress it can cause employees to experience. *Understimulation* can occur in jobs which involve repetitive work and underutilization of skills. The emotional responses to these jobs are apathy, boredom and reduced levels of motivation (Caplan *et al.*, 1975). Behavioural responses are likely to be less well organized than they would have been at higher levels of stimulation. Many studies have shown that people who do repetitive work also face increased risks of stress-related illnesses (e.g. Ferguson, 1973). Cox (1980) has suggested that the effect of repetitive understimulating work on health occurs through what he termed an *emergency stress response.* This occurs when someone performing a repetitive task has to readjust his or her attention suddenly because it had drifted away from the task. He argued that because of the increased physiological 'wear and tear' these adjustments involve, the higher frequency of attentional shifts inherent in repetitive work was detrimental to health. More specifically this 'wear and tear' seems to come from elevations in heart rate and noradrenaline levels—a hormone associated with hardening of the arteries.

Many people at work face the opposite problem—having to cope with too much stimulation. *Overstimulation* can be as stressful, if not more so, than understimulation. Perhaps the classic example of a job in which large amounts of variable information have to be coped with is air-traffic control. The health costs in terms of ulcers, skin disorders, hypertension, and respiratory complaints have been well documented (Martindale, 1977; Rose *et al.*, 1978).

Numerous studies have demonstrated the damaging effects of overload on managers. Working long hours is actually a coping strategy used by many managers. Quick *et al.* (1990) cite the comments of a fairly typical manager who would 'read every night or work every night and bring home a briefcase full and really feel guilty if I didn't'. But long hours and excessive workloads inevitably lead to stress-related problems such as increased alcohol and cigarette consumption, depression, low self-esteem, and coronary heart disease.

While managers can exert some control over their workload—for example, by delegating or rescheduling—jobs which combine overload with low control are experienced as particularly stressful. Carrère *et al.* (1991) studied urban bus driving, an example of an occupation which combines overload with low control. They measured the hormones associated with blood pressure and coronary heart disease (adrenaline and noradrenaline) and found drivers had about twice the amount found in other blue-collar and office workers. While not enough is known about the effects of this heightened hormonal activity, this may account for the much higher risk of coronary problems among bus drivers. Other studies have also found the combination of overload and low control a particularly stressful one (e.g. Mackay and Cooper, 1987).

Type As and type Bs

Even though occupations vary in the stress-related health risks they carry, it is now accepted that individuals similarly differ in their proneness to stress-related health risks. As early as 1868 a German doctor, Von Dusch, noted that people who developed coronary heart disease (CHD) were often excessively involved in their work. In 1943 another doctor, Dunbar, noted that his CHD patients could frequently be characterized by compulsive striving, self-discipline, and an urge to get to the top through hard work. In the late 1950s, Friedman and Rosenman began a series of studies on managers in a range of companies. In an early study, fifty accountants were monitored for six months. Blood samples were taken every fortnight to gauge their cholesterol levels, which were then compared with their diaries where they reported the amount of stress present in their work and homes. With other factors such as diet and exercise held constant, they found cholesterol levels went up and blood coagulation times went down during periods of stress. In 1959 Friedman and Rosenman made their most controversial contribution to the understanding of the relationship between stress and heart disease. They operationalized a behaviour pattern, termed type A, which they believed encapsulated what Von Dusch, Dunbar, and others had observed in their CHD patients. This behaviour pattern, they argued, carried a risk of CHD independent of all other known risks. Individuals who fall into the type-A category display:

1. A strong and sustained drive to achieve poorly defined goals they have set for themselves.
2. An intense desire to compete.
3. A desire for recognition and promotion.
4. Involvement in numerous and varied activities which have deadlines.
5. Habitually fast completion of physical and mental functions.
6. High levels of mental and physical alertness.

In extreme instances type-A behaviour involves tense facial and body muscle tone, rapid body movements, hand- or teeth-clenching, excessive gesturing and explosive speech characteristics. Conversely, the type-B individual displays less striving, aggression, hostility, and competitiveness, and is in general more relaxed. While these are extremes, most people do in fact fall into only one of the categories, 40 per cent being type A and 60 per cent type B (Glass, 1977).

A large body of evidence has been accumulated which has confirmed the association between type-A behaviour and CHD. One series of studies observed a sample of over 3,500 men over a fifteen-year period. Of the twenty-five deaths caused by CHD, twenty-two had been classified as type As. This yielded a risk factor in the type-A group for CHD some six times larger than that for type Bs (Rosenman *et al.*, 1975). Why does type-A behaviour carry such an increased risk of CHD? Chesney and Rosenman (1980) argued that some behaviours in the type-A constellation are more predictive of CHD than others. They saw four facets of type-A behaviour as particularly predictive of CHD:

1. *Time urgency*: type As feel time passes too quickly.
2. *Their competitive and hard-driving style* makes type As work harder and faster than type Bs, even when no deadline is present. Type As seem to impose deadlines on themselves. This enables type As to maintain and even enhance their performance on multiple tasks compared to a fall in performance by type Bs.
3. *Suppression of symptoms*: though type As work harder and faster than type Bs, they report less fatigue and complain less. In fact, hard work and self-imposed deadlines seem to reinforce their suppression of symptoms since it is only at times when the pressure has eased that symptoms are experienced.
4. *Hostility and aggressiveness* are thought to be the facets of type A behaviour which best predict CHD. Type As are more impatient, aggressive, and irritable with others. When provoked, type As are much more hostile than type Bs in similar circumstances (Carver and Glass, 1978).

The motivational basis for type-A behaviour is thought to be their 'need for control'. Type-A behaviours are elicited in situations in which type As feel challenged, under pressure or threatened. It is at these times that differences in blood pressure, heart rate, and adrenaline level are observed between type As and Bs. Carruthers (1980) tentatively suggested that adrenaline accelerates the ageing of the cardiovascular system and so increases the CHD risk.

In a work-oriented society, type-A behaviour is not seen as a clinical problem. If anything it tends to be rewarded. Measures of type-A behaviour are positively correlated with occupational status, though, interestingly, type Bs are most prevalent at the top of organizations (Friedman and Rosenman, 1974). Byrne and Rheinhart (1989) provide data which suggest it is the willingness of type As to devote their own time to the organization rather than their competitiveness or speed and impatience which is the key to their success.

Healthy type As are obviously a great asset to organizations, given that their hard-driving style may be necessary to cope with the work environment. For example, Rose *et al.* (1978) found type-A air-traffic controllers had higher rates of stress but the largest single chronic illness in the sample, hypertension, was suffered by type Bs. This finding is consistent with the view that stress results from a mismatch between an individual and the work environment. Air-traffic control, a type-A job, produced more stress-related illness in type-B controllers.

Type As' increased risk of CHD, however, often confronts them with the choice of either curtailing their ambitions and accepting positions of lower status with less responsibility, or learning to face challenges without eliciting health-damaging physiological responses. We will now examine some of the recent developments in occupational stress management which provide type As and others suffering stress-related problems with the second option.

Occupational stress management

The costs of stress-related problems to an economy are substantial. Absence illness, accidents, and staff traumas can be the direct or indirect result of stress. Whilst it is difficult to calculate the exact costs, Schrears *et al.* (1996), estimated that about 30–50 per cent of absenteeism can be attributed to stress. And correlations between measures of stress and health whilst seemingly modest, in the order of about .3, probably underestimate the relationship because of the presence of the individual differences described in earlier sections.

Interest in stress management has burgeoned in recent years. Numerous consultants and trainers now deliver stress-management programmes of varying degrees of usefulness to individuals and organizations. There is now even an institute for those who are involved in stress management to become members of. Stress management has become big business.

Individuals are, of course, not passive recipients of workplace pressures. If we are left alone we develop our own characteristic coping strategies. These, like trainers' programmes, vary in effectiveness from the useful to the downright harmful. A commonplace example of the latter is caffeine consumption. Whilst most of us use caffeine to some extent, too many coffee breaks in response to work pressures, particularly if combined with significant domestic consumption, can lead to increased irritability, anxiety, tension headaches, and sleep loss. These will only serve to compound the problems.

The strategies individuals adopt have been explored by a number of psychologists (Folkman and Lazarus, 1980; Moos and Billings, 1983; Dewe, 1991). Essentially, individuals adopt one of these strategies:

1. Appraisal focused
2. Problem focused
3. Emotion focused

In the first individuals may undertake a conscious *logical analysis* of what is troubling them. This might, for example, involve examining causes and effects or thinking about what has changed in their life recently (Butler and Hope, 1995). Or it could involve *cognitive redefinition*. This is where individuals accept their situation but attempt to find something positive in it. *Cognitive avoidance*, where individuals cope by denying the problem, for example by forgetting it exists, can often be less conscious.

In the second, problem-focused strategies, individuals actively tackle the problems causing their stress. This can involve *obtaining guidance* by talking the problem through with friends or family. It might involve taking *direct action*. One form of effective direct action identified by Bunce and West (1996) in work groups was *role innovation*. They found individuals who had innovated in their roles by introducing new skills or procedures demonstrated improvements in work-related stress. Some individuals tackle the problem by *developing alternative rewards*, substituting rewards which had been difficult to obtain with rewards which are more readily obtainable.

The third, emotion-focused, strategy might be adopted if it seems little can be done to modify the problem. Here emotional defences are engaged which help individuals manage their anxieties. First, by *affective regulation* individuals try to avoid paying attention to them—perhaps best summed up as showing a 'stiff upper lip'. Secondly, by *resigned acceptance* individuals can stoically accept the situation and expect that the worst is likely to occur. Thirdly, by using *palliatives* such as smoking, daydreaming, taking a day off, or overeating, individuals may find their problems more tolerable. Finally, individuals can attempt to cope with their emotions through *emotional discharge*—'letting off steam'. This form of coping, however, can involve behaviour—such as spreading rumours, losing one's temper, being over-critical, damaging property and violence—which can actually increase the problems an individual faces.

This classification emphasizes the distinction between active and passive coping strategies—changing the environment or distorting one's view of reality. Investigations of the relationship between coping strategies and stress outcomes have demonstrated that individuals using the active appraisal or problem-focused strategies experience fewer harmful physical and psychological outcomes than those using the passive avoidance methods (e.g. Quick *et al.*, 1990; Bunce and West, 1996).

Classifications like the one above provide those involved in stress counselling with a useful conceptual framework for exploring an individual's coping strategy. The availability of simple pencil and paper tests identifying an individual's coping strategy provide individuals with helpful, objective feedback facilitating awareness and the development of more effective responses to stress.

Interventions in the worksite can have an organizational or individual focus. This distinction has sometimes been characterized as *primary* or *secondary*: organizational methods are designed to remove the source of the stress while secondary methods enable methods enable individuals to cope with it better. Table 2.1 describes some of the types of stress-management programmes and techniques available to organizations and individuals.

As can be seen from Table 2.1 there is a considerable range of interventions possible. Often interventions will include an educational component covering the concept of stress discussed earlier in this chapter—what stress is, the appraisal concept, what causes stress,

---

Organizational focus

Organizing the work task and the work environment (improving communications, autonomy, participation, defining work roles and ensuring manageable workloads);

Applicant screening and selection;

Career guidance;

Continuous training;

Promotion and transfer screening;

Mentoring and coaching;

Courses aimed at management to improve management skills and generally and specifically the ability to recognize the symptoms of stress in others;

Sick-leave policy;

Staff attitude surveys;

Career and succession planning strategies.

Individual focus

Specific medical examination before appointment;

Stress education covering nutrition and weight control, smoking, alcohol and caffeine reduction;

Fitness and exercise training;

Support after traumatic events;

Individual counselling;

Assertiveness training;

Biofeedback;

Positive self-talk;

Imagery training;

Progressive muscle relaxation (see Box 2.1).

Table 2.1 Worksite stress-management interventions

and how it manifests itself. This can constitute the intervention itself but more normally is the introduction to one of the more specific techniques outlined in the table.

Physical exercise, fitness, and nutritional advice were initially offered by organizations in the context of general health-promotion programmes. But evaluation of these programmes also found them to be extremely useful for individuals as a method of coping with stress. For example, in an early study of NASA employees the researcher found after a year of regularly using exercise facilities provided on the site, individuals taking part in the programme reported less stress and indicated they felt able to handle work pressures more effectively (Durbeck *et al.*, 1972). Subsequent research has confirmed the beneficial effects of exercise.

Selye (1975) suggested the reduction in stress produced by exercise stems from what he called the *cross-resistance effect*, whereby the increased strength of one bodily system or process has an impact on another bodily system or process, and thus affords organisms some physical protection from environmental stressors.

Biofeedback, progressive muscle relaxation, meditation, and imagery training are all methods of controlling arousal and inducing relaxation. Biofeedback involves measuring pulse, blood pressure, or the activity of sweat glands and providing immediate feed-

Box 2.1 Progressive muscle relaxation

Whilst relaxation is an obvious antidote to stress, for many individuals relaxing is actually quite difficult. We know we *should* relax but many of us do not know *how to*. Progressive Muscle Relaxation (PMR) is thus a useful stress-management skill as it teaches individuals the 'how to'. It was developed in the 1920s by a doctor, Edmund Jacobson. Studying electrical activity in muscles Jacobson noticed many individuals had a considerable level of activity or what he termed residual tension even when they were asked to sit and relax. Many of us experience this as never really feeling comfortable, even in our favourite chair at home. Jacobson found his technique helped individuals achieve total muscle relaxation. PMR is based on the finding that if muscles are tensed they return to a more relaxed state when the tension is released. The technique, once acquired and practised, produces a profound, refreshing, and pleasant sense of relaxation. Jacobson believed his technique also helped reduce psychological tension—mental relaxation following on from physical relaxation. An additional benefit of PMR is that it helps individuals become more aware of their muscular tension, i.e. individuals start to notice which muscles tend to get more tense than others, which tend to stay tense, and which are more difficult to relax.

Ideally PMR should be practised for twenty to thirty minutes twice a day. From my experience of running these sessions with groups of managers one problem can be that individuals fall asleep. To reduce the risk of this avoid PMR for an hour after eating. To avoid cramp it is also best not to try PMR if the room is cold and your muscles are tired.

The basic technique is:

1. Separately tense an individual muscle group.
2. Hold the tension for roughly five seconds.
3. Release the tension slowly and at the same time say silently, 'Relax and let go'.
4. Take a deep breath.
5. As you slowly breathe out say silently 'Relax and let go'.

This can be applied to any of the muscle groups in turn (head, neck, shoulders, arms and hands, chest and lungs, back, stomach, hips and legs, and feet) and to the entire body.

A PMR session starts with participants getting as comfortable as possible and loosening any tight clothing. Legs should be slightly apart. Slowly open your mouth and move your jaw from side to side. Now let your mouth close keeping your teeth slightly apart. As you do this take a deep breath and then slowly let the air slip out. When you are tightening one part of your body try to have all the other muscles limp and loose.

Individuals develop preferences for whether they work up or down the body. But generally a PMR session would start with tensing and relaxing all the muscles in the body at once and then moving on to each of the muscle groups in turn.

Total Body PMR

First tense every part of your body. Tense your jaw muscles, eyes, arms, hands, chest, back, stomach, legs, and feet. Feel the tension all over your body . . . hold the tension briefly and then silently say, 'Relax and let go . . . ' as you breathe out . . . let your whole body relax . . . Feel a wave of calm come over you as you stop tensing. Sense the relief.

Gently close your eyes and take another deep breath . . . notice the tension as you hold your breath . . . Slowly breathe out and silently say 'Relax and let go . . . ' Notice the sense of relaxation. Let yourself drift more and more with this sense of relaxation . . . As you progress you will exercise different parts of your body. Become aware of your body and its tension and relaxation. This will help you to become deeply relaxed on command.

Shoulders PMR

Tension in the neck and shoulders is very common. PMR for the shoulders is thus particularly important. First shrug your shoulders up trying to touch your ears with your shoulders. Feel the tension in your shoulders and in your neck. Hold the tension . . . Now relax and let go. As you do this, feel the shoulders becoming more relaxed. Take a deep breath. Hold it, then silently say 'Relax and let go' as you slowly breathe out.

Notice the difference, how the tension is giving way to relaxation. Move your right shoulder up trying to touch your right ear. Feel the tension in your right shoulder and along the right side of your neck. Hold the tension . . . Now, relax and let go. Take a deep breath. Hold it, then silently say, 'Relax and let go' as you slowly breathe out.

Next move your left shoulder up trying to touch your left ear. Feel the tension in your left shoulder and along the left side of your neck. Hold the tension . . . Now relax and let go. Take a deep breath. Hold it, then silently say 'Relax and let go' as you slowly breathe out. Feel the relaxation pouring into the shoulders. As you progress through your other muscles you will become looser and more and more relaxed.

This basic technique can be applied to the other muscle groups. Here is how these muscles are tensed. Follow each tensing with steps 1–5 above.

Head	Neck
1. Wrinkle your forehead	1. Push your head back into your chair.
2. Squint your eyes tightly.	2. Bring your head forward to touch your chest
3. Open your mouth wide.	

Head

4. Push your tongue against roof of your mouth.
5. Clench your jaw tightly.

Arms and hands

1. Hold your arms out and make a fist with each hand.
2. One side at a time, push your hands down into the surface where you are practising.
3. One side at a time, make a fist, bend your arm at the elbow, tighten up your arm while holding the fist.

Stomach

1. Tighten your stomach area.
2. Push your stomach area out.
3. Pull your stomach area in

Neck

3. Roll you head to your right shoulder.
4. Roll your head to your left shoulder.

Chest and lungs

1. Take a deep breath
2. Tighten your chest muscles.

Back muscles

1. Arch your back.

Hips, legs, and feet

1. Tighten your hips.
2. Push the heels of your feet into the surface where you are practising.
3. Tighten your leg muscles below the knee
4. Curl your toes under as if to touch the bottom of your feet.
5. Bring your toes up as if to touch your knees

PMR, whilst very effective, does require a good deal of commitment (up to an hour each day). But it does repay practice and effort. For example, individuals who have acquired the technique can relax muscles differentially, enabling them to carry on using needed muscles, for example using those required to drive a car but reducing tension in un-needed ones such as facial muscles. This enables skilled PMR users to relax muscles as soon as they notice them becoming tense. This means that once the technique is acquired it is possible to utilize it in a wider range of environments, helping to replace tension with relaxation throughout the day.

back. With practice individuals can gain some degree or control over these. Relaxation techniques such as PMR or imagery training are methods designed to help individuals gain control of their internal stress response. More details of PMR are provided in Box 2.1. In imagery training people try and quiet their minds down by imagining being in a restful place. Techniques of positive self-talk (concentrating, for example, on reasons to be optimistic), assertiveness training, and time management aim to enhance an individual's appraisal of a situation and analysis of the resources he or she has available to meet job demands.

One key question is obviously the extent to which any of these techniques transfers to the workplace. For example, the control an individual acquires over his or her physiological arousal in an off-site setting seems to be easily disrupted by stressors present at work. Additionally, considerable commitment is required to acquire relaxation techniques like PMR and then to continue practising them both inside and outside the workplace.

Even when worksite programmes appear able to produce reductions in self-reported and objectively measured levels of stress, it is often difficult to establish why the improvements have occurred (e.g. Murphy, 1996; Bunce, 1997). The fact that many programmes use more than one of the methods in Table 2.1 makes it difficult to disentangle the effects of any one of them.

Research on worksite stress-management programmes also indicates that control groups often show as many changes on physiological and self-reported psychological measures of stress as the experimental groups. This implies that a number of the effects, over and above the specific factors being tested for, are operating to reduce stress levels. These might include non-specific but common elements of training, such as sitting in a comfortable position, the intention to relax, a credible training strategy, and motivation due to self-selection into the study.

It is clear, however, that individually focused programmes are effective in reducing both physiological and psychological manifestations of strain (Bunce, 1997). Unfortunately, it is difficult to identify what precisely the active ingredients of the programmes have been. This is because there seems to be amongst single technique approaches a good deal of what is termed outcome equivalence. In other words, on the majority of outcome measures little variation exists between different treatment approaches. This is partly because of common components unrelated to the technical content of the programme, but some of the outcome equivalence can also be attributed to very poor research design which, with a few notable exceptions, plagues stress-management research.

What has also recently emerged from stress-management research is the fact that the use of multi-method approaches in which two or more techniques are combined appears to be superior in producing more consistent and positive effects than single technique approaches (Murphy, 1996). This is particularly the case in the methods employing contrasting techniques, for example by combining arousal reduction and personal skills training through role-play techniques. These results suggest that the effects of combining techniques are multiplicative rather than additive.

Although currently it is difficult to say exactly why worksite stress-management interventions work there is at least evidence that they do. Additionally, it is clear that the reduced absenteeism and other benefits related to reductions in stress more than repay the costs of such programmes to organizations. One early study suggested the cost–benefit ratio was as high as 1 : 5—each £1 spent was equivalent to £5 saved (National Institute for Occupational Safety and Health, 1987).

The major criticism individually oriented programmes face comes from writers who argue that organizations can use these methods to adapt employees to poorly designed work environments and so avoid the need for more radical reorganization. Instead they suggest more attention should be given to the strategies in the first part of Table 2.1 which reduce the prevalence of objective stressors in organizations by increasing communication, participation, autonomy, and training.

Although this represents a valid criticism there are at least two reasons why the need for individually focused occupational stress-management programmes remains. First, many stressors cannot be designed out of organizations: for example, deadlines like the end of a financial year. And secondly, many organizations are unwilling to change their structure and practices, which means individually focused stress-management programmes are the only way of reducing occupational stress and improving employee well-being.

Whilst the distinction between organizational and individual strategies has been emphasized, the most effective approaches may well be those which straddle the two domains. These will be interventions at the organizational level which empower individuals to target the stressful aspects of their environments for themselves. Such strategies could, for example, include providing increased autonomy and thus enhancing an individual's ability to identify ways of innovating adaptively in his or her role.

Conclusion

Whilst we have dealt exclusively with stress in this chapter it is a subject which resonates with many of the themes and issues which appear throughout this book. Stress is, as we have seen, the outcome of some of the dominant characteristics of modern market economies—uncertainty, high demands, and low control. And it is not, as sometimes suggested in the media, restricted to certain occupational groups, such as executives in high-pressure jobs. In fact, some of the most stressful jobs are those where demands are high and control is low—urban bus driving, for example. Nor is stress simply 'out there'; rather it is the result of an interaction between an individual's emotional, intellectual, social, and physical resources and the demands on him or her. But, as we have also seen, some organizational arrangements, particularly those characterized by uncertainty, are more likely to be experienced as stressful.

We are not passive recipients of environmental demand. Indeed, Selye—the 'pope' of stress research—believed that some stress, what he termed 'eustress', was actually beneficial. It motivates us to get things done and not make mistakes, which fits with the idea of us functioning best under moderate stimulation (although what constitutes moderate varies significantly between individuals, as we will see in the next chapter). Individuals develop their own coping strategies, some more effective than others, and increasingly organizations are using stress-management techniques to encourage effective coping. These can be *primary*—dealing with the source of the problem through better work design—or *secondary*—providing individuals with enhanced coping skills.

These reduce the need for what Murphy (1996) described as *tertiary* programmes, which are those which essentially take place in hospitals and out-patient clinics.

Because the links with other areas of research are increasingly being recognized, stress will become a more central topic in the future. For example, those involved in work design recognize that one of the effects of the new manufacturing initiatives could well be increased problem-solving and attentional demands (often combined with low control) on operatives. Similarly, those involved in job satisfaction research now recognize stress as an extreme indication of low job satisfaction. Whilst these researchers traditionally focused on the relationship between their measures of satisfaction and productivity or staff turnover, a key outcome variable now is as likely to be stress and poor mental health.

What would seem to be both important and urgent is for a new generation of stress-management research. With a few notable exceptions this area of research has been undermined by sloppy design, poor specification of the technical content of a programme, and inadequate sampling and measurement. What future research needs to do is identify what the active ingredients of stress-management programmes are. Some careful research producing hard empirical evidence might help reduce some of the cynicism about the value of such interventions which makes training directors and managers often reluctant to purchase worksite stress-management programmes. This means for many employees tertiary programmes are the inevitable consequence of a lack of worksite provision.

Study questions for Chapter 2

1 Is stress a stimulus or a response?

2 Is there a 'stress prone' personality?

3 How can roles become stressful?

4 Is too much or too little stimulation at work inherently stressful?

5 Is stress largely a white collar/managerial problem?

6 Could stress largely be designed out of most jobs?

7 What makes worksite stress-management programmes more likely to be effective?

Further reading

Cassidy, T. (1999) *Stress Cognition and Health*. London: Routledge.

Crandall, R. and Perrewé, P. L. (eds.) (1995) *Occupational Stress: A Handbook*. Washington DC: Taylor and Francis.

Frankenhaeuser, M., Lundberg, U., and Chesney, M. (eds.) (1991) *Women, Work and Health: Stress and Opportunities*. New York: Plenum Press.

Goldery, C. and Breznifz, S. (eds.) (1993) *Handbook of Stress*, 2nd edn. New York: Free Press.

Karasek, R. and Theorell, T. (1990) *Healthy Work: Stress, Productivity and the Reconstruction of Working Life*. New York: Basic Books.

Kets de Vries, M. F. R. (1995) *Life and Death in the Executive Fast Lane*. San Francisco: Jossey-Bass.

Lazarus, R. S., and Folkman, S. (1984) *Stress Appraisal and Coping*. New York: Springer.

Meichenbaum, D. (1997) *Treating Post-Traumatic Stress Disorder: A Handbook and Practice Manual for Therapy*. Chichester: Wiley.

Schabraig, M. J., Winnubst, A. M., and Cooper, C. L. (eds.) (1996) *Handbook of Work and Health Psychology*. Chichester: Wiley.

3 Individual Differences

Summary points and learning objectives

By the end of this chapter you will be able to

- understand the notion of the normal distribution and factor analysis;
- define the concept of personality;
- describe the main dimensions of personality identified with factor analysis;
- understand the main contributions of Freud and his followers to our understanding of personality;
- identify ways in which psychodynamic concepts are relevant to an understanding of workplace behaviour;
- describe some of the ways in which our social learning affects our personality;
- define intelligence and indicate how psychological and common-sense definitions of intelligence are different;
- understand the concept of G;
- distinguish between general and special abilities (aptitudes);
- discuss the impact of differences in intelligence on effectiveness at work.

Introduction

While many psychologists attempt to identify processes which are common to all individuals—the way information is processed and stored, for example—others are preoccupied by the differences they observe between people. In general, because of the practical applications in clinical, educational, and work settings, the study of individual differences has concentrated on two areas: personality and intelligence.

Common to the study of both are a number of key assumptions. The first is that although individuals are *unique* they are also *consistent*; character and intelligence are developed early and remain much the same throughout adult life (Costa and McCrae, 1997; Eder and Mangelsdorf, 1997). Thus, the bright, sociable child should become a bright, sociable adult. Secondly, although differences between individuals' intellectual capabilities and personalities seem bewilderingly complex, there are, in fact, just a few *underlying dimensions* along which these attributes vary. And finally, reducing the com-

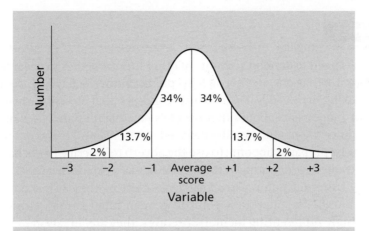

Figure 3.1 The typical curve of a normally distributed variable
Normally distributed variables produce this characteristic bell-shaped curve. With a measure of dispersion—the standard deviation—it is possible to calculate the proportion of the population falling above or below a particular point on the scale. It can be seen that 68 per cent of the population fall within +1 and −1 standard deviation of the average score for the population.

plexity of observed differences between individuals is usually achieved by making the assumption that individual differences are *normally distributed* (Figure 3.1).

The idea that the normal distribution—which had been shown to apply to physical characteristics such as height and weight—could also be applied to psychological attributes was first suggested by Francis Galton (1822–1911). By assuming a normal distribution, psychologists can use sophisticated statistical techniques which both identify connections between aspects of personality or intelligence and describe an underlying set of personality or intelligence *factors* which explain the observed associations.

In the workplace the study of individual differences is useful in at least two ways. First, a sounder basis for the prediction and understanding of behaviour can help those whose jobs involve dealing with other people. Secondly, it is important to have the best possible match between the people's personalities and intellectual abilities and their jobs, since a bad match leads to poor performance and stress. Thus the ability to identify and measure the individual differences associated with high job performance enables organizations to select and recruit individuals with these attributes.

In this chapter we will examine the extent to which psychologists have managed to identify the key dimensions of personality and intelligence and what relationships these dimensions have with job performance.

Personality

We at all times need to develop accounts of other human beings in order to make sense of their current behaviour or to be able to predict future behaviour. To do this, often without realizing it, we develop and use concepts that describe their personality. Normally our judgements about other people's personalities are based on their behaviour. For instance we might say, 'she behaved *conscientiously*'. If she often behaves like this we might be prepared not only to use the adverb to describe her behaviour but also to employ the adjective *conscientious* to describe her as a person. Eventually, we may find ourselves—by using the noun *conscientiousness*—inferring the existence in her of something called a *trait*. The important point to bear in mind is that, although traits are nouns, seemingly representing mental structures, they are, in fact, *dispositional concepts* which reflect a person's characteristic behaviour.

Psychologists define personality as *the relatively enduring combination of traits which makes an individual unique and at the same time produces consistencies in his or her thought and behaviour.*

Normally, if asked to produce character descriptions we would be unlikely to apply the same traits to each person, since some would appear highly relevant to some people but not to others. Each individual would probably elicit a unique set of traits. This is termed an *idiographic* description. This type of description also occurs in certain professional contexts, psychiatry for example, where each patient's character is explored in considerable depth. Many psychologists, however, use what are termed *nomothetic* descriptions where a trait is applied universally. The advantage of this approach is that it enables standardized assessments of groups of individuals such as job applicants, to be made.

In this section we will examine three perspectives that have made significant contributions to our understanding of personality.

Firstly, from the nomothetic perspective, we will describe some dimensions of personality produced by a statistical technique known as factor analysis. Secondly, we will outline the model of personality developed within the idiographic tradition by Sigmund Freud. His view of the developmental processes which shape people's personalities from childhood has been both controversial and influential since its appearance eighty years ago. And finally, returning to the nomothetic perspective, we will examine some personality dimensions proposed by psychologists who believe that *social learning*—the learning that occurs through interaction with others—has effects that are permanent enough to be considered part of a person's personality.

Personality factors

A major influence on personality research in recent years has been *factor analysis*. This is a sophisticated statistical technique which, its proponents claim, helps identify the basic underlying building-blocks of personality. Although there are misgivings about the technique (e.g. Gould, 1981) it has none the less driven much of personality research in the last fifty years. Indeed, some psychologists would argue that the only way to describe personality differences scientifically is with concepts derived from factor analysis.

A factor analysis of personality begins by collecting data from a large sample of individuals. Data could be 'self-report', i.e. responses to questionnaires, or objective, e.g. performance on a test of detail consciousness such as a proof-reading exercise. It could also include what Cattell (1967) referred to as life data such as ratings of academic achievements.

The next step is to identify what associations exist between the various measures. This is achieved by calculating the correlation between two sets of scores. A correlation coefficient indicates the strength of any linear relationship between two measures. It varies from +1.00, a perfect positive relationship in which individuals' position on one scale corresponds exactly with their position on the other, through 0.00 where there is no relationship between subjects' scores on the two measures, to −1.00, a perfect negative relationship in which the subject's position on one scale is the opposite of his or her position on the other (Figure 3.2). Thus, for example, there may well be a positive correlation between the behavioural measure of party-going and the trait scale patient–impatient, subjects who attend numerous parties also tending to rate themselves as impatient.

The third stage of a factor analysis is the construction of a *correlation matrix* in which the correlation between each of the behavioural measures or rating scales is plotted against all the others used in the survey (Figure 3.3).

A factor analysis then attempts, by using some sophisticated mathematics, to identify the smallest number of *factors* that need to be postulated to explain the pattern of associations found in the correlation matrix. Factors are given names by examining which of the original behavioural measures or rating scales correlate best with the factor—although some researchers prefer to invent names for their factors to remind us that we are dealing with statistical abstractions that may not necessarily correspond exactly to the psychological make-up of individuals or our existing language system.

An example of a questionnaire based on a factor analysis of personality data can be found in Box 3.1. Current orthodoxy is that much of the variation we observe between each other's personalities can be 'explained' with just five factors. Indeed, there is now intense interest in what is termed the *big five*. Many psychologists see the big five as an important integrating taxonomy—a common language for those involved in personality research and its applications in clinical, educational, and occupational settings (Wiggins and Trapnell, 1997).

Extraversion–introversion

Nearly all of the popular multi-dimensional questionnaires in some way measure extraversion–introversion. Even outside the factor-analytic tradition this has long been seen as a key difference between individuals (Jung, 1927; James, 1907). The extravert is essen-

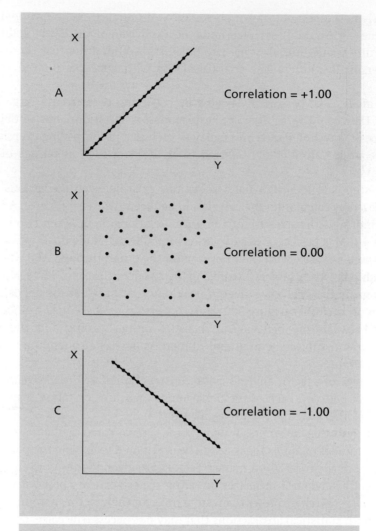

Figure 3.2 Correlation representing the association between two variables

In A and C, subjects' scores on variable X and Y are perfectly correlated (directly in the former and inversely in the latter). In B, however, there is no relationship between individuals' scores on the two scales.

tially sociable, energetic, socially confident, and cheerful, whereas the introvert is more quiet, self-contained, serious-minded, and somewhat aloof.

Extraversion–introversion, as with the other four factors, is a dimension which is assumed to be normally distributed. In other words, whilst there are individuals at the extremes of the continuum most of us are in the middle—ambiverts—who from time to time can demonstrate the characteristic behaviours of either extreme.

Tests	2	3	4	5	6	7	8	9
1	0.4	0.6	0.0	0.1	0.1	0.1	0.1	0.1
2		0.4	0.4	0.3	0.4	0.1	0.2	0.1
3			0.1	0.0	0.2	0.1	0.1	0.1
4				0.3	0.6	0.0	0.1	0.1
5					0.4	0.1	0.1	0.2
6						0.0	0.0	0.0
7							0.5	0.4
8								0.4

Figure 3.3 An example of a correlation matrix
The outlined figures represent significant correlations between scores on tests; three groups of correlations indicate the presence of three underlying factors (based on Guilford, 1967).

Box 3.1 Five-factor inventory

Instructions
Below is a list of adjectives. Read each adjective and tick the description which fits you best.
SD = Strongly Disagree; D= Disagree; N = Neutral; A = Agree; SA = Strongly Agree.

	SD	D	N	A	SA
1. Carefree	[4]	[3]	[2]	[1]	[0]
2. Sociable	[0]	[1]	[2]	[3]	[4]
3. Realistic	[4]	[3]	[2]	[1]	[0]
4. Courteous	[0]	[1]	[2]	[3]	[4]
5. Neat	[0]	[1]	[2]	[3]	[4]
6. Inferior	[0]	[1]	[2]	[3]	[4]
7. Jolly	[0]	[1]	[2]	[3]	[4]
8. Systematic	[4]	[3]	[2]	[1]	[0]
9. Argumentative	[4]	[3]	[2]	[1]	[0]
10. Structured	[0]	[1]	[2]	[3]	[4]
11. Anxious	[0]	[1]	[2]	[3]	[4]

	SD	D	N	A	SA
12. Serious	[4]	[3]	[2]	[1]	[0]
13. Artistic	[0]	[1]	[2]	[3]	[4]
14. Self-centred	[4]	[3]	[2]	[1]	[0]
15. Disorderly	[4]	[3]	[2]	[1]	[0]
16. Happy	[4]	[4]	[2]	[1]	[0]
17. Communicative	[0]	[1]	[2]	[3]	[4]
18. Broad-minded	[0]	[1]	[2]	[3]	[4]
19. Co-operative	[0]	[1]	[2]	[3]	[4]
20. Conscientious	[0]	[1]	[2]	[3]	[4]
21. Nervous	[0]	[1]	[2]	[3]	[4]
22. Gregarious	[0]	[1]	[2]	[3]	[4]
23. Cultured	[0]	[1]	[2]	[3]	[4]
24. Sceptical	[4]	[3]	[2]	[1]	[0]
25. Methodical	[0]	[1]	[2]	[3]	[4]
26. Worthless	[0]	[1]	[2]	[3]	[4]
27. Private	[4]	[3]	[2]	[1]	[0]
28. Experimental	[0]	[1]	[2]	[3]	[4]
29. Cynical	[4]	[3]	[2]	[1]	[0]
30. Restless	[4]	[3]	[2]	[1]	[0]
31. Confident	[4]	[3]	[2]	[1]	[0]
32. Energetic	[0]	[1]	[2]	[3]	[4]
33. Inquiring	[0]	[1]	[2]	[3]	[4]
34. Popular	[0]	[1]	[2]	[3]	[4]
35. Determined	[0]	[1]	[2]	[3]	[4]
36. Angry	[0]	[1]	[2]	[3]	[4]
37. Cheerful	[0]	[1]	[2]	[3]	[4]
38. Traditional	[4]	[3]	[2]	[1]	[0]
39. Calculating	[4]	[3]	[2]	[1]	[0]
40. Committed	[0]	[1]	[2]	[3]	[4]
41. Disheartened	[0]	[1]	[2]	[3]	[4]
42. Pessimistic	[4]	[3]	[2]	[1]	[0]
43. Imaginative	[0]	[1]	[2]	[3]	[4]
44. Hard-headed	[4]	[3]	[2]	[1]	[0]
45. Unreliable	[4]	[3]	[2]	[1]	[0]
46. Optimistic	[4]	[3]	[2]	[1]	[0]
47. Dynamic	[0]	[1]	[2]	[3]	[4]
48. Pragmatic	[4]	[3]	[2]	[1]	[0]
49. Considerate	[0]	[1]	[2]	[3]	[4]
50. Productive	[0]	[1]	[2]	[3]	[4]
51. Helpless	[0]	[1]	[2]	[3]	[4]
52. Active	[0]	[1]	[2]	[3]	[4]
53. Curious	[0]	[1]	[2]	[3]	[4]

		SD	D	N	A	SA
54.	Forthright	[4]	[3]	[2]	[1]	[0]
55.	Disorganized	[4]	[3]	[2]	[1]	[0]
56.	Self-conscious	[0]	[1]	[2]	[3]	[4]
57.	Independent	[4]	[3]	[2]	[1]	[0]
58.	Theoretical	[0]	[1]	[2]	[3]	[4]
59.	Manipulative	[4]	[3]	[2]	[1]	[0]
60.	Perfectionist	[0]	[1]	[2]	[3]	[4]

Interpreting your score

Add up your total score for each factor.

Your Extraversion score is the total of your score on questions—
2, 7, 12, 17, 22, 27, 32, 37, 42, 47, 52, 57.

Your Neuroticism/Stability score is the total of your score on questions—
1, 6, 11, 16, 21, 26, 31, 36, 41, 46, 51, 56.

Your Openness to Experience score is the total of your score on questions—
3, 8, 13, 18, 23, 28, 33, 38, 43, 48, 53, 58.

Your Agreeableness score is the total of your score on questions—
4, 9, 14, 19, 24, 29, 34, 39, 44, 49, 54, 59.

Your Conscientiousness score is the total of your score on questions—
5, 10, 15, 20, 25, 30, 35, 40, 45, 50, 55, 60.

To interpret your score, tick the box corresponding to the high, average, and low score range. Remember this is necessarily a very rough estimate of your position on these factors. And the implications of score depends very much on other variables such as organizational culture and job demands.

Compared with others your responses suggest:

	High (31 or more)	Average (25–30)	Low (0–24)
Extroversion	Sociable, outgoing, happy-go-lucky, lively, and energetic. You like to have a lot going on at any one time.	Your willingness to be outgoing depends very much on the situation and who you are with.	Your general preference is your own company or to be with a small circle of friends or family. You prefer to focus on one activity at a time.
	High (25 or more)	**Average (15–24)**	**Low (0–14)**
Neuroticism	You experience strong feelings which you may sometimes find difficult to channel effectively. You can be tough on your-	You have a reasonable ability to keep your feelings in control, and generally you are able to keep a sense of perspective.	You have an ability to cope well with pressure. Your presence during times of crisis can be reassuring for others. You may run

	self and can allow small things to get under your skin.		the risk of seeing too unaffected and 'laid back' at times.
	High (30 or more)	**Average (25–29)**	**Low (0–24)**
Openness to experience	You have a strong intellectual curiosity. You like new ideas. You enjoy taking a broad analytical approach to problems.	You attempt to balance an interest in ideas with the practical demands of the situation. Reasonably change-oriented but you do not believe in change for its own sake.	Your focus is very much more on the practical and immediate require-ments of a situation. No one would accuse you of day-dreaming or of losing touch with what is going on around you. You may sometimes run the risk of getting too bogged down in detail.
	High (36 or more)	**Average (30–35)**	**Low (0–29)**
Agreeableness	Tender-minded, easy to work with, accepting and tolerant of those around you. A natural 'team player'.	Reasonably friendly and trusting of those around you, but there are people you find more difficult to relate to.	Hard-nosed, tough-minded, and some-times unforgiving. You prefer to keep individuals at 'arms' length'. Others would say you do not suffer fools gladly.
	High (40 or more)	**Average (31–39)**	**Low (0–39)**
Conscientiousness	Dependable, hardworking, you have a strong sense of obligation and duty. You expect a lot of yourself and try to live up to the expectations others have of you. You have a strong need for order and predictability in your environment.	Reasonably conforming, self-disciplined, and organized, but there are times when you are willing to overlook a system or procedure if it does not seem to be serving a purpose.	You are a free-wheeling individual who can be highly individualistic in approach. You prefer to figure things out as you go along rather than make detailed plans in advance. You can tolerate change, unpredictability, and ambiguity in your environment.

Extraversion–introversion is a broadly based factor and inevitably, over the years, there have been disagreements between factorists about exactly what specific traits correlate with it. Hans Eysenck (1916–1997) a fierce, lifelong advocate of factor analysis, had 'the need for stimulation' at the core of his extraversion factor. For Eysenck, extraverts differed from introverts because they were more 'stimulus hungry'. They therefore sought out environments which provided the level of sensory stimulation they needed to remain alert. This would be manifested behaviourally in a number of ways. Extraverts would be more sociable, preferring to go to a party than read a book. They would be more active, engaging in a variety of social and physical activities. But alongside this affiliativeness and 'liveliness' there was, for Eysenck, an impulsive, risk-oriented facet to extraversion. Extraverts were thus likely to be less responsible and less self- and emotionally disciplined. More recently, the affective or emotional content of the dimension has been seen as the core of the factor. In this more current conception, the traits correlating with the factor are seen as sharing a common positive emotional component. The extravert is now seen in more positive terms. The Eysenckian extravert was potentially unreliable, poorly adapted, and 'under socialized'. The current view, perhaps partly reflecting shifts in normative assumptions about socially desirable behaviour, is that extraversion is indicative of an individual's adaptation to life. Extraverts are seen as more effectively engaged with the world than introverts. They essentially have more capacity for joy and pleasure.

The traits now seen as defining extraversion are:

1. *Venturesomeness*—extraverts are more socially confident than introverts. This means they are more socially adventurous and thick-skinned. This, for example, enables them to project themselves more confidently in groups or when with unfamiliar individuals. Being more confident they enjoy change, excitement, and variety, meeting new people for example, more than their more introverted peers.

2. *Affiliativeness*—extraverts are more warm, friendly, and attentive than introverts, who may appear relatively detached, cold, and aloof by contrast. Whilst introverts prefer more 'arms' length' dealings with others at work, extraverts tend to prefer closer involvement. The strong affiliative element of extraverts means they tend to have a wide range of friends. The affiliative needs of introverts are normally met by a smaller circle of friends and family.

3. *Energy*—extraverts tend to prefer to have too much rather than too little to do. Whilst introverts prefer to focus on one task extraverts prefer to have a number of projects and activities on the go at any one time. Extraverts therefore enjoy work which provides variety, for example, opportunities for travel or multi-tasking.

4. *Ascendance*—extraverts, being more confident and affiliative, tend also to be more assertive than their more introverted peers. This enables them not only to come through more strongly in groups, not minding being the centre of attention, but also to get behind their opinions with some vigour. Extraverts, therefore, tend to be more dominant than introverts.

The extraversion–introversion factor thus provides a useful way of summarizing a range of important traits which tend to go together. Whilst the factor is statistically well defined it represents a *description* rather than an *explanation*. What is required is a theoretical rationale for the factor. We need to answer the question, where does it come from and so what more fundamentally does it psychologically represent?

For Eysenck the answers lay in our biology and ultimately in our genetic make-up. He saw an individual's position on this dimension as essentially representing his or her level of *cortical arousal*. This could be thought of as the mental equivalent of muscle tone. The cortex, the conscious, thinking part of our brain, is kept alert by being sprayed with signals from, in evolutionary terms, a much older part of our brain, the ascending reticular activating system (ARAS). Eysenck argued that extraverts have a sluggish ARAS, introverts an overactive one. This means introverts are more receptive to incoming signals. Extraverts therefore require more going on around them for their brains to function adequately. This also means extraverts are more likely to habituate to stimuli and have what are termed micro-sleeps—switching off for a few seconds. To remain alert extraverts need to shift their attention to a number of sources of stimuli. Conversely, introverts who are already reasonably alert need less going on around them and so are less prone to switching their attention.

Eysenck argued that much of the impact of this *physiological* difference on *psychological* differences between individuals arose from its effect on 'conditionability', introverts being more receptive and easier to condition than extraverts. This implied introverts are constitutionally more likely to assimilate through conditioning, the rules, obligations, and attitudes of their social environment. Conversely, the impact of socialization on extraverts is attenuated by their weaker conditionability. Extraverts are therefore less likely to acquire conforming and conscientious behaviour patterns than introverts. The connection between physiology and introversion–extraversion has not been straightforwardly established. Streslau and Eysenck (1987), reviewing a number of studies, were able to find some support for the hypothesized relationship, but other studies and reviews have provided inconsistent support (e.g. Claridge, 1970; Green, 1997).

With many ways of assessing the activity level of the cortex some physiological measures have supported Eysenck's position more than others. This suggests that the interaction between our physiology and our level of extraversion is the result of several underlying biological components arranged and integrated in a way which is not yet fully understood (Green, 1997). But whilst the precise links between this factor and our physiology are not currently clear, extraversion, whatever its roots, none the less accounts for a considerable proportion of the differences we observe between personalities.

Neuroticism–stability

The second of the 'big five', like extraversion, appears on virtually all factored questionnaires. Again, it should be remembered this factor is also normally distributed, most of us sitting in the middle of the dimension. High scorers on neuroticism scales report a high level of 'negative affect'. This means they are more prone to worry or anxiety and are more likely to perceive themselves as having physical symptoms such as aches and pains.

The more specific traits correlating with the factor are:

1. *Anxiety*—many psychologists distinguish between state and trait anxiety. It is the difference between being anxious right now and often being anxious. High scorers tend to experience both forms of anxiety to a greater extent than low scorers.

2. *Tenseness*—perhaps because of the presence of high state anxiety high-scoring individuals tend to be much more tense and irritable than their lower scoring peers.

3. *Low self-esteem*—high scorers tend to be less self-assured than lower scorers. This means that at work they are less complacent, less arrogant, and less convinced of the social and intellectual resources they have to deal with problems.

4. *Guilt-proneness*—alongside the low self-esteem is a tendency to be more self-critical and self-blaming. When things go wrong high scorers tend to blame themselves more than they blame those around them. Failure for high scorers is therefore more painful than for their more self-assured peers.

5. *Emotional control*—high-scoring individuals experience strong complex feelings which they sometimes find difficult to channel effectively. This means alongside their irritability high scorers can get very frustrated and perhaps lose their tempers. At work this can cause high scorers sometimes to give up rather than confront difficulties.

6. *Irrationality*—the strong negative feelings experienced by high scorers can sometimes mean they get a distorted view of reality, finding it difficult to keep things in perspective. Little problems can take on an importance out of all proportion to their objective reality. This may also make high scorers overly mistrustful of others, and cause them to misread social cues and become suspicious of other people's motives.

7. *Shyness*—the heightened anxiety experienced by the high scorer may load onto social encounters. This might mean there is a degree of fear attached to ordinary social encounters making the high scorer more stiff, self-conscious, and less socially fluent than his or her lower-scoring colleagues.

8. *Moodiness*—the negative affect associated with the factor can mean the high scorer is more subject to considerable mood swings, shifting from feelings of self-pity and depression to having much more positive feelings about life.

Neuroticism–stability has also been seen as having its roots in our biological and genetic make-up. Eysenck saw the factor as a psychological manifestation of the stability of an individual's automatic nervous system (ANS). The ANS is the part of the nervous system not directly under conscious control which carries a number of reflex activities; it is also involved in certain emotional responses. Some individuals inherit a *labile* ANS which responds vigorously to stress and also takes some time to return to its baseline. In addition, they will experience more spontaneous activity, that is, shifts in activation which are not clearly attributable to external events. Conversely, some individuals are born with a *stabile* ANS, characterized by a weaker response to stress, a more rapid return to baseline, and less spontaneous activity. This means individuals with a labile ANS are constitutionally more prone to developing the traits described above. However, the activity of the automatic nervous system and the individual's level of neuroticism–stability do not seem to be as tightly coupled as Eysenck argued. Indeed, some of the coping mechanisms discussed in the last chapter represent important intervening processes moderating the relationship between outside threat and the activity of the ANS.

Conscientious–expedient

This broad underlying factor emerges out of associations between smaller traits such as obedience, persistence, impulse control, planning and organizing, perfectionism, and integrity (honesty). It is a very well-established factor appearing on most factored questionnaires. The high scorer's behaviour, perhaps as a result of familial conditioning, is dominated by the need to live up to other people's and self-imposed expectations. High scorers therefore have a strong sense of obligation and duty. As Hogan and Ones (1997) suggest, high scorers will 'show up for work on time, complete assignments accurately, mow their lawns and keep a balanced cheque book.' Low scorers have less concern with living up to other people's expectations and usually also have fewer self-imposed standards. This makes them more individualistic. They pursue their own agendas and are more willing to overlook or ignore the rules which constrain other people's actions.

In being more concerned with rules, high scorers tend to adopt a more systematic and procedural approach to work. They prefer orderly, predictable environments where there are clear targets, performance strategies, and work roles. Low scorers are less organized, plan less, preferring to figure things out as they go along. They tend to be more flexible and responsive, coping better with turbulent environments and 'fuzzy' work roles.

This fundamental difference in responsiveness to external obligation appeared very strongly in research conducted by the author on a large student population. Out of a number of other predictors of academic success, such as intelligence and previous achievement, conscientiousness was the best single predictor of the likelihood of getting through year one of a degree course. High scorers were those who, when presented with a conflict between social and academic demands, reconciled it by choosing to do what was formally required of them. Low scorers with weaker impulse control, given the choice, for example, between writing an essay or going to a party, often chose the latter, paying the price later in higher failure rates (Rhodes, 1983).

In a work setting low scorers can also adopt fairly expedient strategies. This can make them sometimes seem ill prepared. They are also irritated by rules and regulations or what they see as 'red tape'. Low scorers enjoy finding loopholes—ways of getting around rules. Conversely, the downside of being too high on this factor can be inflexibility, a tendency to play it too much 'by the book'. Additionally, particularly when under pressure, high scorers may feel they cannot do things to their own very high standards and can start to become overly perfectionistic and obsessional. None the less, a high score on this factor is seen as one of the most consistently useful predictors of performance across a wide range of jobs (Barrick and Mount, 1991).

Open to experience–closed to experience

Consistently in factor-analytic studies, a dimension emerges from a broad constellation of traits, which although variously labelled essentially differentiates those who actively seek out new and varied experiences from those who are more closed to experience. Although regularly appearing in studies this factor has none the less been the most difficult to pin down and to describe exactly the meaning of high and low scores. There are, however, enough common themes in the factor descriptions across studies to provide a reasonably satisfactory description of it. High scorers would typically be artists, poets, or indeed anyone with a rich inner world. They have highly developed aesthetic interests which set them apart from low scorers. This concern with the arts and the world of ideas is why the factor has sometimes been called *culture*.

A high scorer tends also to be more analytical and intellectual in their approach to life and work. This has meant the factor has also been labelled *intellect*. It has been seen as the manifestation of intelligence in the personality domain. And indeed there is a correlation between tests of intelligence and openness. But there is more to this factor than intelligence. As McCrae and Costa (1997) point out, open, intelligent individuals are not only able to grasp new ideas but actually *enjoy* doing so, whereas intelligent low scorers, i.e. those more closed to experience, can have highly developed interests but these tend to be in narrow fields. The hallmark of open individuals is the diversity of their interests.

The impact of this difference is noticeable when I am running courses on personality assessment in companies. The course lasts five days and consists of a theoretical element at the beginning of the week followed by practical case-study work. An individual's position on this scale indicates which part of the course he or she will enjoy most and when I might need to work harder to maintain motivation. High scorers prefer the front end, the theoretical component. They enjoy the novel concepts and different ways of looking at personality. Given the choice they would spend longer on elaborating the theoretical and conceptual material. Conversely, low scorers prefer the more practical case-studies. Indeed, to keep the motivation of low scorers high during the theoretical element numerous practical examples are used to illustrate the relevance and concrete application of the theoretical material. Similarly, referring back to the theoretical material retains the motivation of high scorers during the practical case-study work.

Whilst high scorers are potentially more imaginative and creative problem-solvers, low scorers are more practical individuals. Low scorers are more 'hands on' at work with a more down to earth and often more productive approach. However, being too low scoring can mean it is difficult to step back and take a broader more conceptual overview of a problem. But having a very high score can conversely involve being too abstracted, too detached, and not sufficiently grounded in the more practical, immediate, and mundane elements of work. Whilst this factor represents a fundamental way in which our personalities differ not much is understood about where it comes from. At present it is unclear whether an individual's position on this scale is a manifestation of genetic inheritance or conditioning (McCrae and Costa, 1997).

Agreeable–hostile

The fifth factor captures differences in an individual's style of interacting with others. High scorers tend to be good-natured, empathic, co-operative, trusting, and mild-mannered. Low scorers are more irritable, mistrustful, headstrong, tough-minded, and hostile. This factor thus has enormous implications for the quality of an individual's relationships with others. It may therefore seem to have a highly evaluative component—high score, good; low score, bad. There would seem to be few advantages to having a low score. But in some environments low scorers can be highly effective. Their suspiciousness, for example, means they are not easily fooled. They tend not to accept what others tell them at face value. They are better placed to deal with potential or actual conflict. To some extent they expect the worst of others so are not overly disappointed when others let them down. Their urgency and irritability means they are more concerned with getting things done than with the quality of their relationships.

However, the 'prosocial' behaviour of high scorers makes them natural 'team players'. For example, one study of a number of machine crews found high score behaviours such as helping others, sharing expertise, acting as a peacemaker, and keeping in touch with others had a significant impact on performance and the quality of work (Podsakoff *et al.*, 1997). In fact, the highly adaptive nature of agreeableness has led to some speculative explanations of this factor which sees evolution as the process through which it was developed and reinforced to increase the chances of inclusion in the group and therefore survival.

An important finding is the high degree of stability of this factor. An individual's position on this scale seems highly consistent from childhood onwards. This suggests there may well be fundamental biological mechanisms producing the differences captured by this factor. One suggestion is that it reflects how well an individual deals with negative feelings psychologically. However, this is one line of research among a number of neurological and neurochemical mechanisms currently being explored. The limited evidence available on the heritability of some aspects of agreeableness provides further support for the idea that there may well be an inherited biological basis for this fundamental difference in our orientation to other people (Graziano and Eisenberg, 1997).

Many psychologists believe that, taken together, these five broad factors provide an adequate account of the *structure* of personality. However, even within the factor-analytic tradition there are dissenting opinions. Eysenck, for example, over a number of years, developed and tested a three-factor model. This incorporated extraversion and neuroticism but posited a third, psychoticism. He argued that agreeableness and conscientiousness correlate negatively with psychoticism and so are essentially simply facets of his psychoticism factor. Handley's Insight Inventory, also based on factor analysis, uses four broad factors. Whilst Eysenck, Handley, and others have used less than five factors, Raymond Cattell (1916–1998) developed the widely used sixteen-factor model of personality. In Cattell's model the big five appear, to some extent, but are broken down into smaller, somewhat intercorrelated factors. Cattell argues that broad global factors like the big five lose a good deal of more specific information. For example, introversion–extraversion can, as we have seen, be divided into a number of related factors such as affiliativeness, liveliness, social confidence, openness, and group orientation (Factors A, F, H, N, and Q2 in Figure 3.4). Whilst the correlation between these factors will mean an individual who is high A should also be high F and H and low N and

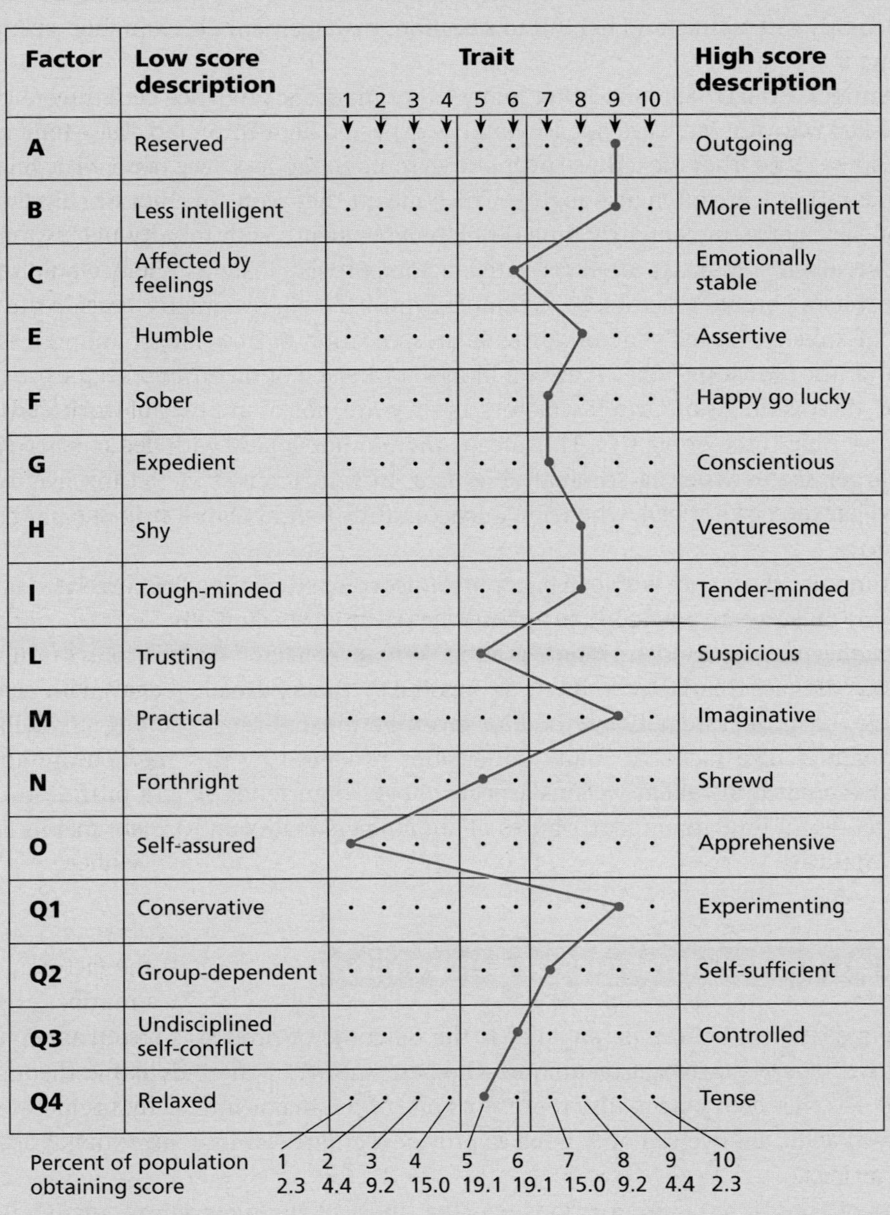

Factor	Low score description	Trait										High score description
		1	2	3	4	5	6	7	8	9	10	
A	Reserved	·	·	·	·	·	·	·	·	·	·	Outgoing
B	Less intelligent	·	·	·	·	·	·	·	·	·	·	More intelligent
C	Affected by feelings	·	·	·	·	·	·	·	·	·	·	Emotionally stable
E	Humble	·	·	·	·	·	·	·	·	·	·	Assertive
F	Sober	·	·	·	·	·	·	·	·	·	·	Happy go lucky
G	Expedient	·	·	·	·	·	·	·	·	·	·	Conscientious
H	Shy	·	·	·	·	·	·	·	·	·	·	Venturesome
I	Tough-minded	·	·	·	·	·	·	·	·	·	·	Tender-minded
L	Trusting	·	·	·	·	·	·	·	·	·	·	Suspicious
M	Practical	·	·	·	·	·	·	·	·	·	·	Imaginative
N	Forthright	·	·	·	·	·	·	·	·	·	·	Shrewd
O	Self-assured	·	·	·	·	·	·	·	·	·	·	Apprehensive
Q1	Conservative	·	·	·	·	·	·	·	·	·	·	Experimenting
Q2	Group-dependent	·	·	·	·	·	·	·	·	·	·	Self-sufficient
Q3	Undisciplined self-conflict	·	·	·	·	·	·	·	·	·	·	Controlled
Q4	Relaxed	·	·	·	·	·	·	·	·	·	·	Tense

Percent of population obtaining score	1	2	3	4	5	6	7	8	9	10
	2.3	4.4	9.2	15.0	19.1	19.1	15.0	9.2	4.4	2.3

Figure 3.4 Cattell's sixteen personality factors

Each individual is profiled on the basis of his or her answers to a questionnaire which takes about thirty-five minutes to complete. Scores for each factor are assumed to be normally distributed, here divided into ten, thus 38.2 per cent of the population fall within the middle band. Since a large amount of data on various occupational groups is available, Cattell's personality factors are used widely in selection and vocational guidance. As well as being predictive of job performance, the profile has also been used to build effective staff and managerial teams. The profile shown here belongs to one of the authors.

Q2, many individuals do not follow this pattern. And it is 'out of place' scores which are particularly interesting and helpful in selection, management development, and counselling.

Heather Cattell (1989) found that many of her marriage guidance clients were low A, i.e. lacked warmth, but were not as would be expected high Q2. In fact these individuals were low Q2, i.e. they lacked warmth but were none the less very dependent on their partners. They were often also high L, which meant they were, in addition, highly critical of their partners. Similarly, in a development setting with managers I have found smaller, albeit somewhat intercorrelated factors, provide insights which would simply get lost using broader factors. For example, whilst the big five might indicate the presence of anxiety, Cattell's factors provide an indication of how longstanding it is and whether the individual takes it out on himself or herself or on others.

The disadvantage of Cattell's factors is they are not as robust mathematically as the larger big three or big five. This means they do not appear with the same clarity as the larger scores when factor-analysing data. In fact, interest in the big five can be traced back to Fiske (1949), who tried unsuccessfully to find Cattell's more complicated structure.

Ultimately, the choice between big, 'pure' uncorrelated and smaller correlated factors depends on subjective judgements about the nature of personality and the context in which the personality description is used. Whatever factor descriptions are used it remains the case that factor-analytic as opposed to 'theory driven' techniques currently provide the most systematic method for investigating differences between individuals' personalities. The fact that many dimensions produced by this method are able to improve predictions about various aspects of behaviour lends weight to the view that they represent fundamental attributes of human personality and are not merely statistical artefacts.

Freud and the dynamics of personality

Many researchers believe personality is the outcome of processes too dynamic to be captured by any statistical technique. The best known of these dynamic theorists is Freud. His theory of personality represents one of the major intellectual achievements in psychology, and we can only hope to provide a glimpse of its complexity, scope and applications.

One of Freud's basic propositions was that most of the material in our minds was housed in what he termed the *subconscious*, a vast repository which for most of the time was inaccessible to us. What was available to individuals in the conscious mind represented just the tip of the iceberg (Figure 3.5). Between the conscious and subconscious mind lies the *pre-conscious*, similar to what we would usually term the 'back of our minds'. Here information is more readily available than if it were in the subconscious. Appointment times or the chores for a day are examples of the sort of items which might be stored in the pre-conscious.

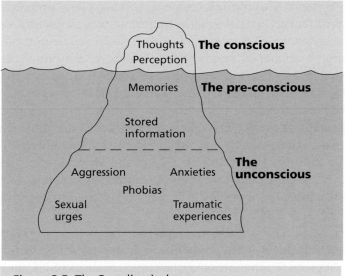

Figure 3.5 The Freudian iceberg

Freud also proposed a tripartite structure for personality, consisting of *id*, *ego* and *superego*. The id is driven by a fixed source of instinctual 'psychic energy' which fuels two innate *drives*: sex and aggression. (It should be noted that what Freud meant when he employed the term 'sex' was very different from its current meaning. Freud meant the term to include all forms of sensual experience and certain 'sublimated' substitutes such as friendship.) The id operates on what Freud termed the *pleasure principle*: it seeks immediate gratification of impulses produced by its two drives.

The social world, however, is not organized in a way that makes this possible; its demands are housed in the ego. Using the *reality principle*, the ego strives to relocate the id's impulses to times or activities in which their gratification is possible. Freud saw the ego as existing only partly in the conscious mind, much of it, like the id, being housed in the subconscious and preconscious.

The superego is also concerned with control of the id and further restricts the range of situations in which the id can be gratified. It differs from the ego in that it incorporates values and morals. Whereas the ego may restrict gratification of the id to a range of feasible situations—for example, the release of aggression in contact sports only—the superego further restricts the range to situations which are morally acceptable as well. This, for example, may mean that boxing is dropped from the set of contact sports in which aggressive impulses are gratified because it is found morally unacceptable, whereas fencing is continued. The superego, also, is not wholly conscious since it is acquired through a long process of internalizing parental and societal values.

Freud's theory of personality set the scene for a struggle between the id and the superego for control of the ego. The superego will contain various negative prescriptions forbidding behaviour of certain sorts, often leaving little room for the gratification of basic desires sought by the id. This conflict, besides absorbing a large proportion of the fixed amount of 'psychic energy' available to the individual, was assumed, if severe, to result in abnormal behaviours such as are found in obsessional and neurotic disorders.

Freud proposed a number of ways in which the subconscious mind develops mechanisms which enable individuals to live with these conflicts. They have the general label of *defence mechanisms*. The principal defence mechanism is *repression* or motivated forgetting. Extreme instances involving a total loss of memory (amnesia) are often traceable to a single traumatic event. Freud believed the memory of the event was not lost but buried with other details of the individual's identity in the subconscious. The material can become available again through associations, dreams and psychotherapy. In less extreme cases of repression, memories of painful past experiences are kept out of consciousness or can lead to forgetting to do things loaded with anxiety, like visiting the dentist.

Another way in which individuals can be protected from their anxieties and conflicts is through *projection*. This defence mechanism achieves its defensive function by projecting the problem on to other people. For example, feelings of inferiority can be projected on to other people assumed to be of lower status. Other defence mechanisms include *reaction formation*, in which the individual develops a trait which is the opposite of the original predisposition (for example, sexual preoccupations are transformed into exaggerated prudishness); *denial*, where an individual struggles not to notice potentially ego-threatening events; *regression*, during which an individual retreats into the behaviour patterns of an earlier stage of development; and *displacement*, where an individual redirects unacceptable impulses.

One of the major determinants of people's personalities, in Freud's view, is what happens in early childhood when the conflicts between the id and the outside world first occur and when methods for dealing with them are first acquired. Freud believed childhood could be divided into *stages* corresponding to the principal sources of physical pleasure for children. The adult personality, he believed, contains residues of the conflicts experienced at each one. If, however, conflicts were experienced which were not satisfactorily resolved at the time, the individual becomes *fixated*, progresses no further and displays the cluster of traits associated with that stage.

Since the mouth is the primary source of satisfaction of the very young infant's bodily needs, the infant begins life in the *oral* stage. The infant is also assumed to derive pleasant physical stimulation from sucking. Freud suggested that oral fixation stems from too much or too little oral gratification. Too much gratification produces the oral-optimistic character, characterized by dependent and trusting attitudes. Too little gratification creates the oral-pessimistic personality in which the individual is sarcastic, caustic or even sadistic.

Freud suggested that at about 2 years old, as control of the muscles employed in elimination is acquired, the focus of pleasure shifts to the anus, since pleasant sensations can now be derived from the expulsion or retention of faeces. He therefore termed this the *anal* stage. It is at this point that the outside world begins to oppose the id. The conflict for the child is between parental authority, in the form of toilet training, and gratification of the desire to retain or eliminate the faeces. Fixation here occurs through strict or too weak toilet training. Toilet training that is too severe produces the anal or obsessional personality in which the individual is excessively neat, pedantic, orderly and controlled. Conversely, where toilet training has been too weak the child may become untidy and sloppy in adult life.

Interestingly, some support for the presence of the oral and anal personalities comes from factor analysis. There is a certain amount of irony in this as some early advocates of factor analysis, such as Hans Eysenck, were extremely critical of Freud, seeing his work as essentially unscientific. The oral and anal personalities to some extent resemble the agreeable and conscientiousness dimensions described earlier. Their presence as factors does not, of course, imply Freud was correct about the way these differences develop in people.

At about the age of 4, children enter what Freud termed the *phallic stage*, as he believed the child's sensual experiences were essentially penetrative and thus masculine in character. Freud suggested that in this stage, to avoid the guilt associated with the experience of attraction towards the parent of the opposite sex, the child begins to identify with the parent of the same sex. During the *latency* period, which begins at about the age of 5 and ends at puberty, the id appears to be relatively quiescent. Finally at puberty we enter the *genital stage* where we leave behind the self-centredness of childhood and begin to seek pleasure through satisfactory sexual relationships.

Freud's analysis of personality and behaviour has attracted a great deal of criticism. People in Freud's time, during the culturally restrictive Victorian era, found the explanation of behaviour, particularly infant sexuality, very difficult to accept. The theory has been dismissed as unscientific. One view is that for a theory to be scientific it must generate testable propositions so that it can in principle be disproved. The number of non-observable concepts in Freudian theory and the difficulty of generating specific testable propositions for it has meant many psychologists, especially those who advocate factor-analytic methods, consider the theory worthless.

Recent criticism (e.g. Webster, 1995; Masson, 1992; Irrigaray, 1993) has ranged from the work of Freud endorsing culturally prescribed gender identities, and thus the inequalities these involve, to the idea that Freud's views are essentially theological views dressed up as psychology. Whilst some feminists have seen Freud's views as phallocentric and over-emphasizing the role of the father, others have suggested that Freud, in laying bare the way culturally prescribed gender identities represent a thin, precarious layer on top of a much more complex underlying unconscious reality, is potentially very liberating for women (Minsky, 1996).

Despite the range of criticisms, many people have continued to develop and use the Freudian theoretical framework, believing it to be a powerful tool for the exploration of human personality and behaviour in the workplace (e.g. Kets de Vries, 1995).

Personality dimensions and social learning

Locus of control

One problem with Freud's analysis of personality development which many of those who are currently developing the theory have sought to rectify is his neglect of the effects of interacting with the social world. Many personality theorists believe that the social learning that occurs when interacting with siblings, peers, parents and teacher produces cognitive changes in individuals which are sufficiently enduring to be considered as stable personality traits. Two traits identified by social learning theorists have been found to be particularly useful in predicting behaviour in a variety of contexts.

First, *internal vs external locus of control* represents the extent to which people have built up the generalized expectation that they can exercise control over their environments. If our experience of the world teaches us that we can influence events, we tend to acquire an internal locus of control. If, however, the environment seems to be largely beyond our control we develop an external locus of control (Rotter, 1966). An extreme example of this type of learning would be if a child experiences the death of a parent at an age when he or she cannot understand why this should happen. The child may therefore come to believe that he or she has very little control over events. A great deal of research suggests that the locus of control we develop has important implications for behaviour in later life. For example, Brown and Harris (1978) found that depressives were far more likely to have lost a parent before the age of 5 than non-depressives. In occupational settings, research has found that internals tend to achieve higher status and incomes than externals, who in turn are more likely to feel that their workload is high and their working conditions are poor. Because internals tend to believe that they have control over the outcomes they experience, they believe that there is a connection between their performance at work and their reward level, and thus they are more easily motivated than internals, who feel there is less connection between effort and outcome.

Because locus of control is produced by people's experience of the world, it is not a completely unchanging aspect of personality. Significant changes in the control people can exercise over their environment may produce changes in their locus of control. At work, for example, experiencing participative decision-making procedures may cause a shift towards an internal locus of control in employees.

McClelland and need for achievement

Secondly, differences in social learning were also seen as the explanation of variation in David McClelland's dimension, the *need for achievement* (N-ach). A considerable amount of research carried out by McClelland suggests that the learning that fixes an individual's portion on this dimension occurs early on in life and so can be considered as a relatively stable feature of personality. Child-rearing practices and the father's occupation were seen as combining to influence the child's level of achievement motivation. Families producing high N-ach children tended to stress self-control, high standards, and individual initiative and independence, whereas low N-ach children came from families which emphasized compliance, dependence, a collective orientation and getting on with others.

One of the most interesting aspects of McClelland's work was his attempt to show that the general level of achievement in individuals was linked with economic and technological growth in society as a whole. Children who have grown up in cultures and families that stressed achievement are more likely to engage in entrepreneurial activity in adult life. In *The Achieving Society* (1961), McClelland put forward his well-known hypothesis that increases in achievement motivation spread throughout a society precede periods of economic and technological innovation. One notable form of evidence for this was to derive measures of achievement imagery found in children's books in different cultures at different times. He found that the amount of achievement imagery predicted economic activity in the society a generation later.

Cassidy and Lynn (1989) have identified seven factors which go to make up McClelland achievement motivation. Table 3.1 indicates the factors and items used by Cassidy and Lynn to assess them.

Factor	Example item	Yes	No
Work ethic	I like to work hard	Y	N
	I get bored if I don't have something to do	Y	N
Acquisitiveness	It is important for me to make lots of money	Y	N
	The most important thing about the job is the pay	Y	N
Dominance	I think I would enjoy having authority over other people	Y	N
	I think I am usually a leader in my group	Y	N
Excellence	I hate to see bad workmanship	Y	N
	There is satisfaction in a job well done	Y	N
Competitiveness	It annoys me when other people perform better than I do	Y	N
	It is important for me to perform better than others on a job	Y	N
Status aspiration	I like to be admired for my achievements	Y	N
	I like to have people come to me for advice	Y	N
Mastery	I prefer to work in situations that require a high level of skill	Y	N
	If I'm not good at something I would rather keep struggling to master it than move on to something I may be good at	Y	N

Award yourself two marks each time you circled a yes, then total your score. People on average will score about sixteen. If you have scored more than twenty, your N-ach is high. If you have a score of less than twelve, your N-ach appears to be low. However, because of the small number of items on this scale results should be treated with considerable caution.

Table 3.1 An example of an N-ach scale adapted from Cassidy and Lynn (1989)

Many researchers have found McClelland's concepts useful in exploring other achievement-related issues such as women's achievement. This research typically uses a projective test known as the Thematic Apperception Test, which requires subjects to write a story about an ambiguous figure, thus prompting them to project their own personalities on to the image in order to provide it with meaning. The story is then analysed and scored for the degree to which achievement imagery is present. For men, early research found that this measure of achievement motivation predicted achievement behaviour reasonably well. For women, however, the results were more complex, inconsistent, and puzzling. There was often no correlation between the achievement imagery a woman used on the test and her achievement behaviour. One intriguing explanation was that women who do want to achieve also acquire through social learning a fear of success (Horner, 1972). This conflict between need for achievement and fear of success creates tension, anxiety, and stress in women whose need for achievement is high. The stress will only be reduced by radical changes in the social learning that occurs in females during childhood and adolescence.

More recently, McClelland has, as will be seen in the next chapter, been in the forefront of the 'competence revolution'—the attempt to identify in explicit behavioural terms key differences between excellent and indifferent performers. Need for achievement—the desire for success and accomplishment—is for McClelland a key competence which needs to be built into assessment procedures.

Clinical approaches

So far the discussion has focused on concepts which are useful for describing the normal range of personality. But a number of consultants, particularly those operating at very senior levels in large organizations, utilize concepts from clinical traditions within psychology (e.g. Kets de Vries, 1993, 1994, 1995). These clinically oriented concepts provide the starting-point for exploring dysfunction within individuals, groups, and organizations. They describe behaviours which can undo a managerial career if not identified or have disastrous effects on a group or organization's perception of reality or culture. Specifically, these concepts provide the tools for exploring the 'inner theatres' of senior managers in order to understand relationship or performance difficulties on development programmes. Perhaps the most well known of these is the programme run for senior managers by Kets de Vries at INSEAD—the international business school.

One influential clinically oriented framework was developed by Theodore Millon, an American clinical psychologist. Millon (1990), like Eysenck, believes there is much to be gained from building bridges with the physical and biological sciences. Unlike Eysenck, he casts his net much wider to include not only psychology but also evolutionary theory, chemistry, population biology, ecology and ethology. Additionally, from the psychological sciences he borrows from psychoanalysis and social learning theory. His theory is thus an impressive synthesis of existing sources. The evolution of our species—basic adaptive and survival mechanisms which have developed personality at the most fundamental level—can be considered across three broad dimensions:

Active vs. Passive
Pleasure vs. Pain
Self vs. Others

These relate to whether an individual takes the initiative as opposed to reacting to events, whether he or she is motivated towards pleasure or pain, and whether the self or others are seen as the main source of social reward. An individual's position on each of these dimensions is seen as a function of his or her biology and coping strategies acquired through social learning. Combinations of these dimensions produce the nine different personality types outlined in Table 3.2.

1. Detached Personalities (Schizoid or Avoidant)
The hallmark of detached personalities is lack of warmth. They appear to others as cold, aloof, humourless and lacking in empathy. They have few friends and are distant even with relations. The roots of this may be early childhood experiences such as loss, rejection or critical parenting. The extremes of this personality style are termed schizoid or avoidant.

2. Dependent Personalities
Lacking in self-confidence, dependent types see themselves as weak and inadequate. At work their passivity means they want others to assume responsibility for them. They need others around them to make things happen and will thus absorb a good deal of a supervisor's time. The psychological roots of this style are either overprotection or frustrated dependency needs during childhood.

3. Histrionic Personalities
This personality style is characterized by a desperate need to attract attention. Thus histrionics can be flirtatious, seductive, approval-seeking and self-dramatizing. For these reasons they tend to change their 'fronts' to maintain others' interest. Histrionics pay little attention to detail and so tend to lack organization and judgement. The origins of this appear to be an inability to capture the attention of parents as a child.

4. Narcissistic Personalities
Superficially, narcissists can appear extremely charming or even charismatic. However, a longer acquaintance changes this perception to one of arrogance, egotism and lack of consideration for others. Narcissists are capable of ruthlessly exploiting others for their own ends while managing somehow to justify their behaviour to themselves. They are preoccupied with their own success or brilliance but also envious of others. When criticized they react with rage or humiliation. Above all, narcissists feel they are exceptions. The psychological roots are parents who have not created a secure sense of self-worth in the child. This may occur, for example, if the child has been 'loved' because he or she possesses a particular talent or quality.

5. Aggressive (Sadistic) Personalities
Aggressive personalities take pleasure in dominating, humiliating and possibly even brutalizing others. They believe themselves to be unsentimental, competitive and tough-minded. They may be able to mask their personality at work, but may give themselves away through vindictively persecuting another employee. Their dominance makes them quite rebellious employees. However, their competitiveness and brutality may well be rewarded through promotion. The psychological basis of this style is the aggressive belief that attack is the best form of defence.

6. Passive-Aggressive Personalities

The hallmark of these personalities both occupationally and socially is resistance to demands for performance. They seem to be unable to decide between responding actively or passively towards others. Thus, they passively accept a request, for example, from a spouse or manager and then express their resistances by not accomplishing the task. In personal relationships this means passive-aggressives are seen as unpredictable. At work, when their defiance is manifested in forgetfulness, inefficiency, lack of attention to detail or the occasional outburst, they underachieve and may well be seen as a problem. The psychological basis for this behaviour is thought to be conflicting and confusing parental behaviour. Passive-aggressives never really learn as children what behaviour works, and in adult life they end up with a pessimistic negative feeling that nothing ever really works for them as adults either.

7. Controlling Personalities (Obsessive-Compulsive)

The basis of this personality is the need for control. Controlling types are happiest operating systems where the performance requirements are clear and the method of achieving these requirements is known. They want their world to be orderly and predictable and thus tend to be rigid and inflexible. They place a very high value on authority and will be highly deferential in the presence of a superior but contemptuous and hostile towards subordinates. Controlling types tend to be hard-working perfectionists often to the point where they afford themselves very little opportunity for recreation. Their conformity and conscientiousness are thought to be the result of reaction formation against oppositional, rebellious and self-orientated feelings. They resolve the conflict between their basic hostility towards others and the fear of punishment by developing the opposite traits of conformity and passivity.

8. Paranoid Personalities

A high sensitivity to pain is thought to be the psychological basis for the paranoid personality. Paranoids are overly concerned with potential threats to their self-esteem. This often means they misread other people's behaviour, construing it as critical or rejecting. Their favourite defence is projection, blaming others for their own faults, which makes them overly hostile and contemptuous towards others. They are difficult to live or work with. Their great sensitivity puts them constantly on the defensive and makes it difficult for them to relax. The origin of this degree of sensitivity may lie in having had extremely intrusive parents, making it difficult for the child to establish any degree of autonomy.

9. Masochistic Personalities (self-defeating)

In common usage masochism has a sexual connotation. In Millon's typology the term has a much broader meaning. The masochistic individual prefers pain to pleasure. This leads to self-denial, self-blaming and self-sacrificing behaviour. By demonstrating their worst characteristics, masochists encourage others to take advantage of them. When others do take advantage, masochists respond with anger followed by guilt. There has been considerable speculation about the origins of this personality. Social learning theory suggests masochists have internalized the 'badness' they used as a child to get a reaction from their parents. Another possibility is some anomaly in the wiring of the cortex.

Table 3.2 Millon's nine personality types

The nine types described in Table 3.2 can be considered to be on a continuum and are found in varying degrees throughout the population. It is also possible for an individual to be a 'hybrid', demonstrating aspects of more than one personality style: for example, narcissism with control creates a mixture which, organizationally, can be very successful. Millon has developed a test designed to assess these characteristics in the 'normal' population (Psychological Corporation, 1993). The implications of each type for managerial effectiveness are described later in the chapter.

Intelligence

Conceptions of intelligence

The concept of intelligence has probably attracted more public attention and aroused more controversy than any other in the field of individual differences. This is partly because it has affected more people's lives than any other psychological construct. The old tripartite educational system of grammar, secondary and technical schools formed the basis of public education in Britain in the period between 1944 and 1971; and this was founded on the assumption that the ability of a child to benefit from a grammar school education could be predicted at the age of 11 from his or her score on an intelligence test. Similarly, many large organizations believe an individual's ability to perform in professional or administrative roles can to an extent be predicted from an intelligence test score. Controversy has particularly surrounded the use of test scores to support arguments about the heritability of intelligence and its distribution in different racial groups (e.g. Howe, 1997; Rushton, 1997).

While the use and abuse of intelligence tests and test data aroused a level of concern that spread to the general public, another important debate was taking place between academics about what the term itself actually meant. Sternberg (1985) has provided a useful classification of conceptions of intelligence. He suggested the major distinction is between *explicit* and *implicit* theories. The former are 'based on data collected from people performing tasks presumed to measure intelligent functioning'; whereas implicit theories are based on intuitive assumptions about the nature of intelligence.

Explicit theories can be based either on dimensions of intellectual abilities that have emerged from factor analysis, such as verbal comprehension or spatial reasoning, or on assumptions about the cognitive processes that contribute to intelligent functioning. The former differ in the number of factors they propose, ranging from one (Spearman, 1927) to one hundred and fifty (Guildford, 1982). The latter differ in the level of cognitive processing that they use to explain intelligence. Cognitive processes assumed to represent the basis of intelligent functioning have included:

1. The *pure speed* of an individual's information-processing measured by simple reaction time experiments.
2. *Choice speed*, an individual's ability to make a quick choice between two simple stimuli measured by choice reaction time experiments.
3. *Speed of lexical access*, the time taken by an individual to retrieve information from long-term memory.
4. *Speed of reasoning processes*, an individual's speed at higher-order information-processing, such as completing a series of numbers.

Thus, both types of explicit theory develop tests which are assumed to isolate and provide measures of the important aspects of intelligence. Implicit theories have included:

1. The power to generate accurate responses.
2. The ability to use abstract thinking.
3. The ability to adjust to the environment.
4. The ability to adapt to new situations.
5. The capacity for knowledge and knowledge possessed.
6. The capacity to learn or to profit by experience

Because psychologists are mainly interested in measuring intelligence, they have preferred to use the more quantifiable explicit theories. Thus, although in this section we will describe only explicit theories, we should stress that implicit theories dominate the assessment of intelligence in everyday life—during the conversations and interviews we have at work, at college or in informal social situations it is implicit theories that we use to make inferences about other people's intelligence.

Measurement of explicit intelligence factors

Of the explicit theories, those based on factor-analytic techniques have been highly influential in the field of intelligence research. Unlike personality which, as we have seen, can be broken down into a number of factors, there is a considerable amount of agreement that a large proportion of the variance in intelligence scores can be accounted for by a single, large factor: G. This general factor permeates all our intellectual activity, determining to a large extent how well we do on spatial, verbal, numerical, memory and other types of test. G seems to account for just over half the observed differences in test scores in a group (Vernon, 1971).

The belief in a general intelligence factor can be traced back to the work of Spearman (1904). He used a technique of factor analysis similar to that used by Eysenck in personality research, which extracts factors independent of each other. G was produced by the correlations of scores on all ability tests. Individuals who did well on one type of test tended to do well on all others. There was, however, a certain amount of variance specific to each test. So, for example, an individual's score on a vocabulary test was determined firstly by his or her level of g and secondly by his or her standing on a factor specific to that test.

As we have already seen, it is possible to use factor analysis to provide a larger number of less independent factors. Some researchers have therefore preferred to break G up into a number of more specific abilities. Thurstone (1938), for example, described what he termed seven *primary abilities*:

1. Spatial ability.
2. Verbal reasoning.
3. Perceptual speed.
4. Numerical ability.
5. Memory.

6. Verbal fluency.
7. Inductive reasoning.

Though tests devised to measure individuals on each of these factors will provide more specific information about their abilities, test scores on each will tend to be inter-correlated. Vernon (1971) proposed that by deriving different types of factorial solution from test data, a hierarchical model of intellect can be constructed which identified four levels of ability: G; major group factors (verbal–educational ability and practical–mechanical ability); minor group factors; and specific factors (Figure 3.6).

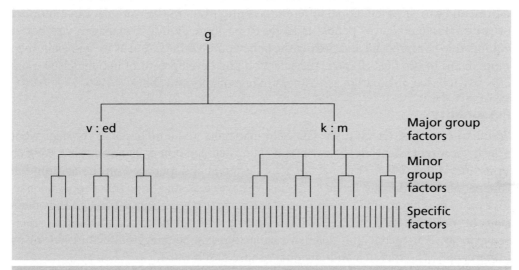

Figure 3.6 Vernon's model of the structure of human abilities
Source: Vernon (1971)

In a sense, then, as far as explicit theories are concerned, the question of how best to describe the structure of intellect is a technical question: what is the most compelling factorial solution to a set of data? With the availability of cheap computational facilities it has become easier to explore the various methods of factor analysis and so some agreement has recently developed about what requirements a factorial solution to test data should meet (Barret and Kline, 1980). Applying these criteria had produced a refinement in the notion of G: fluid ability, Gf, and crystallized ability, Gc. Essentially, the distinction represents the difference between an individual's reasoning *processes* (Gf) and the outcomes or *products* of these processes (Gc). Thus, tests which measure an individual's ability to solve problems or respond to novelty, tests of 'abstract' reasoning for example, provide measures of Gf, whereas tests which measure knowledge acquisition, tests of vocabulary for example, provide measures of Gc. Logically, then, Gf is the precursor to Gc, and since performance on tests of Gc will also have some reasoning component, measures of Gc and Gf tend to be somewhat inter-correlated.

The Gf and Gc constructs have become the factors which many contemporary psychometricians believe account for a large proportion of the variance in scores on any aptitude or attainment test. It is this two-factor theory which currently dominates research and test construction. For example, the development of the latest British Army Recruit Battery was based on this model of intelligence (Collis *et al.*, 1995).

Personality and intelligence in the workplace

If we turn now to look at the application of the above concepts of intelligence and personality in the work setting, an understanding beyond the 'common sense' area of the nature and causes of individual differences is important in the workplace in a number of ways. Management of people is likely to be more skilful if managers are better equipped to comprehend and predict the behaviour of others. And as we will explore in more detail in the next chapter, the selection and development of individuals is more effective if based on accurate assessment of personality and ability.

Personality

Freudian concepts, for example, can help managers and employees to consider what may be occurring beneath the surface of their own and others' behaviour (e.g. Kets de Vries and Miller, 1984). Organizations are designed and managed on the assumption that people act rationally. Freud's view, as we have seen, suggested that people's behaviour often falls short of this ideal. One of the ways this can occur is through the operation of defence mechanisms, which protect individuals from threats to their self-esteem. This means that defensive behaviour can be triggered by an event or by other people who threaten an individual's sense of self-worth.

The increased threat to our self-esteem at work caused by pressure for performance, fear of failure and the presence of authority figures means we may utilize the most powerful of defence mechanisms—projection—to protect our egos. This enables us to externalize any difficulties we may be having at work. For example, we can blame poor supervision or unhelpful colleagues rather than accept the part personal inadequacies have played. By projection we can off load unacceptable feelings of inferiority and inadequacy.

Two features of projection increase the difficulties of individuals using this defence mechanism. First, if we project difficulties onto other staff we will not only blame them for our problems but also tend to treat them with contempt or even hostility. This obviously may cause a deterioration in relationships. Secondly, projection makes it very difficult for individuals to perceive that their own inadequacies have contributed to their current problems. This means people may resent and ignore advice or counselling from colleagues or superiors.

Ego strength is important in determining an individual's ability to cope with the daily wear and tear of working life. Individuals with high ego strength are able to cope with the frustrations and obstacles which confront them at work without losing their tempers or giving up. Karson and O'Dell (1976) liken individuals with low ego strength to tyres with little tread—a 'blow out' at some stage is inevitable, for example when small problems assume a significance out of all proportion to the threat they actually pose.

The workplace is also where we are likely to meet higher levels of formal authority than were experienced at school or college. Any conflicts people have had with previous authority figures, such as teachers or parents, are likely to be transferred to the workplace if they were not resolved at the time. So according to Freud we can unknowingly transfer our feelings towards earlier authority figures to our current managers and supervisors. Additionally, Freud believed that people are largely unaware of the intensity and ambivalence that may be locked up in their feelings towards authority figures. When transference occurs, individuals may cope with these feelings by 'acting out'. This means that a relatively minor event in adult life can cause a quite disproportionate amount of either hostility or affection to be displayed or experienced in the presence of an authority figure. Doctors and psychiatrists are regularly faced with patients experiencing inappropriate feelings towards them through transference. Managers ought similarly to be aware of this possibility.

Both of the social learning variables we described earlier offer interesting insights into behaviour in the workplace. David McClelland claimed that by adding two further personality dimensions, the need for power (N-power) and the need for affiliation (N-aff), he would be able to identify the relative importance for each variable to high job performance in particular types of management (McClelland and Burnham, 1976). People who are high in N-ach, for example, set themselves very high standards of personal performance. A surprising consequence of this is that although they make very good entrepreneurs, they do not make particularly good managers. This is because they feel they are the most competent person to do a job and tend not to delegate as often as they should. In addition, McClelland demonstrated that effective managers are higher in N-power than N-aff (McClelland and Boyatzis, 1982). In short, they enjoy the exercise of power more than they enjoy being liked by colleagues and subordinates. However, he found that managers had also to possess a considerable amount of self-control to be effective. Without self-control a high need for power channels energy into attaining personal rather than organizational goals. For example, a manager may suppress information which indicates the line of action he or she has chosen is incorrect (Fodor and Smith, 1982).

Internals differ from externals because they believe they make things happen rather than things happen to them. This difference occupationally is clearly an important one. And indeed there is a good deal of evidence to suggest that locus of control is related to a wide range of organizational variables: occupational level, income, perception of job characteristics, perceived autonomy, perception of working conditions, job satisfaction, occupational advancement, and performance (Spector, 1986). In terms of these variables this research indicated that organizations are best staffed by internals. They tend to perceive their workload as manageable and so tend to experience less stress. Furthermore, they perceive a connection between their effort and their performance, and so are more easily motivated and more satisfied with their jobs. This appears to be particularly important in sales occupations. The belief that rewards are contingent on one's own performance in internals motivates prospecting and insulates the salesperson from rejection. The locus of control dimension can account for as much as 25 per cent of the differences between employees' motivation and productivity.

As we saw, an individual's locus of control, though believed to be stable enough to be considered as an aspect of personality, is not completely fixed. This means that if organizations allow people more control over their work, job satisfaction and motivation are likely to be increased and stress reduced. As we shall see later, a theory of motivation (VIE) focuses on increasing an individual's perceptions of control. Similarly, an important approach in designing work to increase motivation and job satisfaction involves using groups, which are afforded a greater degree of autonomy over the way work is performed.

The relationship between Millon's typology and managerial effectiveness has been extensively researched by Kets de Vries (1989). He has found many of the self-destructive tendencies in each of Millon's personality styles can ultimately undermine a manager's ability to cope with the psychological forces present in the leader–follower relationship. These forces will be discussed more fully in Chapter 8. Table 3.3 summarizes the managerial or leadership potential of each personality style.

Style	Leadership potential	Followership potential
Narcissistic	very high	low
Aggressive	high	low
Paranoid	high	medium
Histrionic	medium	high
Detached	medium	medium
Controlling	high	high
Passive-aggressive	low	high
Dependent	very low	high
Masochistic	very low	high

Table 3.3 The relationship between Millon's personality typology and leadership potential

Eysenck, as we have seen, suggested an individual's standing on the introversion–extraversion dimension reflected how 'stimulus-hungry' he or she is. The significance of this for workplace behaviour is that individuals differ in the sort of work environment they are constitutionally best equipped for. Introverts appear to be able to cope with jobs which provide low levels of stimulation. On vigilance tasks, where attention has to be focused for long periods of time on a single stimulus source, a radar screen for example, most people are subject to a *performance decrement*. As we pointed out earlier, signals are missed and signals which did not occur are reported. Introverts, however, display far less deterioration over time in performance on vigilance tasks. Conversely, extroverts tend to prefer and be better at jobs where the work is complex and varied. Knowing an individual's position on this dimension can therefore help predict what kind of task he or she will prefer and perform well.

The neuroticism–instability dimension essentially indicates an individual's emotional stability. Therefore jobs like selling, which routinely involve a good deal of rejection, may not be suitable for people scoring high on the N scale. Rejection would reinforce the low opinion that high scorers tend to have of themselves and could ultimately lead to depression.

Intelligence

Because occupational status is a fundamental form of achievement in any industrial society, and the basis of most other aspects of consumption, we might assume that such status is determined by an individual's intellectual capacity. But access to professional and managerial occupations largely occurs through achievements in higher education. This means we first need to consider the relative importance of intelligence in gaining access to higher education. In fact, social class and the type of school an individual attends are better predictors of his or her chances of going on to higher education than intelligence (Halsey *et al.*, 1980). The relationship between intelligence and occupational status, therefore, is not a simple or direct one.

What intelligence does seem to do is set a threshold for entry into occupations which makes access to higher-status jobs difficult for people with low scores. Large-scale research on army recruits in the Second World War found that the median IQ scores increased and the range of scores decreased with increasing occupational status. Thus, the median score for accountants was 128 with a range from 94 to 154 while the median score for labourers was 88 with a range of scores from 46 to 145 (Harrell and Harrell, 1945). Some researchers have argued that even this relationship can be questioned. They argue that this simply reflects the way the concept of intelligence has been operationalized. Psychologists, they argue, have wittingly or unwittingly developed intelligence tests to measure an individual's ability to function in high-status jobs. In other words, part of what has come to be meant by intelligence is the likelihood that an individual can function at certain levels in the occupational structure.

If there does not seem to be a simple association between measures of occupational intelligence and status, what relationship does IQ have with actual performance in a job? The average correlation between test scores and some measure of job performance appears to be about .5. However, the relationship between the two seems to vary according to whether the job is professional, intermediate (e.g. clerical) or routine. Performance in professional jobs appears to have little to do with intelligence test scores. As we suggested earlier, intelligence seems merely to set a minimum level below which entry into an occupation is difficult. Above this level, however, performance in a job is unrelated to intelligence. Fiedler and Leister (1977*a*) have argued that effectiveness is determined not only by a manager's intellectual capacity but by a number of other personal attributes and aspects of the work environment. They suggested that poor relationships between manager and staff, a manager's lack of experience and motivation, and his or her inability to cope with uncertainty all reduced the strength of the relationship between intelligence and effectiveness. This implies, for example, that the knowledge which comes with experience has to be present before the intellectual ability to manipulate information can be used to predict a manager's effectiveness. Fiedler and Leister (1977b) have supported this by demonstrating that the relationship between IQ and managerial effectiveness dropped from .36 with experienced managers to .15 with inexperienced ones.

In intermediate occupations, where there is a wider range of intelligence than in professional and managerial jobs, a fairly strong relationship between test scores and measures of job performance has been observed. In routine jobs, however, there again appears to be little relationship between the two, presumably because the reduced variety and autonomy and increased automation of routine work leave little opportunity for intelligence to affect the level of performance. However, despite a good deal of research to suggest that IQ is not a powerful predictor of job performance, there remains a widespread belief among managers that intelligence is directly related to high and low achievement in the workplace, which ensures that IQ tests continue to be included in selection procedures for a wide range of occupations.

Conclusion

In this chapter we have covered some of what is known about the nature of two fundamental human attributes—personality and intelligence. Psychology, as we have seen, has provided useful accounts of the underlying architecture of each. And, particularly in the development and application of factor analysis, we have seen psychology at its most 'neutral', 'scientific', and 'objective'. A repository of concepts and knowledge about the fundamental ways we differ and the impact of these differences in the workplace now seems to exist.

But some readers may well have found the content of this chapter somewhat distasteful. You may possibly feel that in all the concern to reduce the complexity of personality and intelligence to a few underlying dimensions (exemplified best by factor analysis) the fundamental uniqueness of individuals has been lost. In other words, this 'reductive' approach has seemed largely about depersonalizing and pigeonholing individuals.

There is, it should be stressed, no attempt here to deny the fundamental uniqueness of human beings. All that is being claimed is that in some important ways people are reasonably consistent; and that it is possible to identify the basis for this consistency. In any event, as we will see in Chapter 6, we have, at the back of our heads, our own personal 'index system' which we use to make sense of each other. In that chapter you will also encounter the argument that there are 'no such things as traits'. This argument holds that people behave too inconsistently to infer the existence of these stable underlying entities. We would not deny the impact components of situations—roles, rules, and goals, for example—have on our behaviour. But we would argue there is sufficient evidence—biogenetic, factor-analytic, and developmental—to make a good case for the existence of traits. We do not want to take up extreme situationalist or traitist positions, but as evidenced by the inclusion of both, we treat them as useful and complementary perspectives.

Given this body of knowledge about individual differences one obvious question arises: why is this repository of seemingly useful concepts not utilized more? One example of this historical reluctance in the UK was the demise, in the 1970s, of the main organization responsible for distributing measures of intelligence and personality. This lack of interest is, to an extent, not surprising. We are all familiar with the subject-matter of this chapter—personality and intelligence—and managers can often feel experts in the subject. Indeed, over the years of working as a psychologist in organizations I have met many managers who can use their experience of people to make astute judgements about someone's suitability for a post. But this ability—rather like some darts players' computational competence—does not always generalize to other contexts, such as predictions about the individual's likely performance in different job grades or his or her suitability for development. One common problem I encounter is that culturally we tend to confuse *ability* and *achievement*. Whilst there is a connection between the two it is not as close as many seem to assume. Achievements such as skills and academic qualifications may have been a struggle for individuals or easily acquired. They can represent the ceiling of someone's ability or a platform for future progression. The context-free 'explicit' concept of intelligence presented in this chapter does much to help separate out the two and enable an individual's potential to be considered independently. Similarly, the concepts of personality discussed in this chapter represent considerable improvements on some of the more everyday categories we tend to apply to each other. (A technique for identifying the concepts you currently use can be found in Chapter 6.)

Whilst historically there may have been a reluctance to utilize concepts drawn from psychology, the economic pressures to take these concepts more seriously will increase. As Charles Saatchi, who built one of the largest advertising agencies in the world, once said: 'the assets of this organization go up and down in the lifts'. Human capital, a factor increasingly recognized as critical to the success of an organization, is also the most elusive. It is, as we saw in Chapter 1, possible to develop human capital. But in this chapter we have also seen there are fundamental human attributes which can underpin an individual's ability to contribute effectively in a particular role either now or in the future.

In the next chapter we take exploration of individual differences one further step and examine in detail how organizations can assess them. And we will describe evidence about the relative effectiveness of the range of assessment methodologies available to individuals and organizations.

Study questions for Chapter 3

1 Are factors inventions rather than discoveries?
2 To what extent is the 'Big Five' account of personality an unhelpful oversimplification?
3 Is Freud essentially fiction?
4 Is the only way to describe personality scientifically to use factor analysis?
5 What relevance do Freudian concepts have to the workplace?
6 What is 'G'?
7 An individual's ability can be captured best by assessing his or her level of G—discuss.
8 Can intelligence be improved?
9 What impact do differences in intelligence have on effectiveness at work?

Further reading

Brunas-Wagstaff, J. (1998) *Personality: A Cognitive Approach*. London: Routledge.

Ceci, S. J. (1996) *On Intelligence.* London: Harvard University Press

Cooper, C. and Varma, V. (eds.) (1997) *Processes in Individual Differences*. London: Routledge.

—— (1999) *Intelligence and Abilities*. London: Routledge.

Ewen, R. B. (1997) *An Introduction to Theories of Personality*. London: Lawrence Erlbaum Associates Inc.

Gardner, H., Kornhaber, M. C. and Wake, W. K. (1996) *Intelligence: Multiple Perspectives.* London: Harcourt Brace

Howe, M. J. A. (1997) *I.Q. in Question: The Truth about Intelligence*. London: Sage.

Matthews, G. and Deary, I. (1998) *Personality Traits*. Cambridge: Cambridge University Press.

Pervin, L. A. (1996) *The Science of Personality*. New York: Wiley.

Rushton, J. P. (1997) *Race, Evolution and Behaviour*. New Brunswick: Transaction.

Sternberg, R. J. and Grigorenko, E. (eds.) (1997) *Intelligence, Heredity and Environment.* Cambridge: Cambridge University Press.

—— (1997) *Thinking Styles*. Cambridge: Cambridge University Press.

Webster, R. (1996) *Why Freud Was Wrong*. London: Fontana Press.

4 Assessing Individual Differences

Summary points and learning objectives

By the end of this chapter you will be able to

- describe the reasons assessments occur in organizations;
- understand why accurately identifying a job's demands is important;
- describe different approaches to identifying person requirements;
- describe the advantages and disadvantages of the concept of competence;
- describe different assessment methods;
- understand the advantages and disadvantages of each method;
- understand the concepts of reliability and validity;
- describe what is known about the reliability and validity of different assessment methodologies.

Introduction

In the last chapter we explored some of the fundamental human attributes which differentiate us as unique individuals. In this chapter we will look at how these concepts are taken out of academic settings and applied in organizations. We will first seek to answer what purposes assessments serve at work. You may associate assessment with 'point of entry' selection. But increasingly assessments are used for a variety of reasons. To some extent the increased use of assessment stems from fundamental changes in the relationship between employers and the employed and the increasing flexibility required as job demands change more rapidly—issues which will be examined elsewhere in this book. One key issue we will examine in some detail is how job and person demands are identified. For assessments to be of any value they have to be focused on the attributes individuals need to possess in order to cope with a job's demands. And some of the legal difficulties employers have found themselves in have stemmed directly from not having an adequate and defensible description of the role and of the human attributes required to function competently in it. The main purpose of this chapter is to examine the various assessment methods available to organizations and particularly their strengths and weaknesses. The key question for any assessment methodology to answer is: what is the status of the information it generates? And we will conclude the chapter by looking at recent evidence which seeks to answer this question.

Why assess?

Nowadays, individuals are likely to experience assessment throughout their careers. In fact, one of the future developments in organizations will be more frequent use of assessments as job characteristics change more rapidly in response to turbulent market conditions (Cooper, 1997). Accurate, focused assessments help individuals involved in screening, selection, succession planning, career planning, team building, management development, and counselling.

Screening

Organizations faced with large numbers of applicants will need to use some form of screening procedure to identify candidates to be put forward to the next stage in the process. For example, the United Kingdom's 'Fast Track Civil Service' entry receives about 10,000 applications each year. Candidates' scores on a qualifying test determine whether they proceed to the next stage. Similarly, one high street retailer in the United Kingdom with the same number of applications each year scores application forms for evidence of achievement, responsibility, leadership, and motivation. Some organizations—if numbers permit—might use a brief ten to fifteen minute interview to screen applicants.

Selection

Appointing the wrong person is usually a costly mistake for an organization; and being in the wrong job is usually a bruising experience for the individual. Accurate assessment helps reduce the 'error-rate'—taking on individuals who turn out to be unsuccessful and turning away people who would have been successful.

Succession planning

What happens when key individuals retire or leave? The author recently ran a series of assessments in a major financial institution with individuals who were one level below the Board of Directors. This was prompted by the realization that within five years most of the current Board would have retired. Assessment in succession planning is about helping individuals and organizations identify the gaps between current skills and abilities and what is required at the next level up. Accurate identification of gaps enables development to be effectively targeted.

Career planning

Whilst historically the demands for accurate information about individuals have come from organizations (as in the examples above) individuals can benefit from high quality information about their abilities and strengths and weaknesses, particularly at branching points in careers, such as entry to the labour market or transition from one job or career to another. The organizations this author works for carry out many thousands of assessments each year, providing individuals with a better understanding of their abilities and potentially enabling them to target or create opportunities which better match their strengths. Whilst career planning is often carried out on a one-to-one basis *career review workshops* run for groups of individuals in organizations are increasingly common. These provide 'time out' to consider the questions, where am I now and where do I want to be? Assessment helps identify what abilities and attributes individuals currently have to get where they want and what else they might need to develop to help get them there.

Redeployment

Accurate information about abilities and potential is particularly useful when an individual's job in an organization disappears but where potentially there are other opportunities within the organization which he or she might be suited to. For example, I recently carried out a redeployment project in a vehicle manufacturer. The site involved assembly and manufacturing of some parts, but the company took the decision to source parts from one of its factories overseas and expand the assembly side of the site. Assessment was welcomed by the trade unions on the site who were concerned that redeployment decisions might be driven by favouritism rather than merit. The assessment also provided an opportunity for the skilled operatives involved in manufacturing parts to consider whether they really would be able to cope with the more routine, machine-paced, and repetitive nature of assembly work.

Team building

Information about individual differences within a team can help identify, explore, and resolve performance and relationship issues. For example, Patrick Handley's 'Insight Inventory' provides focused information on some key individual differences which impact on the way an individual communicates with others and responds to pressure (Handley, 1988).

Management development

The starting point of a development programme has to be an accurate assessment of the individual's abilities and personality and how these might interact with current or future job demands. Such an assessment provides a neutral, objective framework for exploring relationship and performance issues and devising a focused *personal development plan*.

Equal opportunities

Assessment can, if carried out properly, increase equal opportunities. Objective information about abilities and skills can confront stereotyped assumptions. For example, when working in a bank carrying out assessments for promotion, the data I generated clearly undermined existing sexist assumptions about the promotability of female staff. Because women in this bank tended to start their careers earlier they had fewer academic credentials than their male counterparts. However, assessments of ability demonstrated differences in academic attainment were not related to scores on ability tests. The potential to progress was evenly distributed between the sexes.

Getting it right—defining job demands

The first step in any effective assessment process has to be accurately identifying what the job demands actually are. This can be achieved using *quantitative*, questionnaire-based procedures or *qualitative* interview and observation approaches, or as is sometimes the case, a hybrid of both.

Quantitative

In the United States there has been a long tradition of identifying job demands with standardized questionnaires. These produce a *job profile* by statistically identifying the distinctive characteristics of a job when compared with other jobs. The use of standardized questionnaires to identify job demands in the United States has been driven by a concern to produce job profiles which are legally defensible (Uniform Guidelines on Employee Selection Procedures: EEOCC, 1978). Subjective judgements about job demands and the abilities and traits required for effective task performance can become the basis for litigation. 'Defensible' job and person specifications have also become a requirement in Europe. Some major employers have found themselves having to defend selection decisions because there was no clear link between the assessments candidates undertook and the job's demands (Wood, 1997).

The two most widely used standardized job-profiling questionnaires are the PAQ, Position Analysis Questionnaire (McCormick *et al.*, 1969) for non-managerial jobs, and the MPJFI, Managerial and Professional Job Functions Inventory (Baehr, 1987) for managerial jobs. MPJFI comes out of two decades of research at the Human Resources Centre at the University of Chicago. Generating an MPJFI job profile involves jobholders or individuals familiar with the job—such as their managers rating the importance of a number of activities to the job. Baehr's questions refer to underlying or 'generic' job requirements which occur in a range of managerial and professional jobs. Examples of MPJFI questions are included in Figure 4.1.

MPJFI describes jobs along sixteen factors Baehr identified using factor analysis initially in a large sample of private- and public-sector managerial and professional employees. The MPJFI questionnaire usefully has two response modes: importance and ability. The importance inventory produces a profile for the job. The ability version plots

Rate the importance of each activity to
the job. Make two separate sets of judgements.

Answer all statements (Tick the appropriate box)

Scale headings (diagonal): Little or none · Less than average · Below average · Above average · More than average · Outstanding

113. Developing and maintaining a general interest in innovation and needed change. ....

114. Providing the technical leadership on a project. ....

115. Accepting the responsibility for the effect of organization decisions on the security and careers of individuals. ....

116. Helping to build co-operative relationships within the work group. ....

117. Analysing the causes of breakdowns in operations with a minimum of delay. ....

118. Encouraging employees to use personal protective equipment. ....

119. Actively seeking feedback on communications sent to others. ....

120. Evaluating the decision-making ability of others. ....

121. Accepting personal responsibility for disciplining poor performers. ....

122. Seeking and utilizing feedback from others regarding one's own developmental needs.

123. Attending workshops on problems and challenges presented by changing legislation on personnel practices. ....

124. Alerting the organization to changing cultural values and their possible impact on its future. ....

125. Entertaining important representatives from outside the organization. ....

126. Helping to formulate the overall mission of the organization. ....

Figure 4.1 Examples of managerial and professional JFI questions

an individual's perception (relative to others) of his or her ability to cope with each of Baehr's sixteen dimensions. The disparity between an importance and ability profile provides a useful framework for discussing training and development needs.

The meaning of the scales is as follows:

1. *Setting organizational objectives.* Formulating the overall mission and goals of the organization; setting short and long-range objectives which are significant and measurable and which incorporate future predictions; and evaluating alternative structures for future organizational operations.
2. *Financial planning and review.* Making economic decisions and managing capital assets; establishing a budget and independent controls to assure that the budget is met; maintaining accurate financial records using up-to-date procedures.
3. *Improving work procedures and practices.* Analysing, interpreting, and evaluating operating policies; initiating and formulating improved procedures and policies within the organizational structure; ensuring that new procedures are installed smoothly.
4. *Interdepartmental co-ordination.* Understanding and co-ordinating the problems and work activities of different departments within the organization; using informal

communication lines as well as work committees to gain and disseminate information across the organization.

5. *Developing and implementing technical ideas.* Originating technical ideas and designs; translating technical ideas into feasible solutions to organizational needs; leading technical projects and writing appropriate reports; helping the organization adjust to and evaluate technical changes.

6. *Judgement and decision-making.* Analysing incomplete information to make decisions; being flexible in non-routine decisions; acting upon decisions concerning resource and workforce allocation; accepting responsibility for the consequences of both one's own and one's subordinates' decisions.

7. *Developing group co-operation and teamwork.* Encouraging and building workgroup relations which will lead to better exchange of ideas; improved decision-making; more open communication; higher morale and sense of purpose; recognizing destructive problems and conflicts within the workgroup.

8. *Coping with difficulties and emergencies.* Efficiently working under pressure; effectively handling unexpected problems; day-to-day crises; emergency situations; quickly analysing operations breakdown and setting priorities for action.

9. *Promoting safety attitudes and practices.* Taking responsibility for the identification and elimination of job safety and health hazards; promoting and communicating safety practices and regulations to employees; investigating possible job-related accidents and illnesses.

10. *Communications.* Monitoring and improving both external communications channels and internal upward and downward communication lines; developing, testing, and seeking feedback on one's own communication skills; conducting effective meetings.

11. *Developing employee potential.* Evaluating employees' present performance and potential in order to create opportunities for better utilization of their abilities; examining and responding to employee dissatisfactions; assisting others in overall career development.

12. *Supervising practices.* Clarifying subordinates' job functions and responsibilities; motivating employees while maintaining discipline and control; seeing that subordinates maintain established standards of performance and accepting personal responsibility for those who do not.

13. *Self development and improvement.* Formulating self-improvement goals using feedback from others to help assess one's own strengths and weaknesses; improving one's own skills by participating in developmental programmes and by assuming new positions; co-ordinating personal career goals with organizational needs.

14. *Personnel practices.* Ensuring that the organization adheres to UK equal opportunity policies and is aware of the legal framework for selection and development of minority group applicants.

15. *Promoting community–organizational relations.* Staying informed on community, social, economic, and political problems and their relevance to and impact upon the organization; accepting responsibility for the ongoing relationship between the

organization and the community; actively seeking information from and disseminating information to the community about the organization.

16. *Handling outside contacts.* Promoting the organization and its products to outside contacts and clients; handling and entertaining long-term clients, suppliers, and visitors so as to convey properly the organization's relationship with them; expediting client/customers' special requests and handling their complaints about the organization.

An example of an MPJFI profile is given in Figure 4.2.

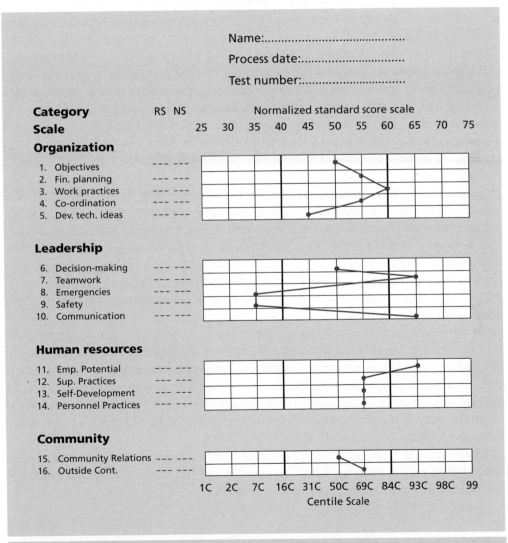

Figure 4.2 A MPJFI profile (see Box 4.1)

In a selection setting what PAQ or MPJFI data enables is a clear link, that is all too often missing, to be made between what attributes of an individual are assessed and what the job actually requires. Thus assessment becomes more focused, making the resulting selection decisions more resistant to legal scrutiny (see Box 4.1).

Qualitative

Less structured procedures are often used to elicit information about the job's demands and the human attributes necessary for effective performance. These include: interviews with jobholders, their supervisors, co-workers, subordinates, or others familiar with the job; observation and analysis; or when possible actually doing the job.

Job analysis interviews are normally 'in depth'; lasting between one and two hours. Whilst often conducted on a one-to-one basis, they can also be conducted with a *focus group* consisting of individuals who are job experts—i.e. are effective jobholders or are managers. The focus group will 'brainstorm', i.e. think up as many job characteristics and human attributes required for performing the job as possible, without critically evaluating them. Interviews and focus groups are unstructured methods of obtaining a wealth of 'context rich' information not available by other means. What can assist in generating this information are techniques such as the Critical Incidents Technique (Flanagan, 1954) or the Repertory Grid Technique (e.g. Stewart and Stewart, 1981). Both are ways of helping to focus an individual's thinking and articulate key job or person characteristics.

Critical Incidents Technique was the product of research in the Second World War aimed at helping to identify specific reasons for success or failure, for example in bombing missions. But the technique transfers well to organizational settings. It involves questioning individuals about times when things went particularly well or particularly badly. Questioning focuses on identifying actual incidents or 'behavioural events'. If enough data is collected categories of incidents begin to emerge. For example, in carrying out a job analysis using this technique at one level below the Board of Directors in a financial institution I realized many of the times when things went particularly well or badly were when other people either did or did not appreciate the impact of their actions on other parts of the business. This led to the formation of a key job demand labelled 'organizational awareness'. Similarly, carrying out a critical incident analysis with a sample of team leaders in a large automotive concern, it seemed many of the events characterizing times when things went very well or very poorly related to the ability to work with other teams. Thus one key requirement of team leaders was the inter-coordination of teams.

Repertory Grid Technique (described more fully in Chapter 6) can be used to elicit either job or person characteristics. An example of a job analysis interview which utilizes all of these approaches can be found in Box 4.2.

Box 4.1 Defensible assessments

One assignment illustrating the use of job-profiling instruments such as the MPJFI involved designing the assessments for the selection of a European training manager for an American multinational manufacturing company with production facilities scattered across Europe. The sensitivity of American companies to the possibility of litigation or other forms of challenge to selection decisions meant that the link between the job demands and the assessment activities had to be very explicit and objectively derived. Copies of the importance version of the MPJFI were distributed across Europe to the other training managers. Responses were then averaged to produce a profile for the job. The most distinctive characteristics of the role when compared with the MPJFI database was on factors 7, 10, and 11 (see Figure 4.2). This indicated that when compared with other managerial jobs the key to effectiveness in this role was the ability to communicate effectively at meetings, influencing and persuading. Specifically this involved pushing training further up other managers' agendas by increasing awareness of the contribution training could make to the range of problems they were confronting. This involved not only stating views but obviously also getting them to 'stick'.

The assessment activities which flowed from this profile were interactive. Candidates were given opportunities to demonstrate their ability to influence and persuade. For example, in one exercise candidates were given complex briefs which they were given some time to analyse. Each of the briefs involved complex organizational scenarios which all had training implications. Each candidate had a different scenario but one which was of equivalent difficulty to those of other candidates. After the analysis time was up each candidate was able to chair a meeting. They were asked to introduce themselves, explain the problem, and then suggest what their proposed solution was. Observers rated the ability of the candidate to analyse the problem, propose a solution and get this to stick. Some candidates had the ability to grasp the subtleties of the problem and propose effective solutions but had little ability to get the group to accept it. Other candidates demonstrated a modest ability to grasp complex organizational problems and recognize their training implications but were very good at gaining acceptance of inferior and unworkable solutions. The candidate who was appointed had both the ability to analyse problems, propose training solutions, and gain acceptance for these.

Box 4.2 A qualitative job analysis interview

This interview can be used with the job incumbent or his or her manager. It is also possible to run this interview with groups of 'job experts' such as senior managers. Interviewing groups of senior managers, for example a Board of Directors, about the work of their Regional Directors can in itself be useful, as it sometimes becomes clear during the interview that quite different understandings of the role are present in the room. With some managers some of these questions, particularly those which involve trying to extract 'constructs' (see Chapter 6 for more detail and a fuller construct exercise) can seem odd. But if the purpose of the questions is made clear, i.e. that it is simply a technique which helps them identify and describe key underlying differences in jobs or individuals, these feelings disappear and in fact managers find the interview interesting and helpful.

1. Can you describe in a couple of sentences the major outputs of your/the target job?
2. Right, if (response to Q1) is/are the major output(s) can you tell me how these are achieved—what skills do you think are involved in achieving this/these output(s)?
3. You are possibly familiar with the Pareto principle—80 per cent of results coming from 20 per cent of effort. If this were to apply to your/this job what would this 20 per cent be?
4. (If with the incumbent) Can you think of a day when you went home thinking you had really achieved something? Can you tell me what happened?
5. (If with the incumbent) Can you think of a day when you went home feeling the day had been particularly difficult? Can you tell me what happened?
6. (If with the incumbent) Can you think of some colleagues doing a similar job as yourself in the organization? (It is useful to have some pieces of card to write names on.) If the individual is concerned about confidentiality, initials or some other way of preserving anonymity can be used. In some contexts—i.e. when looking at similarities and differences between jobs at a similar level—job titles rather than individuals are used. Try to get about ten names or job titles, one on each piece of card. Laying three in front of the interviewee (or on a flipchart if with a group) ask: Can you tell me one important way in which any two individuals (or job titles) are different from a third? These constructs can be usefully probed in order to put more behavioural flesh and context on them—How do you know when someone is . . . can you give me an example . . . what are the implications for the business of someone being X rather than Y? Repeat four or five times with different combinations of names or job titles.
7. If interviewing the target job's supervisor ask: Can you think about your best (target job). You do not need to say who it is but tell me what is so good

about him/her? Can you give me an example, an event which demonstrated this attribute?

8. Again if interviewing the supervisor repeat question 7, only this time looking at a particularly difficult incumbent. Once more probe to identify 'critical incidents'.

9. (If appropriate) What did you find most difficult about moving up into your current position? What advice would you give to anyone being promoted into your (job grade)?

This interview can last between one and two hours. It provides context-rich insights into the nature of the job and differences between excellent and indifferent performers which more quantitative questionnaires will not pick up. By collecting enough data from a series of interviews the critical job and skill demands can be identified.

Competences

A popular way of crossing from job demands to the attributes individuals need to cope successfully with them is the concept of competence. The definition of a competence is: 'an *underlying* characteristic of an individual which is *causally* related to *effective* or *superior* performances' (Boyatzis, 1982). The distinction is often made between *differentiating competences* which distinguish superior from average performers and *threshold competences* which are required for adequate or average performance.

Competences can be traits (e.g. self-assertion, stress resistance), motives (e.g. need for achievement), self-concept (attitudes and values), technical or expert knowledge, cognitive abilities (intelligence), or behavioural skills (e.g. 'active listening'). As Spencer *et al.* (1994) suggest, a competence is 'any individual characteristic that can be measured or counted reliably and that can be shown to differentiate significantly between superior or average performers, or between effective and ineffective performers.' Identifying competences involves similar processes to job analysis. The process is defined in Figure 4.3.

The twenty competences developed by Spencer *et al.* (1994) as most commonly associated with success in technical/professional/managerial and senior executive level jobs can be found in Box 4.3. The competences found in this box straddle the distinction between management and leadership which will be explored more fully in Chapter 8. Clearly the competences will vary in the extent to which they differentiate between the excellent and the indifferent in any given organizational context. And the problem with a generic list like this is that in some jobs, the key competences can be quite specific—in senior jobs within central and local government, for example, political judgement and sensitivity are critical, which is somewhat different to organizational awareness in this list, as they involve much more than simply learning and understanding power

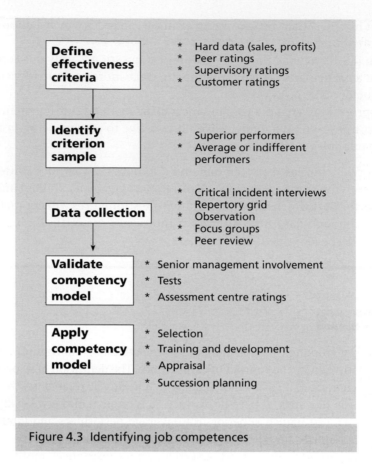

Figure 4.3 Identifying job competences

relationships. Another criticism of this list might be that it is too lengthy. By using factor analysis (described in Chapter 3) we might be able to correlate importance ratings for competences in a large number of jobs and identify which competences are essentially manifestations of the same 'thing'. Conversely we could argue it is not detailed enough, particularly in the area of, for example, leadership. Compare these competences to Gary Yukl's dimensions in Chapter 8, which provide a more fine-grained analysis of leadership skills. But a list like this provides a useful starting-point and can mean the exploratory stages involved in identifying them can be cut short if an organization feels it can work with a set of generic competences.

The impact of the 'competence revolution' has been enormous. For example, in the United Kingdom the Management Charter Initiative uses the language of competences to structure its courses and prescribe what is required of an effective manager (MCI, 1997). The appeal of competences was in seeming to offer a common language for describing the key attributes required for effective performance. This language was as relevant for those drawing up job advertisements, making selection decisions, or devising development plans for individuals. Competences were also accessible, since they

Box 4.3 The twenty most widely used competences

I. *Achievement cluster*	Tech./Prof.	Mgr.	Exec.
1. Achievement orientation Acting to improve performance, do a task better (faster, more efficiently, at lower cost, etc.) by committing oneself to accomplishing challenging objectives, or competing against a self-defined standard of excellence. This standard of excellence may be one's own past performance (striving for improvement), an objective measure (results orientation), the performance of others (competitiveness), goals one has set, a unique accomplishment (an 'entrepreneurial' new venture promoting a new product, service, procedure, etc.), or doing something new (innovation).	✔	✔	✔
2. Concern for quality and order Acting to minimize errors and maintain high standards of quality by checking and monitoring data and work, and by developing and maintaining systems for organizing work and information.	✔	✔	
3. Initiative Taking self-directed or self-motivated initiative to do more than is expected or required in the job, act before being required to by events, to improve job performance, avoid problems or find or create new opportunities.	✔	✔	✔

II. *Helping service cluster*	Tech./Prof.	Mgr.	Exec.
4. Interpersonal understanding Understanding, interpreting and responding to others' concerns, motives, feelings, and behaviours; accurately recognizing strengths and limitations in others.	✔	✔	✔
5. Customer-service orientation A concern with helping or serving others; efforts (including initiative and tenacity) to discover the customer or client's needs, and to meet those needs. 'Clients' may include internal staff, such as a boss or downstream department, students, or actual external customers.	✔	✔	

III. *Influence cluster*	Tech./Prof.	Mgr.	Exec.
6. Impact and influence Acting to have an impact on others (individuals or organizations), to influence or persuade others.			

III. Influence cluster	**Tech./Prof.**	**Mgr.**	**Exec.**
[Specific intents to develop others' abilities or to meet others' needs are scored on the Developing others and Customer-service scales. Use of positional power to influence others' behaviour, with little concern to persuade them to willingly agree or comply, is scored on the Directiveness scale. Impact and influence covers all types of impact.]		✔	✔
7. **Organizational awareness** The ability to learn and understand the power relationships in one's own or other organizations (customers, suppliers, etc.). This includes the ability to identify who are real decision-makers and the individuals who can influence them; and to predict how new events or situations will affect individuals and groups within the organization.			✔
8. **Relationship building (networking)** Acting to develop and maintain a network of contacts, both inside and outside one's own organization, with people who may be able to supply information, assistance, or support for work-related goals. This includes efforts to build or maintain friendly relationships with people who are, or might someday be, useful in achieving work-related goals.		✔	✔

IV. Managerial cluster	**Tech./Prof.**	**Mgr.**	**Exec.**
9. **Directiveness** The intent to make others comply with one's wishes where personal power or the power of one's position is used appropriately and effectively, with the long-term good of the organization in mind. It includes a theme or tone or 'telling people what to do'. The tone ranges from firm and directive to demanding or even threatening. Attempts to reason with, persuade or convince others to comply are Impact and influence, not Directiveness.		✔	
10. **Teamwork and co-operation** The intention to work co-operatively with others, to be part of a team, to work together, as opposed to working separately or competitively. For this competence to be effective, the intention should be genuine. Teamwork and co-operation may be considered whenever the subject is a member of a group of people functioning as a team.	✔	✔	✔

IV. *Managerial cluster*	Tech./Prof.	Mgr.	Exec.
11. Developing others A genuine intent to foster the learning or development of others with an appropriate level of need analysis. Its focus is on the developmental intent and effect rather than on a formal role of training. It requires a genuine intent to develop others with some thought or effort and does not include routinely sending people to formal training programmes.		✔	
12. Team leadership The intention to take a role as leader of a team or other group. It implies a desire to lead others. Team leadership is generally, but certainly not always, shown from a position of formal authority.			✔

V. *Cognitive, thinking/problem-solving cluster*	Tech./Prof.	Mgr.	Exec.
13. Technical expertise The motivation to expand and use technical knowledge or to distribute work-related knowledge to others.	✔		
14. Information seeking The extent to which a person collects and uses information relevant to work-based problems or opportunities, gets several opinions or inputs, or investigates issues and known facts before making decisions.	✔		
15. Analytical thinking The ability to break complex problems (or processes or projects) into component parts and consider or organize the parts in a systematic way; e.g. make systematic comparisons of different features or aspects; set priorities on a rational basis; identify time sequences, or causal If, then relationships.	✔	✔	
16. Conceptual thinking The ability to see patterns or connections between situations that are not obviously related; identify key or underlying issues in complex situations; or use creative, conceptual, or inductive reasoning to develop novel concepts.	✔	✔	✔

VI. *Personal effectiveness cluster*	Tech./Prof.	Mgr.	Exec.
17. Self-control; stress resistance Acting to keep one's emotions under control and restrain negative behaviours when provoked, when faced with opposition or hostility from others, or when working under conditions of stress.	✔	✔	✔

VI. Personal effectiveness cluster	Tech./Prof.	Mgr.	Exec.
18. Self-confidence Expressing belief in one's ability to accomplish a task and select an effective approach to a task or problem. This includes confidence in one's own ability expressed in increasingly challenging circumstances, confidence in one's own decisions or opinions, and the ability to handle failures constructively.		✔	
19. Organizational commitment; 'business-mindedness' Acting to align one's behaviour with the needs, priorities, and goals of the organization; putting the organization's needs before one's own; acting in ways which promote organizational goals or meet organizational needs.	✔	✔	✔
20. Flexibility Acting to adapt to and work effectively with a variety of situations, individuals or groups. The ability to understand and appreciate different and opposing perspectives on an issue, to adapt one's approach as the requirements of a situation change, and to change or easily accept changes in one's own organization or job requirements.		✔	✔

required no specialist, i.e. psychological, knowledge to apply. And being written in the language used by an organization they recognizably related to a specific context.

However, there are a number of problems with the notion of competence. First, at a general level there is some confusion about what the term actually means. The fluidity of meaning inherent in the Boyatzis and other definitions lends itself to confusion. They have a Humpty-Dumpty quality—they can mean whatever the user intended them to mean. One critic has even suggested they are nothing more than a trendy word for the term skill.

Woodruffe (1993) has provided some useful suggestions for tightening the term up. He points out that there are essentially two ways the term has come to be used in organizations—areas of competence and competence. Essentially, this distinction is between task characteristics and person variables. An area of competence might be financial forecasting. But competences are the behaviours an individual needs to display in order to cope with this part of the job. A competence here might include analytical thinking. Woodruffe suggests the term competence should be restricted to the qualities of people and not tasks. He argues some of the confusion is the result of this failure to distinguish between areas of competence and competence itself. This leads to the problem—when assessing people against competence requirements—known as 'double counting'—

when a piece of behaviour can be counted towards two 'competences', thus artificially inflating an individual's assessment.

A second problem arises when competences are assumed to have some explanatory value. Competences are convenient ways of summarizing and describing clusters of behaviour, nothing more. They do not possess the explanatory value of some psychological concepts such as intelligence or aptitude. This becomes particularly apparent when using competences for development. A low rating in a competence dimension leads to a discussion about a development strategy for the individual. But the competence dimension provides no explanation of why the individual is low. And this problem is compounded by competences being an amalgam of traits, abilities, and motivations. It is not clear whether the apparent lack of competence in the area is something which is, for example, deeply rooted in their personality—the result of biological or social learning differences, or whether it was an absence of motivation causing the individual to be uninvolved in the assessment and unwilling to display the behaviour associated with that competence.

Thirdly, there is a tension in competence models between their generality and their specificity. If a competence model is too general, important information can be lost. For example, the competence 'communication' might mask important differences between an individual's written and oral effectiveness. But, conversely, too long a list of competences means fine distinctions which *conceptually* seem to be helpful *empirically* in practice get lost. An example might be trying to rate a candidate on the analytical and conceptual thinking competence during a group exercise. In a list of fifteen competences used by a retailer I found assessments of competences were very highly correlated. Assessors were, given the level of correlation, clearly not able to make the distinctions between relatively similar competences.

Fourthly, competence models can run the risk of prescribing current requirements without considering how they might change in the future. To avoid this, involvement of senior management is crucial to ensure some competences relate to what might confront the organization in the future. For example, in working with a building society it was clear from directors that the future would involve further rationalization of lending institutions, customization of products, and more collaboration with other organizations such as supermarkets. These changes in the organization's environment and the ability to adapt to them would need to be reflected in any competence model developed for senior managers.

Finally, Du Gay *et al.* (1996) argue that competences exercise an insidious form of control over individuals. They locate competences in a much broader historical context, suggesting they serve economic and organizational imperatives—to redefine managers and managerial work. From this perspective competences present a way of changing the relationship between the organization and the individual. They are thus a central relay mechanism mediating social structures and individuals. Historically, loyalty and compliance were the qualities valued in managers. In the 'new managerial work' entrepreneurial qualities are emphasized, redefining the relationship between organizations and managers in market terms (i.e. reviewed regularly through assessment and either renewed or terminated). They argue that competences exercise control by encouraging individuals to turn themselves into projects. Individuals need to develop a style of life and a relationship to themselves which maximizes the worth of their existence to themselves. Individuals assume the status of being the 'subject' of their own existence. The promise of competences for organizations—capturing the most elusive of resources, the human one—has meant that the failures associated with attempts to operationalize the concept have been ignored by organizations.

Du Gay's arguments are important as they remind us of the wider economic and historical context in which competences appeared and the deeper social functions they may serve. These broader issues of managerial control and managerial careers are discussed more fully in Chapter 12. Despite all of these criticisms, conceptual, methodological, empirical, and political competences are currently the concepts which many readers will be assessed against at various points in their careers.

Assessment methods

Interviews

Though the most widely used method—particularly in the selection process—the interview has, for a long time, had a number of fierce critics who claim it is of little use in predicting actual job performance or is even potentially discriminatory (e.g. Wood, 1997; Silvester and Chapman, 1996). However, there is some evidence which shows that, under some circumstances, the interview can be a reasonably good predictor of job performance—at least as good as other more expensive methods—and can provide accurate assessments of key psychological variables (e.g. Anderson, 1997). For example, one review of a number of studies found interview ratings of candidates correlated strongly with measures of their G-general ability (Huffcutt *et al.*, 1996). These more encouraging findings have to some extent helped recently to rehabilitate the interview as a useful method of assessing individuals.

But to be effective the interview has somehow to minimize the effects of a number of processes which can radically undermine its usefulness. First, the interview has to contend with the *general* problems which reduce our capacity to perceive and gauge others accurately in all situations.

1. *Impression formation*. We tend to make judgements about others very quickly and tend to ignore information which later contradicts our first impression. This is because we seem to have an 'index system' at the back of our head which we characteristically apply to others in order to make sense of their behaviour (a technique for accessing your own index system can be found in Box 6.1, Chapter 6 where this aspect of social perception is discussed in more detail). I have met many managers who are quite proud of their ability to assess quickly ('I knew as soon as she walked through the door her face would fit . . . '), and who had considerable faith in these judgements.

2. *Halo effect*. If we perceive certain key traits, we tend to judge all other aspects of the individual according to whether we have judged the person favourably or unfavourably

on these traits. A negative halo effect which drives down ratings of individuals is sometimes referred to as the *horns effect*. Both represent considerable problems as they can drastically reduce the accuracy of an assessment, and they can occur in any assessment setting from selection to performance reviews. Whilst halo effects can reflect personal preoccupations such as neatness or accent, some general ones do seem to exist. For example, Marlowe *et al.* (1996) found clear evidence of gender and attractiveness having an impact on ratings of suitability, particularly amongst less experienced managers.

3. *Stereotypes*. Ready-made generalizations about members of social categories can distort judgements about individuals. Stereotypes are most likely to be used if, for one reason or another (time constraints, ability, prejudice) an interviewer is unable or unwilling to do the amount of information gathering and processing required to develop an accurate assessment of the individual. The practical effect of a stereotype is that the interviewee is no longer a unique, differentiated individual but simply a member of a social category who is assumed to possess certain characteristics.

4. *Limited capacity*. The brain is not a particularly good processor of a lot of information arriving simultaneously. During an interview the interviewer can be flooded with information—verbal and non-verbal. Interviewers cope the way we do more generally in life—by attending selectively, i.e. processing fully some information at the expense of other information. Alongside these basic limitations on information processing other physiological factors can further reduce the amount of information processing going on. The number of evaluative categories—the size of the 'index system' referred to above—can be fairly small, and our attentional beam can drift through boredom and fatigue, particularly if interviewing a number of individuals.

5. *Idiosyncrasy*. Our index system—the evaluative categories we use—may reflect our own interests and attitudes. In other words, to some extent our assessments of others can reveal as much about our own preoccupations, commitments, and projects as the individual being assessed.

In addition to these general problems of person perception, the interview faces a number of *specific* problems which can, if not corrected, further undermine its usefulness. These include:

1. *Primary and recency effects*. In a selection setting interviewers seeing candidates across a morning or afternoon tend to have far more vivid memories of the first and last candidate they see. This is because the memory traces of middle-order candidates have suffered more interference than those at the beginning and end of the session.

2. *Strategy*. Again, in selection settings some interviewers can adopt particularly ineffective strategies with candidates. This can be the result of anxiety or inexperience. One strategy known as the 'tell and sell' means interviewers tell the candidate about the job and then sell the idea he or she is well suited to it. This means any genuine mutual exploration of whether the candidate is right for the job and vice versa simply does not occur.

3. *Interviewees*. Some people are better at being interviewed than others, and this skill may have little to do with the ability to cope more generally with the job. Many

individuals realize the selection interview is essentially an elaborate social game with rules and set pieces and have effective stock answers to some of the absurder questions interviewers can sometimes ask—'What are your strengths and weaknesses?', 'Where do you see yourself in five years' time?'

4. *Like me.* To be effective interviewers need to be aware of the tendency to view very favourably candidates who seem to possess similar characteristics ('That is exactly how I would have answered that question at his age!').

5. *Contrast effects.* Judgements about individuals can be affected by the quality of previous candidates. For example, a really difficult interview with candidate A can mean the assessment of a somewhat more talkative candidate B is highly inflated.

6. *Negative information.* In selection settings, with a large pool of candidates to see, interviewers can, wittingly or unwittingly, come to view the task as primarily a rejection procedure. This means the interviewer searches for reasons to reject a candidate. Negative information about candidates therefore becomes disproportionately weighted. One negative piece of information, such as failing an exam, can wipe out the positive evidence, such as good work experience.

7. *Ethnocentric bias.* One problem interviewers face is somehow taking into account differences in *attributional styles of interviewees* (Silvester and Chapman, 1996). We have already encountered the idea of differences in attributions—the way people explain their own and others' behaviour—when describing locus of control in the last chapter. But whilst locus of control is a cognitive personality variable used to explain some differences between individuals, it is possible that general differences in attributional style exist between cultures. For example, if questioned about achievements, an individual from a collectivist culture might emphasize group effort. The attribution of a European or North American interviewer might be one of low internal motivation. Differences in attributional style may well be a potent source of discrimination in the interview.

8. *Self-delusion.* It is easy to fool ourselves about the value of our interviewing. Most managers see themselves as 'good at interviewing'. And there are a number of possible reasons for this perception. There are two interwoven strands in an interview: information gathering and rapport-building. Many interviewers tend to concentrate on rapport-building at the expense of the information gathering element. In other words, the social encounter has been reasonably warm and friendly, but at the end of it very little concrete information is now available which was not already known from the references and application form. This is compounded by a tendency to avoid probing—asking awkward and sensitive questions. There seems to be a moral obligation to accept an individual's 'front'—their definition of themselves (see Chapter 6). To do otherwise seems to break a fundamental 'rule' of social life. This means candidates can make claims about themselves which will not be subjected to much continual scrutiny. But the feeling that the encounter has been reasonably warm and friendly perhaps deludes us into feeling it has been a success and means that we rarely take into account the above defects.

Ross and Nisbett (1991) suggest the general effect of these person perception problems is to reduce our 'conservatism' and 'charity'. In other words, we seem to be willing to ascribe characteristics to individuals (conscientious, sociable, intelligent, etc.) on the basis of very little evidence. We rarely withhold judgement. Moreover, the judgements are often quite negative. They offer some interesting insights into why we are prone to such errors. They argue that our forebears spent their working and domestic lives with intimates: siblings, parents and spouses. Ascribing qualities to intimates was reasonable since there were massive behaviour samples to infer traits from. By comparison an interview provides us with a relatively minute behaviour sample. But we are stuck with a trait language which, they claim, is more appropriate for use among intimates.

Clearly, these general problems of person perception and those which are more specific to the interview format present interviewers with significant difficulties which need to be overcome. One response has been to make interviews more systematic. There are a number of methods of making interviews more consistent; the two main ones are: *situational interviews* and *behaviour description interviews*. Situational interviews involve presenting candidates with identical hypothetical scenarios and rating responses according to a predetermined format. For example, 'a machine guard has come off, you cannot get in touch with the maintenance engineer, the production team are saying they will not work with it, it is the night shift, switching the line off loses £100,000 worth of production, an industrial injury risks a fine, possible damages and bad publicity—what do you do?' In behaviour description interviews interviewees are asked to identify real situations from their past which are job relevant. For example, 'how did you motivate a difficult member of your team?'

Common to both is the introduction of more structure. Candidates are asked the same questions with the same coding used to assess responses. And research demonstrates structured interviewing is much more effective at predicting future job performance. Whilst some unstructured interviews can predict only about 4 per cent of the differences which emerge in actual job performance, structured approaches can do as much as nine times better at 36 per cent (Anderson, 1997).

So why are unstructured approaches to interviewing not more common? Dipboye (1997) provides six reasons:

1. Structuring interviews makes it more difficult to sell a job to good candidates.
2. Interviewers do not enjoy the restrictions of a more structured process.
3. Whilst structured approaches help answer the 'can do—will do?' questions, they seem less useful when exploring the third key question—'will fit?'
4. Structured formats can be perceived as less fair by both interviewers and candidates.
5. Unstructured interviews give the interviewers more power—they are freer to ask questions they feel are important.
6. Interviews also serve an 'expressive' function. They provide interviewers with opportunities to convey symbolically information about the organization. This expressive function of an interview is less easily achieved in a more structured format.

Interestingly, differences in intelligence seem to be more important to interview ratings in an unstructured format. This is presumably because more intelligence is required when negotiating a route through the looser format and achieving a higher rating than through the more structured version (Huffcutt *et al.*, 1996).

But the evidence for structured interviews is, despite some of their limitations, persuasive. Structuring the process means questioning is not only more consistent but is also related more straightforwardly to the job demands.

Another response to the difficulties inherent in interviewing is to emphasize the need for interviewers to be trained. Like other social skills, effective interviewing depends on the ability to progress smoothly through the encounter, on sensitivity to cues, and on developing a rapport with another person. Progressing smoothly through an interview is established by the behaviours outlined in Table 4.1. What is noticeable is that many of

Behaviour	Example	Comment
Open question	Why did you leave your first job?	Used for opening up an area for discussion
Closed question	You need to give a month's notice to your present job?	Used to clarify details or give an anxious candidate an easy question to reduce his or her nervousness
Advisement	Let's move on to your time at university	Used to guide the thoughts and feelings of the candidate
Reflective listening	So you're saying that you've achieved everything you can in your present company	Used when attempting to capture the thoughts and feelings behind what the candidate has said. Also a powerful method of conveying acceptance. Is possibly the most difficult interviewing skill
Interpretation	You seem to enjoy having to respond quickly to difficulties	Used to communicate the interviewer's perspective on what the candidate has been saying
Process disclosure	I feel you are not being as open as you perhaps could be	Used occasionally by the interviewer to reveal how he or she is reacting to the candidate at that moment, thus giving the candidate a chance to comment on the interviewer's reaction
Biographical disclosure	Yes, that happened to me when I moved down from the North	Used to reduce the asymmetry and formality of the interviewer–candidate relationship
Summarizing	So for the last five minutes you have been telling me . . .	Allows the interviewer to check his or her understanding of what has been said and provides the interviewee with an opportunity to alter the interviewer's opinion
Probing	Could we go back to your time with . . .	Enables the interviewer to pursue claims made by the interviewee

Table 4.1 Key interview behaviours

them do not occur in ordinary conversations. Behaviours such as summarizing are crucial to the information-gathering element of the interview but they are unlikely to appear in an interview unless an individual has been trained to use them. Interview training focusing on these behaviours and on how to avoid the problems outlined earlier are now commonplace, involving videotaped practices, feedback, and coaching.

By making individuals aware of their own attributional biases, the need to remain open, to be more systematic, and to be more self-critical, decisions based on interviews can be as effective as those based on other methods (see Box 4.4).

Biodata

An abbreviation of biographical data, this technique involves identifying what biographical characteristics predict outcomes such as length of stay in a job and training performance. Biodata information ranges from concrete variables, such as length of stay in previous jobs and marital status, through to softer attitudinal areas, such as opinions about teamworking.

Biodata can be as powerful a predictor of behaviour as pencil and paper tests. But it can involve a considerable initial investment by the organization, as a study has to be commissioned to identify what, if any, biographical predictors exist. To be sufficiently robust a reasonable sample has to be available. I have carried out a number of biodata assignments for organizations, each of which has involved coding and analysing information from over a thousand employees' application forms. However, once the critical characteristics and their weightings have been identified, the ongoing cost is minimal.

The predictive power of biodata is assumed to arise from past experiences and behaviour shaping future experience and thus behaviour. It is undoubtedly a powerful technique. For example, in one of the studies referred to earlier the biodata formula was able to predict correctly eighty-five times out of a hundred whether an applicant would stay in the company more than two years. Intriguingly, in this study one of the usual predictors of tenure, average length of stay in previous jobs, operated in the opposite direction to what was expected. Usually an individual with short previous tenure repeats this in future posts. Similarly, long previous tenure predicts subsequent lengthy tenure. In our study this did not appear. Long tenure elsewhere predicted a brief spell with this organization. This confirmed the 'gut feeling' of some senior managers that they were losing individuals with a wealth of experience and background.

This example actually indicates one of the problems with biodata. The circumstances which caused those with long track records with other companies to leave (essentially, in this instance, lack of support) would be changed as a result of the biodata study. Thus, the prediction that long previous tenure indicates an unacceptably short stay would probably not hold in a year's time. Generally, biodata cannot be expected to last more than three years.

As well as being volatile it can be seen from this example that biodata tends to be very job and organization specific. What characteristics predict performance or tenure in one job grade probably could not be used to predict these outcomes in others. In

Box 4.4 Self-awareness questionnaire

Like all social skills interviewing is enhanced by self-awareness. This questionnaire provides you with a framework for reflecting on what went well and less well. For each of the questions you answered 'no' or 'uncertain' to, consider the following questions. What happened? What could I do to improve this? What might be difficult about achieving this improvement? But what would the pay-off be?

		Yes	No	Uncertain
1.	Did I relax the individual initially?	☐	☐	☐
2.	Did I progress smoothly from the opening to the exploratory phase?	☐	☐	☐
3.	Did I ask open questions?	☐	☐	☐
4.	Did I direct the interview effectively?	☐	☐	☐
5.	Did I summarize at points?	☐	☐	☐
6.	Did I avoid leading questions?	☐	☐	☐
7.	Did I probe effectively?	☐	☐	☐
8.	Did I avoid discriminatory questions?	☐	☐	☐
9.	Did I make sufficient notes?	☐	☐	☐
10.	Did I remain open until the end of interview?	☐	☐	☐
11.	Did I balance positive and negative information?	☐	☐	☐
12.	Was I aware of any contrast effects?	☐	☐	☐
13.	Did my questions relate to the job demands?	☐	☐	☐
14.	Did I get the talking/listening balance correct?	☐	☐	☐
15.	Did I provide the individual with sufficient information about the job, organization, rewards?	☐	☐	☐
16.	Did I have a clear interview structure and objectives?	☐	☐	☐
17.	Did I appear unanxious, patient, and attentive?	☐	☐	☐
18.	Did I explain what would happen next?	☐	☐	☐
19.	Did I conclude the interview effectively?	☐	☐	☐
20.	Did I get the information gathering/ rapport building balance right?	☐	☐	☐

Adapted from Guirdham (1995)

practice this means if organizations decide to invest in biodata, each job grade requires a separate study.

However, despite these drawbacks biodata is one of the most cost-effective selection techniques. With some exceptions, notably the life insurance industry and the 'fast track' of the British Civil Service, biodata is at present underutilized in Europe.

Psychometric tests

Getting more 'value' from an interview, as has been seen, is partly achieved by making the interview more structured and standardized—in other words more like tests. The key features of psychometric assessments are as follows.

1. *Standardized test materials and administration procedures.* Everyone is given the same questions in the same order. The only exception to this is when questions are administered on a computer. Some programs are 'adaptive'—they work out that certain questions would be too difficult or easy and skip them. The test is administered in the same way. This consists of an introduction and a script. The script takes individuals through the examples and, ideally, ensures everyone is clear what is expected of them. Before reading the script the administrator should have spent a few minutes ensuring the group is standardized in terms of their *motivation* and *expectation of success*. This is achieved by ensuring individuals understand why the test is being used, how it fits into the assessment process, what weight is put on it, what relevance it has to the job, and the availability of feedback (e.g. Fletcher, 1997).

2. *Standardized scoring procedures.* Unlike an unstructured interview, responses to psychometric tests can be scored straightforwardly. In ability tests responses are either right or wrong. On personality tests responses demonstrate a preference for one type of behaviour.

3. *Standardized interpretation procedures.* Individuals' scores are interpreted in the same way. This can be done through *norm referencing*, *criterion referencing*, or *content referencing*. With norm referencing the individual's score is interpreted by identifying its position along the normal distribution curve (discussed in the last chapter). The curve is not necessarily the general population. It might represent the distribution of scores, for example, in a representative group of senior managers. There are different ways of expressing an individual's position under the curve. In the UK percentiles are commonly used—the proportion of individuals performing as well or worse than this particular individual. Thus the 80th percentile means only 20 per cent of this group would be expected to do better. Percentiles have a number of problems. They exaggerate small differences in the middle of the distribution. A meaningless two or three score difference between individuals—perhaps the result of unlucky or lucky guesses—becomes a 20 or 30 percentile difference. Conversely, they understate differences at the extremes—a 10-score difference might put individuals on the same percentile. Worst of all, they endow tests with a spurious air of accuracy. Since, in reality, all tests or administration procedures are not perfect, each score is effectively a sample. Like all samples they contain error and are effectively only estimates. This means that probabilistic statements need to be made—expressing the score between a range of percentiles which

takes into account the error associated with the test. For example, 'there is a 95 per cent chance that Camilla's ability lies somewhere between the 70th and 95th percentile when compared with other senior managers.' However, in my experience organizations prefer a single percentile, thus treating the score as a 'perfect' score rather than an estimate. The error inherent in test scores is handled more effectively by methods more popular in North America—stens and stanines. These divide the curve up into ten and nine broad bands, respectively, giving individuals an indication of their relative status rather than a 'precise' position under the curve.

Norm referencing answers the basic question—where is this individual relative to others? *Criterion referencing* answers an equally important one—is this what we would expect to see in an individual likely to be successful in the job or on this training programme? Answering this question involves researching the relationship between test and job or training performance. This enables the calculation of 'cut scores', i.e. scores below which the individual is unlikely to succeed.

Content referencing adds to the information value of psychometric assessments by interpreting the pattern of performance. For example, in an assessment of numerical reasoning it is possible to have technique and reasoning questions. Two individuals can arrive at the same score through very different routes. One individual has lapses in technique but when in possession of one can go on to reason with it. Another individual may have plenty of techniques but find it difficult to reason with them. In normative terms they are identical but there are very different implications for each pattern of score.

These standardized procedures are what makes psychometric assessment distinctive. But what is a test? Essentially, anything which provides a quantitative assessment of a psychological attribute or attributes can be counted as a psychometric test. Thus, the distinction between a physics test and a mechanical reasoning test is that one measures knowledge—how much physics teaching an individual has been exposed to—whereas the other should measure the more pervasive and fundamental psychological attribute, which, for example, will determine the extent to which an individual profits from physics teaching in the first place.

Tests commonly used include the following:

1. *Dexterity tests*. For employees whose work involves manual skills such as soldering, wiring, or fitting, tests of fine or gross eye–hand co-ordination are useful. As well as selection applications, dexterity tests are often used to establish the effect of industrial injury to assess damages or to identify progress in rehabilitation programmes.

2. *General ability tests*. Historically, as was discussed in Chapter 3, a great deal of emphasis has been placed on tests of 'g' or general ability. The assumption that intelligence is one 'thing' has meant one score has sufficed as an indication of an individual's ability. More appropriately nowadays, general ability tests are used where jobs are non-routine, analytical, and complex to give an indication of how well individuals cope with novelty—'learn the ropes', 'grasp essentials', and 'think on their feet'.

3. *Aptitude tests*. The notion of 'multiple intelligences'—individuals being more complex bundles of ability which are not necessarily consistent—has encouraged the use of tests of more specific abilities such as verbal, numerical, spatial, and mechanical.

4. *Critical thinking tests*. The most widely used tests in managerial and supervisory jobs assess this 'crunch skill'. Critical thinking tests simulate situations where managers are presented with persuasively or even emotively argued reports prepared by people who probably know more about the subject than they do. For example, for a pharmaceutical company a manager might have a number of reports each arguing for funding of clinical trials of their product. To be effective the manager must be able to suspend emotions and prejudices and deal with the reports on their own logical merits. Do the conclusions follow from a thorough analysis? Are the reports littered with hidden assumptions? Are the inferences solid? In short, are these strong or weak arguments?

5. *Personality tests*. Where interpersonal skills such as selling, influencing, motivating, or team working are important to job performance, responses to personality questionnaires can provide clues about how applicants will cope with these demands. Personality questionnaires will also provide data on more general personality issues such as coping with stress, rigidity, attitudes to authority, and creativity.

6. *Personal qualities*. A number of widely used tests do not fit easily into any of the above categories. These include the more focused occupational tests of, for example, customer service or team-working skills. In North America there has been a long tradition of assessing integrity—i.e. honesty—and these tests are beginning to be a feature of assessment in Europe (e.g. Rust, 1997).

Tests have two technical criteria to meet before they are useful in occupational assessment: *reliability* and *validity*. The concept of reliability addresses two questions. First, is the measure self-consistent? In other words, to what extent does each test item measure the same variable? This is sometimes termed *internal reliability*. Secondly, does the test yield the same score for an individual on retesting (assuming the trait or ability is itself stable)? This is often called *test–retest reliability*. Internal reliability can be calculated by correlating scores for each question with those for each other question. The average correlation indicates the extent to which questions are measuring the same thing. Alternatively, scores on one half of the test can be correlated with scores on the other half. Test–retest reliability is measured by establishing the extent to which scores obtained on two administrations of a test are similar. To reduce the chances of subjects remembering their answers from the first sitting, the interval between testing seasons should be at least a month.

Normally we would expect test scores to possess test–retest reliability and not be subject to fluctuations. Reliability coefficients (in other words, the correlation between test scores at time 1 with test scores for the same group of subjects at time 2) of about .7 or better are usually expected in tests used in occupational assessment.

The validity of test scores is equally important. A test is said to be valid when it measures what it purports to measure. This means that differences between individuals' scores actually reflect differences on the variable being measured. First, if a test looks like it measures what it claims to measure, it is said to have *face validity*. This is important because if individuals can see that a test seems to be measuring relevant attributes, they are more likely to co-operate with the tester (e.g. Fletcher, 1997). Face validity therefore increases the acceptability of tests in the selection procedure. Secondly, when scores on a test correlate well with scores on other tests of the same attribute, the test is said to possess *concurrent validity*. For example, if scores for a group on a new IQ test correlate well with the scores on other IQ tests, we can be reasonably confident that the new test is measuring intelligence. Concurrent validity does not, however, imply *criterion validity*, the ability of a test to predict real-life performance. The criterion validity of an aptitude test used in employee selection would be its ability to predict some aspect of job performance.

Validity is usually expressed as a correlation coefficient. For example, one of the authors was employed to conduct a study of the relationship between a test and sales performance. Figure 4.4 indicates the scatter of results obtained. The diagonal line represents the line of 'best fit' for the data. The scatter represents a correlation of about .5. If the organization decides that in future it wants to employ people who are likely to sell more than 45 units per month, 'cut-off' scores on the test can be established by extrapolating across to the line of best fit and dropping down.

If these fifty individuals were now to apply for their jobs, what use would the test be?

In the top right-hand corner we have our *true positives*. These are people whose performance we would correctly predict. They have 'passed' the test and have turned out to be successful in the job.

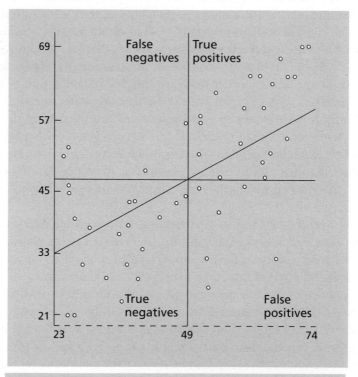

Figure 4.4 Deriving a cut-off score from a validity study

In the bottom left-hand corner we have the *true negatives*. These are individuals who 'failed' the test and whom we have predicted currently would not perform adequately.

In the bottom right-hand corner are the *false positives*. These are individuals who have 'passed' the test and who would therefore be recommended. However, they do not succeed in achieving the sales targets.

In the top left-hand corner we have our *false negatives*. This group would be the most hard done by. Their score on the test suggests they would be unsuccessful, but if given the chance they would succeed.

Out of the fifty individuals, we have made eleven errors using this cut-off point. This represents an error rate of 22 per cent. This is much better than could be expected by chance and would have significant financial implications. Of course, with only fifty individuals the results are at this stage tentative and would need to be revalidated as more data became available.

One major issue with criterion validity is what is known as the 'criterion problem'. In the example above the performance criterion was a straightforward one. Individuals are either putting business on the books or they are not. But with many jobs no such 'hard' data is available. Many validity studies use 'soft' criteria like supervisory ratings to assess the validity of a test. These criterion scores may themselves be problematic, undermined by halo effects and the other problems of person perception described earlier.

Incremental validity is the extent to which test 2 increases the overall predictive value of the assessment over and above test 1. For example, working on a help-line dealing with hardware and software problems might require a high level of intelligence. The individual has to be able to get to grips quickly with what the problem might be and see a solution. But alongside this he or she has to be able to give callers the confidence to try to fix a problem themselves. Thus, a measure of sensitivity would provide incremental validity to a measure of intelligence.

Finally, it is sometimes difficult to find a measure against which a test's criterion value can be assessed. In these situations the test's *construct* validity is measured instead. This involves generating a number of hypotheses about the test variable as a construct or concept and then finding evidence to support or reject these hypotheses. For instance, to demonstrate the construct validity of a measure of job satisfaction we might hypothesize that high scorers would have less absenteeism, be less inclined to leave the organization and show higher levels of job performance. Low scorers should be absent more often, should be more likely to leave and should demonstrate poorer work performance than high scorers.

Test usage in the UK has grown enormously in recent years. Surveys indicate about 70 per cent of large employers use some form of psychometric assessment, although among smaller employers (below 25 employees), where the bulk of the population work, the figure is much lower at around 15 per cent (e.g. White and Doyle, 1997). Inevitably, a great deal of controversy has accompanied this explosion of interest. Like any other assessment technique its value varies enormously. For example, poor test administration which irritates and confuses, or where the administrator even manages to enhance anxiety, will undermine the value of the best constructed test. Generally speaking, ability and aptitude tests provide high status information. Individuals either get questions right or wrong and the total can be interpreted straightforwardly. But, their usefulness still rests on whether they ultimately relate to the job's characteristics.

Much more problematic are personality tests whose validities and reliabilities are much lower. And, if anything, their use is more widespread than would be supported by the evidence for them. Some critics have even claimed that what evidence does exist in manuals can be illusory, because statistical techniques such as correlation and regression capitalize on chance associations.

There are a number of reasons why validities for personality tests are much lower. First, the status of the information is initially much lower than with ability tests. Responses to questions such as 'I make friends easily' force individuals to fall back on their self-concept—'me as a friendly person–me as a less friendly person'. And this self-concept might not stack up with how others see them.

Secondly, individuals can distort responses. Motivation to do this may be particularly high if the test is part of a selection process. Individuals will want to present themselves in the best possible light so will tend to increase their affiliativeness and reduce their neuroticism. Many tests, however, have ways of identifying the degree of distortion present. On many scales, such as tough-minded vs. tender-minded, it is not clear what a socially desirable response would be. Good test administration seems to reduce markedly the degree of distortion—i.e. emphasizing there is no right or wrong profile and that distortion can be detected. Some research suggests distortion is much less of a problem than is initially imagined and tends to be a manifestation of other traits such as conscientiousness and anxiety (e.g. Ones *et al.*, 1996).

Thirdly, correlation indicates the presence of linear relationships. With personality we might expect some relationships to be curvilinear. For example, a low level of dominance produces a poor ability to close sales. But customers might find very high scorers too 'pushy' and 'overbearing'. The middle range scorers will therefore be associated with 'higher sales'. While there clearly is a relationship this would not show up in a correlation coefficient and thus the personality test would not seem to be a 'valid' predictor of performance. As Jones and Poppleton (1998) point out, we need more sophisticated statistical models to capture these more complex interactions.

Finally, for a whole range of technical reasons (e.g. poor reliability, inadequate sampling, poor criterion measures, absence of a normal distribution on the criterion measure, etc.) the average maximum correlation between a personality test and a criterion—unless conditions are particularly favourable—is about .3 (i.e. explaining about 10 per cent of the variation between high and low performers). In the light of this Warr (1997) suggests we should be pleased with a validity as low as .2 against this maximum.

Clearly, what is required of users of personality tests is sensitivity to these epistemological and empirical difficulties. In other words, personality data has to be treated as highly tentative—based on self-report and in need of corroboration from other more concrete forms of evidence. This sensitivity can be in short supply. As an expert witness I have had to comment on a personality report produced by a consultant which was written as if it were all true rather than as a set of inferences requiring corroboration. In some parts of Europe these problems are less likely to occur. For example, in much of Scandinavia only psychologists have access to personality tests, and in Holland the ethical code for psychologists means candidates have the right to challenge the contents of a report *before* it reaches the selection panel.

Perhaps most worrying of all is the use of what are called 'quick and dirty' tests: five-minute personality tests requiring individuals to indicate which adjective is most and least like him or her. These tests yield scores which are mathematically interdependent—so, for example, as you go up the sociability scale you go down the other scales. The construction of these forced choice or *ipsative* tests with their interdependent scales makes it impossible to compare meaningfully individuals on a scale-by-scale basis. Their use in selection procedures, to make comparisons between individuals, is thus not appropriate. But this limitation is often overlooked.

In the United Kingdom, where non-psychologists have access to personality tests, the British Psychological Society has attempted to raise standards by giving credentials to test users. The level-A certificate is obtained by demonstrating competence in test usage to a psychologist. Theoretically this ensures a minimum level of understanding of the importance of reliability, validity, and proper administration among test users. The level-B certificate attempts to provide a baseline of understanding of personality theory.

It is possible to accuse the Society of combining naivety and optimism in their attempts to introduce credentials into the UK market. The naivety arises because there is inevitably a tension between the commercial imperatives of test publishing and a credentialing system which represents a considerable barrier (up to eleven days training) to access, particularly when this barrier to access can be criticized for being too 'academic', elaborate, and prescriptive (e.g. Jones and Poppleton, 1998). The optimism ignores the reality that individuals with credentials are just as likely to be confronted by organizational pressures which can encourage bad practice—for instance, using raw scores instead of normed scores, or not taking into account test error, and thus over-interpreting small differences between candidates, and even testing in corridors. These are all examples I have encountered among trained individuals. It is also optimistic to ignore the difficulty of delivering a full appreciation of the limitations of psychometric data in a relatively brief period of training (e.g. Rees, 1996).

Assessment centres

The term 'assessment centre' refers to a method rather than a place. The objective of an assessment centre is no different from other techniques already described: 'to obtain the best possible indication of a candidate's actual or potential competence to perform at the target job or job level' (Woodruffe, 1993). The assessment centre approach, however, is to combine a range of assessment techniques to give the fullest picture possible. While assessment centres will utilize interviews and tests, the critical and perhaps defining feature of the method is the use of work simulation. Work simulations can be written or interactive. An example of a written simulation is the 'in-tray' exercise. Typically, the individual is told he or she has just returned from holiday or is going on holiday this evening. A tray full of faxes, memos, letters, and reports has to be read and acted on. The way the applicant prioritizes and demonstrates incisiveness, sensitivity, market awareness, customer orientation, or other competences identified as important to effective job performance can be rated.

Interactive exercises can be in groups or on an individual basis. Group exercises might involve assigning individuals roles—for example giving each participant the opportunity to lead a discussion on a specific problem for fifteen minutes—or assigning no roles, as in group problem-solving exercises. One-to-one interaction exercises provide participants with opportunities to display a range of competences. For example, in an assessment centre I deliver in an insurance company, a professional actor plays an employee who has been the subject of a complaint from a customer and from some co-workers. Participants have to confront the behaviours which have caused the complaints but not in a way which will demotivate the employee.

Assessment centres vary in length. They can last half a day or run up to five days. The first assessment centre in the UK was the War Office Selection Board, designed during the Second World War to improve officer selection. Its direct descendant, the Civil Service Selection Board, lasts for two days for participants with a third day for assessors to 'wash up'—i.e. evaluate the information and make decisions. Assessment centres in both the UK and USA were developed originally to improve selection procedures. But nowadays they are as likely to be used as part of an employee development programme; hybrid centres combine both objectives—making selection decisions and identifying development needs (e.g. Shipton *et al.*, 1998).

Assessment centres are intense, gruelling experiences which normally provide both the applicant and the assessors with valuable insights into suitability or areas for development. The presence of work simulations has the benefit—particularly in selection—of giving participants a 'feel' for the job and helps some applicants to realize they would not be suited to the job or organization.

Assessment centres represent the Rolls-Royce of assessment techniques. They are expensive to build, usually involving consultants developing custom-made exercises. They are also expensive to run. The assessors observing and rating candidates' performance are usually senior managers who will therefore be away from their jobs for the duration of the centre. Whilst having the drawbacks of the Rolls-Royce they also have its advantages. Assessment centres have repeatedly demonstrated they are the most powerful and robust of selection techniques. And, like the car, a well-run assessment centre can give participants a very favourable impression of the organization.

Most organizations using assessment centres try to make them as collaborative as is possible: in other words, something being done *with* rather than *to* individuals. When being run for development this is easier as, on some exercises, rolling feedback—reflection and review of performance immediately after the exercise, perhaps even involving some coaching, becomes an important part of the process. Most of the data on participants' reactions to assessment centres has indeed shown favourable reactions to them. Participants typically rate them as fair and valid. But their thoroughness and intensity can mean that unsuccessful applicants are more likely to suffer a reduction in their self-esteem, competitiveness, and motivation than if rejected with procedures which involve less psychological engagement. This underlines the crucial importance of sensitive, supportive feedback after the assessment centre.

Conclusion

Organizations and increasingly individuals benefit from accurate assessments of their abilities and competences. And, in future, as job roles and job characteristics change more frequently as organizations respond to external pressures, assessment will become a more pervasive feature of organizational life. We have, in this chapter, seen that the overall aim of any assessment of an individual is to obtain accurate and job-relevant information to enhance decision-making, for example, in selection and promotion or developing a targeted and individually tailored development programme.

As we have seen the notion of competences is now a common approach to translating job characteristics into person requirements. But, the notion of competence tends to roll up distinct psychological factors—traits, abilities, and motivations—into one category. This can be particularly problematic when considering development issues. And it has been suggested that the notion of competence and a concern with more continuous assessment of individuals throughout their careers serves other functions. Managerial work is now redefined in more market and entrepreneurial terms with key competences such as innovativeness and market awareness being used to assess individuals. And in so doing it is suggested that this fundamentally changes the relationship between the manager and the organization to a more contractual one. Loyalty and compliance are no longer critical to an individual's career. Instead assessment against key competences becomes the method of determining whether the relationship between the organization and the individual is continued or terminated.

A key question when using one or more of the assessment methods discussed is to keep in mind the relative status of the information each provides. And the central criteria here were reliability and validity. High status information will have both these qualities.

A number of studies using a technique called *meta-analysis*, which enables the results of numerous studies to be combined, have provided an indication of the average criterion or predictive validity of various assessment methods. The results of some of these studies can be found in Figure 4.5. When interpreting this figure, square the correlation coefficient to indicate how much of the difference in performance is 'explained'. Thus, ability tests seem to do best, explaining about 25 per cent of job performance. Personality tests, at best, explain about 9 per cent.

We did not include a discussion of graphology in this chapter because its use tends to be fairly limited, apart from in France and French-speaking Belgium. In the UK estimates of usage vary between 1 and 3 per cent of organizations and these tend to be

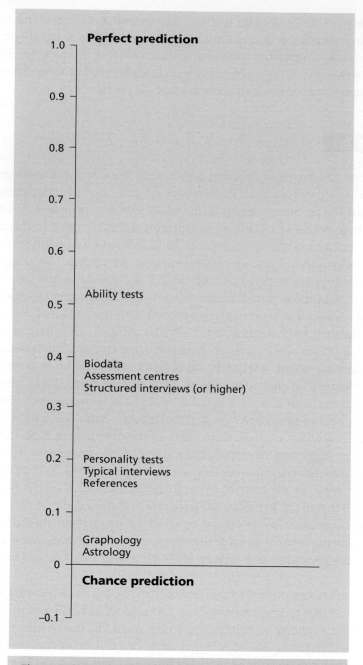

Figure 4.5 Better than chance? Accuracy of prediction using various methods. Compiled from various meta-analytic sources

subsidiaries of French organizations (Driver *et al.*, 1996). Graphology, a technique which stretches back to the 16th century, is based on the idea that handwriting traits manifest personality traits. Whilst ratings of personality based on handwriting samples by graphologists seem to be quite reliable, i.e. graphologists agree with each other, there is no evidence of the validity of the technique (e.g. Tapsell and Cox, 1997).

Assessment centres often achieve validities as high as .68—for example when predicting whose career will advance fastest. But one surprise in this table may be why, at about .4, assessment centre predictions of performance are not higher. This is because assessment centre ratings can be dragged down by subjective processes. I have, for example, argued on more than one occasion with assessors who were prepared to discount two days' worth of positive evidence because a candidate's shirt was not well ironed or tie was slightly askew. In addition, there can often be organizational politics surrounding particular participants. An extreme instance of this was an assessment centre for the chief executive of a large organization I delivered when two of the assessors had received a payment of £80,000 from one of the candidates. Unsurprisingly, they were not particularly interested in the results of the assessment! And this statistic includes all the poorly designed and delivered centres where decisions are rushed and competences are unclear or inappropriate (e.g. Wigfield, 1997).

Ability tests do well in meta-analytic studies. But tests, like assessment centres, can be undermined by poor administration and interpretation. The components of good test usage are generally never all present and sometimes none of them are (Fletcher, 1997).

Indeed, focusing simply on validity has restricted discussion of equally important aspects of assessment processes—their fairness and the rights of individuals being assessed. The concern with validity reflects who, historically, the beneficiaries of assessment procedures were: organizations. Increasingly, individuals will expect to benefit from assessments—irrespective of the setting (e.g. unselected applicants), and will have the right to challenge the content of assessment reports. Perhaps, the biggest challenge facing those designing and delivering assessments is how to reconcile an increasing concern with the defensibility of assessments with rapid organizational change. Legal defensibility requires hard evidence derived from the lengthy processes of job analysis and validation. But by the time a job is analysed and the assessment procedure validated by determining statistically the relationship between assessment ratings and job performance, circumstances may have rendered the original job analysis obsolete. The answer to this conflict may be in making assessment processes more open, participative, and transparently fair, and hence less liable to legal challenge.

Study questions for Chapter 4

1 Why might individuals encounter assessments more frequently than has historically been the case?

2 Discuss the differences between quantitative and qualitative approaches to identifying job demands. Which are more effective?

3 Why is a job analysis an important component of the assessment process?

4 To what extent is competence a Humpty-Dumpty term—meaning whatever people want it to mean?

5 To what extent is the interview the most socially desirable assessment technique but the least effective?

6 Can the effectiveness of the interview be improved?

7 Should the use of personality tests in selection be made illegal?

8 What are the advantages and disadvantages of assessment centres?

9 What might cause an assessment procedure or decision to face legal challenge and to what extent can the possibility of such challenge be minimized?

Further reading

Anderson, N. R. and Herriot, P. (eds.) (1997) *International Handbook of Selection and Assessment*. Chichester: Wiley.

Dubois, D. (1993) *Competency-Based Performance Improvement: A Strategy for Organizational Change*. Amherst, Mass.: HRD Press.

Herriot, P. and Pemberton, C. (1995) *New Deals: The Revolution in Management Careers*. Chichester: Wiley.

Iles, P. (1999) *Managing Staff Selection and Assessment*. Buckingham: Open University Press.

Jackson, C. (1996) *Understanding Psychological Testing*. Leicester: BPS Books.

Kline, P. (1993) *The Handbook of Psychological Testing*. London: Routledge.

Woodruffe, C. (1993) *Assessment Centres: Identifying and Developing Competence*, 2nd edn. London: IPM.

5 Motivation and Job Satisfaction

Summary points and learning objectives

By the end of this chapter you will be able to

- describe content theories of motivation;
- describe process theories of motivation;
- understand the differences between content and process approaches;
- describe the effect of knowledge of results and goal-setting on motivation;
- define the concept of job satisfaction;
- describe ways of assessing an individual's affective response to work;
- describe the job characteristics and variance models of job satisfaction;
- detail the characteristics most commonly associated with job satisfaction;
- understand what is known of the relationship between job satisfaction and other variables such as gender, personality, class, and age;
- describe the relationship, as far as it is understood, between job and general life satisfaction;
- describe the predictive value of job satisfaction and objective workplace variables such as absenteeism, turnover, and productivity.

Introduction

In the years following the Second World War, western industrialized societies experienced increasing prosperity and relatively full employment. Developments in housing, welfare and education policies both reflected and fostered the rising expectations of people in post-war society. In this context employers were faced with a workforce which could, if dissatisfied, change jobs relatively easily. This led to an interest in what creates a stable and well-motivated workforce, and in particular to an interest in the concepts of *motivation* and *job satisfaction*. Nowadays, though relatively full employment is no longer a feature of the labour market, because of its practical implications (particularly productivity and labour turnover) interest in motivation and job satisfaction has persisted. Indeed, there are still a great many occupations where employers experience difficulties in obtaining skilled staff, where the demand for such types of labour is high and the problems of attracting and maintaining a stable workforce continue.

In this chapter we will examine research which has sought to identify the conditions which create a motivated and satisfied workforce.

Needs at work

Motivational theories can be divided into two categories, termed *content* and *process*. Content theories assume that all individuals possess the same set of *needs*. These theories tend to be heavily prescriptive in nature, since by assuming people have similar needs they are also recommending the characteristics that ought to be present in jobs. Process theories, on the other hand, stress the differences in people's needs and focus on the cognitive processes that create these differences.

Content theories

Although content theories are based on the assumption that we can attribute a similar set of needs to all individuals, theories within this category differ in their accounts of what these needs are. Maslow (1954) outlined what is perhaps the most influential of the content theories. He suggested there is a *hierarchy of needs* up which people progress. Once individuals satisfy a need at one level in the hierarchy, it ceases to motivate their behaviour; instead they are motivated by the need at the next level up the hierarchy. Thus, at first individuals are motivated by physiological needs such as hunger and thirst. If conditions are such that these needs can be satisfied, security needs such as the need for shelter and protection become the major influence on an individual's behaviour. A favourable environment allows an individual to progress from behaviour activated by these *deficiency needs* to behaviour which reflects what Maslow termed *higher-order needs*.

As can be seen from Figure 5.1, this progression ultimately leads to behaviour motivated principally by the need to realize one's full potential, which Maslow termed the need for *self-actualization*. Maslow, however, believed that because of the uneven distribution of satisfying work only a small proportion of the population reached this level. Thus, self-actualization is for most of us a need which will motivate our behaviour throughout our lives.

Although not originally intended as an explanation of motivation in the workplace, Maslow's idea of a hierarchy of needs has, none the less, been enthusiastically adopted by many management theorists. It was seen as offering a number of predictions about what motivates people in societies offering relatively full employment. When jobs are scarce, employees are motivated solely by deficiency needs. When jobs are readily available, and deficiency needs are easily satisfied, social needs become important motivators in the workplace. This means organizations will have to provide opportunities for employees to satisfy their social needs, for example by providing company sports and social facilities. Once social needs are met, intrinsic aspects of work, the amount of

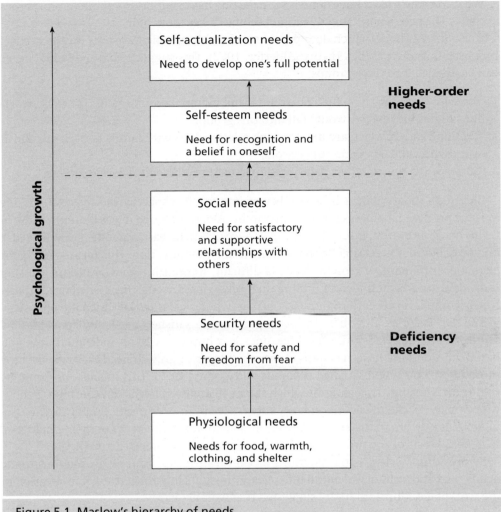

Figure 5.1 Maslow's hierarchy of needs

challenge, responsibility and autonomy it offers, become increasingly salient to employee motivation. Thus, the theory suggests that employees will always tend to want more from their employers. Having satisfied their subsistence needs, they strive to fulfil security needs. When jobs are secure they will seek ways of satisfying social needs and if successful will seek the means (increased autonomy, participation, responsibility) to the ultimate end of self-actualization.

Though many found the idea of a hierarchy of needs appealing, we should stress that the notion has not had much empirical support. In fact, Maslow had not intended his ideas, based on his observations of patients, to be used as a theory in the traditional sense of the term. Consequently he provided no operational definitions of the variables he described, which has made measurement of their relative strengths difficult.

What Maslow's ideas have done is to make one basic, important point: in prosperous societies the need for self-actualization becomes a key motivator.

One content theory which does provide reasonably reliable measures for the needs it proposes is known as ERG theory (Alderfer, 1972). This suggests that individual needs can be divided into three groups:

1. *Existence needs*, which include nutritional and material requirements. At work, working conditions and pay would fall into this group.
2. *Relatedness needs*, which are met through relationships with family and friends and at work with colleagues and supervisors.
3. *Growth needs*, which reflect a desire for personal psychological developments.

Alderfer's theory differs in a number of important respects from Maslow's. While Maslow proposed a progression up a hierarchy, Alderfer argued it was better to think in terms of a continuum, from concrete (existence needs) to least concrete (growth needs); and he believed it is possible to move along it in either direction. This means that if, for example, fulfilment of growth needs is difficult, *frustration regression* occurs, causing individuals to concentrate on fulfilling their relatedness needs. Unsatisfied needs therefore become less rather than more important, whereas Maslow assumed the opposite.

The two theories also differ in the importance of satisfied needs. Whereas Maslow argued that when satisfied a need becomes less important to an individual, research based on Alderfer's ideas has found that relatedness or growth needs actually become more important when satisfied (Wanous and Zwany, 1977). This means, for example, that team working arrangements which satisfy relatedness needs can continue to motivate employees and are not necessarily superseded by growth needs. Employers, according to Alderfer, are in this sense more easily able to satisfy the needs of their employees. In general, tests of the two theories have tended to favour Alderfer's predictions.

By breaking Maslow's and Alderfer's broad variables up, a number of more specific needs can be identified which can offer clearer insights into the nature of motivation in the workplace. Mumford (1976) suggested that workers have:

1. *Knowledge needs*—work that utilizes their knowledges and skills.
2. *Control needs*, which are satisfied by the provision of information, good working conditions and high-quality supervision.
3. *Psychological needs*, such as the needs for recognition, responsibility, status and advancement.
4. *Task needs*, which include the need for meaningful work and some degree of autonomy.
5. *Moral needs*—to be treated in the way that employers would themselves wish to be treated.

Mumford's assumption, therefore, was that employees did not simply see their job as a means to an end but had needs which related to the nature of their work.

A second theory which makes the same basic point is known as Herzberg's *two-factor theory* (Herzberg *et al.*, 1959). The original research for this was based on interviews with 200 accountants and engineers using what is known as the critical incidents technique. This involves asking interviewees to talk about occasions when they felt either particularly satisfied or particularly dissatisfied with their jobs. Two sets of incidents seemed to emerge from these interviews. One involved achievement, advancement, recognition, autonomy and other intrinsic aspects of work. Because these represented sources of satisfaction they were called *motivators*. The second set of incidents concerned working conditions, salary, job security, company policy, supervisors and interpersonal relations. This set, termed *hygiene factors*, were described as sources of dissatisfaction by the sample. Job satisfaction and dissatisfaction therefore appeared to be caused by different sets of factors. The presence of motivators in the workplace caused enduring states of motivation in employees. Their absence, however, did not lead to job dissatisfaction. Hygiene factors, on the other hand, produced an acceptable work environment though not increased satisfaction or involvement with a job; their absence (e.g. low pay), however, caused job dissatisfaction. Thus motivators reflected people's need for self-actualization, while hygienes represented the need to avoid pain (Table 5.1).

Motivators	Hygienes
Responsibility	Supervision
Recognition	Salary
Promotion	Work environment
Achievement	Company policies
Intrinsic aspects of the job	Relationship with colleagues

Table 5.1 Herzberg's two-factor theory of motivation

As well as describing employees' needs, the theory goes a stage further and indicates how people's jobs can be redesigned to incorporate more motivators (Table 5.2). And not surprisingly, a theory which describes both what motivates employees and how jobs can be changed to achieve a well-motivated workforce has attracted a great deal of interest from managers seeking ways of motivating staff and from academics testing Herzberg's propositions.

Support for the two-factor theory has been mixed, however. The independent effect of motivators and hygienes has been questioned, and at least one study has demonstrated that both can be related to job satisfaction and dissatisfaction (Schneider and Locke, 1971). By using accountants and engineers, who have fairly lucrative occupations, Herzberg might have introduced a middle-class bias into his research. A wider sample of the working population might have produced a somewhat different list. The validity of the critical incidents technique has also been questioned. First, it has been argued that people tend to externalize explanations of failure and internalize explanations of

Principles	Motivators involved
Increasing employees' autonomy while retaining accountability	Responsibility and achievement
Increasing the accountability of employees for their own work	Responsibility and recognition
Providing employees with a complete natural unit of work	Responsibility, achievement and recognition
Making performance feedback available to employees	Recognition
Introducing new and more difficult tasks to employees' work	Growth and learning
Assigning employees specific or specialized tasks at which they can become expert	Responsibility, growth and advancement

Table 5.2 Herzberg's principles of vertical job loading

success. In other words, interviewees would tend to relate their successes to the exercise of their personal initiative, but see their problems at work as a reflection of other people's or organizational inadequacies. Thus the two distinct sets of factors could simply reflect this tendency rather than a genuine division in the motivational properties of the incidents interviewees talked about. Secondly, there may well be a gap between what people are prepared to admit motivates them and what actually motivates them. This could account, for example, for pay appearing as a hygiene factor.

Despite criticisms of the ideas of Maslow, Alderfer and Herzberg, their notion of a self-actualizing or growth need has had considerable influence on management theory and to an extent on management practice. Before these content theories were popularized there were two 'models of man' on which management theory and practice could be based. There was the model of *rational economic* man and that of *social* man. The former would expend effort to the extent that it was in his or her economic interests to do so. The latter searched for affiliation and supportive relationships in the workplace, and thus effort was significantly influenced by the collective work rate. (Later we shall see how these different approaches to human motivation have produced very different approaches to the design of work and the style of supervision employed in a workplace.)

One notable attempt to illustrate the connection between different models of motivation and managerial practices was made by Douglas McGregor in *The Human Side of Enterprise* (1960). He pointed out that a consequence of assuming people behave like rational economic beings is the belief that they require either reward or coercion to motivate them. McGregor called this model of motivation *theory X*. Autocratic managerial styles are the logical result of translating theory X into managerial practice. Instead, McGregor advocated managerial strategies based on *theory Y*, which uses the self-actualizing model of motivation proposed by Maslow and Herzberg. Theory Y has at its centre *complex man*, possessing a bundle of social and self-actualizing needs, who, given the appropriate conditions at work, can show high levels of responsibility and self-direction. Complex man does not avoid responsibility, but because of the routinization of work and high levels of external supervision is generally provided with a working environment which offers little opportunity to exercise or develop it. The role of management from this perspective, then, is to create the conditions in which this reservoir of hitherto untapped human resources can be utilized.

Process theories

What all process theories have in common is an emphasis on the role of an individual's cognitive processes in determining his or her level of motivation. One major process theory, *equity theory*, assumes that one important cognitive process involves people looking around and observing what effort other people are putting into their work and what rewards follow for them, and comparing this ratio with their own. Individuals can also compare their effort–reward ratio to one which they experienced at another point in time. Equity theorists assume that this *social comparison process* is driven by our concern with fairness or equity. We perceive effort and reward not in *absolute* but in *relative* terms (Adams, 1965). When people perceive others enjoying a similar ratio of inputs (effort, qualification, skill level, seniority) to outcomes (pay, advancement, fringe benefits) to themselves, they experience equity. When people perceive a ratio of inputs to outcomes that either favours other people (underpayment) or themselves (overpayment) they experience inequity, which is assumed to be a sufficiently unpleasant experience to motivate changes in either behaviour or perceptions, or both (Table 5.3).

	Myself	Yourself
Equity	Inputs (100) / Outcomes (100)	Inputs (100 / Outcomes (100)
Inequity (Underpayment)	Inputs (100) / Outcomes (100)	Inputs (100) / Outcomes (125)
Inequity (Overpayment)	Inputs (100) / Outcomes (125)	Inputs (100) / Outcomes (100)

Table 5.3 The conditions of equity and inequity described by Adams (1965)

In one notable experiment, Adams and Jacobsen (1964) tested a number of predictions from this theory. To induce equity and inequity in people they set up a fictitious publishing company and advertised vacancies for students to do proofreading. One group of students was told that they were not qualified to earn the going rate but would still be paid it. Theoretically this should induce feelings of inequity. Another group was told they were not qualified to earn the going rate and would earn a lesser rate, which should be experienced as equitable. Finally, a third group was told they were qualified to earn the proofreading rate and would earn it. This again should be experienced as equitable. Results supported equity theory predictions: not only did the first group produce better quality work, they also worked harder than either of the other groups.

Most subsequent studies, however, have found that predictions from equity theory are supported best in conditions of underpayment, since the threshold for experiencing overpayment is high and feelings of overpayment do not appear to last very long. This is perhaps because we find it easier to rationalize why we should be overpaid than underpaid.

Additionally, if the feeling of underpayment is shared by enough people in a workplace, collective industrial action can occur. Managers involved in wage-setting therefore have to be careful to avoid setting wage rates which cause people to feel underpaid relative to others within the same plant (internal inequity) or to comparison groups outside the organization (external inequity).

Although rates of pay are a common cause of perceived inequity, and thus industrial disputes, conflict can be caused by perceived inequity in what is termed the *effort bargain*. Employers and employees may have quite different ideas about the intensity of labour that constitutes 'a fair day's work'. Employers naturally feel that, having paid the wage, they should decide what is a suitable level of effort from workers. Workers for their part fear that if the employer has control of effort intensity he may be tempted to increase it arbitrarily to an inequitable level, which they will resist if they have the power to do so.

Baldamus's classic study *Efficiency and Effort* (1961) remains the most thorough analysis of what is involved in the effort bargain. He points out that in a stable employment relationship the two sides will in effect have struck a bargain, in which the employee's total effort is exchanged for pay and other returns. He draws attention to the fundamental role of 'custom and practice' in industrial relations in determining in equitable effort–reward ratio. A variety of factors will affect effort, the pace and intensity of work, and the individual worker's experience of fatigue and monotony. Reward is comprised chiefly of pay but convivial working conditions, job security, interesting work and reasonable supervision may be involved as well. With so many factors the effort bargain can only be established over time by custom and practice.

In addition, he suggests the effort bargain is potentially unstable. When established there will be a balance between effort and reward. Should any of the elements change, however, the relationship may begin to be perceived as inequitable by one or both of the parties. Baldamus defined situations in which the wages–effort exchange deviates from previously accepted standards under the notion of 'wage disparity', which he suggests is 'the very centre of industrial conflict'. Of course, workers may fail to notice any change that has taken place, or they may be aware of it but unable to do much about it, or they may accept the change as equitable. During periods of high unemployment, for example, workers' expectations tend to adjust to their reduced labour market power, and they may put up with conditions they would previously have found unacceptable. None the less, if an effort bargain is disrupted it may lead directly to conflict as one side or the other attempts to force a renegotiation. Moreover, Baldamus adds, modern industry is dynamic: managements are continually looking for higher productivity, workers' opinions on a fair return for their effort may change, and there are changes in the wider environment which have an impact within the firm. Inflation, for example, undermines the effort bargain by tipping it in the employer's favour, because it reduces the value of wages while the employee still puts in the same effort.

Research (Summers and Hendrix, 1991; Dornstein, 1989) in real rather than laboratory settings supports Adams's original predictions and confirms equity theory as one of the most useful frameworks for understanding work motivation.

The key role of employees' perceptions of their jobs is underlined again in the *valence, instrumentality and expectancy (VIE) theory*. This explanation of employee motivation has been popular since the publication of Vroom's study, *Work and Motivation* (1964). He argued that what was crucial to motivation at work was the perception of a link between effort and reward. Perceiving this link could be thought of as a process in which individuals calculated first whether there was a connection between their effort and their performance (expectancy), then the probability that valued rewards (valences) would follow from high performance (instrumentality). The *motivational force* of a job can be calculated if the expectancy, instrumentality and valence values are known (Figure 5.2).

The motivational force of a job is attenuated by the individual's abilities, traits, role perceptions and opportunities. This implies, for example, that although a person might

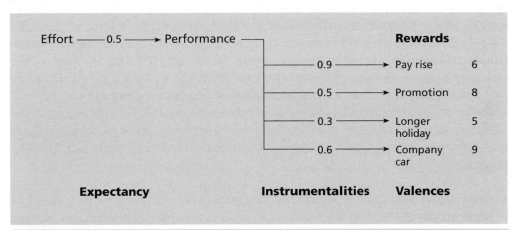

Figure 5.2 The VIE model of motivation

In this example the individual perceives only a 50 per cent change of increased effort leading to increased performance. She has ranked four rewards on a +10 to a −10 scale and has estimated the probability of increased performance producing each of these desired rewards. The motivational force of the job—the effort she is willing to expend on it—is calculated by adding the products of the valence × instrumentality calculations and multiplying the total by the expectancy value. Thus (.9 × 6) + (.5 × 8) + (.3 × 5) + (.6 × 9) = 16.3 × .5 = 8.15. This figure can be used to predict some criterion of job performance—a supervisor's assessment, for example, or if available, more reliable measures, such as sales figures for sales staff.

be motivated to perform a particular task well, he or she may be restricted from doing so by his or her abilities. In addition, opportunities for the exercise of effort also vary and thus affect the impact of an individual's motivational force on his or her achievement. Recession, for example, makes the task of selling more difficult whatever an individual's motivational force.

In summary, VIE theory stresses the rational–cognitive aspects of an individual's work motivation. The theory predicts that jobs which produce low levels of motivation will be those where aspects of job performance are out of the worker's control. In machine-paced assembly tasks, for example, we would find that expectancy and instrumentalities have low values. In fact, one of the desired outcomes may even be machine breakdown.

VIE theory is supported best by studies which attempt to predict the tasks on which an individual will work most and least hard. Prediction coefficients for this type of study are usually between .5 and .6. Attempts to use VIE measures to predict which person will work hardest in a group or on a particular task are less successful, producing coefficients of .3 to .4 (Eerde and Thiery, 1996). In one study, however, though the validity coefficients averaged out at .52 for the group, individual coefficients varied from $-.08$ to $-.92$. Thus, for some individuals behaviour could be predicted quite well from the VIE measures, whereas for others they were unable to predict performance (Muchinsky, 1977). This might suggest when VIE measures are not predictive of behaviour it is unconscious or irrational processes which have motivated individuals.

There does not seem to be any reason, however, to suggest behaviour not predicted by VIE measures is irrational. As we saw earlier, social rationality is highly complex; the subjects who performed best in the Adams and Jacobsen experiment did so because they felt they were being overpaid relative to their qualifications. Our perceptions and calculations are therefore not solely concerned with the future, predicting the value of our own efforts; we also look sideways at others and often alter our performance according to internalized norms about what is fair and unfair in terms of effort and reward.

The main contribution of both types of process theory has been to highlight the effects of cognitive and perceptual processes on objective work conditions. It suggests that managers need to pay attention to four main aspects of their subordinates' perceptions:

1. They need to focus on the crucial expectancy values—employees must perceive a link between their effort and their performance. This may mean improving training so that effort is utilized more efficiently, providing guidance and ensuring sufficient support for high performance is available, for example by ensuring adequate machine maintenance.
2. Managers should determine what outcomes an employee values. It may well be that employees value recognition and praise more than they do economic reward.
3. They need to link the reward that subordinates value to their performance, since this reflects the simple psychological truth that people are likely to repeat a response if they have been rewarded for doing so.

4. Managers finally need to ensure that wage rates are not set at a level which employees perceive as inequitable.

Knowledge of results and goal-setting

Imagine you are set an essay question by a tutor, you are a highly motivated student, you read around the question and carefully prepare an answer. What happens to that essay after you have handed it to your tutor can determine whether you remain highly motivated. Similarly at work, what happens after a particular response may be important to the maintenance or enhancement of motivation. What is required in both cases is what is termed *knowledge of results*. Management theorists have, for some time, pointed to the motivational properties of this type of feedback to employees, and have explored ways in which information systems in organizations provide it (e.g. Guirdham, 1995).

Despite a wealth of research highlighting the positive motivational benefits of knowledge of results, many organizations still provide employees with little or no information about their performance. Often this is because information systems tend to be designed for management functions (accounting, planning, production) and use data that may be incomprehensible to employees.

In some organizations knowledge of results is provided only where performance has fallen below some optimum level. In such cases of 'management by exception' managers exert their authority only when performance is poor, and appear on the shopfloor only when something has gone wrong. This is because many managers are reluctant to feed back positive information since they feel that they would be congratulating staff for doing what they are paid to do. Feedback in these contexts therefore tends only to occur when output is significantly less than satisfactory and management comes under pressure to improve it.

Even within management, sometimes key performance data are available only to the Board or a small group of senior managers. I have, for example, worked as a consultant in an organization where one of the motivational problems amongst junior and middle managers was lack of feedback on the profitability of specific contracts. Paradoxically, senior managers were concerned to develop junior and middle managers' financial and commercial awareness, i.e. their understanding of the impact of their decisions on profitability. But they were unwilling to disaggregate financial data to reveal how specific contracts were performing.

This example highlights one of the difficulties of harnessing the motivational properties of knowledge of results. Although feedback can have considerable impact on both motivation and learning, implementing feedback systems can often have wider organizational implications. Feedback can affect the relationship between employees and management or, as in the example above, senior and other managers, by disrupting existing authority structures.

Harnessing the motivational properties of feedback is an important supervisory or management skill. Guirdham (1995) suggests for feedback to be effective it needs to be:

1. *generally positive*: reward is more effective than punishment;
2. *well timed*, as soon as is possible, but constant feedback is not necessary; fortnightly can be as effective as weekly;
3. about behaviour the individual has some *control* over;
4. *specific* rather than general: examples of specific incidents are more useful than vague generalizations;
5. about *publicly observed* behaviour, i.e. not based on revelations or secrets;
6. *sensitive* when dealing with negative feedback: it is very easy to trigger an individual's defence mechanisms, which means the individual will lose any potential benefit.

A number of techniques reduce the possibility of defence mechanisms operating. The *feedback sandwich* uses a positive introduction and conclusion to make the negative information more palatable. A *causal analysis* encourages individuals to identify potentially negative consequences of their behaviour themselves. For example, when you did X what effect did it have? Was that the effect you wanted to have? What could you have done that would have produced the effect you wanted? It also helps to appear *open*, for example, 'it seems to me . . . ' or, 'do you think it would be better?' rather than being dogmatic and seemingly overly evaluative.

The positive motivational consequences for employees of accurate information on work performance being available can be further enhanced by a practice known as *goal setting* (Locke, 1968). Goals direct effort and provide guidelines for deciding how much effort to put into each activity when there are multiple goals. To be effective the goal or goals need to be made reasonably specific. Goal-seeking theory also asserts that a positive linear relationship (given an adequate level of ability) exists between goal difficulty and performance. In other words, harder goals lead to more effort and performance than easier ones. However, very difficult goals at the limits of a person's ability will not produce higher levels of performance. Over the last thirty years there has been an impressive amount of research supporting the difficulty–effort relationship.

Another strand of goal-setting theory has been the effect of participation on performance. Participation is assumed to have its effect because it increases an individual's perception of control and fairness in the process. This has been challenged by some researchers who suggest that if a goal is difficult and individuals have the ability it should motivate regardless of the level of participation. There is a degree of support for both positions. This inconsistency can partly be explained by the conduct of the research—for example, whether it was undertaken in a laboratory or in a work setting (Yearta *et al.*, 1995). And sometimes the effect of participation can be complex. For example, in the study of pizza delivery drivers cited in Chapter 1, one group of drivers was asked to choose a goal. They chose stopping at road junctions. The other group was assigned this goal. Both groups increased the percentage of times they stopped at junctions. But in the participation group non-targeted behaviour (signalling and seat-belt use) also went up whereas they actually went down in the other group (Ludwig and

Geller, 1997). In addition to some mixed support for the motivational effect of participation in goal setting some other gaps exist in the theory. For example, it is not clear
whether the motivational effect of goal setting extends to goals more than a few months
away (Yearta *et al.*, 1995).

In general, however, goal setting like knowledge of results provides some useful
guidelines for individuals dealing with the day-to-day problems of motivating others.
Put together they suggest, first, individuals are motivated by clear and reasonably frequent feedback on performance, particularly when positive; and secondly, motivation is
increased by setting specific and difficult goals. Participation may increase staff's commitment to the process and can make it less likely that unreasonably high goals, which
could be counter-productive, are set.

Job satisfaction and well-being

Few concepts in applied psychology have attracted as much interest as job satisfaction.
Many popular and academic writers have become increasingly critical of the work performed by a large proportion of the working population, seeing in the workplace a part
of society which had neither kept pace with improvements in living standards nor
accommodated the rising expectations of the post-war period. Factories were, they
argue, often dirty, noisy, dangerous places which offered little satisfaction for the needs
we described in the preceding section. And clerical work too often lacked any intrinsic
satisfaction, even though this was due to the routine nature of the work and declining
status and pay rather than to poor conditions. Managers found themselves facing the
behavioural consequences of this central problem in the experience of work: costly
levels of staff turnover, absenteeism and poor industrial relations. More recently, the
scope of research has broadened considerably. Job satisfaction is now examined in the
wider context of overall well-being exploring the dynamic and complex relationship
between general life satisfaction and satisfaction with work.

What is job satisfaction?

If people claim to be satisfied with their jobs, what do they mean? They are usually
expressing something more like a feeling about their job rather than their thoughts
about it. Seeing job satisfaction as essentially an *affective* rather than *cognitive* response
means the concept can be placed more squarely in a broader mental health context.
Given the effects of lack of job satisfaction on mental health this enables useful links to
be made with other areas such as stress research (e.g. Wall *et al.*, 1997; Haynes *et al.*,
1997). Another benefit of placing job satisfaction in this broader context is the availability of measures used to explore an individual's well-being. These can be usefully
applied to assess an individual's affective response to his or her job.

Peter Warr and his colleagues, at the Institute of Work Psychology in Britain claim a two-dimensional model best captures the range of affective responses to work (e.g. Warr, 1998). Central to this model is the horizontal axis—feelings of high or low pleasure. In addition to the level of pleasure individuals feel is the degree of arousal or activation they experience. This two-dimensional model indicates both the *content* of an individual's feelings, and their *intensity*, as represented by the distance from the mid-point (see Figure 5.3).

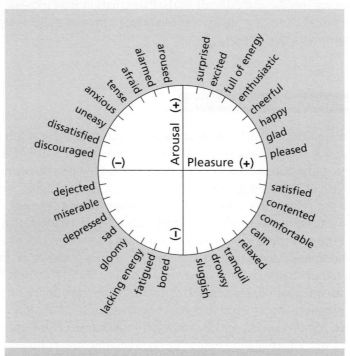

Figure 5.3 A two-dimensional view of well-being

This two-dimensional model generates three measurement axes which can be used to research systematically the effects of various job characteristics on an individual's feelings (e.g. Haynes *et al.*, 1997). Axis one is the horizontal, pleasure–displeasure, dimension. Axis two (anxiety–comfort) and axis three (enthusiasm–depression) combine elements of pleasure and arousal by running through the mid-point. An individual's position on each axis can be assessed using a number of standard questionnaires (see Figure 5.4).

Whilst Warr's two-factor model provides useful 'broad' affective outcomes at work, more specific models have been developed. For example, Daniels *et al.* (1997) statistically identified five affective factors (anxiety–comfort, depression–pleasure, positive affect, kindness, and anger) which they claim can capture better the subtleties of emotional experience at work. Whatever model is used, seeing job satisfaction as more than a

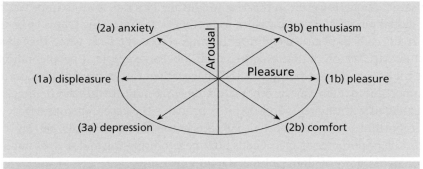

Figure 5.4 Three axes for the measurement of well-being

simple pleasure–displeasure response considerably enhances the sophistication and quality of research examining the relationship between job demands and feelings.

Global and facet satisfaction

In many studies axis one, pleasure–displeasure has been assessed with just one question: 'How satisfied are you with your job?' This approach measures what is termed overall or *global* satisfaction. Another approach has been to ask people to express feelings about particular aspects or *facets* of their job. The rationale for this is that people may be upset by an overbearing supervisor but be fairly happy with their salary and workmates.

Breaking the global concept into its constituent facets can be done conceptually or statistically. In the conceptual approach, researchers can either use their own hunches and investigations about what the significant facets of a job are, or adopt a particular theoretical framework which specifies a set of facets in advance. Sometimes the specific nature of the organization or occupation in which the job satisfaction research is being conducted means the former is preferable. Wallis and Cope (1980) found the relevant facets of job satisfaction for nurses included the feeling of being needed by the patients, the way hours of work are organized, the adequacy of the in-service training received, and the pay compared to others outside the hospital.

The statistical method of deriving facets involves using techniques, such as factor analysis, to reduce large quantities of questionnaire data to a few underlying general dimensions usable in a range of occupations. Factored multifaceted questionnaires measure dimensions such as satisfaction with the organization, pay, promotion prospects, supervisors, the nature of work itself, and co-workers.

Some researchers, while deriving measures of facets of job satisfaction, also like to combine these to produce a global measure. This raises the question of whether the predictive validity of a global job satisfaction measure can be improved by weighting facets which subjects have indicated are important to them. In some cases there appears to be a clear justification for doing this. For example, in the study of nurses' job satisfaction cited above, the feelings nurses experienced on the occasions when they thought they had 'got through to patients' were found to be very important to their overall level of the job satisfaction. However, in practice weighting does not seem to improve the ability of a global job satisfaction measure to predict behaviour. This seems to be because people are already implicitly weighting the importance of a facet when they give a rating of their satisfaction of that aspect of their job. For example, if people indicate that they are highly satisfied or highly dissatisfied with their rate of pay, the chances are that pay is important to them. On the other hand, if people indicate they are neither satisfied nor dissatisfied with their supervisors, it is probably the case that supervisory style is not an important component of their job satisfaction. In other words, getting a person to weight the importance of a facet adds little new information and so does not improve the predictive validity of global job satisfaction measures.

Whilst facet measures may indicate specific issues in organizations which need remedying, scores on such scales tend to be intercorrelated. As Warr (1996) points out, scores on one facet scale—the nature of work undertaken in particular—are highly correlated with other scale scores and with a global response. In fact, Wanous *et al.* (1997), reviewing a large number of facet studies, suggests the correlations between global and facet scores are so high that a single global question, although assumed by many researchers not to provide a sufficiently robust estimate of an individual's job satisfaction, is clearly an acceptable alternative to longer questionnaires.

Theories of job satisfaction

In this section we will examine two widely used theories in contemporary job satisfaction research. One theory stresses the individual, subjective nature of job satisfaction. It assumes that individuals can differ in their perceptions and experience of similar jobs. The other proposes that there are important objective features of the jobs people do which give rise to job satisfaction. Both provide important insights into either why some jobs are experienced as satisfying while others are not, or why some individuals find particular types of work dissatisfying while their colleagues doing identical jobs are satisfied with their work.

Variance theory

Variance theory is based on a simple idea: if you want x from your work then you are satisfied to the extent that it provides you with x. The major problem for variance theorists is defining what it is that people want from their jobs. One way of solving this is to borrow concepts from motivation theory so that variance in what is wanted and what is available from a job occurs: for example, in the extent to which self-actualizing needs can be fulfilled. This means that by borrowing from motivation theory some researchers can specify in advance the variations in work satisfaction that employees could meaningfully report in their jobs. Another approach assumes the relevant variances depend on the nature of the work and thus differ from occupation to occupation. This provides a more flexible framework with which to analyse problems of low job satisfaction within occupations.

Either approach, specifying in advance the relevant facets of job satisfaction or identifying them through investigation, enables researchers to establish whether there are significant individual differences present in reported levels of job satisfaction or whether there is a high degree of consensus among staff about what aspects of work lead to high levels of satisfaction and dissatisfaction. By identifying what aspects of a job give rise to high and low levels of satisfaction, managers are better placed when considering what changes can be made to improve job satisfaction.

Job characteristics

If variance theory suggests the causes of job satisfaction are subjective, the job characteristics model suggests the opposite: the causes of job satisfaction are to be found in the objective characteristics of a job. This view was first outlined by Hackman and Oldham (1975). Their model has inspired thousands of research papers and its key concepts still provide the foundations of much job satisfaction and job characteristics research (e.g. Parker *et al.*, 1997; Munz *et al.*, 1997).

Hackman and Oldham suggested jobs differ in the extent to which they involve five core dimensions:

1. *Skill variety*. The extent to which they require the use of a number of different skills and talents.
2. *Task identity*. The extent to which they require the completion of a whole, identifiable piece of work.
3. *Task significance*. The degree of impact they are believed to have on other people inside and outside the organization they are situated in.
4. *Autonomy*. The extent to which they provide freedom, independence and discretion in determining such things as work place, work breaks and allocation of tasks.
5. *Task feedback*. The extent to which they provide clear and direct information about the effectiveness of performance.

They suggested that if jobs are designed in a way that increases the presence of these core dimensions—for example, by combining tasks and opening feedback channels—three critical psychological states can occur in employees.

1. *Experienced meaningfulness of work*. This is determined by the level of skill variety, task identity and task significance.
2. *Experienced responsibility for work outcomes*. This is determined by the amount of autonomy present.
3. *Knowledge of results of work activities*. This is determined by the amount of feedback present.

According to Hackman and Oldham, when these critical psychological states are experienced, work motivation and job satisfaction will be high. Furthermore, behavioural outcomes, such as the quality of work and attendance, may also be improved. Hackman and Oldham did, however, include one personal attribute in their theory termed *growth need strength* (GNS), which they believed moderated the extent to which the critical psychological states could be experienced. If an individual has little need for growth it is unlikely that he or she will experience the critical psychological states strongly. The relationship between the theory's concepts is illustrated in Figure 5.5.

Hackman and Oldham constructed the *job diagnostic survey* (JDS), a questionnaire completed by employees to provide measures for each of their variables. They believed that it was possible to combine these measures to produce what they termed the motivating potential score (*MPS*), for a job using the formula:

$$MPS = \frac{\text{Skill variety} + \text{Task identity} + \text{Task significance}}{3} \times \text{Autonomy} \times \text{Feedback}$$

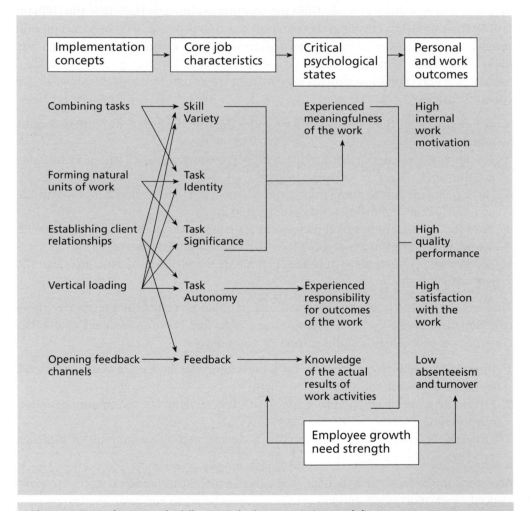

Figure 5.5 Hackman and Oldham's job characteristics model
Source: J. R. Hackman, G. R. Oldham, R. Janson, and K. Purdy (1975), 'A New Strategy for Job Enrichment', *California Management Review*, 17: 57–71.

Since the first three core dimensions contribute to the same critical psychological state, they are averaged. As scores on measures of the other two dimensions are multiplied and not added, low scores on either produces a low *MPS* value. If no autonomy or feedback is present, the *MPS* value is zero.

Thus, the theory encompasses not only job characteristics and job satisfaction, but also work design principles, psychological studies, and motivation. The attraction of such an ambitious model has been amplified by its clear specification of concepts and relationships between them and a readily available measuring instrument. Particularly well established are the relationships between job characteristics and job satisfaction. One meta-analysis, where a large number of studies were examined, found impressive average correlations with job satisfaction: task variety .32; task significance .38; skill variety .41; autonomy .46; feedback .41; motivating potential .53 (Loher *et al.*, 1985). But perhaps, almost inevitably given its breadth, support for the entire model has been less impressive. Its main contribution has been in focusing attention on the effect of job characteristics on affective states and in providing a number of key research concepts.

Although the breadth of Hackman and Oldham's model was impressive in hypothesizing relationships between core job characteristics and critical psychological states, the range of job characteristics it included was actually relatively narrow. For example, management practices and supervisory style were absent. More recently, the range of job characteristics included by researchers has broadened. The ten best established characteristics, i.e. those consistently correlating with employees' affective states, have been assembled by Warr (1998):

1. Autonomy—absence of close supervision, discretion.
2. Opportunity for skill use—skill utilization.
3. Externally generated goals—job and task demands, workload, role demands, role conflicts.
4. Variety—skill variety, task variety.
5. Environmental clarity—feedback, role clarity, information about the future, absence of job insecurity.
6. Availability of money—income level, financial resources.
7. Physical security—noise and temperature level, good working conditions, safety.
8. Supportive supervision—effective leadership.
9. Opportunity for interpersonal contact—quantity and quality of interaction.
10. Valued social position—wider social evaluations of job status.

This list of characteristics represents a useful generalizable set of predictor variables in job satisfaction research. What is currently developing is a better understanding of how these characteristics shape an individual's affective response for work.

Warr (1987) for example, proposed a *vitamin model* of job satisfaction. In other words, too much or too little of some of these characteristics can be harmful. And indeed there does seem to be some evidence of this (e.g. de Jonge and Schaufeli, 1998). For example, too much or too little of category three—workload, category two—skill use, category four—variety, category five—clarity and category nine—interpersonal contact, can be associated with low levels of satisfaction.

Researchers have also explored whether job characteristics operate independently, additively, or synergistically. In the *demands–control* model (e.g. Wall *et al.*, 1996; Karaseck, 1979) low levels of autonomy are combined with high levels of demand. In other words, high demands on individuals are not harmful in themselves. Another line of research explores the specific effects of job characteristics on an individual's affective response (e.g. Haynes *et al.*, 1997). For example, externally generated goals seem to have more effect on anxiety—axis two in Figure 5.4—than on the other two. Autonomy, however, is more strongly related to axis one—job satisfaction—than to anxiety or depression.

An example of an organization attempting to increase the motivation and job satisfaction of staff using some of these ideas can be found in Box 5.1. Clearly, job characteristics have a strong impact on job satisfaction. And the categories outlined above provide the key concepts in current job satisfaction research. Interestingly there is a good deal of resonance between what has emerged from the job satisfaction research and studies which have attempted to discover what in general causes people to enjoy their lives. To date probably the biggest and most systematic project to explore this broader question has been led by Professor Csikszentmihalyi based in the Universities of Chicago and Milan. He suggests that the commonalities underlying enjoyment are the conditions which cause what he terms *flow*. Not to be confused with the passive idea of 'going with the flow' this kind of flow is, in fact, quite the opposite—when we are most integrated with ourselves and focused on a task.

The conditions of flow are:

1. A challenging activity that requires skills—doing things which are goal-directed, bounded by rules, and require the investment of psychological energy.
2. A merging of action and awareness—a classic characteristic of optimal experience is when individuals become so involved in what they are doing that activity becomes automatic and they stop being aware of themselves as separate from the actions they are performing.
3. Clear goals and feedback—in a flow experience goals are normally clear and feedback immediate.
4. Concentration on the task at hand—while flow is present an individual is able to forget all the less pleasant aspects of his or her life.
5. The paradox of control—flow experiences involve a sense of control, or often lack a sense of worry about losing control. A key characteristic of flow experiences is the freedom to determine the content of consciousness. Thus the individual is not addicted to a sense of control to the point where this dominates his or her thinking. Control in flow experiences tends to be more about the possibility rather than the actuality of it.
6. The loss of self-consciousness—flow experiences are said not to obliterate the self but what slips below the threshold of awareness is the *concept* of self. Being able to forget

Box 5.1 D-I-Y job satisfaction

Competition in do-it-yourself retailing has increased considerably in recent years, as consolidation in the market led to a fierce battle for market share. Whilst there is little retailers can do to differentiate themselves on product (a tin of white emulsion, the equivalent of baked beans to a food retailer, is much the same wherever it is purchased) there was much that could be done to gain competitive advantage by improving customer satisfaction. Do-it-yourself outlets are notoriously unwelcoming; their vast warehouse-sized floor spaces house a usually indifferent but not normally visible staff.

At Do It All, one of the major players in do-it-yourself retailing in the UK, senior managers recognized the opportunity to improve market share and profitability through improving customer service. More enthusiastic customers mean repeat visits and higher in-store spending. But senior managers recognized also that 'you cannot treat your customers better than you treat your folks'. This is sometimes termed the service–value cycle, where employee motivation, loyalty and commitment lead to customer loyalty and satisfaction, which lead to increased profitability, which can in turn lead to increased employee motivation, loyalty, and commitment. Do It All started by reorganizing the work in a strategy they termed Participative Design—meaning staff were able to participate in discussions which involved the redesign of their work. Work redesign was focused on six key characteristics—autonomy, opportunity for learning, variety, supportive team climate, experienced meaningfulness of work, and a meaningful career path. These characteristics were most easily achieved by reorganizing work around teams. Each team was responsible for one area of the store. Once the team members have reassessed how they will work together they are given the responsibility of managing themselves. As one store manager said: 'We thought we were doing fine but that is because we were looking at the store from the manager's point of view. Once we looked at the store through the eyes of the customer we realized why we needed to change the way we manage'. And as another pointed out 'because staff are dealing with customers every day staff have the ability to put themselves in the customer's shoes'. Anecdotal reactions from staff have been positive; as one employee stated 'the store is much better now . . . I like the fact you are accountable for your own area, you take more pride in it . . . it's one of the best ideas put in place, it's down to the responsibility and accountability which we now have.' Her manager similarly had responded positively to the change: 'It's fun to come to work these days. Everyone is involved with running the store and taking responsibility. We have improved our standards . . . the best results definitely come from working this way . . . the store manager's role becomes more of a contact one to facilitate the self managed teams . . . people deliver to expectation and give what they think you expect of them.

The difference with this style is that people come to understand for themselves what needs to be done. Then they do the job to their and the customer's expectations.'

More systematic analysis of staff attitudes to these changes has confirmed the anecdotal data, finding a marked improvement in attitudes, but also revealing a more complex picture. Questionnaires were administered at the start of the project and six months later. On every repeated statement, all 15 of which were positively worded, there was an increase at the second stage of the research in the proportion of people who strongly agreed. The proportion who slightly agreed also increased in the majority of statements.

Examples of such shifts are shown in the table. Thus whilst there was a significant increase on global job satisfaction on some of the facets, career opportunities and understanding how the job contributes to the whole store showed little change. And the data show that on many of the questions dissatisfaction runs at between 20 and 40 per cent. Obviously for Do It All these are the early stages of the project, but the data does illustrate some of the complexities of attempts to increase motivation and satisfaction. For example, in re-designing work around teams the need for supervision was reduced, which seemed from the data to have an impact on the perceived opportunity for career development. We explore some of the theoretical and practical issues of work redesign more fully in Chapter 11.

	Stage 1		Stage 2	
	Agreed strongly %	Agreed slightly %	Agreed strongly %	Agreed slightly %
I am allowed to make full use of my my abilities	19	35	24	40
I enjoy my job	35	37	44	37
My work gives me satisfaction	23	39	29	40
My job provides enough variety	22	32	25	40
I feel valued at work	15	32	22	37
My ideas are valued	12	30	16	40
There are good career development opportunities	10	29	13	25
I understand how my job contributes to the whole store	51	32	55	32

who we are if only temporarily appears to be potentially very enjoyable and an important component of the flow experience.

7. The transformation of time—in flow experiences the passage of time is very different.

The conditions of flow can be present in the workplace and, as can be seen, there is a degree of overlap between these and Warr's nine categories. Flow and job satisfaction are most likely to occur when there is challenge, feedback, and skill usage present. But for Csikszentmihalyi the focus is more on the internal psychology of enjoyment rather than on the detail of objective task characteristics. The key for him is the ability to control consciousness. This means individuals who have the ability to gain control over their attention can experience flow doing any structured activity. They are thus able psychologically to transform the work they are doing. For example, he cites instances of individuals in his research experiencing flow when engaged in seemingly repetitive work such as soldering, where there would appear to be little skill variety.

Whilst outside the traditional job satisfaction research there is none the less much interest in how flow experiences can be built into work and training (e.g. Haworth, 1997).

Correlates of job satisfaction

As well as the theories we have just examined there have also been attempts to establish whether specific variables such as gender, age, personality, or occupational status are predictive of job satisfaction. There has also been considerable interest in the complex relationship between an individual's job satisfaction and satisfaction with other aspects of his or her life.

Gender

In Chapter 18 we explore the broad pattern of differences between men and women's experience of work and the labour market. Given the differences described there, i.e. women on average being in lower paid and lower quality employment, it may seem surprising that women report similar levels of job satisfaction to men. In fact, in Britain there is some evidence that women report significantly higher levels of job satisfaction (Clark *et al.*, 1996).

It may well be that women, despite having strong psychological attachment to work, have lower expectations and therefore employ different social comparison processes to men when evaluating their jobs. There is some evidence that job characteristics have a different impact on men and women. For example, autonomy seems to be more important for men's job satisfaction than women's (Pugliesi, 1995), whereas supportive supervision has more impact on women's job satisfaction than men's (Mottaz, 1986).

Age

Whilst for many years no relationship between age and job satisfaction was consistently identified there now seems to be a growing amount of evidence that there is a relationship. Perhaps we would expect the relationship to be linear, i.e. older workers reporting higher levels of job satisfaction than younger workers. But the relationship appears to be more complex than this. Recent evidence suggests the relationship is U-shaped (e.g. Birdi *et al.*, 1995; Clark *et al.*, 1996). Very young workers report higher levels of satisfaction than those in their late 20s. Job satisfaction seems to rise again, with older workers reporting higher levels of job satisfaction. In one study, eighty control variables which might cause the age effect, such as pay and prospects, were included in a sophisticated statistical analysis, but a significant age effect persisted. In other words, age itself rather than variables associated with it has a direct impact on job satisfaction. It may well be that changes in expectations and the comparison processes used across time are responsible for this U-shape. Young people may report satisfaction not only because of the novelty of work but also because of the background of youth unemployment. However, in their late 20s expectations of work may rise and individuals compare themselves with peers who may well have found more attractive jobs. Improved general well-being and the possibility that social comparison processes may be less important may account for the rise in job satisfaction in older workers.

Personality

In Chapter 3 we described the concepts of extroversion and neuroticism. Whilst these were characterized as traits, i.e. general predispositions, they can also be manifested in more specific *states*—positive affect and negative affect (PA and NA). These are independent of each other. High positive affect is marked by feelings of excitement and enthusiasm. High negative affect is characterized by feelings of fear, anger, sadness, and guilt. Neuroticism and extroversion, with their associated affective states, provide the psychological context in which people experience their work, i.e. a generalized tendency to experience positive and/or negative feelings. And, indeed, strong relationships exist between measures of PA and NA and job satisfaction. The median correlation between PA, NA, and job satisfaction is .31 and $-.26$, respectively. In other words, there do seem to be important differences between individuals seemingly captured by the PA and NA concepts which to some extent shape an individual's experience of work.

Social class

Job satisfaction has tended to be the research domain of psychologists. Their concern has tended to focus on individual variables like personality or in plant factors such as job characteristics. Sociologists have suggested that out-plant factors can be linked with job satisfaction. One classic study of car assembly workers in Luton found that, although they performed repetitive, semi-skilled work at individual work stations, they expressed a general satisfaction with the work (Goldthorpe *et al.*, 1968). During interviews the assembly workers expressed what the researchers described as a calculative, instrumental orientation to work tasks, workmates, and the company. The researchers tentatively linked this instrumental attitude to work to a number of out-plant factors. Workers tended to be young and married with high financial commitments. Luton was a new community and so had a population with no familial links there. Generally the assembly workers had experienced downward social mobility relative to their fathers who had been skilled men. These out-plant factors, the researchers concluded, might in turn cause the assembly workers to construe the term 'job satisfaction' not as 'deriving pleasure from a job' but as 'the practicality of a job'. If the wages were relatively high, which they were, the job was seen simply as a means to a high standard of living.

The Luton study is a useful reminder to psychologists that explanations of job satisfaction which focus exclusively on in-plant variables ignore a whole range of important contextual variables such as socio-economic status which might cause different groups of workers to construct different meanings as to what constitutes a satisfactory job.

Job and life satisfaction

The extent to which job and life satisfaction are connected has long been a question which sociologists, from Marx and Engels onwards, have attempted to answer. For psychologists, the presence of underlying, general traits with their related states—PA and NA—and the centrality of work in modern industrialized societies would make it surprising if there were no statistical relationship; in fact, the relationship is a moderate one, at .35 (Tait *et al.*, 1989).

What reduces the strength of the relationship is the range of other factors influencing life satisfaction. And, as the Luton study shows, orientations to work vary considerably. For individuals more involved in work the general well-being–work well-being correlation can be higher. But even amongst those who are highly work-involved the correlation between general and job well-being is not necessarily high. Multiple role conflicts can be one of the prices paid by those whose work has a greater centrality. And multiple role conflicts can radically undermine job satisfaction. Warr (1998) has summarized the research findings to date graphically (see Figure 5.6).

The double headed arrow between general and job well-being indicates the mutual causation of the two. The effect of general well-being on job well-being is, however, possibly stronger than the other way around. Solid lines represent causal links, while dotted lines represent indirect effects. For example, NA has a direct and indirect effect: its indirect effect is by virtue of its impact on an individual's perceptions of his or her work or non-work environment.

Behavioural correlates of job satisfaction

So far we have discussed the meaning of job satisfaction and the ways in which it has been explained or predicted, but for many years the key issue was the practical one: what are the implications of job satisfaction for workplace behaviour? The common-sense assumption is that if people are content with their work, this will be reflected in behaviour which is favourable for the organization. In short, the behavioural correlates

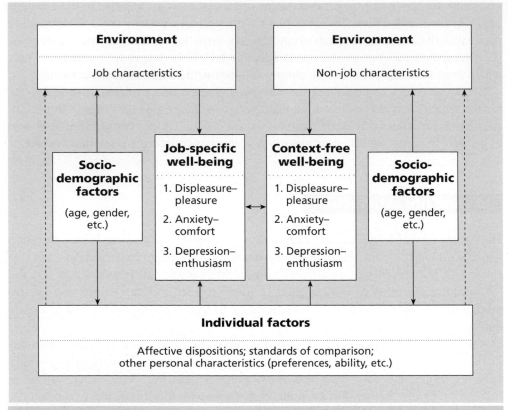

Figure 5.6 Watt's model of employee well-being and its determinants

of job satisfaction should be higher work performance, lower absenteeism, and lower staff turnover. This highly plausible assumption was what fuelled a good deal of interest in the concept in the first place. Yet, as we shall see, an enormous amount of research focused on the practical implications of job satisfaction has failed to establish a strong direct link between job satisfaction and workplace behaviour.

Job satisfaction and productivity

Estimates of the job satisfaction–performance relationship vary according to the occupational group being studied. For managerial and professional groups, studies average the correlation at .31; for white-collar workers the figure is more modest at .24; and with other groups lower still at .15 (e.g. Podsakoff *et al.*, 1996). The choice of performance criteria also affects the size of the relationship. For example, George (1991) found the relationship between job satisfaction and a 'soft' measure of performance—supervisory rating—was .26. Against the 'harder' criteria—sales performance—the relationship was only .1.

The strongest implication of much of the research is that the two variables, job satisfaction and performance, are relatively independent of each other. There seem to be at least two possible reasons for this. The first is that in many jobs variations in satisfaction cannot lead to variations in productivity. In machine-paced assembly work, for instance, the speed of the production line is constant whatever the level of job satisfaction of people working on the line (although in some instances it is possible to express low satisfaction through sabotage). Secondly, even when correlations do appear, the associations may be spurious, since both may be associated with another factor. In other words, job satisfaction and productivity may well have largely separate causal paths: one set of factors (e.g. investment in technology) determines productivity, another set (e.g. perceived equity of rewards) produces job satisfaction.

Some researchers, on the assumption that the most significant source of satisfaction is doing a job well, have even suggested the relationship is conceptualized better the other way around: high productivity leads to high job satisfaction. The implications for management seeking higher productivity are quite considerable. The common-sense view suggests that management should be concerned with improving job satisfaction for employees as this leads to higher productivity. The reverse view, that high performance leads to high job satisfaction, if true, means that management simply needs to reward past levels of high performance to increase productivity. In short, much of the psychological evidence suggests that for a range of reasons a satisfied worker is not necessarily a productive one. As we have seen although there is a link between job satisfaction and performance this link tends to be at best a modest one.

But recently, researchers at the Centre of Economic Performance at Sheffield University in the UK posed a slightly different question. If the relationship between individual performance and job satisfaction is seemingly weak, is there a stronger relationship between job satisfaction for the workforce as a whole and the organization's productivity and profitability? To answer this question they collected data from 42 manufacturing companies and over 5,000 employees who responded to questions on a range of variables such as satisfaction with co-workers, autonomy, variety, hours of work, recognition, promotion prospects, pay, physical conditions, and responsibility.

To avoid the methodological problem associated with many studies which collect satisfaction and performance data at the same moment in time making it difficult to know what causes what, the researchers looked at profits a year later. But given that company performance can be relatively stable and that high job satisfaction may be driven by the organization's high performance and the increased prospects for promotion, pay, and job security which follow from this, the researchers took additional precautions. They statistically took out the effects of company performance for the three years before the job satisfaction data was collected. They then looked to see if they could still predict performance three years later. This meant the researchers were really looking at whether the collective satisfaction of a company's employees could explain a change in productivity and profitability over the following year rather than the effect of company performance on job satisfaction.

Even with these stringent precautions variations in job satisfaction accounted for 11 per cent of the changes in company performance. No other factor they examined, such as competitive strategy, technology, market share, and Research and Development strategy, had as strong an effect on company performance. When the researchers probed their data deeper still they found the job satisfaction of those who described themselves as non-management who did not work on the shop-floor seemed to be the most important in predicting company performance.

West and Patterson's (1998) research represents a significant and authoritative study which seems to have provided a definitive answer—at least for the manufacturing sector—to the question of whether employee attitudes impact on performance. But as we have seen their model works not at the individual but at the workforce level. Increased workforce satisfaction leads to higher productivity and then to greater profitability.

But if we now know these links exist, how do they come to be there? West and Patterson suggest the answer lies in employee co-ordination and team-working. Where the level of satisfaction is generally high employees may be more motivated to engage in 'pro-social' behaviours and make extra effort to help other departments and functions. Less satisfied workers may in contrast 'hoard' their resources and focus on their own performance. Over a year the thousands of instances of helping out accumulate to make a substantial difference to productivity and performance. In addition more satisfied workers can control the negative impact of less satisfied individuals.

Whilst methodologically and conceptually West and Patterson's research is both rigorous and persuasive some of their more detailed findings none the less make depressing reading. They visited 110 manufacturing sites with an average of 230 staff. In more than half of the firms the average job cycle-time (i.e. the time it takes to complete a task) was ten minutes or less; in 25 per cent the average job cycle-time was one minute or less. As we have seen from earlier studies, it is the intrinsic aspects of work which are the most important sources of satisfaction. And indeed West and Patterson's own work confirms this. The sheer level of monotonous and deskilled work is clearly counterproductive given West and Patterson's general findings of the relationship between satisfaction, productivity, and profits.

In a sense their data indicate the gap between the rhetoric or 'hype' expressed as 'our people are our greatest asset' and the objective characteristics of much work. But whilst their work gives the lie to the rhetoric it also underlines the profound truth of the statement.

Conclusion

The centrality of work in modern market economies has made an understanding of the psychology of motivation and job satisfaction a key component of business and management education syllabuses, and the writings of Maslow and Herzberg are routinely included on other programmes. For example, in the UK motivational programmes for the long-term unemployed include a session on Maslow and motivation followed by a brainstorming session for participants to work out how they might fulfil their higher-order needs while living on unemployment benefit. If anything, the work of Maslow and Herzberg has become too commonplace. It now suffers to some extent from being taught as if it were 'true' rather than as a set of sophisticated and problematic speculations about the nature of human motivation.

Certainly the body of research and writing covered here does seem to explain and account for the major causes of differences between jobs and individuals in the amount of motivation and job satisfaction they cause and experience. As we have seen, content theories suggest there are basic, underlying human needs, which jobs need to provide opportunities to fulfil if they are to motivate individuals. Process theories suggest the possibility of differences in perceptions which might lead to higher or lower states of motivation. They stress the cognitive dimension of motivation. Here motivation is not so much the outcome of need fulfilment but of social comparison processes. We are motivated if we are able to look over our shoulders or perhaps back into our own past and feel we are being rewarded (in the full sense of the term) adequately. We also attempt to calculate the instrumentality of our actions, i.e. the extent to which we feel effort leads to increased performance and ultimately to some valued outcome. And as we have seen the least motivating environments are those where we feel no such connections exist. This state is particularly prevalent amongst the long-term unemployed. Here individuals may feel that however many letters they write no interviews or job offers follow, and it is obviously crucial for people working with unemployed groups to ensure that individuals retain a sense that they do have some control over the outcomes they experience and do not acquire learned helplessness.

In job satisfaction research we have seen there is a good deal of understanding about the key characteristics of jobs which lead to 'positive affect' in individuals. Although the relationship between measures of job satisfaction and behaviour at work, such as absenteeism and productivity, is a complex and indirect one.

But, given the insights provided by this research, the obvious question to ask is why so much of what characterizes people's experience of work is at odds with the contents of this chapter? Csikszentmihalyi, for example, talks of the possibility of experiencing flow—an 'optimal psychological experience'—in the workplace. And yet the experience of work for most individuals is that time at work is essentially wasted—at best a means to an end, at worst stressful and damaging. Similarly, Hackman and Oldham and more recently Warr and others have highlighted the importance of autonomy in people's work. But the reality for most is that autonomy and discretion are concentrated in the hands of the few.

The reasons for this gap between the ideal of people who are motivated, self-actualizing, and have a strong sense of the connection between their efforts and the outcomes they experience, receiving constructive feedback, supportive supervision, and experiencing high levels of job satisfaction and the real nature of work for many is the substance of the latter half of this book.

Whilst the original impetus for motivation and job satisfaction research stemmed from a practical concern with increased productivity there has in recent years been a change of emphasis. Attempts to increase performance have now been set in the wider context of alternative work design which we will examine in Chapter 11. Job satisfaction research has now broadened and is driven by a more general concern to explore the effects of work on mental health and the dynamic relationship between work and life satisfaction.

Study questions for Chapter 5

1 What are the differences between content and process theories of motivation?
2 Does Maslow's theory of motivation tell us more about American society in the 1950s than the fundamental nature of human motivation?
3 What are the motivating characteristics of work?
4 Is pay a motivator or a hygiene factor?
5 What is job satisfaction?
6 Are some people more likely to be satisfied with their work?
7 Are some jobs more likely to produce job satisfaction?
8 Why are measures of job satisfaction not very predictive of outcomes in the workplace?

Further reading

Chimiel, N. (1998) *Jobs, Technology and People*. London: Routledge.

Csikszentmihalyi, M. (1992) *Flow: The Psychology of Happiness*. London: Rider.

Haworth, J. (1997) *Work, Leisure and Well Being*. London: Routledge.

Howard, A. (ed.) (1996) *The Changing Nature of Work*. San Francisco, Calif.: Jossey-Bass.

Kahnerman, D., Drener, E., and Schwarz, N. (eds.) (1998) *Understanding Quality of Life: Scientific Perspectives on Enjoyment and Suffering*. New York: Sage.

McClelland, D. C. (1985) *Human Motivation*. Cambridge: Cambridge University Press.

Munro, D., Schumaker, J. F., and Carr, S. C. (eds.) (1997) *Motivation and Culture*. London: Routledge.

Wagner, H. (1999) *Human Motivation and Emotion*. London: Routledge.

Section 2

Groups and Work

Groups and Work

In Section One the fundamental unit of analysis was the individual employee. While psychological properties people bring to the workplace are obviously important, by the early 1930s psychologists realized that several important workplace phenomena could not be satisfactorily explained if the individual employee remained the basic unit of analysis. These psychologists suggested that to advance the understanding of workplace behaviour the focus of research would have to shift from individual to group process.

What had prompted this realization was the Hawthorne studies, a series of experiments conducted by a group of psychologists in a large electrical components factory over a fifteen-year period. The studies suggested that work groups were a fundamental unit of social organization which possessed properties that existed independently of their members. Perhaps the most important conclusions of the Hawthorne researchers were that groups were capable of causing profound changes in their members' perceptions, beliefs, attitudes and behaviour.

The results of the studies were popularized by a management writer, Elton Mayo, who believed management had a lot to gain from an increased awareness of the social dynamics of the workplace. He believed there was a fundamental paradox between the technical accomplishments of modern industry on the one hand and the social incompetence he claimed existed among managers on the other. Thus, Elton Mayo and a group of his colleagues began what became known as the *human relations movement*. They believed that their research and writing offered management the opportunity of increasing their behavioural sophistication, and therefore their effectiveness.

Because much of the initial material produced by the human relations movement was based on a rather paternalistic social ideology, in which managers were assumed to act on rational criteria while workers were seen as motivated by unconscious social 'sentiments', much of it is now discredited. None the less, Mayo and his associates did establish the agenda for what social aspects of the workplace merited detailed attention. In this section we have used the agenda the human relations movement provided but have expanded it where recent developments in psychology and sociology have added items of interest.

In Chapter 6 we examine the nature of social interaction. Since much of our time at work is spent interacting with other people, an analysis of what occurs during social encounters is particularly useful, especially if it offers insights into why some individuals are better than others at dealing with people. This analysis thus provides the theoretical foundations for training programmes which develop the social skills required for successful performance in a job.

The social group, as we suggested above, is a fundamental form of social organization and an analysis of its structures and processes is essential to an adequate understanding of workplace behaviour. In Chapter 7, in addition to examining the effects of group membership on individuals we consider in some detail the research and the movement that began the interest in work groups: the Hawthorne studies and the human relations movement.

Leadership in the workplace was another traditional concern of the human relations movement. The view of human relations writers was that supportive leadership leads to high-performing work groups. In Chapter 8 we close the section by summarizing and commenting on the vast amount of leadership research undertaken by psychologists to test this and other propositions about what constitutes effective leadership. We conclude with a discussion of some leadership training programmes that have been developed by using some of the psychological insights about the nature of effective leadership which have crystallized out of this research.

6 Social Interaction

Summary points and learning objectives

By the end of this chapter you will be able to

- describe the notions of dramaturgy and impression management;
- understand how individuals construct and monitor personal fronts;
- understand how fronts are manifested in organizations;
- describe the features of social situations;
- understand the notion of personal constructs;
- describe the kinds of information available about others during interaction;
- understand the reasons for attributional errors in social life;
- describe the notions of open, closed, and defined situations;
- describe how rules and interaction differ in each kind of situation;
- describe the components of social skill and how it differs from other skills.

Introduction

In Section 1 we examined attributes of individuals such as personality and intelligence which can be referred to when explaining or predicting behaviour. Though individual differences are undoubtedly important, it is now time to consider other complementary perspectives. In this chapter we will examine the basic processes underlying the activity between people in everyday social settings. The concepts of *dramaturgy* and *social skill* will be central considerations here. The former highlights the expressive and symbolic aspects of social interaction. Writers who have explored the dramaturgy of everyday life have argued that the statistical systems of exploration and classification involved in the study of individual differences are static, and so cannot capture the dynamic and creative aspect of our social activity. The concept of skill, you may remember, embraced both cognitive control of actions and automated behaviour. This implies that we may be unaware of the considerable cognitive achievement our automatic social responses represent. The concept also forces us to consider what kinds of modelling and categorization are involved in social interaction and so helps to explain, for example, how changes in social competence occur over time and why some individuals perform better than others at jobs which involve social skills.

Dramaturgy and impression management

A central theme of this perspective involves our ability to engage in *impression management*. The social world is seen as a stage on which 'actors' constantly create and recreate their social selves according to their conceptions of what it is to be a social person (de Waele and Harré, 1976). Interactions between actors are characterized by each monitoring his or her own performance and the performance of others. Personality, from this perspective, is the internal resources an actor can draw upon to construct a 'social face'. Indeed the personality theory of the future may focus on the goals and competencies that go to make up these resources (Harré and Gillet, 1994). Thus personality is seen as a form of social intelligence.

Harré used the term *persona* to describe the social face we present to others. He saw persona production as a kind of intellectual puzzle. Actors have somehow to select the correct persona or range of personas for a given situation. Cialdini (1988), for example, found the highest-earning waiter would constantly change his face according to the type of customer he was serving. With families he was warm and homely, with dating teenagers he was haughty and intimidating. And with the older, lone female customers he was solicitous and confidential. Actors have to be able to recognize, create or define the social situation they are in and possess some knowledge of the rules of behaviour within it. Being able to recognize a solution does not guarantee that actors will give good performances, however. They may be able to define a situation correctly, for instance, but not have an adequate supply of personas to draw upon to act appropriately within it.

Goffman (1971) has also attempted to capture the creative and expressive aspects of our social behaviour. He particularly emphasized the symbolic aspects of our self-presentational activity. He saw social encounters as comprising a manipulation of both *sign activity* (verbal and non-verbal behaviour) and *sign equipment* (props such as clothes). Actors manipulate these symbolic aspects of social interaction in order to project definitions of themselves on to situations. This self-definition is termed a *personal front*. Social interaction involves a constant monitoring of our own and other people's personal fronts. To do this, we make comparisons between what Goffman called *the given* and *the given off*. The former are the more controllable aspects of sign activity, particularly verbal behaviour; while the principal source of the latter, less controllable, portion of sign activity is an actor's non-verbal behaviour. Of course, other people are not unaware of being monitored and will attempt to control these aspects of their own sign activity. We, in turn, are aware of the possibility of this kind of manipulation. Individuals differ in the extent to which they monitor their behaviour and other people's reaction to it. Some people seem to be consistently conscious of engaging in impression management and their success in doing so. In others, self-monitoring is less marked.

For these individuals the use of what is termed 360-degree feedback is particularly useful. This provides individuals with information about how others below, above, and at the same level in the organization view them. The feedback is usually based on responses to a standardized inventory such as the Insight Feedback style questionnaire (Handley, 1988). Self-awareness and understanding the impact of one's front on others appears to be an important managerial attribute. For example, Church (1997) in a large sample of managers, found self-awareness—measured by the similarity of self-perceptions and the perceptions of others—consistently differentiated high- from low-performing individuals.

When we monitor others we also expect a correspondence between the *appearance* and *manner* of the other's personal front. Our appearance is determined by our choice of sign equipment, such as style of dress. Our manner indicates the part we want to play during an encounter and is the result of our sign activity: for example, the tone of voice we use. Though we constantly monitor the personal fronts of others, it remains true that we rarely, if ever, attempt to discredit the definitions people present of themselves. Goffman suggested this is because there is a moral obligation or social rule that we should accept other actors' self-definitions. Breaking this rule by damaging the integrity of another person's front severely disrupts interaction and is likely to cause considerable embarrassment.

Goffman argued that individuals often project fronts for tactical reasons without really believing in them. For example, at work a front may be adopted in order to gain some reward, such as a coveted appointment or promotion. Assuming the individual does not drop the front, it may be some time before the individual believes it has anything to do with what he or she feels is 'the real me'.

The adoption of particular fronts is often encouraged by organizations. This is because fronts symbolically convey and dramatically highlight information which might otherwise be unapparent. The formal suit of the executive, for example, gives the impression that tasks will be carried out in a similarly reliable and discreet manner. Goffman claimed that there were at least two disadvantages of preferred fronts as far as organizations were concerned. First, some executives will get their jobs because they 'look the part' rather than through genuine managerial talent. Secondly, getting on in an organization may be determined by the extent to which individuals can manipulate their sign activity and sign equipment to imitate the personal fronts of their organizational superiors. In both cases, impression management can become more important in the struggle for authority, status and power than competence and accomplishment.

According to Thompson (1961), impression management in the workplace involves at least four personal fronts:

1. *Superior*. Impression management here is concerned with the projection of competence, sincerity, poise and activity.
2. *Subordinate*. Employees in subordinate roles have to project loyalty to company and superiors, deference and dependability.
3. *Specialist*. Those engaged in specialist positions have symbolically to convey dedication to their speciality and disinterest in the organizational power game. They therefore appear incorruptible, concerned only with the truths revealed by their speciality.

4. *Lower participants.* Employees with little or no chance of moving up the hierarchy have to display activity even when there is little or no work to do. Though loyalty is not expected, compliance is. By projecting innocence and limited competence they can maintain their aura of compliance when they transgress rules and legitimately reduce their contribution to the organization.

Thus, from the dramaturgical perspective, much of an individual's activity at work or in other social situations involves symbolically conveying through sign activity and sign equipment aspects of the personal front he or she has adopted. However, it has also been pointed out that side by side with the expressive, self-presentational goals of social interaction that Goffman, Harré and others highlight, social situations also usually involve more specific task-related goals such as selling, negotiating or interviewing. Therefore, the likelihood of successfully attaining a goal in a social situation depends upon a dynamic combination of interpersonal skills (chiefly impression management) together with the more straightforward technical skills. This combination we would define as *social skill*.

Social skill

The skills we deploy in social situations appear to involve developing understandings of three aspects of social interaction: the social situations we must interact within, the person(s) with whom we interact and the components of the 'interactional work' which enable us to attain our goals in social encounters.

Understanding social situations

Understanding the nature of a social situation is essential to a competent social performance in it. If we are unable to perceive what behaviour ought to be used in a particular social situation, we are unlikely to achieve whatever goals we may have been pursuing. How, then, do individuals develop a comprehension of situations? This has proved difficult to answer. Social scientists have to be careful not to develop inadequate conceptual frameworks to describe social situations, or they risk creating a gap between the characteristics of situations as described by social researchers and as experienced by people themselves. Argyle (1994) suggested we should characterize situations as discrete entities, each having its own goals, rules, elements, concepts, settings and roles.

Goals Social situations, as we have already proposed, provide opportunities for the attainment of goals, both expressive and task-related. Individuals often pursue more than one goal and these can interfere with or assist one another. For example, a supervisor may pursue an expressive goal (to be accepted as an approachable person) and a task goal (such as co-ordinating group activity). An important part of social skill is balancing the demands of expressive and task goals.

Rules Perhaps the most important aspect of any social situation are the rules which guide individuals' goal-directed behaviour. Argyle defined rules as the shared beliefs which dictate which behaviour is permitted, not permitted, or required. In social situations our understanding of the rules regulates our conduct, enabling us to respond to cues and predict the likely effect of our actions. Hence social situations seem to contain two clusters of rules. One cluster contains universal rules present in all social situations, such as: use a common language or signalling system; make interaction pleasant (e.g., do not embarrass others); and prevent aggression (i.e. be polite). The second cluster applies to specific social situations; for example, do what the doctor says when in the surgery.

In selling, the universal rules which are present alongside situation-specific ones include: show mood control; listen to objections and do not get into arguments ('win the argument, lose the sale'). In interviewing, situation-specific rules include: show evidence of preparation, give focused answers, relate job to future career goals, use positive language, display self-confidence and self-awareness. Gallois *et al.* (1997), found there was a strong relationship between the extent to which candidates broke rules and assessments of their 'hirability'.

Another classification of the rules operating in social situations suggests there are the following:

1. *Interpretative rules*. These provide criteria for interpreting and labelling events in the social world. For example, interpretative rules operating on football terraces define what constitutes 'provocation' from a supporter of the other team.
2. *Prescriptive rules*. These indicate what ought to be done in response, once a situation has been interpreted and understood. In this sense, prescriptive rules also reflect the moral concerns and values of participants in the situation.
3. *Non-generalizable rules*. These are 'one-off' rules created on the spot when routines produced by the more stable rules are interrupted. Non-generalizable rules reflect the fact that social situations are often quite complex, and established rules can rarely cover all the variations and possibilities.

Breaches of prescriptive rules are often seen as 'mistakes' by other participants and usually call for an 'explanation'. For example, if a supervisor is overly critical of one of his or her team and breaches prescriptive rules about what constitutes fair feedback, the team might 'explain' the behaviour by labelling him or her as 'stressed'. Breaches of rules drastically reduce the chance of a successful outcome to an encounter. In some occupations such as law and medicine a breach of a rule by a practitioner may end his or her career.

Thus the action of rules can be as important in the prediction and explanation of behaviour as trait or ability profiles. From this perspective our effectiveness is determined by our awareness of what rules are present in an encounter and our ability to construct an adequate persona. But the impact of rules on social situations varies. At one extreme there are ceremonial or ritual occasions. These are termed 'closed situations' as they have a fully rule-guided character. At the other extreme there are much more fluid situations—such as informal evenings at home. In these more 'open situations' some rules do operate but there are no fixed goals or prescribed interactional routes for individuals. The workplace occupies a middle ground. Behaviour is to a degree rule-guided, but a certain level of ambiguity exists about how participants' goals are realized. It is in these 'defined situations', with their mix of goals and possibilities for different interactional routes through encounters, that social skills are particularly important.

Repertoire of elements The attainment of goals in situations appears to involve a specific repertoire of 'acts' or 'elements'. Each situation defines a specific repertoire of elements as meaningful and others as inappropriate. Elements can be divided into verbal categories, verbal contents, non-verbal communications, and bodily actions. For example, in negotiations the verbal categories would include: offer, accept, and reject. Verbal contents would contain information and settlement points. Non-verbal elements would include: looking, frowning, and smiling. Bodily actions would involve various body postures and perhaps walking out. Knowing the repertoire of elements appropriate to a situation is crucial to a skilled or competent social performance in it.

Concepts We acquire skills by actively abstracting concepts which appear to have some explanatory utility for the system we are attempting to integrate with. Concepts provide us with the categories which enable us to reduce the complexity of incoming stimuli. In Chapter 1, we cited an account of a production manager whose goal of increased efficiency was achieved by conceptualizing the costing and production system and making cross-references between them. Concepts are also the bases of our comprehension of social situations, other people and social interaction. Professional social skills like selling, supervising, interviewing, negotiating and psychotherapy each involve a specialized set of concepts in addition to the general stock of concepts.

Environmental settings Environmental psychologists have explored for some time the effects of the physical layout of furniture, barriers (e.g. filing cabinets), the amount of privacy, personal space and crowding on psychological variables such as arousal, interaction, self-evaluations and aggression. For example, props are often used to divide offices up into 'pressure' and 'semi-social' areas. The pressure area, usually around the desk, is where formal interaction 'in role' occurs, with the occupant of the office taking the lead. The 'semi-social' area, perhaps around a coffee table, provides the opportunity for less formal interaction. Skilled managers are able to select the area of their office most appropriate for the type of interaction they expect to have during a meeting. Similarly, a skilled selection interviewer uses the semi-social area to obtain biographical information from a candidate and can further reduce the formality of the situation by sitting at right angles to the candidate rather than directly opposite. Props can also symbolically convey information about personal attributes such as status, competence, and affluence.

Roles Social interaction occurs within the context of a social world structured by the relations in which people stand to one another. Such a structure means that we are able to see order in other people's behaviour, and to predict their likely responses. This in turn reflects the fact that much behaviour involves people enacting social *roles*, for we would define a role as the normal way for people to behave in given situations. At home, for example, the relations of marriage and parenthood give rise to the familial roles of wife, husband, father, mother, son and daughter. At work, the division of labour and distribution of authority create roles like supervisor, manager and worker.

The most important aspect of this structure of relations is the *expectations* that others have of appropriate behaviour within a role. In fact, roles are defined by *the set of expectations that others have of the role incumbent's behaviour*. Some expectations are made explicit by legislation: for example, parents must feed their children and protect them from physical and moral danger. Mixed with whatever legal expectations exist are the cultural assumptions about appropriate behaviour within a role. Both legislation and cultural assumptions are subject to modification.

It is often difficult for us to recognize the profound effect roles have on our behaviour or that they are part of an external social structure, defined by other people's expectations. This is because we experience social roles not as something external to ourselves, but as personal properties. We manage to translate the set of external expectations about our behaviour in a role into a corresponding set of psychological properties such as beliefs, values, attitudes, prescriptions (I ought to) and proscriptions (I ought not to).

This is referred to as *internalization* of expectations, and can result in major changes in an individual's behaviour. Roles are internalized during *role episodes*, which refer to the whole of the process of perceiving others' expectations of us. These involve:

1. The initial expectations of others of what behaviour is appropriate in a role.
2. Communicating these initial expectations to the new occupant of a role. In the workplace this may involve formal procedures such as training or induction courses, or can occur informally by observing others occupying similar roles.
3. Developing a set of initial assumptions about what behaviour is expected.
4. Testing one's own initial assumptions about appropriate role behaviour by performing tasks.
5. Feedback from others on the extent to which performance matches their expectations.

Finally, we must distinguish between the role itself and *role behaviour*. The main point here is that, although the role itself is structured (like the script in a play), behaviour in a role can be modified by the expressive concerns of individuals (like an actor interprets a part). A new manager, for example, may want to be the most popular or the most innovative in the firm. In this way, roles provide an arena for the interplay of the practical requirements we have to meet and our own expressive concerns.

Comprehending other people

In our discussion of general skills in Chapter 1, we saw that skilled individuals develop a *model* or inner representation of the dynamics of the system they are interacting with. This enables them to predict the future states of the system and responses of the system to their actions. The models were based on conceptual categories developed to translate 'raw data' from sources into 'action-relevant inputs'. The categories contained in their models mean that skilled workers could quickly 'read the face of the system' by sampling information from time to time, and so update their models of the state of the system. Therefore, in social interaction we need to construct 'models' of others in order to predict their reactions. In some work-related situations, such as selection interviewing and psychotherapy, constructing a model of the candidate or patient is the principal goal of the encounter. In other situations, supervising of selling for example, developing an adequate understanding of the member of staff or customer plays an important part in the effectiveness of an individual's performance.

Though comparison with skilled activity is useful, since it makes us consider what categories or 'sampling strategies' people use, there are some important differences between social and practical skills. First, the uncertainty presented by people can be very considerable, because individuals can change and they differ in terms of their attitudes, beliefs and goals. Secondly, we have to include in our model what model the other person may have of us.

How, then, do we build these models? People we interact with provide us with a continuous flow of data, both verbal and non-verbal. Language is the symbolic system through which a great deal of our practical and expressive activity is achieved. Argyle's work, however, has demonstrated the importance of 'non-verbal channels' as a source of information about the feelings and attitudes of others towards us. Even when contact occurs through speech alone, as when talking on the telephone, we use features of speech such as accent, changes in tone, pauses and variations in tempo to complement our understanding of the speaker and what he or she has said.

Our attention across verbal and non-verbal channels is as selective and organized as perception in other skilled activities. What we attend to is determined by the 'categories' we use to model others. These, in turn, are often related to the purpose of the encounter. The categories you would employ to model someone you have just met at a party are likely to be different from those employed by a supervisor to model a new subordinate. Whatever categories are employed, much of our attention will be directed towards non-verbal aspects of the other's performance since these also provide us with feedback about our own performance.

There are a number of potential sources of non-verbal information provided by others during social interaction. The most important source is the *face*. As Argyle (1994, p. 26) stated, 'the face gives a fast-moving display of reactions to what others have said or done, and a running commentary on what the owner of the face is saying'. We are able to identify with reasonable accuracy eight emotions and cognitive reactions from the faces of others: happiness; surprise; fear; sadness; anger; disgust; contempt; and interest. We should, however, not forget that the face muscles are under voluntary control. This means that, although a rich source of emotional and attitudinal data is available, facial expressions are very often a mix of wanted and unwanted movements: for example, a polite smile in the bottom half of the face and a frown in the top half.

Gaze performs a number of non-verbal communication functions. We gather information from the faces of others with brief gazes aimed mainly around their eyes. The gaze of other people provides an important additional source of information about their attitudes and feelings towards us. High levels of gaze can indicate a range of feelings towards us from love, through interest, to hate. Argyle and Cook (1976) reviewed gaze studies and found high gaze from another person could indicate the other is: interested in you, of low status, attempting to dominate you, extrovert, and not embarrassed. In some contexts, correctly decoding gaze is extremely useful. For example, Goodfellow (1983) described how the skilled teacher could decode the slightest gaze from a pupil to detect whether anything was amiss, and whether the pupil was being mildly mischievous or malicious. Decoding gaze became less accurate in encounters between people from different cultures, because the use of gaze varies considerably across cultures. This means gaze can become the source of considerable embarrassment and misunderstanding in cross-cultural encounters. Negotiators involved in selling to foreign clients need to be able to decode correctly the level of gaze being received and display the appropriate level of gaze within the context of a particular culture.

Additional sources of non-verbal information include *body posture* and *body movement*. Though these do not usually provide specific information about the attitudes or emotions of others towards us, they can indicate their general emotional state or mood. In some contexts where a person is being judged (such as a selection interview), they may attempt to suppress indicators of mood, and here *non-verbal leakage* can provide an indication of how relaxed, anxious or confident the person is. Skilled interviewers can use leakage, such as excessive lower body movements, to make a guess about the nature of the candidate's feelings on the subject, and if necessary return to the subject later in the interview. Mood is often contagious. An awareness of the role played by body posture and movements in conveying information about mood is important in professional contexts since it reduces the risk of contagion occurring. The sales person, for example, needs to be aware of the mood being signalled by his or her body posture or movements when dealing with customers. If it is not positive it is likely to be 'caught' by customers. The selection interviewer similarly needs to be careful he or she does not catch the mood (particularly anxiety) of the candidate.

Appearance often provides us with a rich source of information about others, particularly when little other information is available, for example before a meeting or interaction begins. Although aspects of the other's personal front are highly controllable, they are none the less often assumed to be an important source of information about attitudes, allegiances, status or class. In addition, appearance can be used in an active mode to convey highly specific messages. On the football terraces, for example, minor differences in the way scarves are tied, the precise type of footwear and the length of the trousers people wear all contribute significantly to the models football fans construct of each other (Marsh, 1982).

Personal construct theory

Given all these potential sources of information, how do we make inferences about others? As we suggested earlier, the *filtering* and *selection* from among these inputs is determined by the categories we employ. This was the basic assumption of Kelly's (1955) personal construct theory, which provided a useful way of exploring how individuals comprehend people and events. Constructs are 'bi-polar adjectives' with which individuals organize their perception of the world and provide it with meaning. Examples of the types of constructs used in daily interaction are intelligent–dull, friendly–unfriendly, autocratic–democratic, stable–unstable, and promotable–unpromotable.

Individuals seem to develop stable preferences for using particular sets of constructs in characterizing themselves and others. When we first meet people the constructs we use are mainly about *role*, *appearance*, and *behaviour*. As more information becomes available, for example during the course of an interview, we modify our model to include more 'psychological' constructs, such as those about personality. Indeed, an important determinant of an interviewer's skills is the ability to remain open to fresh information rather than developing a fixed model of an individual early on in the interview which can be overly affected by appearance.

The meaningfulness of any construct to an individual is determined partly by the range of contexts in which he or she is willing to apply it, and by what is termed its *implicative potential*—the number of specific inferences the individual can make from the construct to others in his or her construct system. A rather extreme illustration of this comes from one of the authors' work with a recruitment agency. The assignment involved identifying ways of improving the way they categorized clerical work and clerical workers to get better matches between the two. In one office many clerical job seekers' files had purple dots on them. This it emerged indicated this clerical worker had a poor complexion. The employee coding individuals in this way clearly had an important (for her) construct, good complexion–poor complexion. Its implicative potential included another one in her system—acceptable to employers–unacceptable to employers.

According to personal construct theory, the structure and content of an individual's construct system are what determines his or her ability to make a variety of distinctions between people and their personalities. People organize their behaviour in the light of the constructs they have available to them. Box 6.1 provides you with an opportunity to identify some of the constructs you use when making sense of other people.

The simplest feature of a construct system which can be considered is how *elaborate* it is. The more constructs an individual can employ in a situation the more able he or she will be to make inferences about the other's personality and motives. The more elaborate a construct system is, the more an individual is able to construe an interaction from different perspectives and make inferences about the attitudes of others involved (Neimeyer and Hudson, 1985). Professional social skills such as interviewing, selling or negotiating are supported by a stock of valid constructs enabling relevant predictions to be made about other participants. But as the earlier example illustrated, a preference for particular constructs may reduce the validity of our models of others.

Box 6.1 What are your constructs?

What constructs do you employ to make sense of other people? This exercise provides a method of accessing the 'index system' you have at 'the back of your head'. This exercise is best undertaken in pairs.

1. Take a piece of card or paper. Tear or cut it into ten pieces each large enough to write a name on.
2. Think of ten individuals. This exercise works best if you are accessing one set of your constructs. This means try and use individuals from just one area of your life—those you work with or for, those who report to your, or perhaps, if you are involved in interviewing, candidates. If you are studying full-time use fellow students, friends, or family.
3. On each piece of card or paper write one name. If anonymity or confidentiality are considerations—perhaps because your colleague will know some of the individuals, use initials, first name, or code word.
4. Hand each other your ten names. One of you is now responsible for eliciting the other's constructs. This is done by taking three names from the pack and placing them in front of the other person. You then say: 'Tell me one important way in which any two are the same and different from a third'.
5. Note down on a piece of paper what the individual says, for example,
      Tall–short
6. Pick these three names up and place them at the bottom of the pile. Now take another three placing them in front of your partner and repeat the question.
7. You should be able to elicit about twelve constructs before your colleague 'runs out'. At twelve (or less—see note (a)) swap over. The person providing constructs now has his or her partner's names to elicit and note constructs.

Notes:
(a) While you should be able to get twelve there is no shame in getting less, and indeed one of the first learning points may be precisely that we have and use a limited set of constructs. If you feel your partner is beginning to run out, for example, if you notice repetition, stop. There is no point forcing your partner to say something. This is unlikely to reveal anything about how he or she characteristically differentiates between individuals.
(b) Constructs can be about anything. There is no assumption here that they need to be psychological. However, they should, as the question suggests, be a distinction which you believe is important.
(c) You may find your partner finds it easy to say why two are similar, but they may occasionally struggle to say how the third is different. When this happens you may need to prompt in order to help your partner tighten up his or her thinking and say how the third differs. This may involve some exploration about what the construct is about.
(d) This exercise is a simplified version of Kelly's 'repertory grid'. The technique has a number of applications—counselling, identifying training needs, and constructing person and job specifications.
(e) Some questions which help focus a discussion about what constructs emerge are found at the end of this chapter

Constructing other people adequately is also facilitated by what Kelly (1955) termed *commonality*, namely the extent to which there is overlap or similarity between the constructs and construing processes of oneself and others. This is because similarity between one's own constructs and those of another person make it easier to understand their psychological processes. Commonality has been found to be a good predictor of friendship formation among groups of individuals (Duck, 1998).

Having an overlap or commonality with other people's construct systems does not always guarantee comprehension. A person may possess very similar constructs and construing processes to others but may still make little or no attempt to understand them. At this more complex level, where we have to take into account people's motives and wishes, comprehending the other involves what Kelly termed *sociality*. This is the deliberate attempt to subsume the construing processes of the other into one's own construct system. Sociality does not necessarily involve commonality. A manager, for example, may be able to subsume a subordinate's construct system without their respective construct systems being similar. Commonality, however, as we have already suggested, does increase the probability of success of attempts to subsume the construct system of others.

Kelly saw sociality as the key to viable social relationships: 'to the extent that one person construes the construction processes of another, he may play a role in a social process involving the other person'. In occupational settings, sociality is essential to skilled social performance. In selling, for example, sociality enables predictions to be made about what aspect of the product or service will be the most attractive to the customer and enable the salesperson to anticipate the customer's information-processing capacity. In supervision sociality provides a supervisor with an idea of how subordinates will treat instructions. Sociality is not always one-way or asymmetrical: most social situations, particularly in a professional setting, involve some degree of mutual construing. But not everyone is aware that mutual construing occurs in social encounters. Some people model others often quite elaborately but do not comprehend that others are also modelling them. Some people model others but assume others have a fixed and fully established model of them. The hallmark of social skill is when we actively develop models of others while assuming they are actively modelling us.

Ross and Nisbett (1991) described some of the attributional errors resulting from failing to take another person's construal into account. As they point out:

the real source of difficulty does not lie in the fact that human beings subjectively define the situations they face, nor even in the fact that they do so in variable and unpredictable ways. Rather the problem lies in their failure to recognize and make adequate inferential *allowance* for this variability and unpredictability. (p. 82)

This failure has important effects on our ability to comprehend others. Because, rather egocentrically, we assume our construal of the situation is 'correct', we believe others' construal will be similar. This leads to what is termed the *false consensus effect*. Assuming others possess similar constructions of events means we explain apparently deviant behaviour in others in terms of unusual and extreme personality traits rather than different construals of the situation.

Thus, in one experiment described by Ross and Nisbett, subjects were asked to help with a study into 'communication techniques'. If they were prepared to help (they could opt to sign up for a later study) they would have to walk around the campus for thirty minutes with a sandwich board with the message 'Eat at Joe's'. Subjects were asked to give their own decisions about whether to participate, and to estimate other people's decisions. The false consensus effect appeared in subjects assuming the majority of their peers would make the same decision as they had. The choice to participate or not depended on the subjects' construal of (*a*) what the experiment was about (conformity, uptightness, being a 'sport'); (*b*) the reaction of their peers; and (*c*) the reaction of the experimenter to a refusal.

These subtle differences in construal of the situation determined the decision to sign up or not. But both 'compliant' and 'non-compliant' subjects confidently attributed extreme personality traits to explain the other group's behaviour. As Ross and Nisbett concluded, not making adequate allowance for differences in construal is ultimately a failure: 'to recognize the degree to which . . . interpretations of the situation are just that—constructions and inferences rather than faithful reflections of some objective and invariant reality' (p. 85).

As we have seen, personal construct theory suggests that we actively construct models of one another. It also suggests this process can go wrong. We have already seen the lack of commonality, sociality and adequate constructs reduces the probability of a valid model of the other being constructed.

There are two other ways in which a model's validity can be reduced: *pre-emption* and *circumspection*. Pre-emption, the cutting short of construing processes, is seen when there is lack of time, willingness or capacity to construe others. When construing is pre-empted the model is constructed out of stereotypes and ready-made generalizations. In contrast to this, circumspection involves the excessive construing of others and a consequent failure to commit oneself to a particular view of or lines of action with them. Circumspection is triggered by the uncertainty and ambiguity which other people's behaviour or personalities contain. Attempting to cope with this uncertainty can, as with neurotic thought, cause individuals to become 'preoccupied with' or 'lodged in' construing. Social skills depend on an ability to strike an appropriate balance between the pre-emptive and the circumspective construing of other people.

Interactional work

The concept of skill is particularly helpful when examining the 'interactional work' which constitutes much of our social life and through which our practical and expressive goals are attained. Like other skilled work, interactional work possesses a hierarchical structure, and therefore offers a number of possible units of analysis. Words form up into sentences, sentences construct social acts (demanding, asserting, complying, rejecting, etc.), social acts build up into episodes (a group of social acts characterized by some internal homogeneity such as an introduction) and episodes form encounters (interviews, sales negotiations, team briefings, etc.). This building up of encounters out of words is termed *concatenation* (Harré, 1992). Achieving goals in social situations therefore depends on the ability to build up and progress through social encounters. As we shall see, progress has been made in describing how this is achieved.

Open sequences If we use the types of situations described earlier (closed, open, and defined), we can consider the skills required for competent interaction in different types of situation. 'Open' situations seemingly involve neither prior goals nor specific interactional routes for participants. For example, simply talking to friends in a chance encounter usually involves no specific objectives or sequences of interaction. In these situations discourse is relatively unplanned, lacking forethought or organization. Sequences of interaction in open situations involve what is termed *reactive contingency*: that is, each participant simply responds to what the previous contributor has said.

Even in these seemingly 'open' situations it is possible to discern some rules operating to shape sequences. At the simplest level, participants have to co-ordinate their contributions. *Turn-taking* is achieved using principles acquired at the earliest stages of the development of interactional competence. Young children capable of only one- or two-word utterances take turns to make their contributions, which to the annoyance of many a parent they tend to repeat until the other participant has acknowledged what they have said. Schieffelin (1983) for example, found 30-month-old children attending to each other's contribution and sustaining interactions of over twenty-five turns. In adulthood, the conventions for indicating a desire to retain, obtain or hand over the role of contributor are usually so well learned that we are unaware of them. Analyses of interaction show individuals signal a willingness to hand over the role of contributor by pausing, gazing at each other at the end of a contribution or asking a question. Gaze at the end of a contribution is used not only to signal a willingness to hand over the floor but also to gain feedback on how others have reacted to a contribution. Keeping the floor involves not pausing, not looking at others at the end of sentences, using certain gestures and raising one's voice. To take the floor, a participant needs to listen for what Sacks *et al.* (1974) described as 'transition relevance space'. At these points in the interaction an individual uses particular grammatical constructions as 'place-holders' which give him or her time to construct a well-formed proposition.

In addition to turn-taking, participants in conversation also appear to adhere to other rules:

1. Quantity. Contributions should be as informative as possible without providing too much information.
2. Quality. Contributions should be true or have sufficient evidence to support them.
3. Relevance. Contributions should be relevant to what has preceded them.
4. Manner. Contributions should be clear, unambiguous and organized.

Orderliness also appears at the level of the social acts performed by contributors. Clarke (1983) discovered that subjects could rearrange into the correct order cards containing single contributions taken from informal sequences of interaction. More importantly, they could do the same for a set of cards on which the various social acts constituted by these contributions had been written. The orderliness of subjects detected among social acts was between pairs such as question–answer, offer–accept, request–comply and reject–reason. These sequences are known as *two-step* sequences. The ability of his subjects to recognize orderliness in interaction at the level of both social act and sentences led Clarke to suggest that there was a 'grammar' or 'syntax' of social acts analogous to that of languages. One such rule, which enables people to perceive orderliness, reflects generally held beliefs about sustaining harmony in social interaction. For instance, if an individual is to sustain a pleasant exchange, he or she must provide a reason after refusing an offer because of a general belief that offers should be accepted, even when acceptance involves inconvenience.

Although two-step sequences are observable in many interactions, there do not seem to be regularities in associations between two-step units in most situations. Sequences of more than two acts are generated by the persistence over time of an individual's goals. In the relatively unplanned discourse of open situations, the goal of a participant is often simply to establish and sustain what are termed *discourse topics* (a concern or a set of concerns). If an individual wants to sustain a discourse topic, he or she needs to match a contribution to the preceding utterance of the other person. This produces sequences termed *topic-collaborating sequences*. If, however, an individual wishes to continue the flow of discourse but change the topic, the previous contributor's last utterance can be used to create a new discourse topic. These sequences are termed *topic-incorporating sequences*. New discourse topics can also be introduced by 'breaking and entering': that is, by creating discontinuities in the dialogue. This can be done either by introducing a new discourse topic which has already appeared in the 'discourse history' or negotiating a completely new discourse topic. The skills required to sustain or negotiate new discourse topics in open situations include: securing the other's attention; articulating utterances clearly; providing sufficient information for the other to identify objects, people or events (referents) included in the discourse topic; providing sufficient information for the other to understand the relationships between referents of the discourse topic; locating and attending to sources of misunderstanding ('repair work'); and shaping utterances taking into account what is termed the other's 'presupposition pool', and estimation of what the other person understands ('recipient design').

Defined sequences Interaction in defined situations, such as between incumbents of organizational roles, involves more than merely attempting to draw on each other's presupposition pools to sustain discourse topics. At least one participant will invariably have an objective. This may be to provide the other with information, sell the other something or make a selection decision. Utterances are, therefore, preceded by more forethought and planning than in 'open' situations, and discourse is relatively planned. One feature of this is the *four-step* sequence, produced by a goal of one participant persisting after the other's response, as in the following example:

A Interviewer (question)	Why do you want to leave your present job?
B Candidate: (inadequate response)	I would rather not go into that.
C Interviewer: (accounts for question)	I think we really do need to know why you have decided to leave our major competitor.
D Candidate: (adequate response)	I felt the company no longer offered me the challenges I'm looking for.

Here, the interviewer's goals of ascertaining the candidate's reason for leaving persists from A through B to C. Sequences structured by the goal of one participant only possess what Jones and Gerard (1967) termed *asymmmetrical contingency*, one participant responding according to the objectives of the other.

In encounters between individuals occupying specific roles, it is usually the case that both participants have goals. Encounters in these 'defined' situations may still be relatively under-identified for participants in a number of ways. The precise nature and variability of the other's objectives or initial construction of the situation may not be known. No routine sequences of interaction are built into defined situations so a strategy for dealing with the encounter has to be worked out. This means participants have to establish a *working consensus* of what type of situation they are involved in. This then provides the stable ground on which they can base a strategy for interaction.

The ambiguity and unstructuredness that still reside in defined situations make social skills an important determinant of effectiveness in them. To establish a working consensus of a situation individuals need to be able to construe the construing processes of others. As Singleton (1983, p. 291) pointed out, 'in the case of social skills reality is not only physical events, it is also the schemata in other people's minds which control their attempts to communicate'. An individual, therefore, must be able to detect, absorb and recreate the schemata or models which lie behind the initial statements of other participants. As we have seen, the complexity of an individual's construing was related to his or her ability to construe a situation from another's point of view. In selling, for example, the ability to imagine being the customer enables a salesperson to understand the customer's needs.

Establishing a working consensus of a situation is also assisted by a degree of commonality between the participants' construct systems. An individual's willingness to share constructs increases the likelihood of this commonality between constructions of a situation being achieved. By sharing constructs, individuals allow others to check to what extent their models of the situation map on to each other. If, for example, a manager's and subordinate's constructions of a situation do not map on to each other reasonably well, interaction is unlikely to get very far and some form of conflict or opposition may ensue. Sharing constructs allows the other to accept, elaborate, modify and return the model until the models map on to each other sufficiently well for a working consensus of the situation to have developed.

Having established a working consensus, participants can develop a strategy for dealing with the encounter and for achieving their objectives. At this stage skilled communication requires the same skills as those required in 'open' situations. To move nearer to our goals our contributions must possess good recipient design. The skilled communicator is sensitive to cues provided by the listener which enable utterances with good recipient design to be constructed. Increasing sensitivity to these cues is now central to training programmes in many areas where professional competence depends on social skills. For example, sales training once consisted of requiring salespeople to rote-learn scripts. In other words, training was based on an implicit model of simple asymmetrical contingency in interaction—a one-way communication from the salesperson to the customer. Nowadays, however, sales training emphasizes the importance in successful selling of sensitivity to cues from customers.

In selling, as in other areas where professional social skills are employed, an accurate estimation of the listener's ability to process information is crucial. The skilled salesperson is able to provide screened and selected information at a pace which matches the customer's ability to assimilate it. One device known as 'checkback', where agreement is sought from a customer (e.g. 'don't you agree?'), enables the salesperson to ensure that he or she is working at the same pace as the customer. If checkback indicates that a customer's pace has been exceeded, the salesperson would need to engage in 'repair work', locating and attending to the points when the customer was lost. Checkback is also thought to increase the commitment of a customer to the salesperson's objectives.

Listeners can also be lost by asking what are known as *closed questions*, which require simple definitive answers. The importance of avoiding these closed questions has been stressed in situations as diverse as selling and psychotherapeutic interviews. The closed question often creates a hiatus which allows listeners to disengage from the discourse. A further way listeners are lost is when statements threatening their self-esteem or self-concept are used. This means *tact* is an important component of social skill, since it protects the feelings of listeners and so retains their attention. Argyle (1983, p. 51) defined tact as 'the production of socially effective utterances in difficult situations'. In selling, for example, a salesperson needs to transform 'do you have the authority to order?' into 'do you normally decide on the ordering or do you leave that up to someone else?'

Tact is also a component of a crucial skill in professional and occupational settings, namely dealing with objections. In modern complex organizations people's objections and grievances often stem from real conflicts of interest, and may not be readily handled even by tactful negotiation. But in many cases objections that result from disappointments or misunderstandings can be resolved. For example, an effective sequence for handling grievances in line management is: search, probe, handle, and restructure. For instance, a subordinate claims she is not able to use her skills fully. By searching and probing on the basis of her statements, her supervisor establishes the source of the grievance is actually her feeling that she should have been promoted by now. Handling and restructuring involve carefully readjusting her expectations in line with a more realistic time-scale for acquiring the experience necessary for competence in a promoted post. In selling, one commonly used sequence for handling objections is: welcome; restate; overcome; and continue. For example, an objection is welcomed by the salesperson: 'I can understand how you feel, Mr Jones.' It is restated to enable the salesperson to confirm precisely what the objection refers to: 'You're unhappy about using the magazine because you don't believe it is reaching 25,000 potential customers.' The salesperson can then overcome the objection by giving more information: 'As I mentioned earlier our circulation is fully controlled so we can guarantee who is receiving it.' If the customer accepts this response the salesperson returns to the point before the objection occurred.

The ability to progress smoothly through an interactional sequence in pursuit of a goal appears to be crucial at all levels of interaction in social encounters: sentences, social acts and episodes. The generally held beliefs about sustaining harmony in social interaction and presenting pleasant fronts operate at all these levels. These are outlined in Box 6.2.

Social encounters, particularly in defined situations, need to have the practical purpose of the meeting sandwiched between episodes in which a harmonious social relationship is established, for example, by recalling the last meeting, and then re-established perhaps by arranging a future meeting. This gives rise to the common five-episode structure for encounters: greeting, establishing relationship, central task, re-establishing relationship, and parting. Some individuals find the transitions in front required to move from practical to expressive episodes and vice versa particularly difficult. It is at these points where we have to negotiate a shift in the definition of the situation (Guirdham, 1995).

Episodes are themselves built up out of two-step and four-step sequences. For example, the central task containing the practical purpose of a sales encounter can involve (1) gaining interest (2) identifying the customer's needs (3) selling the benefits of a particular item or service to the customer (4) welcoming the customer's objections, and (5) 'closing' the sale. High-selling sales staff are able, by developing a good rapport with the customer, to move smoothly through episodes involved in the central task and are thus more likely to close a sale.

Like other skilled activity, then, social skills involve a smooth progression towards a goal. This means responses should be well timed and in the correct order. An appropriate sequencing of responses for socially skilled behaviour ultimately depends on the validity of the models we construct of the people we interact with and of the social situations in which we find ourselves.

Box 6.2 Five rules for constructing effective fronts

The goal of social skills training is helping individuals communicate and work more effectively together. There are a number of specific social skills which individuals might need to demonstrate at work. These include influencing, motivating, counselling, coaching, and interviewing. All of these are more easily accomplished if you attempt them from behind an effective front. This is not as easy as it may seem. This is because we can, quite unwittingly, undermine the effectiveness of our fronts by providing others with easily misread information. The introvert, for example, with lower levels of eye contact may appear uninterested. An assertive individual can appear insensitive by unwittingly appearing to put down someone else's opinion. A highly conscientious person can unknowingly be seen as nitpicking and dismissive. This means it is important to learn how to suspend, if only temporarily, these behaviours. Psychometric tests such as the Insight Inventory can provide a useful starting point for identifying why communication or relationships are not always as effective as we would wish. Inventories such as Insight can help in establishing what short-term shifts in your front might be helpful. In general the most effective front is the one others are more likely to like. This means:

1. *Displaying consistency*: do not project a front which you cannot maintain throughout the interaction.
2. *Display liking* for the other individual(s): whilst difficult for some to achieve, this is the most effective way of eliciting approval from others.
3. *Display agreement*: this is particularly important for those who find 2, above, difficult. Particularly effective is the 'spontaneous expression' of a similar attitude.
4. *Display interest*: sometimes termed 'stroking', this can be achieved verbally or non-verbally. Non-verbally, gaze and attentive listening are particularly effective. This may have the consequence of helping to find something which makes it easier to demonstrate liking.
5. *Display a degree of self-disclosure*: too much early on is counter-productive but too little can be seen as defensiveness, mistrustfulness, and a lack of openness.

These rules might seem manipulative but remember the goal is simply to enable you to be a more effective team member, colleague, fellow student, or supervisor.

Conclusion

In this chapter we have examined the view that social behaviour is fundamentally characterized by individuals engaging in impression management. From this perspective people are creative, expressive beings who convey information about themselves in a variety of verbal and non-verbal ways. By constructing 'fronts' individuals project definitions of themselves as particular kinds of individual. This to a large extent imposes a moral obligation on others to accept this front. They also attempt to regulate definitions of the situations they are in. But alongside these attempts to construct effective fronts is the constant monitoring by others of the success or otherwise of our impression management.

What this approach offers is an explanation of social behaviour located much more squarely in the cognitions and discourses of individuals. Understanding social behaviour is about understanding the rules which shape human conduct. As Harré and Gillet put it,

the psychological is not reducible to or replaceable by explanations in terms of psychology, physics or any other point of view that does not reveal the structure of meanings existing in the lives of the human group to which the subject of an investigation belongs. (1994, p. 20)

Kelly's construct theory examined in this chapter is hence central to this perspective since it elucidates the meanings individuals construct of the people and events they encounter.

The approach outlined in this chapter represents in many ways a radical departure from mainstream psychology. For example, its implications for personality theory are considerable. It suggests that stabilities in behaviour are not the result of inherent personality differences but of people behaving similarly in similar situations. In other words, the consistency is in the situation, not the individual. Some have gone as far as to say there are no such things as traits i.e. stable underlying consistencies in behaviour. It might, however, still be worth studying because personality constructs form part of our construct systems and therefore help to make sense of ourselves and others. Personality exists, from this perspective, only because we think it does. To dismiss traits altogether, as some have, is probably to go too far. But in emphasizing the importance of situations, language, rules, and cognitions as important determinants of social behaviour, this perspective does much to correct the historical over-reliance on traits and individual differences as the principal explanatory basis of behaviour.

Study questions for Chapter 6

1 'The key defining characteristic of social life is impression management'—discuss.

2 From your own experience of working in organizations or studying in institutions, can you give examples of some 'fronts'. Are some more 'successful' than others and why?

3 What are the components of social situations?

4 It is the features of social situations rather than trait profiles which determine an individual's behaviour—discuss.

5 How do we comprehend other people we interact with?

6 If you undertook the construct exercise—consider the following questions:

   a) Did you manage to get twelve and if you did was it a struggle towards the end of your list?

   b) What are they about—personality, behaviour, attitude, ability, role, status, appearance? Are they a mixture of these or do they tend to be concentrated on one of these categories?

   c) Of your list is it possible to see any underlying constructs? In other words, is it possible to reduce the list to perhaps three or four 'super-constructs' and what would these be?

   d) Are you surprised by any of your constructs?

   e) Are they similar to your partner's? And if so, why might this have occurred?

7 In what way is social skill different from and similar to other types of skill?

8 To what extent is it possible to improve social skills?

9 The notions of dramaturgy and impression management suggest our behaviour is not sufficiently consistent to infer the existence of stable underlying traits—discuss.

Further reading

Argyle, M. (1994) *The Psychology of Interpersonal Behaviour*, 5th edn. London: Penguin.

Burns, T. (1992) *Erving Goffman*. London: Routledge.

Duck, S. (1998) *Human Relationships*, 3rd edn. London: Sage.

Goffman, E. (1971) *The Presentation of Self in Everyday Life*. London: Penguin.

Guirdham, M. (1995) *Interpersonal Skills at Work*, 2nd edn. London: Prentice Hall.

Harré, R. (1993) *Social Being*, 2nd edn. Oxford: Blackwells.

—— and Gillet, G. (1994) *The Discursive Mind*. London: Sage.

Rosenfield, P., Giacalone, R. A., and Riordan, C. A. (1995) *Impression Management in Organizations*. London: Routledge.

7 Group and Intergroup Behaviour

Summary points and learning objectives

By the end of this chapter you will be able to

- describe two reasons for group formation;
- describe categories of group membership;
- discuss the concept of team roles;
- explain the development and impact of group norms;
- understand key aspects of group process;
- describe the concept of synergy;
- describe the concept of groupthink;
- understand the concept of group polarization;
- discuss why teamworking does not always improve productivity;
- describe the concept of reflexivity;
- understand the possible causes of intergroup competition;
- understand the profound influence of the Hawthorne studies.

Introduction

In the workplace much of our social behaviour occurs in a group context. In this chapter we will explore the effects of our group membership on our social behaviour. Managerial interest in group working arrangements has increased dramatically in recent years. Collective working arrangements at work are now commonplace—the project group, the Corporate Management Team, the Quality Circle, the Production Team, and the shift 'crew'. The notion of employee involvement which we will critically examine in Chapter 11 also presupposes some form of collective or group identity. The concern with groups is seen also in job descriptions and job advertisements, which now refer explicitly to an ability to work well in a team as an essential personal attribute. (Incidentally, in this chapter we will use the terms team and group interchangeably. On close inspection of the terms there seems to be no important difference between the two.)

So managements increasingly use teams to arrange work around; and this is done in the expectation teams deliver more than individuals—the sum is more than the total of its parts. Team working has for this reason had conferred on it an almost mythical status as a panacea for motivational and performance problems. One important function of this chapter will therefore be to examine more critically the claims for the benefits of team working. In the psychological literature going back over a century it has been clear that groups often do not perform as well as the same number of individuals working alone. For example, as long ago as the 1890s a French agricultural engineer, Max Ringelmann, found that a group pulling on a rope exerted only about 75 per cent of the force these individuals produced working separately. Groups have also been responsible for disasters such as Chernobyl and errors of judgement such as the 'Bay of Pigs fiasco'—a bungled attempt in 1961 to overthrow Castro's army in Cuba.

There is then an important gap between the 'hype' about teams—exaggerated expectations of what they are able to deliver—and what is often the reality. But some of the processes which promote or undermine group effectiveness are well understood and documented, even if not always applied to the workplace. We will examine this research in some detail.

However, the first task of this chapter will be to build a good understanding of groups and group functioning. We will thus explore some of the basic features of groups and teams. Why do groups form in the first place? What structures do they develop? What processes shape interaction between team members? How do groups relate to one another? Good intergroup co-ordination can make the difference between a smooth and effective production process and one characterized by conflict and poor performance. If group identity can be a basis for conflict with other groups and manifested, for example, in prejudice and discrimination—how might we reduce such conflict?

All of the current interest in teams and team working has its origins in some research carried out near Chicago in the late 1920s through to the early 1940s, and no discussion of teams at work is complete without reference to what became known as the Hawthorne studies. This research had a profound effect on management thinking and identified very vividly both the positive and negative (from a managerial perspective) qualities of group working arrangements. We will conclude the chapter with an examination of these classic studies.

Why do groups form?

Although there is no straightforward answer to this question, at least two main assumptions about the basis for group formation have been put forward. Some writers stress the *functional* reasons for the existence of groups, such as joint action on a task; face-to-face interaction or mutually dependent relationships. Fiedler's (1967) useful typology of work groups, for example, is based on the nature and intensity of interaction necessary for task accomplishment:

1. *Interacting groups.* Members are interdependent and need to co-operate and co-ordinate their actions to accomplish the group task.
2. *Co-acting groups.* Members work together on a common task but do so relatively independently.
3. *Counteracting groups.* Individuals work together for the purposes of negotiating and reconciling conflicting demands and objectives. Performance is measured by the acceptability of the solution to group members.

This typology reflects the extent to which group members' behaviour is determined by group structure and processes. The impact on members' behaviour, values, and attitudes of interacting and counteracting groups is far greater than in co-acting groups because of the increased intensity of interaction they involve.

Whilst the functional basis for group formation is at the heart of Fiedler's typology, other writers have emphasized the *psychological* processes which cause groups to form: the perception of a shared identity, and attempts to fulfil needs for affiliation, recognition, and self-assertion. In other words, groups form because they provide individuals with opportunities to fulfil fundamental human needs. Whilst many of the needs groups fulfil are conscious, some writers have stressed the role unconscious processes have in providing the basic psychological context for group membership (e.g. Bion, 1959; Kets de Vries and Miller, 1984).

While Bion's work was with small therapeutic groups, some psychologists working in organizations argue that his ideas are equally relevant to the workplace. Bion suggested that parallel to the 'functional' group exists another one. Individual members contribute to and draw quite unconsciously from this parallel group. And it is this second group which can give the functional group its powerful, emotional climate. Bion and others believe this second group is essentially regressive in nature. This is because it involves some very primitive, childlike emotional mechanisms such as dependency, projection, and denial. This other group can—by acting as a 'collective ego'—distort reality and sometimes operate in ways which are quite at odds with the effective performance of the functional group.

This other, unconscious group, Bion termed the *basic assumption group*. It is basic because it is essentially regressive in nature and seems to be operating on the basis of unconscious assumptions about what the group is or should be trying to achieve for its members. In organizations the basic assumption group can permeate a range of activities—from casual conversations by the vending machine to the way decisions are made. It recreates and reinforces itself, for example by utilizing chance events such as accidents. It generates the shared fantasies which provide the psychological environment—the myths, the distortions, the shared perceptions of reality out of which organizational culture is created.

Bion argued that groups operate at any one time with one of only three basic assumptions.

1. *Fight–Flight.* The basic assumption here is that there is an enemy 'out there' against which the group has either to defend itself or escape from. Groups operating with this

basic assumption are either avoidant or paranoid. With avoidance there is a strong sense of external threat, and as a defensive–adaptive response there are excellent relationships between group members. There are good, efficient internal systems. But this group has its 'head in the sand' as there tends to be inadequate monitoring of the external environment.

By contrast in the paranoid mode the group has a similar sense of threat, but a much more competitive and aggressive attitude towards it. Here there is much more scanning of the environment—an excessive concern with competitor activity. There is also an element of projection—i.e. misreading the intentions of other groups and splitting—creating a sharp divide between allies and enemies. But this charged emotional climate also creates commitment, conviction, and energy amongst group members. This can lead to rather impulsive decision-making. The lack of reflection and deliberation can also produce a poorly conceived strategy for the group.

2. *Dependency*. The group here comes together as if to be taken care of by someone. In organizations three scenarios can be manifestations of this basic assumption (e.g. Kets de Vries and Miller, 1984). The first is characterized by strong faith in a charismatic leader. Members believe this individual has talent and ability and can be depended on to take care of them. This can provide the leader with considerable freedom. He or she is able to take risks and challenge existing strategies and ideology. Another scenario is when the leader has gone but the dependency assumption persists. Here the leader's 'bible' is crucial. It enables members to extend the presence of the leader into the present by rigidly adhering to past practices and procedures. In the third scenario there is a takeover by a parent organization, customer, or supplier. This might revitalize the group by breaking up bureaucratic practices which have become embedded during the second scenario. But the shift in power, control over resources, and restriction of decision latitude can ensure dependency continues.

3. *Utopian* (originally termed 'pairing'). The basic assumption here is a person or idea will deliver the group from its anxieties and difficulties. In this group there is much anticipation and fantasy. In fact, so much psychological energy is invested in the future that pressing current problems (cash flow, order book) might be overlooked. Group tensions are low in anticipation of this shared future, and thus there is a highly collaborative and democratic approach to decision making. This basic assumption supports a good deal of creativity and innovation.

The main problem of utopian groups is that while goals—this ideal future state—are clear, means of achieving them are much less so. Utopian organizations are best exemplified by research-oriented companies. Sometimes they can lack pragmatic individuals in production, marketing, and finance who can turn innovations into commercial reality. Or if there are practical individuals in the group they may lack the influence to get other members to have an equal concern with the means of achieving group goals.

Bion would argue that at any one time groups are characterized by just one basic assumption. The group can stay with this basic assumption or move on to another one perhaps because of external events. What is both fascinating and in a sense disturbing about Bion's ideas is that group life is characterized by such a limited range of basic assumptions. These basic assumptions are both powerful and unconsciously shared. For Bion groups form because of basic emotional states and assumptions present in all of us. They form out of unconscious 'hard-wired' preconceptions of what groups are about and what they can provide us with. From this perspective our 'groupishness'—the answer to why groups form, is with us from birth. There is a biogenetic basis to group formation rooted in our evolutionary development as a species.

Whilst not all psychologists would agree with Bion's psychodynamic, unconscious, and innate explanation of group formation all would agree with him that groups enable the interweaving of a complex mix of functional and psychological forces. And for this reason our various group memberships play a fundamental role in our lives and the development of our social identities.

Group structure

The structure of a group reflects the basis of group identity—and indeed the very fact that we can speak of a group at all rather than merely a number of individuals. For a structure reflects the established patterns of behaviour that are distinctive within a particular group. Structure constitutes a distinctively *social* aspect of group life, and may act as an objective constraint on members' activity. One important aspect of structure consists of the different *categories of membership* that the different individuals making up the group occupy.

1. Early on in a group's history a *group leader* will often emerge because he or she is perceived by other members as the most competent at the functional requirements of the leadership role. The division of status and authority between group leaders and followers that this implies is an important dimension of group structure. Bales and Slater (1955) suggested these functional requirements were related both to the group's task and to the group's socio-emotional requirements. Behaviours associated with the task include co-ordinating, initiating contributions, evaluating, information-giving, information-seeking, opinion-giving, opinion-seeking, and motivating individuals. Behaviours associated with the group's socio-emotional requirements include reconciling differences, arbitrating, encouraging participation and increasing interdependence among group members. One individual may be perceived by the group as capable of meeting both the socio-emotional and task requirements of the leadership role. In some groups, however, two leaders may emerge, each with perceived competence in one of these leadership functions.

2. Group *members* can be defined as individuals who have accepted group goals as relevant and recognize an interdependence with other group members in the achievement of these goals. Acceptance of group goals is associated with an individual's needs (subsistence, dependence, affiliation, dominance) and the extent to which his or her social identity is derived from membership of the group. Individuals can also decide whether to accept group goals on the basis of a rational estimation of the utility of group membership.

3. Sometimes, however, an individual's personal goals conflict with the group's goals; and if he or she is not prepared to modify his or her personal goals, dissatisfaction with the group becomes almost inevitable. The individual is then identified as a *deviate*. Group members will usually attempt to increase the deviate's acceptance of group goals. Indeed, persuading a deviate to accept group goals can absorb a considerable proportion of a group's time.

4. If deviates resist group pressure and continue to reject group goals, the group will eventually give up on them and they are left alone by other group members. They become *isolates*. Though they may be tolerated because their output is required, they are unlikely to be included in activities which do not directly involve the task. In extreme cases group members may seek not only the psychological isolation of such individuals but their physical isolation too.

An enormously influential typology of group structure—the bedrock of innumerable management development courses and team-building events—was developed by Meridith Belbin (1981, 1993). In fact, Belbin's team roles are a particularly good example of academic research bridging the gap between theory and organizational practice. The model's success is, to some extent, explained by its accessibility. It requires no specialist knowledge of group dynamics or group theory to use, and it is readily available. A pencil and paper questionnaire forms part of Belbin's original text. Additionally, alongside Belbin's own commercially available software, team-role profiles are routinely generated by software supporting the two major personality tests used in occupational assessment. Belbin's model is now so widely disseminated it has become the *lingua franca* of team work.

Belbin's model was based on a mixture of observation, personality, and ability data. He proposed that alongside any functional and technical expertise individuals bring to a team, differences in personality and ability give rise to styles of behaviour and thinking which predispose people to one or other of his team roles:

1. *Co-ordinator*. This is the person who attempts to establish the goals and agenda of the group. He or she will allocate roles and responsibilities and sum up the feelings and accomplishments of the group. Assertiveness, affiliativeness, and conscientiousness drive the behaviours of the co-ordinator.
2. *Plant*. Essentially the plant is the ideas person. Plants thus tend to be more innovative and to search for possible changes in the group's approach to its problems. They tend to be intelligent, introverted, and imaginative.
3. *Implementer*. This is the team member who converts ideas and objectives into practical operational procedures. Implementers tend to be task-oriented, conscientious, and affiliative.
4. *Monitor evaluator*. This team member analyses problems and evaluates the contributions of others. Those around the monitor evaluator may feel he or she pours scorn on their suggestions. Monitor evaluators tend to be sober, introverted, and shrewd.
5. *Shaper*. Extraverted, tense, and defensive, shapers are anxious to prioritize and structure the group's activities.

6. *Teamworker*. Affiliative and not overly dominant, teamworkers focus on the interpersonal behaviour of team members. They encourage participation, arbitrate, and
harmonize.

7. *Resource investigator*. Extraverted, imaginative, and stable, resource investigators identify ideas and resources in the external environment which are available to the
group.

8. *Completer*. This team member is keen to complete the tasks to the deadline.
Completers identify areas which need more work and possible oversights. Anxiety
and conscientiousness are the traits driving this team member.

9. *Specialist*. This individual is focused on providing specialist knowledge and skills.
Specialists tend to be single-minded and self-motivating.

Whilst some of the influence of the team roles model stems from its availability,
much of it comes from its highly prescriptive nature. Belbin provided managers, consultants, and trainers with a good deal of straightforward advice on how team effectiveness is improved. In other words his model provides a way of describing teamwork
and of improving it. He suggests teams work best if there is:

1. A match between an individual's responsibilities and his or her 'natural' team role.

2. A spread in mental ability—the plant needs at least one other member to bounce
ideas off, but if everyone in the team is very bright the team can spend too much time
arguing and so not agree any effective solutions.

3. An ability to identify and adjust imbalances in the group.

4. A strong plant to produce ideas for the team.

5. A good co-ordinator to show patience, command, seek out ability, and elicit trust.

6. A range of team roles available to the group.

Belbin suggests particular team roles are important at different stages of a group's life.
At the beginning of its existence when needs are being identified the presence of strong
shapers and co-ordinators is crucial. Later on, when the group needs to follow through
on some of its ideas, completers and implementers are vital.

Surprisingly, given the model's widespread use, there is only sparse empirical support for it (e.g. Senior, 1997; Fisher *et al.*, 1998). In addition, assigning an individual his
or her team role is not unproblematic. The measures of team roles have poor psychometric properties—reliability and validity (e.g. Furnham *et al.*, 1993), and from experience of working in organizations, team roles are sometimes 'over-interpreted'. They can
be seen as set in stone—fixed, rigid attributes of individuals. This can encourage
labelling of individuals. Consultants, trainers, and managers can put too much weight
on an individual's team-role profile, ignoring other more concrete forms of evidence.
Perhaps most worrying, given its psychometric properties, is the use of the team-role
questionnaire in selection.

But to be critical of Belbin's model is in some ways to miss the point. Despite these
criticisms, the model has taken on a life of its own and an influence out of all proportion to its empirical support. Its main benefit—the main 'payoff' for trainers and con-

sultants using it, is as a *heuristic*—as a way of thinking and talking about team and individual effectiveness. It provides team members with 'permission to talk'. In other words, a neutral, non-evaluative framework for discussing their own and other people's contributions to the group. And in doing so, can help resolve performance and relationship issues which are becoming a barrier to effectiveness.

Group norms

Groups have their most significant impact on our behaviour through the operation of *norms*. Indeed, many social psychologists believe that behaviour in groups can be understood only in relation to the norms that are operating within it, since they represent the *expectations* within the group for appropriate behaviour of group members. As these expectations are external to each member, norms are thus part of a group's structure. It is often hard for individuals to realize the impact the expectations of others have on their behaviour (as it was in the similar case of roles, discussed in Chapter 6) because norms become part of their psychological make-up, affecting their attitudes, values, beliefs and behaviour. Guirdham (1995) suggests that there are four norms which are generally present at work.

1. *Fairness*. We have already seen in Chapter 6 how equity operates as a motivator. In the context of group norms we generally expect other group members to behave equitably. If they do not, we either get distressed or attempt to punish them.
2. *Reciprocity*. This implies that if A does something for B, B has a duty to do something for A. This norm helps in initiating contacts since, if A is polite to B, there is a duty on B to be polite to A. But as Guirdham points out, in business settings the operation of the reciprocity norm is problematic. This is because individuals can assume there are ulterior motives for the others' actions. For example, if when running an assessment centre for a senior appointment I am willing to accommodate an extra candidate without quibbling or charging more, this can be interpreted by the client as trying to keep goodwill. The client can therefore feel under no obligation to reciprocate by, for example, offering another assignment. The operation of the reciprocity norm requires a great deal of knowledge about how it works in particular organizational or social settings. It is therefore unwise to expect too much of it.
3. *Reasonableness*. Guirdham claims most people in business expect each other to behave reasonably, by, for example, not exploiting or withholding payment from suppliers and therefore taking excessive credit.
4. *Role expectations*. The pressure on individuals to live up to the expectations other people have of their roles has the force of a norm.

A group's norms do not occur by accident; they represent the interaction of social, historical, and psychological processes, and they are thus resistant to change. In Chapter 5, for instance, we discussed an example of the historical development of group norms when considering the effort bargain at work, which we saw emerged from a normative consensus about what constitutes a fair ratio of effort to reward. Although norms are generated out of the practical activity of groups and are embedded in their experiences and history, when necessary groups can also generate norms very quickly.

If a group suddenly faces very different demands, or conditions are such that it is necessary to form a new group, then the ability to generate norms quickly may well be essential to the group's survival. Industrial disputes provide a number of examples of sudden changes in circumstances. If, for instance, a union with no previous experience of strike organization enters a dispute with an employer it has suddenly to generate norms quickly in order to carry out the numerous activities necessary to maintain and enhance the strike (e.g. striker welfare, picketing, support services for pickets, dealing with the media, and fund-raising).

The principal way in which group norms are absorbed is through observation. At work, for example, a new employee will estimate the norms for attendance, workrate and dress from the group's modal behaviour—that is, how most people in the group behave. Group members also observe the extent to which an individual's behaviour matches the group's norms. Norms usually include a degree of tolerance and specify a range of acceptable behaviour, known as the *zone of acceptance*, so that members will take action only if another member's behaviour falls outside this range. For example, in the Hawthorne studies which we will be discussing in greater detail later in the chapter, the norms included: (1) not 'rate-busting' (turning out too much work); (2) not 'chiselling' (turning out too little work); (3) not 'squealing' (telling the supervisor anything detrimental to the group). Anyone who deviated from these norms was subjected either to sarcasm and ridicule or to a physical penalty—a harsh blow to the upper arm—known in the plant as 'binging'. These sanctions generally ensured conformity to group norms. Groups thus wield an enormous amount of power over their members.

Group processes

We now turn to the *process* of interaction within groups, which refers to the manner in which group action is constructed on a continuing basis. Unlike structure, process emphasizes changes in the flow of activities; indeed group processes indicate how structures become established and how over time they may change. Process also points to the subjective perceptions of group members and their active involvement in group life.

Cohesiveness

Cohesiveness can be defined as the complex of forces which gives rise to the perceptions by members of a group identity. The cohesiveness of groups has a major impact on their functioning. Its most important effect is on the *potency* of group norms—that is, the extent to which norms determine behaviour within a group. The cohesive work group can develop norms that present management with major problems, for example by enforcing conformity to a workrate far below what is considered acceptable by management. Equally, they can be a great asset to management, for example by having norms which prescribe a willingness to put in additional effort when required. Not surprisingly, then, sources of groups' cohesiveness are of considerable interest.

A proportion of any group's time will be spent on what are termed *process issues*, such as getting to know other members and resolving any interpersonal difficulties. And if the problems arising from process issues are successfully dealt with, the group will be a reasonably harmonious and cohesive social unit.

What characterizes group process depends on the length of time a group has been in existence. Generally, groups go through four stages—forming, storming, norming, and performing—each with different process issues members have to deal with.

1. *Forming*. Group process at this stage is about exploring and resolving the very fundamental parameters of the group's existence. These include what the group is trying to achieve, what resources it has, how much time is involved, how often it will meet, and how individuals will co-operate with one another.
2. *Storming*. Group process at this stage may involve a degree of conflict. Sharp disagreements can emerge on goals and strategies. Additionally, at this stage individuals are still establishing their relationships with other members and working out their degree of attachment to the group. Group process may be so destructive at this stage that the group does not survive. However, groups that do have defined or redefined their task in accordance with members' needs.
3. *Norming*. The experience of storming can raise awareness of the need to develop a more cohesive way of working together. Group process at this stage may still involve conflict. But members in this period are developing a more positive orientation to the task and each other. Norms for more collaborative and co-operative arrangements begin to emerge.
4. *Performing*. At this stage process issues are about achieving group goals. Divisions of labour emerge as members take on more specific functions. The increased orderliness and structure can mean group process at this stage becomes more formal.

An important factor enhancing or reducing a group's capacity to progress successfully through these stages is the *stability* of its membership. At first sight we might assume frequent changes in membership would reinstate some of the more problematic elements of group process, reducing cohesiveness and effectiveness. And indeed there is some evidence for this (e.g. Clegg and Fitter, 1978). More recently, with complex decision-making groups it seems that some instability can be useful. In these groups new members can act as 'consultants', providing fresh information and insights (e.g. West, 1996; Rogelberg *et al.*, 1992).

The *attractiveness* of group membership is also an important ingredient in the creation of a cohesive group, since the more attractive a group is to its members, the more they will desire its continued existence and work to make it a cohesive social unit. The attractiveness of a group is partly determined by its *composition*. Members of a group have to get along with each other, which may be difficult if they are very different in status, values, attitudes, abilities, or interests. At the same time, if group members are too similar, some of the benefits of group cohesion will be lost. For example, if members all have similar views, a range of alternatives is unlikely to be considered. Moderate heterogeneity in a group balances the requirements of cohesion and productivity (Jackson, 1996). Group attractiveness is also influenced by the extent to which its members are *dependent* on it either to satisfy their psychological needs or to achieve their goals.

As we will see when discussing intergroup behaviour, a group's relationships with other groups have an important effect on cohesiveness. *Competition* with other groups causes a group member to perceive other members as more similar than they actually are (Turner, 1982). This increases solidarity within the group and the willingness of group members to co-operate with one another.

While the primary importance of cohesiveness, as we stated earlier, lies in determining the impact of a group's norms on its members, membership of such groups has been found to have a number of other important effects on group members and group functioning. Perhaps the most important of these is the beneficial effect a cohesive group has on its members' psychological state. In fact, this aspect is utilized by psychotherapists who treat their patients in groups. Positive identification with a cohesive group enhances an individual's self-concept and self-esteem, while supportive interpersonal relationships reduce anxiety and satisfy a range of ego needs. These benefits do not, however, always occur. Inexperienced psychotherapists may, for example, not be able to prevent one member's self-esteem being damaged if they are victimized by other members of the group. However, most therapists feel the benefits of using cohesive groups outweigh the potential disadvantages.

Synergy

If we consider decision-making within groups, or committees in organizations, the common-sense view of committees is that they take a great deal of time to produce poor-quality decisions. Much of the research on groups, however, reveals the opposite, that in most conditions groups outperform even their best member. This phenomenon of groups has been termed *synergy*.

This occurs because discussion within groups generates more alternatives than individuals, tends to eliminate inferior contributions, averages out errors, and supports creative thinking. This means groups invariably have the edge over other individuals in situations where accuracy is a priority, errors are expensive and time is relatively cheap.

Hall's 'Lost on the Moon' is useful for demonstrating the synergistic qualities of groups (Hall, 1971). This begins with each member being asked to imagine being lost on the moon and having to decide on the priority of items he or she would include on a journey back to the mother-ship. Members are then asked to achieve a consensus of opinion on the ranking of items. When a consensus has been achieved, individual and group rankings are compared to a ranking produced by NASA experts. The group's ranking is usually superior to any of the individual rankings. More recently techniques have been devised which actively promote synergy in decision-making groups. Stepladdering (Rogelberg *et al.*, 1992), for example, involves members taking turns to present their perceptions of the problem and potential solutions. The constant verbalization and reiteration of the problem increases communication, the active evaluation of ideas, and reduces the pressure to conform.

Reflexivity

A cohesive group is not necessarily an effective group. Cohesiveness may determine the impact of group norms on its members and can affect how pleasant group membership is. But it is not consistently a good predictor of performance. Michael West and his colleagues at the Institute of Work Psychology in the UK, suggest that much of the gap between the 'hype' about the benefits of cohesive teamworking and the reality can be explained by the notion of *reflexivity*. West (1996) defines this essential ingredient of group process as 'the extent to which group members overtly reflect upon the group's objectives, strategies and processes, and adapt them to current or anticipated . . . circumstances' (p. 559).

Reflexivity can be considered as existing along two parameters: task and social. Indications of reflective task processes include reflection on:

group objectives—are they appropriate, clear, valued; are members committed to them?
group strategies—are they detailed enough, has the group considered alternatives, a likely time-span, their effectiveness?
group processes—how are decisions to be made, how much support is there for innovation, how much feedback is available to the group, how will members interact?
environment—what are the wider implications of group activities, for example on the ecology, local community, organizational objectives? What are relationships with other groups to be? What is the likely impact of technology?

Indications of reflexivity on the social dimension of group life include reflection on:

social support—how much mutual support do members provide each other?
conflict resolution—how do members resolve conflict? Are these methods effective? Could more effective ways of handling conflict be developed?
member development—do members provide support for each other's development within the team? Are members encouraged to acquire new skills and learn from each other's experiences?
team climate—what do members do to ensure working in the group is a pleasant experience?

Non-reflexive groups therefore fail to articulate important process issues which affect effectiveness. They tend to react to situations as they exist at the moment—for example, by assuming organizational objectives are 'givens', immutable constraints which need to be worked with rather than at (e.g. Allen, 1996). Non-reflexive groups are more prey to the defensive routines such as denial and projection discussed at the beginning of this chapter.

Conversely, reflexive groups are more likely to be questioning and critical of group or organizational activities and objectives and prepared, if necessary, to attempt to change them. They may even become the 'whistle-blowers' in organizations (e.g. Hartley, 1996).

Box 7.1 Reflexivity questionnaire: how does your team function?

Exercise 1

To measure levels of task and social reflexivity in your team, ask all your team colleagues to complete this questionnaire without consulting each other about the answers. Add the scores for task reflexivity and social reflexivity separately, i.e. add all team members' scores for the task element and then all team members' scores for the social element. Reverse score negative questions. Divide both totals by the number of people completing the questionnaire. At the bottom of this box are the values against which you can determine whether your team's scores are high, low, or average compared with the scores of other teams. Indicate how far each statement is an accurate or inaccurate description of your team by writing a number in the box beside each statement, based on the following scale of 1 to 7:

Very inaccurate 1	2	3	4	5	6	Very accurate 7

(a) Task reflexivity

1. The team often reviews its objectives. ☐
2. We regularly discuss whether the team is working effectively together. ☐
3. The methods used by the team to get the job done are often discussed. ☐
4. In this team we modify our objectives in light of changing circumstances. ☐
5. Team strategies are rarely changed. ☐
6. How well we communicate information is often discussed. ☐
7. This team often reviews its approach to getting the job done. ☐
8. The way decisions are made in this team is rarely altered. ☐

Total score ☐

(b) Social reflexivity

1. Team members provide each other with support when times are difficult. ☐
2. When things at work are stressful the team is not very supportive. ☐
3. Conflict tends to linger in this team. ☐
4. People in this team often teach other new skills. ☐
5. When things at work are stressful, we pull together as a team. ☐
6. Team members are often unfriendly. ☐
7. Conflicts are constructively dealt with in this team. ☐
8. People in this team are slow to resolve arguments. ☐

Total score ☐

Scores	(a) Task reflexivity	(b) Social reflexivity
High	42–56	48–56
Average	34–41	40–47
Low	7–33	7–39

Reproduced with the very kind permission of Professor Michael West.

What encourages reflexivity? Turning inwards and confronting inadequacies or obstacles is not necessarily a pleasant experience. What seems to encourage it are difficulties with or interruptions in the normal functioning of the group. Interruptions could include new members, shocks, surprises, and interference from senior managers. Difficulties might include changes in market conditions, problems with machinery, or time allocation and use. Whilst interruptions and difficulties usually provide the 'critical incidents' which prompt reflection, West suggests that success can encourage reflexivity. Non-reflexive groups will accept success unquestioningly whereas reflexive ones are more likely to consider what caused it.

The proposition that reflexivity predicts group effectiveness is well supported. For example, studies of problem-solving groups find that those which spend time considering how to go about tackling the task are more effective than those which do not explore performance strategies (e.g. West and Anderson, 1995).

For West much of the potential of teamworking in the workplace goes to waste. Group process is often too similar to what Bion observed in his therapeutic groups—primitive, defensive, and ultimately counter-productive. West's prescription is to focus on reflexivity as the process through which greater effectiveness is achieved. In this sense he has provided the agenda for the large number of consultants and managers who take 'time out' with teams on team-building events. The group has to be able to come away with a better understanding of its own task and social processes and how these might be improved. Although to some extent a crude method of addressing some of these subtle, complex process issues, West has helpfully developed a questionnaire which facilitates this process (Anderson and West, 1996; Anderson and West, 1994). A version of this questionnaire is provided in Box 7.1.

Group innovation

Innovation is now recognized as the key to economic survival in a globalized and competitive market-place. And much of the interest in reflexivity is in its contribution to encouraging innovation in groups. West and Farr (1990) suggest four factors need to be present to enable groups to innovate.

1. *Vision*. In innovative groups there is more likely to be a shared understanding of the group's goals.
2. *Participative safety*. Participation in group discussion reduces resistance to change. If groups have norms which encourage members to provide ideas, for example by rewarding rather than punishing contributions, then innovation is more likely.
3. *Commitment to excellence in task performance*. This norm creates a culture of 'constructive controversy' where members are constantly reviewing and improving working practices.
4. *Support for innovation*. To make change happen there has to be support. This can come from the members' mutual encouragement and co-operation or from the organization providing resources. The success of Japanese quality circles when compared

with western attempts to use the technique may come from the presence of a manager in the Japanese quality circle. This increases the upward influence of the group and the likelihood of support for the group's innovations.

But as West and Altink (1996) point out these factors do not occur simply because teams are put together. The degree of reflexivity required to develop, maintain, and enhance these norms is high. And this can only be achieved if teams are trained and developed effectively.

Groupthink

One notable disadvantage of groups which are highly cohesive but not reflexive is that their decision-making ability can be drastically reduced by what Janis (1972) termed *groupthink*. He defined this as a deterioration of mental efficiency, reality testing, and moral judgement that results from in-group pressures. In other words, the pressures of conformity that can arise in highly cohesive groups reduce reflexivity, clouding members' judgement and their ability to reach a correct decision. Interestingly, Janis illustrated this notion with a detailed analysis of the ill-fated attempt by the Kennedy administration to invade Cuba. Janis claimed the decision which instigated the Bay of Pigs fiasco in 1961 was the result of groupthink. He claimed all the symptoms of groupthink were present in the advisory group, comprised of President Kennedy, his cabinet, and other senior staff, which took the decision to invade. They became convinced of their *invulnerability*—they assumed that since they were all exceptionally able they could not possibly fail. They believed that the 1,000 Cuban exiles, outnumbered 140 to 1, really could beat Castro's army. Group discussion was characterized by a collective *rationalizing away* of information contrary to the group's beliefs. The group also believed they were *morally correct* in what they were doing, thus giving them a right to interfere with Cuba's sovereignty. This belief stemmed in part from the inaccurate *stereotyping* of the Cubans that occurred within the group—they believed, for example, that the Cuban people would flock to the support of the exiles. Janis argued that *self-censorship* prevented people in the group from expressing dissent, since group members feared being seen as disloyal. This process was reinforced by what he termed *mindguards*, who protected the group from information and individuals that would disrupt the consensus. More recently Reason (1987) has argued decisions by the operators responsible for the catastrophic accident at Chernobyl to experiment with one of the reactors was the product of groupthink.

Janis believed, however, that groupthink was not inevitable even in cohesive groups. Members of such groups can avoid it by actively searching out information, irrespective of whether it is contrary to the group's opinion. The group can also assign the role of 'devil's advocate' to one member to ensure alternative solutions are proposed and discussed. When trust is present in cohesive groups, conflict does not damage relations between members and will ultimately yield more productive solutions.

Group polarization

Another common-sense assumption about groups is they are inherently more conservative than individuals when it comes to taking decisions that involve risks. Again research evidence appears to undermine this. A substantial number of early studies show groups tend to make more extreme decisions compared to the same decisions made alone by individual group members. Since the group seemed to shift towards risk in its decisions it was called *risky shift*. More recently, however, a number of studies have demonstrated groups could also show the opposite tendency, a *caution shift*. Nowadays it is generally accepted that what is termed *group polarization*, the tendency for group decisions to be more extreme than those of individuals, is responsible for both sets of findings.

Why should groups produce more extreme decisions than individuals? One suggestion is that there is a *diffusion of responsibility*, where individuals, feeling they will not be held wholly responsible for a decision, are willing to take riskier decisions. Another explanation is that *social comparison processes* are operating (Goethals and Darley, 1977). Here group members, attempting to present themselves in the best light, not only endorse the predominant cultural value but, by comparing their views with others, attempt to endorse it at least as much as everyone else. Thus group decisions become more extreme in the direction of the prevailing social attitudes. This would explain, for example, why groups tend to take riskier business decisions but more cautious decisions about whether an individual should marry. In the former, as entrepreneurial qualities are valued in a wider context, each member will adopt an entrepreneurial stance to ensure the approval of other members; in the latter, caution stems from beliefs about the dangers of broken marriages. Another explanation proposes that *information exchange* and *persuasive arguments* are a major cause of the polarization of views in groups (Burnstein, 1983). In juries, for example, a juror starts off with a fairly moderate view about the defendant's innocence or guilt. After listening to the information and arguments presented by other jurors, he or she becomes convinced of the defendant's guilt or innocence. In other words, group discussion creates a bandwagon which everyone eventually will jump on.

It is no doubt the case that all four processes operate in groups to produce the polarization phenomenon.

Group decision-making in organizations

As we have mentioned, decisions in occupational and organizational situations are very frequently taken within a group context. Meetings, committees, project teams and so on are important decision arenas. Similarly, at the very highest level, decisions can frequently be traced to a senior corporate group. Even though organizations typically have chief executives who exercise the largest single influence, a plural executive system is still the locus of much of the real power.

This means that the processes discussed above take on a major significance (particularly since a common-sense understanding of groups, as was also mentioned, is not a very reliable guide). The overwhelming advantages of group-based decision-making that were summarized in terms of synergy—the breadth of experience brought to a problem, the benefits of discussion, emergence of new ideas—may be offset in certain circumstances by phenomena like groupthink and polarization. Hence, it is vitally important that people in organizations remain aware of the potential problems, and of the group processes that can cause both excessive conformity or highly extreme decisions to emerge.

Intergroup behaviour

Groups do not exist in isolation; they are usually embedded in a network of relationships with other groups. At work, there are a variety of groups representing different functional, professional, departmental and economic interests. Though not inevitable, it is often the case that when such divisions between groups become salient, conflict follows. An analysis of the reasons for increased competitiveness in intergroup behaviour is important, because if we know what processes are involved we are more likely to be able to derive feasible solutions to intergroup conflict. In the wider arena of public policy, where issues such as racial or sexual discrimination occur, this could mean the difference between success and failure in reducing intergroup divisions.

Two main explanations of intergroup conflict have emerged, and they reflect the two different bases of group formation we identified at the beginning of this chapter. The first stems from the assumption that groups form for functional reasons (Sherif and Sherif, 1982). Functional theorists believe that if groups have a functional basis, group conflict must be the result of a group perceiving another group as a threat or a potential threat to its goal attainment. For example, if a firm's management pursues the goals of low unit costs and high volume, while labour seeks high wages and shorter working hours, then according to functional theory intergroup conflict is highly likely.

The second explanation is known as *social identity theory*, which assumes groups form through the perception of a shared social identity (Tajfel, 1978; Turner 1991; Brewer and Miller, 1996). Social identity theorists argue that an individual's self-concept is made up from his or her personal identity, which derives from a unique combination of personality and intelligence traits together with an identity created by membership of various social groups. They argue further that our self-evaluation, and thus our self-esteem, are a function of the *positive distinctiveness* (attributes which are valued by members and are thus used to make comparisons between one's own and other groups) we perceive in the groups to which we belong.

The implications of group membership for an individual's self-evaluation mean that when people perceive positive distinctiveness in other groups they can do one of three things: (1) join the outgroup; (2) redefine the elements of the status comparison so as to change their own perception of negative distinctiveness into positive distinctiveness (e.g., 'Black is beautiful'); or (3) compete to change the relative position of the outgroup on the significant status dimension(s). The third strategy will lead to conflict between the two groups when the status dimension is a valued resource such as power or money.

The competitiveness involved in intergroup behaviour is reinforced by the effects of ingroup membership on the perception, attitudes and ultimately behaviour of ingroup members. The perception among individuals of membership of a common group causes members to stereotype themselves. They see themselves as less differentiated than they actually are on dimensions such as goals, personality traits, status, motives, attitudes and values. This process, termed *depersonalization*, enables ingroup members to perceive themselves as a cohesive social unit. This depersonalization of ingroup members does not occur to the same extent as it does to outgroup members who are seen as completely undifferentiated. The need for a positive social identity also means that ingroup members are likely to perceive larger differences between themselves and outgroup members than actually exist. In addition, there is likely to be what is termed *ingroup favouritism*, ingroup members tending to favour each other over outgroup members. This can get to the point where it is unjustified and unreasonable and becomes *ingroup bias*. At this point perception of the outgroup has little basis in truth. Ingroup members tend to remember only negative information about the outgroup. Attributions about the outgroup also tend to be made on the basis of 'illusory correlations'—that is, accidental pairing of events which are perceived as supporting inferences about the outgroup.

How, then, is intergroup conflict resolved? A functional theorist would argue that the solution of intergroup conflict lies in contriving conditions in which shared goals can be perceived. This is based on the assumption that *superordinate goals* will create a *superordinate group*; an example of this would be reducing conflict between managerial groups by drawing attention to outside competition and thus a threat to the shared interest of survival. A modification of functional theory suggests it is not so much the practical goals which members seek to attain that are the basis of group formation but the social interaction task-related activity necessarily involves. This modification has produced a solution to intergroup conflict known as the *contact hypothesis*, which predicts that increased social interaction between ingroup and outgroup will break down the intergroup division. An example of this approach is the desegregation of schools in the United States by bussing schoolchildren of one ethnic group to school, where they mix with children of another group. In a famous series of studies testing the functional and contact hypotheses, two groups of boys in a summer camp were made to compete in a number of events, resulting in a considerable amount of intergroup hostility. In the final series of events, groups had to work together to achieve common goals in one event and join forces to compete against a group from outside the camp in another. Both the co-operative task interaction and the threat from outsiders reduced the intergroup hostility that had been established (Sherif *et al.*, 1961).

Though in some instances increased contact and the perception of superordinate goals can successfully reduce intergroup divisions, social identity theorists claim that in many cases this is unlikely to occur, and even where it does, the change in attitudes is not necessarily transferred to other situations. Thus at work, for example, the presence of rewards contingent on management and labour working together for a common goal can provide individuals with precisely the justification they need for their co-operation with the out-group, so leaving their private attitudes to the outgroup unchanged. For social identity theorists one solution lies in increasing the availability of social identifications that cut across existing divisions, thus enabling superordinate social groups to emerge. Appeals to identify with the nation or the organization, and the use of slogans and symbols to rein-force this, are examples of attempts to create superordinate social identifications.

In the previous chapter we discussed the effect of differing construal of a situation on decision making. Differences in construal can be a consequence of group membership. For example, studies of pro-Arab and pro-Israeli groups watching news reports demon-strated virtually no overlap in their reaction to the reporting. Both sides were convinced the other side had been favoured by the media. More fundamentally, groups seemed to disagree about what they had actually seen. Judgement of the object and the object of judgement had been affected.

In the context of negotiation, Ross and Stillinger (1991) have shown this produces what they term *reactive devaluation*. The very act of offering a proposal to an outgroup seems to reduce the attractiveness of the proposal to the outgroup and change its mean-ing. Thus a group offering a compromise will probably be disappointed when its offer is rejected by the outgroup. The outgroup can then be accused of bad faith. Reactive deval-uation is a major cause of the mistrust and misunderstanding which often occurs in the negotiation process. What these studies suggest is that both sides fail to recognize the extent to which each side is responding to a subjectively different proposal. Thus what is seen as a fair and reasonable compromise by the ingroup may well be seen as self-serving and trivial by the outgroup.

Unfortunately, individuals' group-based construals seem to remain intact even when new social identifications are contrived that cut across existing boundaries. Social iden-tity theorists believe that a history of conflict at the societal level leads to a general belief that boundaries between groups are immutable. Secondly, the biases in social percep-tion caused by group membership (e.g. self-stereotyping, accentuation of differences between ingroup and outgroup) mean that the chances are that the new social identification will not be perceived (Brewer and Miller, 1996).

For social identity theorists the answer lies in uncovering what factors in situations trigger intergroup behaviour rather than interpersonal behaviour. The salience of group memberships seems to be related, first, to how secure the status differential is between the groups; if it is secure its salience will not, in most situations, be high. Secondly, within a specific setting, the relative proportion of members of each group seems to influence the salience of group behaviour. The most hostility between groups seems to occur between a minority group with a positive self-image and a majority group with a negative self-image.

Thirdly, in real world settings there is often more than one identification present—political, gender, religious, and social. Any two persons may share membership in one but have differences in others. These *cross-categorizations* appear to dilute the salience of any one categorization (Brewer and Miller, 1996). Finally, what might reduce the salience of group membership is an individual's self-esteem. Low self-esteem can enhance the importance of group identification as a means of achieving positive social identity (Fein and Spencer, 1997).

This suggests reducing intergroup conflict at work can be achieved by:

1. Emphasizing the superordinate goal of total organizational effectiveness. Initiatives such as 'right first time' can increase awareness of goals which are common to groups.
2. More social contact and communications between groups. The cross-functional group—increasingly common in organizations—helps achieve this. These groups draw individuals from marketing, production, sales, finance, and customer services to help identify quality, inter-coordination and performance issues.
3. Reducing the salience of group membership by rotating employees between groups or departments. This would also encourage empathy between groups.
4. Ensuring groups do not have to compete for valued resources. Organizations need to provide adequate resources to enable the team to achieve its targets or objectives. Workgroups should never be put in the position of competing for some scarce organizational resource. Emphasis should be on pooling resources and rewards.

In many situations, individuals clearly have a choice between intergroup and interpersonal behaviour. In negotiations, for example, the relationship between the parties built up over a number of years is often highly valued by each party. At the same time, at an intergroup level, each negotiator is a representative of a group which seeks to achieve distinctive objectives and this usually serves to force groups apart. The necessity of having to treat others as members of a separate group can cause considerable embarrassment during negotiations. One skill in negotiations is the ability to enhance interpersonal or intergroup aspects of the situation. Achieving compromise is more likely if the interpersonal aspects of the situation—friendships—are emphasized. Conversely, increasing the importance of the intergroup division, for example by meeting in separate rooms with occasional contact between a nominee from each group, results in a victory for one side only.

In sum, then, functional theorists can indicate how conflict can be reduced, but only in the range of situations in which intense goal differences are not present. To account for conflict which still occurs, particularly where intergroup behaviour is involved in a wider social context, it is social identity theory which provides the necessary conceptual framework. However, at present, social identity theory provides no solutions to intergroup conflict, a fact which serves to remind us of the salience of our group memberships in society and the enduring effect they have on our perceptions, beliefs, attitudes and behaviour.

Hawthorne and the human relations movement

The emphasis on social interaction and group dynamics we have been exploring in this and previous chapters reflects very much the modern concerns in the study of behaviour at work. But during the early stages of its development, in the 1920s, occupational psychology relied heavily on a crude 'mechanical' model of human behaviour. Individuals were regarded as acting in isolation and responsive only to 'rational' economic and physical stimuli. A great deal of research was preoccupied with ways of increasing workers' productivity.

There was a consensus among the researchers and managers of the day that an individual's work rate was determined by factors such as temperature, humidity and illumination. Other aspects of the work situation, such as payment systems, patterns of rest breaks and the length of the working day, also played a part in determining a worker's output. The demand for scientific research into the effects of these factors led to the founding of the National Institute of Industrial Psychology in Britain and the Psychological Corporation in America.

However, in the late 1920s this picture was to change radically; and we will conclude by looking at the research which is normally credited with having brought about this transformation, the so-called *Hawthorne experiments*.

In 1927 the Western Electric Company invited a group of researchers from Harvard University to help the management continue their investigation of factors affecting worker productivity at their Hawthorne plant near Chicago. What prompted this invitation was some rather curious findings which had emerged from studies that had taken place in the plant over the preceding three years. The company wanted a definitive answer to a seemingly simple question: what is the relationship between illumination and productivity levels? A group of engineers from the American Academy of Sciences was hired to provide the answer. They ran a series of studies which manipulated illumination levels and recorded output. To their surprise they found that output seemed to increase both in control groups where illumination was constant and in experimental groups when illumination was lowered. In one study illumination was cut to an amount which represented the amount of light available on a moonlit night, but output was maintained and the employees reported no eyestrain and claimed they actually felt less tired than when working under bright lights.

The Harvard researchers assumed the failure to relate illumination and output could be attributed to the fact that the engineers were not systematic enough and took only one variable into account. They believed that if they selected a small group of workers and placed them in a separate room away from the disruptive influences of other employees and departmental routine, they would succeed where the Academy of Sciences' researchers had failed.

The researchers began their first series of experiments, the so-called relay assembly test room experiments, with a group of six female employees. They selected women who reported they would be happy to work together, and who were equivalent in the level of skill they possessed so that differences in performance could not be attributed to a skill difference within the group. They also chose a routine task, assembling telephone relays, which required no machinery, so that an individual's output would be determined by her performance alone. The women were placed in an observation room with one other person, an observer, whose task was to record output data and maintain a friendly atmosphere in the room.

The researchers then set about posing the questions that were typical of the day: what is the effect of temperature, humidity, health, number of rest breaks, length of working day, method of production and payment system on output? They manipulated these variables in a long series of experiments, changing the pattern of rest breaks, hours worked, etc. and monitoring the effect on output. What the studies showed were major increases in output achieved by the group under virtually all conditions. Even when original conditions were restored production frequently still went up, and this of course totally contradicted the predictions of the 'rational man' model of behaviour.

Though the relay assembly experiments continued for five years, quite early on the experimenters reached a tentative explanation of their striking results. This is now recognized as a turning point in the development of psychology applied in the workplace and it continues to exert an influence on management theory and practice some eighty years later. What the experimenters gradually realized was that none of the variables which were commonly associated with increases in productivity could explain their findings. What had come into existence in the relay assembly test room was a *social system*. According to Elton Mayo, the person responsible for popularizing the results and developing the implications of the research into a social and managerial philosophy: 'what actually happened was that six individuals became a team and the team gave itself wholeheartedly and spontaneously to cooperation in the experiment' (1943, p. 73).

In other words, the women had become a social group demonstrating the kinds of process which we discussed earlier in this chapter. This does not, however, explain why their output norms were high. To do this the experimenters pointed to what had become known as the *Hawthorne effect*. In fact, nowadays it is more common to distinguish two Hawthorne effects. The first effect is that the mere knowledge of being an experimental subject changes behaviour from what it would otherwise have been. The distortion in behaviour can easily undermine the value of social scientific research. The second is produced by friendly supervision; the observer in the relay assembly experiment had become a trusted friend of the women, allowing the new social organization to develop, which, in turn, had imbued their working lives with new meaning.

The Hawthorne studies continued for twelve years and included a mass interviewing of 21,000 Western Electric employees, observation of a group of men in a bank wiring room (discussed in Chapter 11) and extensive personnel counselling. What was so important about these studies was that although some British industrial psychologists had drawn attention to similar findings (Myers, 1924; Cathcart, 1928), here for the first time was a large body of evidence shaking the settled managerial conventions of the time that workers were wage-pursuing automata (Bendix, 1956). The social organization of the workplace and its implications for effective management were spelled out to a large audience. Thus managers were urged to use the studies to master the nature of the social reality they operated in:

We have failed to train students in the study of social situations; we have thought that first class technical training was sufficient in a modern and mechanical age. As a consequence we are technically competent as no other age in history has been; and we combined this with utter social incompetence. (Mayo, 1943, p. 120).

The Hawthorne studies marked the beginning of the human relations movement, a tradition in management which stresses the importance of social factors at work. For human relations theorists, the role of management is to provide organizational environments in which employers can fulfil the social needs of their employees, thus providing work with the meaning routinization has taken out of it, and tap employees' desire for co-operative activity. This can be done through team-building, supportive supervision, increased communication and opportunity for participation in decision-making and counselling. Thus, human relations theorists assume that, to the extent managements have insight into the skills to manipulate these social factors, they will be able to harness their employees' social needs to managerial ends.

We will not devote more space here to an account of this vitally important school of thought, because in a sense much of what is discussed in this and certain other chapters reflects human relations interests. The application of group dynamics, the concern with leadership and accounts of work motivation and satisfaction, dealt with elsewhere in this book, are all central issues in human relations research.

However, it is appropriate finally to indicate some of the adverse reaction that this approach has attracted. A number of criticisms have appeared of the Hawthorne studies (Rose, 1975; Rice, 1982) and of the human relations movement in general (Braverman, 1974; Hill, 1981). Carey (1967), for example, argued that the studies were so flawed in terms of the experimental methods employed that their conclusions cannot be regarded as supported from the evidence. In one sense, though, this does not matter. The vitality of the Hawthorne studies now stems not from any academic merits but from their all-round influence on the management process.

For this reason, much of the criticism of the human relations movement has focused on its impact on *management practice*. And here Bendix's noted *Work and Authority in Industry* (1956) has been highly influential. Bendix argues, for example, that Mayo and his colleagues were too preoccupied with group process, often to the exclusion of organizational factors like the impact of managerial power, and wider social factors in the labour market. Sometimes this put the research in rather a dubious ethical position, since the managerial motives for commissioning the research tended to be ignored. Sometimes, too, it led the researchers to adopt paternalistic attitudes towards workers: workers were regarded as being irrationally motivated by social and affectual interests. In contrast, management were seen to act on the basis of rational economic criteria reflecting the drive towards efficiency. Secondly, Bendix and others have pointed out that in reality human relations ideas have found only limited acceptance. In particular, the claim that they have 'superseded' previous mechanical models of man is very much overstated. In fact, the basis of managerial control in industry, as represented by modern methods of production control, remains those very same mechanical models. And thirdly, even where these ideas have been influential, the claim that they represent a new 'humane' approach is likewise largely untrue: they really represent simply another strategy of organizational control. Bendix, for instance, argued that the human relations movement has provided a new 'verbal dress' for managers who have little sympathy for its message, and who pursue the traditional authority-based relationship between themselves and their employees.

That said, however, the human relations movement has affected certain specific areas of management, such as personnel practices and management training, even if this is far less true in the central area of managerial responsibility. Moreover, there has been an enduring influence on modern thinking about the managerial role, and about the directions in which that role might be performed and made more progressive. As we will see in the following chapter—the pervasiveness of these ideas has ensured that the human relations tradition has had some influence on managerial policies, albeit not as much as the Hawthorne researchers once envisaged.

Conclusion

The conclusion which flows from much of the evidence examined in this chapter is that groups and teamworking arrangements have complex effects on individuals' perceptions, attitudes, and behaviour. And many of these are not beneficial either for individual group members or the organizations they work for. This is because, as we have seen, group membership can cause distorted perceptions of reality. The social identities our group memberships give rise to can be at the root of our willingness to stereotype and discriminate against non-group members. In addition, competitiveness with other groups, encouraged by a strong group identity, can be dysfunctional if, for example, both groups are part of the same organization. Co-operation can be replaced with factionalism and obstructiveness whenever separate group identities are invoked.

Within a group, the dependency and conformity which group membership can encourage stifles originality and innovativeness—qualities now increasingly crucial for economic survival. Many of the worst errors of judgement which were at the root of notable disasters such as Chernobyl and the Bay of Pigs have come from group decisions. Group cohesiveness—often seen as a positive quality of groups—in these instances produced a setting where no one member was prepared to introduce contrarian thinking into the discussion in order to confront and challenge a consensus building up which they disagreed with. And the norms which shape members' behaviour can, as has been shown from the Hawthorne studies onwards, sometimes operate against the interests of senior management.

Yet the promise of groupworking remains. Teams and teamworking are still seen as the best way of marrying the fulfilment of fundamental individual psychological needs with the managerial requirement for more flexibility, less 'down time' as members cover for each other's absences or variable work rates, and more self regulation by team members, reducing the costs of supervision. For this reason, as we will see in Chapter 11, the workgroup remains the focus of efforts to redesign work.

The army of consultants and trainers running team-building events are also sustained financially by the apparent promise of groups. However, the scepticism about what can amount to little more than 'awaydays' for teams is often justified. As we have seen what needs to occur is a close examination of key group processes—those about how tasks are accomplished and how members relate to each other, and this is not necessarily a pleasant psychological experience. If this 'reflexivity' is developed then the rhetoric about groups might become more of an organizational reality.

Study questions for Chapter 7

1 In what, if any, ways are groups more effective than an equivalent number of individuals?

2 Why do groups form?

3 To what extent is 'cohesiveness' in groups a 'good thing'?

4 What groups do you belong to—of these which has more impact on your attitudes and behaviour—and why?

5 In what ways do groups behave differently to individuals?

6 'Money spent on team building is not necessarily money well spent'—discuss.

7 What is the contribution of Belbin's model of team roles?

8 What causes conflict between groups and to what extent can the possibility of conflict be minimized?

9 Why were the Hawthorne studies so important?

Further reading

Brewer, M. B. and Miller, N. (1996) *Intergroup Relations*. Buckingham: Open University Press.

Hare, A. P., Blumberg, H. H., Davies, M. F., and Kent, M. V. (1996) *Small Groups: An Introduction*. London: Praeger.

Hartley, P. (1997) *Group Communications*. London: Routledge.

Kernberg, O. F. (1998) *Ideology, Conflict and Leadership in Groups and Organizations*. London: Yale University Press.

Sprears, R., Oakes, P. J., Ellemers, N., and Haslam, S. A. (eds.) (1996) *The Social Psychology of Stereotyping and Group Life*. Oxford: Blackwell.

West, M. (1994) *Effective Teamwork*. Leicester: BPS Books.

—— (ed.) (1996) *Handbook of Work Group Psychology*. Chichester: Wiley.

—— (1997) *Developing Creativity in Organizations*. Leicester: BPS Books.

Wetherell, M. (ed.) (1996) *Identities, Groups and Social Issues*. Buckingham: Open University Press.

Worchel, S., Francisco Morales, J., Paez, D., and Deschamps, J. C. (eds.) (1998) *Social Identity: International Perspectives*. London: Sage.

8 Leadership

Summary points and learning objectives

By the end of this chapter you will be able to

- detail the psychological attributes which seem to predict leadership effectiveness;
- describe how leadership emerges and is maintained in groups;
- discuss the ways in which leadership style differs in individuals;
- discuss the impact of cultural norms on leadership style;
- describe the key situational factors influencing leadership effectiveness;
- understand the way leadership style interacts with the situation;
- understand the notion of charismatic and transformational leadership;
- describe approaches to improving leadership skills in individuals;
- distinguish between leadership and management.

Introduction

Why can some managers and supervisors gain the best efforts of their staff while others are only able to obtain a moderate amount of co-operation, or even attract open hostility? Obviously organizations are keenly interested in the answers to this question. Their hierarchical structure means that organizations continually have to face the problem of selecting and training people to assume positions of authority over others. At every level in organizations and in every department there will be groups of subordinates under the control of superordinates—in other words, there will be leadership situations.

The term 'leadership', however, often conveys a rather more glamorous image than that of the mundane world of work. Leaders like Napoleon, Gandhi, and Churchill emerge from a broad political context rather than an occupational setting. Authority is vested in them because of their personal gifts and abilities and the charismatic qualities they possess, or at least so we imagine. The example of such leaders gave rise to the earliest attempts at psychological research on the topic: the so-called trait theory of leadership. This assumes certain people are born with a set of key personality characteristics, or traits, which make them 'natural leaders'—indeed, this view of leadership is sometimes termed an 'implicit' theory, or the 'great man' theory of leadership.

In this chapter we shall see that the search for these traits has proved relatively fruitless. But there has, none the less, been a resurgence of interest in traitist approaches—particularly those emphasizing the 'charismatic' basis for leadership. Inconsistent support for a trait explanation of leadership effectiveness prompted many academics to study not what sort of person the effective leader is, but what he or she actually does. In other words, the *behaviours* of leaders becomes the focus of interest. This research has given us a reasonably clear idea of the main dimensions of leadership behaviour. What has been more difficult is the discovery of strong relationships between these dimensions and organizational variables such as productivity, job satisfaction, and staff turnover. The recognition that no one pattern of leadership—'one best way'—consistently produced high effectiveness led to what are termed *situational* or *contingent* theories of leadership. These predict that key features of the situation—such as the motivation and competence of subordinates—interact with a leader's style to determine its effectiveness. We will examine two theories which attempt to predict which styles 'fit' which situations. One theory assumes leaders' styles are relatively fixed—reflecting deep-seated motivational and temperamental differences. To achieve a good fit leaders need to change situations to match their style. The other assumes leaders can shift their style relatively easily and thus change their style to fit the situation.

The difference 'charismatic' individuals appear to be able to make, for example, in seeming to be able to realign and remotivate struggling organizations, or more spectacularly when they 'go wrong' and take an organization down with them, has caused a resurgence of interest in charismatic leadership and we will explore the psychological basis for this form of leadership.

The acid test of leadership theory is its practical relevance, and we will conclude with an examination of the extent to which almost a century of research has translated into effective training programmes.

Leadership as an attribute of the individual

At first sight the relationship in the heading of this section seems plausible and confirmed by personal experience. The relationship seems further supported by the study of great leaders throughout history. This view of leadership suggests it resides in traits or attributes of the individual. In any situation where leadership is appropriate, the person with the largest number of desirable traits emerges as the leader. In organizations this would represent an ideal state of affairs. Having located these traits and developed assessments which would measure them, selection and development would become a fairly simple mechanistic affair. Not surprisingly, the search for these 'desirable traits' has produced an overwhelming amount of research.

Personality traits

There is a fair amount of consensus about which traits correlate with leadership effectiveness. Of the big five personality features discussed in Chapter 3, meta-analytic studies have found effective leaders are often high scorers on *conscientiousness* (i.e. are reliable, hard working, dependable, achievement-orientated, and concerned with quality and standards). They also score highly on *extroversion* (i.e. are lively, socially confident, and affiliative), *openness to experience* (are willing to accept fresh evidence, see beyond the immediate and obvious), and *agreeableness* (not antagonistic). Effectiveness is also associated with scoring low on neuroticism (stability, coping with pressure, and good 'reality testing') (Barrick and Mount, 1991). But remember this represents correlational evidence and there will be many effective leaders who do not possess these qualities. Henry Ford, for example, notoriously did not allow any modifications to occur to the Model T for a number of years, despite evidence of losing market share, and even vandalized a modified vehicle produced by his engineers. And Churchill suffered from his 'black dogs'—bouts of depression. In working with senior managers, I have noticed it is often precisely neurotic inner tensions and anxieties which motivate some highly successful individuals to succeed. Failure for a somewhat neurotic manager is far more painful than for his or her more self-assured colleagues. Thus as with all correlational evidence there are important exceptions to the general trend in the results.

From a similar perspective based on working with senior managers and chief executives, Kets de Vries (1997) argues that the *sine qua non* for effective leaders is a component of agreeableness—empathy—the ability to connect emotionally with others, perceive, respond to, and manage the emotional needs of subordinates. It is empathy which enables individuals to build the network of allegiances and alliances deemed crucial to success in middle and senior management. It is lack of empathy—manifested by vindictiveness and excessive criticism—which has undone many a managerial career. But as this is correlational evidence and the correlation is not a perfect one it is likely we will have all encountered seemingly effective and successful managers who are also emotionally illiterate.

Another trait which has been linked to effectiveness is humility—the opposite of hubris. Excessive grandiosity leads to an inflated sense of importance and a distorted sense of reality. This can lead to dramatically impaired decision-making. A startling illustration of this is provided by Hayward and Hambrick (1997) in their study of 106 large acquisitions. They found chief executives who were 'infected' with hubris overestimated their ability to manage firms they were targeting for takeover. This meant paying far too much for the target company. They found the greater the recent praise for the chief executive (objectively assessed by counting the number of newspaper and magazine articles), the larger the overpayment. In effect, each highly favourable article resulted in a 5 per cent overpayment. For the average acquisition this meant each article cost a $48 million overpayment. Hubris meant some chief executives had literally come to believe their own press—at a significant cost to shareholders.

A related quality which also helps maintain good judgement is a sense of humour. This enables individuals to cope better with pressure and not allow their thinking to become preoccupied with pessimistic scenarios. As well as assisting good reality testing, humour provides a way of introducing difficult truths into group thinking and thus avoiding the problems of groupthink described in Chapter 7. The trait which has attracted the most attention in recent years is charisma—regarded by many as the essence of leadership and the 'missing ingredient' of much leadership research. The volume of research charisma has generated merits a separate section.

Intelligence

Part of a leader's task is to manage complexity. We would expect their ability to do so to be to some extent determined by their intelligence, and strong social beliefs about intelligence mean intelligence tests are consistently used in management selection. This promotes what is sometimes reported as the 'faith validity' of intelligence tests, i.e. an unquestioning belief in the usefulness of intelligence tests in managerial selection and a strong preference for employing high over low scorers.

But some studies have found connections between measures of intelligence and leadership effectiveness as low as zero. The median of such studies is a modest positive correlation of .2. The discrepancy here between what we tend to believe and the empirical evidence has led some researchers to attempt to explain the absence of a stronger relationship. We have already encountered one such attempt in Chapter 3, when we discussed Fiedler's hypothesis that a series of screens (intervening variables) moderated the effect of a leader's intelligence on his or her effectiveness. Further support for the view that intervening variables moderate the effect of a leader's intelligence comes from Podsakoff *et al.* (1996). In a meta-analytic review of twenty-two studies, they found such variables as the staff's professional orientation, ability, experience, and training and whether the workgroup was cohesive or not could effectively neutralize or substitute for a leader. In other words, these contextual variables had more impact on measures of effectiveness than differences between leaders.

In a classic study Ghiselli (1963) suggests the relationship is curvilinear: correlations are reduced if relationships are not linear. To test this idea he sorted a sample of managers into high-, medium-, and low-IQ groups. He found managers in the high and low bands were less likely to be successful in their positions. This implies an optimum level of intelligence is one high enough to cope with the organizational and human complexities of leadership, but not so high that he or she is regarded as being 'on a different wavelength', 'overly intellectual', or finds it difficult to relate effectively to less gifted individuals.

One refinement of the notion of intelligence has come from Jaques (1989). He argues that in an organizational setting what is important is not so much an individual's 'g' but his or her *cognitive power*, which is defined as the maximum scale and complexity of the world an individual is able to cope with. Jaques argues cognitive power is central to the understanding of differences in leadership ability. This is because it determines an individual's *time horizon*—the maximum time-span of a task an individual can comprehend and work with. The further up an organization they rise, the more individuals need cognitive power, as they have to think about tasks which make take years instead of months or days to complete. Cognitive power is seen as largely independent of 'g' (and education, gender, or class) and is an ability developed much more gradually during an individual's career. However, it seems unlikely that cognitive power as defined by Jaques could be as independent of 'G' as he claims, and it probably represents one important manifestation of the interaction between 'G' and an individual's organizational experiences.

Motivation

Attaining a leadership position and being effective in it might be not so much a reflection of intellect or personality but of an individual's needs or motivations. Leadership from this perspective represents individuals projecting various psychological needs on to organizational settings. Conversely, being dependent on a leader could represent a regressive state—a desire to return to a period in our lives when we were completely taken care of. In Leonard Gordon's factor-analytic research on interpersonal values, leadership consistently emerged as a factor alongside five others—support, conformity, recognition, independence, and benevolence (Gordon, 1993). In other words, the desire to be in a leadership position and have control and authority over others does seem to vary significantly between individuals and meaningfully represent a dimension along which individuals can be assessed.

Further support for the existence of fundamental motivational differences comes from large-scale organizational surveys carried out in the 1970s. Bass *et al.* (1979) surveyed over 3,000 middle managers. Respondents were asked to rank eleven life goals. A clear set of preferences emerged, the most preferred goals reflecting self-actualization needs (self-realization and independence). A middle band related to affection, security and competence. Least preferred were prestige and wealth. Though all managers had emphasized 'higher-order' needs, the goals dealing with assertiveness and accomplishment were more often emphasized by faster-climbing managers, whereas those dealing with comfort were chosen by those with slower rates of promotion.

Similarly, Hofstede (1978), using factor analysis to identify underlying motivational dimensions in the ranking of life goals by 65,000 IBM employees, found two factors that explained 54 per cent of the variations in rankings. One factor stressed comfort rather than accomplishment, the other stressed assertiveness and leadership as opposed to service.

Both these studies echo Maslow's theory of motivation described in Chapter 3 and the personality constructs operationalized by McClelland described in the same chapter. Competing for senior managerial positions is, from these perspectives, a manifestation of intense needs for accomplishment and growth. This is the reason McClelland makes the Achievement Orientation (see Box 4.3) the first in his list—an overarching or meta-competence without which many of the others do not appear in an individual. As Zaleznik (1977) pointed out, leaders are different to managers. Leaders appear to have goals which are embedded in their natures. This enables them to put energy into projecting their goals in the form of visions for organizations which excite others to work towards turning these into reality. Managers, in contrast, have goals which are derived from external sources (i.e. the expectations of others). Goals for managers are thus impersonal; they do not come from within their own psychological make-up. And the large-scale studies of Bass and Hofstede would support the idea that fundamental differences in the motivational make-up of individuals are mapped on to organizational life, resulting in differential rates of progression.

Two contrasting lifestyles were identified by Bray *et al.* (1974) after studying the progress over eight years of 400 managers in a large American company. These reflected motivational differences in the sample similar to those found in the other studies. They described those who tended to gain in occupational interests and in whom self-actualization needs seemed pre-eminent as 'enlargers'. These individuals were less concerned with friends, parents, family and recreational or social activities than with work. They were more likely to move away from their home towns and stressed the importance of innovation and change in their approach to organizational problems. This contrasted with the 'enfolder', in whom the 'lower-order' security and comfort needs were strongest. They were more likely to stay in their home base and to maintain long-term friendships. They were much less likely to engage in self-improvement activities, but did not lose their interest in recreational and social activities to the same extent as the 'enlarger'. Bray *et al.* found these differences were associated with rates of advancement, 'enlargers' being more successful than 'enfolders'.

What may seem surprising is the lack of evidence suggesting that a need for money and wealth is a key component of the motivational make-up of successful managers. Some managers do in fact express a strong interest in pay. The evidence suggests a manager's position in an organization determines the extent to which wealth is a dominant need. Interest in pay tends to be stronger lower down the managerial hierarchy, whereas intrinsic aspects of work and a spiralling search for challenge seem to motivate successful senior and middle managers.

The search for associations between the personal attributes of leaders and effectiveness has been a major objective of leadership research, but inconsistencies in research findings have led some to question how much of the variation in leadership effectiveness is explained by individual differences. For example, one landmark study, reviewing fifty years' worth of research, concluded 'the evidence suggests that leadership is a relation that exists between persons in a social situation, and that the persons who are leaders in one situation may not necessarily be leaders in other situations' (Stogdill, 1948).

Ralph Stogdill's review did not rule out the possibility of trait variables explaining some of the difference in leadership effectiveness. His review did, however, encourage researchers to broaden the scope of research to include features of the situations leaders find themselves in. But Stogdill and others were clear that the omission of trait variables from any model of leadership was as unacceptable as the study of them to the exclusion of all other classes of variables.

The emergence and maintenance of leadership

Although leadership positions in formal organizations are assigned to individuals on the basis of experience, seniority or expertise, there are many situations at work where leadership emerges without formal sanction. There are many individuals in the workplace who lack formal status but who none the less are perceived as leaders. Many researchers have been interested in how these people acquire leadership roles in groups. The examination of group interaction reveals that the people who become leaders tend to participate early on in group discussion (Hollander, 1978). Being the strong silent type is not a successful strategy. Initially the person who emerges as leader is the individual who does the most talking. The quantity of a person's contributions seems to indicate to other group members his or her intention to take a leadership role. The quality of contributions, however, dictates whether the individual remains acceptable as leader, since it determines the extent to which an individual is seen by other members as competent and contributing to group goals.

Group members seem to look for two types of competence. First, they look for what is termed *socio-emotional* competence. People who are perceived as possessing this are those who appear to be aware of and can influence group relations and cohesion. Socio-emotional competence covers a broad cluster of behaviours. More specifically, West (1997) suggests that an important part of a leader's socio-emotional competence is the ability to encourage reflexivity, as discussed in the last chapter. Similarly, Kets de Vries (1997), argues that the most important socio-emotional behaviours are those which support the charismatic role of the leader, i.e. those which empower, energize, and provide a vision.

Secondly, groups identify the level of *task competence* in individuals. In other words, leaders have to be able to demonstrate they can contribute to the problem-solving capacities and effectiveness of the group. As we have seen in Chapter 4 these task competences can be broken down into more specific competences (such as planning and organizing) or areas of competence (e.g. specific technical competences, such as financial planning).

An interesting distinction has been made between actual and perceived competence. This distinction is similar to that made by Goffman (1971), who argued that the maintenance of the correct 'personal front' enables relatively incompetent individuals to be perceived as competent. Price and Garland (1981) manipulated perceived competence by informing subjects that the leader was either highly competent or relatively incompetent. This had a marked effect both on the willingness of subjects to comply with the requests of the leaders and on the ratings of the leaders' effectiveness, subjects being less willing to comply with leaders perceived as relatively incompetent and rating them as less effective.

Emergence as a leader has also been associated with the extent to which individuals are able to behave with *spontaneity*. People who initiate a wider range of activities within the groups or attempt to develop wider opportunities for individuals to participate are more likely to emerge as group leader. The converse of spontaneity is *contagion*, the extent to which an individual is influenced by others. The skilful leader is able to balance the needs for spontaneity and contagion. Indeed, an individual emerging as group leader is related to the perception by group members of an appropriate balance between the two in his or her behaviour. Unsuccessful initial attempts at leadership may be the result of too much spontaneity and too little contagion—for example, attempting to take the group off in a direction which is not acceptable to group members. On the other hand, the individual who displays no contagion may be seen by group members as simply pursuing the dictates of self-interest.

Having gained the leadership role, a leader may need at some point to initiate activity that does deviate from group norms. This is made possible by earning what are termed *idiosyncrasy credits* (Hollander, 1958). The leader acquires these by being perceived as displaying competence on the group task and conformity to group norms. Maintaining credits is crucial to survival in the leadership position. It appears that once individuals have acquired the leadership role they may have less latitude to deviate from particular role obligations (Hollander, 1961). This seems to be because leaders have to negotiate with group members a trade-off between being allowed to deviate from general group norms (e.g. hours of work) and conforming closely to other norms such as promoting group cohesion and task performance.

The research on leadership emergence supports the view that what is important is not so much what people are but what they actually do. In the next section we will examine some attempts to identify the key dimensions of leadership behaviour.

Leadership style

Consideration and initiating structure

In 1945 Shartle instigated the Ohio State University Studies to investigate the nature of leadership behaviour and its relationship to various criteria of leadership effectiveness. He and his associates began by collecting a list of 1,800 phrases which described leadership behaviour. These were then placed into nine different behavioural categories. Of the initial items only 150 fell into only one category. These items formed the first questionnaire designed to assess aspects of leadership behaviour (Hemphill, 1950). Two independent factors emerged when data collected by using the questionnaire was subjected to factor analysis (Halpin and Winer, 1957).

The inter-correlations producing the first factor, *consideration*, were among items like 'exhibits concern for welfare of group members', 'appreciates good work', 'is easy to approach', 'responds to suggestions', and 'obtains approval of actions'. The inter-correlations producing the second factor, *initiation of structure*, reflected associations between such leader behaviours as 'maintains standards', 'meets deadlines' and 'defines in detail objectives, methods of work and roles'. Two tests, one for subordinates, the leader behaviour description questionnaire (LBDQ), and another for supervisors, the leader opinion questionnaire (LOQ) were then constructed to provide measures of supervisors along each dimension.

The identification of these two dimensions of leadership behaviour and the development of measures enabling supervisors to be measured on each prompted a great deal of research assessing their reliability and validity. A classic study of the effects of interactions between the scales on two organizational variables, grievance rate and turnover rate, established that quite complex relationships existed between the scales and these organizational variables (Fleishman and Harris, 1962). Some of the results are

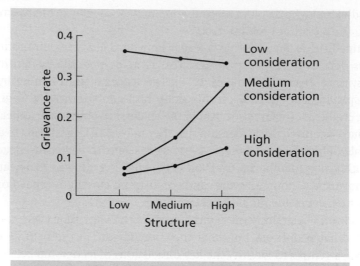

Figure 8.1 The interaction between structure, consideration, and grievance rate

Source: E. A. Fleishman and E. F. Harris (1962), 'Patterns of Leadership Behavior Related to Employee Grievances and Turnover', *Personnel Psychology*, 15: 43–56.

illustrated in Figure 8.1. As the graph indicates, being low in consideration generates most grievances and is not compensated for by being low in structure. For supervisors medium in consideration, grievance rates were determined by their level of structure. In general a supervisor's level of consideration is positively related to employee satisfaction with the organization and to measures of group and organizational cohesiveness. Initiation of structure, on the other hand, in general negatively correlates with absences, grievance and staff turnover (Science Research Associates, 1989).

It rapidly became clear, however, that the effects of consideration and structure on the variables of productivity and job satisfaction were moderated by intervening variables such as the type or size of the work unit. For example, an early study by Fleishman and Harris (1955) found that merit ratings for supervisors by their managers were positively related to their level of structure in manufacturing departments but negatively related for supervisors in service departments. Similarly, Schriesheim and Murphy (1976) found that the supervisor's initiation of structure was positively related to subordinates' job satisfaction in large work groups but negatively related in small groups. A number of other aspects of the workplace—the nature of the task, skill differential between supervisor and subordinates—also appear to alter the relationship between effectiveness and the two types of behaviour. At present we do not have a complete understanding of how the relationship between a leader's behaviour and his or her effectiveness is modified by organizational variables.

Some researchers have pointed out that, although assumed to be conceptually distinct, empirically the scales used to measure initiating structure and consideration do not appear to operate independently. A number of studies have shown that the scales can correlate with each other. In other words, managers who are high on one scale tend to be high on the other. This has led to the claim that we can also describe leaders along one general activity factor, termed *motivation to manage vs. laissez-faire management*. Laissez-faire or inactive managers are unwilling to accept responsibility, give directions or provide support. They tend to act not so much on their own initiative but in response to specific requests from their staff. There is some evidence that the level of a leader's activity is an important explanatory variable (Bass *et al.*, 1975). Inactivity in leaders is consistently negatively related to productivity, subordinate satisfaction and group cohesiveness (Stogdill, 1974).

While some people have suggested that the Ohio dimensions can be collapsed into one general activity factor, others have stressed the very opposite, that two dimensions are not enough. Bass (1981) argued that by using only two factors much specific information about a leader's behaviour is thrown away. For example, a moderate score on the initiation of structure dimension may mask certain specific difficulties a leader has, such as maintaining work standards. To counter this, some techniques of factor analysis have produced as many as twelve factors describing leadership behaviour. In practical applications, such as counselling, selection or leadership training, where information about a manager's leadership is required, it may well be important to have available a more detailed description of leadership behaviour.

One of the main problems in interpreting the results of research using the Ohio dimensions is that much of it is of the concurrent correlation type. This means that data on leader behaviour and organizational variables are collected at one point in time. We are not able to tell from the results whether high performance has caused high consideration or vice versa; each is equally plausible. This makes studies of the effects of changes in leadership behaviour and organizational variables over time particularly valuable. Unfortunately, these studies are few and far between. One series of studies, however, has collected data on leader behaviour, subordinate satisfaction and production at different points in time and across a wide variety of industrial settings (Greene, 1975, 1979). The results suggest that considerate leadership was causally antecedent to increased subordinate satisfaction. But it also seems that changes in the productivity of the subordinates resulted in changes in leadership behaviour. An increase in productivity caused an increase in consideration and a decrease in initiation of structure. In other words, there is an *interaction* between leadership behaviour and group output variables. Leaders affect the behaviour of their staff who, in turn, affect the behaviour of their supervisors. Additionally Smith and Peterson (1988) provide evidence suggesting items on the leader opinion questionnaire are culturally specific:

> ... it could well prove to be the case that leaders in organizations from all parts of the world do indeed need to attend both to the task in hand and also to the maintenance of good relationships within the work team. But *how* this is to be accomplished in each setting will be dependent upon the meanings given to particular leadership acts in that setting. A supervisor who frequently checks up that work is done correctly may be seen as a kind father in one setting, as task centred in another setting, officious and mistrustful in a third. (p. 100)

However, despite methodological problems, there are two reasons why initiation of structure and consideration are still widely used concepts in leadership research. First, the availability of a reliable, easily administered, and inexpensive measure of them means that data on the leadership style of individuals or groups of supervisors can be gathered quickly. The scales provide useful summaries of underlying consistencies in behaviour. As a psychologist working with leaders of workgroups, being able to identify an individual's position—relative to other managers—along the two dimensions provides a useful platform for a discussion. In one instance, a store manager of a major retailer, whose maximum initiation of structure score was combined with a minimum score on consideration, responded by saying 'at least they know when I am coming!' But the scores usefully focused the discussion on the implications of his leadership style—not least of which was around a 300 per cent staff turnover rate in his store—way above the norm in the organization. Secondly, the validity of the measures—their ability to account for some of the variance in criterion organizational variables such as productivity and turnover—indicates the Ohio researchers have identified two key dimensions of supervisory behaviour.

The democratic leadership style

One of the most interesting questions raised by leadership research is how the forms of authority experienced by individuals in organizations correspond to how it is exercised more broadly in society. In most industrialized societies there have been increases at least in expectations for openness, access to information, collaboration, communication, and consultation (e.g. Gastil, 1997). These expectations and the democratic ideals they stem from can mean there is a stark contrast between these normative assumptions about authority and the way authority is exercised in organizations.

This contrast was originally highlighted after the Second World War by the social commentator Daniel Bell. As he put it:

> the problem of leadership is shaped by the fact that while we live in a society of political democracy almost all basic social patterns are authoritarian and tend to instill feelings of helplessness and dependence. . . . our factories, hierarchical in structure, are, for all the talk of human relations programs, still places where certain men exercise arbitrary authority over others. (1948, p. 375)

Not surprisingly, a large amount of research has investigated how this 'problem of leadership' can be resolved. For example, the University of Michigan has conducted several hundred studies involving over a quarter of a million people. The dimension at the heart of these 'Michigan Studies'—democratic–autocratic leadership—is perhaps the most complex construct in the leadership literature. It refers to the way in which decisions are taken; whose needs in the organization are met; and what characterizes the relations between leader and follower, for instance, how much coercion is present.

Many of the studies used the framework developed by Likert (1961) to capture these aspects of leader–follower relations. Likert proposed four 'systems' of relationships in large organizations which reflected an organization's position in the democratic vs. autocratic dimension:

1. Exploitative autocratic;
2. Benevolent autocratic;
3. Consultative;
4. Democratic.

Leadership in systems 1 and 2 emphasizes the *legitimacy* of managerial authority, for example by providing no opportunities for consultation between staff and management. Relationships between leaders and subordinates are formal in system 1. Managers will treat subordinates in an aloof, cold and in extreme instances hostile manner. The chief distinction between systems 1 and 2 involves the nature of control. The benevolent autocrat prefers to control by using rewards; the exploitative autocrat uses more coercive and punitive methods of control. Power in systems 1 and 2 organizations is concentrated at the top with no consultation with subordinates.

The emphasis of leadership in systems 3 and 4 is on the creation of supportive, friendly interpersonal relationships based on trust, participation and two-way communication between follower and leader. The organizational goals of high output and high standards are no different to those in systems 1 and 2, but in systems 3 and 4 the aim is to achieve these objectives by team working and the leader's encouragement of the group members' best efforts, for example by obtaining and making constructive use of subordinates' ideas on improving work methods. Subordinates are also able to influence or determine their performance targets during group goal-setting sessions. In order to study organizations with these different systems of management, Likert developed a measure known as the *profile of organizational characteristics* (POC). This included the range of variables embraced by the democratic vs. autocratic dimension—how decisions are taken, whose needs are met, what characterizes the relations between leaders and subordinates, and how much coercion is generally present in the leader–subordinate relationship. Likert was thus able to establish what position an organization occupied along the autocratic vs. democratic dimension.

Likert was completely in favour of system 4 management. His prescription to organizations to move towards system 4 was not just a political campaign. He claimed that such a shift had a positive impact on organizational effectiveness. These effects could occur in any type of industry and range from improvements in employee motivation and job satisfaction to increased productivity. Research had produced correlations of the POC measure with organizational performances ranging from .3 to .6. Likert found that a period of five years may be required for improvements to appear. But moving to system 4 is not easy. It involves massive shifts in an organization's culture and behaviour of managers.

Like the Ohio research, democratic leadership also emphasizes behaviour over position and authority. So what behaviours would a manager need to display to be defined as a democratic leader? There seem to be five behavioural clusters (e.g. Gastil, 1997):

1. *Clarifying*—democratic leaders need to make clear their accountability for decisions, their lines of authority, power, agenda, and motives.
2. *Reducing*—democratic leaders need to reduce privilege and status differentials (such as separate dining facilities), hierarchies, inequalities, and concentrations of power.

3. *Distributing responsibility*—democratic leaders seek the maximum participation of others by devolving responsibility and empowering individuals.

4. *Developing others*—empowering individuals involves ensuring others are equipped to deal with their responsibilities. This might mean individuals need developing in confidence, self-esteem, or analytical ability. The democratic leader needs to set high but reasonable standards and 'demand' that others accept their responsibilities. Developing others can involve 'mentoring' and 'coaching' individuals. However, the leader should avoid charismatic behaviour which encourages dependency and regression.

5. *Facilitating*—at the heart of democratic leadership is productive, participative decision-making. The democratic leader is aware of group process and thus encourages reflexivity (West, 1996). For example, he or she will focus on the task but also create participative safety—i.e. a congenial atmosphere which supports free discussion. However, he or she is also capable of enforcing norms—for instance about resolving conflict—when necessary.

This list indicates democratic leadership requires both considerable skills and commitment—personal and organizational, and it may well be no one individual in a group can display all these behaviours and the role is filled by more than one individual. As can be seen, being a democratic follower requires maturity and active participation and is, in many ways, as demanding as being a democratic leader. But being managed in a way which encourages emotional and intellectual skilling rather than deskilling is more likely to fulfil fundamental psychological needs, such as those for power, achievement, and application.

One of the major criticisms of democratic leadership is that in some settings the style is simply not appropriate. Democratic leadership can, because of its emphasis on deliberation and participation, be much more expensive and slower than autocratic and directive styles. Gastil's (1997) decision-tree for democratic leadership (see Figure 8.2) indicates when it is feasible and when other options are more appropriate. Democratic leadership raises very fundamental issues about the nature of power and control in organizations. Indeed, a criticism of democratic leadership is that in some instances it has been used manipulatively, for example, to fend off demands for unionization. We will return to explore these broader issues of power, authority, and control in Chapter 16.

Leadership style and nationality

Democratic leadership is a style actively prescribed by some for ethical, psychological, political, and economic reasons. Another question leadership research has attempted to answer is the extent to which cultural norms, born out of historical experience, also prescribe certain leadership styles. For example, has the Economic Union created a homogeneous approach to leadership. Is there a European leadership style?

A study conducted by the Cranfield School of Management in the UK suggests, as yet, there is not. Questionnaire data from 600 top managers across Europe were subjected

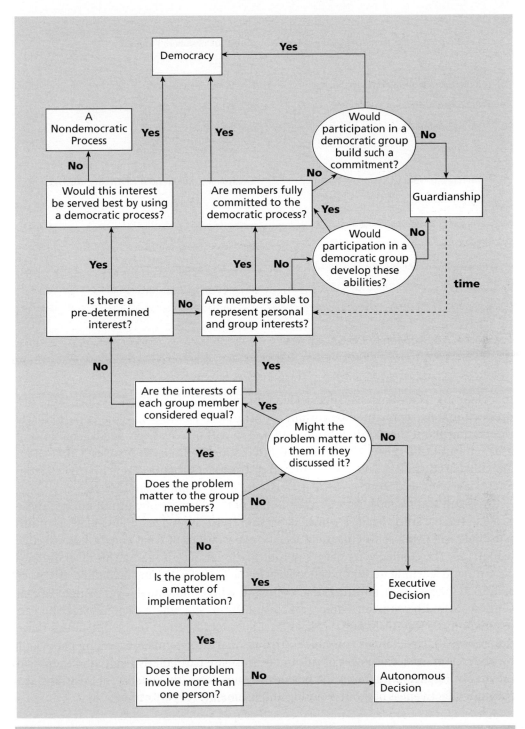

Figure 8.2 Decision tree for democracy and democratic leadership

Leading from the front (UK, Ireland, Spain)

Charisma

Reliance on individual's leadership ability

Rules and procedures hinder performance

Self-motivation

Dominance

Consenus (Sweden, Finland)

Team spirit

Effective communication

Attention to organizational detail

Open dialogue

Consensual decision-making

Managing from a distance (French)

Lack of discipline

Pursuit of personal agendas

Strategic/conceptual thinkers

Ineffective communication

Ambiguity

Towards a common goal (Germany, Austria)

Valuing functional expertise

Authority-based leadership style

Clear roles of responsibility

Discipline oriented

Identify with systems and controls

Figure 8.3 European Leadership Styles

to a rigorous factor analysis. This yielded four relatively distinct styles which were disproportionately represented by certain countries (see Figure 8.3). What is particularly interesting about the Cranfield study is that even within a relatively small geographical area, cultural differences clearly give rise to distinctive leadership styles. Other more globally based studies have also identified distinctive Germanic, French, Anglo-Saxon, and Asia-Pacific leadership styles (e.g. Hofstede, 1991; Trompenaars, 1993).

Cross-cultural research serves to remind us of the diversity of cultural norms. These provide the backdrop against which leadership styles are judged. Individuals in multinationals will bring some culturally specific expectations of what constitutes effective leadership. The challenge managers in multinationals face is taking this diversity into account and learning to respond effectively in the face of it. Having facilitated groups of senior managers in a multinational company where individuals were Anglo-Saxon, Chinese, Scandinavian, Germanic, French, and Latin, and where each manager had an opportunity to lead the group, I can, at least anecdotally, attest to the difficulties these differences in expectations can cause. Attributional errors—misinterpreting behaviour by underestimating the power of cultural norms—are particularly likely, and these will inevitably impact on a range of business issues from the quality of relationships through effectiveness of group working and ultimately on performance.

Fiedler and Task vs Relationship oriented leadership

Stogdill's review of the trait literature encouraged a recognition of the part situational variables played in the explanation of leadership effectiveness. Although much of the subsequent empirical research included situational variables, little theoretical development occurred to assist in the explanation of results of this more broadly based research. However, the publication of Fred Fiedler's *A Theory of Leadership Effectiveness* (1967) ended this atheoretical phase of leadership research. Fiedler presented an elaborate theory that attempted to account for the contingent nature of leadership effectiveness.

Fiedler began by distinguishing leadership behaviour from leadership style. Leadership behaviour is the specific response a supervisor makes in a particular situation. Unlike most other researchers Fiedler believed that leadership style—consistencies in the pattern of responses across different situations—was a relatively fixed feature of individuals which reflected a supervisor's motivational make-up.

He proposed that leadership style is fundamentally characterized along a dimension termed *task-oriented leadership vs. relationship-oriented leadership*. He developed an instrument, the *least preferred co-worker* (LPC) scale, which provided a measure of an individual's position on the dimension and by implication his or her motivational make-up. The LPC score is derived by a supervisor describing on a number of bipolar adjectival scales the person they have found the most difficult to work with. Thus, a supervisor would rate the least preferred co-worker along eight point scales like friendly–unfriendly, intelligent–unintelligent. A high score is obtained by placing least preferred co-worker towards the positive end of each scale. Fiedler interprets the high-scoring supervisor as an individual who is concerned with establishing good interpersonal relations, more considerate and lower in anxiety. High scorers are also more 'cognitively complex', since they are able to separate out evaluations of the least preferred co-worker's job performance from evaluations of his or her personality and ability. The high scorer acquires self-esteem not through intrinsic satisfaction of a job well done, but through the recognition by others of his or her competence. A low score is acquired by denigrating the least preferred co-worker, describing him or her as unintelligent, lazy, and unfriendly. This is thought to reflect a lack of concern with personal relationships and by implication more concern with the task. The low scorer is presumed to be less cognitively complex than the high scorer, being unable to differentiate work performance and personality. Successful task performance is the principal source of satisfaction for the low scorer. Both high and low scorers are concerned with the task and interpersonal relationships. The high-scoring supervisor is concerned with the task in order to achieve successful relationships. The low-scoring leader is concerned with interpersonal relationships in order to achieve successful task performance. Fiedler argued that low-scoring and high-scoring leaders differ in behaviour most when the satisfaction of their needs is threatened.

Fiedler's second task was to construct a satisfactory method of describing and measuring leadership situations. An important feature of leadership positions, he argued, is the extent to which the authority of the leader is legitimized by the organization. Does the leader have the power to hire and fire? Are there large differences in status and rank? This feature of leadership situations he termed the leader's *position power*, and a checklist was devised to provide a measure of it.

The second feature of leadership situations which he sought to describe was the *task structure*. Some tasks are routine and have one route to a single solution, while others are less straightforward. He classified task structure using four dimensions: goal clarity, the degree to which the goal requirements are clearly ascertainable; decision verifiability, the degree to which it is possible to know whether a solution is correct; goal path multiplicity, the number of possible routes to the goal; and solution specificity, the number of possible solutions.

The third feature of the situation that Fiedler built into the model was what he called *leader–group relations*. If leader–group relations were good, the leader was accepted, group members were loyal and communication was easier. Fiedler devised an instrument (the group atmosphere score) which yielded a measure of leader–group relations.

These aspects of the work situation Fiedler presumed captured the essential features of leadership situations. Research on a large number of work groups in a variety of work settings showed that the relationship between a supervisor's style and his or her effectiveness was mediated by the leadership situation. Thus the final task for Fiedler was to describe and explain the interaction between leadership style, the leadership situation and the leader's effectiveness.

In order to identify the pattern of this interaction Fiedler simplified his concept of a leadership situation by combining the three measures of it (position power, task structure and leader–group relations) into one representing the *favourability* of the situation to the leader. To do this Fiedler assumed that the most important determinant of situation favourability was leader–group relations followed by task structure and position power. He then divided each of these three measures into two on the basis of the median point that had been identified for each scale by his research. By combining each of the three, now dichotomized, dimensions in their order of importance he created a dimension comprised of eight ($2 \times 2 \times 2$) octants representing situational favourability. Thus, according to Fiedler the most favourable situation was one in which leader–group relations were good and task structure and position power were high. Conversely, the least favourable situation for a supervisor was one in which he or she faced poor leader–group relations, low task structure and low position power.

Fiedler then plotted each of his research studies by placing them on the horizontal dimension according to what octant they fell into and on the vertical axis according to the correlation found between the supervisor's LPC score and his or her team's effectiveness.

To summarize the interaction between leadership style, situational favourability and effectiveness, Fiedler drew a line connecting the median correlations of studies in each octant (Figure 8.4). Fiedler found that low LPC leaders were most effective when the situation was either highly favourable or highly unfavourable. In situations of moderate favourability, high-scoring supervisors performed best. This represented an important

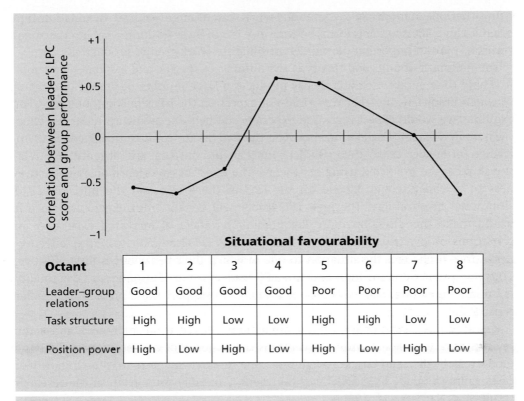

Figure 8.4 The relationship between situational favourability and leaders' LPC score
The bow shape was formed by joining the median correlation for studies in each octant between LPC scores and group performance
Source: Fiedler (1967).

Octant	1	2	3	4	5	6	7	8
Leader–group relations	Good	Good	Good	Good	Poor	Poor	Poor	Poor
Task structure	High	High	Low	Low	High	High	Low	Low
Position power	High	Low	High	Low	High	Low	High	Low

correction to the prevailing human relations view that relationship-oriented supervision was always preferable.

Fiedler explained his conclusions by arguing that, since high and low LPC leaders seek to satisfy different needs, situations that threaten the satisfaction of those needs will trigger very different behaviours in each. In situations of low favourability the group is best served by directive and structuring leadership and the needs of low LPC leaders are more likely to produce these behaviours. In jobs where there is a low level of task structure, for example where the goals are not clear or the number of possible routes to a solution is high, directive and structuring leadership may be welcomed by group members in order to reduce their frustration and anxiety.

Conversely, highly favourable situations where jobs are routinized, the position of power is high and leader–group relations are good provide an environment in which the low LPC leaders' needs are not threatened, enabling them to relax and become less structuring. Highly favourable situations produce very different behaviours in a high LPC supervisor. Since there are already good relations, they become more involved and structuring, which, since the task is already highly structured, is likely to be resented by group members.

In situations of moderate favourability where conditions are mixed, the relationship-oriented high LPC scorer performs better, since it is in these positions that interpersonal relations play an important part in determining the work group's productivity.

The hallmark of any good theory is the number of specific and testable predictions it is able to generate. Fiedler's theory produces a large number of predictions, many of which predict results that we would not expect on the basis of common sense. For example, we would expect increased experience to be associated with increased effectiveness in a leader. Correlations between the two do not confirm this (Fiedler, 1970). Fiedler (in Fiedler *et al.*, 1975; Fiedler, 1982) points out that the absence of a relationship can be predicted using his theory. The effect of experience on the effectiveness of a leader would depend on the LPC of the leader and the initial level of situational favourability. The high LPC leader will benefit from experience since it would make this situation more favourable. The effect of increased experience in conditions of low situational favourability for low LPC leaders is to reduce effectiveness, since it changes the situation to one in which their behaviour is least effective. Converse predictions for high and low LPC leaders occur if situational favourability is initially moderate. Some evidence is available to support these predictions (Fiedler *et al.*, 1975).

Research has also supported other predictions derived from the model, and many reviews have found that despite exceptions the majority of studies support the basic model (e.g. Fiedler and Garcia, 1987). But some research suggests that the minority of cases falling outside the model can represent a sizeable proportion of the research results (e.g. Nathan *et al.*, 1986).

Given the scope of the model it is hardly surprising that it has received mixed support. There is no doubt, however, that there are some specific problems with the model. Some studies have shown LPC scores are not as fixed as Fiedler envisaged and may not be independent of group performance (e.g. Katz and Farris, 1976). This implies changes in group performance may lead to changes in a leader's style. Similarly, Smith and Peterson (1988) argue that supposedly independent aspects of the model are confounded. For example, they argue that LPC scores overlap with leader–group relations and thus leadership style and situational favourability are not at all independent. They suggest that group performance also affects leader–group relations. Perhaps the major problem with the model lies in its attempt to capture all of the differences, subtleties, and complexities of leadership behaviour in one, essentially personality-based, measure—task vs. relationship orientation.

However, Fiedler's attempt to explain the nature of leadership effectiveness represents a considerable advance in leadership theory, and his basic finding that the effectiveness of a leadership style was contingent on the situation remains a view which most psychologists and leadership trainers will still subscribe to.

Hersey and Blanchard—high probability leadership

Hersey and Blanchard's (1988) model of leadership draws extensively and effectively from the work of the founding fathers of leadership research a generation earlier—Fred Fiedler, Ralph Stogdill, Edwin Fleishman, and the other early Ohio researchers. In taking the elements of research which have conceptually and empirically stood the test of time and critical scrutiny they provide a fairly robust model which currently represents the 'state of the art'.

They follow Ralph Stogdill in assuming leadership effectiveness is the result of an interaction between the person and the situation. Based themselves at Ohio State University they borrowed the two concepts originally developed there—initiation of structure and consideration. Like the original Ohio researchers they also assume these scales are conceptually and empirically distinct—i.e. it is possible to be high or low on both, or high on one and low on the other. The most distinctive aspect of Hersey and Blanchard's model is how they conceptualize the situation. This was the fundamental problem faced by Fiedler—how to capture and measure the key characteristics of situations leaders find themselves in. Hersey and Blanchard believed the key situational issues faced by leaders were the competence and motivation of followers. This they operationalized as the 'readiness' or 'maturity' of followers. Readiness is therefore not an evaluation of followers' traits, values, the group atmosphere, or power differentials but more straightforwardly an appraisal of how well an individual or group is likely to perform a specific task.

By combining high and low relationship and task behaviour Hersey and Blanchard created four leadership styles: delegating, participating, selling, and telling. Using data from various sources they plotted a curve representing what they called the high probability style. Like a high probability tennis shot this curve indicates which style is most likely to be successful for a given level of follower readiness. In effect, the curve indicates where the highest style-effectiveness correlations appear (see Figure 8.5). The key difference between Fiedler's situational leader and Hersey and Blanchard's is choice. Fiedler assumes leadership style is the manifestation of relatively fixed motivational and temperamental differences. Hersey and Blanchard, in contrast, assume leaders have control over what leadership behaviour they display.

Hersey and Blanchard's prescription to leaders thus appears simple:

(a) diagnose the readiness level of the followers for a particular task;
(b) provide the appropriate leadership style for that situation.

Accomplishing the first accurately may involve breaking a job down into more specific tasks as competence and motivation are likely to vary for elements of more complex multi-faceted jobs. Hersey and Blanchard's model is avowedly *cognitive*. At its heart is the cognitive skill of a leader to diagnose follower readiness accurately. The unstated assumption here is that leaders are rational and want to diagnose follower readiness and change their behaviour accordingly. Leaders, they assume, are well intentioned.

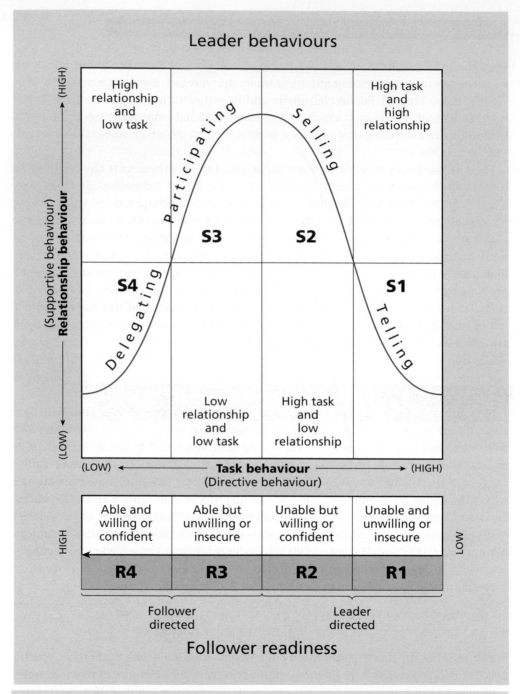

Figure 8.5 Situational leadership

They are in the business of creating 'win–win' situations for themselves and their followers.

But as we have seen in Chapter 3, sometimes our behaviour falls short of this rational ideal, and leaders confronted by the loneliness and pressures of very senior positions can get caught up in a web of emotional processes, leading to impoverished reality testing. Settling scores, vindictiveness, jealousy, grandiosity, or the many other ways of projecting inner conflicts on to others all make leaders less than willing to create 'win–win' situations. The biographies of leaders are littered with examples of individuals not coping well with the 'demon' of irrationality—we have already mentioned the example of Henry Ford, who refused to allow any modifications to the Model T for nineteen years, despite competitors catching up with and overtaking the model's market share. On being shown a slight modification by engineers he flew into a rage and ripped the car to pieces. As a psychologist working with Chief Executives and senior managers I have also witnessed the effects of irrationality on relationships and task performance. However, assuming that rationality and goodwill are present, Hersey and Blanchard's model provides an effective synthesis of some important strands of leadership research. The model's simplicity means that the psychological insights it incorporates can be transmitted in a short training session. And the presence of well presented and packaged supporting exercises, inventories, videos, and games, means the model now forms the basis of a significant proportion of leadership training.

Charismatic or transformational leadership—the return of the 'great man'

Charles de Gaulle once commented: 'In the designs, the demeanour, and the mental operations of a leader there must be always a "something" which others cannot altogether fathom, which puzzles them, stirs them and diverts their attention.' This mysterious 'something' that some leaders have to inspire their subordinates to do things beyond their capabilities and into sometimes unquestioning compliance seems to have been lost in the theories and research discussed so far. The feeling that the romance, mystery, and even the subject-matter of leadership have been lost in abstract conceptualization has caused a resurgence of interest in what is termed charismatic or transformational leadership.

Burns (1978) was the first leadership researcher to write extensively about charisma. He starts with the distinction between managers and leaders. Managers are power holders who have, by virtue of their position, the capacity to influence others. But for Burns leadership requires something else. To be leader the individual must be able to 'induce followers to act for certain goals that represent the values and motivations—the wants and needs, the aspirations and expectations of both leaders and followers' (p. 19). This he described as transformational leadership. In what he describes as transactional leadership there is simply a mutual exchange for economic or political reasons between leader and follower. In transformational leadership a deeper, more powerful process is present. Here one or more persons engage with others in such a way that leaders and followers raise one another to higher levels of motivation and morality.

The differences between transformational and transactional leaders have been described in more specific terms by a number of authors (e.g. Conger, 1991; Bass and Avolio, 1993; Kirkpatrick and Locke, 1996). These authors suggest the core components of transformational leadership seem to be:

1. *Charismatic communication style*—transformational leaders are able to engender trust and respect. Their communication style both motivates and intellectually stimulates followers.
2. *Communicating a vision*—transformational leaders set challenging goals for followers, and these usually cause followers to question traditional approaches, values, and beliefs.
3. *Implementing a vision*—transformational leaders are able to energize their followers and focus their efforts on achieving goals.
4. *Individualized consideration*—transformational leaders give followers the feeling they are treated as unique individuals. Treatment is fair but is perceived as different from that received by others.

Conger (1991) in particular emphasized the role of language in the charismatic leadership style. He argued that organizational cultures and educational systems discouraged individuals from acquiring the communication skills necessary to sell themselves and their messages. He suggested two communication skills that are the linguistic hallmarks of charismatic leadership—framing and rhetorical crafting. Framing is about defining the purpose of the organization in a way which creates emotional excitement and a sense of confidence. Rhetorical crafting involves using metaphor, rhythmic devices, and allowing emotions to surface, for instance through non-verbal channels. Whilst quite often politicians have these skills very few managers have.

The impact of these differences on the approach to managerial responsibilities is considerable (see Table 8.1). As can be seen from the table, transformational leadership equates with adaptive change, whereas management is about smooth implementation of existing policies. Both processes are clearly important, although organizations facing up to change will place a high premium on identifying transformational leaders. Interestingly, on measures of transformational leadership women score significantly better than men (Bass and Avolio, 1994), a fact which has considerable implications as uncertainty and change increasingly become the norm.

Whilst some have treated it as such, charisma is not really a trait. What is central to the notion of charisma are the two-way processes of projection and transference discussed in Chapter 3. As long ago as 1939 when the world was beginning to descend into war and nations lined up behind charismatic leaders, Freud suggested that leadership also operated as a symbolic unconscious level. Leaders represent the return of the 'primal father' with whom, like the father of our own early childhood, it is easy to identify. As Freud suggests, 'we know that in the mass of mankind there is a powerful need for an authority who can be admired, before whom one bows down, by whom one is ruled

	Leaders	Managers
Creating agendas	Establishing direction Developing vision of future Developing change strategies	Planning/budgeting Developing plan Developing timetable
Building networks	Alignment of people Inculcating vision in persons/teams	Organizing/staffing Developing Staffing, delegation, and monitoring policies
Execution	Inspiring Energizing others to overcome barriers	Controlling/problem-solving Monitoring and taking corrective action
Outcomes	Potentially revolutionary changes Order out of chaos	Order and predictability Key results expected by significant others

Table 8.1 Kotter's comparison of leadership skills and management
Source: Adapted from Kotter (1990).

and perhaps even ill treated' (1939, p. 109). More recently, as Kets de Vries (1993) points out, 'leaders are partly defined by the desires of their followers. A great potential for distortion exists.' Leaders are therefore, from a Freudian perspective, a prime target for the process of *transference*.

Leaders benefit from a kind of psychological confusion about who they are as they become mixed up in the follower's mind with significant individuals from his or her childhood. And while transference stimulates our dependency needs, another process identified by Freud—projection—enables us to attribute the leader with our own desires and fantasies. The elation experienced by the followers of charismatic leaders is partly the result of being able to rid themselves of prohibitions. The Leader becomes their conscience.

From this perspective all leadership is potentially charismatic. Some leaders, however, are more aware of these processes and may actively encourage them. By speaking directly to a follower's unconscious through metaphor, simile, simple language, and stark contrasts, some leaders can harness the processes of transference and projection. Many organizations have either benefited from or have been rescued by constructive forms of charismatic leadership. However, many spectacular crashes—de Lorean, for example—are the result of the dark side of charismatic leadership. While some leaders can use these processes constructively, others are ultimately destroyed by them.

From theory to practice

The acid test for leadership theory has to be its practical relevance. Leadership training is now offered by a large number of consultancies and internal training departments, and sessions designed to improve leadership skills are now commonplace components of management education and development programmes in educational settings.

To what extent has leadership research enhanced our understanding of what skills managers need to display to be effective? We have seen that leadership research has essentially provided us with a composite picture of effective leaders. On the one hand, they need to display interpersonal sensitivity, whilst on the other handling effectively the practical demands of the task. They are also, according to situational theory, sensitive to key contingency variables and able either to modify the situation to suit them or select an appropriate leadership style to suit the situation. They are also effective team builders—able to enhance the reflexivity of the groups they are members of. Their decisions are accepted because they are perceived as competent individuals by other group members; and because they have encouraged participation in decision-making, there is more commitment and support for decisions. As we have seen, effective leaders are continuously negotiating their role with subordinates. From this perspective, group members exchange their compliance in return for the leader meeting their needs. These can include dependency needs. Some leaders may, wittingly or unwittingly, cause their followers to project their hopes and feelings onto them. This can work constructively, motivating achievement; or it can cause regression into dysfunctional dependency characterized by the emotional and intellectual deskilling of followers.

Sensitivity training and teambuilding

In order to meet the group's needs a leader must first be able to perceive them. As we have seen some psychologists have argued *empathy* is therefore one of the basic building-blocks of leadership skill. Therefore, the development of a leader's sensitivity to others has been a key area in leadership training. A number of techniques have been developed to do just this. The first of these and perhaps the most notorious is the T-group (T for training). Developed in the late 1940s, a T-group consists of about 12 trainees and one trainer. The usual factors such as agendas and work roles which guide interaction in the workplace are absent. The task of the trainees is to interact and then at points analyse what has occurred in the group—for example what roles have emerged, who is participating and who is becoming dependent on whom. The trainer throws the burden of keeping the interaction going almost entirely on the group, intervening only occasionally to reflect on what is occurring in the group or to encourage participation. Supporters of T-groups believe this sequence of interaction, analysis, and feedback promotes:

1. An increased self awareness;
2. An increased awareness of the needs of subordinates;
3. An increased desire to share information;

4. An increased desire to reach decisions participatively;
5. A shift towards less formal styles of interaction with subordinates;
6. A reduction in assertive and directive leadership behaviour.

A number of studies of the effects of T-groups suggest they do in general produce the desired outcome. However their popularity has declined considerably. They are intense psychological experiences and require a great deal of skill from the trainer. Some critics claim the technique is simply *unethical* because it may invade individual privacy, disrupt an individual's defence systems, and pressure group members to conform. In addition, trainees may be required to assume that the trainer's values are superior to their own. While some people undoubtedly find T-groups a powerful psychological experience, the emotional stress involved can produce casualties in the group, trainees sometimes actually requiring psychiatric help afterwards. In reply to these criticisms supporters of the technique claim the benefits make the small amount of stress and damage it may cause acceptable.

In an effort to reduce the variability of the effects of T-groups caused by differences in the skill of trainers, sensitivity training has become more standardized, and is now able to be delivered by much less skilled and experienced individuals. These typically involve group problem-solving exercises or working in pairs on interpersonal issues. Though not as powerful an experience as a T-group, these team exercises, particularly when combined with feedback from trainer and peers, similarly give leaders an indication of the way they respond in groups and of the impact of their behaviour on other people.

One problem both the unstructured T-groups and the more standardized exercises face is demonstrating that the learning which occurs in the group is *transferable* to the workplace. Some critics have suggested that trainees can have difficulty perceiving a link between the learning of abstract social-psychological concepts and practical problems in their workplace. In response to this, both T-group trainers and those using more standardized approaches increasingly complement group work with exercises such as role-playing based on trainees' current problems. For example, in my organization we conduct diagnostic interviews with senior managers to identify 'critical incidents' from which we can construct role-playing scenarios which link the more abstract learning in the group with more concrete day-to-day work problems.

Situational leadership

Leader-match training Fiedler's contribution to leadership theory has been immense and attempts have been made to translate his insights into a leadership programme. You may remember the distinctive feature of Fiedler's leadership theory is his conceptualization of leadership style. Whereas Hersey and Blanchard assume it is possible for a leader to change his or her style according to the situation, Fiedler believes that leadership style is a reflection of relatively permanent personality and motivational variables. If Fiedler is correct it would be easier to teach leaders how to change the situation than how to change themselves. Fiedler and Chemars (1984) developed a training programme called *leader-match training* to enable leaders to do just this. The first stage of the programme is the assessment of where a leader is on the task-oriented–relationship oriented dimension. This indicates what sort of situation the leader is likely to be most effective in. A leader is then taught how to assess the favourability of a work situation and how to change the situation to suit his or her leadership style. Support for this approach comes from a number of studies in which performance evaluations of leaders were taken from two to six months after the course (Fiedler and Mahar, 1979). Performance ratings of 423 leader-match-trained leaders were compared with ratings of 480 leaders in control groups. The results indicated leader-match trainees had significantly higher ratings than leaders in the control groups.

The value of leader-match training, however, is doubted by a number of researchers. We have already seen that the notion of fixed leadership styles has been questioned. In addition the 'match' between leadership styles and leadership situation was based on the median correlation of effectiveness and style in the original studies. In some octants along Fiedler's dimension of situational favourability, the median result masks a considerable range in the size and direction of correlations between leadership style and effectiveness. But it does seem that by focusing on the key concept of situational control Fiedler's trainees were able to increase their understanding of how to maintain the appropriate balance between their leadership style and situational control, and their heightened sensitivity to these issues did seem to lead to increases in effectiveness.

Hersey and Blanchard Although less well academically supported, Hersey and Blanchard's variant of situational leadership benefits from considerable commercial support. Both authors market a number of products which help provide stimulating and effective learning for managers. Videos, tests, and exercises all help increase a leader's ability to assess accurately their followers' readiness and select an appropriate leadership style. An example of a situational leadership game can be found in Box 8.1.

Box 8.1 The situational leadership game

Try these questions either on your own or competitively. If the latter you can form into groups or pairs. Read the situation and decide which of the actions you would take. If doing this competitively, if the other team or individual declares an action you then have a minute to decide on your course of action. Refer to the answers to score your responses. Try not to look at the answers— better still cover the answer page with a piece of paper.

Continue through the five situations. The highest score is the winner.

Scores 10–8. Excellent. You clearly understand the principles of situational leadership. You are able to vary your style according to the situation and competence of your subordinates.

Scores 7–5. Reasonable. You have some understanding of the principles of situational leadership, but you should read the rationales on the questions where your score was low and ensure you understand why your score was less than perfect.

Scores 5 and less. You tend to approach the leadership function using only one style. From a situational leadership perspective you need to be able to vary your leadership style to ensure it matches your subordinates' motivation and competence.

For the full board game—an excellent way of learning the principles of situational leadership—contact Management Learning Resources, P.O. Box 28, Carmarthen, Dyfed, SA31 1DT.

Situation	Action
Situation 1	
Your group has been dropping in productivity during the last few months. Members have been unconcerned with meeting objectives. Role defining has helped in the past. They have continually needed reminding to have tasks done on time. The group is relatively new to the job.	A. Emphasize the importance of deadlines. B. Involve the group in problem-solving. C. Individually talk with members and set goals. D. Do what you can to make the group feel important and involved.
Situation 2	
Recent information indicates some internal difficulties among your followers. The group has a remarkable record of accomplishment. They have effectively maintained long-range goals. They have worked in harmony for the past year. All are well qualified for the task.	A. Avoid confrontation; don't apply pressure. B. Make yourself available for discussion without pushing for completion. C. Make your feelings about goals clear and do all you can to help in goal completion. D. Act quickly and firmly to correct and redirect.
Situation 3	
You have been considering instituting a major change. Group members have tended to resist change that they did not initiate. They have a fine record of accomplishment. They respect the need for change.	A. Make things pleasant for followers through involvement and reinforcement of good contributions. B. After discussing results, you reset standards. C. Intentionally do not intervene. D. Be willing to make changes as recommended, but maintain performance standards.

Situation 4

Your group had responded well to your spelling out tasks specifically and dealing firmly with those members who did not demonstrate appropriate behaviour. Lately, this style has not been achieving results.

A. Take steps to direct followers towards working in a well-defined manner.

B. Try out your solution with followers and examine the need for new practices.

C. Be careful of hurting boss–follower relations by pushing.

D. Let followers work it out.

Situation 5

You have been considering making major changes in your organizational structure. Members of the group have made suggestions about needed change. The group has demonstrated flexibility in its day-to-day operations.

A. Allow the group to formulate its own direction.

B. Incorporate group recommendations, but see that uniform goals are maintained.

C. Allow group involvement in goal setting; don't push.

D. Redefine goals and supervise carefully.

Answers

Situation	Scores	Your score
1	A = +2	
	B = −1	
	C = +1	
	D = −2	
2	A = +2	
	B = +1	
	C = −1	
	D = −2	
3	A = +1	
	B = −2	
	C = −1	
	D = +2	
4	A = +2	
	B = +1	
	C = −1	
	D = −2	
5	A = 0	
	B = +1	
	C = +2	
	D = −2	
	Total score	

Rationales for scoring

Situation 1

+2 This action (HT–LR) provides the directive leadership needed for this inexperienced group.

−1 This action (HR–LT) is appropriate for working with people of average readiness, but at present this group does not have the ability to take responsibility or experience to engage in significant problem-solving.

+1 This action (HT–LR) may be appropriate if the group begins to demonstrate some ability to meet deadlines and accomplish tasks.

−2 This action (HR–LT) tends to reinforce positively the group's present inappropriate behaviour and, in the future, the leader may find members engaging in work restriction or other disruptive behaviour in order to gain attention.

Situation 2

+2 This action (LR–LT) best allows the group to derive its own solution to the problem.

+1 This action (HR–LT) is appropriate if the problem continues since it involves interpersonal relationships.

−1 This action (HT–HR) may be appropriate if the problem intensifies; however, at this point the problem is not goal clarity or goal completion. The group has already demonstrated ability to meet deadlines and accomplish tasks.

−2 This action (HT–LR) would be too abrupt with a group at high levels of readiness. The problem is one of interpersonal relationships not direction and task accomplishment.

Situation 3

+1 This action (HR–LT) provides an environment in which a group at this readiness level will feel free to participate and provide some input to the change process.

−2 This action (HT–LR) is inappropriate since the group has demonstrated ability to produce results; the problem is one of implementing a major change.

−1 This 'hands-off' action (LR–LT) is appropriate for working on a day-to-day basis with a group at high levels of readiness but not when a leader has to make an intervention to implement a necessary change. While participation is appropriate, some direction is needed.

+2 This action (HT–HR) involves the group in the change process, but maintains some structure by having performance standards.

Situation 4

+2 This action (HT–LR) provides the directive leadership needed for this group to work in a productive manner.

+1 This action (HR–HR) may be appropriate if the group begins to develop and demonstrates some ability to meet deadlines and accomplish tasks.

−1 (HR–LT) Worrying about boss–follower relations at this time tends to reinforce the group's present inappropriate behaviour and, in the future, the leader may find the group engaging in work restriction or other disruptive behaviour in order to gain attention.

Situation 4

−2	This 'hands-off' action (LR–LT) only increases the probability that this behaviour will continue.

Situation 5

0	This 'hands-off' action (LR–LT) is appropriate for working with this group on a day-to-day basis, but not when a leader has to make an intervention to implement a major change.
+1	The relationship behaviour in this action (HT–HR) is appropriate in developing and implementing a change with a group within the goals of the total organization.
+2	This action (HR–LT) best demonstrates consideration and focuses group involvement on developing the change.
−2	This directive action (HT–LR) is inappropriate for a group that has demonstrated flexibility in its day-to-day operations; the problem is one of implementing a major change.

Reproduced with kind permission from Paul Roberts, Management Learning Resources.

Skill training

Much leadership training is now based on *skills theory*. Leadership skills such as information-gathering, interviewing, counselling, negotiating, motivating, and using feedback are assumed, like other social skills, to be organized hierarchically with a cognitive component ultimately governing behavioural responses. The leadership trainer therefore divides the training programme equally between improving the ability of trainees to develop adequate cognitive models of their staff and work situation and developing the behaviours associated with the skill through practice and feedback. For example, to improve trainees' skill in motivating staff the trainer would spend a session exploring theories of motivation with trainees using motivational theories to identify possible 'blocks' in organizations which reduce the inclination to work and 'boosters' which improve motivation.

In the next stage the trainer role-plays a member of the trainee's staff and is interviewed by the trainee, who uses the concepts acquired in the first session to guide the interview. This is followed by a feedback session in which the trainer and other trainees comment on the effectiveness of the interview in terms of how effectively the subordinate's current motivational state was diagnosed and to what extent the interview would have increased his or her motivation. Further practice interviews are arranged for the trainee on the basis of these comments and suggestions, and the procedure is repeated until the trainee's performance is considered satisfactory. Many other variants of this approach are possible. For example, in my organization each cognitive session and role-play is followed by a 1 : 1 mentoring session with the leader in order to establish how well the learning has transferred to the workplace. Trainees are also encouraged to keep a diary to record their experiences and to take every opportunity, such as lunch breaks, to discuss the issues raised by the skills training with other trainees.

A number of typologies have been developed which specify the nature and number of managerial skills the training needs to focus on. These differ in terms of the broadness of the skills they describe. We have seen the Ohio scales provide extremely broad behavioural categories. Others such as Alban-Metcalfe (1984), describe extremely specific 'micro-skills' which may be more useful in developing very particular competencies. A useful 'middle-range' typology was developed by Gary Yukl (1989) who describes leadership skills which are neither too specific nor too broad and which can be used as the basis of a 'leadership skills audit' to identify strengths and areas for development. Yukl provides a questionnaire to measure the relative presence of these leadership skills in supervisors and managers. What is particularly useful about Yukl's typology is that it does not concentrate solely on face-to-face interaction but emphasizes the key skills of networking and of negotiating a social order. The typology is set out in Table 8.2.

Conclusion

In this chapter we have explored the range of attempts to develop a better understanding of the dynamics of leadership and create training programmes which harness these insights. Human relations theorists have established a tradition which emphasizes an increased awareness of self and of group dynamics. They would argue the relationship-oriented style of leadership which emerges from an increased sensitivity to group dynamics, for example the ability to increase the reflexivity of a group, is preferable and more effective. In contrast, situational theorists assume that a leader's effectiveness is a result of the interaction of the leader with a situation. They train supervisors to analyse their own behaviour and leadership situation and to change aspects of either to produce a better fit. Skill theorists bring the insights of skill theory—clear specification of behavioural outcomes and an emphasis on practice and feedback—to develop a leader's ability to comprehend his or her staff and use these macro-cognitive changes to develop the micro-behavioural responses involved in skilled leadership. Each will persist and continue to be developed, and in their different ways will contribute to achieving the aims of the human relations movement set out some sixty years ago; to increase social skill and insights into the social dynamics of the workplace among supervisors and thus to reduce the level of social incompetence in the management of organizations.

Perhaps the main concern many have with leadership research is the extent to which it avoids broader issues of power and class. Leadership research, as we have seen, tends to locate power in the interpersonal skills of individuals and in the 'micro-environments'—situational contingencies they operate within. There is no sense of the presence of the social structures which cause organizational life often to be characterized by deeply entrenched power hierarchies. This criticism is essentially that an area of psychological research has overlooked or ignored the issues and debates within another area of the social sciences—sociology. Obviously, within this book we attempt to avoid this mistake by examining these broader parameters of control and authority within

Building relationships

Networking: Socializing informally, developing contacts with people who are a source of information and support and maintaining relationships through periodic interaction, including visits, telephone calls, and correspondence, and attendance at meetings and social events.

Supporting: Acting in a friendly and considerate manner, showing sympathy and support when someone is upset, listening to complaints and problems, looking out for someone's interests, providing helpful career advice, doing things to aid someone's career advancement.

Managing conflict and team-building: Encouraging and facilitating constructive resolution of conflict, fostering team-work and co-operation, and building identification with the organizational team or unit.

Influencing people

Motivating: Using influence techniques that appeal to emotions, values, or logic to generate enthusiasm for the work and commitment to task objectives, or to induce someone to carry out a request for support, co-operation, assistance, resources or authorization; also setting an example of proper behaviour by one's own actions.

Recognizing and rewarding: Providing praise, recognition and tangible rewards for effective performance, significant achievements, and special contributions; expressing respect and appreciation for someone's accomplishments.

Making decisions

Planning and organizing: Determining low-range objectives and strategies for adapting to environmental change, identifying necessary action steps to carry out a project of activity, allocating resources among activities according to priorities, and determining how to improve efficiency, productivity and co-operation with other parts of the organization.

Problem-solving: Identifying work-related problems, analysing problems in a systematic but timely manner to determine causes and find solutions, and acting decisively to implement solutions and deal with crises.

Consulting and delegating: Checking with people, before making changes that affect them, encouraging suggestions for improvement, inviting participation in decision-making, incorporating the ideas and suggestions of others in decisions, and allowing others to have substantial discretion in carrying out work activities and handling problems.

Giving–seeking information

Monitoring operations and environment: Gathering information about the progress and quality of work activities, the success or failure of activities or projects, and the performance of individual contributors; also, determining the needs of clients or users, and scanning the environment to detect threats and opportunities.

Informing: Disseminating relevant information about decisions, plans and activities to people who need it to do their work, providing written materials and documents, answering requests for technical information, and telling people about the organizational unit to promote its reputation.

Clarifying roles and objectives: Assigning tasks, providing direction in how to do the work, and communicating a clear understanding of job responsibilities, task objectives, deadlines, and performance expectations.

Table 8.2 Yukl's typology of management skills

organizations in later chapters. Readers will therefore benefit from the individual focus of leadership research and the broader sweep of sociological accounts.

Even within psychology some see leadership research in a similarly negative way. Some psychologists, for example, have argued that leadership research fosters notions of dependency—the regressive childlike need to be taken care of by someone more powerful. In other words, the leadership literature promotes our emotional and intellectual deskilling by encouraging—particularly in transformational leadership—the notion of a divide between those who can lead and those who can only follow. In doing so leadership research may even, unwittingly, psychologically legitimize the power structures sociologists criticize it for ignoring.

Study questions for Chapter 8

1 Are leaders born rather than made?
2 To what extent are the main traits associated with effective leadership well established?
3 What is the difference between a leader and a manager?
4 What features of the situation interact with a leader's style?
5 To what extent does leadership research support the idea of 'one best way' in leadership style?
6 Is charisma a trait?
7 To what extent is it possible to be a democratic leader?

Further reading

Bass, B. M. and Stogdill, R. M. (1990) *Handbook of Leadership*. New York: Free Press.

Burns, J. M. (1978) *Leadership*. New York: Harper and Row.

Gardner, H. (1997) *Leading Minds*. London: Harper Collins.

Georgiades, N. and MacDonell, R. (1998) *Leadership for Competitive Advantage*. Chichester: Wiley.

Grint, K. (ed.) (1997) *Leadership: Classical, Contemporary, and Critical Approaches*. Oxford: Oxford University Press.

Kets de Vries, M. F. R. (1989) *Prisoners of Leadership*. Chichester: Wiley.

—— (1993) *Leaders, Fools and Impostors*. San Francisco, Calif.: Jossey-Bass.

Komaki, J. L. (1998) *The Operant Model of Effective Supervision*. London: Routledge.

Kotter, J. P. (1996) *Leading Change*. Boston, Mass.: Harvard Business School Press.

Pauchant, T. C. *et al.* (1995) *In Search of Meaning*. San Francisco, Calif.: Jossey-Bass.

Section 3

Patterns of Work

Patterns of Work

The focus in earlier parts of this book has been on the psychological processes acting on individuals and their immediate environment in workgroups. Factors in the historical, social, and economic environment—the wider context in which work is carried out—were not really considered in their own right. In the chapters in Section Two where we examined motivation to work, the improvement of workgroup experiences, and job satisfaction, we took for granted the reasons why these alternative forms of work organization were needed in the first place. However, it is now necessary to retrace our steps and think more thoroughly about the nature of work in modern industrial society. We turn to a *sociological* analysis of work and the broader structural and processual factors affecting workplace behaviour.

In Chapter 9 we begin by looking at the basic forces that shape work and define an industrial economy like our own. This rests on an examination of the classical writings on work of Marx and Weber, the basis of much modern thinking. Other important variables which resurface throughout the following chapters, notably technology and skill, are located within this framework. In addition, the theories and concepts of a modern master, Foucault, are examined. Foucault has probably informed debates about work more than any other recent writer—particularly as regards the nature of power in modern industrial economies—and there are important continuities with the classical writings. In one way or another all adopt a historical approach, and emphasize emerging forms of work organization.

Modern forms of administering work, under the approach developed here, are seen essentially as structures of control and authority. Hence the question of workplace conflict is integral to the account. However, people react to constraint in complex ways. The account of the employment relationship in Chapter 10 therefore emphasizes patterns of consent as well as conflict. Industrial social science has usually confined itself to the study of informal conflict based on workgroups, leaving trade-union action to be the subject-matter of industrial relations. To an extent, however, this is an artificial distinction, and both types of conflict are examined here.

The strict division between jobs described above is the basis of control and efficiency in organizations, but it has produced the kind of fragmented, routine work associated with many of the problems of industry. Hence the movement to provide alternative work designs. In Chapter 11 we close the section by describing and evaluating these attempts to 'humanize' the workplace. Though social scientists began with a narrow focus on motivation and job satisfaction, many have broadened their scope to include technological and social features of the workplace—changes in job content, provision for group working, and levels of participation. However, this is also an area that over the years has been much affected by fashions in management thinking, and we review the current popularity of trends towards employee 'involvement' and 'empowerment'; we also consider the progress that has been achieved in providing work environments that are humanly fulfilling. Finally, work redesign as a topic is unusual because of its strong associations with one particular company; the fame of the Volvo experiments has provided a series of models of good practice in redesign, and we conclude the chapter with a case-study of the Swedish car company.

9 Work—The Classical Approach

Summary points and learning objectives

By the end of this chapter you will:

- be aware of how the *classical writings* of Marx and Weber inform an understanding of the nature of work;
- be aware of the contribution of *Foucault* to modern debates;
- understand a range of *basic concepts* and concerns in the analysis of work: alienation, rationalization, the labour process, technology, control and power;
- appreciate the importance of a *historical* approach for understanding modern work systems;
- see the basis in classical writing of *current debates* that have sprung up around these issues.

Introduction

Questions about the nature of work in modern society have to begin by asking about the main concentrations of employment and the types of work that most people do. A cursory examination of the occupational skills structure shows what is perhaps an obvious point, namely that 'lower-level' jobs, in services and industry, constitute the main groupings of employment. These are primarily jobs with a low content of skills and relatively poor pay. The upshot is that the experience of work for a great many people is of jobs which are uninteresting and offer little in terms of a career or hope of advancement.

Of course, this picture needs to be qualified; certainly there is a great deal of *variation* in work. Although the largest single categories of employment are unskilled manual and low-grade service work, many people have satisfying professional or managerial jobs, while others exercise technical or manual skills. There is also an important *subjective* element. People experience work in different ways; and what may be an unrewarding job, done out of pure necessity, to one person, might be perfectly satisfactory to someone else. In a time of persistent unemployment and when recession constantly seems to threaten, it can be argued that people's expectations of work change: in more straitened times perhaps many people regard any job as a good job.

None the less, it remains to true that as far as objective factors are concerned, a high proportion of work probably affords little in the way of individual fulfilment or hope beyond the immediate present. In order to understand this we need to develop an analysis of the forces shaping the jobs performed by the bulk of employed people.

Of the various ideas that need to be taken into account the theory of *alienation* developed by Karl Marx is of central importance. The notion that modern conditions of work produce alienated labour has long been influential, both directly on our understanding of work and in terms of the alternative theories it has evoked. The legacy of Marx means that we now have a much more detailed understanding of the analysis of work as a *labour process*.

Another of sociology's founding fathers, Max Weber, also attracts lasting interest. Weber's influence has been immense and one of his main contributions was his analysis of bureaucracy. This will be discussed later in Chapter 14, but behind his theory of bureaucracy lay the conviction that this particular form of organization represented the most rational expression of economic order, and Weber's ideas concerning the *rationalization* of labour are pertinent to our discussion here.

In this chapter, then, we shall first examine the basis which exists in classical theory for an analysis of the work process. We will then briefly turn to historical developments, and to the rise of modern systems of work organization. We go on to single out *technology*, which has been regarded as having a distinctive impact of industrial growth, though at this stage discussion is confined to the classical 'political economy of mechanization'. Finally, we conclude by examining the work of the French social scientist Foucault, who, although a more contemporary figure, in certain respects continues these classic themes, and who has played a major role in defining the nature of current debates about to work.

Marx, Weber, and the critique of labour

Alienated labour

Alienation is one of the formative concepts that have helped us understand the nature of industrial society; for Marx it encompassed the whole of his theory. Alienation represented the underlying 'law of motion' of capitalism and the central condition of that society. It is important, however, to know how Marx's ideas developed, as alienation is a concept that has been misunderstood and misused. In particular, it became commonplace to equate alienation loosely with feelings of 'dissatisfaction' with work. Marx's usage was very different. For him alienation was a concrete process of social change, though one which certainly affected people's subjective experiences.

Central to Marx's approach was a 'materialist' view of labour as the basis of human society. The transformation of the natural world through shared labour, initially out of the physical needs for survival, brings the social and cultural world into existence. This is true of all societies, but in advanced ones labour is carried out under definite 'relations of production', and here the institutions of political power shape the forms of useful collective work. Within capitalist class relations, in particular, the creation of a material and social world becomes a distorted and degraded activity. Human labour becomes alienated labour, an idea Marx first put forward among his early writings in the *1844 Manuscripts* (1975, pp. 279–400).

What constitutes the alienation of labour?

Firstly, the fact that labour is *external* to the worker, i.e. does not belong to his essential being; that he therefore does not confirm himself in his work, but denies himself, feels miserable and not happy, does not develop free mental and physical energy, but mortifies his flesh and ruins his mind. . . . His labour is therefore not voluntary but forced, it is *forced labour*. It is therefore not the satisfaction of a need but a mere *means* to satisfy needs outside itself. Its alien character is clearly demonstrated by the fact that as soon as no physical or other compulsion exists it is shunned like the plague. (1975, p. 326)

Marx set out a number of dimensions of alienation, describing the impact of class relations on work and on the wider human community. Firstly, workers are divorced both from the *product* of their labour and from the *process* of production. In other words, the product and the manner in which work is performed are controlled by the employer by virtue of his ownership of capital. The fact that labour is 'external' to the worker, a mere means to an end, follows from this. These economic factors have social consequences in that *people become alienated from themselves*. The forces that strip work of its creativity in effect remove from it the truly human element, reducing workers virtually to the level of animals which produce only out of instinct or for immediate need. Also, a broader social alienation occurs: *people stand in an instrumental relationship to one another*, defined in terms of the economic power they command rather than their worth as human beings.

Marx contrasted the might of capital—the huge accumulation of private property, the development of a central state, the private ownership of cultural and artistic products—with the impoverishment of the mass of working people. When people lack control over their own labour, the material things people themselves have created confront them as hostile entities. They become subject to the industrial and technological systems others have designed and built, and they are powerless in the face of market forces. Alienation thus produces the unequal and polarized society in terms of which Marx viewed modern industrial capitalism. He saw in 'this whole system of estrangement' a supreme irony. For at just the point in history where the powers of science and industry conferred a degree of mastery over society's enemies—the natural world (disease, shortage of food) and fear of superstition—so the class divisions in capitalism negated these achievements for the majority of people. Humankind fell victim to itself.

The labour process

Until fairly recently, a commonplace criticism of Marx had been that he gradually abandoned his earlier 'humanistic' concern with alienation for the strictly 'economic' analysis found in his later writings, notably in *Capital, Volume 1*. However, it now tends to be acknowledged that he did not reject the idea of alienation. Rather, he focused more narrowly on 'the act of production within labour' and developed an account of alien-ation within the work process. We shall briefly explore some of the main ideas from this approach (for a more detailed account, see Thompson, 1989, pp. 38–64).

At the heart of Marx's theory of the labour process—and for him the defining feature of capitalist society—was the emergence of the wage relationship and of labour as a *commodity*. When labour itself is bought and sold on a market of exchange, it becomes a cost of production, an object of commercial investment, and this underlines the dehuman-ization of work. Commodity-status also points to the essential insecurity of much mod-ern employment. Certain things can improve a person's chances of a job (qualifications, trade union protection) but in the end society provides no natural right to work.

However, labour is unique in being an active human commodity. While it contains great potential for productive work, workers may resist their exploitation. In this con-text, Marx suggested that the exchange between capital and labour is not a simple exchange of wages for work. Rather, the employer first buys the *labour power* of the worker, expressed as an agreement to work for a certain time, and it is then the employer's responsibility to convert this potential into real labour—to set employees to work, in other words. The notion of labour as a 'variable' or 'potential' input to produc-tion draws attention to the struggle for control of the labour process, and to the employer's motivation to intensify the use of labour.

Thompson (1990) has identified four key features of labour process theory. First, the importance of the employment relationship as the basic producer of wealth. The employer–worker relationship is the basic class relationship, and changes here provide the main 'motor' of change in the rest of the economy and society. Secondly, the employment relationship is highly dynamic. Competing capitalists have to seek ever greater rates of profit, and hence the labour process will continuously be transformed in pursuit of greater productivity. Thirdly, capital is compelled to increase its control over labour. The means of control exist outside the labour process, and the degree of control over labour is never total—none the less, a generalized 'control imperative' within the work process does exist. And fourthly, the employment relationship is a relationship both of production and of exploitation. Though it contains aspects of co-operation, conflict remains an endemic and structural feature.

In sum, Marx's analysis points to the divisive nature of the capitalist labour process. Pre-capitalist work processes, he pointed out, were limited in their productivity and in the extent of the control of any ruling group by the need to rely upon handicraft skills. Effort and efficiency were subjective factors held in check by the worker. In pre-indus-trial society, where people had control of their working lives to a much greater extent, the historical record shows that a much greater value was placed on creative leisure, and work and leisure were closely integrated (Marx, 1974, p. 381). However, all this began to change under a capitalist economy. The alienation of labour from production then became the root cause of industrial conflict, representing the real basis of broader social conflicts and the massive inequalities of wealth and power that characterize mod-ern industrial societies.

Weber and rationalization

Modern thinking on work has also been greatly influenced by Max Weber, whose ideas on rationalization have implications that are similar in many ways to the Marxist idea of alienation.

Weber regarded the spread of rational behaviour as the central dynamic of western capitalist societies. In the transition from pre-industrial society, religious and mystical paradigms for coming to terms with the world declined and gave way to secular forms of explanation based on empirical science; this culminated in the market economy and the rise of industrial capitalism. In particular, the impact of rational criteria on economic action was for Weber the decisive factor which distinguished modern industrial capitalism from more traditional forms of society.

In the last resort the factor which produced capitalism is the rational permanent enterprise, rational accounting, rational technology and rational law, but again not these alone. Necessary complementary factors were the rational spirit, the rationalisation of the conduct of life in general, and a rational economic effect. (Quoted in Lee and Newby, 1983, p. 189)

This 'spirit of rationality', which pervaded economic and social life, was especially apparent in the ways in which work was administered and organized. Rationality here refers to the use of formal procedures (capital accounting, systematic management, corporate planning, etc.) in the control of economic enterprises. The point Weber emphasized was that only formal administration provided the basis for operations to be *calculable*. Being able to plan ahead with some degree of certainty is an essential requirement when large amounts of resources have to be committed. Both the massive level of provision in the modern state and the increasing size and complexity of modern industry require that organizations meet forecasts and perform predictably. This would be so, Weber argued, whether in a capitalist market economy or a centrally to planned socialist one.

Calculative logic was not, however, the only attribute of a modern society. Here Weber contrasted *formal* with *substantive* rationality. Formal rationality referred to the calculation of economic means, discussed above, while substantive rationality referred to the persistent intervention of human ends and values. The two rationales were 'always in principle in conflict', since human needs are not necessarily met by rational calculation (Weber, 1964, p. 185). This viewpoint was the cause of an undercurrent of profound pessimism in Weber's thought, for although he stressed the effectiveness of rational administration, he believed that this mode of action would inevitably spread to and rule all areas of social life. In this, Weber was author of a fundamental criticism of modern society: the fear of all 'ultimate values' eventually becoming submerged in a society dominated by the cold logic of formal decision-making.

The spread of formal rationality entailed 'the concrete appropriation of economic resources by owners' (Weber, 1964, p. 247). The calculability of large-scale enterprise and the autonomy of workers were, Weber stressed, polar opposites. To the extent that formal rationality was enforced, the worker had to be completely excluded from any role in the authority structure of the firm. For Weber, this was the upshot of inevitable technical developments. Technical efficiency depended upon managements having 'extensive control over the selection and modes of use of workers'; any 'rights to participate in management' in practice led to 'irrational obstacles to efficiency' (p. 247).

From a historical point of view, the expropriation of labour has developed since the sixteenth century in an economy characterized by a progressive development of the market system, both extensively and intensively, by the sheer technical superiority and actual indispensability of a type of autocratic management oriented to the particular market situations, and by the structure of sheer power relationships in society. (1964, p. 247)

For Weber, then, rationalization in the modern world meant the transformation of human relationships into impersonal exchanges under the compulsion of technical rationality. The normal, spontaneous qualities of human society are obliterated as work organizations concentrate on the *means* to achieve economic goals, while the goals themselves may become increasingly meaningless. Rational conduct ultimately produces a society that

is bound to the technical and economic conditions of machine production, which today determine the lives of all the individuals who are born into this mechanism, not only those directly concerned with economic acquisition, with irresistible force. Perhaps it will so determine them until the last ton of fossilized coal is burnt. (Weber, quoted in Salaman, 1981, p. 59)

Emerging forms of work organization

Another central concept in analyses of work is that of *control*. We saw above that conflicts of interest between employers and employees bring about a fundamental problem of the control of labour. From this it follows that work is often designed for the chief purpose of facilitating control, and that the historical development of forms of work organization is to be understood in terms of employer's strategies to secure control in changing circumstances.

Of course, controls inside the workplace cannot be divorced from wider legitimation of managerial authority that derives from the ownership of capital. The threat of dismissal to workers is the ultimate sanction behind managerial authority. The freedom to dispose of assets (which may involve threats to close a plant, or to transfer production) can also be decisive. None the less, the authority delegated to management by virtue of the legal rights of ownership is not in itself normally sufficient. In addition, there are important structural controls of labour which derived from the basic form of work organization, the modern factory.

The factory system

Throughout the seventeenth and eighteenth centuries in Britain, the system of production of the feudal and mercantile era underwent radical transformation, culminating in the Industrial Revolution of the 1780s. Independent producers in agriculture and in handicraft industries came under the sway of capitalists, and production was being organized on an increasingly large scale. All paths led to the development of the factory as the fundamental form of organizing production.

None of this denies the purely economic and technical advantages of the factory system. Vastly improved economies of scale were possible, as was the later application of machinery and the new power source, steam. Also, in the developing markets of the nineteenth century, goods of a comparable quality and specification were in demand, a type of output only possible where methods could be standardized. Yet, as Marglin (1974) has pointed out, it was only as this system gradually came to predominate, and technical improvements were diverted exclusively into it, that its economic advantages came to be fore. The prime motive behind the *initial* development of the factory system was enhanced control.

The very fact of work being performed in organizations is itself a control of labour and the basis of other controls. In the preceding domestic system there were limits on the extent to which work could be regulated. With individual tasks dispersed over different households, and even communities, cottage systems were capable of developing only fairly rudimentary forms of control, and employers were often more interested in the profits to be gained from trading off occupational communities (supplying them with materials and selling the finished products) than they were in organizing production itself. But with the advent of the factory all this changed. When workers were gathered under one roof, their activities could be tightly supervised, tasks could be assigned, output accurately measured, and times of attendance checked.

In terms of the industrial discipline that could be imposed, a *division of labour* was also crucial in forging the link between efficiency and control. The splitting up of work into specialized functions, organized by department and section, raised the productive powers of labour at the same time as it enabled the central control of the labour process. Most observers of the early factory system were surprised by the extreme fragmentation of work, which was qualitatively different from anything that had gone before. Marx spoke of the worker being transformed into a 'detail labourer', with the factory itself becoming the 'collective labourer' where tasks were integrated. Before Marx, Adam Smith had focused specifically on the division of labour as the basis of economic prosperity. Indeed, he begins *The Wealth of Nations* with a detailed account of the productivity gains attendant on 'a proper division and combination' of operations. 'The different operations into which the making of a pin, or of a metal button, is subdivided, are all of them much more simple, and the dexterity of the person, of whose life it has been the sole business to perform them, is usually much greater' (1982, p. 113). However, Smith had mixed feelings about this form of work organization: while he marvelled at its contribution to productivity, he was not blind to the less desirable social consequences. He saw, as did Marx, that the fragmentation of work was the chief cause of labour becoming a degraded activity—a fact no less true of the 'manufactories' of the eighteenth century than of today's assembly lines.

Modern management and Taylorism

Another aspect of work organization that reflects the class nature of production involves the *intensification* of work. Marx, on this point, distinguished the 'formal' from the 'real' control of labour. Nineteenth-century capitalism inherited a labour process based on artisan production, and in the early factories previously independent crafts-men became wage workers. Marx referred to this as formal subjugation, because at this stage labour still retained its craft nature. Real subjugation arose, Marx suggested, when capital began transforming work itself from its archaic forms.

The Factory Acts of the 1840s and 1850s were an early impetus to labour intensification. Previously there had been very little legal control of employment condi-tions; but the Acts placed a limit on the length of the working day, and on other abuses like the use of child labour, which encouraged employers to concentrate on raising pro-ductivity. Marx notes that employers' interest in *efficiency* greatly increased from that time forward (1974, pp. 442–51).

Still, for most of the nineteenth century the means to increase productive intensity had not progressed much beyond the basic controls of the factory itself. During the last quarter of the century, however, modern methods of the systematic control of labour came into use. These originated in the scientific management movement pioneered by the American, F. W. Taylor. Beginning in the 1890s, Taylor developed a 'science of work', the methods of which involved the detailed study of work processes with a view to increasing efficiency and labour productivity. Tasks were carefully observed and broken down into component actions, which were then measured on the basis of standard times—hence the more popular name of 'time and motion' study.

The far-reaching effects of scientific management, or 'Taylorism', for work in con-temporary society have been widely recognized. Weber, for example, spoke of the Taylor system as the pioneer of the application of rationalized methods of work (1964, p. 261). More recently, Braverman in his influential study *Labor and Monopoly Capital* (1974) has been particularly important in drawing attention to the general principles of scientific management that Taylor set out, and to their implications for the 'degra-dation' of work.

First, Taylor recommended the most detailed division of labour that was practically possible: relatively complex tasks should be split up into the maximum number of sub-tasks. He insisted that the skills which had built up within a workforce—skills of hand and eye, knowledge and experience—should be absorbed within the management func-tion and converted into formal procedures. Management should assume 'the burden of gathering together all of the traditional knowledge which in the past has been pos-sessed by the workmen and then of classifying, tabulating, and reducing this knowledge to rules, laws, and formulae' (quoted in Braverman, 1974, p. 112). Taylor also recom-mended the 'divorce of conception from execution'. All thinking about work—planning, securing of supplies, maintenance of equipment—should be managed by a specialist staff. The worker should simply have to execute the task in hand, or become an 'opera-tor', to use the modern term. Thus Taylor stressed that 'All possible brainwork should be removed from the shop and centred in the planning or laying out department' (Braverman, 1974, p. 113). Abercrombie and Urry (1983) have usefully summarized the 'Taylorist strategy for capital', and the manner in which it transformed existing labour practices, as follows:

... as long as workers knew more than their managers, then management would have to persuade the workers to cooperation. This could clearly be seen in relation to piecework—since management did not know how long in fact it took to do each piece of work; it was rational for workers to ... restrict output. Taylor realised that the only long-term solution to this from the viewpoint of capital was to devise a new system of capitalist control that would overcome the rational tendency for workers to restrict output ... this could only be achieved by transforming the very form of knowledge possessed by workers. (p. 101)

The advantages to employers of adopting such a strategy are overwhelming. Labour is cheapened by reducing its skilled component, the flexibility of labour is increased by simplifying tasks, and there is a great potential for generally streamlining production. Unnecessary tasks can be eliminated, physical layouts improved and work speeded up. Taylor himself conducted thousands of consultancy exercises in his time and often achieved notable increases in output and productivity. Above all, with work designed by staff specialists and integrated within a production plan, management's control of production was intensified in a way which hitherto had not been possible.

Not least important was the *ideological* aspect. Systematic measurement and methods of standardizing tasks, it was claimed, made this a 'scientific' study of work. Standards of effort were argued to have been arrived at by purely rational methods. At bottom this claim was spurious because, as critics have to pointed out, work study is always dependent upon agreed notions of what is a fair and reasonable pace of work (Baldamus, 1961; Braverman, 1974, p. 86). Nevertheless, managerial authority has been legitimized to an important degree because of the 'neutral' language of scientific management.

Finally, it is important to consider the *historical context* in which scientific management was introduced. Allied to industrialization in the United States, there was a rapid growth in the size of the economy and labour force. America industrialized on the basis of the then new technologies, like steel, chemicals and mass production. Littler (1982) points to the labour crisis created in these new industries as workers entered jobs lacking any traditional standards of pay and effort. In this fluid situation, scientific management represented an employers' initiative to establish a formal system of discipline, one which they very definitely controlled.

Littler has also stressed that Taylorism was chiefly important for extending *direct* managerial control. Up to the 1880s, the most common form of shopfloor organization was based upon the authority of subcontractors and supervisors. Labour masters, gang bosses and foremen were powerful figures in the early factory system recruiting workers and organizing payment and discipline. However, with economic growth, these personal and informal methods of control became a barrier to efficiency. Taylorism helped to eliminate such systems of internal contracting, and provided a form of industrial discipline that enabled owners to employ labour directly.

Like all aspects of industrial development, these methods were adopted unevenly. Their concrete impact varied widely, and other methods that modified Taylor's original system were developed. Yet Taylor's doctrine was taken up enthusiastically in the United States, and by the 1920s and 1930s had spread to continental Europe and Britain. In important respects, this started the process of diversification into specialist functions, such as production control and industrial engineering, which laid the basis of modern management as a rational system of administering work.

Technology and work

So far we have seen how a wide range of developments account for the rise of individual societies. They include the spread of market relationships and the growth of the money economy, the organization of work in the shape of the factory system, employment as the dominant relationship of production, and generally rational modes of thought and action. Of all such preconditions, however, the one that is linked most directly with industrialism itself is *technology*. This is because advancing technology can be identified with the high rates of *change* that are a defining feature of modern societies. It was essentially the Industrial Revolution, and the first development of machinery which came with it, which brought about the rapid pace of innovation we are now familiar with. Since then the *technical* aspect of change has continued to provide a powerful symbol of conditions that we think of as 'modern'.

Commentators on the early industrial scene, like Marx and Adam Smith, perceived the close link between technology and the way in which work is organized. The imposition of the factory system, with its concentration of the labour force and intricate division of labour, actually made possible the development of machinery. Complex and skilled craft work had to be reorganized along rational lines before it could be mechanized. Hence a dynamic relationship exists between work structuring and mechanization, the one progressing under the impetus of the other. Both Marx and Smith had mixed feelings about the factory system, recognizing that the massive increases in the productive powers of labour seemed to go hand in hand with the subjugation of people to work. Marx in particular was preoccupied with mechanization (1974, pp. 351–475) and his critique remains the basis of many more recent attacks on modern technology. He believed that the fiercely competitive nature of capitalism compelled employers to force up productivity, and that mechanization was their chief means of doing this.

In its fundamental form, conflict between technology and labour rested on the constantly changing relation between technical capital (machines, plant, equipment) and human capital (living labour). Marx believed that the overall trend favoured an expanding technology. Although many modern economists would disagree—recognizing that industrial economies are becoming increasingly capital-intensive, but not accepting that this necessarily occurs at the worker's expense—Marx believed that over the long term capital intensification diminished the contribution of living labour.

Marx detailed a number of aspects of the 'strife between workman and machine'. Machinery was the great leveller, reducing any special techniques and skills needed in work, so that human labour was rendered interchangeable and easy to substitute. In this is found a central theme of labour process theory, that capitalist work organization has a long-run tendency to produce 'homogeneous' labour. Not only did machinery displace labour, it created actual unemployment. Marx thought that the rate at which labour was displaced by machinery would always outpace the rate at which new work was created via general economic expansion. Hence the tendency of capitalism to generate a 'reserve army' of unemployed people was in large part attributed to technological advances. Marx also stressed the enslavement of workers to machines, particularly in terms of the perpetuation of working hours. This is because machinery, especially complex machinery, runs the risk of becoming obsolete even before it is worn out. Hence employers will be anxious to have it used intensively to extract its full value before obsolescence takes over.

In short, Marx believed that under pressure of existing class relationships machinery played a key role in the alienation of labour. Much of this still rings true, and is especially consistent with the economic problems of recessionary times. Modern ideas about the 'capital-deepening' effects of new technology have led to fears that economies are now so capital-intensive and productive that unemployment has become a structural feature, and of course being unemployed and unable to participate in the market economy is an obvious expression of alienation. We also find concern being expressed about the change to highly intensive forms of production. Just-in-time and other 'Japanese' systems (discussed more fully in Chapter 20) now dominate world manufacture, and in them workers are under pressure to be ever available and wholly committed to the company regime.

The highly negative view of technology that these arguments present is in certain ways justified. We have seen that some of the very first observers of emerging technology in the Industrial Revolution were scathing. Modern observers tend to see more possibilities for benefit and improvement, but these are often precarious and vulnerable to economic forces. And while alternative technologies exist (as we will see in Chapter 11), they too are usually uncertain and subject to the vagaries of labour markets. Set against these forms of labour displacement and intensification there are some far more positive views of technology—perspectives which do not just grudgingly admit benefits but see modern technologies as a liberating force. These reflect common-sense views about the progressive role of technology and they continue to inform discussion. So any impression of a closed debate would be much mistaken and whole new debates on the themes introduced above have opened up in recent years. New technologies and the wave of applications of microelectronics in particular have revived questions about the influence of technology on work. However, an account of this will be deferred for later chapters; for the present we will round off this chapter with a consideration of the work of the French social scientist, Michel Foucault.

Foucault and disciplinary power

Like Marx and Weber, Foucault was interested in the nature of power in society and the analysis he developed has been extremely influential—though difficult to 'place' in the sense of locating it in a tradition or tracing its predecessors. While there obviously are similarities and links with other writers, his theory is the product of a singular approach. Nevertheless, Foucault measures up to the standards of classical writings in so far as his theory is both profoundly historical and operates at the broadest social level.

The view of power that we derive from an analysis like that of Marx, and to a lesser extent Weber, is essentially structural. It reflects a dominant set of interests, or a regime of ideas, that is somehow imposed on the majority. For Foucault the weakness of structural approaches is that they fail to distinguish the realities of power, and have yet to catch up with the changed nature of power in 'post-modern' society. The approach developed by Foucault has stressed a *disciplinary* notion of power. This is a distinctive and unusual theory but one certainly worthy of attention.

Foucault begins by identifying older, archaic forms of power, which he calls *sovereign power*. In traditional society this emanated from the monarch, but the main point is that sovereign power is institutional in nature; it stands outside those under power and is imposed as a kind of superstructure. In *Discipline and Punish* (1979), Foucault develops this theme in a historical analysis of criminality. It may seem curious to take 'deviant' behaviour as a starting point, but the punishment of crime is seen as a generalizable 'political tactic'. Up to the eighteenth century, punishment involved elements of torture and public spectacle; the stocks, the chain gang and the public exhibition of prisoners were normal. The point about such punishments, Foucault argues, is that they were symptoms of a particular kind of power. A policy of terror and atrocity against the wrongdoer represented the sovereign exacting vengeance and was designed to make people aware of that power.

Foucault goes into considerable detail on this point (including grisly descriptions of public executions) in order to demonstrate the total contrast with modern forms of power. During the eighteenth century and by the beginning of the nineteenth, 'the great spectacle of physical punishment disappeared' and was replaced by imprisonment. Large-scale projects of prison building were accompanied by programmes of rehabilitation. This, says Foucault, was the beginning of the disciplinary age. Whereas sovereign power was external, brutal and dramatic, disciplinary power is mundane and based on the surveillance of behaviour. In one sense this idea is not new. It was certainly part of the Weberian tradition to emphasize indirect and 'rational' forms of control. Weber was concerned with the 'iron cage of bureaucracy', and with modern systems of calculation that submerged all natural and localized human relations. But with Foucault we see a broader development of these ideas, and disciplinary power identified as the basis of modern forms of stratification.

The movement from one project to the other, from a schema of exceptional discipline to one of a generalized surveillance, rests on a historical transformation: the gradual extension of the mechanisms of discipline throughout the 17th and 18th centuries, their spread through the whole social body, the formation of what might be called in general the disciplinary society. (1979, p. 209)

Under Foucault's conception of power there is no centre, no superstructure, no imposition from above. Instead power is *systematic* in the precise sense of being integral to all social relationships. Disciplinary power is insinuated in daily routines, it involves the 'meticulous observation' of action and the 'penetration of regulation into even the smallest details of everyday life'. The principles of disciplinary power are those of the enclosure of personnel on functioning sites (factories, hospitals, prisons) and the partitioning of behaviour. The full range of modern organizations contain many differences of appearance, but they share the same underlying programmes of power and a common parent in the prison: 'prisons resemble factories, schools, barracks, hospitals, which all resemble prisons'. Other instruments of disciplinary power that Foucault was interested in include procedures like the examination, the investigation, and systematic training. These constrain human motivation into 'collectively useful aptitudes' through the organization of occupations and professions (also aptly called disciplines).

They contribute to what Foucault called the *normalizing judgement*. The process of normalization is 'one of the great instruments of power' in modern society; it involves the establishment of limits of accepted behaviour, standards to be achieved. Those who comply may be rewarded, but anyone falling outside the routines is automatically defined as deviant. These techniques of control, if in the form of distributions of attainment, will by their very nature exclude some participants. The ones who are bottom of the list, or in the last quartile, are defined as the unpromotable, the ignorant, the incapable.

The panoptic schema and power/knowledge

Foucault conjures one particularly compelling image of disciplinary power: the *Panopticon* of the English social reformer, Jeremy Bentham. This was an architectural design the principle of which was a circular building with an observation tower at the centre. The outer perimeter was divided into cells with windows facing out for light, and inward so that each space could be constantly observed. Bentham devised the Panopticon as the basis of prison design, and although largely forgotten today the idea had a considerable impact on the great nineteenth-century projects of penal reform. Foucault was struck by the sheer economy of the Panopticon, the way in which 'just a gaze' could hold sway over a mass of individuals. It represented a 'technology of power designed to solve the problems of surveillance' (1980, p. 147).

. . . the major effect of the Panopticon is to induce in the inmate a state of conscious and permanent visibility that ensures the automatic functioning of power. So to arrange things that the surveillance is permanent in its effects, even if it is discontinuous in its action; that the perfection of power should tend to render its actual exercise unnecessary; that this architectural apparatus should be a machine for creating and sustaining a power relation independent of the person who exercises it; in short that the inmates should be caught up in a power situation of which they themselves are the bearers. (1979, p. 201)

Of course, Bentham's design was impractical—a fixed observatory could hardly accommodate the divisions of labour and communications networks found in modern organizations—and Foucault was well aware of this. But he saw the Panopticon as a kind of image or metaphor of disciplinary power. A key aspect of the panoptic image is the *visibility* of the prisoner. The basic function of a centre of observation, Foucault suggests, is fulfilled by modern institutions like the training of professional and educational institutions.

This idea has been translated into organizational terms in studies of the accounting function. Accounting has become the universal language of business, and accountancy an extremely influential corporate profession. The reason that accountants are so central to managerial power, it is argued, is that they make the implicit visible. The potential for activities in organizations to be concealed is enormous. How do managers know that the operations they are supposed to be supervising are working to plan? Accounting provides the techniques for achieving this. Accountants are able to evaluate inputs and outputs and aggregate complex activities into money flows, and so enable management to evaluate business performance. In this vein Miller and O'Leary (1987) have stressed that accountants assist in the social construction of the 'governable person'. In industry the production of disciplined work forces has usually been attributed to groups like supervisors and production engineers; but accountants too produce standards of effort and contribute to normalized assessments that are the basis of rational power.

Foucault was interested in the role of 'experts' of all kinds. Experts themselves have gone through lengthy training which reproduces in them aspects of disciplinary power; they then become active agents who produce normalized judgements of others. As Burrell points out; 'Today, a "normalizing" function is performed by a whole series of subsidiary authorities who swarm around the "disciplines". For example, educationists, psychiatrists, psychological experts, members of the prison service and magistrates all form parallel judgments of the "cases" coming before them' (1988, p. 227). However, there is more to this than just the monitoring of activity. Foucault employed the term *power/knowledge*. Note, it is not power *and* knowledge, in the sense that we would all recognise of 'knowledge giving power'. For Foucault the relationship between knowledge and power was more intimate and dynamic; experts actually create the categories with which they establish factual knowledge.

Of central importance here is the idea of 'discourse'. This refers to the specific languages of occupations and professions—the sales talk, the technical jargon and so on. Professional discourses are an independent source of power, such that experts 'through their talk' can define situations and create key areas of knowledge. Thus if the psychiatrist diagnoses a person (as schizophrenic, say), the attachment of the label will empower psychiatric professionals with control over the patient as regards incarceration and treatment. But the central item of knowledge (the patient is schizophrenic) and the category itself (schizophrenia) were created by the discourse of the profession in the first place.

Parallel power

As well as arguing that modern organizations are all 'alike' in sharing an underlying power dynamic, Foucault also argued for the 'difference' and distinctive origins of organizations. Burrell (1988, p. 227) points out that Foucault was concerned not with generalized power but with parallel centres developed around specific social problems.

Foucault's historic research into areas like medicine, psychiatry and criminology showed at what point the spark of disciplinary power jumped from one area to another.

Moreover, penal organizations themselves had antecedents, and in tracing these Foucault uncovered an entirely new set of historic connections. Curiously enough they derived from the social responses to disease. The reaction to the leper in early medieval times was one of exclusion; the later reaction to the plague involved detailed regulations for the containment of the disease in any village it had struck, very much akin to disciplinary power.

This enclosed segmented space, observed at every point, in which the individuals are inserted in a fixed place, in which the slightest movements are supervised, in which all events are recorded, in which an uninterrupted work of writing links the centre and periphery, in which power is exercised without division, according to a continuous hierarchical figure, in which each individual is located, examined and distributed among the living beings, the sick and the dead—all this constitutes a compact model of the disciplinary mechanism. (1979, p. 197)

These two 'projects'—'the leper and his separation; the plague and its segmentations'—Foucault suggests were merged in the great 'carceral' institutions of the nineteenth century—the prisons, approved schools, asylums and workhouses. The new distributions of power for 'correcting the abnormal' then became the model for the divisions of labour in productive organizations. In particular, the problem that industrial capitalism poses is that of the use of mass labour. Owners effectively have to entrust their wealth (technology, materials, etc.) to workers; hence, Foucault points out, the strong emphasis in early capitalism on morality—strict timekeeping, abstinence, a fair day's work—and the creation of crime and criminals as separate categories. This contrasted with the 'amiable tolerance' of crime that characterized earlier centuries (1980, p. 41).

In a sense this represents a similar approach to Weber's. Weber saw the modern organization as deriving from a particular type of social control, the bureaucracy, and traced its historic antecedents. (He was much interested in the ancient Chinese civil service, military organization and church as precursors of bureaucracy.) With Foucault the parallel issue was the control of deviancy. He noticed the rise of the carceral institutions of the eighteenth and nineteenth centuries, and in writing their history indicated some of the origins of modern organizations.

Debating Foucault

The above analysis clearly departs from many conventional views of power, and in recent years a good deal of criticism has been levelled at it (Gane, 1986; Hoy 1986). There is in Foucault's theory no central motivation to power by some identifiable body—a ruling class or dominant interest. Instead, power becomes a web of social relations, a set of strategies, 'a mechanism that no one owns' (1980, p. 156). Such an analysis often appears descriptive and lacking in satisfying causal explanations. For example, there seems to be no explanation of the transition to a disciplinary mode; we are told simply that society lost its taste for physical punishment some time around the turn of the nineteenth century (Foucault, 1979, p. 14). Likewise Foucault's method of spotting analogies and similarities between very different organizational forms—the containment of the plague, prisons, factories—may seem rather far-fetched. However, there is little point in regarding these as criticisms of Foucault. We have to accept him on his own terms. Foucault belonged to a stream of thinkers (allied to Weber and the phenomenologists) for whom no ultimate 'causality' exists. Models of cause and effect may be appropriate for the natural sciences, but not for the social world. Instead, we look for symbolic connection and collectively defined 'problems' to which society seeks 'solutions'. This is the message behind Foucault's search for historic antecedents and exotic organizational forms: there are no mechanical causes, only circular processes of response that go back indefinitely. Nor does it do any harm to stand the accepted wisdom on its head from time to time, which Foucault certainly does. Rather than always regarding economic institutions as self-sufficient, his focus shifts to 'deviant' models of power. Bringing the periphery to the centre in this way frees up the analyst and greatly enriches understanding.

A more damaging critique of Foucault centres on his *pessimism*, which in social science inevitably tends to be linked with determinism. The central issue with Foucault is not economic exploitation but the domination of behaviour. Exploitation for profit is at least human and understandable, but there is something chilling about the 'mechanism that no one owns'. The paradox is that, while Foucault's analysis is supposed to oppose structural solutions, his use of incarceration as a motif for human existence is gloomy and deterministic in the extreme. His theory seems to be about 'a global unity of domination' (Burrell, 1988, p. 277).

Foucault's admirers have replied to these critics by challenging the suggestion that his conception of disciplinary power appeared to preclude all forms of human resistance. Here Knights and Vurdubakis (1994) address the specific criticisms that Foucault seemed to leave no 'space' for resistance to occur, nor allow for any particular agents of resistance, nor provide any overarching morality to give reason to resistance. These writers argue that Foucault does not in fact represent disciplinary power as a monolithic regime, but that power relations are 'multiple and have different forms'. They point out that for Foucault power apparatuses are always localized (in the prison, the asylum, the factory) which was reflected in his historical approach—Foucault advanced no general theory of power but only forms of power in 'particular socio-historical settings'. In any one locale, forms of power from different contexts can overlap, Knights and Vurdubakis point out, and they can be 'power' in one context and 'resistance' in another. Thus, power and resistance call each other into being: power gives rise to resistance, while the 'discovery' of sites of resistance can be the justification for new power relations.

Foucault himself denied the charge of pessimism. He accepted that his analysis implied that no one can ever 'step outside' disciplinary power, but not that this meant domination was inevitable. 'To say that one can never be "outside" power does not mean that one is trapped and condemned to defeat no matter what' (1980, p. 141). Disciplinary power does not always take a negative form nor do power relations take the sole form of constraints and punishments; resistance itself is a form of (countervailing) power.

Thus Foucault makes no assumptions about the passivity of those under power, rather the exercise of power encourages the emergence of counter-strategies designed to cope with it. Resistance is part of the power relation:

there are no relations of power without resistance: the latter are all the more real and effective because they are formed right at the point where relations of power are exercised; resistance to power does not have to come from somewhere else to be real, nor is it inexorably frustrated through being the compatriot of power (1980, p. 142).

Indeed, power and resistance can be intertwined in unexpected ways so that resistance can even *assist* the rule of disciplinary power, more so than passive acceptance. (In the case of psychiatry, for example, resistance in the form of patients denying they are ill, or refusing medication, is taken as a symptom of the complaint.)

Whatever one makes of the positions in this debate, we would argue that there remain unresolved tensions in Foucault's thinking. Thus when he was setting forth his ideas on disciplinary power he did appear to argue that, though power relations are elaborated in many locations, they share the same basic mechanisms. Also Foucault (like Weber) had strong liberal and humanist instincts, and was deeply worried by insidious forms of control. But he was at once too optimistic and too pessimistic. He was too optimistic in assuming that sovereign power had been superseded by the 'gentle way to punishment'. Plenty of brutal regimes survive around the world, and power based on property still determines much social inequality. He was too pessimistic in assuming that disciplinary power penetrates all social relations. What Foucault gives us, however, is a new language of power, one that captures the subtle and internalized constraints in modern bureaucratic situations. How many of us have felt this sort of pressure when waiting for the results of an exam, or on realizing that our department's performance is worse than others? The complex and 'literary' method employed by Foucault succeeds where more structural theories of power might obscure these intricacies.

Conclusion

This chapter has presented the classic concepts that provide the language and set the parameters from which contemporary discussion of work and organization has evolved. The notions of alienation and rationalization together point to the problems of productive work being overshadowed by the institutions of capital. This is not to say that the theories of Marx and Weber were always in agreement. There remain deep divisions between them. None the less, the similarities in their conclusions are also striking. They both sought the causes of the development of capitalism in the dynamics of production, and saw capitalism as a specific way of appropriating labour within distinct institutional forms. Both gave full credit to capitalism's enormous productive powers, but at the same time saw deep-rooted conflict between rational and irrational forces. These classic sources are an essential basis of understanding, and studies of industrial organization often revisit them for fresh inspiration.

With Foucault it would be going too far to trace a line of development from Marx and Weber, but as we have indicated there are similar concerns especially with Weberian analysis. The attention focused on indirect and 'insidious' forms of control as the crucial aspect of modern times; the abiding dilemma of an apparently pessimistic analysis combined with a delight in human subjectivity, and an interest in distant historic forms—all are shared with Weber. And in tune with classic theories Foucault may rightly be said to be concerned with the forces that shape industrial societies.

Some of the ideas will seem dated while others are still fairly easy to apply. The idea of productive efficiency, for example, was early detected by Marx in terms of the shift to intensive forms of control; Weber feared it as the reason why rational bureaucratic forms of organization would eventually dominate social life; and Foucault was concerned with the sheer efficiency of modern types of surveillance. This is clearly a theme that has stayed with us. The newcomer economies (Japan and the Pacific rim countries) have transformed the global economy, and they have all competed by ratcheting up accepted levels of industrial productivity. Yet common to each of the above writers was a challenge to accepted notions of productive efficiency as an almost moral criterion of the modern age.

By the same token, ideas that now seem out of date may also have contemporary echoes—particularly if we are prepared to interpret the ways in which they can re-emerge in different shapes and forms. Marx is perhaps the most problematic, since his theories can appear less and less relevant in the privatized and apparently heavily individualized economies in which we now live. Nevertheless, as noted above, many ideas that were fashioned as industrialism was emerging ring true today. Alienation, for instance, has a broader interpretation in terms of people losing control of their lives and becoming absorbed in the priorities of industrialism. Certainly one of the key features of modern work systems that critics have pointed out is a sense of labour being required to make this kind of totalizing commitment, and whole national economies needing to be focused on production. This notion of sacrifice and the invasiveness of modern economic structures was also, in different ways, central to the writings of Weber and Foucault. Similarly, the so-called factory system seems to apply only to manufacturing, while we are aware of trends in the expansion of services and new kinds of employment that do not seem to fit the historical mould. Yet the 'factory system' can also be a much more generalized way of regulating work. In many new white-collar jobs, and even technical and professional work, we can see these conditions being reproduced; and while there are efforts to dissolve centralizing patterns of employment, in other ways they reappear in new forms.

Finally, the ideas that have been raised in the chapter continue to feed modern debates. Technology, as we have said, is an abiding theme and one we return to. Likewise, new systems of work organization have emerged that dictate the current directions in which industrial economies are moving, and we devote a later chapter to these ideas as well. However, the labour process theme has been perhaps the most influential and long-lived of contemporary debates. This continues the basic arguments about the nature of work that were pioneered by the classic writers, and it is to this we turn in the following chapter.

Study questions for Chapter 9

1 Weber was said to have been engaged in a life-long 'debate with Marx's ghost'. What do you think the conversation was about?

2 Can we apply an idea like alienation to modern social and economic conditions, or is that diluting the concept too much?

3 In their various ways, Marx, Weber, and Foucault all struggled with the *pessimistic* direction their theories lead. How did they address this problem?

4 In what ways can work systems be thought of as systems of control?

5 It has become a common criticism of modern work forms that they reproduce 'insidious' as opposed to direct forms of control. What is meant by this?

Further reading

Burrell, G. (1988) 'Modernism, post-modernism and organizational analysis 2: the contribution of Michel Foucault', *Organization Studies*, 9/2: 221–35.

Dobb, M. (1963) *Studies in the Development of Capitalism*. London: Routledge and Kegan Paul.

Foucault, M. (1984) *The Foucault Reader*, ed. P. Rabinow. Harmondsworth: Penguin.

Giddens, A. (1971) *Capitalism and Modern Social Theory*. Cambridge: Cambridge University Press.

Gordon, C. (ed.) (1980) *Power/Knowledge: Selected Interviews and Other Writings 1972–1977 by Michel Foucault*. Hemel Hempstead: Harvester Wheatsheaf.

Gospel, H. (1983) 'The development of management organization in industrial relations: a historical perspective', in K. Thurley and S. Wood (eds.) *Industrial Relations and Management Strategy*. Cambridge: Cambridge University Press.

Hughes, J. A., Martin, P. J., and Sharrock, W. W. (1995) *Understanding Classical Sociology: Marx, Weber, Durkheim*. London: Sage.

Littler, C. R. (1982) *The Development of the Labour Process in Capitalist Societies*. London: Heinemann.

Littler, C. R. and Salaman, G. (1984) *Class at Work*. London: Batsford.

Sakolosky, R. (1992) 'Disciplinary power and the labour process', in A. Sturdy, D. Knights, and H. Willmott (eds.) *Skill and Consent*. London: Routledge.

Thompson, P. (1989) *The Nature of Work*, 2nd edn. London: Macmillan.

10 Conflict and Consent in Work

Summary points and learning objectives

By the end of this chapter you will be able to

- detail the elements of *conflict* and *consent* that make up the employment relationship;
- trace the course of the academic *labour process debate*;
- understand the ways in which *gender* affects the labour process;
- appreciate researchers' long-standing interest in *cultures of resistance* in the workplace;
- distinguish the notion of *structural* conflicts of interest, and that of *subjectivity*, as contrasting approaches to employment relations;
- see how a critical sociology of *industrial relations* has viewed collective conflict;
- appreciate how the changing *political climate* has affected strategies of industrial conflict.

Introduction

We have seen how, from workers' point of view, rationalized labour practices can mean a constraining and unstable work environment. There can be a sharp discrepancy between the degree of freedom and dignity workers believe they deserve, and the control that employers think is necessary for authority to be maintained. Therefore industrial conflict, and resistance on the part of workers, remain constant features of the workplace. However, the emphasis on structural constraints and formal control provides only a partial view. Relationships between workers and managements are more complex than this. Work is a central part of people's lives even in jobs that apparently allow little discretion. Indeed, if production is to go ahead at all there has to be some level of co-operation between the sides of industry, and workers require some autonomy if their initiative is to be counted on. Thus, as well as conflict, there are degrees of consent, working arrangements, and patterns of accommodation. All these aspects of the employment relationship have attracted the attention of researchers.

Running through these efforts has been the so-called *labour process debate*. We referred in the previous chapter to Harry Braverman's account of Taylorism. But the publication in 1974 of Braverman's *Labor and Monopoly Capital* sparked off a major debate concerning the impact of these forms of work organization. For more than two decades labour process theory has influenced critical thinking about the nature of work. And its echoes continue right down to the present as the debate renews itself with questions about new technologies and the formation of new social identities in the workplace.

The original focus of Braverman's theory was the alienating aspects of capitalist relations of production and the structures of control inherent in modern work systems. But Braverman was less interested in how conflicts of interest between employers and workers translated into actual behaviour and the experience of people in the workplace. Labour process theory subsequently has opened up precisely these areas of interest. The emphasis on people as active subjects in the labour process implies the detailed study of forms of worker resistance, as well as the positive aspects of workers' contribution to production goals. It has also focused interest on the ways in which gender affects how work is organized. The study of gendered social identities has helped to explore the mutually defining notions of men's and women's workplace experience.

However, explorations of conflict and the employment relationship have not been the concern of the labour process debate alone. Other strands of social science theory, drawing on industrial sociology and industrial relations, have also looked at changing patterns of control and resistance. They have shown how workers' opposition may be informal and confined to covert activity, or it can be formal in the sense of being openly accepted and even part of a recognized bargaining arrangement. Trade-union organization in particular provides an important basis of opposition. The recognition of a union can immeasurably strengthen workers' resistance—though in the global industrial relations climate of recent years argument rages around the continued role of conflict as a labour strategy.

In this chapter, then, we follow the path of the labour process debate: the original statement of the theory, the critique of its apparent omissions, and current expansion of the debate. We explore recent stages of debate which have brought together aspects of the subjectivity of workplace relations, such as resistance and consent as well as gender issues. Academic debates are never tidy things, however, with clear-cut stages and boundaries, and intertwined with this there are other accounts of independent workplace resistance, workgroup cultures, and industrial conflict at the collective level.

The labour process debate

Braverman focused particularly on the notion of *skill* in work. The controversial view he put forward was that the contemporary labour process is characterized by a progressive 'degradation' of work. He focused particularly on craft and trade skills, seeing systems of management like Taylorism as methods of degrading and deskilling this type of work. Zimbalist, one of Braverman's main supporters, summarized the argument as follows:

There is a long-run tendency through fragmentation, rationalization and mechanization for workers and their jobs to become deskilled, both in an absolute sense (they lose craft and traditional abilities) and in a relative one (scientific knowledge progressively accumulates in the production process). Even when the individual worker retains certain traditional skills, the degraded job he or she performs does not demand the exercise of these abilities. Thus, a worker, regardless of his or her personal talents, may be more easily and cheaply substituted for in the production process. (1979, p. xv)

Braverman partly intended his argument as a challenge to a view which had become the accepted wisdom in organization theory, namely that Taylor's ideas had been 'superseded' and no longer determined management methods. This orthodox view held that the Human Relations Movement (discussed in Chapter 7) heralded a more sophisticated approach to the design of work, one that recognized the human needs of workers and supplanted the coercive Taylorist methods. Braverman's answer was that this was mere wishful thinking, a confusion between what academics were recommending and what employers were doing. In his view a visit to any modern organization would show that, far from being superseded, Taylorist methods are institutionalized. They have been refined over a long period and form the basis of modern systems of work control.

Braverman was not alone in taking this interpretation of Taylorism. Others have pointed out that the main impact of human relations has been as a type of ideology, while scientific management represents the practice. Braverman himself quotes the noted management writer Peter Drucker, who stressed that while human relations has had a fairly limited influence, Taylor's methods determine 'the actual management of the worker and work' (1979, p. 88). Also, other Marxist writers, independently of Braverman, have focused on the concept of deskilling. They have viewed Taylorism as a kind of weapon or offensive that represents a distinct stage in the development of employment relations; skills are seen as the only form of 'capital' possessed by workers, and the loss of skills as a new stage of alienation (e.g. Allen, 1975). Braverman's contribution, though, was to address these issues forcibly, and to make a timely intervention when the shortcomings of certain conventional explanations were becoming obvious.

The critique of Braverman

Braverman's thesis was not received uncritically, however, and the years following the publication of *Labor and Monopoly Capital* saw a growing critique of his work (e.g. Littler, 1982, 1990; Littler and Salaman, 1982; Storey, 1983). A number of these challenges can be summarized as follows.

First, the 'universal deskilling' thesis attributed to Braverman was held to be inaccurate since a range of more subtle processes also occurs—such as reskilling (the growth of wholly new skills) and upskilling (the enhancement of existing skills). In effect, critics argued, Braverman had idealized and romanticized the image of the craftworker as a survivor from some pre-industrial past, implying that skills in a modern context exist merely as a residue from those times. However, it has been pointed out that technological and industrial development is constantly bringing new skills, specialisms, and entire occupations into being. (We need only think of a highly skilled industry like computing, which did not exist 40 years ago, to see the truth of this argument.) Thus if industrial capitalism itself can create new skills there can be no simple deskilling process.

Secondly, Braverman was criticized for too narrow a focus on employment relations and the workplace. This crude form of materialism ignores what has been called the full circuit of capital—the effect of capital markets, activities like investment and finance, and the role of the state and political action. There is no reason to suppose that these factors are any less important for change in industrial society than relations of production (MacInnes, 1983; Kelly, 1985).

And thirdly, when these broader elements are taken into account, they reflect a great deal of variation and diversity in the industrial cultures and labour-market patterns of different regions or countries, or historical time periods. Countries like Britain and America have, it is true, been criticized for running down the skills of national workforces, but this situation is not universal. Other countries—examples that spring to mind are northern European countries like Germany and Sweden—have much stronger records of encouraging worker competence and investing in skills.

In this sense, his critics have accused Braverman of taking a one-dimensional view of work organization. They argue that any unilinear change from skilled craftwork to rationalized labour is not borne out by the record. However, in addition to such contextual factors, the basic understanding of the employment relationship that lies behind these broader elements has also been criticized. Braverman is accused of having a schematic model of class relations, one defined by objective forces and a fixed range of behaviours. This deterministic approach makes little allowance for *subjectivity* in the labour process—the diversity of behaviour that people as social actors engage in, and the fact that social consciousness is shaped by a range of identities and allegiances. Given these criticisms, in recent years labour process researchers have explored the mechanisms of workplace control, emphasizing the diversity of relationships between workers and managements.

For one thing it has been argued that *managerial strategies* towards labour are oversimplified in the Braverman thesis. Braverman insisted that control and deskilling typify the capitalist labour process, whereas his critics have suggested that there can be no single imperative. In particular, Taylorism is only one of the strategy choices that managements have at their disposal. A well known alternative that has been identified is that of 'responsible autonomy'. This allows workers to act independently, retaining some control over production, but assumes they will also act 'responsibly' and in line with management's own goals. Originally a Tavistock concept, responsible autonomy came out of the classic experiments on job redesign, and was deemed to reflect wholeness of task and the multiple skills which were the basis of work reform (Trist and Bamforth, 1951; and see Chapter 11). Subsequently the idea was popularized by Friedman, who contrasted it with strategies of 'direct control' like Taylorism. Friedman suggested that RA and DC strategies were generic types that encompass the range of specific strategies that management might adopt towards labour. They reflect the tension between the need to gain co-operation from those who actually perform work, and the need to enforce industrial discipline. He argued that a trend towards responsible forms of control could be detected in practices like job enrichment and instances of relaxation in competitive pressure (Friedman, 1990).

Braverman has also been criticized for effectively writing workers out of the equation. In particular, he offers no analysis of, nor seems to reserve any place for, *workers' resistance*. He has been criticized for assuming the employing class is all-powerful and the working class passive. What is being emphasized here is the need to reassess the significance of actions like strikes, sabotage, and output resistance which might hitherto have been regarded as limited defences adopted by workers, or simply as troublesome for efficiency. On the contrary, these are important elements shaping the relationship between workers and employers. The employment relationship must be conceived of as an interaction between employing and working classes.

Summarizing these more recent explorations in labour process theory, Sturdy *et al.* point out that 'unqualified reference to deskilling as the major tendency in the development of the capitalist labour process is now untenable' (1992, p. 4). The degradation of work need never reach crisis point, because other choices are continually expanding and emerging. There may be a shift towards less direct strategies of control, while industrial capitalism generates technologies that have the potential for skill creation, and workers themselves are an active force in grasping and developing these opportunities.

Deskilling reassessed

While these criticisms are certainly persuasive, they are perhaps uncharitable to Braverman. In its own right, *Labor and Monopoly Capital* was a deliberately polemical book and not meant to satisfy the methodological criteria of social science. This needs to be recognized when his ideas are detached from the mainstream of Marxist thinking of which he was a part. Braverman's critics are academic social scientists for whom comprehensiveness of description and understanding are all-important. Braverman by contrast was a labour activist; he wrote within the same tradition of political economy as Marx, and with Marx shared a selective emphasis on the 'objective' aspects of class relationships. It would be a nonsense to suggest that activists of this kind somehow forgot about workers' resistance; it was simply that 'resistance' was not something they theorized.

It may also be true that Braverman's critics have distorted his argument somewhat. Braverman did allow for more complexity than the 'crude deskilling thesis' usually laid at his door. Jermier *et al.*, for instance, point out that Braverman was writing at a time when debates and academic positions were quite different. Any opposition he had to 'subjective' accounts of workers' experience was aimed at conservative studies of job satisfaction and worker consciousness, which were widespread at the time and carried out by managerialist social scientists. A more careful reading of Braverman's work reveals numerous insights into subjectivity. He was certainly aware of the 'subterranean stream' of hostility towards alienating forms of work, and the complexities of 'habituation' to control that characterized real work processes (Jermier *et al.*, 1994, pp. 4–5).

The deskilling thesis has also been defended in more specific terms (see e.g. Zimbalist, 1979; Hill, 1981). It is suggested that the various types of managerial control should not all be seen as equal in significance, nor should responsible autonomy be regarded as an alternative to direct control. Rather, managerial strategies which share control with workers usually operate within an overall policy of direct control. Braverman's admirers also argue that he did not overstate the impact of scientific management (indeed, that it would be virtually impossible to do so). While there certainly were barriers to the diffusion of Taylorist methods, and methods other than Taylor's were developed, it would be mistaken to lose sight of the broader pattern of change. Despite variations in the spread of such systems, in the world's dominant economies like the United States and Japan these principles have spread rapidly, and the growth of formal labour policies and bureaucratic structures has meant highly rationalized forms of management. Thus Thompson (1989, p. 136) has argued that the case for 'responsible' strategies being equated with those based on direct control is not sustainable. The long-term trend is that of a shift towards direct control in central areas of industrial employment. Thompson uses the term 'systematic management' to refer to the trend towards rationalized and bureaucratic control (1989, p. 126).

Nor has there been any shortage of research broadly confirming Braverman's position. Studies that find overwhelming evidence of deskilling in different sectors and organizations continue to appear. O'Connell-Davidson (1994), for example, looked at white-collar rationalization in a privatized utility. This is a sector in which new private owners have often radically changed employment cultures. In this case an existing manual system was replaced with automated office systems with the explicit aim of centralizing control. Management had always known that clerks possessed a great deal of detailed knowledge, and the new structure sought to 'fragment, standardize and simplify' the clerical task. The aim was to reduce 'the organization's dependence upon any individual clerk's experience and acquired knowledge'. Resistance was manifest in several ways (refusal to train within teams, and minor acts of sabotage like overloading the screens) but there were limits. The computerized systems could trace entries to individual clerks. Moreover, official opposition fizzled out despite a majority ballot for strike action—a classic case of a poorly led union, in which a largely female rank-and-file felt intimidated by male-dominated leadership. Thus, despite workers' 'strong desire to resist', O'Connell-Davidson counts this as a clear-cut case of deskilling.

In fact, the specific example of clerical deskilling has provided quite a lot of support for the deskilling thesis (not all of it intentional). While industrial deskilling has proceeded for many years, real opportunities for productivity gains are increasingly found in the office. A number of accounts of clerical and white-collar work have sustained a classic Braverman scenario: a traditional 'craft' skill among clerks—the possession of detailed knowledge of files and the ability to locate and process information—being destroyed by centralizing information technologies. Rather ironically, some of this empirical work has been conducted by researchers who, in other contexts, have argued that the deskilling thesis needed refining (e.g. Crompton and Reid, 1982; Storey, 1986).

Workplace control and resistance

Still, it remains clear that any comprehensive account of work must cover the areas referred to by Braverman's critics. Consideration of the active role that workers play—the resistance to control, as well as the skills and forms of co-operation that are exercised in the interests of production—has made a valuable contribution to our understanding of workplace relations. Before coming to this point, however, it will be useful to retrace our steps and look at other accounts, because the labour process debate has no monopoly on issues like control and resistance. We can refer to separate traditions of exploring the *cultures* generated within groups in the workplace, and also those who have pointed out that individual and group resistance has a *structural* aspect that stems from the clash of material interests.

Workgroups and work cultures

The collective resistance of workers is behind much informal action in the workplace and has fascinated researchers from the earliest days. Given the power of the managerial hierarchy to dispense or withhold rewards, open acts of defiance expose individuals to reprisal. But resistance based in the group can be difficult to pin down. Workgroups may generate distinctive cultures of resistance based on informal relations or some sense of shared occupational identity, such as a craft ethic. Workgroups often develop common values and a sense of their own history. They may share distinctive ways of communicating, such as a repertoire of sayings and jokes. Such a culture—frequently the expression of past struggles with management—can form a basis of unity and continuing resistance to formal controls.

The classic study of workgroup resistance, first discussed in Chapter 7 above, is the famous Hawthorne research (Roethlisberger and Dickson, 1943). Management at the Hawthorne plant had been frustrated in their efforts to raise production in a section where electrical assemblies were wired up—the so-called Bank Wiring Room—and the researchers were called in to try to resolve the problem. They discovered the existence of a strong group culture which enforced an output norm. Workers in the section perceived management's standards—arrived at by Taylorist methods—to be outside their control and liable to be raised arbitrarily. Consequently they restricted output to a level they regarded as reasonable, one that did not undermine their own pay and job security, and one that slower members could keep up with. The researchers discovered the pressure that such groups can bring to bear on members to conform to common norms. In this case positive sanctions involved acceptance into the friendship cliques, while negative sanctions meant ridicule and ostracism for anyone who broke ranks and tried to 'bust' the agreed work-rate.

In this study, completed over 60 years ago, are found a number of elements that set the agenda for studies of workgroup resistance: different forms of control being applied by management but matched by the efforts of those under control to create space for themselves; the ingenuity of workers and the surprising effectiveness of their strategies in the face of highly constraining work systems; and the moral dimensions to the claims of both sides over the 'fairness' of work effort. However, the Hawthorne studies were also a product of their time and took for granted certain managerialist assumptions. The prevailing view was that group resistance stemmed from workers' misunderstanding of management's intentions. Indeed, the choice of language itself was value-laden, and disapproval was implicit in the very notion of workers 'restricting' output. The widespread acceptance of this biased view has been traced to the Hawthorne research and the Human Relations Movement which followed it. These interpreted 'output restriction' in terms of the social requirements of sustaining a group structure. Workers' desire for group membership was contrasted with managers' rational criteria based on technical efficiency. However, such conflicts of interest may be genuine, not merely an irrational response by workers. Workers' behaviour is really a response to managerial control and best understood as a counter-attempt to assert workers' own control (Lupton, 1963, p. 6; Burawoy, 1979, p. x).

During the 1950s and 1960s some celebrated studies followed up these concerns. They argued that so-called restrictive practices are not just defensive and oppositional, but usually reflect attempts by workers to impose their own definitions of a fair day's work. Interestingly, they came up with the finding that a recognized agreement (albeit a purely informal one) often exists. Lupton's research in an electrical components firm, the noted study *On the Shop Floor*, showed how an equitable balance between wages and effort can develop. Workers and supervisors colluded to 'fiddle' earnings and work allocation in a complex system. The 'fiddle' was 'a quite stable adjustment of the discrepant goals of management and workers' (1963, p. 6). Similarly, Donald Roy's classic studies showed the conscious manipulation of payments systems. In one case, Roy (1952) observed that output restriction stopped short of the point where jobs would have been retimed and pay rates cut. In another (1954) study operators, inspectors, and supervisors co-operated in informal practices to 'fix' a fair job rate.

Manual workers are not the only occupational group to have to cope with imposed controls. Professional and white-collar employees increasingly find their status and conditions under attack, and it is possible to see in such groups the same kinds of collective responses. Pettigrew's (1973) well-known account of the implementation of a computer network in a large retailing firm provides a good example of group solidarity among professionals. The programmers in the company initially had a good deal of control over the computer installation—this was the very early days of commercial computing before there was a hierarchy within these occupations—which provoked management to cut down their influence. The programmers responded in various ways: by attacking the competence of the 'analysts' whom management brought in to dilute and fragment their work, and by habitually withholding their most important resource: information. They kept details of programmes in their heads, and always explained procedures to managers and analysts in highly technical jargon. These varied and imaginative tactics grew out of a strong collective identity developed in the face of the hostility that was encountered from management.

The ways in which systems of control are adapted depend to some extent on the work context—in particular the room for manœuvre that market pressures, technology, and work organization allow. Patterns like the 'fix' and the 'fiddle' were developed by skilled workers who retained considerable discretion on the shopfloor, and professional groups possessing key skills can also often exploit employers' dependence on them. Where this kind of discretion exists informal relationships do not always subvert formal goals. Workers can adapt in ways that support the organization, and instances in which workers take the initiative to get a job done reflect co-operative elements in the employment relationship. In contrast, in work settings under much tighter constraints, or based on work-pacing technologies, there is usually less scope to manipulate managerial controls, and workers' resistance may take a more defensive form. Even here, though, the extent to which workers can find space for themselves and exercise some autonomy is often surprising.

Conflict and control

Conservative social science, as already noted, has usually interpreted the point-of-production resistance of workers as a problem of poor communications, of managers and workers being unable to understand each others' point of view, or as some other type of human relations difficulty. But other more critical writers have long argued that the tension between managerial control and workers' resistance involves a clash of real interests, as well as being a structure that is dynamic and changing. For example, Goodrich's (1975) classic concept of a 'frontier of control' has been an influential way of visualizing the employment relationship. The boundaries of control are seen as continually shifting as one side or the other gains ascendancy; workers or management may gain control of some aspect of operations, but the struggle may simply move to another level or another area. Managerial control and the degree of power management has to direct work are always relative to the countervailing power possessed by workers.

Structural perspectives like this have continued to inform the labour process debate. For example, Edwards (1990) has developed a comprehensive account of workplace conflict and resistance. He suggests that 'structural antagonism' might be a better term than conflict, because conflict can imply that workers and managers are constantly and visibly at war. In reality a perpetual struggle for control in work is not always obvious or observable. The tactics workers adopt are versatile and often covert, so that an intimate knowledge of a workplace might be needed in order to be aware of resistance going on. Nor does resistance have to be manifest to be effective. The threat of resistance being offered if some change were to be initiated may be enough to maintain the status quo.

Structural antagonism, Edwards argues, lies at the root of the capital–labour relation and arises from a clash over the distribution of surplus. It does not determine behaviour so much as create the pre-conditions for action: 'workers and employers respond to these pressures and in so doing develop traditions and understandings that are used to interpret relations with each other. Their struggles stem from the exploitative character of the capital–labour relation, but they have an autonomy' (Edwards, 1990, p. 126). Thus, managers do not have total strategies of control, nor do workers only resist.

Day-to-day interaction involves many behaviours, including forms of consent and co-operation. Nevertheless, Edwards insists on the primacy of the antagonistic relation and that consent is not on a par with conflict. Domination by employers and the subordination of labour remain the typical form of production relations. So while the labour process has a relative autonomy, the struggle between capital and labour is still the main dynamic shaping the employment relationship.

Other recent research has also explored the control–resistance dialectic. A number of studies show people working in regimes of tighter monitoring and control (Turnbull, 1989; Sewell and Wilkinson, 1992; Dawson and Webb, 1989; Delbridge *et al.*, 1992). Modern systems like lean production and teamworking invariably adopt the softened language of employee and customer care. But while this is the rhetoric, the reality of cost cutting suggests that traditional attempts to homogenize labour have not been superseded (Pollert, 1996; O'Connell-Davidson, 1994). Indeed, much evidence suggests that new work systems may bring changes but have not transformed the basics of the workplace, and exist alongside old-style labour management and attitudes (Hodson, 1989).

In this context, McKinlay and Taylor's (1996) study of an electronics plant highlighted a particularly intense form of control: peer review. This was a system based on production teams and regular sessions of internal scrutiny. Individual members would be assessed by the group, their performance praised or admonished, and their grades decided by mutual scoring. The researchers stressed that, with individuals required to demonstrate 'a positive attitude', intense psychological pressures were generated in the groups. They likened the internal controls of peer review to the systematic discipline and surveillance famously discussed by Foucault (see the previous chapter for an account of Foucault's power theory). These insidious forms of control are thought to be more effective because more difficult to resist; they replace direct coercive control with self-control, and are perceived as legitimate, even natural. Peer review (which was coupled with strict selection and a non-union environment) was this type of 'microscopic disciplinary process'. Nevertheless, McKinlay and Taylor caution against exaggerating the power of Foucauldian-type controls. People still 'seek to prise open spaces for individual dissent, and remain capable of collective opposition, however limited in scope and duration'. In the production teams the tension between social aspects of group membership and the punitive aspects of mutual scoring, undermined the groups' effectiveness. Workers resented the intimidation and being forced to judge their teammates. They 'quickly learnt to subvert the surveillance objective' by means of trading scores—a way of ensuring they gave each other favourable ratings, or at least avoided unfavourable ones.

The implied critique of Foucault's imagery is that insidious control is actually not that subtle, nor are people always taken in by these forms of internal discipline. Others too have found little evidence of workers being deceived by participation schemes, again the reason being that true participation is rarely on offer (Tausky and Chelte, 1991). As emphasized above, internal controls are not necessarily alternatives to direct control, but in reality may be implemented in conjunction with more coercive methods.

Subjectivity and the labour process

Labour process researchers have recently suggested that workplace resistance still has not been fully explored, and that our understanding of important aspects of this phenomenon needs to be taken further. Thus Jermier *et al.* (1994) argue that we need to document the 'spirit of refusal' that survives in everyday resistance at work, and in particular that a full blown theory of resistance is still missing. What is required, they say, is a proper idea of the subject—a notion of how a sense of identity is formed even within constraining work systems. This would include sexual identity and gender, as well as notions of self-esteem. Paradoxically therefore (given resistance as our starting-point), the place of work in people's struggles to form and sustain their ideas of self may include something approaching a moral commitment to work.

As noted above, the subjectivity of management groups raised the possibility of strategies that rely on areas of accommodation between management and workers—which in turn raise the issue of *consent* within the employment relationship. Workers have certain resources even in the most restrictive circumstances: the power to disrupt production and withhold co-operation, but also the practical abilities and know-how on which employers depend. Hence the active role of groups in employment relations involves degrees of co-operation and consent as well as struggle on the part of workers.

Until recently studies of workgroup resistance have been an accepted part of labour process theory. We saw above that such studies have a long pedigree (particularly in the American tradition of detailed accounts of shopfloor culture). They often take place in the classic setting of the male manual worker, and stress the ingenious practices and tricks that evolve as workers seek to make space for themselves, or are able to subvert work controls and turn them to their advantage.

Continuing this tradition was Michael Burawoy's *Manufacturing Consent* (1979), a major empirical study of the politics of the shopfloor. This was an insider account of skilled manual work based on the researcher's own experience in an engineering workshop. Burawoy posed the question: Why do workers work as hard as they do? He observed an often frantic pace of work and workers exceeding production targets by wide margins. Coercion or payment alone did not explain this. Instead 'an element of spontaneous consent' was involved. Burawoy interpreted shopfloor behaviour as a set of games, the overall game being that of 'making out'. What he meant by this was the whole question of people surviving and prospering in demanding work environments. In the case he studied, it meant all of the 'angles' and subtle strategies that workers employed to maximize earnings. The basis of this consent was the work culture itself.

the shop-floor culture revolves around making out. Each worker sooner or later is sucked into this distinctive set of activities and language . . . In my own case, it took me some time to understand the shop language, let alone the intricacies of making out. It was a matter of three or four months before I began to make out by using a number of angles and by transferring time from one operation to another. Once I knew I had a chance to make out, the rewards of participating in a game in which the outcomes were uncertain absorbed my attention, and I found myself spontaneously cooperating with management in the production of greater surplus. (Burawoy, 1979, p. 64)

The building of workplace consent happened via the absorption of workers in this culture, and via the sense of status and identity that came with being an experienced operator.

However, lately this tradition has come under fire from some labour process writers who have argued that it undervalues both resistance and consent. They suggest that it limits worker behaviour to rituals and forms of self-expression which may delay and harry management but which are really only defensive responses, not a direct challenge to managerial control. Notions like 'making out' confine workers' creative presence to that of minor skirmishes. They reflect low levels of accommodation with work rules, and deny a larger engagement or more active input into organizational life (Marchington, 1992; Jermier et al., 1994; Collinson, 1994).

Indeed, if the active subject becomes the focus of attention, 'resistance' and 'consent' become two sides of the same coin. Employees' efforts to claim a rightful place in work, one that reflects a sense of personal worth, may mean 'resisting' managerial priorities, but to the employee (and perhaps to other stakeholders like industrial courts or the media) it may appear as a progressive reform of working arrangements. Here, for example, Collinson (1994) emphasizes the 'overlapping character of consent, compliance and resistance' that becomes evident once the detailed experiences of groups in the workplace become the focus of attention. 'Whether specific practices are best defined in terms of resistance or consent or both will be determined by the particular power relations and by employees' subjective orientation, commitments and indeed motivation and determination' (1994, p. 50).

The consent/resistance dialectic

Various types of consenting practices have been explored in recent years, one being the idea of informal co-operation. This is not just an optional extra but crucial to economic success; firms need more than a kind of grudging consent from workers, they need active compliance in production. Thus the informal skills that workers develop in so-called unskilled jobs have always been counted on by employers. Recently these have been reappraised by labour process theorists. In an influential article, Manwaring and Wood (1985) highlighted what they call *tacit skills*, and were anxious to redress the tendency to devalue or ignore these aspects of subjectivity within work settings. Many workers relate positively to the production process via tacit skills—the tricks of the trade, the co-ordination of hand and eye, the ability to operate socially. Much of the pride and satisfaction that can be derived from jobs defined as unskilled or semi-skilled comes through exercising these forms of discretion.

In this context, Sturdy (1992) has also sought to challenge the 'neglect of the subject' that is common in accounts emphasizing the constraints of routinized work. He stressed instead unpredictability and variability in behaviour. People's behaviour is not always defined by objective circumstances—whether this is passively complying with rules or inventing routines and games to subvert rules. Sturdy investigated the clerical structures in two insurance companies. These were large processing centres, with departments covering life and pensions and general insurance such as motor, home, and accident; and clerks were dealing with the full range of customer enquiries, claims, and new proposals. In particular he found a practice identified as work 'shifting' which demonstrated a kind of productive self-discipline. It referred to workers' habit of wanting to 'shift' their work, to get it out of the way. This positive desire to 'get their work done' reflected the immediacy of the task: a batch of files coming in brought the response of wanting to get it completed. A sense of satisfaction, of having 'had a good day', derived from the experience of being able to clear your desk. And, conversely, frustration was caused by being held up in various ways—by open-ended customer enquiries, computer breakdowns, other people not completing their end. Sturdy points out that this is the exact opposite of work avoidance (like the output resistance of the Hawthorne studies), and he insists that shifting involved a positive type of clerical consent, not simply compliance with the managerial regime. Sturdy also rejects the view that shifting in any way reflected the stereotype of clerks as deferential and compliant workers. Indeed, other forms of resistance were rife, and the insurance clerks entertained some highly cynical views about management's competence. Nor was shifting solely a form of consent but incorporated resistance to management-imposed schedules as well. This was not therefore an escape from work but an 'escape into work' and represented a positive claim on work.

In another study, Collinson (1994) also showed how the realities of worker behaviour often blur the distinction between consent and resistance—how certain types of 'resistance' can involve workers exploiting new areas of knowledge and creating a deeper engagement with the organization. Collinson was first sceptical of the value placed on the traditional class- and gender-based work culture. The all-male shopfloor that engages in familiar kinds of ritualized opposition—manipulation of the bonus scheme, concealing information, holding back output—is based on suspicion of management and hostility to the company. This was dubbed 'resistance through distance' and Collinson was critical of any tendency to exaggerate or romanticize it, instead stressing its 'limited effectiveness as a means of dissent'.

This particular oppositional strategy simultaneously incorporated elements of compliance and consent that severely threatened the possibilities and effects of resistance. It failed to challenge and thus actually reinforced the commodification of labour and managerial control. By merely seeking to secure a degree of personal discretion and autonomy in and around the edges of their formally controlled and commodified position, these manual workers resisted in ways that simultaneously accommodated themselves to the sale of their own labour power. (Collinson, 1994, pp. 36–7)

This was contrasted with the case of a female employee of an insurance company who had been the victim of discrimination—not gaining a deserved promotion due to her service being interrupted by a pregnancy. She challenged the firm and, with the help of a (female) union official, successfully fought the decision in internal hearings, exposing inconsistencies in the firm's case. 'Resistance through persistence', Collinson claims, was a more effective and successful strategy. It meant the employee gaining knowledge of the firm's own procedures, and over a lengthy period courageously resisting attempts at intimidation. Resistance through persistence meant the employee seeking 'greater involvement in the organization and to render management more accountable by extracting information, monitoring practices and challenging decision-making processes' (1994, p. 50). In this way, Collinson draws attention to types of resistance that stem from an ambition for a proper organizational role and greater involvement in work.

Gender in the labour process

The diversity and subjectivity of labour processes are also influenced by a range of social identities and in particular that of gender. The traditional setting of the labour process debate—indeed of much discussion of the workplace—has been *gender-blind*. The taken-for-granted assumption has been of a 'typical' male workforce and a work situation of permanent employment, often in manual industries. But this has always been a mis-reading of the realities of work, and is increasingly so as labour forces differentiate and new work forms emerge. By ignoring gender, traditional labour process analysis has ignored the ways in which both men's and women's work experiences are shaped. Indeed, the paradox is that while labour process theory has tended to assume a male workforce, the experiences of workers as men—and masculinity as a specific issue—have only recently begun to be explored. In reality, the redistribution of skills (whether positively or negatively) is not simply a function of objective forces, nor does it affect all equally. Gendered work roles filter and mediate the pressures of the labour process in complex ways.

Employers take advantage of gender-divided skills to lower the value of women's labour and submerge their abilities. Also, certain of the characteristics of male labour (a kind of macho toughness) can be exploited via its in-built tendency to glorify work pressure. On the other hand, gendered identities can be the basis of resistance. The traditional male-oriented trade-union and work culture are obvious examples, while there may be a different range of solidarities amongst female workforces and occupations.

In this context, Gottfried (1994) has looked at the kinds of non-traditional workplaces, which are increasingly becoming the norm and which tend to employ high proportions of female labour. These were firms in the American temporary help sector (THS) that hire out temporary, part-time, and sub-contract workers often in clerical or retail jobs. This part of the new service economy is characterized by discontinuous work performed in changing locations. Hence the focused, bureaucratic control of the typical organization is not evident, and controls are 'dispersed into an overall system'. Much responsibility is devolved to workers themselves. This type of control is effective because THS workers do not have the same employment rights as permanent workers. The 'threat of disposability and absence of job rights' means that the willingness to work unsupervised can be made a condition of employment. Gottfried also stressed that the stereotypes of 'women's work' become part of these control mechanisms. What has been called emotional labour exploits supposed female qualities, such as glamour and charm, just as other forms of labour might exploit physical strength or effort.

> [Emotional] production is present in THS firms which commodify workers by selling not only a set of competencies but also a gendered subject to a client in the same way that a manufacturing firm subcontracts standardized parts from a supplier. When clients purchase the labour power of a temporary worker, they expect a person whose conduct and demeanour conform to organizational norms. (Gottfried, 1994, p. 114)

Not being part of any stable collectivity, and having a weak labour-market position, THS workers are vulnerable. Nevertheless, they do assert their individuality, albeit less visibly and more defensively. Gottfried records forms of individuality in dress code, examples of working-to-rule (e.g. refusal to use initiative in tasks like copy typing), and the exploitation of clashes of interest between the agency and the client firm. The broader point Gottfried stresses is that because their organizational and market power is different, women's and men's experiences of resistance are different. Women's resistance may be covert and fragmented, and linked to social and domestic networks. Nevertheless the importance of everyday acts of opposition should not be overlooked.

Research has also stressed the ways in which men's and women's work roles are *mutually defining*. For many male occupations, the status and character of the job is an integral part of the occupants' separate identity as men. The supposed male qualities—strength, endurance, the ability to stand the pressures of work—are not self-contained attributes but exist only in contrast with supposed female attributes. This is particularly so in skilled manual or technical work. Men's sense of themselves is tied in with the possession of skills, but technical skills have always tended to be a male preserve, defined by the exclusion of women. A process like deskilling, therefore, can be doubly destructive. It means an erosion of job status and separation from aspects of work that define masculinity—a crisis of identity for male workers as men, as well as loss of occupational standing.

However, as Baron (1992) has pointed out, the situation is more complex even than this. Because there are no fixed gender identities, 'gender' is not a mechanical means of determining and pursuing a group's interests. Newly gendered identities are constituted afresh as circumstances change, and in open-ended and unpredictable ways.

> The view that men shape work to protect their gender interests assumes that gender is monolithic, rather than multidimensional and internally inconsistent. The view also assumes that men are omnipotent—that they know what their gender interests are and that they have the power to construct the world the way they want. But these very questions require documented answers. Research needs to question male power, rather than assume its existence, and to examine its limitations and its variations. (Baron, 1992, p. 71)

In her own historical research in the US printing industry, Baron looked at the Linotype revolution of the 1880s and 1890s, and employers' attempts to feminize the occupation. The 'gendered terrain' on which employers and (male) workers fought involved how the newly mechanized work would be defined. The employers' strategy was to argue that mechanization (particularly the new keyboarding) meant that work now demanded intellectual skills and dexterity and dependableness (female attributes). The male-dominated print unions based their opposition on the argument that this work was unsuitable for women: Linotype work was exhausting and demanded physical endurance. Baron showed too that other technologies emerging at the time separated the hot-metal type setting from type justifying and distributing, but these were never adopted. Instead the Linotype, which integrated these operations, was embraced by craftworkers precisely because they could claim the dirty and hot work as natural men's work. (This was also, incidentally, a fascinating example of how social/gender factors actually affected the outcome of a technological change.)

The sting in the tail was that, having been forced into adopting a narrow definition of their skills, men were caught up in much tougher work regimes. For while the print workers believed that by protecting the boundaries of their work they were protecting their identity as men and their occupational integrity, in fact they had no guaranteed control of wider definitions of skills. The subsequent period saw employers enforcing much higher levels of productivity and work speed.

Box 10.1 Varieties of conflict in the employment relationship

Because it is human behaviour, opposition to the constraints of the workplace varies in many ways. Resistance can be openly recognized or covert; it can be spontaneous or organized. Conflict can be based on actions taken by individuals, action by groups, and action at the level of formal organization. The great diversity of industrial conflict is also a reflection of the tactical nature of the response. Interests are mobilized and the players use forms of resistance that are appropriate in changing circumstances. What makes sense in one situation may not in another. Industrial conflict can even be initiated by management. Look at the range and levels of conflict and discuss how they overlap and interact.

- Spontaneous resistance and sabotage; whistleblowing;
- Workgroup resistance and counter-cultures;
- Industrial conflict and firm-specific disputes; strikes, go-slows, work-to-rules;
- Large-scale demonstrative strikes, political action.

Industrial conflict and industrial relations

The above account has focused on the subtle ways in which different social identities shape the labour process. However, workers' interests are also mobilized on a broader front, and industrial conflict includes strikes and other kinds of action, as well as the role of trade unions as workers' representatives. All resistance has a basic role in shaping the effort bargain, and to an extent there is a continuum between these types of conflict and more informal ones. Much strike activity is based on resistance by groups of workers, while the strength of any union in the final analysis rests on its members' resolve to oppose managerial control at the point of production. Still, without the support of effective trade unionism, individual and informal resistance may have strict limits. In focusing on the *collective* character of disputes we are moving to a level of analysis that covers a wider economic and political framework. Outside the confines of the labour process, factors like public opinion, the economy, and government policy on industrial relations cannot be ignored.

Conflict in the employment relationship has had an important influence on theories of industrial relations. The orthodox approach to the subject involved a *pluralist* perspective. This viewed employers and unions as both possessing roughly equal power. Their interests may clash in some areas (so the model implied) but the terms of the relationship were negotiable. However, the weaknesses of this approach have long been recognized. To view workers and employers as equal partners in a contract lacks any sense of the sharp inequalities of power dividing them. Moreover, there are difficulties if industrial conflict becomes a major issue. A pluralist perspective sees conflict as a temporary breakdown in job regulation and emphasizes the resolution of disputes. The model therefore has a place for conflict, but evidence of a powerful opposition of interests between employers and workers is more difficult to accommodate.

Understanding industrial conflict

The problems with conventional pluralist ideas prompted a more radical sociology of industrial conflict. This sees industrial relations as part of a totality of social relations. The labour process and wider employment context are important here, while a unifying theme is an overall view of *power and control* in industrial societies. It is also important to assume that conflict is a reasoned response of one type or another, or a form of *social action*. This means an emphasis on the different versions of events that industrial conflict invariably produces. What the workers might think is a lively practical joke, management may regard as sabotage; what workers might see as intensification of their labour, management may regard as an improvement in flexibility, and so forth. As impartial observers, it is important that we take account of all 'definitions of the situation' and are prepared to understand events as participants themselves experience them.

Implied here is a definite change of emphasis from pluralist-type accounts. While they focused narrowly on the formal institutions of industrial relations and the legalities of the employment contract, now the motives and actions of the groups involved in workplace relations become the focus of attention. It is how they perceive and define events, and how their consciousness forms and changes, that is decisive. This means looking beyond conventional explanations. In media accounts of industrial conflict, for example, the cause of a dispute will usually be attributed to the issue over which work relations broke down. We tend to think of disputes being brought about by specific disagreements—over pay, for instance. However, explanation needs to be more holistic than this. We need to distinguish the events that precipitated the action from issues which form the background to any given dispute, while the broader social context of conflict also needs to be considered.

A model account of how these levels of analysis may be linked up is provided by Gouldner's (1955) classic *Wildcat Strike*. This traced the course of an unofficial stoppage in a small American factory that produced plasterboard. The plant, a major source of employment in a small community, had been operated for years under what Gouldner termed an 'indulgency pattern' of management. Here the relations between managers and workers were tolerant and involved loyalties and commitments over and above the mere exchange of wages for work. However, the corporation that owned the plant regarded it as being inefficiently run and brought in a regime of tighter discipline. New machinery was introduced which meant an unpredictable pace of work, and there were changes in the management and supervisory structure with popular men demoted and unpopular men promoted. All in all the 'indulgency pattern was subjected to a crippling attack, and workers' hostility rapidly mounted' (p. 28). As events came to a head a quarrel broke out between the union steward and a production engineer, who was himself closely associated with the efficiency drive and the focus of much tension. It was this which sparked off the strike.

By dwelling on this complex chain of cause and effect, Gouldner indicated that the strike could only be understood against the background of changes in the employment relationship. The employer's intention to retake certain areas of discretion was seen by the workers as the contravention of a rule which was regarded as fair and legitimate by most people in the plant, including many in management. Thus the strike came as no surprise to those involved. The researchers, the workers, management, and union officials all 'saw it coming' and regarded the strike as a wholly understandable outcome.

This brings us to the broader context of conflict. Factors operating at this level are remote from the event but predispose different groups to act in certain ways, and hence define the limits of other causes. The underlying cause of conflict is the distribution of wealth and power, itself a reflection of deep class divisions in society. Within the workplace, inequality and conflict are inextricably bound up, irrespective of the relationship between particular managements and workforces. Wages are part of the employers' costs, which they must seek to minimize, and workers experience a ceaseless downward pressure on living standards. It is only by exerting pressure themselves, using whatever means are at their disposal, that they are able to sustain wage levels and general conditions. Thus the returns going to labour and capital are not simply allocated by the hidden hand of the market. They stabilize as the outcome of conflict.

The social response to strikes

Though industrial conflict comes in many shapes and sizes, there can be little doubt of the massive amount of attention focused on one of its forms. Strikes are a dramatic type of conflict (or at least they can be portrayed as dramatic events) and public opinion tends to be firmly fixed upon them. This is important because public opinion has a crucial influence on the climate in which industrial relations are conducted. The popular perception is that strikes cause severe economic disruption, yet this needs some explaining as it bears little relation to the facts. The impact that strikes have on production tends to be greatly exaggerated. While the economy can be damaged by certain groups of workers, relatively few actually have this kind of muscle. Also, strikes account for an almost negligible amount of lost time compared with total hours worked by the employed population, and when compared with other causes of lost production such as sickness and industrial accidents.

Why then the outcry about strikes? In his thorough analysis of industrial conflict Richard Hyman (1989) put forward two main reasons. First, the role of the news media in forming public opinion is very important. Certainly research has detected an element of straightforward bias in the reporting of strikes. Managers are often portrayed as reasonable and responsible, and greater authority is attributed to their views, while strikes are seen as 'problems' created by workers. But simple bias is not a complete answer. The way in which news is produced also needs to be taken into account. News cannot just be seen as information about events transmitted to the public in some unproblematic way; in a very real sense news is manufactured. The raw material of events is processed—selected, edited, dramatized, presented—by the professionals who run the media. Ultimately it is their values that shape the version of events the public receives (Edwards, 1979).

In seeking to present strikes as 'newsworthy' an artificial image of industrial relations is often conveyed. News coverage tends to reduce the complex process of strikes to a single issue. (In terms of our model, only the precipitating causes tend to be brought out.) It is only if a strike stays in the news for a long period that anything of its history or underlying causes will emerge—and then only in the 'quality' press, rarely on television or in the tabloids where most people obtain their information. Hence workers' demand for jobs with reasonable pay and security may command public sympathy but not necessarily widespread legitimacy, and those on strike may simply appear as troublemakers causing dissent unnecessarily. Employers, by contrast, can call on powerful ideological forces to legitimize their interests. They need only announce a general aim of improving efficiency or international competitiveness and their case is virtually made for them.

However, this still leaves unanswered the question why strikes are presented as they are. This brings us to the second of the points Hyman raised. He suggested that the public clamour over strikes reflects their political repercussions rather than any direct economic impact. Strikes, in other words, represent a challenge to *managerial authority*. Even though very few strikes create a real crisis of control in firms, any strike, no matter how short-lived, contains the seeds of a deeper threat. As Hyman (1989, p. 157) puts it, it is hardly surprising 'that those who exercise managerial authority typically resent this limitation on their autonomy, and are sometimes haunted by the fear that strikes may escalate into an explicit challenge to the minority control of industry'. The edifice of organizational power represents the rights of ownership delegated to management. Thus, when the control of labour is thwarted by industrial action, ultimately the employment relationship itself is being undermined. As this is the basis of a capitalist industrial society, we can see why the disruption of authority in industry should be regarded as being so critical.

New patterns of industrial action

As well as the above rather generalized analysis, patterns of industrial conflict reflect other causes and influences. The changing political climate of collective organization covers a range of 'corporatist' factors—whether trade unions are included in or excluded from influence by government, the social welfare traditions in particular countries, and differences in industrial climate and culture. Also, changes in the structure of employment and what is the 'typical' workplace may affect the nature and level of conflict.

Throughout the 1980s and 1990s the impact of long-term recessions, or weak economic recoveries, has compelled employers to cut labour costs, at the same time as persistent unemployment has shifted the balance of market strength in their favour. Another factor has been global competitive pressures. These have induced workers to accept stricter disciplinary codes and work reorganization and to embrace the realities of the marketplace. As a result, throughout the recent period there have been significant changes in global and European strike patterns. Patterns differ from country to country, but the commonly held view is that there has been a general decline in strike rates, ushering in a new era of industrial peace and 'maturity' in industrial relations (Edwards, 1992, 1995).

In Britain, for example, in the 1990s, strike activity fell to historically low levels. The public perception was that the country had been 'strike prone' but that during the 1980s and 1990s all that changed. With measures to curb trade-union power the country's strike record became internationally competitive, and certainly the link between the weakened state of the labour movement and a rapid decline in industrial action seemed clear enough. The Thatcher administrations of the 1980s broke with the postwar consensus on employment, and became willing to use unemployment as an instrument of policy. Successive Conservative governments also extended the interventionist role of the state, legislating to restrict strikes and supporting activity. In this period of 'realism' trade unions became preoccupied with ensuring that any action they contemplated was lawful, while the immediate concern of many of their members moved towards job security (Hyman, 1989).

However, while strike data lend some support to the prevailing public opinion, they belie any simple notion of the 'reform' of an excessively strike-ridden country. As Table 10.1 shows, during the 1980s Britain came just below the middle in a ranking of strike days per 1000 employees—above some major competitor countries (Germany, France, Japan) but below others (Italy, Spain, Canada). And while strikes in Britain declined during the 1980s, this was part of an international trend and Britain's relative position actually worsened slightly. Only in the 1990s did the country fall below the OECD average on recorded strikes.

The situation confronting workers may have emerged with great clarity in Britain but the rise of free-market thinking has been worldwide. The declining trend of strike activity can be detected in many of the economically developed nations (though by the

	Annual averages of working days not worked per 1,000 employees; Selected OECD countries, all industries and services.		
	1986–90	1991–5	1995
Italy	315	183	65
Spain	602	469	169
Canada	429	159	130
Australia	224	130	80
United Kingdom	137	24	19
France	111	94	302
Germany	5	17	8
Sweden	134	50	182
United States	82	42	50
Japan	5	3	
OECD average	161	75	93

Table 10.1 International comparisons of labour disputes 1986–1995
Source: *Labour Market Trends* (London: HMSO), April 1997, p. 130.

later 1990s this trend had started to reverse, and most OECD countries saw strike rates rising again). Table 10.1 shows that in countries such as France, Germany, Sweden, and Japan, which have always tended to have low strike levels, conflict remained low, while the likes of Australia and the UK have joined the low-strike countries. Long-term strike-prone countries like Italy, Spain, and Canada also saw some downward drift but certainly not always consistently. Nor does industrial peace necessarily betoken a resurgent management. Germany, the powerhouse of Europe, is typified by sometimes residual strike levels punctuated by massive disputes. Indeed, a number of researchers have cautioned against any simple reading of the statistics.

Edwards and Hyman (1994) argue that in Europe a longer historical view, over the whole post-war period, shows the decline is not all that marked and the 'downswing is not a secular trend'. Only Austria shows a progressive decline in its strike record since the 1950s, and only in the UK did the 1980s and 1990s stand out as a time of historically low levels of disputes. France and Italy show little variation over the decades; in Germany the pattern fluctuates; and in Sweden industrial conflict rose in the 1980s. Moreover, the nature of strikes seems to have changed significantly. Patterns remain diverse but new meanings and new locations for industrial conflict emerged in the 1990s. Gall (1997) has challenged the consensus that conflict has declined in significance and has characterized the decade 1986–95 in terms of 'a growth in industrial strife'. In particular, the character of disputes in this period was dominated by the 'demonstrative' strike. Gall points to the paradox of a decline in strikes specific to plants or employers, alongside explosive growth in short duration national stoppages often meant as political protests. Italy, Spain, Greece, France, and Germany have all seen these large-scale stoppages. They indicate workers caught up in wider-level events including public-sector cuts, the pressures of meeting European Union criteria, and shakeouts in major industries like autos.

Industrial relations and the labour process

Nevertheless, if we return to firm-specific conflict, the changing political climate has paralleled a raft of changes in the nature of the workplace. Information technologies and flexible work patterns have been brought in across many firms. Investment from newcomer economies—like Japan and Pacific rim countries—has apparently meant the importation of new management practices. The new workplace itself may be a greenfield site, employing new 'human resource management' practices that demand altered relations with trade unions, or even union exclusion. Workforces may be feminized, employed on different contracts, in smaller workplaces, and with career and partnership deals with management.

As a result, it has been suggested there has been a permanent decline in the tendency for workers to pursue their interests collectively. Action like strikes is neither appropriate nor effective in the current climate. Commentators have interpreted these changes to mean a shift from traditional forms of collectivism to *individualism* as a means of pursuing interests. For example, Edwards (1992) speaks of a reshaping of the pattern of disputes. He points to a sea change in the relationship between employees and managements in which policies 'aimed at the worker as an individual' have taken precedence. Similarly, as Bacon and Storey (1996) argue, the demands from the new workforces are for a trade-union response tailored to specific needs.

The real challenge of HRM in mainstream companies is that it threatens to deliver for the individual what the union cannot. Trade unions need strategies and policies whereby they are seen to be pushing for individual development. (Bacon and Storey, 1996, p. 70)

Rather than the old 'pay and strikes' agenda, Bacon and Storey suggest, the union movement has to redefine itself to serve this broader pattern of rights and advancement. The upshot has been to effectively sideline conflict as the first weapon of employee protection.

Others, however, have wondered whether there is as much continuity as change in current work settings. Ackers *et al.* (1996) have stressed the need for a careful sifting of the evidence before concluding that sweeping changes are under way. They point out that some of the most detailed studies have been carried out in American transplants (i.e. the mainly Japanese multinationals located in the USA) as these are among the longest established of the new workplaces. Reviewing these studies, they suggest that industrial relations based on union–management partnership deals has been limited, while traditional union influence over pay and conditions has continued; and there is still plentiful evidence of informal and individual resistance. Similarly, with fashionable practices like human resource management, employee involvement, and teamworking, much traditional conflict and worker grievance exists alongside them rather than being eliminated by the new methods (see also Hodson, 1989).

Explorations of this train of thought have pointed out that the impact of changes in recent years has sometimes been contradictory and has given rise to possibilities for *union renewal*. Arrangements that have been intended to curb union power have produced opportunities for regeneration based on more democratic and decentralized forms of unionism (Fosh, 1993). Leaner, devolved management structures have meant that bureaucratic unions have had to develop more responsive structures of their own (Fairbrother, 1996). And legalistic requirements, like the need to ballot members, have put unions in touch with their own membership in ways they never were, and have helped bring about the involvement and participation of the union rank-and-file. Thus 'individualism' and 'collectivism' need not be polar opposites or alternatives; there is nothing to prevent unions from providing services for members as individuals while still pursuing collective action.

In this sense, too, Kelly (1996) has questioned so-called *social partnership* models of the employment relationship. These suggest that, in the new industrial relations climate, unions have had to give up traditional forms of militancy and build more accommodating and moderate relations with employers. Flexibility and teamworking, employee involvement and commitment, and no-strike deals are all part of the new HRM agenda. They reflect the demise of the strike weapon and the recognition of productive efficiency as the common ground for worker–management partnership. Kelly, however, is sceptical of social partnership, and argues instead that 'the general case for militancy is more compelling than the case for moderation' (p. 98). He identifies the use of industrial action as a key element of militancy, and he provides several arguments for continued militancy: that in reality employers do not want a genuine 'partnership' with labour but remain hostile to true power sharing; that there is little evidence of employers actually promoting areas of shared interests (e.g. health and safety, training); and that among unions that have retained a militant stance there is often a growth in membership and evidence of the successful protection of members' interests.

What we observe is that employers have sought to reassert power over their workforces to enable the pursuit of profit-restoring measures. The misleading rhetoric of human resource management and social partnership should not blind us to the continuing antagonism of interests that characterizes the employment relationship. (Kelly, 1996, p. 99)

Thus belief in the demise of industrial conflict may be premature. It is in any case misleading to 'read off' from the current situation a collapse of workers' resolve to take independent action; and it would be an exaggeration to speak of the collapse of militancy, or infer that over the long term resistance cannot be maintained. Much depends on the determination to defend jobs and conditions. Above all, the changes of the present period mean that the full extent of developments in employment patterns remains an open issue.

Conclusion

In this chapter we have followed the twists and turns of the labour process debate. All sides recognize Braverman's 'creative rehabilitation of Marx's own theory of the labour process' (Burawoy, 1979, p. xiii) and see the employment relationship as exploitative and productive. But there are important differences of emphasis, particularly between a structural versus a subjectivist approach.

With a key topic like consent and tacit skills, for example, some researchers have emphasized that people cannot build their work identities on a sense of exclusion; consenting practices based on informal skills, like knack and dexterity, represent important ways in which people stake a claim to their jobs and express their individual subjectivities. On the other hand, a crucial political dimension seems to be missing from tacit skills, and a structural perspective draws attention to the limits of consent. We see this in Manwaring and Wood's (1985) example of the worker who 'had to pick up twenty-six bolts and washers out of a pallet and place them on the front cover of the engine. After six months he would always automatically pick up the right number' (1985, p. 178). This kind of 'skill' would hardly improve the worker's marketability, and while he may gain some satisfaction real benefits go to the employer in terms of productivity gains.

Similarly, the weight that is assigned to conflict differs sharply. Researchers stressing the subjects of social action have been concerned with the totality of market and work relations. For them any account of the labour process that claims to be comprehensive has to include positive elements of skill and consent, as well as the subjectivities of social and gender identity. These are 'as much a condition of the reproduction of capital' as are the forms of workplace conflict that Braverman emphasized (Sturdy *et al.*, 1992, p. 1). Structuralist researchers, on the other hand, tend to privilege conflict, seeing it as the driving-force behind change in industrial capitalism. In this sense, Edwards has concluded that

conflict in the shape of structural antagonism is a basic feature of any exploitative mode of production, and consent, tacit skills, the negotiation of order and so forth have to be understood as shaping how this antagonism is developed and not as principles which can totally counteract it. (1990, p. 147)

Some of the same echoes are picked up in the discussion of collective conflict. Debate there centred on change versus continuity. Whether the industrial relations scene had irrevocably changed, and industrial action and militant unionism are now submerged in a new labour–management accord; or whether the root causes of industrial disputes, in the commodity status of labour and the constraints of managerial authority, continue to hold sway.

The debate probably comes down finally to a difference between the structuralist (and mainly Marxist) writers who argue for a long-term trend towards the degradation of work, and others who argue that the changing nature of work is a spontaneous and uneven process. These positions are difficult to reconcile. It is hard to impose a single interpretation on anything so complex as industrial and occupational change. Moreover, the dilemma may be unresolvable in any practical way, since it ultimately rests on more fundamental debates in the social sciences. What is more important is to emphasize the deeper understanding of work that the labour process debate has led to.

The research that has come out of the critique of Braverman represents a major advance. It has focused attention on historical and comparative forms of work organization, as well as the current realities of the workplace.

Study questions for Chapter 10

1 What was distinctive about Braverman's account of work relations, and what prompted early scepticism about his thesis?

2 How do workers exercise discretion, and create space for themselves, in constraining workplace regimes?

3 How does a structural perspective on the employment relationship explain workplace conflict?

4 What is the evidence for consent in the labour process and employees' positive accommodation to workplace rules?

5 How would you distinguish structural from subjectivist images of the labour process?

6 'Most analyses of the workplace have used gender as a synonym for women' (Barrow). Why would this be a misleading assumption?

7 Why is such a fuss made about strikes when they seem to have little direct economic impact?

8 What are the arguments for and against the view that industrial conflict is neither appropriate nor viable in the modern political-economic climate?

Further reading

Ackers, P., Smith, C., and Smith, P. (eds.) (1996) *The New Workplace and Trade Unionism*. London: Routledge.

Baldamus, W. (1961) *Efficiency and Effort*. London: Tavistock.

Benyon, H. (1984) *Working for Ford*, 2nd edn. Harmondsworth: Penguin.

Burawoy, M. (1985) *The Politics of Production*. London: Verso.

Edwards, P. K. (1986) *Conflict at Work: A Materialist Analysis of Workplace Relations*. Oxford: Blackwell.

—— and Scullion, H. (1982) *The Social Organization of Industrial Conflict: Control and Resistance at the Workplace*. Oxford: Blackwell.

Edwards, R. (1979) *Contested Terrain: The Transformation of the Workplace in the Twentieth Century*. London: Heinemann.

Friedman, A. (1977) *Industry and Labour: Class Struggles at Work and Monopoly Capitalism*. London: Macmillan.

Hyman, R. (1988) *The Political Economy of Industrial Relations*. London: Macmillan.

Jermier, J. M., Knights, D., and Nord, W. R. (eds.) (1994) *Resistance and Power in Organizations*. London: Routledge.

Knights, D. and Willmott, H. (eds.) (1990) *Labour Process Theory*. Basingstoke: Macmillan.

Sturdy, A., Knights, D., and Willmott, H. (eds.) (1992) *Skill and Consent: Contemporary Studies in the Labour Process*. London: Routledge.

Thompson, P. (1989) *The Nature of Work*, 2nd edn. London: Macmillan.

Wood, S. (ed.) (1989) *The Transformation of Work?* London: Unwin Hyman.

Zimbalist, A. (ed.) (1979) *Case Studies on the Labour Process*. London: Monthly Review Press.

11 Alternative Work Design

Summary points and learning objectives

By the end of this chapter you will be able to

- detail the *techniques* of job redesign and employee involvement;
- distinguish the *principles* behind meaningfully redesigned work;
- discuss the organizational and market *constraints* that affect the implementation of these techniques and principles;
- review the *historical* development of work redesign;
- understand the *critical debates* that have raged around contentious issues like worker autonomy and empowerment;
- distinguish the modern phase of *employee involvement* and its links to the new managerialism;
- understand the importance of the changing *social and economic context* in which methods of job redesign and employee involvement have been implemented.

Introduction

The expectations we have of employment in industrial society include social rewards as well as purely economic ones. Yet the human needs of people in work are very often frustrated by jobs, many of which make little or no allowance for individual commitment or the exercise of skills and initiative. The modern design of work is traced back to a period from roughly the 1890s through to the 1920s, and the pioneering figure of F. W. Taylor (and following him the Gilbreths and others) who set down the principles of the 'scientific' study of work. Taylor's ideas decreed that workers behaved in an individualist manner, motivated by monetary rewards, and that jobs should be fragmented and tightly controlled and measured. Partly this was meant to cut down worker fatigue and create a newly efficient and streamlined work process, but the outcome was an approach to job design that was ignorant of the social aspects of work. Taylorism (discussed in detail in the previous two chapters) became the basis of a powerful management movement which fed beliefs and myths that workers were only fit for, and indeed wanted, repetitive jobs. The world neatly and handily divided into a responsible and energetic minority, destined for management, and the mass fitted by nature for routine labour. Listen to Henry Ford writing in 1924:

Repetitive labour—the doing of one thing over and over again and always in the same way—is a terrifying prospect to a certain kind of mind. It is terrifying to me. I could not possibly do the same thing day in day out, but to other minds, perhaps I might say to the majority of minds, repetitive operations hold no terrors. In fact, to some types of mind thought is absolutely appalling. To them the ideal job is one where the creative instinct need not be expressed. The jobs where it is necessary to put in mind as well as muscle have very few takers—we always need men who like a job because it is difficult. The average worker, I am sorry to say, wants a job in which he does not have to put forth much physical exertion—above all, he wants a job in which he does not have to think. (Henry Ford, quoted in Berggren, 1993, p. 203.)

However, the legacy of Taylor is now widely perceived as containing many drawbacks. The human issues of routinized, deskilled labour are seen as problems in their own right, while the dissatisfaction experienced in work may have wider economic repercussions. Poor productivity and quality, the 'withdrawal' from work manifest in absenteeism and labour turnover, as well as types of industrial conflict have all been linked to alienation from work.

The attempt to address these problems and to organize work along more human-centred lines has long been the concern of reforming groups, social scientists, and socially aware employers. Social psychology has made a contribution to these efforts which goes back at least to the Hawthorne experiments (see Chapter 7). The 'discovery' of group factors marked the beginning of the Human Relations Movement and theories about social behaviour in work. Indeed, in different ways the theories of motivation and group dynamics reviewed in chapters 5, 6 and 7 have all been concerned with the question of appropriate occupational rewards and work settings.

Interest in the social and economic benefits of participative work structures covers a wide spectrum of possibilities. The involvement of employees in high-level decision-making (worker representatives on the board of directors) or participation in the financial aspects of the company (share ownership schemes) are two examples. And of course determining decisions about pay and working conditions is already widespread in the industrial relations arrangements for collective bargaining. These are all forms of employee participation. But for a number of years much interest in this area has focused on changing the actual jobs that people perform, and devising a response to the type of job design that divides and constrains labour. In this chapter we will be looking at the redesign of work—the context in which an interest in 'enriched' work emerged and took shape, and how these issues have adapted to employee empowerment and involvement in more recent market conditions.

Techniques of work redesign

Researchers in this area initially singled out three main dimensions along which the jobs of individuals or groups can change. These reflect the functional aspects of the work performed (variety), a political or power dimension (autonomy), and the level of meaning that people are able to invest in work (completeness of task). Analytical dimensions such as these are important as they provide objectives for work design and a set of criteria by which we can assess redesigned jobs.

- *Variety*. This refers to the complexity and differentiation of work. An increase in task variety and the multiplicity of skills exercised should improve the content and quality of a job, increasing its interest for the individual and reducing the monotony and routine of work.
- *Autonomy*. This refers to the degree of control that people have over their jobs. Lack of autonomy is typical of much machine-paced or assembly-line work, and is regarded as a main cause of job dissatisfaction. Conversely, work experience can be greatly enhanced by the introduction of 'higher-level' tasks which involve a degree of discretion and responsibility, and by the group allocation of work and the self-selection of groups.
- *Completeness of task*. Many routine jobs reflect the imposition of extreme divisions of labour. This creates highly fragmented, meaningless work and means that people are unable to see any sense in what they do. To reverse this trend, effective redesign needs to create 'whole' tasks that are more identifiable and meaningful, and based on integrated work cycles.

Two basic approaches to the redesign of work involve rotating the jobs that workers do and enlarging individual work tasks. *Job rotation* does not actually mean changing the work itself, but it permits a greater variety for individuals by moving them between jobs. In practice, managers often use this method without necessarily having a formal system of rotating workers at regular intervals. They may simply ensure that particularly unpleasant or monotonous jobs are shared, and that certain workers are not allocated to them permanently. Secondly, *job enlargement* involves merging a number of simplified tasks to form a single task with an extended range of work. In mass assembly industries, for instance, this often means that cycle times (i.e. the time taken to complete a single cycle of a repetitive task) are not allowed to fall below some stipulated minimum level, so there is a limit placed on the extent to which jobs can be subdivided.

However, each of these methods is thought to be inadequate as a basis for genuinely humanizing work. Job rotation merely redistributes existing work, and job enlargement involves regrouping unit tasks rather than seeking to improve the work itself. At best, it has been argued, these methods make cosmetic changes. At worst they may bring about an actual deterioration in working conditions. If job rotation is used chiefly to create a more flexible workforce, workers may find themselves being moved from job to job without being consulted. This may disrupt the rhythm of work and threaten job security if workers become interchangeable. Similarly, the enlargement of jobs sometimes merely results in an intensification of work. People often cope with monotonous jobs by mentally 'switching off' to some extent, but work that involves a whole series of repetitive tasks may require much closer attention. The most unpleasant and taxing jobs are often those that are monotonous and also demand high levels of attention.

The 'enrichment' of work

There are, however, other methods regarded as more meaningful ways of redesigning work. Two of the most important ones are *job enrichment* and the provision for *group working*. The basic purpose of job enrichment is to introduce responsibilities or additional tasks into a job which genuinely do make it more of a complete occupation. Many routinized production jobs can be enriched by the inclusion of tasks such as machine maintenance, elements of inspection and quality control, or machine-setting. It may also be possible to arrange for workers to obtain their own materials, or to deal with communications with other departments. Changes like these can enhance workers' skills and enable them to deal with complete tasks rather than highly fragmented ones. Thus, instead of similar degraded tasks being combined together, genuine job enrichment means that a certain amount of planning and control is introduced into the work—tasks which otherwise would have been the responsibility of supervisors or specialist types of workers.

Secondly, group working has many potential advantages. There are manifest social and psychological gains in working co-operatively with others, rather than on isolated tasks; also many of the requirements of job enrichment can be built into the group context. Group tasks by their very nature tend to be based on complete operations and involve greater complexity and variety than fragmented tasks. Groups can be self-regulating, reducing the need for supervision and increasing members' perception of control. Furthermore, it is relatively easy to allow for job rotation and the fair allocation of tasks within a group system of working—indeed it can be beneficial to allow group members to arrange this for themselves.

The socio-technical systems approach

The application of group theory to the work situation has been greatly advanced by the researchers of the Tavistock Institute of Human Relations. Their distinctive approach, developed in a series of classic studies in the British coal-mining industry and later in the Indian textiles industry, stressed an active involvement on the part of researchers in diagnosing firms' problems and proposing long-term solutions.

The Tavistock's interest in work groups began in the late 1940s when one of their researchers, Eric Trist, investigated the reasons for the failure of mechanization in coal-mining to bring about improvements in productivity and for the poor state of industrial relations in the industry. Before mechanization, coal had been extracted by small teams of miners. Each shift team worked in a section of the coalface, miners shared all the tasks in the coal-getting cycle, and pay was distributed according to group consensus. These shift teams became highly cohesive social units which helped them deal with the dangerous and difficult conditions in which they worked (Trist and Bamforth, 1951).

However, the arrival of new technology (conveyor belts and coal-cutting machinery) transformed the old methods, and also seemed to require different social relationships. With the new method, each shift consisted of a large group of miners under a supervisor; the team was divided into specialists, and an elaborate pay structure led to a status hierarchy developing among miners. The production and industrial relations problems caused by these changes included co-ordination difficulties as shifts were unable or unwilling to clear work left by the previous shift, and problems of control due to miners' resentment of being supervised.

Trist recognized the central problem of the impact of technological advances on traditional group working practices. Any solution would have to involve 'the general character of the method so that a social as well as a technological whole can come into existence' (Trist and Bamforth, 1951). This line of thought led to the concept of work organization as a *socio-technical system*. It implied that the work setting has to be seen in terms of two inter-related systems: a social and a technical system, each with its own independent properties. And while optimizing the overall system does usually mean sub-optimal states for each component, ideally the costs would be balanced out so that no one system carried them all (whereas what had occurred in mining was that optimization of the technology had led to a severely sub-optimal state in the miners' group relationships).

The Tavistock researchers carefully observed how particular groups of miners had adapted to the changed conditions. They noted that on certain coalfaces groups emerged naturally that managed to utilize the new technology under modified working arrangements. Using these observations the Tavistockers developed a 'composite' method in which miners were divided into shift teams. Within each self-contained team, practices were adopted such as the miners acquiring skills in all phases of the work-cycle, and choosing what shift they worked on and the task they wanted within each shift. These modifications reduced the co-ordination and supervisory problems, as well as satisfying miners' socio-psychological needs for more meaningful work and satisfactory relations with other miners.

The first direct application of Trist's socio-technical principle came with research conducted by A. K. Rice in an Indian textile mill (Rice, 1958). As with the mining study, mechanization had disrupted an established work pattern. The introduction of automatic looms had deskilled jobs and turned workers into machine-minders, the effects of which had nullified any expected productivity gains. In this context, Rice helped to introduce a group working system, later extending it to non-automatic weaving. Both systems were based on small groups of workers, self-regulating and self-led, and performing all the tasks of weaving. This resulted in steady improvements in output and quality of cloth. Rice also stressed the very high value that workers placed on these co-operative working arrangements. Once they had been given the opportunity to reorganize themselves into secure groups, workers showed great determination in making the new system successful.

The model of production as a socio-technical system provided a framework within which Rice included a broad range of factors. For example, he noted that workers' attachment to the group system was strengthened by elements of Indian culture, particularly the tradition of collective working in family-based cottage industries. In addition, the enhancement of work had meant that jobs became more demanding, and Rice was very clear about the responsibility of management to provide adequate training and technical support for the new groups.

Box 11.1 Socio-technical principles

This attempt to set out the key elements of the socio-technical approach is no authoritative reading of socio-technical principles. Nor does it bother to state the obvious, namely that redesigned work has to meet common standards of variety, autonomy, and completeness of task. The point simply is to try to single out what socio-technical theory has contributed to our understanding of (meaningful) work redesign. Because while socio-technical theory represents the 'classic approach', in some ways it has never been bettered by other more fashionable and current ideas.

- Job redesign cannot exist in a vacuum. The Tavistockers' open systems model of organization suggested that wider factors, like culture and the management of group boundary conditions, have to be taken into account if changes are to be sustained.
- Meaningful redesign must be interactive. Employees' involvement should amount to more than just passive consent. Changes should be evolutionary, with inputs from all parties, rather than being a set of abstract principles.
- Meaningful redesign must be holistic. Workers' input and socio-technical principles have to be represented throughout the redesign process—particularly in the early stages when decisions are taken that have a constraining influence further down the line.
- Social partnership is possible. A balance can be struck between the social criteria of responsible work and the technical/economic criteria of productive effectiveness.

Interestingly, in a follow-up study, conducted some 15 years after Rice's original research, Miller (1975) confirmed the importance of these aspects of the work context. Miller found that in automatic weaving production had reverted to individual methods, while in the non-automatic sheds the group system had survived remarkably intact. He explained this by the different impact of increased work pressure on the two production systems. Workers' strong attachment to the groups made them resilient over the long term, but under excessive pressure some of the groups had been unable to adjust. Here, a failure of management to continue to provide support and protection for the groups had accounted for the collapse of group working.

Tavistock principles can be applied in their fullest form on new, 'greenfield' sites where the technology is not already established. Innovation is all too frequently obsessed with the technological side, while the human aspects are considered only as an afterthought. The concept of production as a socio-technical system implies that *both* subsystems are equally important. For example, Klein (1981) has described the design of a new plant for the confectionery company, Trebor. Because of strong company interest in the human side of work, she was able to examine the social consequences of particular layouts with the design team. This resulted in the building of an impressive factory, with single-status facilities, pleasant surroundings and a group-based production process. As Klein was at pains to emphasize, the different groups involved (architects, equipment suppliers, management) were not always in harmony, and the involvement of a social scientist was no automatic guarantee of a human environment. Amid the 'welter of activities' a number of important choices as to how work might be organized were lost. Nevertheless, it remains true that the work process is more likely to be optimized where choices can be made which adapt the social as well as technological aspects.

Autonomous work groups

The great virtue of the Tavistock approach has been in extending the range of variables that are seen to affect workers' attitudes and performance. It has thus greatly increased the *scope* of work design. But although the socio-technical approach has been extremely useful and influential, it has not evolved into a general theoretical framework. The practical concerns of investigators have usually caused them to focus on the particular workplace under investigation, and to adopt 'action' methods in order to intervene at each stage to try to improve different aspects of performance. These factors have made it difficult to define more general guidelines for the design of work. In short, the breadth of socio-technical theory has been achieved at the cost of precision.

By the 1980s, however, psychologists were attempting to develop precise definitions of group variables. In particular, they proposed 'autonomous work groups' as a useful model, both theoretically and for the practical purpose of introducing changes in the workplace. This was seen as a compromise between the very narrow job characteristics model, based on individual motivation, and the more diffuse socio-technical systems.

The autonomous work group needs to be distinguished from the more ordinary co-acting group, where the main impact of membership on individuals is through higher levels of interaction (see Chapter 6). The crucial difference between the two types of group is the means of *control*. Co-acting groups are controlled externally, whereas autonomous work groups are to a large extent self-regulating, either removing the need for supervisors or greatly reducing it.

For example, Kemp *et al.* (1983) investigated job design on a greenfield site, where they were able to use several control groups so that plant and shift factors could be eliminated. Groups of eight to twelve operatives had been established, and responsible work roles included job allocation, the resolution of local production problems, organizing work breaks, contacting other departments and training new recruits. When compared with control groups, the researchers were able to show that greater job satisfaction, perceptions of higher job complexity and improved leadership style were successfully established in the experimental groups. However, workers' commitment to the firm and their work motivation remained the same. In other words, this carefully designed experiment showed both that beneficial changes may be brought about, and also that the effects are rarely simple when a broad range of variables is measured.

Box 11.2 Natural workgroups and meaningful alternative design

The whole notion of the 'expert' design of work would hardly be necessary if jobs were skilled and responsible in the first place. However, the notion of some original state of traditionally skilled work, while it may seem far-fetched, can be expressed in the idea of *natural work groups*.

This doesn't necessarily mean some primal state, but simply work organization that is not predominantly management inspired nor the creation of design specialists. In such cases the ways in which tasks are performed will have evolved over time through the local control of labour. The 'natural' way of doing a job invoked common-sense understandings of work and shared tasks that emerge spontaneously. It reflects a task organization that is an outflow of workers' skills and abilities, as well as the logic of the job itself. Such a basis of satisfying and productive work has a potential for alternative design that has rarely been recognized.

In this context some of the classic research is worth revisiting. The early Tavistock studies, undertaken by Trist and Rice, were much concerned with new job designs derived from established work patterns. Trist's pioneering studies placed central importance on traditional groups. The 'single place' method of mining was a system of shared tasks based on the multi-skilled miner and a natural sequence for coal-cutting that required very little formal organization. These working arrangements were shattered by the arrival of mechanized coal-cutting, but on some coal-faces methods evolved that withstood the changes. This form of 'composite' self-regulation embodied many elements of single place working while still absorbing the higher levels of mechanization.

In this classic case, therefore, the original impetus came from workers' own design of work. The Tavistock researchers paid close attention to long-term changes and working practices that preceded the automated systems they were called in to investigate. Indeed, the researchers spent long hours with their notebooks just observing how composite methods emerged. In most modern textbooks, however, you get no sense at all of this independent work culture. The role of natural workgroups in these famous experiments is largely forgotten and the Tavistockers themselves are simply said to have designed the new systems.

The idea of natural workgroups also reveals something of the paradox at the heart of job redesign. There is often a strong resemblance between work that has been (meaningfully) redesigned and the choices people make when they plan and organize their own work. The classic Tavistock cases certainly had this kind of 'cyclical' element— work that was redesigned in order to inject skills and discretion that ironically had been there in an initial stage of collaborative production. Obviously not all cases are living examples of work adaptation in this sense, nor can all problems be tackled by recapturing 'lost traditions'. But the key point is that employees' commitment to new working arrangements can only be guaranteed if their interests are allowed to take shape independently, however that is achieved. Meaningful alternative design had to be an interactive process rather than an abstract rationale applied by outside experts.

Source: R. Fincham (1989) 'Natural workgroups and the process of job design', *Employee Relations*, 11/6: 17–22.

The constraints on work redesign

Numerous programmes of work redesign have been initiated. The most widespread and systematic developments have undoubtedly been those in Scandinavian companies, such as Volvo, Saab-Scania and Norsk-Hydro, but other major companies like ICI, Phillips and Fiat have also pursued work redesign as an element of employee policy. Individual case studies have often shown impressive results. Changes in working conditions and improvements in various criteria of performance and worker satisfaction have all been reported. However, this apparently sound body of research and practical application is now being assessed much more critically.

Part of this criticism has arisen from a re-evaluation of the *evidence*. Although the record is impressive at first sight, under scrutiny the research methodology of many case studies turns out to have been flawed (Kelly, 1982). For example, there have been tendencies to report only positive findings and to accept managerial assessments of success rather than seek objective measures. There has often been a marked failure to allow for a 'novelty effect'—the possibility that improvements in workers' satisfaction may arise out of the newness of change rather than changes in the working arrangements themselves. Thus, few experiments verify whether improvements are sustained over the long term. Related to this, the problem of 'compensatory rivalry' occurs if other plants within a company, or other departments, get to hear of a particular job redesign project, and their own performance suffers because they feel they have been overlooked. This may lead to the performance of the experimental group being artificially inflated. Finally, it may be impossible to isolate the effects of job redesign if, as sometimes happens, a whole package of changes is implemented at one time.

A second general criticism concerns the wider influence of job redesign. Again, the record of research and the support of major companies is superficially impressive, and there has been an acceptance of work humanization at the level of public policy. None the less, the true impact of all this has been far less significant. Many of the programmes have in fact never progressed beyond the experimental stage, and have often been discontinued after a short period. Similarly, many schemes have implemented cosmetic changes, despite claims of far-reaching job enrichment.

One of the main reasons why so much research in this area has not conformed to sound methodology is because many case studies have been carried out by paid consultants. Even research conducted by academics is often part of a consultancy exercise and far from being independent. Under such circumstances, where management calls the tune, researchers may be under pressure to short-circuit proper empirical procedures and to come up with positive findings. This gap between theory and practice can only be explained by taking seriously the context in which work restructuring is conducted. Only so much can be specified by the techniques of work redesign. In reality, it is *how* the techniques are implemented, and whether they are sustained over time, that often decides the success or otherwise of projects. Work systems are not set in concrete but depend on the organizational and market environment in which they are implemented;

and the full range of group variables, as well as wider environmental factors, have to be considered.

The work group context

The more detailed experiments that occupational psychologists have developed include a range of factors which can influence work design, and which determine whether any benefits will be sustained (Slocum and Sims, 1980; Wall, 1980; Kemp *et al.*, 1983).

Box 11.3 The quality of whose working life?

This interesting and rather humorous piece of research was done by David Guest and his colleagues while they were looking at a project to improve the 'quality of working life'. The company concerned was attempting to redesign the work process to make it more interesting for workers, more varied, more meaningful, and so on. Management was very enthusiastic about the scheme. They had implemented it on an experimental basis, and they regarded it as being highly successful and beneficial in terms of its impact on the nature of employees' jobs and their positive experience of work.

Guest and his colleagues decided to look at the workers' opinions of the scheme, in order to get a more rounded set of views of its success, and what they found was quite startling. They distributed a questionnaire to the workers asking about their knowledge of the scheme and their feelings about it. The findings showed that, first, only about 50 per cent of workers even knew that any kind of new scheme was in existence. Secondly, only about half of those who acknowledged that there was a scheme in existence correctly identified it, only about half again thought that it made any difference. And only about half of those thought that the changes had been beneficial to them.

So here was a situation in which management had put a scheme into operation which they regarded as being both important and beneficial. But there was a yawning gap between managers' and workers' perceptions of the change. The workers, whose jobs it was supposed to benefit, were mostly unaware of any change having taken place; and only a small proportion (it was less than 10 per cent) regarded the change as being positive and significant.

The implications of such a finding are considerable. In this particular firm, workers and managers inhabited different worlds, with relatively poor communications channels between them. And what was an important 'reality' for managers was practically unknown to the bulk of employees. The failure to elicit workers' opinions and involve them in the change process would almost certainly damage any chances of success.

Source: D. Guest, R. Williams, and P. Dewe, 'Workers' perceptions of changes affecting the quality of working life', in K. Duncan, M. Gruneberg, and D. Wallis (eds.) *Changes in Working Life*, Chichester: Wiley, 1980.

1. *First-level managerial practices*. It is clear that the behaviour of supervisors is critical in determining the value of autonomous work groups to an organization and to group members. Drawing on the leadership behaviour dimensions of 'initiating structure', 'consideration' (see Chapter 8) and 'tolerance of freedom', Wall and Cordery (1982) argued that if autonomous work groups are to be successful—indeed if the groups are to enjoy a measure of true autonomy—then supervisory practice has to change in the direction of more freedom, less initiating structure and more consideration.

2. *Group composition*. While the group has to possess task-relevant skills, these alone are not usually sufficient for effective performance. To utilize pooled resources, process problems also have to be minimized. We saw in Chapter 6 how cohesiveness within a group can be undermined if members are too dissimilar in status, values and abilities. Hence, effective personal and work outcomes are more likely with moderate heterogeneity in group members.

3. *Norms and performance strategies*. Discussions of how work can be accomplished can cause anxiety in group members and this too can lead to group process problems. Members may avoid discussing appropriate ways of performing group tasks, and develop strategies either as a habitual response or by accident. Autonomous work groups may, therefore, need to be encouraged to develop norms which support the exploration of various performance strategies.

4. *The general work setting*. Good group design, in terms of task, composition and supervisory practices, can be reinforced or undermined by a number of contextual factors. For example, the reward system and the performance targets need to be planned appropriately. Effective task behaviour must be adequately rewarded, and performance targets must be both challenging and realistic, if good work group design is to be enhanced. Management also has a key role in ensuring that teams are provided with enough information to enable members to distinguish between flexible performance targets and targets which act as real constraints on behaviour. Without such detailed information, the group may develop ways of working based on inaccurate perceptions of an organization's requirements. Finally, the pattern of relationships between a group and other groups may affect the outcome of autonomous working arrangements. A balance has to be achieved between integration and differentiation: too much integration of effort between groups may lead to a loss in group identity; too much differentiation may result in damaging levels of competition.

The organizational context

In addition to the immediate context of work groups, the economic demands for profitability in organizations and established technological practices impose very powerful constraints on what may be done to improve work. Much of the work humanization literature, it has been suggested, has overlooked or underestimate these realities of organizations.

Job design An important though often unacknowledged factor constraining work *re*design is the process by which work is designed in the first place. Particularly with complex mass assembly, the production jobs that workers perform have to be seen not as discrete tasks but as the final link in a long chain, beginning in the original design phase and continuing through product and process development. In these early stages little or no consideration will have been given to the human needs of the workers who will eventually carry out production. As Child (1984, pp. 38–9) has pointed out: 'heavily capitalized mass production plant . . . has generally imposed the greatest constraint upon work restructuring'. Inflexible production processes, where individual tasks are highly integrated, can prevent all but the most superficial of changes in the assembly stages.

Furthermore, while we may assume that programmes of work redesign are based on human criteria, in reality the reverse is often the case: the rationale of job design may continue to constrain attempts to humanize work. Thus, in a survey of work design programmes in Europe, Lupton and Tannner (1980) found that production engineers initiated the majority of projects, and efficiency-related goals were uppermost. This was despite the fact that projects were mostly publicized in terms of the benefits for workers.

Organizational power structures Organizational hierarchies in reality are structures of deeply entrenched power, and this has also proved to be a major constraint on work humanization. The attempt to transfer control to shopfloor jobs may well threaten the status and security of the managers and supervisors who exercise that control, and in several instances where apparently promising schemes have been abandoned it has been because of the wider repercussions for organizational power. Indeed, to the extent that work redesign really is significant, we should expect it to cut across the existing divisions of power.

One of the commonest causes of failure in programmes is resistance from supervisors. An early experiment carried out in the Norwegian company Norsk-Hydro clearly illustrated this problem. The firm's intention was to enrich workers' jobs by the inclusion of some basic supervisory tasks, which would also allow the foremen to devote more time to forward planning. However, the foremen perceived the changes rather differently. They saw the bread and butter elements of their jobs being taken over by workers, and being compensated for by some vague activity, planning, of which they had little experience. Consequently, the foremen resisted the scheme in its early stages and, faced with their disapproval, management called it off. However, by this time the workers had begun to respond positively to the changes and were disappointed when they had to return to the old ways of working. Thus at the end of the day, management were back where they started, but with a suspicious supervisory group and a disgruntled workforce.

The constraint of organizational power is also frequently the explanation behind the common paradox of projects being abandoned because they are 'too successful'. The strict demarcation of power within organizations means that even seemingly small changes may be widely disruptive, particularly if they set off demands that managers feel unable to meet or which threaten their control.

Employee involvement and empowerment

The movement towards more enriching work of the 1960s and 1970s highlighted methods like autonomous workgroups as the basis of groundbreaking new patterns of organizing and designing jobs. However, as we saw, the reality was that autonomous work was never really implemented—certainly not much beyond the project stage, and not beyond the boundaries of individual companies. But by about the mid-1980s a new wave of thinking about employee relations took shape based on the empowerment and involvement of employees in the workplace, and which has many surface similarities to the old autonomy movement.

Employee involvement (EI) embraces a wide range of programmes, some of which are connected with employees' control over (redesigned) work. Marchington *et al.* (1992) define what they call 'the EI mix' to include initiatives such as house journals, suggestion schemes, employee attitude surveys, and team briefing; also included are quality circles, customer care and total quality initiatives, and team working. Clearly some of these are not particularly significant, while a few (like suggestion schemes and attitude surveys) have been around a long time. Nevertheless, some initiatives are more innovative and may involve aspects of redesigned work. Empowerment in particular is a repackaging of elements of job enrichment enabling employees to use their skills more effectively. It means responsibility for production being pushed down to the factory or office floor, which has implications for employee participation and the design of jobs. Empowerment is thus often an aspect of wider restructuring and the move to flexible and less bureaucratic organizational designs.

Marchington *et al.* make clear the main characteristic of EI is that it is management sponsored. The involvement of workers means involving them in the goals of the company and obtaining commitment and loyalty. Rather than being part of a pattern of co-determination, or the sharing of workplace power, EI is about 'enhancing employee contribution to the organization'. For this reason, much of EI works at the level of communication, and is based on information about company policies and plans as a means of getting employees to identify with them. For instance, one very popular and widespread EI technique, team briefing, divides the workforce into groups which meet on a regular basis (usually monthly) to be briefed on various items of company news. This provides a network of downward communications for companies, as well as a means of gauging employee opinion on specific issues.

EI is also closely linked with many of the fashionable, or even 'faddish', elements of new management thinking. Recognizing the importance of the customer, for example, is an aspect of competitiveness that many firms feel compelled to adopt; the empowerment of employees to take decisions about customer service, and enhancing their motivation to do so, are then seen as crucial. Similarly, new approaches to personnel that go under the banner of 'human resource management' are all about treating labour strategically, as an asset rather than a fixed cost; and this means actively defining the contributions that employees make. Strategic HRM sees workers as 'a human resource to be

nurtured and developed, thus engendering a wider commitment to the organization'
(Ackers and Black, 1992). In addition, many organizations have taken up the idea of
change at the 'cultural' level. They seek to alter the climate of attitudes and adapt the
whole organization to a core set of beliefs and values, often being flexible and market
focused. EI programmes are commonly part of such cultural change given their aim of
transforming employee attitudes.

As Marchington *et al.* (1992) discovered, companies that are alive to these new
approaches are likely to adopt a range of EI techniques. Firms may use a combination
(or even a full mix) of methods, many of them overlapping in the practical detail of their
operation. Customer care and total quality programmes are often implemented under
cultural change, while a focus on 'people' is about engaging the commitment and
loyalty of both the customer and the worker.

In this sense employee involvement, and the commitment of workers to organizational objectives, are products of a new environment—a set of related changes that has
transformed the market situation of companies since the 1980s. Numbered among
these is the intensification of global competition which has forced managements to
explore all the means at their disposal of getting a competitive edge. Much of this competition comes from 'newcomer' economies, like Japan and the Pacific rim countries,
which themselves apparently have work cultures based on attention to detail and
identification with central goals. The production methods (like just-in-time) coming
from these economies are based on workers being locked into a total commitment to
production. Labour-market factors have also contributed. Rising unemployment and
declining trade union power—again features of the 1980s and 1990s—have created a
vacuum into which employers have stepped with direct appeals for worker commitment.

In the new economic climate, and a labour market that favours employers, some
observers have been puzzled by the recent wave of interest in employee involvement. As
with all systems of ideas, interest in them ebbs and flows with circumstances, and work
humanization has been seen as a product of periods of full employment when employers have had to compete for labour. Ramsay (1977) in particular has traced a number of
surges in worker participation since the end of the last century, which invariably have
occurred when conditions have favoured labour—during times of economic growth
and/or less intense competition, when there has been a national drive to stimulate output and productivity, or when the state and employers have been nervous of the power
of organized labour.

All this accords with the decline in the numbers of projects and autonomous working
shown by companies towards the end of the 1970s. The charitable view was that work
humanization was making 'slow progress'. But more critically it was suggested that in
the changed circumstances, with unsettled economic conditions and higher unemployment, employers no longer needed work humanization either as a means of attracting
labour or as a justification of their policies (Ramsay, 1985; Friedman, 1984). In this
sense, the period since around the mid-1980s, which has apparently seen a new desire
to seek improvements in the employment relationship, does not at first sight seem to fit

the pattern. However, numerous researchers have recognized that this revival of interest in participation and involvement has been quite different from periods which have preceded it. The prevailing economic climate would not normally be linked with major examples of employee responsibility and autonomy. And, indeed, modern versions of employee involvement bear little resemblance to actual socio-technical principles, while EI itself is management initiated and not a product of labour-management interaction (Ackers *et al.*, 1991; Ramsay, 1991; Sewell and Wilkinson, 1992*b*; McArdle *et al.*, 1995).

Here Buchanan (1992) has argued that there has been a change in perceptions, on the part of both managers and workers, of the boundaries of legitimate authority. When the idea of giving employees more scope at work was first developed it was seen as inappropriate and risky by managers whose experience had been that of conventional organizations and the direct control of labour. But changed conditions have meant that adaptive organizations and employee initiative are essential for remaining competitive. In new design organizations, Buchanan points out, realistic expectations determine the employment relationship and widen the area of acceptability of organizational goals and employee discretion.

Team working

As we have stressed, several (though not all) EI techniques have implications for redesigned work. Quality circles, total quality schemes, and empowerment are among the most significant. Quality circles are not directly about redesign but are decision-making groups—group working arrangements which involve workers meeting, perhaps at the end of a shift, to discuss the day's problems and ways of improving production. Nevertheless, they can be integrated into new work designs and used for tapping into employees' detailed work experience. Quality circles were helpful for gaining the levels of continuous improvement in working practice necessary for total quality initiatives, though they were linked with the first wave of total quality management in the 1980s (Marchington *et al.*, 1992, p. 6). More recently *team working* has been a key technique used in the drive for total quality. As an EI method it relates more specifically to worker responsibility, as well as bringing into play the group technology long associated with job redesign.

Some rather critical case studies of team working have drawn attention to the paradox of individual employees being required to take responsibility for quality while real decisions are taken elsewhere. Common features of these studies have included workers being responsible for driving down errors and for programmes of work intensification, much closer monitoring of output and defects, and various 'behavioural' factors entering into workers' security and advancement (Sewell and Wilkinson, 1992*b*; McArdle *et al.*, 1995).

Pollert (1996), for example, looked at the introduction of team working in the food industry. This was definitely a deskilled environment, with workers doing assembly line-type jobs such as packing and the care of automated machinery, but teams were at the heart of a new empowerment culture. The old extended supervisory hierarchy had been flattened and new team leaders invested with responsibilities for team building and motivation. Pollert stressed that team working was all part of the tough industrial relations climate since the 1980s, and that it complemented skill and task flexibility and the obsession with removing demarcations and bureaucratic barriers. Her assessment was that, as a form of participation, team working was an artificial exercise given the constraints of repetitive production. It had not challenged or displaced the old divisive forms of work but simply reinforced them. 'For the majority of employees the "flexibility" of team working is limited to job rotation, greater integration of quality control into production, cleaning up around the production area and work intensification' (Pollert, 1992, p. 186). Workers themselves were generally cynical about the teams, seeing them as an excuse for cost cutting and team briefing as a form of brainwashing. Paradoxically 'team working' and management-appointed team leaders could also disrupt existing production groups and structures of work relations, because team composition and team boundaries were often quite arbitrarily drawn. Also there were important gender implications that reinforced the divisions between men's and women's work. Team working for men, who were engaged in the production end of the process (food mixing, preparation), did involve some level of task and social exchange; but for women doing the really repetitive jobs like packing and sorting, team working was next to meaningless.

In another case, McKinlay and Taylor (1996) describe a microelectronics plant that they dub the 'factory of the future'. Self-managing teams, in which members learned and rotated all tasks, were at the heart of a distinctive pattern of labour regulation, while a 'management sanctioned team ideology' replaced bureaucratic control. This was not skilled work, but neither was it degraded routine labour; the products were sophisticated components and they were fabricated on high-tech production lines. Interestingly, in this industry, McKinlay and Taylor point out that the gender balance had changed in recent years: electronics had witnessed a shift from female-dominated mass assembly to a masculinization of production, and over 80 per cent of workers in this particular plant were men.

The researchers describe a number of noteworthy features of the case. In particular, teams took on a disciplining and policing function via a practice of peer review. Members were required to rate each other on various production and attitudinal dimensions and to assess the behaviour of individuals. Though few organizations have actually taken team working this far, peer review formed the basis of an intensive system of internal controls. Looked at another way, what was being exploited, whether consciously or not, were the kinds of group processes like 'groupthink' that we describe in Chapter 7, and the disturbing power of groups to control and modify members' behaviour. In the event, the teams became increasingly variable and erratic, and the research revealed 'a deep and pervasive distrust of peer review' (p. 293). As the system of mutual scoring became increasingly punitive, and their dislike of it hardened, workers developed practices of 'trading' and equalizing scores. Hence the group processes unleashed by management were gradually tamed.

Evaluating employee involvement

Individual case studies like these have also been more widely supported. For example, a survey of some 4,500 trade-union activists carried out by Waddington and Whitston (1996) reached a cautious conclusion on employee involvement. These researchers found that teamworking had been introduced in up to 12 per cent of enterprises, though techniques that had less impact on power relations (e.g. team briefing) were more widespread. However, work intensification was in no way rolled back or diluted by these changes, and control remained 'the overarching objective of management practice at the workplace' (p. 174). Findings like these suggest that social partnership strategies—which express the conviction that managements' goals of performance can be reconciled with an interest in more fulfilling work—are still constrained by the conflicts inherent in the employment relationship. Waddington and Whitston argued there was little evidence to support the view that industrial relations had become more consensual during the period of EI and that 'us and them' attitudes were still the main agenda.

That said, other aspects of research findings have been more positive. Marchington *et al.* (1992, p. ix) found broadly favourable employee attitudes towards involvement, while in some case studies the workforce endorsed the new company culture. Thus, McArdle *et al.* (1995) found that employees in an electronics plant consistently reported more job satisfaction and relished the new ways of working, despite the added responsibility and intensification. McKinlay and Taylor (1996) found that, while employees resented the practice of peer review, groupworking itself was popular. In both these instances extraneous labour-market factors partly explained the acceptance of the new regimes: huge job cuts and closure threats had led to high levels of job insecurity in one case (McArdle *et al.*), while in the other a rigorous selection procedure was in place in order to find workers whose attitudes fitted the company image (McKinlay and Taylor).

Nevertheless, the internal regulation that many feared would be the outcome of EI regimes in reality often rebounded on itself. In certain cases (McKinlay and Taylor, Pollert) researchers showed that the familiar need for employee or trade-union interventions to make controls work was evident, and that intensive team-based discipline simply fell apart. Thus, managerial policies were not the all-embracing systems they purported to be, and workers still exercised their own forms of determination over the labour process. In this vein, Ackers and Black (1992, p. 188) saw EI as a potentially neutral space which employees and their representatives can use 'to express more positive views about the way work is organized and management manages.'

Conclusion

How, then, should we assess the possibility of the meaningful redesign of work? Should these methods be dismissed as ineffective, or even as a management 'con trick'? In his classic study, *Labor and Monopoly Capital* (1974), Braverman anticipated modern doubts by portraying involvement in just this way, as a kind of seductive ploy

allowing workers to move from one fractional job to another, and have the illusion of making decisions by choosing among fixed and limited alternatives designed by a management which deliberately leaves insignificant matters open to choice. (Braverman, quoted in Marchington *et al.*, 1992, p. 10)

In the modern economic order, the power of managements and markets has meant that 'involving' employees is now subsumed in the right to manage—hence the evidence that few of these initiatives impact on real decision-making. Clearly, if these sorts of criticisms are taken seriously, work redesign and employee involvement cannot be taken at face value.

For one thing, despite claims to the contrary, jobs are rarely designed at the expense of *managerial control*. Indeed, restructuring itself may be a tactic of control. Schemes may convey the impression that firms are concerned with employee welfare, and redesigned jobs may devolve a limited amount of discretion, while management remains only marginally committed to change. Thus surveys have found increased control and work intensification rather than unalloyed benefits for workers (Kelly, 1980; Waddington and Whitston, 1996). The methods may further be used as a means of undermining trade-union organization. Redesign schemes should allow for workers to participate in planned change, yet they may partially be intended as a way of diverting workers away from their trade-union representatives.

Efforts to humanize work and involve workers can also be seen as serving an *ideological* purpose. Rather than necessarily being part of management practice, or having any real impact on the work process, these ideas are more concerned with deflecting criticism and with a firm's outward image. They are part of a new range of management techniques that exploit a human relations language and insidious forms of psychological pressure and manipulation. In the commitment culture of the modern firm, workers are meant to find fulfilment in identifying with corporate goals and in contributing their loyalty and skills.

Despite these criticisms there remains a certain amount of guarded optimism concerning work redesign, though the gains looked for are more modest. Work restructuring programmes have left behind a residue of change in some workplaces. And even if this has not been dramatic, the designers of work systems are at least aware of the arguments against fragmented, highly repetitive jobs, and there are some signs of a move away from strictly Taylorist methods towards more broadly based workflows. If 'job satisfaction' has been seen as a cheap alternative to making real improvements in working conditions—the latter of course means capital expenditure and may involve independently recognizing workers' interest—it is now known that meaningful work redesign needs to be adequately resourced. The careful design of projects, the assessment of repercussions, and the sustained backing of all the main players are basic requirements. Given this kind of commitment, we know that improvements in worker fulfilment and performance can be brought about.

Indeed, the debate has moved on in recent years. An awareness of the constraints on alternative design brought awareness of redesign as a practical exercise. It cannot rely on ideal circumstances but is carried out in firms that have to contend with real pressures for profit and efficiency. These concerns have been the impetus behind more pragmatic approaches. Kelly (1985), for instance, has argued that the shaping of work always contains choices, and that sufficient 'political space around the issue of work organization' exists for meaningful job design practices to operate. Similarly, Manwaring and Wood (1985) point to the 'tacit skills' that people possess, even in jobs defined as unskilled. Frequently taken for granted, even by employees themselves, tacit skills reflect the informal knowledge that is the basis of efficiency and co-operation, and which keeps breaking through no matter how constraining the work regime. More recent detailed case studies affirm this basic scenario, and indeed that high commitment regimes like team working can be self-defeating.

These considerations show that the tensions inherent in employment relationships don't go away. On the one hand, opportunities for workers' own design of work continue to exist—particularly where trade unionists and workers make serious attempts to bargain over job design. It is further suggested that some market trends are on the side of work reforms. With firms having to respond to demands for complex and high quality products, skills have to be redistributed in ways that encourage workers' commitment to production. Managerial motives are likely to reflect the need for more flexibly designed systems as much as the desire to control labour. On the other hand, now that it is possible to take a longer perspective, the contrasts between modern 'employee involvement' and the older socio-technical and human-centred approach seem stark indeed. EI fits a hierarchical structure of workplace power and bears little real resemblance to the participative, democratic, socio-technical model.

Work redesign theory continues to move off in new directions. In particular, attention has fastened onto wider comparative considerations. The kind of approach we have been used to, based on the expert design of work, has given way to interest in the institutional circumstances in which different models and approaches may be realized. Thus, the application of socio-technical principles has long been associated with Sweden, and a distinctive Scandinavian/Swedish model of co-determination in work design is now well documented (see the Volvo case study in the Appendix). At the other end of the scale, a stream of innovations that has come to dominate world production derives from 'Japanese' models based on variants of just-in-time production. Lean production, Toyotaism, and the like are strongly linked with forms of commitment and participation that we associate with EI. The work traditions on which German and north European economies are based seem different again. While job redesign has tended to take for granted a past break with high-trust forms of work, approaches that are identified with Germany stress a continuity with craft traditions. These themes will be picked up and further explored in Chapter 20, where we will see that the qualitative value of human labour, and workers' capacity to find solutions to production problems, are still points at issue.

Study questions for Chapter 11

1 What are the various techniques of work redesign and how meaningful are they as ways of redesigning work?

2 What are the benefits of 'group technology' in redesigning work and in what ways can it be applied?

3 The first principle of job redesign is that there are no principles of job redesign. How might this paradoxical claim be true?

4 The benefits of human-centred work seem self-evident. Why then has it proved so difficult to apply in practice?

5 How have the pragmatic constraints of labour markets affected the nature of employee involvement?

6 Consider the priorities of human-centred work and the socio-technical approach, and compare these with the priorities of employee involvement. What are the similarities and differences?

7 'It is tempting to dismiss moves towards employee involvement as just another ruse constructed by management to encourage workers to engage more freely in their own exploitation' (McArdle *et al.*, 1995). Discuss this criticism.

Further reading

Ackers, P., Smith, C., and Smith, P. (eds.) (1996) *The New Workplace and Trade Unionism*. London: Routledge.

Berggren, C. (1989) 'New production concepts in final assembly—the Swedish experience', in S. Wood (ed.) *The Transformation of Work?* London: Unwin Hyman.

—— (1993) *The Volvo Experience: Alternatives to Lean Production in the Swedish Auto Industry*, Basingstoke: Macmillan.

Blake, R. R., Martin, J. S., and McCarse, A. A. (1989) *Change by Design*. New York: Addison Wesley.

Buchanan, D. and McCalman, J. (1989) *High Performance Work Systems: The Digital Experience*. London: Routledge.

Hanna, D. P. (1988) *Designing Organizations for High Performance*. Reading, Mass.: Addison Wesley.

Kelly, J. E. (1982) *Scientific Management, Job Redesign and Work Performance*. London: Academic Press.

Knights, D., Willmott, H., and Collinson, D. (1985) *Job Redesign: Critical Perspectives on the Labour Process*. Aldershot: Gower.

Marchington, M. (1992) *Managing the Team: A Guide to Successful Employee Involvement*. Oxford: Blackwell.

—— Goodman, J., Wilkinson, A., and Ackers, P. (1992) *New Developments in Employee Involvement*. Manchester School of Management UMIST/Employment Department.

Robertson, I. T. and Smith, M. (1985) *Motivation and Job Redesign: Theory and Practice*. Wimbledon: Institute of Personnel Management.

Sandberg, A. (1995) *Enriching Production: Perspectives on Volvo's Uddevalla Plant as an Alternative to Lean Production*. Aldershot: Avebury.

Scott, A. (1994) *Willing Slaves? British Workers under New Management*. Cambridge: Cambridge University Press.

Appendix to Chapter 11
Case study: Volvo and work redesign

Robin Fincham

In 1993 and 1994 the Swedish car company, Volvo, shut down its plants at Uddevalla and Kalmar bringing to a halt a history of developments that had come to represent some of the most advanced thinking in work design. The closures dealt an undoubted blow to the work humanization movement and were greeted with great dismay by proponents of human-centred work (A. Sandberg, 1993, 1995; Cressey, 1993). For more than two decades the Swedish car industry as a whole developed widely publicized projects based on socio-technical methods and worker autonomy, and Volvo in particular had become justly famous for reforming the assembly line, the classic symbol of alienated labour. The company's long pedigree of group-based methods (Gyllenhammar, 1977*a*, 1977*b*) included many operations—passenger car assembly, trucks, engine production—where they introduced autonomous work groups and achieved increases in cycle times and worker responsibility. But it was at Kalmar and Uddevalla that the most dramatic progress had been made. It is hard to overstate the importance of the plants, both as a testbed for alternative job design and as a potent image of what can be achieved in partnership between managers and workers.

Kalmar and reformed production The car assembly plant, opened at Kalmar in 1974, is probably the best known of all work redesign programmes. Starting from scratch, on a greenfield site, Volvo rearranged straight-line assembly so that a high proportion of work was carried out in a 'dock' system with workers responsible for clusters of tasks. Groups were self-supervising and workers learned all group roles. The car bodies were mounted on self-propelled carriers, or AGVs (automatically guided vehicles), which moved in and out of assembly bays where the work groups were located. Plant layout divided assembly into 20 sections connected in series (giving a basic line system of assembly) but the technology allowed cars to be called up from the main track to be worked on within a flexible time frame. The carriers, a novel feature of the system, made tilting of the body possible so that the underside and inside of cars could be worked on easily.

As Berggren (1989) points out, however, Kalmar was still a compromise between line and dock assembly. The basis of centralized control remained and the development of full-blown autonomous work groups was limited. This meant the Kalmar technology was vulnerable. The buffer stocks between assembly sections gave the workers discretion over line speeds—workers called up and returned cars into the buffer zones rather than direct to the line, which meant that sections could run at different speeds—but equally the removal of buffer stocks could enforce a uniform pace. In fact by the 1980s a much reduced content of work in dock assembly had become the practice in the plant.

Nevertheless, Kalmar had always produced good economic results. For several years the plant was on a par with Volvo's main Swedish car plant, the massive Torslanda plant in Gothenberg, and from the mid-1980s it started to move ahead in critical areas like assembly hours and quality. More significantly, in the couple of years before closure there were dramatic changes in production strategy. From 1990 planners reappraised the plant layout and parallel production and dock assembly returned. As a result, cycle times (which had been between 15 and 40 minutes) increased to as much as one hour in large sections of the plant. According to A. Sandberg (1995), the 'new Kalmar concept' allowed the real potential of the technical system to be realized.

Socialized production at Uddevalla If Kalmar was production reformed, Volvo's plant at Uddevalla, opened in 1989, represented truly revolutionary change. Uddevalla has attracted many superlatives. Berggren (1993, p. 12) calls it a 'transcendant production system'. For Hanke and Rubinstein (1995, p. 182), 'Uddevalla has taken us as far as we have ever been on the road to work without supervision'. The plant has been compared with the main forms of car production, some of which seem to incorporate human-centred work, but which in reality do not measure up to the Uddevalla concept.

Uddevalla's 'enriching production' is fundamentally different from Taylorism and Toyotism, from human, technical and market points of view. In assembly, lean production like Taylorism means repetitive, standardized short cycle jobs. To this comes 'team work' with some rotation and supplementary tasks like inspection and minor repair work as well as contributing to refinement of the standardized procedures. Human-centred work of Uddevalla's type is very different in that it abolishes the line and presents total parallelization of production which allows for advanced customer orientation, interaction between workers and designers, as well as worker autonomy and long work cycles in assembly. (A. Sandberg, 1995, p. 26)

The unique layout of the plant consisted of an automated materials handling centre, surrounded by six independent assembly workshops. Within each of these mini-plants, production teams numbering eight to ten worked on three cars simultaneously. They built complete vehicles on a two-hour cycle. The teams were collectively responsible for job allocation, the scheduling and planning of work, and training; they were supplied with the necessary equipment, including Kalmar-type AGVs that allow the car to tip at angles for easy assembly. Using computers the teams called up parts which arrived silently and smoothly on automatic racked carriers. This system eliminated entirely the serial production of the assembly line. 'The plant combines centralization of the materials handling system with the reconstruction of highly skilled labour intensive assembly, all linked by flexible technology and distributed computer processing power' (Clarke, 1990, p. 4).

As well as technological changes, Volvo devoted huge resources to what Clarke (1990) calls the 'socialization of production'. Working conditions in the plant—noise levels, cleanliness, safety, facilities—were vastly improved compared with conventional car plants. This had also been true at Kalmar, but the company went to enormous lengths at Uddevalla to create an attractive working environment. Rest lounges with fully equipped kitchens and showers were provided; instead of overalls workers wore light tracksuits which they laundered daily, and the company redeveloped all the handtools so that female workers could use them comfortably.

The conditions of whole car assembly also meant that considerable skill levels built up within the Uddevalla teams. Critics of the plant have argued that the need for such skills is actually a barrier to efficiency (Adler and Cole, 1995). The complexity of long cycle times (around two hours to completely assemble a car) is such that the phenomenal dexterity and speed of workers on traditional assembly lines cannot be matched. However, admirers stress that the efficiency gains from repetitive work are more than offset by organization-wide learning. Indeed, Ellegard (1995) has argued that this learning capability was the truly innovative aspect of Uddevalla. The body of knowledge that accumulated in work teams was both a pre-condition of production and the source of the plant's huge potential for improvement. These high levels of collective competence reflect a key element of socio-technical work, namely that the human system as well as the technical system becomes a source of innovation.

Social and market context Changes in production systems do not occur in a vacuum, however, and it is important to look at the social and organizational background as well. To begin with, the nature of the Swedish society and labour market has influenced Volvo (and the country's other car maker, Saab-Scania) to adopt humanized work. In Sweden a history of social democratic government, a strong welfare system, and high living standards have shaped expectations about work. Attitudes towards repetitive work tend to be relatively hostile. The presence of these kinds of social attitudes and a supportive culture has made Sweden fertile ground for imaginative work solutions. Also, residually low unemployment has produced labour-market pressures for work to be designed for workers—rather than the 'normal' situation where with many applying for a few jobs managers have little incentive to make work attractive. The nature of the product and the market niche it occupies are factors too. Volvo cars are sold on safety and quality, and in this type of production human-centred methods are easier to apply than in the high-volume, lower end of the market.

Expectations about work have been supported at an institutional level by groups that have pursued innovative job design. Trade unions in Sweden have high levels of membership, making them key players in industrial policy, and the union movement has long been interested in bargaining about the nature of work. Also, the climate of social democracy has favoured alliances between different sides of industry. The trade unions and the Swedish employers' federation have collaborated over worker autonomy, while government and academic bodies have also participated in the consensus about co-determination. Against this background, there is a very distinctive Swedish socio-technical tradition that has developed further and been more influential than anywhere else in the world.

At Volvo there were some particularly important alliances. During the planning stages of the plants, the intervention of specific groups and individuals was decisive in developing and pushing for the radical vision. Thus Pehr Gyllenhammar, the chief executive for over twenty years, was an enthusiast of work redesign in the company. His power base in his relationship with the unions was a key axis in the developments at Kalmar. Also, at Uddevalla, the trade-union presence, and that of co-opted individuals who strongly identified with socio-technical methods, was crucial in the dynamics of the planning groups (A. Sandberg, 1995, p. 13; Ellegard, 1995, p. 42).

That said, reformed production has only ever accounted for a part of output at Volvo, and only Uddevalla represented fully socialized production. In fact, the company's operations are very varied and span the range from simple Fordism to socialized production. Kalmar and Uddevalla apart, truck and bus production has probably gone furthest in developing human-centred work. This reflects the lower volumes and greater demand for customization in this type of operation. But the car plant at Torslanda is assembly-line based (though quite high levels of team work and other socio-technical methods have been grafted on) and in the main operations outside Sweden, in the USA and Belgium, methods are more strictly Fordist (Berggren, 1993, p. 12).

Thus it would be wrong to think there are consistent policies within Volvo. Plant managers in particular have often been suspicious about giving discretion to workers and have wanted to return to traditional systems of control. Researchers have pointed to divisions between an innovative management culture, sympathetic to ideas about human-centred work, and a more traditionalist camp (A. Sandberg, 1995, p. 13). Thus, while many positive changes are attributed to open-minded management at Volvo, this does not amount to a Swedish 'management style'. Instead, there is a continuous debate about the direction of job design. Of course, noting this variation in policy is no real criticism, as all other major auto manufacturers would be characterized virtually entirely by traditional Fordist attitudes. At least in Volvo there is a debate.

Production strategy and work design The internal political process is much influenced by external economics and the notoriously cyclical market in the motor industry. A company like Volvo—small and heavily reliant on exports—is very sensitive to ups and downs. Both Kalmar and Uddevalla were conceived and built during times of buoyant car sales and tight labour markets. But deepening recession in the industry and rising unemployment in Sweden brought a changed climate, one in which there were already fears for the future of the plants (Hammarstrom and Lansbury, 1991). At the beginning of the 1990s Volvo was planning for cutbacks and rationalization in its multi-plant operations, and this opened up afresh the divisions in management. The tide of opinion as regards the whole programme of enriched work was shifting.

At this point in time a proposed merger with the French car giant, Renault, was taking shape. In fact the talks collapsed late in 1993 and Gyllenhammar resigned when the deal was rejected. The concern was that Renault would have dominated the new company, and Gyllenhammar as architect of the proposal came under fire for making a series of concessions to French ownership. Swedish institutional investors put heavy pressure on the Volvo board to reject the deal out of fears for the future of the national flagship.

In spite of this failure, however, the attempted merger was indicative of the drift of strategic thinking inside Volvo. Renault, like most of the mass car-makers, has pursued a 'Japanese' strategy of lean production, and was uninterested in concepts of human-centred work. Volvo was being urged to rationalize its production, and the turn towards lean methods was part of the process that eliminated humanized work (Berggren, 1995). Following the collapse of the merger, Volvo embarked on a restructuring programme that saw its peripheral holdings stripped out. The cash was used to refocus the group and expand the core businesses of cars, commercial vehicles (trucks and buses), and construction machinery. A strong focus on cost-cutting meant more than 2,000 job losses in 1996 and car production rationalized around the main assembly plants (Simonian, 1996). After the break with Renault, there were joint ventures with Mitsubishi, which reinforced the lean production regime. It was in this context that Kalmar and Uddevalla were shut down.

Uddevalla again Many of the public statements at the time of the closures centred on the plants' productive record. This was attacked from various quarters, while Volvo based its case on the cost benefits of production focused on fewer plants. However, supporters of work humanization have vigorously contested both these claims and argued for the plants' economic (as well as social) viability. On various efficiency ratings Kalmar and Uddevalla were always the equal of conventional plants, and detailed comparisons show they had moved far ahead on specific measures of flexibility and time efficiencies. To some extent, though, these arguments were a diversion and the closures were a simple matter of production policy. Kalmar and Uddevalla were always vulnerable, because they were relatively small (around 700 employees each) and were assembly only (they did not have integrated press and body shops), and they were closed in order to take out capacity at a time when sales had collapsed.

When the problems of overcapacity arose in the early 1990s the power balance inside the company changed. Traditionalist factions in management became actively hostile towards worker autonomy and co-determination, and a coalition of traditional interests within unions and management focused on job security at the Torslanda plant. As Hanke and Rubinstein (1995) put it, 'what mattered was not the plant's performance but the way it was never able to muster the political support it needed . . . Uddevalla closed because it did not have a winning coalition that backed it'.

However, deeper elements of organizational power may have been involved. Observers have hinted at the paradox that the plants may have been shut down partly because of their innovative production—in a sense because they were too successful (Cressey, 1993; Hanke and Rubinstein, 1995). Both plants were on a steep improvement curve at the time of their closure (Engstrom and Medbo, 1995). The Uddevalla concept in particular contained an explosive potential for change, outstripping the incremental or 'continuous improvement' of the Japanese system. Here Berggren (1995) notes that not only were production records strong but an entirely new production concept was emerging. This was 'customer order assembly' and involved redefining the relationship with dealers and delivering customized cars on very short lead times. It was only possible because of the total flexibility of the system, and was beginning to pose an uncomfortable challenge to the major line assembly plants like Torslanda, which could not hope to emulate it.

In conclusion, Berggren (1995) asks the (rhetorical) question, were Kalmar and Uddevalla 'noble experiments' that were doomed to failure once labour and product markets became tougher? The answer is an emphatic, no; they were 'a fundamentally viable model' that matched lean assembly on all conventional criteria, and created new concepts of productive effectiveness and new relationships with the customer. Cressey (1993), too, has cautioned against seeing Volvo's motives as only 'pragmatic responses to external market pressures'. This would absolve management of any choice or responsibility, and imply that worker autonomy and responsible jobs are luxuries that can be afforded only at certain times.

As a postscript, Volvo announced in January 1996 that it was to reopen Uddevalla in a joint venture with the British firm, Walkenshaw Racing. The planned annual output of 20,000 cabriolets and sports cars confirms that Uddevalla is still not part of the mainstream of Volvo's production strategy. However, this unique plant is at least being kept open. Indeed, the fact that production can be switched to quite different models, and productivity sustained at lower levels of output, is a further demonstration of the system's flexibility. So while enthusiasm for humanized work has sunk probably to its lowest point in Volvo, Kalmar and Uddevalla are visible proof of the worth of these methods, and it remains to be seen whether the debate will be renewed in the future.

Case study questions

1 Looking at the Kalmar and Uddevalla projects (especially the latter) which of the principles of socio-technical theory are demonstrated here?

2 What about the development between Kalmar and Uddevalla? In what ways was work design changed?

3 'Although both pride themselves on group work and worker competence, the assembly-line and whole-car assembly are expressions of fundamentally different philosophies' (Sandberg, 1995, p. 16). Discuss.

4 Discuss the argument that work can be humanely designed and match or even exceed the economic performance of conventional systems.

5 How did external labour and product-market factors affect developments at Kalmar and Uddevalla? Were these factors determining?

6 How generalizable is the Volvo experience to other countries, companies, and industries?

References

Adler, P. S. and Cole, R. E. (1995) 'Designed for learning: a tale of two plants', in A. Sandberg (ed.) *op cit*.

Berggren, C. (1989) 'New production concepts in final assembly: the Swedish Experience', in S. Wood (ed.) *The Transformation of Work*. London: Unwin Hyman.

—— (1993) *The Volvo Experience: Alternatives to Lean Production in the Swedish Auto Industry*. Basingstoke: Macmillan.

—— (1995) 'The fate of the branch plants—performance versus power', in A. Sandberg (ed.) *op cit*.

Clarke, T. (1990) 'Automation and craftwork', paper presented to ISA World Congress, Madrid, July.

Cressey, P. (1993) 'Kalmar and Uddevalla: The demise of Volvo as a European icon', *New Technology, Work and Employment*, 8/2: 88–90.

Ellegard, K. (1995) 'The creation of a new production system at the Volvo automobile plant in Uddevalla, Sweden', in A. Sandberg (ed.) *op cit*.

Engstrom, T. and Medbo, L. (1995) 'Production system design—a brief summary of some Swedish design efforts', in A. Sandberg (ed.) *op cit*.

Gyllenhammar, P. G. (1977*a*) 'How Volvo adapts work to people', *Harvard Business Review*, 55: 102–13.

—— (1977*b*) *People at Work*. Reading, Mass.: Addison Wesley.

Hammarstrom, O. and Lansbury, R. D. (1991) 'The art of building a car: the Swedish experience re-examined', *New Technology, Work and Employment*, 6/2: 85–90.

Hanke, B. and Rubinstein, S. (1995) 'Limits to innovation in work organization?' in A. Sandberg (ed.) *op cit*.

Sandberg, A. (1993) 'Volvo human-centred work organization—the end of the road?' *New Technology, Work and Employment*, 8/2: 83–7.

—— (ed.) (1995) *Enriching Production: Perspectives on Volvo's Uddevalla Plant as an Alternative to Lean Production*. Aldershot: Avebury.

Sandberg, T. (1995) 'Volvo Kalmar—twice a pioneer', in A. Sandberg (ed.) *op cit*.

Simonian, H. (1996) 'Volvo takes a long view from atop its cash pile', *Financial Times*, 15 April.

Section 4

Organizational Structures and Systems

Organizational Structures and Systems

The issues dealt with in Section Three were mostly concerned with systematic methods of work organization (like Taylorism) that brought about the rationalization of labour. We considered these as part of the labour process and the employment relationship. But there are other ways of looking at these self-same processes of control that managerial groups exercise over subordinate groups of workers. In particular, there is another aspect of the structuring of work, namely the division of power and authority. This 'vertical' dimension embodies the hierarchies of control which form the basic structure of the modern large-scale organization. Historically, these methods belong to that important period in the last quarter of the last century—from about the mid-1870s to 1900—which saw the emergence of what today we would recognize as the modern industrial economy. In this period industry in America and Europe was transformed. The new work methods emerged against a background of new technologies, like chemicals and steel, together with the new manufacturing and mass production industries. During the 1880s the commercial office and government bureaucracy first appeared. And all these enterprises were being managed on a much larger scale than had hitherto been either necessary or possible. Altogether, an industrial and commercial landscape was taking shape which was quite different from the small-scale capitalism of only twenty or thirty years earlier.

Seen from another perspective, what was happening was the rise of the modern organization. Presthus has summarized this process in America as follows:

Beginning about 1875, social, economic and political trends in the United States prepared the way for the 'organization society', characterized by large-scale bureaucratic institutions in virtually every social area. The master trends included the separation of ownership from management; increasing size and concentration in business; the decline of competition as financial resources required for entry in almost every sector became prohibitive; and the emergence of an employee society (1979, p. 84)

The importance of these changes is easily appreciated. Many of us will spend all or some part of our working lives in large organizations, and we will be their clients and come into other forms of contact on countless other occasions. This should not be exaggerated, because as much as half of total employment is still provided by small firms. Nevertheless, the organizational setting has had a profound effect on the nature of work.

In this section of the book we distinguish the two main approaches to organization. First, in Chapter 12, we look at the critical perspective on organization. This is an approach that in recent years has been radically transformed. The classical writings (largely Weberian) have been reappraised and reinterpreted and a new body of theory and research developed. Much of this centres on the model of organizations as control mechanisms.

This is followed, in Chapter 13, by an account of the managerial approach to organizations—usually referred to as organizational analysis, or simply organization theory. In contrast with the more critical perspective, the emphasis here is on issues of efficiency and effectiveness, and a model of organizations as systems for goal attainment. However, as we will see, organizational analysis need not be 'managerialist' in the crude sense of being unaware of issues of conflict and control—even if these are not given as much prominence as in the more critical accounts.

12 Structure and Control in Organizations

Summary points and learning objectives

By the end of this chapter you will be able to

- outline the principles of Weber's *bureaucratic model* of organization;
- understand the complex ways in which the *formal* model of bureaucracy applies to *real-life* organizations;
- appreciate the social impact of the *rationalization* process;
- evaluate the various *criticisms* of the bureaucratic model;
- trace the *post-Weberian contributions* to our understanding of work and organizations;
- see the culmination of this critical stream in concepts such as *insidious power* and *McDonaldization*;
- discuss the ways in which the control concept helps to define the *nature of managerial work*, and even the possibility of a *managerial labour process*.

Introduction

In the early stages of industrialization, when enterprises were small in scale, the need to plan and administer work presented few problems. But once the size and complexity of plants had grown, administrative structures expanded and came to be seen as existing in their own right. The growth of organizations led to the rise of a separate and distinct managerial structure. Here, for example, Offe (1976) has distinguished what he calls 'task continuous' and 'task discontinuous' types of organization. The former would include things like the small owner-managed firm and the partnership. These are run co-operatively by those who actually perform the work, and planning is simply an outgrowth of the work itself. In contrast, task discontinuous organizations are far more typical of the large-scale modern organization. They have a discrete planning structure, unrelated to those who actually do the work.

Nowadays in all areas of economic life—in industry, government, and public and private services—there are complex and highly developed administrative structures. Such changes reflect the growth of *bureaucratic* forms of organizing work. The concern with bureaucracy is both a very old one and also ultra-modern, as bureaucracies reproduce and extend themselves, and as organizations globalize and find new ways of reaching the consumer and creating demand for their products. These structures, moreover, are set up as a means of pursuing explicit corporate objectives—goals that are not necessarily shared by all of the members. Central organizational processes thus involve the *control* of activities. The mechanisms of controlling behaviour in organizations reflect the structuring of the rewards and deprivations of work. Pay, discretion, and power all increase as one ascends to senior levels, and decrease in the lower ranks.

These themes encompass the concern with the so-called degradation of work, discussed in Chapter 10, which was based on people being denied control of their working lives. And certainly many of the problems of repetitive and insecure work have been attributed to power structures and systematic control in the modern factory and office. However, the control of organizational personnel does not stop short at the factory or office floor. It also applies in varying degrees to the more privileged layers of an organization's employees, and in this chapter we will be discussing how these controlling and rationalizing processes take effect in organizational and managerial structures.

Bureaucracy

Perhaps the defining feature of bureaucracy is that it is solely concerned with the task of administration. It is a purely 'task discontinuous' type of organization. In contrast to other major forms of work, like manual or professional, no concrete task is performed in the bureaucracy. Instead it carries out the task of maintaining a system of records upon which the direction and control of the work of others is based. Typical employees are clerical officers and secretaries. Indeed, the classic example of bureaucracy is the civil service, though other large white-collar organizations (like financial services firms) also have strong bureaucratic elements.

Modern thought on this subject is traced to Max Weber, whose study of bureaucracy has had an enormous influence both on the theory of organizations and on how we understand the impact of organizations on society at large. Weber wrote during the years spanning the turn of the century, towards the end of the period when the modern German nation became consolidated. Unlike the pattern of industrialization in Britain, the German industrial economy developed along highly centralized lines, and one aspect of this was the growth of a huge state apparatus. It was the experience of seeing this central state machine develop and spread that persuaded Weber of the varied implications of the bureaucratic form of organization.

The bureaucratic model

In Weber's (1970) account of bureaucracy the following basic elements were included:

1. *A staff* consisting of a body of employees whose full-time work was to administer the activities of the particular institution. The employee's post carries with it authority over specific areas, but it is a cardinal principle that the incumbent should not overstep the bounds of his or her authority. Such behaviour (for example, the use of formal authority to gain wider influence) might result in various forms of corruption.

2. *A division of labour* which assigns specific tasks to sub-units and individuals. The division of labour in bureaucracies is highly developed: departmental boundaries and individual jobs are closely specified and duties and responsibilities carefully set out.

3. *The hierarchy*, or division of power, involves the ranking of offices to provide clear lines of command. In bureaucracies the hierarchy also is typically very complex, its many levels providing a highly differentiated structure of authority.

4. *Competence* refers to the basis upon which office is held. Factors like luck, favouritism or personal connections should play no part in the position that officials attain; advancement should be decided by expertise and ability alone. Thus organizations have to pay close attention to the process of selection, whereby these qualities can be identified in personnel.

5. *Objectivity* suggests that all dealings within the bureaucracy and with clients should be conducted on the basis of equal treatment according to a procedural routine. The objective conduct of business, free from any personal feelings, is the basis of the reliability of formal administration.

From the point of view of technical efficiency, Weber believed that the above characteristics gave far-reaching advantages, making the bureaucratic form of organization absolutely necessary in a modern economy:

The decisive reason for the advance of bureaucratic organization has always been its purely technical superiority over any other form of organization. The fully developed bureaucratic mechanism compares with other organizations exactly as does the machine with the non-mechanical modes of production. . . . Today it is primarily the capitalist market economy which demands that the official business of the administration be discharged precisely, unambiguously, continuously and with as much speed as possible. Normally, the very large capitalist enterprises are themselves unequalled models of strict bureaucratic organization. (1964, pp. 214–15)

Two things are apparent from this account. First, any large-scale organization will in some measure have a bureaucratic structure. All have a lateral division of tasks and a vertical division of authority, and embrace principles of objectivity and competence. Yet some of these factors may vary quite considerably across different organizations. Some, for instance, may have a relatively relaxed division of labour, with work being accomplished in diffuse groups and with little attention paid to exact responsibilities. In the bureaucratic model, however, these factors are present in exaggerated form. The civil service, for example, has an extremely complex hierarchy, in which close attention is given to differentials covering a whole range of privileges and status symbols.

Secondly, it is obvious that the above factors present too faultless a picture. No real-life bureaucracy meets all of these requirements all of the time. Nor was it Weber's intention to describe actual patterns of behaviour. The model he set out was what he termed an *ideal type*. The word 'ideal' here does not have the evaluative meaning it has in common usage; it refers instead to the pure idea that lay behind the reality. What Weber described was the logical form of bureaucracy, rather than its day-to-day operations.

Nevertheless, in reality organizations do approximate quite closely to Weber's model. People are mostly appointed on the basis of merit, tasks on the whole are clearly allocated, and clients are dealt with impartially. In other ways, the model also represents the *standard* that we expect from organizations. There is normally an outcry if official corruption is uncovered, and we would usually be affronted to be treated according to the personal whim of the official. However, although values of objectivity and competence help to guarantee integrity in public life, and we tend to take them for granted, they are arbitrary and relative like all social institutions. In the historical past organizations were based on quite different rules, where, for example, it was quite normal for an officer-holder to confer privilege on his relatives or favourites.

Authority and rationality

In common with most social scientists Weber was centrally concerned with the problem of social order. Why should people accept the roles allocated to them by some external power, and why do they obey the directives issued on its behalf? There can be many possible reasons. However, if the motives people have for accepting rules reflect only factors like expediency or coercion, Weber reasoned, social order would hardly be stable in the long term. At some basic level there must be a feeling of solidarity with rules. This all-important voluntary element is embodied in a special type of social control, namely *authority*.

The crucial feature of all forms of authority as a basis of social control is that the power of senior officials should be accepted by those under control. The latter should believe that it is right and proper for people in senior positions to issue directives and equally justifiable that their orders be complied with. In short, authority should be regarded as a *legitimate* form of social control.

... custom and personal advantage, purely affectual or ideal motives, do not, even taken together, form a sufficiently reliable basis for a system of imperative coordination. In addition, there is normally a further element, the belief in legitimacy. No system of authority voluntarily limits itself to the appeal to material or affectual or ideal motives as a basis of guaranteeing its continuance. In addition, such a system attempts to establish and to cultivate the belief in its legitimacy. (Weber, 1964, p. 325)

Weber distinguished three types of authority:

1. *Charismatic authority* which is based on the personal qualities, heroic or mystical, of leaders.
2. *Traditional authority*, based on established customs and the right to rule of dominant groups sanctified by such customary beliefs.
3. *Rational authority*, based on the legal occupancy of senior positions by those who exercise authority.

Mouzelis (1975, p. 16), in his thorough account of the Weberian approach to bureaucracy, makes the important point that each of these types of authority gives rise to a different kind of organization. Movements based on charismatic leaders tend to be associated with a temporary and loose type of administrative structure. Traditional authority, vested in the inherited status of a king or lord, gives rise to a more permanent apparatus where officials owe their position to some privilege or contract granted by the superior. Finally, rational authority forms the basis of the modern work organization, and in particular the bureaucracy. Weber was convinced that order was inherent in the bureaucracy's distinctively rational structure, and that this reflected its fundamental importance to industrial society.

We discussed this briefly in Chapter 9, and pointed out that rationality reflects the application of a formal structure of administration as the means of managing complex tasks. Bureaucracy thus permits the calculation and predictability of future outcomes, together with accountability and close control of activities. Bureaucratic authority has advantages over other types since rational action is in evidence throughout the organization, as well as in the organization's relations to its markets and clients. When people perceive that office-holders are competent, that decisions are taken formally, resources are accounted for, and so forth, this upholds the belief in legitimacy. Such beliefs are further supported by the fact that office-holders themselves are subject to the same impersonal rules. The appeal of rationality therefore remains independent of the personal qualities of leaders and so outlasts individuals. Nor is it based on the forces of tradition and habit which may come to be questioned. For these reasons, rational bureaucratic authority should prove to be by far the most stable form of authority.

Finally, all three authority types are themselves ideal types. Thus in real organizations authority will be a mixture of types, and there will always be traces of motives other than the purely rational. Senior management, for instance, are always very careful about projecting the right image, for they know full well that their personal charisma is important if they wish to command authority. Similarly, all forms of authority depend in part upon force of habit; indeed some organizations can be very traditional and hidebound in this respect. As Weber himself put it, all systems of authority rest on a *belief* held by subordinates, and by virtue of which those exercising authority are accepted willingly. The belief is invariably complex and composed of several elements, including habit and personal charisma (Weber, 1964, p. 382). Nevertheless, in a bureaucratic organization one type should predominate, namely the appeal that rational procedures have for the majority of members of the organization.

The critique of bureaucracy

A more obvious meaning of bureaucracy, however, presents a major problem with Weber's account, and that is that it has always seemed at odds with common-sense notions. 'Bureaucracy' in every day terms usually means the exact opposite of the highly rational and efficient system that Weber seemed to refer to. The popular view of bureaucracy conjures up an image of unnecessary paperwork, time-consuming procedure, strict adherence to rules, and unresponsiveness to clients. This critical, common-sense view has formed the basis of a lengthy 'debate with Weber' in which a great deal of modern writing and research has been cast. Later writers stressed various 'dysfunctional' features and the rigid and impersonal character of bureaucracy, contrasting this with the perfect form of administration that Weber appeared to be describing.

The 'ideal type' model of bureaucracy	High degree of internal efficiency. Rational: effective administrative means to corporate ends
The 'effectiveness' critique of Weber's model	Irrational: bureaucracy as 'red tape'; the displacement of corporate ends by administrative means. Inflexible: unresponsive to environmental changes and demends
The 'social' critique of Weber's model	Erosion of individual democratic freedoms. Depersonalization: the 'bureaucratic personality'

Table 12.1 Weber and his critics

It helps to separate out two different themes in this critique (Table 12.1). First there is the suggestion that bureaucracy is actually an *ineffective* form of organization. The question of effectiveness is chiefly a managerial concern (one that we deal with in detail in the next chapter), but for the moment we can note that the emphasis here is on the inability of bureaucratic organizations to achieve their goals in a flexible way, or to respond to changes in their market environment.

This common-sense view of bureaucracy as 'red tape' mounts an explicit challenge to the Weberian notion of bureaucracy as a highly rational means to an end. The criticism centres on the forms of incapacity that emerge in elaborate bureaucratic structures when officials become preoccupied with the administrative process itself. This can happen as a result of an extreme division of labour that allows the bureaucrat to see only a small part of the operation, and also because people's reputations and careers become bound up with established procedures.

Secondly, however, there is criticism that bureaucracy has major *social* dysfunctions. Included here is Merton's (1940) original idea of the 'bureaucratic personality' as a narrow, one-dimensional kind of individual. This basic problem, that large-scale bureaucratic systems produce 'organization men' who are the harbingers of a new kind of bland, conformist middle class, has been a strong theme in critical sociology (e.g. Mills, 1951). In a broader sense this reflects the *depersonalization* of social and economic life. Objectivity was mentioned as a key criterion of rational administration, but objectivity has a negative side. The price that has to be paid is that the quality of human relations, both within the bureaucracy and between the bureaucracy and its clients, becomes transformed into anonymous calculative exchanges.

These socially dysfunctional features have major implications for the erosion of individual freedom. The state bureaucracy is in theory the servant of society. Yet the belief that in some quite straightforward way the state distributes the services to which we are entitled can prove to be rather naive. 'The state' as a principle of government may stipulate this, but in reality the relationship of the state to society is mediated by the bureaucratic machine. At times the individual has little chance of redress against officialdom, and for all practical purposes has to accept the treatment he or she is meted out. Cases of 'bureaucratic abuse' give sufficient grounds for believing that the different departments of the modern state are remarkably autonomous, and that they can and often do appropriate wider powers from their official position. A great many officials of the state—the police, social security officers, welfare officials, immigration officials—in reality have wide-ranging forms of discretions over the way laws are interpreted, and very real power over the members of the public with whom they come into contact.

It now tends to be recognized, however, that these criticisms of the nature of bureaucracy were misjudged as criticisms of Weber. In the first place, it was indeed true that Weber regarded bureaucracies as a highly efficient form of administration. Without efficiency the whole basis of authority in large organizations would have been undermined. And this is certainly at odds with the picture of inflexible, bureaucratic organizations that critics have drawn. Yet, after all, how accurate is their viewpoint? Much of it relies upon appealing to common-sense views, or to anecdotal evidence. By comparison the emphasis on rationality, and the honest fulfilment of contractual obligations, is at least as well founded. If we take a broader comparative viewpoint, compared with organizations in countries where political factors intervene in commercial life far more prominently, the bureaucracies we are familiar with often do seem to be models of efficiency and fair dealing. These positive features therefore form the first impression we receive of bureaucracy, as Weber intended they should.

Secondly, fears about the impact of bureaucracy on society were actually consistent with the viewpoint that Weber held. As we saw in Chapter 9, he was chiefly concerned with much broader issues of *rationalization* as the key historical trend in the development of industrial society. This meant a world dominated by the calculative logic of rational decision-making and the remorseless spread of bureaucratic rationality. It embraced fears of the erosion of individual freedom—and indeed the very efficiency of bureaucracy was what made it a potent threat. Of course, the fear of an overbearing state is as old as the idea of democracy itself, and certainly did not originate with Weber. Yet the idea that bureaucracy poses previously unforeseen problems is no less important today, while the threats that Weber identified when state bureaucracies and business corporations first appeared are more urgent now.

Therefore, considered as criticisms of Weber these points are somewhat irrelevant. The problems of bureaucratic inefficiency and the erosion of democratic freedom were not radical new ideas, even in Weber's time, so he did not develop his 'ideal' model of bureaucracy in a state of ignorance or naivity. None the less, the detailed study of the realities of organizational life and the rising tide of rationality has added much to our understanding of how bureaucracies and other large-scale organizations actually work, and can be discussed now in more detail.

The dynamics of bureaucracy

In the bureaucratic model of organization, social rules govern much behaviour. The rule concept was central to Weber's theory. Rules embody all the key aspects of predictability and control that define modernity. They appeal because they cut across the power hierarchy, seemingly applying equally to all organizational members. Rules imply the existence of procedures for overcoming the problems of uncertainty. They thus serve to reassure in an increasingly complex and diversified world. We have come to value them and have an emotional investment in them. Bureaucracies themselves are often said to be 'rule-bound' in so far as a procedure seems to exist for every contingency.

However, the full complexity of social action in organizations involves much more than just conformity to external rules. Formal authority is not automatically accepted by subordinates. They may resent the imposition of control and resist in whatever ways are available to them. Also, people in authority usually devote considerable efforts to persuasion aimed at shoring up the image of themselves as legitimate office-holders (much the same as the tactics of 'impression management' used by group members, as discussed in Chapter 6). Authority is thus a *dynamic* relationship. Legitimacy can come under threat at any time, or ultimately be withdrawn, and the distinction has to be drawn between official expectations and real behaviour.

The discrepancy between formal rules and actual behaviour reflects the persistent theme of the individual 'making out' in an established, sometimes coercive structure (Burawoy, 1979). We saw in Chapter 10 that resistance to the constraints of Taylorist work design has long been a favourite topic of study. In organizational theory these distinctions are often referred to in terms of the difference between *formal* and *informal* organization.

Informal structure is not so readily identifiable as the formal since it is not officially recognized. Yet informal codes of practice can bind behaviour just as tightly as formal rules. Informal structure includes all of the subtle customs and attitudes, the expectations and unwritten rules that stamp an organization with a specific character or culture. These may involve general patterns like the degree of formality of behaviour that is expected, the deference to those in authority, and the autonomy that people normally have in their work. They also include the real distribution of power—i.e. the possibility of particular groups or individual managers being influential while officially they have no more authority that others at their level. What is referred to as 'learning the ropes' by people newly recruited to an organization means gaining a working knowledge of this informal structure.

Informal actions may serve to undermine rational authority but (as we also saw in Chapter 10) the interplay between formal and informal spheres is complex. In many cases informal action supports formal rules—indeed, organizations would cease to operate without this informal co-operation. Employees often take responsibility on themselves, rather than merely following procedure, and this may involve short-cutting the formal rules. In subtle ways, formal institutions can also exploit employees' willingness to take informal action, and may accept (whether grudgingly or not) informal practices that have become desirable or indispensable. Thus real patterns of action are influenced by many different and sometimes conflicting social rules.

In one way or another the classical studies in the neo-Weberian tradition, such as Blau's *Dynamics of Bureaucracy* (1955), Gouldner's *Patterns of Industrial Bureaucracy* (1954), and Crozier's *The Bureaucratic Phenomenon* (1964), have all emphasized this tension between formal rules and social action. Impersonal rules and social responses are both equally important parts of the total organization.

Thus Gouldner distinguished between the varying content of rules, types of enforcement and the motives which sustained acceptance, as well as the conditions under which the legitimacy of social order might be suspended. Bureaucratic patterns in which conformity had to be strongly enforced were distinguished from the genuine acceptance of authority because interests were widely represented, and these in turn were distinguished from conformity with the form rather than the essence of rules: 'punishment-centred', 'representative' and 'mock' bureaucracies. Similarly, in his study of government recruitment agencies, Blau stressed that competition between employees acted as an important mechanism of control. He too focused on the interplay between formal and informal, seeing in the 'daily operations and interpersonal relationships' the main dynamic of organizational change, namely the continual modification of formal procedures by social practice. Finally, in the rigidly bureaucratic factory that Crozier studied, major problems in an otherwise routine production task were created by machine breakdowns; and this gave maintenance workers who dealt with breakdowns a degree of informal influence, which was reflected in their superior pay and general treatment by management. In this sense, Crozier indicated how an organizational authority structure could in effect become distorted as a result of special powers possessed by particular groups.

Bureaucracy's iron cage

While such studies have stressed the *interplay* between formal rules and social action, in the end this is really a matter for interpretation. Others, who are more radically or perhaps pessimistically inclined, have seen things differently. They have taken Weber's fears about bureaucracy to their limits. Instead of viewing formal and informal spheres as competing rationalities, they have stressed the full extent of formal control. Individuals who come under these controls will invariably put up resistance, but 'making out' in an oppressive bureaucratic environment often has a defensive character.

Insidious or systematic power

One part of the neo-Weberian tradition has stressed the 'insidious' nature of bureaucratic power. Writers like Blau and Schoenherr (1971) have argued that modern power systems may not be coercive in the way that such systems were in the historic past, involving oppressive regimes of supervision. Nevertheless, modern forms of indirect power are perhaps even more effective in constraining behaviour.

Is not the power of control over our lives and destinies that the heads of the military establishment and of giant corporations exercise far greater than the power a Caligula or a Genghis Khan has wielded? This is the paradox: we today are freer from coercion through the power of command of superiors than most people have been, yet those in positions of power today probably exercise more control than any tyrant ever has. (Blau and Schoenherr, 1971, p. 347)

This kind of insidious power, say Blau and Schoenherr, does not involve a 'sinister power elite' and may not even be recognized as power but simply taken for granted. A web of rules and methods of self-control can be highly effective in stifling resistance and maintaining the legitimacy of central authority.

An example of the near complete negation of individual freedom is described in Goffman's famous study of mental institutions, *Asylums* (1968). Goffman emphasized that rules, ostensibly for the benefit of inmates, were in fact used coercively in order to make 'care' a relatively easy task for the hospital staff. He showed how treatment (particularly the issuing of drugs) could be used as punishment rather than cure, and how doctors often withheld treatment until patients had accepted the psychiatric diagnosis of their condition. Furthermore, patients' apparently bizarre behaviour could often be interpreted as attempts to gain a few basic rights (such as a degree of privacy) denied them in the artificial conditions of the asylum. The psychiatric profession usually regarded this as further evidence of the patient's illness. In other words, Goffman was arguing that the true purpose of rules lies in the control of the majority of organizational members for the benefit of the minority in power.

In mental institutions the power of the staff over inmates was greatly amplified as these were what Goffman called 'total institutions', where inmates live entirely within the system (another common example would be prisons). Total institutions are an extreme case of the control that powerful groups exercise. Nevertheless, the issue of control generally lies at the heart of the hierarchical structuring of work.

In Chapter 9 we saw how the French social scientist, Foucault, held a similar view of the 'systematic' qualities of power. Foucault saw power not in the simple, common-sense terms of a structure imposed from above, but in terms of processes that insinuate themselves into all areas of social life. Rather like fluid flowing through the arteries of an organism, power circulates; power relations are elaborated in many locations, and operate through our judgements of others and the bureaucratic procedures with which we control them. Foucault's power analysis in fact divided into two rather different (and some would say contradictory) streams. There was 'parallel power' which stressed the development of different kinds of power relations on different sites, and hence the possibility of countervailing power and resistance. But what he called 'disciplinary power' was the basis of more rigid forms of stratification. His reference to the Panopticon, for example, conjures up an image of the powerlessness of those who are visible inside an enclosed space. Though Foucault is not usually classed as a Weberian writer, the panoptic image comes very close to Weber's 'icy night of polar darkness'. The very fact that resistance is impossible in the Panopticon is what makes the image so arresting: there is nowhere to hide in a cell, nor any escape from the 'disciplinary gaze'. Implicit links can be drawn to modern systems of surveillance, such as new technologies and work systems that automatically record employees' movements.

The type of account Goffman provided can be tied into another of Foucault's ideas, that of *power/knowledge* (and it is no accident that both Goffman and Foucault were interested in 'carceral institutions'—prisons, asylums—as metaphors of modernity). As we saw in Chapter 9, power/knowledge was Foucault's way of representing an extra dimension of power. It is not simply that 'knowledge gives power' but that, with many professions and in many bureaucratic situations, elite groups have the power to actually make the rules and create knowledge itself. When people come within the grasp of the bureaucracy (they become a 'patient', a 'case', an 'inmate') any resistance is interpreted as a sign of the correctness of the original diagnosis. Thus individuals' attempts to cope with oppressive power only reinforces that power. The harder they struggle the deeper in they get. This chilling sense of powerlessness has been at the heart of the critique of modernity.

McDonaldization

One recent and potent image of these social processes is supplied by George Ritzer in his acclaimed study, *The McDonaldization of Society* (1993). Ritzer's analysis is steeped in the Weberian tradition and the idea of the progressive rationalization of social and economic life. He seeks to expand and update Weber's vision by linking it to that icon of popular culture, the fast-food restaurant, and in particular McDonald's. Ritzer's thesis is that 'McDonaldization' is replacing bureaucracy as the model of rationality. It represents the next stage in the rationalization process. The proliferation of fast-food restaurants—the fact that McDonald's is now virtually everywhere—recreates Weber's idea of 'a seamless web of rational institutions from which there is no exit, no escape' (Ritzer, 1993, p. xi).

McDonaldization means that the business principles pioneered by McDonald's are increasingly dominating other industries and activities. Ritzer is not so much concerned with cause and effect here, as with (and this was very much Weber's method) spotting the many affinities between fast food and other sectors of society. Much of his account is devoted to detailing the resonances and echoes that can be found in industries like the media, health, and leisure, as well as activities like sport and politics.

a wide array of social phenomena are linked under the broad heading of McDonaldization. Some have been directly affected by the principle of the fast-food restaurant, whereas in other cases the effect is more indirect. Some have all the dimensions of McDonaldization, but others may have only one or two. In any case, they all are part of what Weber called the rationalization process and what is here, in order to make Weber more timely, labelled McDonaldization. (p. xiii)

McDonaldized industries continue the same basic processes of standardization and rationalization that systems like Taylorism, Fordism, and the assembly line established. Ritzer makes out four specific dimensions of rationalization—efficiency, calculability, predictability, and control—along each of which McDonaldization takes the process to new heights. Thus, the 'dining experience' (with its limited menu and finger foods) is a model of *efficiency*; food preparation embodies all the principles of the assembly line, and the customer him or herself becomes an integral part of the process. Once they have sped through their food, they are 'back in their car on their way to the next (often McDonaldized) activity' (p. 38). *Calculability* is reflected in the emphasis on quantity rather than quality. McDonald's offers the illusion of speed of consumption and large helpings (as Ritzer notes, it is the 'Big Mac' that is pushed at us, not the 'delicious Mac').

Predictability plays on our desire to consume the same thing, over and over again, and to be comforted by the same simple rituals. Like the bureaucracy, which itself works repetitively, the McDonald's franchise is the same wherever you go, it is 'a world that offers no surprises' (p. 99). And, finally, *control* involves the elimination of people from the process and their replacement by technologies and systems. Ritzer reveals McDonald's obsession with regulating down to the smallest detail the preparation of food and replacing humans by machines. Everything possible is outsourced and simplified, to the point where hardly anything is done on site. The fast-food restaurant is a kind of virtual restaurant. Customer behaviour is also obsessively controlled. 'People are moved along in the system not by a conveyor belt, but by the unwritten, but universally known, rules for eating in a fast-food restaurant' (p. 109).

Each of the four dimensions is then the basis of affinities with many other sectors in American society. Thus industrialization of the home kitchen (efficiency) is reflected in a range of kitchen technologies and equipment, like the microwave oven. Microwaveable meals rationalize family life, making the 'home cooked meal' a thing of the past. Also, the emphasis on measurable quantities (calculability) can be found in activities like sport, politics, and television. In television it is the ratings, rather than any notion of the quality of a programme, that determine what the public watches. Politicians worship the opinion polls, and in sport, the rules of games like baseball and basketball have been changed to suit to mass audiences, particularly television. Rather than the subtleties appreciated by aficionados of the game, the demand (as in McDonald's) is for 'great speed and large helpings', for more hits and more points scored.

In other cases, the delivery of services in highly commodified ways (predictability) is increasingly the basis of the mass leisure industries. In the holiday industry, for instance, the package tour is expressly designed to take the uncertainty and challenge out of foreign travel and to reassure consumers with the familiar. In the case of techniques for reducing uncertainty (control) these can be seen in the industries that supply the inputs and raw materials to the fast-food industry, which are dominated by factory farming and intensive animal rearing.

Evaluating the McDonaldization concept Ritzer's main focus remains *food*—in what we physically consume he finds a potent symbol of the incessant consumerism of modern (especially American) life. But the strength of his thesis lies in its breadth and the links to popular culture, particularly the new mass service industries (leisure, media, sport).

McDonald's is part of the modern addiction to entertainment. The fast-food restaurant offers not just the gratification of a basic need (hunger) but diversion and amusement. Ronald McDonald is just as important as the Big Mac. What people are consuming in this environment is a kind of drama, an ever-expanding round of fun. In this, McDonald's shares obvious affinities with the likes of the theme park and the shopping mall. McDonald's is a 'sacred institution' (p. 5) because the public wants this symbolic good. As with all forms of insidious power, it is only partly forced on people: McDonald's is desired as '*the* symbol of the rationalization of America and its coveted market economy' (p. xi).

In this sense, Ritzer extends our understanding by taking a theory that has invariably been applied to the economic sphere, the world of work, and broadening it out. Weber intended his concept of rationalization to have the broadest application, yet he developed it chiefly in the sphere of work—i.e. with the rationalist model of bureaucracy. (The same, incidentally, can be said of Marx, who earlier developed his idea of alienation very broadly, but later focused on alienation from the means of production.) Ritzer by contrast takes the concept of rationalization into the sphere of cultural studies, into the world of consumption rather than production, and in so doing provides a critique of modern and specifically American culture.

Ritzer also supplies a set of sharper criticisms. He points out that McDonald's offers the illusion of value for money, yet the mark-up on individual items is usually hundreds of per cent, and on these profits the global fast-food industry is built. The industry is also a bastion of low-paid, deskilled, Taylorized work; and there are mounting health problems associated with fast food. Given the calorie and fat content, and the mildly addictive nature of salt and sugar with which the food is laced, in a real sense people have become victims of the expansion of these demands.

Most importantly, Ritzer stresses the *dehumanizing* aspects of McDonaldized culture. Here he speaks of the 'irrationality of rationality' reflected in the social costs attached to efficiency, calculability, predictability, and control. Paraphrasing Weber, he raises the spectre of an 'iron cage of McDonaldization' with society increasingly becoming a trap for people, 'their only mobility to move from one rational system to another' (p. 23). The sense in which all these systems are interlocking—the assembly line produces the automobile, the automobile makes fast food possible—produces a vision of McDonaldization as the culminating stage of rationalization.

This kind of fear has animated many science fiction writers and is manifest in such classics as *1984*, *Brave New World* and *Fahrenheit 451*. These works describe a feared and fearsome future world, but McDonaldization is with us now . . . contrary to McDonald's propaganda, and the widespread belief in it, fast-food restaurants and their rational clones are *not* reasonable, or even truly rational, systems. They spawn problems in the health of their customers and the well-being of the environment; they are dehumanizing and, therefore, unreasonable; and they often lead to the opposite of what they are supposed to create. (p. 146)

Ritzer also has an acute eye for the ironies and contradictions of modern mass culture. He notes, for example, that, in the so-called leisure society, corporations have discovered the trick of shifting much of the burden of labour onto the consumer, who has to work harder and harder. McDonald's symbolizes this by having customers clear away their own debris, but in many other cases the concept of 'service' increasingly means self-service. Another irony is that we seem to have become simultaneously hooked on junk food and dieting. In America, Ritzer reports, the dieting and health industry is almost as massive as that of fast food. This seems contradictory, yet both are ways in which the human body is exploited for profit.

Again, the emphasis on quantifiable consumption (the *Big* Mac the *large* fries) seems at odds with the emphasis on *quality* that is everywhere encountered. Mass markets are supposedly a thing of the past, replaced by markets for sophisticated customized goods, while 'quality circles' and 'customer care' programmes ensure that products and services meet the new demands. Yet Ritzer's critique invites us to query all this and ask whether the drive for 'quality' is quite what it seems. And, lastly, there is his squarely placed emphasis on increased rationalization. This is at variance with what virtually all management gurus (as we shall see in the next chapter) argue is happening in organizations. The bureaucracy, they say, has long been fading to extinction and has been replaced by flexible innovative structures. McDonaldization tells us exactly the opposite. The fast-food restaurant as Ritzer describes it is highly bureaucratized and mechanistic, and the society it has cloned is the natural heir of Taylor and Ford, the culmination of a century of rationalizing systems.

All that said, however, there are a number of possible objections and criticisms of the McDonaldization thesis. One is whether it is possible to take the trends that Ritzer identifies and lump them together as instances of a single process: rationalization. Are the mall zombies, the political sound-bites, the bread that tastes like cardboard, Hamburger University, junk-food journalism, and the rest, all cases of the same social condition? Another criticism may be whether Ritzer is being too gloomy and pessimistic about McDonaldization. He sees in the fast-food phenomenon the seeds of the same bureaucratic nightmare that haunted Weber. But is the McDonald's (and the Burger King) on the high street really the harbinger of such a deadly danger? The phenomenal growth of a business like McDonald's, and the proliferation of outlets, depends entirely on a specific business model, namely the franchise. But this is not a model that is widely used, or indeed can be used, in other areas (manufacturing, financial services).

Also, is McDonaldization really the 'master' trend in all of these changes and forms of rationalization? Or is it just one among many? To be sure Ritzer is echoing a popular perception when he singles it out. The 'Mc' prefix has often been used to denote some industry or activity which has suffered the peculiar bureaucratizing and sanitizing impact of the fast-food restaurant. But is this any more than just a handy label? Perhaps the central criticism, though, is that McDonaldization revives a rather worn out model of globalization, one that sees the future as increasingly converging on a single set of (American) values and life-styles. While there may be dangers from US cultural imperialism, Ritzer makes too much of trivial cases of Parisians and Muscovites queuing for burgers. It simply is not true that, as different nationalities and ethnicities around the world develop and modernize, they steadily adopt Western ways. Questions of regionalism and the mixing of cultures are far more complex, and cultural inheritances far more robust, than this.

We will not try to defend Ritzer here but leave the reader to judge. The main point is that this is a thought-provoking book and one of the few accounts that attempts to use the theories of industrial social science in the wider context of cultural studies. In so doing it catches up with many of the trends and changes—the growing importance of consumption, the shift from production to services—that define today's society and economy.

Managerial work and managerial control

Having explored these radical theories of bureaucracy and rationality, it remains to look further at the control concept, because this has been applied by certain prominent researchers to produce an understanding of the nature of management work. They suggest that the notion of control that prevails in the conventional or 'managerialist' literature basically reflects corporate interests. This approach (which we take up in the next chapter) focuses on the kinds of structures that allow managers to regulate their subordinates' activity, with economic performance the end in view. However, a broader notion of control views the whole structure of organizations as a means of controlling behaviour—and indeed beliefs and motivations as well. With the emphasis on constraint and manipulation, this represents a challenge to the conventional view of organization as a system for the attainment of corporate goals. (For early accounts of this perspective see Salaman, 1979, 1981; Clegg and Dunkerley, 1980; chap. 13; Burrell and Morgan, 1979; chap. 11; Storey, 1983; chap. 7.)

In one sense, it is the consequences of managerial *differentiation* that are at issue here. As administrative and bureaucratic structures have grown they have also diversified and very distinctive groupings have emerged—technical, professional, supervisory, corporate. Thus 'management' cannot be seen as a homogeneous or monolithic body, nor is it appropriate to speak as if managers were motivated by a single set of functions (control, planning, etc.). We can illustrate this point by taking an example of just one specialist grouping: supervision. Traditionally it was assumed that supervisors were simply the 'first line of management' (with supervision itself being equated with the lone figure of the foreman). Yet firms often have complex supervisory hierarchies (foremen, general foremen, superintendents) as well as different types of specialist and technical supervisors. To be sure, the drive for 'lean management' in the 1980s was aimed at delayering these structures and reducing the managerial overhead; but the actual extent to which this happened was often limited, and indeed new layers of supervision (teamleaders, for example) seem to have appeared.

The reality is that just as there is an employment relationship between management and workers, there are also significant relations to be studied within management structures. Processes involving political action and conflict, the shifting fortunes of career and occupation, strategies for claiming particular forms of status, and so forth, are all pursued.

A managerial labour process?

One important element of this broad interest in the nature of managerial work has focused on *hierarchical* divisions within management. The argument here is that managers themselves are employees and, with extended and complex hierarchies, they are frequently subordinates as well. Managerial groups are thus subject to pressure and to their own work being degraded and commodified in certain respects, not unlike that of workers. The origins of this approach can be found in Marx's critique of capitalism. Focusing on the conflict between labour and capital, Marx viewed administrative control as an active force in the exploitation of labour. As we saw in Chapter 9, the labour process is seen in terms of the natural control of work of the craftsman being taken over by capitalist control and an elaborate system of supervision. Thus the co-operation of workers in large enterprises is in no way spontaneous or willing, but rather an enforced integration of effort (Marx, 1974, pp. 313–14).

At this point, however, some differences of opinion and emphasis arise. Marxist writers have held to the view of organizations as a control over productive labour. Baldamus, for example, has defined this as follows:

the organisation of industry, with all its complexities and diversities, ultimately revolves on a single process: the administrative process through which the employees' effort is controlled by the employer. This means that the entire system of industrial production will be viewed as a system of administrative controls which regulate quantity, quality and distribution of human effort. (1961, p. 1)

Thus the hierarchy of supervision and management, production planning, and work-pacing technology, indeed the whole edifice of organizational authority, is seen as an artificial structure that alienates the control of work from workers themselves. More recent writers like Armstrong (1989) have confirmed this line of argument, and are suspicious of the notion that managerial work can be seen as a kind of labour process. They stress the importance of retaining the idea of the class-divided nature of capitalist production. A wide differential still separates management from the factory and office floor, and in order to retain an accurate and critical understanding of industrial processes it is important not to lose sight of these differences—nor to blur the distinctions between those who produce and those whose main job is to control.

Others, however, have supported the idea of a managerial labour process as a way of understanding the nature of management work. They stress the growing similarities between managerial work and that of all employees, and that the concept of control also applies within the administrative structure. Thus managers are usually thought of as being in control rather than under control. Yet organizations have extended hierarchies of rewards, status, and power, and with these go varying degrees of commitment. Very senior corporate managers receive such rewards of money and prestige that they identify very closely with organizational goals. But in the middle and lower ranks commitment is much more in doubt. For the employees who make up the bulk of the administration—the junior and middle managers, supervisors, technical specialists—rewards fall far short of those going to top management. Employees in these positions, therefore, constitute part of the organization's problem of control.

In this context Willmott (1997) has pointed to the insecurity of much managerial work. In reality, only an elite of managers occupies a position of privilege and wealth; the majority have little chance of rising into these well-defined corporate groupings. Managers are thus in a 'contradictory' position, being both under and in control; they are 'the targets as well as the agents of exploitation'. Furthermore, as managerial labour is alienated and commodified, we see the majority of managers becoming increasingly concerned with their own well-being and less with the goals of the firm. Thus, Willmott claims, research findings increasingly show that managerial allegiances and commitment are less to their organization, or some mandate from capital, than to personalized and subjective ends like individual careers, families, and managers' professions or occupations. We might add that such a perspective has been given impetus by the trends of the 1980s and 1990s, when downsizing and delayering were dominant, and many observers were suggesting that managerial work had reached a new watershed. The privilege and security of the bureaucratic career has disappeared for many managers. Rather than wielding organizational power, the large majority are powerless to control the corporate processes that affect their working lives (Teulings, 1986).

The nature of managerial control Whether or not managerial work can usefully be thought of as a labour process is still being debated. Of course, some of the constraints of the labour process clearly apply within the administrative structure. Managers and professionals are employees too and may be dismissed if they fail to meet performance standards. But while there is a degree of overlap, the constraints on managers differ in important respects from those that apply to workers. Because workers' effort tends to be controlled by direct and coercive means (like intensive supervision and incentives for output) there is relatively little concern with engaging their loyalty. By contrast, the control exerted over managers is concerned more centrally with their loyalty and commitment. In their case, rewards are not merely an exchange for effort but involve a crucial moral element, so that conformity arises from managers' own internal motivation. In this sense, there is an essential *normative* element to organizational control that secures the self-involvement of managerial groups.

This brings us back to a Weberian-type account and the notion that control, though to some extent enforced, is also in a sense accepted. Managers co-operate in systems of formal authority because of the conviction that they are governed rationally and by the proper discharge of duties, all of which constitutes the basis for organizational legitimacy. The notion of bureaucratic control as 'self-control' reflects the discretion that attaches to managerial jobs at senior levels, the trust that managers enjoy, and the luxury of being held accountable only over the longer term. One of the pioneers of the radical approach to organizational control, Graeme Salaman, has put it this way:

. . . forms of control vary in their effects. Some are highly alienative; others actually encourage normative commitment. The reason for variation in the sorts of organisational control employed for various groups is not only that the sort of work is more or less amenable to this or that form of control. It is also because it would generally be regarded as inapplicable and dangerous to expose senior organisational members in the crucial, decision-making jobs to alienative forms of control, because of the importance of their normative involvement. (1979, p. 129)

Definite features of administrative structures serve to engage managers' commitment. At a fundamental level, because organizations are social systems, a distinctive *culture* develops within them, and like all cultures enforces a degree of conformity. The values and beliefs which make up organizational culture take the form of rules of behaviour, which define informal understandings about how members are expected to act. Secondly, the *division of labour* within management also helps to sustain the central authority. This differs from the division of labour on the shopfloor. As Child (1984, pp. 26–7) has pointed out, workers' jobs tend to be fragmented by Taylorist work practices, giving routine and deskilled operations. But in managerial, technical and professional work, the division of labour is manifest in terms of the *specialization* of tasks. And whereas fragmentation is aimed at removing any discretion or freedom in workers' jobs, with specialization a good deal of discretion is retained. Thus managerial work becomes 'narrow in scope but founded on considerable depth of knowledge'.

As a result, while the division of labour tends to isolate workers, within management the effect is to create departments and units which are interdependent. Within these networks of relationships managers put pressure on one another for greater effort, since they depend upon one another in their jobs. However, the important difference is that here organizational control appears to originate within the management group and does not seem so coercive—although, of course, it ultimately derives from external controls like budgets and output targets. Thus it is common to hear managers complain about such pressure but not to resent it, because 'other people have their jobs to do'.

Professionals in organizations

With growing technological sophistication and the rise of many science-based industries, people with professional training and skills now form an increasingly important part of organizational workforces. Groups like engineers, technicians, and accountants have become much more numerous and central in industrial and commercial organizations. Although such experts can be included simply as part of management, their role in organizations is in certain ways quite distinctive.

As we will see in Chapter 17, the professions are regarded as a kind of occupational control strategy—a means by which groups seek to upgrade the rewards they obtain from employment by gaining recognition and claiming professional status. Occupational groups organize themselves into professions, it is argued, essentially as a way of gaining control over their own market situation and working conditions (Johnson, 1972; Child and Fulk, 1982). What this means, however, is that *organizational structures of control may be incompatible with the occupational controls* upon which the profession bases itself. Thus within organizations the priorities of cost-cutting and tidy administration might be at odds with a professional orientation to 'best practice' in the performance of work. These problems are often made worse because experts and specialists may have relatively little influence within management, despite the importance of their skills. In short, the organizational work setting may deny professionals the autonomy they expect.

Gouldner's (1957) noted distinction between 'cosmopolitans' and 'locals', for example, contrasted professional attachment to wider occupational ideas with the narrower commitment to an organizational career. Similarly, in Burns and Stalker's (1961) classic study of the Scottish electronics industry, the occupational identity of industrial scientists was seen to conflict with many features of their employment context. The scientists became isolated within firms, and found difficulty in fitting into the status conventions. Their identification with technological change caused them to clash with management orientated to more stable operations.

However, it is important not to overgeneralize the conflict between professional loyalties and organizational employment. It is by no means always true that professionals experience organizations as hostile environments. Indeed, one line of argument has suggested the exact opposite, that professional training and work orientations actually resolve many problems of organizational control. Organizations are willing to confer superior rewards and privileges upon employed professionals in return for their 'responsible' approach to work, while for professionals, applying their technical expertise to the problems the organization sets them means that any conflicts are reduced to minor matters. In this sense, Whalley (1986) has referred to production engineers as 'trusted workers'; their occupational socialization and training make them unlikely to engage in acts of resistance or to use their autonomy against the strategic interests of the organization.

Explaining professional status The wide variety of organizational settings that professionals work in has been seen as one way of explaining the differences between occupations that are more or less successful in gaining professional status. Johnson (1972) has referred to three types of occupational control. First, in organizations where professionals predominate (e.g. private practice, universities, research establishments) they usually achieve high levels of status. This 'collegiate' type of occupational control is typical of the senior professions. Secondly, occupations defined by 'corporate patronage' are found within large private corporations, where the employer defines the service, and so shapes the development of the profession over time. Such professions (like accounting, engineering and computing) still enjoy considerable status, although they tend to be 'tied' to a particular employer. Thirdly, 'state mediation' refers to the creation by government of occupations that struggle to sustain their professional status. The ethics of such groups (e.g. teachers and social workers) reflect the rules of the employing agency rather than independent values, and control of the service mainly resides with the state, all of which tends to erode professionalism.

However, the nature of the organizational employer does not by any means account entirely for the variation in professional status. A range of other factors, such as the strength and militancy of the professional body and the demand for particular skills, can have a large effect as well. Within different sectors (private practice, private corporate, public) there is often as much variety in the status enjoyed by professionals as exists between sectors. For example, accountancy is the classic case of an occupation that has been very effective in turning corporate patronage to its advantage, and has successfully upgraded its occupational standing. As Armstrong (1985) has established, the profession has imposed its own language of cost control and formal investment criteria at corporate level, particularly in British companies, which explains the very strong presence the profession typically has in the board room.

Other examples show a more uncertain mix of factors. The computer-skilled occupations (programmers, analysts), for instance, are mainly defined by corporate patronage (in large private-sector institutions like banks) though a degree of collegiality probably exists in the many small software houses that typify this industry. Unlike accounting, this group of occupations has almost no professional development in the shape of a powerful professional body. Rather they have always pursued status by individual strategies based on the acquisition of skills. This has been sustained by a buoyant labour market and ever-expanding demand. The work has become to an extent rationalized, but the demand for new skills and the pace of change of technology has held up. On the other hand, it is not at all clear that the profession has made the journey from isolated technical service to full integration into corporate circles (Friedman, 1989; Fincham, 1996).

What seems clear is that *bureaucratic* work settings impede professional autonomy. Insistence on formal control, a preoccupation with the detail of administration, and rigid divisions of labour all undermine a professional work ethic. Even here though the reality is often more complex. Accounting, as just mentioned, has improved its occupational status mostly in large private-sector corporations run along bureaucratic lines. Similarly, while we tend to associate the state sector with bureaucracy this is not always a hostile environment. Many public organizations operate favourably for professionals. Hospitals within the British National Health Service are a prime example. They represent organizations that have been successfully colonized by the medical professions, doctors in particular. To be sure, the main thrust of government-inspired changes in the 1980s and 1990s was aimed at the 'marketization' of the health sector, which gave increasing powers to NHS managers and potentially upped the bureaucratic character of hospitals, but the moves to absorb doctors in administrative arrangements have largely been resisted. Health-sector professionals are ill at ease with administrative controls, and it is a measure of their power that the medical profession has been able to confront bureaucratic forces and define its own role. Doctors' influence within the NHS has long been seen as the classic example of relatively successful resistance by a profession, and the evidence is that this situation is continuing (Dopson, 1996).

Contrastingly, in other employment settings, the forces of change have been more effective in eroding professional ethics. Local government was traditionally the home of a self-sufficient professional culture in which groups like city architects and town planners were able to define need in client groups and control the delivery of services.

However, managerialist notions have all but replaced the public-service ethos. Though there has been no total loss of professional autonomy, a new strategic managerial role has certainly been ushered in and 'need' is increasingly defined in financial and administrative terms (McNulty and Coalter, 1996). Similarly, universities once provided the model of collegiate values, but academic work has also been impacted by managerialism. An accumulation of power in the hands of university managers has gone hand in hand with declining status and conditions and attacks on academic freedom. Again, academics have certainly not lost control of their work, nor are they entirely innocent partners in their fate, but an erosion of collegiate-type occupational control has certainly taken place (Miller, 1996).

Organizational selection and career

The above forms of control rely on occupational factors, or in some cases reflect the crisis of relations between the state and society of past years. But there is another means of control that represents a generic organizational strategy, consciously and explicitly applied. Selection is the process whereby people are initially recruited into an organization, and continue (as long as their promotion continues) to progress to the inner circles of organizational power. Though there are important technical functions served in choosing people who are competent to perform particular jobs, selection also has a crucial *political* function. The whole of the power structure of organizations rests to a very large extent on the hierarchy as a 'selective mechanism'. For it is vital in ensuring control over personnel that appropriate people are chosen to enter positions of authority. 'Appropriate' here refers to people who will not merely conform to, but actively pursue the goals of the organization, however defined. Thus considerable resources are normally devoted to the allocation of posts; and the procedures of selective recruitment and promotion become increasingly elaborate and formalized the further up the hierarchy one goes, comprising interviews and tests as well as criteria such as track record and past experience.

We might also add that selection automatically implies *rejection*. Thus selection is often portrayed as a 'gatekeeping' function, stressing that unsuccessful candidates are kept out, as well as the successful ones being let in. In this context, Blau and Schoenherr (1971) have emphasized that senior management usually have little need to resort to direct, coercive control because they are able to rely on gatekeeping. Selection ensures that potentially critical groups, which may challenge the settled practice, are simply not allowed entry; they remain as outsiders.

Given the secrecy and confidentiality which surrounds organizational selection, research on the subject is, not surprisingly, rather thin on the ground. However, Salaman and Thompson (1974) have contributed important empirical findings describing the interview procedures used in selecting candidates for officer training in the British army and for selecting management trainees in the Ford Motor Company (see also Salaman, 1979, pp. 187–95). In the army case study, for example, a precisely defined military culture was used as a yardstick for selection. Although the language army selectors used to describe the characteristics they were looking for was apparently rather vague, the selectors themselves knew exactly what they meant. For instance, the capacity in a candidate to remain composed and to present a confident front, even when he had made an obviously incompetent decision, was highly rated, being defined as 'coolness' and 'natural leadership'. The usefulness of such an ability to an organization such as the army, where discipline is of the utmost importance, is readily apparent.

From the employee's point of view, the selection process is experienced in terms of his or her progress, or lack of progress, through the hierarchy—that is, in terms of *career*. Career is a potent form of social control. The prospect of promotion offers huge potential rewards of material gains, prestige, and power. Possibly the greatest appeal is that it resolves the contradiction between extrinsic and intrinsic rewards that appears to be the natural lot of manual workers. If manual workers want higher wages, they usually have to forgo some other reward; they have to work overtime and so lose leisure, or perhaps take on dangerous or unpleasant work, or unsociable hours. With a career, however, increasingly interesting and responsible work is automatically matched by increasing financial rewards.

Career acts as both carrot and stick. If the rewards of promotion motivate management, so too does the fear of failure. Organizations typically are strewn with people who failed to get on, and their fate can be a cruel one in terms of the great psychological pressures that bear upon the unsuccessful. Certainly their presence acts as a constant reminder to the ambitious of the price of being passed over in the promotion race.

Promotion structures therefore engender a particularly intense kind of conformity. Becoming adept at manipulating the organization's belief systems and culture is essential for those with ambition. Learning to interact with colleagues and gaining recognition as an important participant in organizational life are the ingredients of success. The consequences of all this for social control are clear. Such a huge personal investment is involved that a career normally brings about increasing attachment to the organization and its ways of seeing and doing. As Salaman (1979, pp. 140–1) put it: 'When the self is so enmeshed within the organization, the distinction between personal priorities and organizational goals becomes relatively meaningless, and self-control becomes little different from organizational regulation.'

Conclusion

This chapter has explored various radical interpretations of the control concept. The key figure in this was Max Weber, and we saw how Weber's model of bureaucracy has both been widely influential but also widely criticized for creating too idealized an image. This criticism we suggested could be divided into two streams: the first, that Weber underestimated how much bureaucracies encourage conformity and stifle individualism (what we called the social critique); and second, that he ignored the need for organizations to respond to changing environments and markets (the economic critique).

As we argued, much of this criticism is wide of the mark. It reflects a tendency to treat Weber as kind of bench-mark in organization theory, indeed of having originated the very concept of bureaucracy. By taking Weber as the first stage, modern thinking on organizations—which emphasizes flexibility and innovation—can then be neatly contrasted with the strict divisions of labour in his rigid model. But while Weber did pioneer academic theory in this area, the notion of bureaucracy long pre-dates him. Moreover 'bureaucracy' has always had the taint that characterizes its modern usage—that of remote administration, the bureaucrat's arrogant power to ignore democratic processes, and so forth. In this sense, in its own time Weber's ideal type was deliberately oppositional and provocative in describing the benefits of modern organization. And, contrastingly, the modern criticisms of bureaucracy are really not that new.

Whether misplaced or not, the critique of Weber has been extremely fruitful and has led to social scientists' and organization researchers' exploring the informal realities that emerge in real organizations. The response has been for researchers to study unofficial patterns of behaviour and the real-life dynamics of bureaucracy.

Of course, Weber's intentions of identifying the structural features typical in bureaucracy have also been recognized. Weber's genius lay in detecting new and emerging power forms, and the continuing study of these has carried through right to the present. His notion of bureaucracy as an 'iron cage' has been a persistent theme. There have been concerns about 'insidious' forms of power, or, as Blau and Schoenherr (1971, p. 353) put it, 'control that is more dangerous than it seems'. Indeed, the idea of systematic power that pervades organizational life is one of the central concerns of modernity, and was famously voiced by the French social scientist, Foucault. More recently, the interest in 'McDonaldization' has continued these ideas and indeed popularized them. Critics of the McDonaldization thesis have suggested that it reads too much into certain cultural and consumerist trends, but it does attempt to take the new forms of power into up-to-the-minute settings.

Finally, in the last sections of the chapter, we saw how the control concept that occupied us throughout has informed the debate about the nature of managerial work. Control highlights several facets of management that are not picked up by conventional, rationalist theories. The differentiation between groups in management is central. First, there are hierarchical differences that raise issues of conflict and power; and here the vexed issue of a 'managerial labour process' was alluded to—whether the hierarchy should be seen as just that, a continuum with no sharp breaks between 'management' and 'workers', or whether distinctive processes operate in the upper and lower ranks. On the one hand, those arguing for a labour process in management are concerned with the expansion in the lower and middle reaches of management, and the anxieties and insecurity that often define these positions. On the other hand, those arguing for the distinctiveness of different controls tend to see managerial control as basically normative. It relies on internalized obligations to conform and self-inflicted pressures. This led to issues around the recruitment of specialized personnel such as professionals and, what is perhaps the single most important mechanism for controlling managerial behaviour, that of organizational selection. Selection has tremendous power in moulding individual managers' perceptions and motivations to corporate goals, even if the rewards going to senior groups may seem sufficient to explain conformity.

Study questions for Chapter 12

1 What are the features of Weber's model of bureaucracy and what are the criticisms of it?

2 To what extent do the widespread criticisms of Weber do him justice?

3 What do you understand to be the relationship between formal and informal organization?

4 What do you understand as the 'insidious' nature of modern power systems?

5 Discuss the ways in which more recent writers (Goffman, Foucault, Ritzer) have interpreted the new forms of organizational power.

6 What is the critique of modern cultural patterns that the McDonaldization thesis offers?

7 Does the control of a managerial labour force differ from that of groups of manual and white-collar workers?

Further reading

Alvesson, M. and Willmott, H. (1996) *Making Sense of Management: A Critical Introduction*. London: Sage.

Brown, R. (1992) *Understanding Industrial Organizations*. London: Routledge.

Clegg, S. (1990) *Modern Organizations*. London: Sage.

Grint, K. (1991) *The Sociology of Work*. Cambridge: Polity Press.

Hales, C. (1993) *Managing Through Organization*. London: Routledge.

Knights, D. and Willmott, H. (eds.) (1986) *Managing the Labour Process*. London: Gower.

Morgan, Gareth (1997) *Images of Organization*, 2nd edn. London: Sage.

Morgan, Glenn (1990) *Organizations in Society*. Basingstoke: Macmillan.

Reed, M. (1986) *Redirections in Organisational Analysis*. London: Tavistock.

—— (1989) *The Sociology of Management*. London: Harvester Wheatsheaf.

—— and Hughes, M. (eds.) (1992) *Rethinking Organization*. London: Sage.

Ritzer, G. (1995) *Expressing America: A Critique of the Global Credit Card Society*. Thousand Oaks, Calif.: Pine Forge Press.

Thompson, P. and McHugh, D. (1995) *Work Organisations*, 2nd edn. Basingstoke: Macmillan.

—— and Smith C. (1996) 'Re-evaluating the labor process debate', in M. Wardell (ed.) *Labor and Capital in the Twentieth Century: The Braverman Legacy and Beyond*. New York: SUNY Press.

13 Structure and Performance in Organizations

Summary points and learning objectives

By the end of this chapter you will

- understand the basic concepts of *organizational analysis*—system, structure, goal;
- have explored the *systems perspective* and its limits;
- have reviewed the *classical school* of organization theorists;
- understand *contingency theory*, in particular the contingent relationship between organization and technology, and organization and environment;
- be able to evaluate both the *criticisms* and *continuities* in contingency theory;
- be able to evaluate the basic *design choices* available to managers, such as organic, product-based, and matrix structures;
- understand how design choices relate to *contemporary organizational models*, such as lean structures, re-engineering, and the virtual organization.

Introduction

Though there are many different perspectives on organizations, two schools of thought predominate. One focuses on the problems of power in society and how these are experienced in organizations. This corresponds with the approach of the previous chapter, and owes much to the Weberian analysis of bureaucracy. The second is a managerial tradition the concerns of which are efficiency and effectiveness: the design of appropriate structures, and the motivation of groups and individuals to perform in line with stated goals. This derives in part from F. W. Taylor's theory of scientific management and his studies of work administration, as well as broader managerial movements concerned with the principles of effective management.

To a large extent these two approaches have been mutually exclusive, not to say antagonistic. Writers interested in the 'problem' of organization tend not to regard efficiency as an issue of first importance, and those preoccupied with efficiency usually disregard awkward questions about the social and political impact of organizations.

(There are notable exceptions in those who have tackled the problem of integrating the two approaches, or at least acknowledged validity in both sets of claims, e.g. Morgan, 1997.)

However, we will now turn our attention to the managerial approach. Though hardly necessary to justify, the concerns of management merit attention for a number of reasons. Modern organizations produce the goods and services of our material life and the problems of providing these benefits affect all in society. Also, because firms, regions, and nations compete we are all, like it or not, caught up in issues of efficiency and effectiveness. Furthermore, since management has the power to direct activities in organizations, a knowledge of these priorities and objectives is necessary for a wider understanding of organizational behaviour.

In this chapter we will cover the basic ideas of organizational analysis. These reflect the different objectives of organizations and the variety of activities they engage in, with the emphasis throughout on organization as a means of achieving specified economic ends. Particularly influential has been the idea of the organization as a *system*, and the implications of this metaphor for how key concepts (structure, goal) are interpreted. We go on to explore the main developments in *organization theory* itself, together with criticisms and debates that have been at the heart of the renewal and turnover of these central ideas. And, finally, we look at organizational *design* and the continuing interest in appropriate structures and ways of organizing activities.

Organizations as systems

The very word 'organization' suggests a similarity with living organisms, and while there are dangers (which we return to) in taking this analogy too far, it has proved a useful model and one that keeps cropping up in organizational analysis. The parts of an organization—departments, divisions—must integrate their efforts, just as the parts of any living organism are interdependent. Moreover, organizations may be viewed as existing in a competitive environment, as do plants and animals, and they have to adapt to environmental conditions or find their existence threatened.

Organizations have system boundaries in the sense that they may occupy a definite geographical area, although this is not always the case. Government departments and multinational companies, for example, are dispersed over wide areas. None the less, great care is taken in organizations to ensure that the membership is identified and kept under review. Writers who have developed the systems approach, however, have been at pains to emphasize that organizations should not be viewed merely as closed systems; to do this is to adopt a very static picture of how they operate (Elliott, 1980). Organizations have suppliers and clients; and there are wider social and economic forces that affect them, such as the labour market, the community, government legislation and, of course, other organizations. Thus, organizations are open systems, and transactions across the organizational boundary take place continuously, so much so that it can be difficult in practice to define exactly where an organization stops and its environment begins.

Structure and goals

It follows from the systems approach that organizations have a structure—an established set of relationships, with ordered and regularly occurring activities. Because tasks in organizations are almost always interdependent, it is essential that personnel act in a calculable and predictable manner. Hence performance and structure are inextricably linked. And, of course, the desire to improve performance is the underlying reason for studying the management process in organizations. This aim does not refer to the effectiveness of actual decisions taken in given circumstances (which is the central problem of business policy), but rather to the attempt to identify those structures of behaviour which contribute to the achievement of organizational goals.

Reference here is mainly to the *formal* structure of organizations—that is, the official hierarchy of positions, the division of labour and specified operating procedures. This is not to ignore the informal side of organizational activity. We focused on this in the previous chapter, and indeed, as we shall see, organizational analysis has taken serious notice of factors that lie outside the structure of formal authority. But, as Child (1984) has pointed out, only the formal structure is subject to control and planning by management. Thus it remains the fundamental concern of organization theory. In practical terms, the design of an effective structure needs to reflect the objectives of the organization and the context in which it operates. Good management also means anticipating the circumstances that make structural development and adaptation necessary.

There are several distinct but related aspects of organization structure. At its most basic level, formal structure refers to the physical shape of the organization—the distribution of jobs and lines of command—often set out in an organization chart, if the firm in question has one. At a more analytic level we can distinguish two main components of the management structure:

1. The division of labour or function—the division between groups, departments, specialisms, and organizational divisions.
2. The division of power and authority—the division between superordinate and subordinate which forms the organizational hierarchy.

This gives the familiar picture of organizations as pyramidal structures of laterally connected departments and hierarchical levels. Thus, for example, Salaman (1979, p. 61) has defined structure as 'the way in which work is organised and control exercised', a definition in which we can see the twofold emphasis on relationships of communication and authority.

As well as these basic relationships, formal structure is identified with the major areas of managerial responsibility. John Child (1984; chap. 1) has set out in some detail the requirements for the formulation and successful implementation of managerial plans. They include an established procedure for decision-making, with arrangements for the collection of information, the notification of decisions to groups and individuals, and a schedule for meetings. Another important managerial task is the control and co-ordination of activities. Here, operational procedures have to be set down in advance in order to specify areas of accountability and standards of performance; there must be a monitoring system to feed back information on performance to the right authority centres, and arrangements to correct operational activity in the light of any shortcomings. Thus the success and viability of an enterprise depend upon creating the most effective structure of administration, given the circumstances in which the organization is operating—one which distributes the necessary tasks, delegates required authority and controls the outcomes of actions.

In this way the structure of an organization contributes to the goals set by management. Formal structure reflects the fact of goals having been identified and criteria of achievement specified. Indeed, the goal concept is one of the most basic ideas of organizational analysis. It reflects the notion of organizations as purposive bodies that are set up and designed to achieve specific ends. In this sense, Donaldson (1985, p. 7) understands an organization as 'a set of rules oriented towards securing a goal. It is any social system which comprises the coordinated action of two or more people towards attaining an objective'. And, similarly, the subject-matter of organization theory is 'the phenomenon of goal-oriented behaviour'. This also embraces the essential notion of *rationality*. Rational behaviour can most simply be defined as behaviour that logically connects means and ends. It reflects the sense in which organizations define goals explicitly, and define equally carefully the detailed methods to achieve them (i.e. the organization structure). This type of formal rationality, as we saw in the previous chapter, is central to the modern idea of organization.

While some goals refer to broad aims, such as efficiency or the pursuit of profit, these afford little insight into the operations of a specific enterprise, and so more detailed goals are usually of interest. For example, the management of a retail chain specializing in cut-price furniture might well decide that the goal of quality is not its first priority. They may be content to put up with a certain number of customer complaints for a given volume of business. On the other hand, a high-class interior designer would be far more likely to regard quality as a goal that could not be compromised, and might regard a single dissatisfied customer as a threat to future business. Thus, while both firms have the same overall goal of selling furniture for profit, a detailed breakdown of goals and how they are prioritized tells us much more about the different ways in which the two businesses will be run.

Limits of the systems approach

Despite the continued appeal of the systems metaphor there are still drawbacks to this way of visualizing organizations. The inspiration for 'systems thinking' comes mainly from natural science models (engineering, biology, etc.) whereas organizations are social systems. They may have similarities with physical systems, and share some features, but there are also fundamental differences. In particular, the existence of the free-willing subject, and the consequent uncertainty and open-endedness of social behaviour, is something the natural and technical sciences find hard to account for. As a result, the adoption of systems models and their use in organizational analysis can lead to mechanistic and overly rationalist theories.

There are also a number of specific problems with the concept of organizational goals. The idea behind the concept is that the purpose of the division of labour is to break down general goals into specialist ones, which become the goals of designated organization units. These are then recombined, as it were, through the hierarchy and eventually united into the overall objective of the organization. The problem is that while this kind of model may approximate quite well to a physical or technical system—where evolutionary or developmental trends lead to a harmony between sub-systems—it is hopelessly idealized for social systems. The notion of organizations having 'a goal' or single objective is always going to be oversimplified, even if at some levels there is a unity of purpose. The reality is much more likely to be that of *multiple goals*, giving the possibility of goal conflict. The distinct groupings within management bodies—technical staff, production, sales, and so forth—give rise to a variety of legitimate goals, and this is without the informal kinds of conflict and resistance that we know go on as well. These managerial differences were noted in the previous chapter, but for now we can note that such forms of differentiation and conflict are part and parcel of management.

Another problem with the goal concept is that of *reification*. This refers to the tendency of attributing human motives to social institutions—in this case of thinking about organizations as if *they* had purposes and were pursuing goals. Of course, only people in organizations can have goals. Still, it is all too easy to refer to organizations as the active party—to speak of organizations controlling their personnel, learning, adapting to their environments. The danger in viewing the organization as a purposeful entity is that you end up with an abstract and artificial analysis. The people making decisions and the motives behind their actions tend to be concealed. There is the danger of shielding their actions from criticism by implying it was 'the organization' that was responsible—or implying that somehow decisions were inevitable. Thus when analysing 'system outcomes' it is important to be clear that we are talking about the goals officially sanctioned in an organization, not the goals that organizations pursue.

That said, this basic approach of seeing organizations as 'purposive systems', and focusing on their structures and goals, has formed the backbone of organizational analysis from its inception. And in the remaining sections of the chapter we will outline these developments (though, as we will also see, the criticisms suggested here are never very far away).

The classical school

The established theory generally regarded as the starting point of organizational analysis is, as we have said, Taylor's scientific management. This was an approach which gave a decidedly formalistic slant to early theory. Taylor had developed a 'science' of the control of manual work that employers had applied to great advantage; and the first writers on organizations, the so-called classical school, set themselves the task of developing along similar lines a formal theory of administration. Many of them were or had been managers themselves, and they emphasized such practical aspects of administration as the importance of strict specialization in management, and the exercise of strong leadership with clear lines of authority. Henri Fayol, a French engineer, is regarded as the founder of the classical school, and other prominent writers included Gulick and Urwick, Mary Parker Follet, and Mooney and Reiley. (For discussion of the classical school, see March and Simon, 1958; chap. 2; Pugh *et al.*, 1984; Mouzelis, 1975; chap. 4; Clegg and Dunkerley, 1980, pp. 99–106.)

By modern standards their work was probably not very impressive. Their emphasis on the correct 'principles of management' had a slightly archaic flavour, like the search for some magic formula. Concepts were not clearly specified, nor were their claims based on any empirical research. Perhaps their major shortcoming was a failure to take human factors into account (in this they were the true heirs of Taylor) so that an appropriately designed structure was supposed to eliminate all further problems of control and integration. This is something that certainly cannot be assumed away; indeed the central concern of modern organization theory has been precisely those behavioural factors ignored by the classical writers. None the less, the classical school did tackle some of the basic problems of organization design. It cleared a space for organization analysis to develop, and their concerns with formal structure and the functions of management remain valid today.

Contingency theory

After the initial impact of the classical school, interest in organizations shifted to psychological and group aspects (dealt with under the Human Relations school in Chapter 7) and little concern with structure was shown until as late as the 1950s. Then a new line of thought emerged which took a fresh look at structure and at the original focus on the principles of efficient administration. This was the so-called contingency theory. As with many important insights, the idea behind the theory was quite simple, namely that organization structure should be regarded as a contingent variable. In other words, the search of the classical theorists for universal principles of administration was held to be misguided; managers face circumstances which vary, and they must choose whatever structural arrangements are most appropriate in the prevailing context. The proper role of organization theory, therefore, is not to seek any 'one best way' to manage, but to provide insight and guidance for managers to help them formulate responses in the complex situations of organizational decision-making.

The general model implicit in contingency theory assumes that, for an organization to be effective, there must be an appropriate 'fit' between structure and context. Such a model can be set out as follows.

$$\text{CONTEXTUAL FACTORS} \rightarrow \text{ORGANIZATION STRUCTURE} \rightarrow \text{PERFORMANCE}$$

Thus structure is essentially seen as an *intervening variable*, which modifies the effect of contingent factors upon performance, given the context in which the organization operates. Structure is also essentially *adaptive* since it may need to be changed if the context is dynamic and makes demands that alter over time. (For discussion of contingency theory, see Burrell and Morgan, 1979, pp. 164–81; Child, 1984, pp. 217–25.)

Contextual factors embrace all of the given elements which serve to constrain managerial decision-making, so the context may vary over time and from firm to firm in an almost endless variety of ways. However, it has proved possible to isolate some of the most important contextual variables. These include chiefly the type of *technology* an organization uses and the kind of *environment* in which it operates.

Organization and technology

As well as the hardware used in production, the term 'technology' is used to refer to production methods and work organization. Thus technology has become a sort of short-hand term for the general task structure of an organization. A mass production technology, for example, involves large numbers of semi-skilled operatives, and hence the task of labour management and supervision becomes critical. Conversely, science-based technologies generate tasks involving professional and technical skills, and employees with these sorts of ability tend to be self-regulating in their work. Craft technologies are similar in this respect. Thus different production technologies give rise to different systems of tasks, which in turn affect structure.

Woodward Probably the best-known research on the technology-structure relationship is Joan Woodward's (1965) study of manufacturing firms. Woodward obtained measures (some of them admittedly rather simple and crude) of three organizational variables: first, the commercial success of firms; secondly, their production technology (which she classified in three types: technologies that produce single units or small batches, mass production, and process production technologies); and thirdly, certain dimensions of structure (e.g. the number of levels in the hierarchy, the labour intensity and the first line spans of control). These, we can see, cover the three variables in the contingency model above.

Woodward arrived at two major findings. (1) There was a link between structure and technology in that firms in the same technical category (say, all of the unit production firms) tended to have similar organization structures. (2) She then discovered that all three variables—technology, structure, and performance—were related. She found that successful firms in each technical category had structural characteristics near the average for the category as a whole, while the firms with below average success fell in the extremes of the range of structural variables.

This seemed to imply that a given technology 'demands' a particular structure, and firms that obey this 'technological imperative' reap the rewards in terms of organizational efficiency and business success. Moreover, the relationship was clearly a contingent rather than an unvarying one. Thus, for example, in successful mass production firms tasks tended to be clearly defined and the structure bureaucratic. By contrast, in continuous-process firms the technology was often advanced and science-based; firms employed a high proportion of professional and technical staff who required more flexible working arrangements, hence a bureaucratic structure was too rigid and tended to be associated with commercial failure.

Perrow Another influential contingency theorist, Charles Perrow (1970), examined the task structure of different production technologies. Perrow distinguished two basic dimensions of task. First, whether the problems typically encountered in the firm were either well understood, or not well understood. This relates to whether problems are capable of rational solution, and are being solved by the application of known techniques. Second was the degree of variability in the firm's core task: whether there are few exceptional problems, or many exceptions. These two dimensions combined to enable Perrow to distinguish different production technologies, according to the following schema.

	Few exceptions	Many exceptions
Not well understood problems	**Craft**	**Uncertainty**
Well understood problems	**Routine**	**Risk**

Figure 13.1 Perrow's production technologies model

Thus, in *craft* technologies, the problems are unique and only resolvable by the application of human ingenuity and skills, but the pace of work is measured. Such industries are not necessarily traditional or old fashioned; craft-type technologies can be found in extremely modern work settings, such as customized high-tech operations, or in research and development organizations, where time spans tend to be long-term. Secondly in technologies characterized by high levels of *uncertainty* problems again are only resolved via human expertise, but these are also high pressure industries where competition may be intense and the pace of change hectic. The settings Perrow had in mind here were leading edge industries at the highest levels of technical development, such as aerospace and computers.

The next category, *risk*, is like uncertainty in so far as the pressure and pace of change are high, but there are crucial differences between risk and uncertainty. In high-risk industries there may be many exceptions to the rule, but when exceptions occur there are established methods for handling them. A good example here might be the motor industry. High-volume car production is massively complex and automated, but though exceptions occur constantly (breakdowns, process variations) there are also well-defined maintenance and other coping procedures. Finally, in *routine* industries the problems tend to be simple and covered by administrative procedures, and there are also relatively few of them. An example might be the mass production of straightforward products. Thus Crozier's (1964) well known account of the French tobacco industry (see the previous chapter) painted a picture of cigarette production as controlled and predictable and with little competitive pressure, the only elements of uncertainty being mechanical breakdowns.

Implied in Perrow's schema is an increase in the pressures and difficulties of the management task, going from more routine to more uncertain organizational technologies. But this is not a simple linear progression. Craft and high-risk industries, for example, have their own different kinds of managerial problems. What Perrow was able to show was that, at a basic level, managerial responsibilities were contingent upon the organization's task structure. Each had a managerial 'problem' distinctive to its task and technology.

Routine production tasks probably pose the least demanding set of problems for management, though even here managers in bureaucratic work settings can come under hierarchical pressure from above. In craft industries the key 'problem of management' revolves around the value added by these industries residing in the skills of the workforce. Attracting and retaining labour with rare skills, and managing that labour in project teams, is what occupies managerial time and energy. In high-risk industries the management of labour is again the key problem, but there are large bodies of semi-skilled workers, who may be alienated and resistant, so the managerial problem is basically one of control. And, in uncertain production tasks, all the problems of competitive pressures and the difficulties of managing processes at the very highest levels of technical complexity crowd in.

Organization and environment

As we noted briefly above, the systems approach stresses that organizations are shaped by and adapt to their environments. The organization is pictured as existing within a complex economic, political, and social setting: labour markets, supply and product markets, competitors, and so on. The environment is also often seen as a set of concentric rings, which distinguish the more immediate influences (labour markets, competitors, suppliers) from the more distant ones (like the broad industrial culture of a country, or the legislative environment). However, distinctions like these are often oversimplified, with as many exceptions as rules. Thus the state of the national or global economy may be taken for granted when demand is reasonably buoyant, but even mild recessions and downturns can instantly affect certain kinds of businesses. Similarly, for certain individuals and segments in the organization, aspects of the environment will have different meanings. Shareholders may seem a rather distant group to some members, but top executives are likely to feel their presence much more acutely.

Still, the relationship between organization and environment, particularly in terms of potential threats, has been a very influential idea in organizational analysis. Perhaps the most fundamental threat coming from the environment involves the very legitimacy of the organization being called into question. In a sense this is more menacing even than threats of liquidation and closure. Business people tend to take for granted the morality of the marketplace—if their product sells it must be acceptable; if it does not it is simply because a competitor has done better. But threats to organizational legitimacy undermine the ethics of an organization's methods and the value of its product, and can cause a deep crisis of confidence. Many public-sector organizations in Britain, for example, are going through such a crisis under pressure from radical government policies. Central government has imposed a range of changes meant to 'marketize' the sector and bring it under tight financial constraint. This has increasingly confused any clear notion of the service role which has traditionally defined local government's identity and culture. Another example, the giant American tobacco industry, has been under long-term pressure from powerful US health lobbies. By 1997 the industry had been significantly compromised and forced to make crucial admissions, namely that it was aware of tobacco's health risks and addictive qualities. Again (though for very different reasons) these threats to legitimacy caused a deep sense of defensiveness in the industry.

More generally, the environment with which an organization engages (like its technology) is defined by its entry into a particular product market. Once that initial decision has been made environmental pressures—from competitors, from technical change—become part of the context of decision-making. The overall impact of environment is determined by the level of uncertainty that is generated, i.e. whether the environment is stable or the source of rapid and unpredictable change. The more uncertain and complex an organization's environment, the more the organization will need to develop specialized functions to cope with environmental problems, and the more resources it will need to devote to managing the interface with the environment.

Burns and Stalker Burns and Stalker's study *The Management of Innovation* (1961) was an early and very influential piece of research which focused on the organization–environment relationship. These researchers studied the Scottish electronics industry, which underwent rapid expansion in the post-war period under the impact of advances like television and the transistor. With rapid technical change and fierce competition, the firms upon which Burns and Stalker based their research existed in an extremely turbulent, uncertain environment. The researchers sought an explanation of survival and success in such an environment, and they found it in a particular kind of organization structure.

They distinguished two structural types, which they termed 'mechanistic' and 'organic' (1961, pp. 119–25). The mechanistic structure was highly bureaucratic, with a strict division of authority and preoccupation with matters of internal efficiency. By contrast, organic structures were flexible and informal, with a good deal of sharing of responsibility, and lower-ranked staff had considerable influence delegated to them. Of crucial importance was the fact that the organic structure retained a strong sense of direction and commitment which embraced all the personnel.

The distinctive feature of the organic system is the pervasiveness of the working organization as an institution. In concrete terms, this makes itself felt in a preparedness to combine with others in serving the general aims of the concern. . . . The individual's job ceases to be self-contained; the only way in which 'his' job can be done is by his participating continually with others in the solution of problems which are real to the firm. (1961, p. 125)

The organic structure was thus able to adapt to uncertain environments. Indeed, the research showed that firms that survived and prospered in the electronics industry at that time were the ones with organic structures. The firms which floundered (as many did) tended to be the ones with mechanistic structures, their problems arising from their inability to respond to new and unforeseen circumstances.

Once again, however, this was a contingent relationship. Burns and Stalker wished to avoid any suggestion that organic structures are always superior—indeed they can be very expensive in terms of the managerial time taken up in integrating activities. In an environment where there is little need for adaptability the mechanistic structure comes into its own.

Lawrence and Lorsch Another important contingency theory study, conducted by Lawrence and Lorsch (1967), also focused on the internal structures for dealing with external environments. Lawrence and Lorsch examined two key structural variables: differentiation and integration. Differentiation, as we have already seen, refers to the divisions within a management body caused by the range of specialisms and departmental groupings. They defined differentiation as the 'differences in cognitive and emotional orientation among managers in different functional departments' (1967, p. 11). Lawrence and Lorsch stressed that differences in task and occupation were not merely superficial; they give rise to deep-rooted distinctions in attitudes and values.

Different managerial world-views have profound implications for managers' ability to integrate. Integration referred to managers' capacity to act coherently, and was defined in terms of 'the quality of collaboration amongst departments required to achieve unity by the demands of the environment' (p. 11). The researchers stressed that integration is not achieved automatically, via the chain of command, as the classical theorists tended to assume. The differences between functional specialists if not checked led to conflict and a lack of integration. Thus, other things equal, there would be an inverse relation between differentiation and integration: the higher the differentiation, the lower the integration (or the higher the conflict) and vice versa.

The research that Lawrence and Lorsch conducted was a comparative study of organizations, some successful and some less successful, operating in industrial environments with different levels of complexity and uncertainty. They were interested to learn how the most effective organizations coped with the demands of their particular environment.

The research focused on major types of intergroup relations which give rise to recurring problems of integration. It looked at the relationships between production, sales, and research and development departments, and revealed typical patterns of conflict. For example, production managers favoured stable output and low product variation, as these helped them to meet production targets and stay within budget, while

managers in sales desired the exact opposite. Rapid delivery and a high degree of variation helped salespeople to meet customer requirements. Similar problems arose
between production and R&D: development engineers became preoccupied with the
technical problems of product design and were oriented towards long-range planning;
production managers, on the other hand, wanted engineers to be available to solve
immediate practical problems, and their own time horizons were short term. These
kinds of differences caused managers to fail to communicate properly and to be unable
to understand one another's problems.

The obvious answer to the problem of excessive levels of conflict would seem to lie in
reducing levels of differentiation, and only having organizations with homogeneous
bodies of managers. Unfortunately the solution is not that simple. Organizations
require wide-ranging specialist skills if they are to cope with complex environments, as
well as needing to allocate tasks to well-defined sub-units, both of which lead to high levels of differentiation. A contradiction therefore arises: for high performance, high levels
of differentiation are required, but these lead to conflict, which has a deleterious effect
on performance. What this means in practice is that conflict can never be wholly eliminated and the resolution of conflict remains a central issue.

Lawrence and Lorsch identified a range of integrating devices commonly employed
by organizations to resolve conflict. These ranged from simply making an individual
manager responsible for liaison with another department, to practices aimed at the
mediation of relationships with a potential for high conflict. There were also special
integrating groups developed to solve particular problems, as well as highly elaborate
'matrix' structures comprised of intersecting project teams. In addition, Lawrence and
Lorsch reported appropriate forms of motivation, influence, and inter-personal style
among managers which enabled them to understand and accommodate the points of
view of others (p. 80).

Lawrence and Lorsch found that, particularly where market environments were
highly uncertain and turbulent, the most successful organizations had managed to
achieve high levels of integration and high levels of differentiation. This seemed to defy
the rule that integration and differentiation were inversely related, but organizations
could achieve this by means of effective mechanisms for continually resolving conflict.
However, in general 'the most successful organizations tended to maintain states of differentiation and integration consistent with the environment' (p. 134). All organizations had levels of what Lawrence and Lorsch called 'required integration', matching the
context in which they operated. The more powerful integrating mechanisms—which
were also the more costly in terms of managerial time and overhead—were appropriate
only where organizations faced a highly uncertain environment, complex technical
problems, and competitive markets. Otherwise the less sophisticated alternatives were
sufficient to secure economic success.

Criticisms of contingency theory and managerial choice

Organizational analysis subsequently moved away from the consensus of opinion
which made contingency theory the main school of thought in the 1960s and early

1970s, and we should now consider some of the criticisms that have been levelled at it.

First, contingency theory suggested an unrealistic and over-simplified model of managerial activity. For although the theory stressed that there is no *one* best way to manage, it did assume there was *a* best way given a limited number of contextual conditions. The reality, critics have pointed out, is more complex than this. Managers are required to formulate policy and strategy in more varied circumstances than ever contingency theory acknowledged, and in fact there is little convincing evidence that structural designs can be made to 'fit' the context of operations. Secondly, the simple *causal* link between structure and performance has also been challenged. Contingency theory proposed that an appropriate structure gives rise to high performance, but all the empirical research showed (or indeed ever could show) was a *correlation* between structure and performance. The direction of causation was assumed. Critics have therefore suggested that in some cases causality may run the other way. In other words, a more realistic argument may be that it is the initial performance of organizations which determines the kinds of structure they are able to adopt (Child, 1984, pp. 225–30).

A good illustration of this was provided by a company in which one of the authors conducted research. This was a successful manufacturer of surgical equipment, which had adopted a fully integrated management structure. While it was possible that the structure had led to their success, it seemed equally likely that the reverse had happened, that once the company had achieved a dominant market position it then had the resources to develop its matrix structure. This involved a considerable managerial overhead (there was a network of interdepartmental teams permanently established to deal with many specific projects and problems of long-range planning), and it seemed unlikely that any company that had been performing badly would have been able to sustain this level of expenditure as a precondition of success.

A third criticism is that contingency theory plays down the importance of *power*, both the power of strategically placed managers and the power of the organization itself. In this context, Child (1972) has referred to the 'strategic choice' exercised by managers as the 'critical variable in organization theory'. Corporate groups with effective power in organizations have a great deal of discretion; their decisions are not predetermined by context and structure, nor are they without the power to enforce choices which suit their purposes irrespective of constraints placed upon them. Wood (1979) has similarly argued that management policy and the development of the organization's human resources are critical factors, and that firms have the capacity to organize themselves from within, rather than being forced to adapt to technical and market contexts. It would be naive not to recognize that organizations often exercise considerable control over their environments. Large-scale organizations dispose of enormous advertising revenues to stimulate markets, they can exert influence via political lobbying, and much modern technology comes under their control. Indeed, organizations with monopolistic powers over markets and potential competitors are readily able to sustain a poor level of performance, or an inappropriate structure, if they wish to do so for whatever reasons.

Box 13.1 Defining the environment

Robert Scott's (1967) research in New York federal agencies for the blind provides a telling illustration of how organizations in practice may not simply adapt to whatever environment they find themselves in. Scott discovered that 80 per cent of the blind are multi-handicapped, elderly, and black, and that these groups were relatively ignored by the welfare agencies. The agencies were mainly interested in the 'desirable blind'—those who were young, white, and employable—as this group was more appealing to fundraisers and easier to deal with. Agencies competed to attract these people onto their programmes. Ironically, there were only just enough to make their programmes viable, while the large majority of blind people were excluded. The agencies also modified their assistance programmes to keep the desirable blind dependent on them (since they were such a scarce resource) rather than working for the independence of these people in the community. These organizations exercised power not only to broadly influence their environment, but to define it in ways that suited them. The agencies' real environment was the donating bodies and the other agencies with which they competed, rather than the whole population of the blind, which was supposed to be the client group.

Source: R. A. Scott, (1967) 'The selection of clients by social welfare agencies: the case of the blind', *Social Problems*, 14/3; 248–57.

However, while the force of these criticisms has to be accepted, certain points in defence of contingency theory can be put forward. The model linking context, structure, and performance perhaps inevitably involved simplification, but researchers like Woodward and Burns were well aware of this, and in their detailed accounts made a good deal of perceptive comment on the complexity of these relationships. For example, Woodward has frequently been criticized for an order of 'technological determinism' in her work, for suggesting that technology determines organization structure and that human choice plays no significant role. Such criticism is to an extent valid, since she did argue that technology seemed to have an effect on structure and performance of which managers were unaware. However, Woodward also stressed that technology acts only as a *constraint* on behaviour, and that within certain limits conscious choices are exercised.

Donaldson (1985) has offered a vigorous defence of 'the contingency-systems paradigm' against its critics. He argues among other things that contingency theory can take account of organizational change via the notion of systems being disturbed by external pressures but reaching new equilibria. It can also include radical notions of conflict (as we have seen) through the concept of differentiation. Moreover, contingency theory's lasting value is its pragmatism and concern with 'feasible change' (p. 74). Thus the contingency theorists' notion of decision-making as an activity partly constrained, but displaying choice and variability, does not seem unreasonable. As Wood (1979) has suggested, it may be the popularizers of contingency theory who, with 'their limited reading of the work in which they propose to be rooted' (p. 353), are responsible for any oversimplification, rather than the researchers who conducted the classic studies. Certainly this empirical research took our understanding of organization a stage further and their contributions remain important.

Organizational design

The findings of contingency theory as well as the criticisms of it have changed our notions of how managers go about their work, and in particular how they go about designing organizations. Under the classical theory 'design' was never a burning issue as there was supposedly a unified set of management principles. But the contingent thesis of there being 'no one best way' to manage immediately raises the question of different designs. As Butler (1991) has noted, while decision-making has political and informal elements, it still takes place within a set of constraints. Structure is the 'enduring set of decision rules' in an organization, and design involves 'the setting of appropriate structures within which decisions are made and executed' (p. 2). In this sense, the practical outcome of organizational analysis is to inform the selection of appropriate relations between departments and the grouping of sub-units—in short, to equip managers to make informed choices about organizational design. 'The task in designing organizations is to create this organizational setting in such a way as to permit the necessary decision processes to take place effectively' (Butler, 1991, p. xiv).

One fundamental choice lies between organizations that are less rigidly structured, but because of their flexibility can handle levels of uncertainty, versus those that are more bureaucratic and designed for efficiency. Butler (1991) refers to these as 'fuzzy' versus 'crisp' structures. But in fact a number of well-known and influential accounts have focused on this key distinction. A pioneering one was Burns and Stalker's (1961) distinction between organic and mechanistic structures that we reviewed above.

The choice between rationalized versus flexible structures presents itself at many different levels in organizations. The advantages of tight control of costs and labour in a rigidly designed system may be decisive in certain circumstances, but it may be necessary to switch to a more flexible, albeit less efficient, design which can absorb the uncertainties of production if circumstances change. Moreover, even these choices rarely present themselves as simple alternatives. Managers may have to combine different elements of each approach, and they may need to make constant adjustments if the operational or market context changes. Therefore, rather than try to specify structural designs for the functional areas of responsibility, modern theory tends to define the basic choices that managers face and the design principles underlying successful resolution. Frequently such problems are experienced as actual dilemmas that entail the perpetual juggling of different demands.

Control and integration

Child (1984) has drawn attention to two fundamental management tasks—the twin problems of control and integration—which underpin any design decision. These reflect the basic dimensions of any organization structure: the (hierarchical) structure of authority, and the (lateral) division of labour. Both have been discussed before in various guises, but Child provides a useful resumé from the design perspective.

Control refers to the problem of regulating the activities of subordinates. The concept has been detailed at length in this and previous chapters. But control mechanisms typically include standardized operating procedures, job specifications, the monitoring of performance, and the assignment of responsibilities. The basic dilemma of control is that mechanisms for maintaining tight control can be self-defeating. The experience of being closely supervised may demoralize people and make them surrender initiative. It may also engender resistance and give rise to a different kind of vicious circle. On top of problems of motivation, centralized control may cause related problems of inflexibility. Organizations remain responsive to change in part because of power being delegated to those with operational roles. Specialists keeping abreast of innovations in their field, middle managers able to act on their operational knowledge—these strengths keep an organization adaptive. Too rigid a control structure tends to withdraw decision-making capacity from those close to the boundary with the environment.

Strategies aimed at resolving this dilemma need to balance the conditions of the centralization of control and its decentralization. They do this basically by centralizing and decentralizing different kinds of power: the major policy decisions are centralized while operational responsibility is delegated. This kind of loose–tight structure is typical in large divisionalized companies that would otherwise be in danger of becoming mired in bureaucracy (Peters and Waterman, 1982). Thus the structure of multinational companies will embrace a corporate headquarters with authority over things like product development, strategic planning, and major new investment, while the divisions and individual plants remain profit centres and responsible for operational efficiency.

This basic structural design is sustained by corporate management keeping a tight hold of the purse strings. The capital budget will be controlled from the corporate centre, and since important policy decisions always involve capital expenditure, this will effectively keep policy centralized. The plants and divisions are free to run their operations efficiently, but only within an established budget outside which their powers are strictly limited. Thus, within certain limits, this arrangement achieves the best of both worlds: central control over policy and corporate development, and an operational management able to take on-the-spot decisions.

Turning to integration, within any large organization there are enormous problems ensuring that information reaches people in time and in sufficient detail to enable them to co-ordinate their activities. In manufacturing organizations, for example, it is crucial to ensure the efficiency of the supply chain, so that parts are in place when they are needed and the network of suppliers is integrated with production in the main plant.

And in general, in activities like supply, production, and distribution there are logistical difficulties of great complexity involved in getting the inputs of disparate groups integrated in time and space.

Nor is this purely a matter of doing the job as effectively and efficiently as possible. In certain kinds of operations critical areas of value added, and hence the strategic edge of a company, are found in specific areas of integration. In the manufacture of complex high tech products (like certain kinds of instruments systems and computers) the critical areas of production that the company needs to retain under its strategic control are not always in the actual assembly of the product; they may be in areas like quality testing, parts control, and supply chain management.

However, to develop a structure so that people *can* integrate their efforts is one thing, but whether they *will* integrate even given an effective structure may be another matter. In other words, on top of all the technical problems of the dissemination of information and co-ordination of activities, there are often behavioural difficulties of achieving integration. A major cause of conflict in organizations, and lack of integration, involves the communications problems that arise out of the division of labour. Differences in outlook, occupational values, and style of behaviour can become entrenched in organizations and can cause serious problems of co-ordination.

We have seen how this diversity within management—encompassed by the general concept of differentiation—covers many aspects of behaviour. One common source of conflict, discussed in the previous chapter, involves the difference between managers having a professional approach to their work and those with a bureaucratic approach. Another important relationship is that between line and staff management. Line managers, within the central chain of command, and managers of staff or service departments typically have to come to terms with a series of problems if the relationship between them is not to break down. Services that are centralized for economy and control become a scarce resource. Thus service managers come under pressure for quicker and more comprehensive service, while line managers are forced to compete for services in order to meet their own targets.

We also saw earlier in this chapter that contingency theory had a particular interest in behavioural issues. Lawrence and Lorsch (1967) explored three separate dimensions of differentiation: differences in orientations towards time, goals, and interpersonal relations. They showed how difficult it was to integrate the efforts of, say, R&D departments, which have very long time-horizons, with production which may think in terms of minutes and hours. Similarly, departments with very strong orientations towards getting the job done may share little common ground with departments that have more personal orientations. Other important contingency theorists, Burns and Stalker (1961), focused on the relation between technical staff and production, and stressed the difficulties of achieving integration (or in their terms an 'organic' relationship). Technical staff tend to be preoccupied with problems of design and engineering excellence, and may resent having to get involved with mundane production issues. Production staff for their part may have little sympathy for the detail of engineering design and simply want a timely solution. As a result, achieving effective 'design for production' may elude many companies. But Burns and Stalker also showed that successful companies did manage to integrate their efforts in this critical area.

These distinctions between control and integration at the end of the day are to some extent artificial. In practice, any distinction between regulating a set of activities and taking care of lateral integration breaks down and actual managerial behaviour has a more *systematic* character. Nevertheless, analytic dimensions like these are helpful in understanding behaviour. They provide underlying principles when it comes to making design choices and developing appropriate organization structures.

Design choices

The basic functional model represents the first choice design for many large-scale organizations. This structure groups individuals in the most obvious way, with people having similar occupations or functions in the same departments (Figure 13.2). Functional designs are closely associated with bureaucratic structures and, as we have seen, bureaucracy's strict division of labour, formal rules and procedures, and tight accounting and record-keeping can be highly effective. In any enterprise a basic level of rational organization will be necessary. Bureaucracy also has other crucial benefits—for example, the functional departments and hierarchy provide a stable career ladder for staff—which make the bureaucratic model far more attractive and enduring than is often realized or acknowledged.

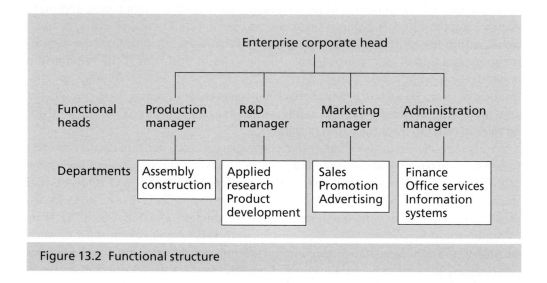

Figure 13.2 Functional structure

Still, as noted in the previous chapter, bureaucracy is probably the most maligned of all organizational forms. We concentrated on the social critique in that chapter, but management thinking has also been critical of the effectiveness of bureaucracy (see Table 12.1). Bureaucratic 'red tape', and the inward focus on internal procedure, was at the root of the problem of the goals of organizations becoming 'displaced' by the pursuit of internal efficiency. Thus, if the smooth-running of an organization becomes the true goal of officials, the stated goals for which the organization was set up tend to slip into the background. The organization may be 'efficient but not effective' in the sense that its processes may be highly streamlined but no longer aimed in the right direction. This sort of shift, from ends to means, can be a familiar experience of dealing with centralized bureaucracies, where the quality of service appears to have been sacrificed to the goal of efficient administration. The kind of absurd rationality that dominates in such organizations has attracted much mordant humour. The (mythical) doctor who announced, 'the patient died but the operation was a success', is just one example of the bureaucratic focus on procedure at the expense of proper objectives.

However, the challenge that has most far-reaching consequences for organizational design relates to organizational change. The contingency theorists we reviewed earlier, strictly speaking, argued that effective design depended on factors like technology and environmental uncertainty, and that a functional structure in itself is no more or less effective than any other. Donaldson (1985, pp. 156–7), for example, claims that the contingency view was 'value neutral' and there was no implication that more or less formalized structures were either good or bad. Rather 'different situations require different sorts of organization for peak effectiveness'. However, there is little doubt that theorists like Burns and Stalker were interested in particular kinds of structures. Even during the hey-day of contingency theory, in the 1960s and 1970s, it was clear that the functional model tended to be rigid and non-adaptive, and that the conditions in which it might flourish were fast disappearing. Certainly today the stable conditions that favour bureaucracies are even scarcer. The global economy reflects an increasingly fast pace of change, and organizations find themselves operating in environments of high uncertainty, complex technical problems, and tight competitive markets.

In this context there is a range of alternative design principles based on cross-functional linkages and more innovative organization structures. The kinds of design choices that have traditionally provided these capacities are among the following (see also Donaldson, 1985, pp. 155–72 and Child, 1984, pp. 88–103 for useful summaries of design types).

The organic model Already discussed at length, this is worth reiterating as it remains one of the most elegant and appealing of alternative models. Strictly speaking the 'organic' structures that Tom Burns found in the Scottish electronics industry of the 1950s were not a distinctive design or organizational type. They were more a set of structural and cultural characteristics—indeed almost a philosophy of organizing—elements of which are found in other alternative models. The organic structure had strong informal networks, fuzzy divisions of labour, a preponderance of verbal communication, and delegated authority—factors which constituted a set of expectations about levels of discretion and how far jobs are predefined. The strength of the model was its capacity to respond flexibly to changes in dynamic and complex environments.

Product-based/divisional structure This structural type involves the skills and occupations needed for a particular type of output—it may be a specific product, but it can also be the product range for a specific market or geographical region—being brought together in a department or organizational division. Product-based structures mean the regrouping of a functional structure, so that instead of, say, all the technical skills, the production skills, and so on being in functional departments, these are redistributed in different divisions (Figure 13.3).

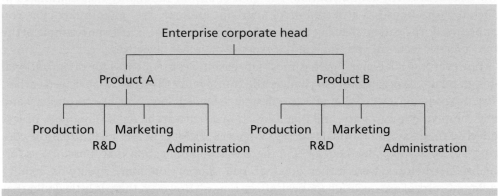

Figure 13.3 Product-based structure

Child (1984, pp. 90–1) points out that organizations often shift to a product-based structure as they expand, and as new product ranges are developed and new markets entered. He describes the case of a steel manufacturer which had taken the decision to diversify into specialist steels. This was a type of production with an extremely high technical specification, but the company initially expanded simply by adding capacity to its existing (functional) departments. However, it soon became apparent that the new products were beyond the capacity of the structure. Production control and quality slipped, and staff in the existing departments were not committed to the new products. Soon the company was falling behind its competitors. At this point, they moved to set up a separate production facility for the new steels, grouped with its own technical and sales back-up. This meant the duplication of these functions in a new division, but justification for this investment was based on the opportunities available.

This example indicates the pluses and minuses of the product-based structure. It can be highly effective, and the only practical choice for companies that are diversifying—and indeed the multi-divisional structure is commonplace among large organizations with a complex product range. However, it does replicate resources, and such structures invariably have to be operated under tight budgetary control that checks the growth in the managerial overhead—making the separate divisions into strategic business units or profit centres.

Matrix structures Matrices allow organizations to simultaneously have two kinds of structure—usually functional and product-based. In these compromise or mixed structures, the normal bureaucratic hierarchy is overlaid with a lattice of product-based

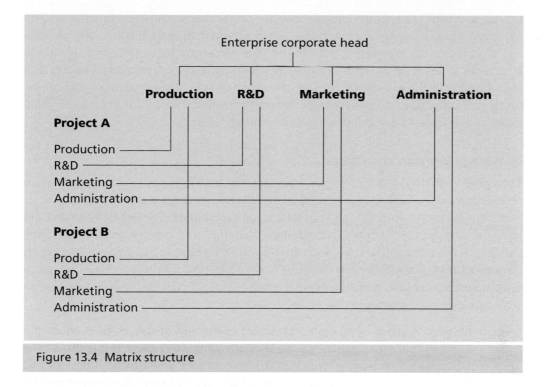

Figure 13.4 Matrix structure

teams or project groups. The matrix thus has dual lines of authority from a divisional structure and a basic functional chain of command. Individuals will belong to a particular department, but will also have membership of a number of teams or project groups. The advantages of matrix structures are that they allow the benefits of grouping specialisms, and the flexibility this brings, together with the benefits of a stable career ladder that comes from retaining a departmental base for the different occupations. As Larson and Gobeli (1987) report, matrix structures were popular during the 1970s and 1980s in many high profile corporations, though the system apparently fell out of favour as its disadvantages increasingly became apparent. The plural chain of command may lead to a confused authority structure (people having several bosses) and power struggles between functional and project managers often ensue. Also the elaborate committee structure can be cumbersome and allow the managerial overhead to get out of hand.

There is in fact a range of variants of the basic matrix (as with most structures) and success and failure seem to depend very much on how the model is implemented. Larson and Gobeli (1987) distinguished three types of matrix—functional, project, and balanced—which refer to where the emphasis lies in the mix between bureaucratic versus project organization. In the functional matrix, the normal hierarchy predominates and project teams may be temporary, few in number, and lacking in influence. The project matrix is the reverse: individuals identify strongly with their teams and project managers have real power over work decisions, with functional managers in the role of service provider. The balanced matrix involves power sharing between functional managers and project managers. Larson and Gobeli surveyed more than 500 American managers with matrix experience, and found over three-quarters of them using these structures (contradicting the belief that they had declined in popularity). The research also found that the full-blown version of the matrix—the project matrix—was consistently rated superior; and even though these organizational forms are stressful for managers and difficult to sustain, they tend to be highly effective.

New organization structures

The above structural types represent basic design choices and principles. However, in recent times the search for better and more effective structures has not slackened. As ever, bureaucracy is both the target of attack and bench-mark. The holy grail that all are trying to achieve is structures that combine the efficiency, control, and occupational stability of the normal hierarchy with an innovative capacity. The emphasis in modern structures is on identifying key business and production processes around which to build new networks and multi-functional teams. Among recent ideas for designing such structures are the following.

Lean structures A series of fashions combined at the end of the 1980s producing a trend towards so-called lean management. These structures were closely linked with the preoccupation with 'downsizing' which drastically cut back white-collar functions and reduced overhead in many organizations, whilst retaining or even increasing capacity. Lean structures in management were also inspired by the lean production model. Essentially a modified version of line assembly, this was built around semi-autonomous teams and designed to meet the Japanese challenge in industries like auto assembly (Womack *et al.*, 1993). Lean management is created by the 'delayering' of bureaucracies and the empowerment of junior positions. In so far as Taylorist practices helped to create cumbersome bureaucracies by transferring responsibilities for planning and control from the shop floor into management, lean structures aim to reverse Taylorism. If forms of discretion are returned to workers, not only are their jobs enriched but management itself is transformed and reinvigorated.

In a sense the interest in lean structures revisits a very old debate. The question of the appropriate shape of an organization's structure has traditionally revolved around the relation between management levels and spans of control (Child, 1984, pp. 58–84). It was once argued that there was a strict trade-off between these two constraints. On the one hand, it was recognized that extended hierarchies carry a range of familiar problems. Communications passing up and down many levels become reinterpreted and distorted, and attempts to formalize communication lead to the usual bureaucratic stranglehold. Also the administrative overhead increases as the organization becomes top heavy with managers. Flatter (i.e. leaner) structures, on the other hand, reduce the number of levels and solve these problems of the over-extended hierarchy. But (for a constant size of organization) the average span of control must then increase, and this will give rise to a different range of problems as managers are unable to control and supervise large numbers of subordinates. However, as Child (p. 68) points out, a number of factors affect this apparent dilemma. Where subordinates' training and competence and their commitment and motivation can be relied on, and where control mechanisms depend on organizational members internalizing the pressures of work, supervision becomes less burdensome for managers.

The lean management movement itself reflects the changing nature of organizational work. Trends like the growth of self-managing teams, and the rising proportion of employees with professional/technical skills, mean that leaner, flatter administrative structures are increasingly the norm. The new flat organizations sharpen the emphasis on team working and the employment of talented and motivated people (Belbin, 1996; Coe, 1997).

Business Process Re-engineering The brainchild of 1990s business guru Michael Hammer, re-engineering advocated radical change and major improvements across a range of production criteria (Hammer, 1990; Hammer and Champy, 1993). Once again, the normal bureaucratic methods and scientific management were the starting-point. Under the re-engineering philosophy, these are seen as breaking down the natural flow of work through an organization and imposing an artificial structure of departments and divisions. The answer is to 're-engineer' the business process. This means starting from basics and showing a willingness to 'obliterate' the old structures and ways. The fundamental task and information flows are redesigned as end-to-end activities. Re-engineering is strongly customer-oriented and also allied with information technology—both of which have inherent process potential. Activities that are customer-driven have little sympathy for red tape and delays that come with functional structuring. Similarly, information flows naturally cut across formal (bureaucratic) boundaries, and can thus be the basis of redesign. Examples of re-engineered solutions are activities like one-stop shopping and direct line financial services—activities in which business is transacted in a single uninterrupted flow, from customer enquiry to final purchase.

The virtual organization These are 'structures' that can be called into existence even though the members of the organizational network are physically dispersed. In fact there always have been virtual organizations of a sort. The professions, for example, are rather like virtual organizations in that they exist as occupational networks giving members a sense of identity via professional associations, conferences, professional publications, and so forth, while individuals work in their separate employing organizations. Another example of a virtual organization might be a consultancy. Consultants are rarely at their desks but perpetually on the move, meeting with clients and working in client organizations. The axis of their work is the consultant–client relationship, rather than the agency itself.

However, there can be little doubt that the recent interest in such organizational structures reflects the development of new technologies—fax, email, teleconferencing, mobile phones—that can provide an effective communications network and obviate the need for a bricks-and-mortar office. The idea that the organization itself may become a virtual reality is tied in with the growing possibilities for homeworking and tele-working.

Conclusion

In this chapter we have seen how systems perspectives, and in particular contingency theory, have been criticized for overlooking aspects of organizational and economic life—how the realities of monopoly control and organizational power represent a challenge to models based on rationalist market behaviour. None the less, the system metaphor remains appealing, and even contingency theory continues to renew certain streams of organizational analysis (e.g. Butler, 1991; Dawson, 1996; Donaldson, 1996). The *structural* perspective of the systems and contingency models insists that the rules of the game and constraints on behaviour prevail, while still taking account of a degree of social and political action. This has great potential advantages. It highlights the dilemmas that lie at the root of all management decision-making—whether to centralize or decentralize, to impose tight controls or more flexible rules—and combines this basic understanding with a practical agenda. The major researchers of the contingency school (the likes of Woodward, Burns and Stalker, Perrow, and Lawrence and Lorsch) explored a range of variables, in the organization and its environment, which attempt to 'fit' organizational arrangements to particular market and productive conditions. The basic theory also provides guidelines and options for organizational design, which attempt to resolve the eternal dilemma between the organizational safety of the bureaucracy and the innovative structures needed in modern environments.

Study questions for Chapter 13

1 Why do organizations need a structure?

2 If the bureaucracy is the most maligned of all organization structures, why then are so many organizations bureaucratic?

3 How does a systems view help us to understand organizational behaviour, and what are its limitations?

4 Discuss the ways in which variation in organization structure depends on contingent factors like technology and environment.

5 How does the concept of managerial choice define the limits of contingency theory?

6 What are the design choices available to a diversifying organization, and what are the advantages and disadvantages of each?

7 Modern organizational designs attempt to combine control with flexibility. How do they do that?

Further reading

Butler, R. (1991) *Designing Organizations: A Decision-Making Perspective*. London: Routledge.

Child, J. (1984) *Organization*, 2nd edn. London: Harper and Row.

Dawson, S. (1996) *Analysing Organisations*, 3rd edn. Basingstoke: Macmillan.

Donaldson, L. (1996) *For Positivist Organization Theory*. London: Sage.

March, J. G. and Simon, H. A. (1958) *Organizations*. New York: Wiley.

Perrow, C. (1970) *Organizational Analysis*. London: Tavistock.

—— (1979) *Complex Organizations: A Critical Essay*. Glenview, Ill.: Scott, Foreman.

Pugh, D. (ed.) (1984) *Organization Theory*, 2nd edn. Harmondsworth: Penguin.

Rose, M. (1975) *Industrial Behaviour: Research and Control*, 2nd edn. London: Penguin.

Thompson, J. (1967) *Organizations in Action*. New York: McGraw-Hill.

Section 5

Organizational Processes

Organizational Processes

If the previous section covered two contrasting perspectives on organizations—the radical and the managerial—they shared a basic *structural* viewpoint. That is to say, they emphasized the constraints that organizational targets and controls exercise, and the patterns of human behaviour that emerge in organizations. However, another basic approach, and one much more favoured in recent years, is to look at behaviour not as structure but as *process* and to emphasize factors of dynamism and change.

In this section, in Chapter 14, we begin with the basic currency of the process view, namely the various theories of organizational decision-making. A number of different readings of organization life have emerged here, though the common feature is a challenge to too rigid a view of the rationality of management decisions. Also in this chapter we consider how these theories have been applied to the central practical problem of management: the management of organizational change.

Chapter 15 looks at a topic that has excited much recent attention, and which has also become established as a key theme in academic and popular management thinking, that of organization culture. The chapter explores the ways in which sociological and managerial interests have shaped the study of culture—one concerned with the expressive and symbolic aspects of organization life, and the other with how culture can be managed in the pursuit of organization goals.

Finally in this section, Chapter 16 examines another area of great recent interest, and one which makes common ground between the radical and managerial approaches. In the study of power in organizations the concept of power is applied to relations within groups of managers. The model of the organization as an arena of bargaining and influence, and the 'Machiavellian' aspect of managerial behaviour, are emphasized.

14 Managerial Processes and Change

Summary points and learning objectives

By the end of this chapter you will

- have reviewed the *critique* of conventional ideas of management rationality;
- have explored the *basic concepts* of the rationality debate, such as *bounded rationality* and *incremental decision-making*;
- have explored the *behavioural theories* of decision-making, and be able to answer the question, What do managers do?
- be able to evaluate the place of *organizational irrationality* in decision-making debates;
- have reviewed *recent models of decision-making* and how these might be classified;
- appreciate the *problematic* and *processual* nature of organizational change, and the centrality of *human agents* in the change process;
- be able to understand individual and organizational strategies for *coping with change* and overcoming *resistance to change*;
- have reviewed models of effectiveness such as *organizational learning*.

Introduction

We focus in this chapter on three related themes that reflect some of the more dynamic aspects of management: decision processes, managerial rationality, and the management of change. Decision-making represents the generalized form of management activity and theories of decision-making are the building-blocks of organization theory. However, decision-making cannot be understood without, at the same time, understanding the nature of managerial *rationality*. Rationality is probably one of the most complex ideas we will come across, and a variety of definitions of rationality lie behind different decision theories. Different writers have expressed preferences across the spectrum from the purely rational to the wholly irrational, with various notions of partial or joint rationality in between.

Once these basic ideas are appreciated, it is possible to move on to explore the practical aspects of managing organizational change. We have already seen, in previous chapters, the importance attached to dynamic organizations and structures and designs that can adapt to changing environments. The modern business climate is increasingly defined by new forms of competition, new technologies, and complex problems for managers to resolve. Thus change management is perhaps the central pragmatic concern of modern theory. Change is the umbrella under which many of the themes we have been considering and will consider—leadership, structure and design, power and culture—come together. Our approach differs from many conventional theories. They tend to stress the practical aspects of the individual coping with change and managements implementing change—setting forth detailed timetables and models of achievement. While we consider these aspects of succeeding at change, our emphasis is on understanding the complex and problematic nature of organizational change itself. This more critical approach stresses social and human aspects and change as an interactive process.

In the chapter, then, we first look at decision-making by exploring the debates around managerial rationality. The 'retreat' from views of 'absolute' rationality reflects the central theme of management writing in recent (and not so recent) years. This permits us to fix more accurately the range of managerial choice and discretion in decision-making. Doubts about rationality have also caused the question to be asked, what do managers actually do? A simple enough query, but one that has been a powerful force in the study of management behaviour and in challenging conventional views of the decision process. A range of models of decision-making are reviewed and classified, again in terms of different dimensions of managerial rationality.

The management of change as a central strategic function is then considered. As already stressed, the problematic and processual nature of organizational change is our main focus. This is followed by more pragmatic models stressing factors like the role of leadership and the means of overcoming resistance to change. Models of organizational effectiveness and organizational learning are finally explored.

Decision-making in organizations

There is a range of technical and mathematical decision theories, but these overlap only in minor ways with the interest in behavioural and organizational theories. This latter focus is not strictly about the success or failure of individual decisions. Rather it is about the relationships between groups of managers and other organizational members engaged in interaction. This may seem relatively trivial yet, when you pause to think, the taking of decisions is actually what is happening when managers interact in this fashion. Indeed, the view of decision-making as a *socially constructed* phenomenon, constrained by the real-life limits of social groups, social structures, and human factors, has long been the inspiration behind managerial theories of decision-making. In particular, there is a constantly renewed debate between a 'social' view that dwells on realities, like the persistence of conflict or the pursuit of self-interest, and a 'rationalist' view which lies behind the more scientific models of organizational behaviour.

The nature of managerial rationality

Rationalism essentially derives from the belief that we can discover laws that govern behaviour. Thus notions of rationality have great appeal when trying to understand a phenomenon like organizations. They are the basis of the belief that people can be controlled and their behaviour regulated and predicted. We saw in Chapter 13 that the systems model—probably the most popular and influential of all organizational metaphors—is inherently rationalist. Systems are seen as being structured and differentiated; they are formally designed for a purpose, and their capacity to adapt to changing environments guarantees their long-term survival. Following from this, ideas of the management task based on factors like planning, control, integration, leadership, and strategy likewise imply rationality at the heart of management.

However, in the previous chapter we also explored the limitations of systems thinking and of systems approaches like contingency theory. These rationalist approaches deliberately restrict themselves to the formally sanctioned aspects of behaviour, since their aim is effective control and design. While they can take account of social factors (such as conflict and power) the extent to which this can be achieved will always be limited. Thus, in spite of undoubted refinements in organization theory since the days of the early writers (see Donaldson, 1985), some of the processes underlying real organizational behaviour are bound to be overlooked or explained inadequately. Rationalist theories have been criticized for overstating unity and consensus in decision-making, for ignoring problems of conflict, and for legitimizing the actions of the powerful and marginalizing the interests of the majority of organizational members. Systems/contingency theories suggest a simple link between human intervention and economic success, whereas the actual relationship is much more tortuous and complex.

Behind these criticisms lies a sense of the problematic nature of the rationality that managerial and organizational structures possess. Conventional management theory implies that decision-making is based on an 'absolute' version of rationality. The idea of organizational goals, for example, suggests the attainment of an ideal state which can be objectively identified and agreed by different groups. We can see this must be true to an extent, otherwise nothing would ever get done in organizations. But equally clearly the view of organizations as structures for the rational pursuit of goals is much too simplistic. Goals may be poorly defined and an inadequate guide to behaviour. The real goals that actors pursue may be subtly different (or indeed very different) from stated goals; personal goals (the pursuit of promotion, power, income, security) may clash with official goals, and goals may change over time or may even be displaced. Similarly, activities like planning and control imply full information, which reflects a rational market choice; yet the reality is that if we always waited for complete information before reaching a decision we would risk never taking a decision at all.

Theories that try to understand how people behave under conditions of uncertainty and incomplete information look very different from rationalist theories. Indeed, critics suggest that managers rarely achieve these ideal forms and that decision-making is never purely rational. They suggest alternative views of decision-making.

Bounded rationality Perhaps the single most influential idea that has explored the deficiencies of human rationality is the concept of 'bounded rationality'. This was developed in a series of groundbreaking publications in the 1950s and 1960s by the American economists and management theorists Richard Cyert, James March, and Herbert Simon (otherwise known as the Chicago School after their association with the University of Chicago), and remains one of the most simple and elegant ideas in this area (e.g. March and Simon, 1958, pp. 137–71; Cyert and March, 1964). These writers criticized management and economic theories of the firm for suggesting that decision-making was optimal and based on absolute rationality. To counter this, they pointed out that in fact decision-making is only rational up to a point. Actual decision-making has a relative character; it is 'bounded' by human limitations and failings and even by 'foolishness and error' (March, 1981).

One of the ideas that Cyert, March, and Simon argued for was that of 'satisficing'. This was a deliberate counter to the conventional idea of optimization in decision-making. Management decision-making, they argued, is rarely optimal in the sense of the best solution being sought and found. In practice, a *satisfactory* solution, one that will cope with the problem in hand, is the most common outcome. The reason, quite simply, is that problem-solving is an arduous activity involving the expenditure of much time and effort. The taking of decisions is best described as a *search process*. Defining alternative courses of action, and testing their relative efficiency, happens only to a limited extent because once a satisfactory solution has been found the search tends to stop.

Another pioneering idea was the notion of *incremental* decision-making. Again, purely rational theories tend to argue that decisions are taken in a series of decisive steps designed to achieve the ideal state envisaged in the goal. And implied in this would be the notion that, when fresh circumstances arise, radical solutions are sought that wipe the slate clean and meet the new demands. The reality, Cyert, March, and Simon argued, was that decision-making proceeds in a series of small-scale or incremental stages, each building on existing arrangements. This again is a much more limited form of rationality, in that the past is acknowledged as both a constraint and a resource which cannot in practice be jettisoned.

As an example of this kind of real-world decision-making, we might consider a common type of organizational decision, to do with the integration of effort, that is found in activities like scheduling, timetabling, and budgeting. Now the rationalistic or optimal method of designing, say, a new budget would be to start from scratch each financial year and cost every item and activity afresh, seeking better alternative suppliers, and so forth. In fact what invariably happens is that last year's budget is taken as the bench-mark and incremental improvements are made—a 5 per cent cut here, a new supplier there. The reality is that creating a totally new budget would entail enormous effort and mean throwing away much that was perfectly acceptable.

Power and politics Cyert, March, and Simon focused mainly on human limitations and on conflict in organizations. It was the fact that there are only 24 hours in the day, that we all have limited talents and energies, and the consequences of managerial differentiation that caught their interest. They did not devote much attention to another aspect of social behaviour, namely the political dimension. Power in organizations in recent years has become a subject in its own right, and one we devote a later chapter to, but it is worth briefly flagging up here.

Power explicitly challenges rationalistic ideas. Indeed, in common-sense terms, when we think of 'rational behaviour' we tend to think of the absence of power. We think of people coming together to solve common problems without any hidden agendas or back-door deals. On the other hand (as we see later in Chapter 16) decision theories based on power argue that decisions 'emerge' from relations of conflict, and reflect the outcome of a power struggle. Where decision-making is decisively political it is only understandable in terms of the pattern of past conflicts and coalitions. Here rationality is entirely relative, reflected in the preferences of cliques as competing 'rationales' of behaviour.

The decision that is ultimately taken, amongst a range of possibles, is the favoured option of the winning interest group. Such a perception of the decision process is quite different from the idea of rational problem-solving. Under the power perspective the decision outcome may or may not be the 'rational' or agreed choice. Factors like goals and environmental constraints are not mechanisms for stimulating action, but have a relevance only as elements in the power game (Pettigrew, 1973; Bacharach and Lawler, 1980). However, as we have said, for the moment we will leave the power concept and continue with theories of decision-making that explore more directly the limitations on organizational rationality.

Behavioural theories of management

The next major challenge to rationalist models came from a group of American management writers headed by Henry Mintzberg, and including the work of figures like Kotter (1982), who favoured the use of observational methods of study. They asked the simple question: 'What do managers do?' In other words, they argued, we know the classical and rationalist models are highly prescriptive, and stress that managers are supposed to plan, control, lead, and devise strategy. So why not actually observe managers' daily activities and see how much of this is true? These theorists used methods that involved following managers around for sample time-periods, and noting down exactly what their interactions with others consisted of. Also diary methods, where managers themselves kept a record of their activities, were a common tool.

Perhaps not surprisingly the research found little evidence of the kind of rational decision-making (planning, controlling, etc.) that was supposed to constitute managers' main tasks. There was little long-term activity, and much reactive decision-making and short-term behaviour. Managers would spend their time making snap decisions and engaging in interactions of a few minutes' duration. Interestingly there was also a great deal of social behaviour—a lot of phoning up of contacts in order to pass the time of day and renew acquaintance, not just as a preliminary courtesy to some business transaction—that is completely ignored by the classical theories of management. In this way, rationality was seen as being limited not only by the exigencies of real-life pressures, but by the need for a degree of 'system maintenance', that is the maintenance of the social groups that form a manager's network of contacts.

Mintzberg's pioneering study, *The Nature of Managerial Work* (1973), presented a searing attack on the notion of managers as rational agents. His point of departure was to note that the 'scientific' pretensions of rationalist theories project various managerial roles—the manager as leader, decision-maker, entrepreneur—but obvious questions about what they actually do are missed out. The irony is that while 'behaviour' features heavily in these theories (behavioural science, organizational behaviour) little real behaviour is observed. The emphasis instead is on quantifiable methods and questionnaires.

Mintzberg's own account was based partly on the limited amount of research then conducted on work activity, and partly on his own intensive study of the work of five chief executives. He stressed the similarity that existed across 'all levels of management from chief executives to foremen' (p. 25). Managers' jobs were characterized by high pressure and an unrelenting pace of work. The activities they engaged in on a daily basis were defined by 'brevity, variety and fragmentation' (p. 31) and appeared to conform to no obvious pattern.

A subordinate calls in to report a fire in one of the facilities; then the mail, much of it insignificant, is processed; a subordinate interrupts to tell of an impending crisis with a public group; a retiring employee is ushered in to receive a plaque; later there is discussion of bidding on a multi-million-dollar contract; after that the manager complains that office space in one department is being wasted. (1973, p. 31)

Mintzberg found that managers had a powerful preference for 'live action' rather than paperwork or working alone. They were also strongly oriented towards informal communication and the garnering of information. At meetings often the gossip and greetings were valued more than the formal proceedings. And managers maintained extensive relationships with wide-ranging groups of business contacts, informants, and experts. Mintzberg also highlighted the aspects of managerial work that contradicted the conventional wisdom: managers focused on concrete issues (and so did very little general planning); they spent surprisingly little time with superiors (so that hierarchical information flows were relatively unimportant), and they preferred verbal media (so an established records system was of secondary interest).

The manager is encouraged by the realities of his work to develop a particular personality—to overload himself with work, to do things abruptly, to avoid wasting time, to participate only when the value of participation is tangible, to avoid too great an involvement with any one issue. To be superficial is no doubt an occupational hazard of managerial work. In order to succeed, the manager must, presumably, become proficient in his superficiality. (1973, p. 35)

Partly it was Mintzberg's wish to challenge the dominant rationalist assumptions that led him to characterize the management process as diverse and prone to disengagement. However, despite appearances to the contrary, we can see that he does not totally abandon the notion of rational behaviour. The important thing for Mintzberg is to understand the nature of managerial work—rather than have some idealized image of it—and within this context behaviour was in certain respects a rational response. In other writers the untidy surface aspects of managerial work are more clearly linked with a degree of purpose which lies beneath. For example, Kotter's (1982) study of American executives found the same kind of aimless behaviour as Mintzberg noted— much executive time spent on non-work conversation, and activities seldom planned in advance—but this apparently ineffective style of management concealed a more rational pursuit of objectives. Internalized plans, or in Kotter's term, 'agendas', were able to relate executives' individual interests with strategic planning. Agendas were not rigid sets of organizational goals, they were a more flexible menu of interlinking objectives; but they did contain the elements of planned and prioritized activities. In addition, loose frameworks of personal contacts or 'networks' extended inside and outside the organization, and supported these intentions. Though informal and social in nature, networks and agendas were key tools in the decision-making of the managers studied by Kotter. They allowed managers 'to react in an opportunistic (and highly efficient) way to the flow of events around them, yet knowing that they are doing so within some broader and more rational framework' (1982, p. 166).

In this way, behavioural theorists have shown that rationality does not have to be applied in an all-or-nothing sense. Our understanding of management rationality can be 'softened' and distanced from the absolute rationality of much conventional management theory, in order to bring it closer to the actual behaviour of managers. But at the same time, there may still be an underlying sense of purpose, or a 'guiding rationality' (Hickson *et al.*, 1986), to what managers do. As Bryman (1984) notes, the 'retreat from rationality', and suspicion of ideas of comprehensive knowledge and optimal decision-making, have resulted in the search for concepts that are more realistic; but the appeal of some sense of rationalism in organizational behaviour remains strong. Thus 'at a time when the literature seems to be rejecting rational conceptions of organization, there is a simultaneous awareness of the theoretical and empirical forms that rationality can assume' (Bryman, 1984, p. 401).

Organizational irrationality

Perhaps the strongest challenge to the conventional view of organizations comes from another group of writers who seek out and emphasize the 'irrational' side of organization life. This is the extreme view that in reality the rules governing decision-making are not rational, even in a relative or bounded sense. They may be formally rational—appealing to some cold internal logic—but they are irrational by any normal standards.

In this context, there are two main aspects of the 'irrationality' argument. First the human limitations that the Chicago School writers drew attention to. When pushed to the extremes of uncertainty and conflict, we see management being characterized by muddle and failure rather than this being a mere constraint on efficiency. Lindblom (1959), for example, speaks of management as an incremental process of 'muddling through' characterized by forms of uncertainty and limited powers of analysis. Cohen likewise proposed a 'garbage can' model of management with a virtually random mix of influences on decisions. He questioned any capacity to prioritize decisions, and negated any capacity to arrive at decision choices via an explicit path. His notion of 'organized anarchy' also mocked the rational model, stressing that organizations are not very 'organized' at all, but are only loosely integrated associations of people living off them (Cohen, March, and Olsen, 1972).

Secondly, though, there is another a view of irrationality that stems from fears that organizations themselves are inherently and deeply irrational—and irrational in the sense that they spawn a version of rationality that is opposed to the rationality of human values and ideals. We have already reviewed this latter belief, in Chapter 12, and shown how it evokes a doomsday image of organizations that has been a continuing thread of criticism. It goes back to Weber's equivocal feelings about the 'iron cage' of bureaucracy, and continues through criticisms of the 'insidious power' of organizations, to present day fears about the 'McDonaldization' of contemporary culture.

One of the sharpest observers of the problematic nature of organizations was Goffman. As we may recall from his account of asylums and the psychiatric profession in Chapter 12, Goffman used organizational irrationality as a key explanatory factor. Where an institution itself is deemed 'irrational' then behaviour within it—which might be regarded as irrational in a normal (or 'sane') context—can become the rational course of action. With patients' and inmates' behaviour, this sense of it being 'rational to be irrational' comes across very strongly in Goffman's study. Goffman delighted in turning the accepted explanations upside down. Thus, the behaviour of patients, which would normally be diagnosed as obsessive or psychotic, was interpreted as rather sane given the conditions in which they had to exist. That context was the asylum, which Goffman classed as a 'total institution'—an organization in which inmates live entirely within the system. The control of such an institution over the lives of inmates is such that there is no escape from rules and the arbitrary power of staff. From their side, the 'care' and 'treatment' that staff gave to patients was reinterpreted by Goffman as punishment (as in the case of drugs regimes). The likes of asylums and prisons cannot simply be equated with the majority of organizations (like work organizations) in which members spend only a portion of their time. However, it remains clear that Goffman intended mental hospitals to serve as a metaphor of organizational irrationality, or perhaps as a proto-typical example in a society increasingly dominated by organizations. Certainly others (such as Foucault—see Chapters 9 and 12) were also attracted to the 'carceral institution' as a symbol of the modern condition.

Strictly speaking, an account of the 'darker' side of organizational irrationality does not belong in this chapter, where the focus has been on managerial problems of ineffectiveness and inefficiency. We have been more interested in writers who follow the Chicago School's emphasis on the limits of rationality. Nevertheless, it is worth cross-referencing the coverage of these deeper organizational disorders (referred to in more detail in Chapter 12) because there is no tidy distinction between the two aspects. Writers who have emphasized the failings of bureaucratic patterns have often been well aware of other aspects of irrationality, and in their accounts the two themes intertwine in practice.

Jackall's moral mazes One of the most significant recent examples of organizations defined in this way is the model described by Robert Jackall. In his seminal book, *Moral Mazes* (1988), Jackall studied corporate life amongst American senior executives. He was concerned with getting under the skin of the modern corporation and finding out the realities of bureaucratic hierarchies. He notes (p. 78) that 'the actual rules for making decisions are quite different from managerial theories about decision making', and that managers themselves were well aware of the rational approach but this formed a kind of rhetoric or way of legitimizing courses of action. Managers knew they had to repeat the rhetoric—while the reality was not only different from this ideal but bore no relationship to it at all. As one manager put it, 'the basic principles of decision making in this organization and probably any organization are: (1) avoid making any decision if at all possible, (2) if a decision has to be made, involve as many people as you can so that, if things go wrong, you're able to point in as many directions as possible' (Jackall, 1988, p. 78). Thus the realities of decision-making, as managers saw it, took into account the likelihood of failure right from the start—again quite different from conventional theories.

This view of decision-making reflected the organization as a hazardous setting for managerial fortunes. The forces contained in organizational hierarchies placed them always on the verge of upheaval, with an 'acute sense of contingency' being managers' constant experience. In short, for Jackall the familiar static picture of bureaucracy was a false image that belied the unstable nature of the corporate career structure. This involved a kind of organizational spoils system. Political alliances, and favours owed by junior managers to seniors, formed a network of precarious pyramids dependent on the outcome of power games. 'Because of the interlocking ties between people, they know that a shake-up at or near the top of a hierarchy can trigger a widespread upheaval bringing in its wake startling reversals of fortune, good and bad, throughout the structure' (p. 33). In this account Jackall is (implicitly) dismissing much of modern management theory—which speaks confidently of rational structures and new flexible organizational forms—and instead returns to an almost archaic notion of organization. He refers to modern organizations as 'patrimonial bureaucracies' (p. 11) with all the features of a medieval court. This is a world where managers have little control over, or even knowledge of, what makes (or breaks) their careers. He describes a world of great complexity, in which arbitrary factors continually intervene, and managers are constantly monitoring all manner of cultural signs in the attempt to guide their actions.

Executives are also prey to the kinds of 'ambiguous expertise' (p. 137) that figures like consultants, public relations experts, and management gurus peddle. Jackall stresses the premium in corporate circles that is placed on being up to date and abreast of the latest thinking. Fresh ideas in a sense are managers' ammunition in the battles they constantly wage against rivals and usurpers. 'Executives trade ideas and schemes and judge the efficacy of consultant programs not by any detached critical standards but by

Box 14.1 The realities of decision-making

In his book, *Moral Mazes*, Robert Jackall recounts a case that illustrates how and why real life decision-making is often very far from the model of ideal rationality. Consider the case of a large coking plant in a chemical company. Coke-making requires a giant battery to cook the coke slowly and evenly for long periods; the battery is the most important piece of capital equipment in a coke-making plant. In 1975 the plant's battery showed signs of weakening and certain managers at corporate headquarters had to decide whether to invest $6 million to restore the battery to top form. Clearly, because of the amount of money involved, this was a serious decision.

No decision was made. The CEO had sent the word out to defer all unnecessary capital expenditures to give the corporation cash reserves for other investments. So the managers allocated small sums of money to patch the battery up until 1979, when it collapsed entirely. This brought the company into breach of contract with a steel producer and into violation of various environmental pollution regulations. The total bill, including lawsuits and federally mandated repairs, exceeded $100 million, although no one is sure of the exact amount.

This simple but typical example gets to the heart of how decision-making is intertwined with a company's authority structure and advancement patterns. As the managers in the company saw it, the decisions facing them in 1975 and 1979 were crucially different. Had they acted decisively in 1975—in hindsight the only rational course of action—they would have saved the corporation millions of dollars in the long run. In the short run, however, they would have been taking a serious personal risk in restoring the battery. What is more their political networks might have unravelled, leaving them vulnerable to attack. They chose short-term safety over long-term gain.

After the battery collapsed, however, the decision facing them was simple and posed little risk. The corporation had to meet its legal obligations, and it had to repair the battery or shut down the plant. Since there were no real choices everyone could agree on a course of action. As one manager says: 'Decisions are made only when they are inevitable. To make a decision ahead of the time it *has* to be made risks political catastrophe. People can always interpret the decision as unwise even if it seems correct on other grounds'.

Source: R. Jackall (1988) *Moral Mazes: The World of Corporate Managers*, pp. 81–4.

what is socially acceptable, desirable and, perhaps most important, current in their circles' (p. 141). Thus external experts exist in a kind of parasitic relationship with organizations. Consultants have a survival interest in producing fresh approaches and newly packaged ideas for the corporate market, and this feeds the need of corporate managers for solutions and a supply of ideas.

Models of decision-making

During the 1970s and 1980s a range of different models of managerial behaviour emerged which attempted to take these earlier ideas a stage further. They sought to explore the specific limits of rationality in detail. Brunsson (1982), for example, stressed the importance of decision-making *ideologies*. Decision-making is so risky and uncertain (a point echoed by Jackall above) that people have to narrow their choices by identifying with sectional 'ideologies' if they are to act at all. The behaviour that Brunsson had in mind is probably familiar to us all, namely the kinds of predictable almost programmed responses that often come from particular occupations or organizational functions. People respond in a scripted fashion rather than analysing situations in depth. In effect, the suggestion is that conventional ideas on rational problem-solving cannot work, as they would produce unwieldy amounts of information and hence inaction—'paralysis by analysis' in the familiar colloquialism—and of necessity people have to act on insufficient knowledge.

Similarly, Staw (1976, 1980; Staw, Sandelands, and Dutton, 1981) focused on the idea of *non-adaptation*. Organizational cultures and forms of behaviour, he stressed, have a determining effect. Organizations become stuck in patterns of formal rules and responses early in their existence and do not change, despite the mounting costs of a misconceived course of action. Managers' careers and reputations, structures of power and authority, and simple organizational inertia, combine to produce a commitment to specific patterns of activity which can be impossible to break out of. Organizational members become adept at managing the appearance of change, while real change is illusory. Given that the ability to adapt to changing environments is one of the central planks of the rationality argument, this was a direct challenge to the systems and contingency theorists. Their claim that a key function of successful organizations is the ability to adapt to dynamic environments is here refuted. Concepts like these recognize the unrealistic nature of theories in which some version of absolute rationality is taken as the basis of individual action. In other more developed decision-making theories some contrasting positions are taken up as regards the nature of management rationality.

Population ecology The population ecology model of Hannan and Freeman (1977) takes its name from the key proposition that a form of economic natural selection operates on populations of organizations. The model contains a similar idea of rationality to that of conventional theories—i.e. that rational processes govern business success—but the key difference is that rationality is not attributed to the individual decision-maker or organization. Within any population of competing organizations, it is suggested, some will emerge on top purely as a result of the nature of economic rivalry. Rationality is thus a property of the economic market not the human agent, and the population ecology model reserves no place for proactive decision-making or executive intervention.

The advantage of this view over conventional theories is that the latter always tend to 'read' certain kinds of managerial behaviour into business success. The tendency is to seek out the successful, high-performing organizations, and then look for types of leadership or styles of decision-making that explain this. Hannan and Freeman suggest that this exercise in hindsight is ultimately misleading and futile. If you look for patterns based on some preconceived notion of success you will always find them, but the reality is that in an economic marketplace some firms will always rise to the top.

Managerial choice As we saw in Chapter 13, Child's (1972) concept of 'strategic choice' was an early and perhaps the most telling direct criticism of contingency theory. But as well as exposing the limitations of the contingent model, strategic choice also provided its own distinctive view of organizational decision-making. Rejecting the effect of contextual factors (technology, environment) as an overly simple solution, Child instead emphasized the capacity of managers to exercise choice over their organization's structure and design, as well as over external market factors. His view thus counteracted the determinism of contingency and systems theories, and argued that managers possess discretion over organization and environment of a strategic kind, and that their decisions are influenced by their own perceptions and values.

Strategic choice introduced a notion of *power* into decision theories—power being the obvious basis of managerial discretion—but it was a distinctive type of structured corporate power. This involved the notion of a 'dominant coalition' of senior managers who embody (and impose) central organizational rationalities. The idea of dominant coalitions occurs in Cyert and March's (1963) critique of the theory of the firm, so it is part of the Chicago School's emphasis on a limited or partial managerial rationality. Power is not seen as being evenly distributed or gradually centralized. Instead, power is discontinuous, and real power is concentrated in the hands of small groups of top managers. The dominant coalition guards its power and in practice is extremely careful of selection into its ranks. Child's use of the concept stressed that these corporate groups effectively determine the pattern of authority in organizations—not necessarily by crudely suppressing competing rationalities, but by shaping specialist goals into transcendent strategic goals.

Resource dependence Rather like contingency theory and strategic choice, there is another influential theory that retains a systematic view of rationality but represents an explicit attempt to marry the idea of a rational system with an element of managerial power. The so-called resource dependence model (Pfeffer and Salancik, 1978) focuses on the exchanges that organizations have to engage in with their environments. But it attempts to do this in realistic terms of the alliances with other organizations that are formed as individual organizations seek to control external uncertainties.

A major element of resource dependence is that of *social exchange*. The rules governing any exchange relationship suggest that partners will want to reduce their own dependency while simultaneously seeking to increase their partner's dependence on them. Relationships also have costs, however, as the partners compete for scarce resources and must share any benefits (though not necessarily evenly). The extent to which any organization can turn the terms of the exchange to its advantage reflects the power difference between partner organizations.

The second key element is an 'institutional' one which looks at actual networks of organizations. As organizational exchanges grow from simple partnerships, the external environment itself is being *constructed* into complex sets of relations including reciprocal linkages in industrial sectors, monopolistic relations, and interlocking shareholdings. The resource-dependence model suggests that these coalitions are the key mechanism (or resource) enabling the organization to control its exchanges with the environment. Forms of rational co-operation and networking with other organizations help to guarantee the flow of accurate information by which the organization can stabilize external threats. Hence resource dependence stresses the organization's strategies of control, the partly co-operative partly competitive networks which modify the organization's exchanges with the environment.

Classifying models

The above brief review of some of the main theories of organization decision-making has revealed a range of different approaches, all reflecting particular views of the nature of managerial rationality. Attempts to classify the different theories have been useful, given the somewhat bewildering variety of approaches, and have tended to focus on two factors: how decisions are determined and the level at which they are made. This has meant theories being positioned on two distinctive criteria: whether we see decisions as the product of an organization structure or of human agency; and whether we see decisions being taken at the micro- or the macro-level (Astley and van de Ven, 1983; Hrebiniak and Joyce, 1985).

Tying this into our own analysis, we suggest that these criteria imply two dimensions of rationality: (1) collective versus individual rationality, and (2) universal versus relative forms of rationality. In other words, first, a structural view of the shaping of organization processes by the task environment suggests an overarching 'market rationality' that effectively defines structure, while an emphasis on human decision-makers argues for the autonomy of individual actors or interest groups in creating and defining what is rational for the organization. Secondly, at a macro-level of analysis, focused on the organization as a system, behaviour is seen as a function of task contingencies and a universal rationality, while micro-level analysis admits a range of relative choices if individuals have limited abilities or if external constraints are overcome (Figure 14.1).

Four theories can be located at the poles of these dimensions. Classical management theory stressed an absolute or universal form of rationality, as well as the function of individual managers to control and lead. The population ecology model also had a strong version of rationality, but this was a property of a collectivity (or population) of organizations. Models that stress power as the basis of decision-making are interested in a kind of micro-politics of organization life, while rationality for them is a purely

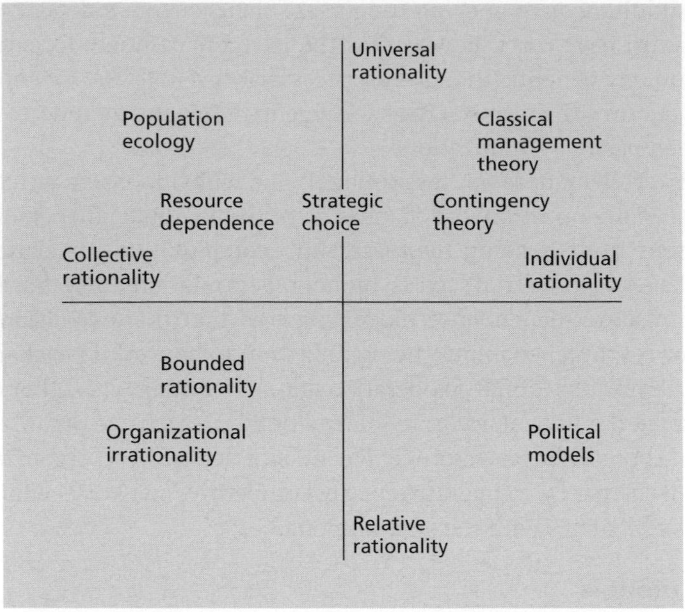

Figure 14.1 Management rationality and models of decision-making

relative kind, namely that of the victor in the power game. Models of organizational irrationality stress the furthest limits on rationality and also that this is a (collective) property of the 'society of organizations'.

In addition, the theories that take a more empirical view need to be located in different positions within the quadrants of Figure 14.1. Though an early revision of the classical school, contingency theory remained closest to the absolute form of rationality. Decisions were still viewed as adapting the organization to its stated goals and hence a systematic view of rationality prevailed. Strategic choice was a reaction against the 'simplest theoretical choice' of functional adaptation, and emphasized instead the power of managers to realize their own preferences. But while 'choice' has a strong political flavour, it remains a theory of rational adaptation since the preferences of the dominant coalition of managers are taken to reflect wider organizational objectives. And in the resource-dependence model we find an essentially pragmatic view of rationality: managers' strategic power bestows the capacity to impose decisions, but wider rationalities also constrain action.

Decision-making debates Of course, classifications are easily oversimplified, not least in terms of the different kinds of theories being described. Theories which simply have different objectives—whether to be deliberately polemical, or to put forward some ideal state, or to attempt an accurate description—are not strictly comparable. For example, models of limited rationality and organizational politics are frequently offered as alternatives to rational models. Yet rational models were not always ignorant of the vagaries of human behaviour. There is little doubt, for instance, that classical writers like F. W. Taylor had an eye for informal activities in organizations, while other 'prescriptive' theories have been quite deliberate about setting aside many real-life behaviours on the grounds that they cannot be formally planned (Child, 1984, p. 4).

Other problems arise in attempting to stand outside the debate. Past discussion has often been distorted by simplistic accounts of theories, or stereotyped assessments of one theoretical position by the supporters of another. For example, critics of contingency theory from the strategic choice camp sometimes portray the contingency view as that of managers being the passive cyphers through which change in the environment acts on the organization's structure (e.g. Wood, 1979). Such an evaluation suggests that contingency theory could not properly understand the links between structure and the management process. But how true is it? Some contingency writers took up a deterministic position, but others tried to show adaptation as the result of managerial decisions (Thompson, 1961, p. 20) and political processes (Burns and Stalker, 1961, p. xii). Even the idea of managers simply 'passing on' environmental pressures is more complicated than it seems. The ability to read and act on market pressures requires a high order of skills and proactive management.

Again, approaches that stress a relative form of management rationality are obviously appealing. To argue that managers possess a wide discretion over organization and environment seems more realistic than the mechanical contingency model. Similarly, the political perspective affords a richly detailed picture of organization life. Yet subjective forms of rationality raise problems from a structuralist perspective. The notion of 'choice' is notoriously problematic. The choices of those in power in organizations may seem like constraints to the less powerful. Also, if choice is detached from the realities of the managerial role, it simply suggests an open-ended and free-ranging version of decision-making. The view of the organization as an arena for the expression of political conflict similarly tends to ignore the constraints of economic life. As Willmott (1987, p. 247) notes, studies (like organizational politics, behavioural theories) that emphasize subjectivity and relative versions of rationality tend to separate management action from the 'institutionally produced rules and resources' that managers use to regulate their exchanges with the environment.

The different views of decision-making, therefore, pose a problem for understanding the basic nature of management and organizational rationality. Many approaches have emerged as products of debate. Choice is plausible partly as a reaction to functionalist accounts, limited rationality as an antidote to optimal decision-making, while the political model is attractive when compared with theories of goal attainment. Some more pragmatic theories seek to satisfy a number of conditions—to take account of human agency within a structural setting, to relate rationality to the political interests of organizational members. Yet it seems inevitable that theories should produce only partial views of the nature of decision-making, not the totality. At the end of the day, such are the complexities of organizational populations and belief systems, that a one-size-fits-all theory is beyond our scope. The richness of organizational life has to be matched with an equally rich array of decision-making theories.

The management of change

Equipped with an appreciation of the nature of managerial work, interaction, and decision-making, we can approach the issue that occupies perhaps the central place in management writing and theorizing, that of organizational change. In today's increasingly competitive and globalizing business environment, the capability of organizations to be flexible and adapt is highly prized and an essential attribute of survival. We saw in the above discussion, and in the previous chapter, that responding effectively to change is implicit in the rational system, and that adapting to dynamic external environments is one of the key elements of rationality. Yet we also saw that organizations are frequently *counter-rational*. Bureaucratic red tape means that organizations can become obsessed with procedures that obstruct the organization's goals. Rationality is bounded by real-life limitations, decision-making is complex and risky, and organizations are political arenas with multiple and conflicting goals. Power can be the motor of change, but it can also allow organizations to pursue idiosyncratic paths and hold out against the pressures of the marketplace. The basic nature of decision-making therefore introduces a range of problems into the change process.

To begin with change can be enormously difficult to get going in organizations. In practice, surmounting the barriers to effective change, and what can broadly be termed *organizational inertia*, is a key concern of management. Carnall (1995, p. 43), for example, refers to various 'blocks' in the change process. These can be emotional blocks if people feel threatened by change and fear the uncertainty associated with it. The way that change is usually presented makes the comfortable assumption that it is always change for the better, but individuals may not see things in this light. They may refuse to confront the need for change and may meet the challenge with avoidance behaviour and evasion. Also, as we saw in Chapter 7, there are collective processes like 'groupthink' which encourage complacency and impair people's ability to evaluate their circumstances.

There are also cultural blocks. Carnall interestingly suggests that in subtle ways our culture may be hostile to change. The ways of thought that promote effective change often involve factors like insight and irreverence towards the establishment; even factors like humour can be helpful in disturbing the existing pattern. Yet these may be regarded as frivolous and may well be frowned upon in normal organizational exchanges.

In this context, Galbraith (1982) has used case-study material to provide a detailed account of the 'pathologies' that occur in real-life organizations. Companies can become bogged down in internal politics, unable to develop the products and services needed to compete with rivals. In one such case, corporate managers were attempting to get a much-needed innovation from a small corner of the firm adopted more widely. But there were numerous barriers to innovation. The main development departments were hostile towards taking on the innovation as it threatened their own projects. Steering extra funds and rewards to the innovators also caused resentment and was regarded as a dangerous precedent. And the innovation itself—which by definition involved uncertainties—was openly disputed by groups hostile to it. The point Galbraith was making is that, while 'innovation' may be seen generally in wholly positive terms, it is nevertheless powerful magic and often difficult for an organization to absorb. It may be easy to argue that bright sparks should be attracted and rewarded, and given the protection to enable them to develop their ideas; but the reality is that innovation cuts across organizational power structures and may be blocked by inertial forces.

Change is problematic

In short, the process of change is no simple phenomenon. This point is worth emphasizing as change tends to be 'objectified' in much of the management literature. It is referred to confidently as if there were no question or problem with the concept, while the 'management of change' has simply been added to the traditional managerial functions of control and planning. The motive for this is clear. The capability for change is massively valued in today's organizations, so that managers are extremely eager to claim to possess the ability and to stake out this particular bit of high ground. Yet in reality change is highly problematic.

The acid test here is to think about an organization that you are familiar with. The management literature will either be describing some organization known to the author, or be referring to theories of change in the abstract; but in your own organization how confident would you be about specifying the nature of change? You probably realize that any ten members would come up with ten different stories about how the organization should change.

Perceiving the need for change itself can be problematic. How would we know change is needed? Again, the management literature is fond of conjuring the image of the 'organization in crisis' where the need for change is instantly obvious. Yet the reality is usually far more mundane. It may not be at all clear whether an organization is doing well or doing badly. What do we mean by 'doing badly'? What measures should be used? Profits? Sales? Market share? Customer satisfaction? What level of performance is satisfactory? And satisfactory for whom? Employees? Shareholders? Customers?

Even assuming that we know change is needed, how easy is it to agree the necessary action? Defining the problem precisely, and seeing it in a unified way rather than from a series of partial viewpoints, presents another level of difficulty. There are many different groups in organizations, and not only do they have different views, but they often inhabit different worlds and attribute different meanings to change. Indeed, another way in which change has become 'objectified' occurs when a dominant view of some change process becomes accepted. In practice (given the power structure in organizations) this tends to be top management's view.

And assuming we get this far, would we recognize change if it happened? This may sound nonsensical, yet because organizational members perceive different realities, whether or not change is perceived at all may vary. This raises the question of the boundaries of change. Where do the boundaries of change fall? Because organizations are made up of people who will be differently affected by change, the impact of change needs to be mapped accurately rather than widely attributed. We need to know who has changed and who has not.

In this vein, the celebrated management guru, Rosabeth Moss Kanter (1919), has registered her suspicion of grand strategies and other kinds of formally planned change programmes. Instead, she recommends that managements must recognize the complexities of the change process. While modern organizations have few doubts about the need for change, the question where to begin does bother them. Organizations, Kanter argues, must be prepared for 'false starts, messy mistakes, and controversial experiments' if their efforts to transform themselves are to bear fruit. Change usually only looks like change (i.e. some definite or radical move) in hindsight, but at the time things are invariably much more uncertain and mundane. She also suggests that the 'prehistory' of change processes needs to be recognized; examples of successful companies may be put forward as models to be copied, but what is often conveniently forgotten is how long it took them to get their procedures in place and the amount of trial and error involved. In a sense, 'change' itself (or at least the image projected in much management writing) is often an imagined story, a projection of some desired state of organizational readiness.

Predictably, retrospective accounts of change processes often distort the real story. Early events and people recede in importance as later events and people take center stage. Conflict disappears into consensus. Equally plausible alternatives disappear into obvious choices. Accidents, uncertainties, and confusions disappear into clear-sighted strategies. Multiple activities disappear into single thematic events. The fragility of change disappears into a public image of solidity and full actuality. (Kanter, 1991)

Change as a social process

As the above discussion suggests, a top-down view that tends to see change as an 'event' is likely to be misleading. Because human agents are involved change is actually a process—a series of interventions by players and other interest groups. Change is interactive and people rarely passively accept their roles according to some predetermined strategic logic. They develop their own strategies and responses, making change open-ended and uncertain.

One of the most influential researchers and writers on organizational change of the past two-and-a-half decades, and one who has married an awareness of the complexities of the change process with pragmatic managerial concerns, is the British academic Andrew Pettigrew. We will look in Chapter 16 at his early work on organizational power, but Pettigrew also developed a broader account showing how cultural mechanisms of change are intertwined with political mechanisms and leadership. In *The Awakening Giant*, his ten-year study of Imperial Chemical Industries, he explored the linkages between organizational politics and corporate culture, and showed the means of managing culture to be subtle and indirect and achieved through the medium of power (Pettigrew, 1985; especially chaps. 10 and 11).

In the period up to 1980 ICI had a 'segmentalist' culture, reflecting the weakness of the corporate centre. The company tradition was for a kind of comfortable continuity in

Box 14.2 The ATM story

Automatic teller machines (ATMs) are the machines situated outside banks which dispense cash and other services. The story of how they were developed by the clearing banks well illustrates the idea of strategic change being an open-ended and unpredictable process.

ATMs were originally seen as a new technology which would cut staff costs. In retail financial services, the costs of employing and training staff like bank clerks are enormous, not to mention the huge cost of maintaining a branch network on expensive high-street sites. So a piece of equipment that would automate the work of the bank teller had great attractions. It was part of the drive towards out-of-branch or remote banking—the relocation of transactions with customers out of the branch and into the street, the home, and other retail outlets.

However, in the event this original strategy didn't work. What happened was that ATMs sparked off a novel pattern of usage of bank branches. Because the machines were so handy, people began to use them for drawing out small sums of money more frequently. But they would still use the branch almost as often as before, as they still had other business to transact. So ATMs did not contribute much towards substituting for branch clerical labour.

Fortunately for the banks, this failure of planned objectives was not a great strategic failure. It could have been, of course, as the development costs of an ATM network are enormous. But customers regarded ATMs as an extremely attractive and valuable new service. Instead of being a cost-cutting technology, ATMs turned out to be a hugely successful *strategic* technology which opened up new markets.

ATM development went through a complex competitive cycle. In the very first stages banks co-operated in what they thought was going to be a relatively small-scale exercise. But when the technology took off, they quickly dissolved these early alliances, and during the late 1970s and 1980s each bank developed its own ATM network in the drive to remain competitive. By the late 1980s, the emphasis shifted towards multi-use cards and being part of an extensive network, and the competitive balance shifted back towards co-operative relations. The evidence suggests, too, that now this technology has indeed become a substantial labour-saver.

What this case illustrates is strategic change as a process. The banks' original assumption was simply that a labour-saving technology would save labour. But they failed to predict that some groups might play an active part rather than passively accepting the technology. Account-holders' own strategies for using the machines transformed what was envisaged as an economic system into the strategic category.

which chairmen served for only a short period, often at the end of their careers, which effectively ruled out any radical changes. Real power lay with the divisions and divisional managing directors. They ran their operations as independent fiefdoms, so that strategic corporate action was next to impossible, and instead the obsession was with short-termism and financial targets. However, between 1980 and 1982 ICI faced a profits crisis and this paved the way for changes at the top, particularly the appointment of John Harvey-Jones as chairman. But the changes that Harvey-Jones implemented did not begin there; the real change process had a much longer history. Pettigrew charts the emergence of a managerial group led by Harvey-Jones that become identified with change. In the decade leading up to the crisis they developed a perception of the inadequacies of ICI's corporate culture and a vision of a more strategic approach. They were able to communicate this vision through a network of contacts and managerial loyalties. Thus Pettigrew identified the problems of getting the need for change accepted, and the fact that change happens only when powerful interest groups line up behind it. These developments in social perceptions precede any planning or action on change (1985, p. 434).

For Pettigrew, then, leadership and the formation of alliances were the springboard of change. Leadership meant using power in order to manage change—or, in his celebrated phrase, politics becomes the 'management of meaning' (1985, p. 44). On the basis of this research Pettigrew developed a model of change that effectively combines a 'stages' approach (i.e. the more conventional kind of framework that sets out the phases through which some ideal change would pass) with a sociological understanding of the complexities of change. As Box 14.3 shows, Pettigrew's model has four principal stages: two early stages in which an awareness of the problem develops and is established as a legitimate alternative throughout the organization; a third stage of acting on these alternative views and actually implementing change, and finally stabilizing the changes over a longer period.

Perhaps the most intriguing aspect of this model is that it reverses the emphasis of the typical positivist managerial model. It compresses the implementation of change into a single stage, whereas in many models this would occupy endless boxes showing different stages in the timetable and phases of development. But the early stages (which in typical models would be squashed into some statement like 'defining the problem') are expanded and strung out. This emphasizes the critical nature of getting the understanding of the problem legitimized organization-wide. Long before change is embarked upon, the work of establishing these social definitions has to be done. In the research we saw how John Harvey-Jones went about changing ICI long term. He worked on developing a 'for change' group—building loyalties and contacts and a vision of change—fully ten years before the actual implementation stage; then when the business crisis broke he was able to move.

Pettigrew also stressed the necessity of this kind of deep cultural shift if change is to be stabilized (1985, p. 434). One of the least acknowledged problems of change is that of the situation lapsing once initial 'changes' have occurred. Because change is not an event but a process it can be reversed. Change is often linked to strong personalities, so

Box 14.3 The process of organizational change

1. THE DEVELOPMENT OF CONCERN by a group of people that existing organizational structures and procedures are no longer compatible with the operating environment.
2. ACKNOWLEDGEMENT AND UNDERSTANDING OF THE PROBLEM that the organization now faces, analysis of its causes, and alternative ways of tackling it.
3. PLANNING AND ACTING to create specific changes in the light of the above diagnostic and objective-setting work.
4. STABILIZING THE CHANGES, which includes how the organization's reward, information, and power systems reinforce the intended direction of change.

Source: A. Pettigrew, *The Awakening Giant* (1985), p. 434

the situation can easily revert back when the initiators move on. Again, this underscores the social and cultural dimensions of deep-rooted change and the importance of the early stages in the model, as well as the significance of leadership. If innovations are to be reinforced they have to be embedded in the historic practices of the organization. (Indeed, Pettigrew showed that while Harvey-Jones's changes were a necessary response to the profits crisis, in other respects the corporate group was uncomfortable with his methods and with the new distribution of power. In several of the company's divisions the old culture re-established itself after the chairman's departure. Ironically, then, rather than being an awakening giant, on Pettigrew's own account ICI seems to have been roused for only a brief period before rolling over and going back to sleep again.)

The human consequences of change

Another problem with a top-down view of change is that it pays scant attention to those immediately affected—or to the extent their viewpoint is taken into account it is often simply to find ways of circumventing any hostility from organizational members. However, for the junior managers, the workers, and technical and specialist employees who have to take on new tasks, learn new skills, and face other uncertainties, coping with change can be a major problem. This is particularly the case during current times, when work transition and occupational upheaval are increasingly common. The issues here reflect people's involvement in the change process and their experience of it, whether they are able to adapt and cope with its undoubted trauma, and whether senior management employ a participative strategy or impose change from on high.

Because change potentially means insecurity and uncertainty, *resistance* may indeed become an issue. People may not see change as change for the better, or may dispute whether it is essential for economic survival; vested interests may emerge and people may become locked into patterns of behaviour. In Chapter 10 we reviewed the collective and organizational face of resistance, but resistance also has human relations and personnel consequences. Many of the problems we have been generally referring to as organizational 'inertia' come down to this kind of resistance, whether overt or silent and grudging.

Hallier (1997), for example, has looked at job changes amongst air-traffic controllers, and focused on the role of middle managers (personnel, unit, and line managers) responsible for implementing change. Air-traffic control has been an occupation with great security and high skill, and also a strong professional and public-service ethos. However, restructuring reflected the growth of a much more commercial climate in the British public sector during the 1980s and 1990s. The changes in job content included deskilling and greater work pressure, greater managerial scrutiny, less consultation over working arrangements, and a greater requirement for geographical mobility. Hallier stressed that in certain respects senior management handed over responsibility for the implementation of change. Hence the discretion of middle managers expanded— not only in implementing the changes, but also in defining how change was presented to the workforce. Middle managers had 'psychological contracts' with both senior management and the workforce. But in the new climate there was no contest as to where their loyalties lay: they sided with the organization and rewrote any informal understandings or concessions with workers. They sought to enhance their status, avoid being linked to poor performance, and concealed worker dissatisfaction from senior management. Workers were 'exposed to a cascade of self protective and opportunistic management behaviours where the interests of decision-makers are placed above those for whom they are responsible'.

In this way Hallier demonstrates the subtle internal politics of change. Middle managers did not just pass these pressures on, but amplified them; they appeared to deny information and take a tough stance where it was not strictly necessary. It was almost as if middle managers regarded change as a rare opportunity to act out senior managers' wishes and demonstrate their loyalty to the organization.

Managing to change Idealistic models of managers sharing information with workers, involving them in decisions, and preparing the ground for change, may simply not square with the secretive and competitive world of the real-life organization. Nevertheless, in terms of personnel and human resource policies, it is necessary for a climate of approval and consent, and even hopefully enthusiasm for change, to be created. Organizations may successfully manage to dispel resistance and inertia by recognizing the truth of the cliché that change means changing people not things. How do they do this?

The necessity of *investing in people* is paramount. Training and staff development are not only about transferring technical skills; they send an important message to a workforce about how the organization values them. In-depth and long-term skills improvement is an opportunity for an organization to convey its culture and develop feelings of commitment.

The specific role of *leadership* is also crucial. Vague reassurances about a brighter future, or bullying about the inevitability of some proposed change, will never overcome people's understandable uncertainty. Instead a full-blown *vision* of an improved position plus practical steps required to arrive at it are needed. Crafting such a vision is a central responsibility of organizational leadership. The organization needs a cadre of people at all levels with the potential to provide this impetus, and the nurturing of this leadership talent is a strategic function of corporate management.

The *acceptance of change* is likewise essential. If this is to happen, and change is to be assimilated, individuals must play an active part in the process. Only then will they feel a degree of ownership. This can be achieved partly through the *involvement* of the workforce. Structures like quality circles and production teams if properly supported help to create an understanding of change processes. People see their own ideas being used as inputs via these mechanisms. This improves the changes, since employee knowledge is being made available, as well as helping to dispel resistance as people become confident in change which they have helped to shape. Possible disadvantages are that these kinds of autonomous groups may take off in directions managers are unable to predict, but this may happen anyway if change is imposed.

Another crucial issue is *information*. People will only accept change if they feel well informed about its progress and how they are likely to be affected. Involvement in workteams obviously achieves this as a matter of course, but other mechanisms for delivering a flow of accurate and timely information are also important. Nor is this question straightforward. There are almost always political considerations about the release of information, and there may be security implications. Secrecy may be inevitable during the early stages of a project. Also managers themselves may be unclear about all the details and may not want to pass on incomplete information for fear of creating misunderstanding. Control over information may be justified in such circumstances. Nevertheless, there is a danger in firms being instinctively secretive. Openness and a willingness to share information are a valuable means of securing change, and firms are well advised to think in terms of establishing, whether formally or informally, an agreed information policy in advance of any upcoming change.

Succeeding at change management

What are some of the models of success in organizations that achieve the ultimate goal of managing change? These tend to be closely associated with the core capabilities we have been discussing: flexible and adaptive organizational designs, committed and talented workforces, a managerial cadre capable of generating drive and vision. However, some of the models and metaphors that have been proposed have defined certain more specific factors.

Effective organizations For example, Carnall (1995, pp. 76–80) suggests that the ability to manage change is what separates the best from the rest in populations of organizations. He distinguishes the effective from the merely efficient organization. Most surviving organizations are able to meet general criteria of efficiency. They are reasonably good at controlling costs and other material resources; they meet basic objectives of profitability and market share; they keep up to date with new systems and technologies; and they maintain a fairly contented workforce. The effective organization, on the other hand, is efficient but is also accomplished at a much higher level of goals, resources, and dynamic structures. And the difference lies mainly in meeting the need for change. While most organizations are good at the basics, the best achieve a shift to a distinctive level of resource development. They maintain a high-skill workforce, which comes from major investment in personnel, and which can respond quickly to changing demand as expertise is in-house. Their staff attitudes and management style are the basis of a well-articulated corporate image and organizational culture. The effective organization's objectives, Carnall suggests, reach beyond the basics and set a standard in levels of organizational adaptability and corporate excellence. This results not only in profitability but also fast growth rates, the penetration of new markets, and a reputation for features like quality and design.

The learning organization A powerful metaphor closely linked with the management of change is the idea that organizations can acquire a 'learning' capacity. Learning in human beings is about being able to detect changing circumstances, modifying past behaviour that has been unsuccessful, and on the basis of this building a repertoire of complex responses and skills. It is essentially 'intelligent' behaviour and linked with distinctive human characteristics like creativity. In the learning organization a variety of analogous factors can be identified.

Openness. The organization has to be open to enquiry and tolerant of criticism and debate. There needs to be a willingness to try new ideas and a lack of defensiveness about the culture. Some organizations, for example, have a practice of preserving an early part of the development process for exploration and questioning; it is recognized that during this stage there will be no rushing to conclusions or pressure to set early objectives. In general it is important that 'failure' should not be wholly a personal issue but a company responsibility. If someone fails at a task, they should not automatically be asked to justify themselves, but questions should be asked about the support they were given and the type of work they were asked to do.

Innovation. The learning organization has an organic structure and culture which permits it to evolve rapidly. It has a deep skill base and the capacity to deal internally with complexity and uncertainty. Innovation often implies high levels of re-investment in research and development, and a powerful sense of the worth of the organization's own products and services.

Strategic orientation. The learning organization cares both for the customer and for its own human resource. There is a clear bias towards the business and the organizational climate is open to external influences. The crucial point about a strategic orientation is that the organization should be responsive to strategic direction and in sympathy with the vision of change created by the corporate group, even though there may be little evidence of formal strategy processes or plans. In other words, the organization is not stuck fast by inertial tendencies that frustrate corporate efforts to innovate.

In one sense, 'the learning organization' is pure metaphor. Learning is quintessentially a human capacity, and organizations are not people. We should resist attempts to

Box 14.4 Safe to fail

In a Scottish retail bank the confidence of staff that trial and error would not be punished reinforced the capacity to innovate. They were a relatively small operation and prided themselves on being nimble, especially in the use of new technology to deliver services. Their remote banking system called PhoneBank was particularly attractive in supporting business. Combined with other services, such as cash cards, it could supply a full banking service without a bricks-and-mortar branch structure.

PhoneBank was developed at a time when the bank was undergoing a change of ownership that itself provided a new climate for innovation. In the late 1980s the bank was acquired from its then owner, one of the large English clearing banks, by an Australian bank. The original parent had treated the bank as their Scottish outlet and had restricted any independent attempts to change the customer or product base. But the Australian bank wished to use them as an entry into the UK market and were keen to promote new strategies.

PhoneBank itself was initiated in pre-acquisition days against the wishes of the English parent. Particularly in the final few years of ownership the bank's autonomy had been eroded by the need to cut costs. But they were firm in the belief that PhoneBank was needed, both as a sign of independence from the parent and as a basis of future developments. The head of Information Systems conceded that he had been sticking his neck out when he developed PhoneBank. When he signed up suppliers, and outsourced major elements of software, the department was in 'a very dodgy situation' given that they were thwarting the wishes of the group. However, he went ahead on his own initiative, and the bank's executive backed his financial authority.

PhoneBank's customer interface drives a range of delivery systems. These range from simple home banking to corporate cash management, direct banking, and speech recognition. It is 'not the most elegant system' but has the virtue of being inexpensive and flexible. It allows wider options and changes without the necessity of overhauling major systems. Senior business analysts contended that the uncertainty associated with the development was contained on a number of levels: the size of the bank, the flexibility of the front-end design, and the continuity with previous systems developments. 'We are small enough to be able to test-bed things without too much consideration as to cost if it doesn't work. Now I'm not saying that we just go into it and say, oh tough, over the wall and try again. But none the less we can take a less serious view if that doesn't work out. The way we designed this, we had the space to fail and move over to something else, so we felt pretty secure.'

reify the organization in any way. Yet there is a sense in which these ideas can be applied. The requirements for organizational learning are that human characteristics should be allowed to flourish in organizations. Bureaucratic tendencies need to be overcome and individual agents as the bearers of ideas and intelligence have to be permitted to emerge and be supported. Conversely the barriers to change, and the inertial forces in organizations, mainly reflect the suppression of the variable and creative factors we associate with the human element.

In this vein, Morgan (1997: chap. 4) has referred to the similar idea of organizations as 'brains'. The human brain is strongly identified with the capacity for intelligent adaptability, so this is another appropriate metaphor if we want to highlight the management of change. Morgan (p. 102) distinguishes several principles of the brain that can be applied to learning organizations—each attesting to the fact that the brain is an organism not a mechanism.

First, the way the brain functions is *holographic*: as Morgan puts it, the whole has to be encoded in all of the parts. The brain constitutes an organic unity in so far as function and memory are distributed, rather than following a strictly divided design. Consequently if parts of the organism are damaged as an entity it can compensate, or recover and relearn lost functions, and can continue working. There is also an element of *redundancy* in the brain. Many of the functions perform multiple tasks, and many individual tasks are capable of being sourced from different sites. Again, this enables the brain to sustain damage and still keep functioning, while redundancy is also a source of creativity as a particular function will be performed from multiple and differing perspectives. (For example, rather than being obsessed with efficiency—which always means cutting out any superfluous provision—many computer programmes these days have in-built levels of redundancy.) There is also a high degree of *connectivity* in the human brain. The network of interconnections between cells and functions is exceedingly dense and rich. This inbuilt complexity is the source of the 'higher-level' functions of the brain such as creativity and intelligence.

Within organizations these kinds of capabilities are replicated by, for example, a high degree of autonomy and multi-skilling in the workforce. This would enable the organization to scan the environment and act on informational inputs in an effective manner. The relatively fuzzy divisions of labour associated with organic structures (Burns and Stalker, 1961) also enhance functions like redundancy and connectivity. They develop cross-functional communication, and encourage people to innovate by exploring and extending the boundaries of their responsibility. Organizations that positively encourage networking and informal communication—with practices like 'management by walking around'—would also improve factors such as the level of connectivity (see the Hewlett-Packard example in the next chapter).

Conclusion

As we have argued in the previous two chapters, any focus on organizations as structures for attaining goals runs the risk of becoming too prescriptive. Managers themselves tend to favour these theories, not always out of naivity or ignorance of the realities of organizational life—they usually know only too well the dangers of failure and the intricacies of organizational politics—but because prescriptive theories help them in their main work of controlling and designing operations. However, for academic purposes, too great an emphasis on goal achievement, or a preoccupation with efficiency, can mean that we are not explaining what organizations are like in action. So while decision-making has often been thought of as a rational process, in reality managers do not act jointly to resolve problems in a purely unproblematic way. Decision-making is a human process constrained by the limits on ability and by the contradictions of social and economic life.

In this chapter various ways of looking at managerial rationality enabled us to distinguish and classify decision-making theories. We can think of rationality as a property of the individual or of social and economic structures. We can also distinguish between strong or 'absolute' versions of rationality—which tend to be the unexamined assumption behind conventional economic and management thinking—and weaker or partial notions of rationality. It is probably true to say (with one or two notable exceptions) that the range of modern theories of decision-making favour the latter, and base their approach on some notion of *joint* rationality. The original formulation of 'bounded rationality' coined in the 1950s is still a contender for the most elegant expression of this concept. At any rate, while the realities of organization life are being recognized, at the same time there is still an attraction to some idea of purpose underlying organizational behaviour. Even in theories that appear to be emphasizing the vagaries of actual behaviour, this kind of residual rationality is usually present.

These considerations helped us to come to grips with possibly the key problem facing organizations in today's business context: the management of change. Following from the account of rationality and decision-making, it was deemed important to explore the problematic nature of change rather than simplistic or idealized change sequences. This places human agents at the centre of the change process. Where change dynamics are in operation, the authority structures that normally contribute to organizational inertia tend to become loosened and unsettled; and in such situations people develop their own strategies, making change open-ended and unpredictable. Thus, if change is to be enthusiastically embraced, management practices need to adjust to this more complex and uncertain context. Leadership and pragmatic programmes, such as organizational effectiveness and organizational learning, must be rooted in the involvement of people in the change process. They must also take in key social processes like the wielding of power and shaping of organizational culture. These latter aspects, however, as well as being part of the management of change, are topics in their own right and we look at them in more detail in the next two chapters.

Study questions for Chapter 14

1 In what ways is a knowledge of managerial rationality useful for understanding the nature of organizational decision-making?

2 What do managers do?

3 In what ways can managerial behaviour be regarded as rational, even allowing for the constraints on rationality?

4 What might lead us to conclude that organizations are irrational?

5 Contrast recent theories of decision-making in terms of the basic picture each supplies of the management process?

6 How does a knowledge of managerial decision-making help us to understand the effective management of organizational change?

7 In what ways is organizational change a problematic process?

8 What are the chief means of overcoming resistance to change?

9 Can organizations learn?

Further reading

Burnes, B. (1996) *Managing Change: A Strategic Approach to Organisational Dynamics*, 2nd edn. London: Pitman.

Butler, R. (1991) 'Learning and change', chap. 10 in *Designing Organizations: A Decision-Making Perspective*. London: Routledge.

Carnall, C. (1995) *Managing Change in Organizations*, 2nd edn. London: Prentice Hall.

Dawson, P. (1994) *Organizational Change: A Processual Approach*. London: Paul Chapman.

Dawson, S. (1996) 'Managing change', chap. 10 in *Analysing Organisations*, 3rd edn. Basingstoke: Macmillan.

Goodman, P. *et al.* (eds.) *Change in Organizations*. San Francisco: Jossey-Bass.

Hales, C. (1993) *Managing through Organisation*. London: Routledge.

Kotter, J. P. (1982) 'What effective general managers really do', *Harvard Business Review*, 60, Nov/Dec, 156–67.

Mabey, C. and Mayon-White, B. (1993) *Managing Change*, 2nd edn. London: Open University/Paul Chapman.

March, J. G. and Simon, H. E. (1958) *Organizations*. New York: Wiley.

Morgan, Glenn (1990) *Organizations in Society*. Basingstoke: Macmillan.

Staw, B. and Salancik, G. (eds.) (1982) *New Directions in Organizational Behavior*. Malabar, Fla.: Kreiger.

Weick, K. (1979) *The Social Psychology of Organizing*. Reading, Mass.: Addison-Wesley.

15 Organizational Culture

Summary points and learning objectives

By the end of this chapter you will

- understand the relation between organizational culture and the *business context*. How does culture contribute to organizational innovation and success?
- appreciate the contribution of organizational culture to the *management of change*;
- understand the *analytic elements* of organization cultures: symbolic, unifying, and holistic;
- understand the *constituent elements* of organization culture, such as stories, myths, heroes, and villains;
- have reviewed some of the *cultural types* in organizations;
- not be too anxious about the *remaining puzzles*. If culture is unifying what about multiple cultures and counter-cultures? Should we take a managerial or an anthropological view of culture? Can culture be managed?

Introduction

The focus on structure in the previous two chapters had the virtue of highlighting the patterns of behaviour that are observable and repeated in organizations. But the structural approach can overlook some important aspects of organizational reality. The qualitative aspect of organizations, what an organization is 'really like', is often poorly captured by structure (particularly formal structure). However, a concept that does try to encapsulate the whole reality is that of *culture*.

Originally an anthropological term, culture refers to the underlying values, beliefs and codes of practice that makes a community what it is. The customs of a society, the self-images of its members, the things that make it different from other societies, are its culture. There are objective factors at work here, in the sense that social beliefs constrain behaviour, but culture is also powerfully *subjective*. It reflects the meanings and understandings that we typically attribute to situations, the solutions that we apply to common problems. Being a 'member of society' means that we have acquired core values through the process of growing up and being socialized. Large swathes of our culture are taken for granted—we are more or less unconscious of the huge fund of meanings and ideas that we hold in common with others. But these social bonds and common knowledge remain integral to our identity and sense of personal cohesion.

The idea of a common culture suggests possible problems about whether *organizations* can be considered as having cultures. Organizations are only one constituent element of society. People enter them from the surrounding community and bring their culture with them. We already have a good many examples of this kind of broader work culture. What are referred to as 'orientations to work' (see Chapter 17) are attitudes that can be understood only by reference to workers' social background. Similarly, in Chapter 11, Rice's classic (1958) study of job redesign in an Indian textile mill showed how workers' responses towards new forms of responsibility very much reflected the work attitudes traditional in the country. And studies of comparative management have shown that managerial practices and values can be very different in different countries. Much of the success of countries like Germany and Japan has been attributed to industrial cultures that foster high levels of performance.

Factors like these would tend to cut across anything that might exist in an organization. None the less, it is still possible to think of organizations as having cultures of their own. Organizations possess the paradoxical quality of being both 'part of' and 'apart from' society. They are embedded in a wider social context, but they are also communities in their own right with distinctive rules and values. They can thus be thought of as 'culture producing phenomena' (Smircich, 1983).

In this chapter we look first at the importance of the business context. An emphasis on values and beliefs might appear to be of mainly sociological interest, yet corporate culture has become one of the great management buzz words. Thus it is necessary to establish what the material gains are perceived to be. What does culture contribute to the bottom line? Secondly, culture is clearly a complex concept, and one we will need to explore in some detail. It refers to the totality of knowledge in an organization or society. But if almost anything is part of culture, the concept runs the risk of becoming vague, a dumping ground of unexplained factors in organizations. So does the concept mean everything and nothing, or can it be defined in more precise ways? Culture is basically substantive; it reflects the beliefs and techniques that characterize *specific* organizations. We therefore need to distinguish the ways in which beliefs are unique to each organization, as well as between different cultural types. Thirdly, we need to review the strengths and weaknesses of the cultural metaphor—in particular the tensions that exist between the idea that beliefs and meanings can be 'managed', and that of culture as a unique set of attributes.

Organizational culture and strategic management

In certain respects culture has long been on the agenda of management theorists. Influential writers like Chester Barnard in the 1930s and 1940s, and Peter Drucker from the 1950s to the present, emphasized the centrality of *values* in the management of enterprises. Management for them always meant more than mere decision-making and

Box 15.1 The Hewlett–Packard way

Enduring values through changing times

Based on the belief that people are committed to doing their jobs well and are capable of making sound decisions, Hewlett-Packard practices a highly innovative style of management known simply as the HP Way.

The HP Way engenders a very open and informal corporate culture. Consistent with this the company has developed a matrix style of organization rather than the more formal pyramid management structure popular among many companies.

It has been our policy not to have a tight military-type organization, but rather to have overall objectives which are clearly stated and agreed upon, and to give people the freedom to work towards these goals in ways they determine best for their own areas of responsibility.

The Hewlett-Packard work environment fosters individual dignity, pride in accomplishment and the motivation to produce quality work. In return the company ensures that employees share in the success which their efforts make possible.

Organizational values

Trust and respect for individuals;
A high level of achievement and contribution;
Conducting business with uncompromising integrity;
Achieving common objectives through teamwork;
Encouraging flexibility and innovation.

Corporate objectives

Profit;
Customer respect and loyalty;
Participating in relevant fields of interest;
Growth;
Helping our people share in company success;
Management that fosters initiative and creativity;
Corporate citizenship and responsibility.

Strategies and practices

Management by wandering around;
Management by objectives;
Open-door policy;
Total quality control.

Source: compiled from company literature.

the planning of procedures. Management meant corporate leadership, which in turn implied motivating people and providing a vision of where the enterprise is going.

Not until as late as the 1980s, however, was culture explicitly identified as the 'something extra' on top of planning and administration. The limitations of conventional ideas of planned change, based on techniques like organizational design and employee selection, are now being recognized. What is the point in changing the staff if new people merely absorb the existing custom and practice? Design and structure are important, but organizations can be successful in spite of poor structures, or fail even if correctly designed. Instead of changing the structure, real change must mean changing the corporate ethos, the images and values that inform action; and this new way of understanding the life of organizations must be brought into the management process. In this context a growing number of companies—Hewlett-Packard, Johnson and Johnson, and IBM are some of the more famous names—have long been known for their avowal of corporate values. Others are following suit and have produced 'mission statements' that combine prescriptions for action with culture.

These point to a number of central aspects of culture. There is an *evaluative* element involving social expectations and standards, the values and beliefs that people hold central and that bind organizational groups. Culture is also a set of more *material* elements or artefacts. These are the signs and symbols that the organization is recognized by, but they are also the events, behaviours, and people that embody the culture. And the medium of culture is social *interaction*, the web of communications that constitute a community. Here a shared language is particularly important in expressing and signifying a distinctive organizational culture. These three elements will be found in many of the definitions of culture.

Success, excellence, innovation

When corporate culture first emerged as a distinctive concept, a cluster of influential writers set out the related ideas and concepts that linked it into the basic notions of how organizations operate successfully, and in particular how they operate in the current climate of unpredictable fast-paced change and fierce competition. They were sometimes interested in culture in its own right, but more often were concerned with broader schemas that situated culture with ideas of innovation, leadership, and organizational change.

Culture and success: Deal and Kennedy As a result of the interest in corporate culture the belief became firmly established that *culture fosters success*. Here, Deal and Kennedy (1982) have argued that culture was the single most important factor accounting for success or failure. Their survey of US corporations found that the firms which were perceived to 'believe in something' or to 'stand for something' were both the strong culture companies and the high performers. The researchers identified four key dimensions of culture.

1. *Values*: the beliefs that lie at the heart of the corporate culture. These should be strongly held and openly supported, because identification with other things (the union, colleagues, instrumental goals) can mean weak or fragmented culture.

2. *Heroes:* the people who embody values. Organizational heroes are the actors who carry culture; by providing role models they assist in getting values widely accepted and adopted.
3. *Rites and rituals:* routines of interaction that have strong symbolic qualities. Whether mundane or elaborate, rites and rituals demonstrate to individuals the expectations that the organization has of them.
4. *The culture network:* the informal communications system or 'hidden hierarchy of power' in the organization. People must be adept at manipulating this if they are to be effective at all.

Culture and corporate excellence: Peters A recent management writer who trades heavily on culture is Tom Peters. Peters co-authored the most widely read of all management books, *In Search of Excellence* (Peters and Waterman, 1982), in which a model is developed of what it takes to achieve corporate 'excellence'. The famous eight prescriptions were distilled out of research with a cross-section of US companies deemed to have that magic quality.

Bias for action
Closeness to the customer
Autonomy and entrepreneurship
Productivity through people
Hands on, value driven
Stick to the knitting
Simple form, lean staff
Simultaneous loose–tight properties

The possession of a unique set of cultural attributes lies behind many of these factors (1982, p. 26). For example, sticking to the knitting means staying close to the core business; we can see that the opposite policy of growth by acquiring unrelated enterprises is likely to dilute corporate culture. Similarly, autonomy is closely related to culture in so far as the freedom to act on one's own initiative is what commits people to central goals. More generally, it is culture which prevents the eight prescriptions from becoming mere platitudes. Everyone knows that 'the customer comes first' or that 'people are our greatest asset', but successful companies make these clichés a reality; they create *specific* customer- and people-orientated climates.

Peters and Waterman also suggest an interesting psychological theory of the link between organizational culture and business performance. Culture can be looked on as a reward of work. We sacrifice much to organizations, and culture is a form of return on effort. Culture provides ordinary people in humdrum jobs with a sense of the significance of their work. People need to find meaning in their lives; culture provides meaning and hence reinforces motivation and morale. It is this that accounts for the 'unusual effort on the part of ordinary employees' (1982, p. xvii) that is the hallmark of corporate excellence.

In his later book, *Thriving on Chaos* (1987), Peters had to deal with the somewhat uncomfortable fact that several of the companies declared 'excellent' in 1982 were experiencing serious difficulties by the late 1980s; some had even gone out of business. His response was to emphasize the market uncertainty of the new economic order. He concedes that he underestimated the seriousness of US economic decline and the threat of competitors (particularly Japan). In this 'world turned upside down' his earlier concept of excellence had proved too static; there are no safe companies. Instead the only prescription is for ceaseless innovation. Interestingly, too, this approach provides a critique of the old systems theories of organization, or contingency theory as presented in Chapter 17. There we noted that in certain contingencies of market stability, bureaucratic companies could be the most effective. Peters disagrees; the idea that there are companies that have little need for flexibility no longer applies. Innovation is paramount. 'The old saw, if it ain't broke, don't fix it, needs revision. I propose: fix it anyway' (1987, p. 3).

Culture and innovation: Kanter Another of the gurus of modern management, Rosabeth Moss Kanter, has likewise focused on the pressing need for innovation. In *When Giants Learn to Dance* (1989) she refers to the growing intensity of global competition as 'the corporate Olympics'—the fact that now there are more competitors than ever, more industrializing nations. The model she develops of 'post-entrepreneurialism' centres on the need for large corporations to retain the flexibility and dynamism of the entrepreneurial roots (teaching the giants to dance). Her earlier book, *The Change Masters* (1984), had also dealt with the cultural changes needed to make large firms innovative, in particular the *implementation* of change and the complex organizational (cultural) processes that go with this. She notes, for example, the paradox implicit in linking culture with change. On the surface, culture has essentially traditional and stable qualities. So how can you have a 'culture of change'? Yet this is precisely what the innovative organization needs.

To manage change as a normal way of life requires that people find their stability and security not in specific organizational arrangements but in the culture and direction of the organization. It requires that they feel integrated with the whole rather than identified with the particular territory of the moment. (1984, p. 133)

Kanter is more concerned than most writers with the problematic aspects of culture. Whereas writers like Peters and Deal and Kennedy dismiss alternative values as 'weak cultures', Kanter takes account of these complexities. She describes a number of cultural types as polar opposites. Some companies have a 'culture of inferiority': a tendency to doubt their own ability, to feel they need to recruit managerial talent from other firms, and to rely on outsiders (e.g. consultants) to create innovation. Contrasted to these are companies with a 'culture of success', reflected in pride in the company, can-do attitudes and a confidence in developing their own managerial talent (1984, p. 92). Another interesting set of cultural types are what she calls cultures of 'age versus youth' (p. 349). Companies in established industrial sectors seem to be more prone to leaving their heads in the sand, seeing little need for change and believing that problems will resolve themselves without being squarely confronted (culture of age). In contrast, newer high-tech industries tend to empower innovators and make it easier for people to question existing patterns (culture of youth). Being a 'young' company has built-in advantages, in so far as innovation and enterprise become the norm for the whole sector.

Culture and the management of change

The above analysis suggests that cultures are resistant to many forms of attempted change, but they can also be amazingly dynamic. In the right circumstances, 'tradition' can be adaptive and self-modifying. Indeed, if real change is to occur in organizations—rather than cosmetic or short-lived change—it has to happen at the cultural level. Given the past failures of management theory, corporate culture therefore has many powerful attractions as a lever for change; the problem is how to get a hand on the lever. The above analysis suggests some pointers.

First, the case has been argued that cultures can be *explicitly created*. Understanding culture and being able to modify it are crucial both to market success for the company and to career success for the individual. You have to work with the culture—or be very much aware of what it takes to change an existing culture. In this sense, successful companies are not shy about promoting their heroes and symbols. Writers like Peters and Deal and Kennedy also dispel any ideas about culture being 'soft'. Strong-culture companies do not generate cosy sets of values that make people committed by making them more content. Such companies are not particularly tolerant of those who reject core values. A strong culture creates powerful behavioural expectations and constraints, more so than any formal structure of procedures and rules.

Second, all of the main management writers are clear that the ability in companies to be culturally innovative is strongly related to *leadership*. Top management must take responsibility for building strong cultures that fit market needs. Deal and Kennedy, for example, supplemented their survey of senior management with biographical material on business leaders, and found that people who pioneer successful companies rarely operate on a narrow economic or administrative front. Rather, they are obsessed with developing values and acting as role models. Similarly, as Peters became aware of the turbulent markets that companies have to survive in, he refined his original eight prescriptions. These became a simplified four-part model centred on *customers*, *innovation* and *people*, all linked via *leadership*. Peters, and other writers too, are strongly drawn to the concept of 'transformational leadership' (see Chapter 8 above). This stresses that the role of leader extends beyond that of the rational analyst. Leaders construct the social reality of the organization for members; they shape values and attend to the drama and vision of the organization. As Peters notes, the leader is 'orchestrator and labeller: taking what can be gotten in the way of action and shaping it—generally after the fact—into lasting commitment to a new strategic direction. In short, he makes meanings' (1982, p. 75).

A third point is that culture is frequently counterposed to *formal rationality*. As Kanter notes, organizations need to be 'conscious of themselves as a culture, not just as a technical system' (1984, pp. 133–4). In this sense culture helps to resolve the dilemma of bureaucracy: formal procedures are necessary for business integrity and planning (Weber was right on this point), but they also stifle autonomy and innovation. Peters especially is highly critical of the 'rationalists' who for so long have dominated management theory and who endlessly recommend complicated systems and technical fixes (reflected in systems like Taylorism). But considerations of culture can hold bureaucracy at bay. The stronger the corporate culture, the less need there is for detailed procedures and rules, because culture itself guides employee action. Thus firms are able to have proper administrative back-up and engage in formal planning without these activities becoming ends in themselves.

Other cultures

As already suggested, the reasons for urgency in the current debate on organization culture reflect to a great extent the new global competition. The period from the mid-1970s has been one of growing uncertainty for firms, with the appearance of new competitor nations, new technologies and new types of consumer demand. In response to a changing environment and business crises, adaptable cultures that are responsive to strategic pressure and corporate guidance have become vital.

According to Morgan (1997, p. 119) a central factor in all this has been the ascent to economic power of Japan. The very differences that are perceived between Japanese culture and ours have highlighted culture as a factor in managerial success. But also the *nature* of Japanese organizational culture, Morgan suggests, focuses on the whole organization, the cultivation of harmonious relations at all levels in the organization, the merging of individual with common goals, and a reliance on worker responsibility. All this contrasts with our own cultural biases. The Anglo-American obsession with bureaucratic systems betrays a tendency to break down processes in mechanical fashion and to seek 'efficiencies in the elements of management'. Under the western (especially American) ethic of competitive individualism, the key metaphor is the game: the obsession with excellence, the need to distinguish winners from losers. Anglo-American production culture is anti-person in other fundamental ways; the ideas of making work systems 'idiot proof' and reducing labour content are endemic to western production values.

This argument may have been oversimplified, however. As will be pointed out in Chapter 20, it was the belief that cultural factors lay at the root of Japanese success that caused western industrialists to despair of ever being able to learn from Japan. In contrast, the later focus on more 'copyable' production principles (the just-in-time system) was what really sparked off interest in Japanese methods. Also, the view of Japanese industrial culture as being rooted in moral qualities of sacrifice may be somewhat idealized. In many ways, Japanese society is just as competitive and individualistic as our own. An alternative view of the Japanese principles of duty and obligation is that these are the means by which large enterprises exploit smaller ones. And an alternative view of the Japanese production ethos is that they are the 'modern masters' of Taylorism.

The most influential American management writers have always been resistant to the 'learn from Japan' movement. Peters, for example, argued that there is no need to look elsewhere for models of corporate excellence; the best American businesses provide these. The problem is that they have been paid insufficient attention (1982, p. xxii).

Later, in *Thriving on Chaos* (1987), he takes the American decline much more seriously. He bemoans the 1980s as a decade of corporate 'madness' characterized by merger mania, asset-stripping and financial corruption. Moreover, the habits of production that the USA persists in (giantism, anti-labourism) continue to put it at a disadvantage with Japan. Despite this analysis, however, Peters still sticks with his original formula: he looks to home-grown exemplars of success, implicitly rejecting arguments about Japan's superior management culture. Similarly, Kanter (1989) was also concerned with the rejuvenation of corporate America, and her models were all local ones. She believed that she saw the beginnings of a tide of change sweeping through American big business, and a number of 'post-entrepreneurial prototypes' exclusively in US firms.

There is no need to delay over this debate. A belief in the importance of a unifying culture, among certain sections of the business community, may well have arisen in the way that Morgan describes. Not only Japan, but also other success economies like Germany and the Pacific rim countries are seen as having cultures that emphasize open communications and the ability to absorb delegated power. It is how these organization cultures are perceived in the minds of managements that is the crucial issue.

Exploring organizational culture

Attempts to define organizational culture have adopted a number of different approaches. Some focus on its *manifestations*—the heroes and villains, rites and rituals, myths and legends that populate organizations. Others emphasize the stocks of collective *knowledge* that members hold. These make up the institutional memory of the organization and make action possible. Culture is also *socially constructed*; it reflects meanings that are constituted in interaction and that form commonly accepted 'definitions of the situation'. Rather than try to cover all this ground in a single statement, however, a better understanding might be gained by sifting out some of the basic attributes to the concept.

Culture is symbolic

We have all had the experience of being asked what the organization we work in is 'really like'. We might attempt to respond in general terms, but if that fails (which it usually does) we start telling stories—we describe a particular person, or recount an anecdote that we feel is somehow typical of the organization. In this sense the stories and legends, which all organizations have, seem to say something deeper; they are the representations of culture.

A symbol 'stands for' something more than itself. The symbol can be many things—a sign, an event, an object, even a person—but the essential point is that a symbol is invested with meaning by us, and expresses forms of understanding derived from our past collective experiences. The sociological view of culture is that organizations exist in the minds of their members. How members define reality is just as important for outcomes as concrete techniques and procedures. Kanter, for example, points out that organizations frequently 'talk up' the emphasis on change. In defining as 'changes' events which may not have been particularly innovative, new definitions of the situation are being created: 'Organizational change consists in part of a series of emerging constructions of reality, including revision of the past, to correspond to the requisites of new players and new demands' (1984, p. 287). In terms of understanding what is going on in organizations, the simple point is that appearances can be deceptive. Situations that seem to have a straightforward function often have a deeper meaning.

It is not entirely clear why symbolic communication is so necessary. Why describe one thing in terms of another rather than directly? Why resort to fables and anecdotes? What is clear, though, is that symbolism plays a major part in daily communication, much more than we usually realize. Symbols are about the *dramatization* of messages and this can be vital for an organization's operation.

Stories The point is well illustrated if we see the communication system of organizations as an unfolding story line. More than any other event, stories show how culture acts as a 'sense-making device'. The collective experiences of people are almost always ambivalent and open to different interpretations. But in a story they are assembled together in a way that rationalizes complex events. There is always a 'line' or a 'point' to a story. Stories are used to manage uncertainty and enable collective action to occur. Indeed, without this dramatizing aspect, organizations could be paralysed by uncertainty. As Boje (1991) points out: 'when a decision is at hand, the old stories are recounted and compared to unfolding story lines to keep the organization from repeating historically bad choices and to invite the repetition of past successes'. Stories are a way of rehearsing complex situations that enable us to check our own understanding with others. Group interests may be embodied in stories, which serve the purpose of advancing those interests and may be used by groups to initiate change. Boje also points out that we should not see stories as static things, wheeled out to prove a point. The enactment or *performance* of the story is the crucial thing: different versions of stories are told in different situations, different actors will have rights over different parts of the story, and getting the story woven into the culture is itself part of the organizational power game. (See also Martin and Meyerson, 1988; McConkie and Boss, 1986; Mitroff and Kilmann, 1975; Wilkins, 1984.)

Culture is unifying

Secondly, culture refers to processes that bind the organization together. In this sense, cultural processes stand opposed to the many forms of conflict that occur in organizations. Although conflict is certainly an ever-present reality, culture represents an equally real and valid alternative face of the organization. Culture then is consensual not conflictual. The idea of corporate culture reinforces the unifying strengths of central goals and creates a sense of common responsibility—which is why it has assumed such an important place in management thinking.

Here we can refer to one of the foremost British management writers, Tom Burns. Burns's early work had stressed organizations as 'plural social systems' that encom-

Box 15.2 The US trip

This is a case example of an organizational story. The background was the purchase of a computer package by a large financial services organization. The company had identified the only package that was really suitable, but there were other potential problems. The supplier of the package was a computer agency that the company had used before and of which it had had a disastrous experience. Not to put too fine a point on it, the agency had made a complete mess of an important project a couple of years earlier. The company was nervous about employing them again because the agency would be doing the conversion programming to integrate the package into the main-frame systems, as well as undertaking future maintenance.

At this point 'the US trip' took place. The parent of the computer agency was an American firm, and because the package was not widely used in Britain a fact-finding trip to the United States had been arranged. The British team held talks there with the agency's top management and visited several user firms that had the package in opera-tion. On returning they pronounced themselves more than satisfied. They stressed that they were initially wary about the cost involved, and about whether an 'expensive for-eign junket' could be justified. But the trip had been worthwhile and one they would repeat in similar circumstances. All their fears about purchasing the package had been removed.

It seems clear, however, that the US trip had developed a kind of ritual significance. It had taken place at a time of uncertainty in an important investment decision. Later, whenever doubts about the purchase were raised, or when managers were being asked to account for their decision, they would say, 'Ah, but there was the US trip', and this single reference stood for a whole bundle of initiatives and effort that went into testing the suitability of the package. It also seems clear that certain aspects of the US trip had been dramatized. This is not to say that any crude lies were told, simply that events had been 'worked over' with benefit of hindsight. The trip had become a story that was retold in order to make sense of an equivocal situation.

Managers made great play of their initial concern about the expense involved, yet it seems unlikely that *at the time* they went about stressing what all this was going to cost and whether it would be of any benefit. Also, the great success claimed for the trip may have been overplayed. In the retelling this was dramatically compared with concerns about the trip's cost; the story line was: 'At first I was doubtful, then I was converted.' Managers actually used the term, 'conversion', as if to suggest a religious experience.

In fact, it was not at all obvious why the trip should have been so reassuring. The com-puter package itself was not the real problem; all parties agreed that it was the best available. It was the supplying agency that caused the worries. The package was to be converted and maintained by the American parent's British operation. The crucial issue, the professionalism of the staff in Britain, could not have been resolved in the United States.

Thus it seems clear that 'the US trip' was referred to partly in a symbolic way to legit-imize a somewhat risky course of action. In the event the gamble paid off; the British staff turned out to be highly professional, and they completed the project on time and to everyone's satisfaction.

passed political as well as rational action (Burns, 1969). But he later turned to the *interaction* of plural systems, 'the working organisation with the political system, the career system and so forth' (1977, p. xi). In his masterly study of the BBC, Burns (1977) anticipated the current interest in organizational culture by several years. Plural systems were integrated at the level of culture, and constituted 'a way of defining the "rules of the game" according to which the internal and external business of the Corporation and all the manifold social intercourse to which this business gives rise should be conducted' (p. xiii).

Burns's famous concept of 'organic' structure (see Chapter 13) was also underpinned by culture. The organic concept stresses the importance of flexible matrix structures, something it shares with quite a few other influential management theories. But though he is usually represented in this way, Burns was trying to convey more than just a non-bureaucratic or flexible approach. Organic structures reflect internalized goals and a deeply held sense of common purpose. This applies especially to workers, and groups like technical specialists, that develop objectives that are often seen as opposing central interests and goals. In an organic enterprise all groups retain a sense of central purpose. This produces an adaptive organization because it enables conventional work habits and authority structures to be modified according to changing demands.

Another important linkage is to organizational *rationality*. This was referred to earlier in the chapter in terms of 'formal rationality': that whole web of procedures, systems and controls designed to make organizational performance predictable and accountable. Yet a more common-sense version of rationality can be related to culture. What people usually mean by 'rational behaviour' is simply the ability of organizational members to work together. If we think of people being able to tackle problems in a reasoned manner, without politicking and without being drawn into hidden agendas, this is what we instinctively think of as acting rationally. The unifying force of beliefs and values held in common lies at the heart of such rational action. Certainly, when managements are advocating strong corporate cultures, this type of exchange is what they have in mind.

Culture is holistic

Culture refers to the *essence*, the *reality* of an organization—what it is like to work there, how people deal with each other, what behaviours are expected. Before the culture concept was widely employed, the term organizational 'climate' was often used; this was vaguer but also referred to the experience of being part of an organization.

One important way in which the holistic character of the organization is expressed is through *rules*. By these, social scientists do not usually mean formally stated and recorded rules (though these can be included); they mean the unspoken, taken-for-granted rules that regulate social conduct. Indeed, the question of what an organization is really like is often followed up with enquiries about the 'rules of the game' or 'learning the ropes'. Because organizations are competitive places, one absolutely vital rule-set for members is that which defines good performance. This is manifest in career rewards like promotions and pay rises. But 'getting on' involves a much wider and more subtle array: being included in discussions, consulted, given good assignments. Making

---

Box 15.3 Organic culture

This apparently trivial case example occurred on a research visit to the Scottish subsidiary of an American electronics multinational.

On first contact the plant's chief executive and the researcher met in the reception area. During this conversation the CE called across to the receptionist to ask for some coffee to be brought. She replied that she had such-and-such a report to finish typing and asked if he could get the coffee himself. The CE said, yes, that report needed to go out quickly, and off he went to get the coffee.

During this brief exchange a total reversal of authority (not to mention gender) roles had taken place. Formal authority had been upended; the boss was acting on the subordinate's initiative. This was not a unique event, nor perhaps should we read too much into it. However, mundane events can often be seen as microcosms of a wider reality. The obvious explanation was that both knew the report was more important than the coffee. But in how many companies would the receptionist have simply 'done her job' and fetched the coffee? And in how many companies would the CE have felt his authority under threat if he had performed the menial task? Perhaps a deeper reality was that the CE and the receptionist had an ever-present sense of company needs, and this shared knowledge enabled them to navigate a potentially difficult situation.

---

it in an organization means learning to navigate in the subtle and dangerous currents that bring these rewards. And the rules of the game can be very different. In one organization success might come from bureaucratic abilities, while in another inputs into some productive enterprise might be the key to success.

This latter type of 'rational' rule is interestingly reflected in Michael Lewis's *Liar's Poker* (1989). An insider account of the 1980s investment banking boom, this book shows the dealing rooms of New York and London as an obsessive and enclosed world, a world of 'hysterical greed and ambition'. The culture of bond-dealing is full of symbols—legends grew up around the main players, epithets were attached to them, they took on heroic or villainous qualities. (Indeed, some of the heroes were also villains—by 1991 the firm that Lewis worked for, Saloman Brothers, had been cited for massive fraud.) The key ritual of Liar's Poker, versions of which are played in most Wall Street firms, is based on players each holding a dollar bill and bidding on combinations of the serial numbers. The game was a potent symbol of the real game: making money.

When you managed a firm, well, sure, you received your quota of envy, fear and admiration. But for all the wrong reasons. You did not make the money for Saloman. You did not take risk. You were hostage to your producers. They took risk. They proved their superiority every day by handling risk better than the rest of the risk-taking world. . . . And if you wanted to show off, Liar's

Poker was the only way to go. The game had a powerful meaning for traders. They believed that it had a lot in common with bond trading. It tested a trader's character. It honed a trader's instincts. A good player made a good trader, and vice-versa. We all understood it. (1989, p. 17)

As we see, in one sense the game *became* the reality: it prevented the skills of the real producers from being submerged by management. Success at Liar's Poker was a flag of status that top management craved as well. Lewis recounts a Saloman Brothers legend in which a senior trader, the 'king of the players', faced down the company chairman in a million-dollar hand of the game. Hence his book is also a kind of homage to the skills of the bond traders. In the final analysis, the rules of success reflected the only thing that mattered—the profit that traders showed on their accounts.

Cultural interconnections We can see that all of the above elements—culture as symbolic, unifying, and holistic—are interlocking. The symbolic nature of culture is unifying. Symbols by definition are based on shared meanings (we would not understand them as symbols otherwise); and since organizational culture is built out of symbolic events it expresses the values and beliefs that members hold in common. Likewise, symbolic/unifying events express the holism of the organization. These processes work through many levels of reality. Culture is rooted deep in unconscious sources, but is also represented in superficial practices and behavioural codes. Indeed, in one way culture has to be mundane as it is reproduced in daily interaction. Because organizations *are* social organisms (not mechanisms) the whole is present in the parts and symbolic events become microcosms of the whole—which is why we often learn what organizations are 'really like' from trivial-sounding incidents.

Classifying cultures?

An initial way of elaborating and exploring the cultures of different organizations is to classify them into types. For example, we saw the polar-opposite types that Kanter developed above, and there have been a number of other such frameworks. One very influential classification scheme, developed by Charles Handy (1986), distinguishes three types of culture stabilized in large enterprises.

1. *Role culture.* This is very similar to the classic Weberian bureaucracy, or to Burns's idea of the mechanistic organization (described in Chapters 12 and 13). Role cultures are highly formalized, they abound with regulations and paperwork, and relations between members are dominated by authority and the hierarchy. A strict division of labour fragments work so that people tend to be reluctant to take on wider responsibilities. Instead, they become obsessed with fulfilling narrow job definitions. Such cultures have the strong disadvantage of being resistant to change, and like many bureaucracies have the tendency to lose sight of their basic objectives and to become preoccupied with day-to-day administration. On the other hand, the tight control of resources is easier under these kinds of culture; indeed, it is what they are intended for.

2. *Task culture.* This is the opposite of the role culture, and similar to Burns's organic type of organization. Task cultures preserve a strong sense of the basic mission of the

organization. They tend to be designed along product-based lines, with the various divisions and groups in the organization devoted to forms of tangible output. Team working is the basis on which jobs are organized; project teams draw on the specialisms needed for task performance, breaking down rigid structures of hierarchy and function. Members' loyalties tend to be oriented towards the work rather than towards formal rules. Obvious advantages of the task culture are that it fosters creativity and is readily adaptable to high-quality services and products. The other side of the coin is that such cultures can be expensive to operate. The control of overheads and the centralization of resources tends to be difficult.

3. *Power culture.* This occurs in organizations with a single power source, which may be an individual or a corporate group. Policy and strategic decisions are centralized, so that a power culture reflects the web of influence that emanates from the figurehead personality or clique. The key power-holders rule through their control of rewards (appointments, promotions, etc.); subordinates defer to power-holders and attempt to anticipate their wishes and attract their attention. Power-holders themselves often adopt idiosyncratic styles of management; things get done by the boss letting subordinates 'into his thinking'. Power structures have the advantage that plans can be formulated and decisions taken swiftly with a single control centre, and the leadership can provide inspiration to sustain a strong culture. On the other hand, if such organizations go wrong, they can go very badly wrong because they depend on the skills and integrity of individuals. Also, a company with a power culture may suffer a crisis of succession when the leadership retires or moves on. This is because central power is jealously guarded and little provision is made for a new generation to take over.

Handy points out in addition that these cultural types are usually tied to particular kinds of organization structure and design. The role culture tends to be linked to the typical pyramid-shaped bureaucratic structure, with formal divisions between functional groups and hierarchical levels. The task structure is associated with flexible matrix structures of management. These contain strong lateral as well as vertical linkages, and groups with overlapping membership. And, finally, the power culture maps on to a web-like communications structure, with the dominant group at the centre and lines of authority radiating out to functional groups and personnel.

The limits of classification Classifications like Handy's can be very useful in analysing real-life organizations; they show us what to look for and highlight key features of the culture. This is especially true if we can find organizations which fit very closely the role, task, and power culture types. What is more likely is that cultures will be a complex mix of types, although even then it may still be possible to see in the organizational culture some of the key dimensions of the classification. For example, the culture of the Wall Street investment banks that Lewis described in *Liar's Poker* could be seen as a mix of two of Handy's types—there was certainly a strong strain of the power culture in a firm like Saloman Brothers, but Lewis (a bond salesman himself) described the traders and salesmen as being basically good at their jobs, so an element of task culture was present as well. The ICI culture (the one that John Harvey-Jones was intent on changing) was also a mix of types. In the lack of strategic direction one might detect a role culture, and the divisions may have been run as power cultures, while power was notably absent from the corporate centre.

Nevertheless, attempts to classify organizational cultures have their limitations. Once a category system is imposed, the diversity of types is constrained and this tends to defeat the purpose of cultural analysis. For example, Handy's different cultural types seem to add very little to the account that was provided by *structure*. The idea of a power culture does have some very interesting aspects and dimensions; but it is hard to see that role and task cultures add much more than, for example, Burns was able to do with his concepts of mechanistic and organic structures. On the other hand, the cultural types that Kanter (1984) developed seem less open to this criticism—probably because they did not imply a fixed classification scheme. Inferiority versus success, age versus youth and so on represented an open-ended set of types that could go on being elaborated.

Culture refers to the unique constellation of beliefs and norms found in each organization, while the categories of a classification scheme are a set of descriptive stereotypes; in themselves they provide little basis for linking different themes and variables. Nor are they particularly sensitive to the symbolic and interpretive aspects of culture. Better approaches focus on actual organizations, attempt to explain how particular cultures arise and are sustained, and link culture to other central organizational processes like power, leadership and the rewards system.

Evaluating concepts of culture

There can be little doubt that cultural analysis has opened up new ways of both understanding and managing organizations. Our understanding of organizations has often been blinkered by the tendency to see our own lives, in the modern science-dominated world, as reasoned and logical, not acted out in dramas, myths and legends. These we associate with ancient history or distant societies. But, of course, people in all societies think of their own behaviour as 'normal' and find it difficult to see the 'magical' elements in daily life. This is doubly true of organizations where conventional theory has long emphasized *rationality*. The primacy of the belief in formal structures and procedures has meant that subjective and symbolic dimensions have tended to be ignored or pushed to the periphery.

Yet cultural analysis brings to centre stage a rich vein of behaviours, and stands on its head much of the conventional wisdom about organizations. Stories, legends and rituals are not insignificant; nor are they 'not supposed' to be there. They are key elements of organizational functioning, and in some cases may actually serve more important objectives than formal decision-making. The cultural emphasis teaches us to think more broadly about organizations and the astonishing variety of value and belief systems, many of which appear to 'work' quite well for the given organization.

Culture also represents one of the few concepts that has had a genuine impact on management thinking. After the many past failures and false dawns of management theory, people at the highest levels in corporations appear satisfied that culture provides at least a partial answer to the perennial question of what accounts for business success. Indeed, it is mistaken to imagine that business has simply borrowed or taken over culture from the social sciences. To a large extent the interest in values and symbolism has developed along its own path in the business world. In taking these concepts over, corporations and management writers have refashioned them. Explicit statements of corporate missions show how companies are reinventing themselves out of the need to compete at new levels.

Conflicting views of culture

However, we need to consider in more depth the different ways in which 'culture' has been used in organization study—in particular the difference between the concern to explain and describe cultural processes, and the managerial interest in relating culture to organizational performance. For example, Wilson and Rosenfeld (1990, p. 233) distinguish two schools of thought on culture, which they call the analytical and the applicable. The analytical school stresses the context and history of the organization and the way that culture acts as a socializing force, controlling the behaviour of members. This approach is concerned with all levels of the organization and with group and informal processes. The applicable school, on the other hand, views culture in terms of commitment to central goals and as a means of managing successful organizational change.

Smircich (1983) also distinguishes a managerial from an analytic approach. The former she criticizes as being a version of systems theory, which views strong internal cultures as means of adapting the organization to external market uncertainties. She argues that treating culture in this way, as a strategy for change, simply means that it will go the way of other failed concepts.

The notion of 'corporate culture' runs the risk of being as disappointing a managerial tool as the more technical and quantitative tools that were faddish in the 1970s. Those of a skeptical nature may also question the extent to which the term corporate culture refers to anything more than an ideology cultivated by management for the purpose of control and legitimation of activity.

In contrast to this, she favours deeper sociological and psychological approaches. Here culture is viewed as a network of interpretations and meanings; organizations are perceived as social constructions, not planned around formal goals, but constituted in interaction around symbols and other expressive representations. Crude functionalism—the view that 'strong cultures' lead to business success—likewise is replaced by a view of culture as a sense-making device, or as a set of practices and understandings for dealing with problems faced in common. For Smircich culture becomes a 'root metaphor'. Organizations are seen not as 'like' cultures or as 'having' a culture, but as *being* cultures. Culture is not an attribute; culture is what an organization *is*: 'organizations are expressive forms, manifestations of human consciousness'.

Corporate culture or corporate image?

These perspectives are not just different ways of looking at the same thing. They are contrasting and conflicting viewpoints. Much of what is rather loosely called 'corporate culture' is really a kind of image of the organization which top management would like to project. This is reflected in the research methods often adopted in this area. Frequently, these consist merely of trawling senior management opinion in a sample of organizations, while explicitly excluding any systematic data from other employees (e.g. Deal and Kennedy, 1982; Child and Smith, 1987). The dangers of an élitist version of culture creeping in are very evident here. And the contrast to the original, anthropological idea of culture, as the gradual emergence of social beliefs and practices in a community of people, could not be greater.

The image of the organization differs according to where you view it from. Many of the 'mission statements' coming out of corporations reflect the official version of culture, which may or may not be the same as the real culture. In this sense, several writers have highlighted the negative faces of culture—the power vacuum at the centre of ICI that Pettigrew revealed, and the cultures of age and inferiority from Kanter. These are certainly not images fashioned by companies to promote themselves, and we might be more inclined to believe them for that reason. Even in companies with a strong ethos of caring for people, the social distance between senior management and shopfloor reality can be very wide. Down among the workforce a culture of employee welfare (team working, productivity through people) may be diluted to a vague feeling of the company as a 'good employer'.

Crucially, the idea of a single corporate culture ignores the *diversity* of groups and interests within the boundaries of the organization. A number of accounts have been at pains to stress organizational culture not as a monolithic concept, but as encompassing the idea of multiple cultures. Organizations are made up of different occupations and professions, different social classes and sexes, and are perhaps spread over different geographical areas. All these can form the basis of distinctive sub-cultures and counter-cultures that compete to define the reality of the organization.

This kind of challenge from below was well illustrated in a giant pharmaceuticals company. Its corporate creed was expressed as a series of statements that started with the ethical (duty to customers, the environment) and proceeded lastly to the economic (profit). The standing joke among employees was that if you wanted to know the company's real creed, simply reverse the order.

Managing culture?

The central problem, then, is whether organizational cultures are indeed 'manageable'. Cultures are hardly planned or predictable; they are the natural products of social interaction, and evolve and emerge over time, the residue of countless events and actions. So is it valid to allow such a notion of culture to give way to a version of managed consensus?

Some management writers certainly provide more sociologically informed accounts of culture. Pettigrew, for example, believes that cultures can be shaped to suit strategic ends, but he is not referring to any kind of corporate brainwashing. What he has in mind is the capacity of organizations to transform themselves from within. He seeks to develop comprehensive models of organizational change that show cultures adapting and being enacted at the level of key symbols by powerful organizational members. Such accounts centre on how shared beliefs interact with the political process, and with new forms of leadership that provide a 'transforming vision'. Morgan (1997) is another writer not averse in principle to tackling managerial problems, but who stresses that this must be combined with a full awareness of the subtleties of culture. Morgan warns against managers rushing to find ways of managing culture and advocates the building up of a sense of commitment among enterprise members, and via that the desired corporate ethos.

Managers can influence the evolution of culture by being aware of the symbolic consequences of their actions and by attempting to foster desired values. But they can never control culture in the sense that many management writers advocate. . . . An understanding of organizations as cultures opens our eyes to many crucial insights that elude other metaphors, but they do not always provide the easy recipe for solving managerial problems that many managers and management writers hope for. (p. 152)

Even accepting these strictures, however, there still exists a tension between the practical goals of management and those of the social scientist trying to understand organizational life. Martin (1985), for example, distinguishes a pragmatic and a purist approach. Some pragmatists are crudely prescriptive, others more subtle, but in the end they see culture as the key to employee commitment and believe that it must be managed. Purists, on the other hand, regard culture as unmanageable by definition; they are sceptical about claims of fundamental cultural changes being managed. Culture is a way of endowing experience with meaning, and any ideas of managing it are both naive and unethical.

Certainly for managers there are strong reasons for wanting to simplify cultural processes. Values of progress and innovation represent the high ground of corporate achievement, and managers not unnaturally want to stake out a claim in this area. There are strong reasons for wanting to identify with programmes of cultural innovation, and this may mean 'objectifying' the recipes for change. To be fair, the more astute management writers are in no way guilty of crudely simplifying culture. But even here there can be tendencies to confuse culture with the images of themselves that corporations seek to promote, or to overemphasize the manipulation of the symbolic elements of organization life.

As a final critical comment, this raises the issue that even if culture can be managed is this necessarily a good thing? Here Willmott (1993) has fashioned a tough challenge to what he calls 'corporate culturalism'. This is the tendency—associated with writers like Deal and Kennedy and Tom Peters—for culture to be promoted as a device for increasing organizational competitiveness. As we saw above, the notion that 'strong' cultures can be developed, which would enhance employee commitment and through that organizational performance, has been very influential. Corporate culturalism is not just a simple fad; it is 'endorsed by a sufficient number of leading management gurus, corporate executives and state mandarins to ensure more than passing influence upon management theory and practice' (p. 516). It has materially affected work in that its basic ideas have been incorporated into change programmes for flexibility, customer care, total quality, and so on. Willmott sees culturalism as a type of organizational rhetoric that attempts to develop self-regulating forms of worker control. This in turn is an element in the historic shift—which we discussed earlier in the book in Chapter 12— identified with arguments about the 'iron cage' of bureaucratic rationality and new 'insidious' forms of power in the post-Fordist economy and society. In this sense, Willmott argues, the background to corporate culturalism is the shift from the direct control of Fordism, towards new work forms that demand control of employee subjectivity and motivation. These seek to develop 'monocultures' which exclude dissent and different forms of cultural expression (sub-cultures or counter-cultures) and only tolerate expressions of commitment to management goals. Thus organizational control is extended by 'colonizing the affective domain' and by promoting a 'monolithic structure of feeling and thought' (p. 517).

Conclusion

Culture spans the range of management thinking, and organizational culture has been one of the most enduring buzzwords of popular management. Yet a concern with culture has also characterized some of the deepest thinking and most influential figures in management theory. Why? What is the appeal of the concept?

Organizational culture is apparently unifying, and this strongly appeals to management's concern with projecting an image of the organization as a community of interests. Also the concept itself promotes an awareness of other industrial and national cultures (Japan, the Pacific Rim) that seem to have been particularly successful in growing innovative work systems. Perhaps most importantly, culture penetrates to the essence of an organization—it is almost analogous with the concept of personality in relation to the individual—and this acute sense of what an organization is—its mission, core values—seems to have become a necessary asset of the modern company. In highly competitive and brand-conscious times, a clear statement of the image and values of a company is now deemed an essential part of its strategic apparatus.

These 'subjective' elements are broadly in harmony with other aspects of current management thinking. Many of the new objectives that organizations have embraced— such as commitments to quality and the customer—are deeply embedded in organizational values. Unlike traditional financial or output goals, something like customer care is all about commitment and the detail of employee behaviour, not something that can be forced on employees or even easily measured.

That said, there are also manifest limits to the extent to which 'culture' can be appropriated within an organizational framework. An organization may appear to have a uni-fying or organic culture, but this may merely be the view from the top. From other van-tage points—from the shop or office floor, the middle and junior strata of management, the different employed professions—the scene may appear more fragmented. What they see may be a set of occupational identities and sub-cultures that may even be the basis of resistance. Relatedly, there is the vexed question of whether or not organizational culture can be managed. Academics interested in understanding and analysing culture tend to say no. On the other hand, the question does not go away, as there are consid-erable rewards for harnessing these potent social forces to corporate goals. While there may be no definitive answer to these questions, the critical and the managerial sides of the debate inform and renew each other, so it remains important to explore both.

More generally, because of the consensual nature of culture, resistance from below and conflict between different groups can be overlooked or played down. But writers like Pettigrew, Morgan, and Kanter, who have taken the cultural perspective a large step forward, have sought to combine the emphasis on shared meanings with precisely such concerns, namely those of power processes in organizations. Power, though, is an issue in its own right, and it is to this we turn in the next chapter.

Study questions for Chapter 15

1 What is the relationship between organization culture and other key organizational concepts: structure, leadership, change, innovation?

2 'If organizational change is to be real change, it has to happen at the level of culture.' Discuss.

3 How does an awareness of other industrial cultures enrich our understanding of the culture concept?

4 How are organization cultures rooted in the symbolic aspects of everyday life?

5 Why is it important to try to classify organization cultures, and what are the limits of classification?

6 Is organization culture just another term for corporate image?

7 How do you reconcile the view of culture as a unifying force in organizations with the idea of organizational sub-cultures and counter-cultures?

Further reading

Administrative Science Quarterly, Special Issue: 'Organization Culture', 28/3, Sept. 1983.

Frost, P. J., Moore, L. F., Louis, M. R., Lundberg, C. C., and Martin, J. (eds.) (1985) *Organizational Culture*. Beverly Hills: Sage.

—— Reis, M., Lundberg, C. C., and Martin, J. (eds.) (1991) *Reframing Organizational Culture*. Newbury Park, Calif.: Sage.

Hassard, J. and Pym, D. (eds.) (1990) *The Theory and Philosophy of Organizations*. London: Routledge.

Journal of Management Studies, Special Issue: 'Organizational Culture and Control', G. Hofstede (ed.) 23/3, May 1986.

Pettigrew, A. M. (1979), 'On studying organizational cultures', *Administrative Science Quarterly*, 24/4: 570–81.

—— (1985) 'Culture and politics in strategic decision making and change', in J. M. Pennings (ed.) *Strategic Decision Making in Complex Organizations*. San Francisco: Jossey Bass.

Reed, M. and Hughes, M. (eds.) (1992) *Rethinking Organization*. London: Sage.

Sackman, S. A. (1991) *Cultural Knowledge in Organizations*. Newbury Park, Calif.: Sage.

Schein, E. F. (1985) *Organizational Culture and Leadership*. San Francisco: Jossey Bass.

16 Power and Organizations

Summary points and learning objectives

By the end of this chapter you will be able to:

- evaluate the *strengths* of the power perspective: its advantages over rationalist approaches, its intrinsic appeal as interesting, positive, and realistic;
- understand power as a *theoretical concept*: Lukes' three faces of power, the nature of organizational power;
- identify the *power resources* that organizational players possess;
- conceive of the organization as a *political arena* and managerial decision-making as a political process;
- understand how *organizational settings* (with structured conflict, hierarchy, career competition) engender power processes;
- understand the power game in terms of the *strategies and tactics* of power.

Introduction

As we saw in Chapter 15, the interest in the organizational culture in many ways represented a challenge to managerialist or systems theories that view organizations as sites of rational decision-making and the attainment of business goals. Over the past decade or so another aspect of organizational theory has also been inspired by dissatisfaction with conventional approaches. This is the concern with organizational power.

The study of power in organizations can present problems. Power, as we will see, is a rather slippery concept, difficult to pin down and define. Power is also one of the major concerns of social theorists, and organizational power (which does have its own distinctive forms) inevitably gets mixed up with the forms of power that occur in wider society. And, as well as understanding the actual arguments, there can be problems in appreciating what point there is in discussing managerial activity in these terms. Managerial work is typically thought of in terms of decisions made on the basis of training and experience (the rationalist view). Within organizations 'politics' is often regarded with great distaste, as the main barrier to getting on with the job. Thus an approach which takes this activity from the margins and places it at the focus of attention—which seems to see organizational activity as nothing other than politics—might seem perverse and hard to accept.

Bacharach and Lawler (1980, p. 1) lead us into the topic of power by suggesting that it occupies the middle ground between two major schools of thought—the contrasting schools of managerial/systems theory and conflict or radical theory. From our discussion in previous chapters this view may seem rather oversimplified. For their part, as we saw in Chapter 13, the managerialists were never quite so naive as to believe that organizations are purely rational and consensual entities. Even the early theorists had a practitioner's eye for problems of workers' resistance, and certainly more recent theory has been able to incorporate issues of conflict within management. Conversely, as seen in Chapter 12, the radical approach obviously does not imagine that conflict in organizations boils over into class struggle, nor does it ignore the fact that organizational life is partly about co-operation. Even Marxist theory is quite clear about the two sides of capitalist enterprise: production happens at the same time as economic exploitation. However, the approach taken by Bacharach and Lawler is at least helpful in setting out the scene. It is useful to look at power as a concept which retains aspects of both the managerialist and radical approaches—power as a radical idea but applied in the context of managerial decision-making. In this sense Bacharach and Lawler suggest a view of organizations as 'politically negotiated orders'.

Adopting this view, we can observe organizational actors in their daily transactions, perpetually bargaining, repeatedly forming and reforming coalitions, and constantly availing themselves of influence and tactics . . . politics in organizations involve the tactical use of power to retain or obtain control of real or symbolic resources. In describing the processes of organizations as political acts, we are not making a moral judgement; we are simply making an observation about a process. (Bacharach and Lawler, 1980, pp. 1–2)

Thus the preoccupation with rationalistic approaches and formal management tasks tends to mean the neglect of processes outside the authority structure. These processes of power and conflict are crucial in shaping managerial activity. We saw in Chapter 13 that formal organization structures invariably contain the means for resolving conflict. However, to represent conflict merely as something that has to be resolved is to fail to explain it in its own right.

In this sense, organizations may be thought of as compromising a dual reality. On one level there is a set of relationships which represent the organization as an *operating system*—these would include the actions of managers in problem-solving, as well as the view of organizations as systems for rational goal attainment. But there is also a parallel system based on the internal *struggle for power*. Much informal managerial activity—the deals and favours that are inevitably a part of real life in organizations—would be included here, as would be the pursuit of self-interest and the defence of departmental interests against other conflicting groups. In this vein, Burns (1969) has referred to organizations as 'plural social systems'.

Business enterprises are cooperative instrumental systems assembled out of the usable attributes of people. They are also places in which people compete for advancement. Thus, members of a business concern are at one and the same time cooperators in a common enterprise and rivals for the material and tangible rewards of successful competition with each other. The hierarchical order of rank and power, realized in the organization chart, which prevails in all organizations is both a control system and a career ladder. (p. 232)

The fact that the political side of organizations has been largely ignored until quite recently, plus the suggestion that power in organizations can actually be the decisive factor in decision-making, has meant that organizational politics is increasingly regarded as a key explanation of managerial behaviour.

Given such a background, a number of fairly straightforward reasons for wanting to study organizational power suggest themselves.

Power is interesting At the risk of seeming trite, the role of power in human affairs has always been intrinsically interesting. To watch a power struggle develop between protagonists can be a fascinating experience. Power-play focuses on the *differences* between individuals and groups, the variety of goals and interests. The power game is also by definition open-ended. Part of its fascination is that we can never be entirely sure about the outcome. No protagonist ever entered the arena in the certainty of losing; nor is there any position so superior that it might not be overturned by subtle tactics.

Power is positive Though 'politicking' in organizations may be resented, power is also about the creative actions of people and the possibilities for organizational change. Anyone who knows organizations knows that little happens unless some powerful group is behind a particular course of action, and that political manoeuvring is always needed to get change under way. The power perspective thus reinforces the importance of managerial skills. It paints a dramatic and perhaps even flattering picture of managers as power-brokers and wheeler-dealers. The Machiavellian image means that power (like culture) is an academic concept of great interest to management audiences.

Power is realistic Power is about how organizations 'really' operate. Often when some course of action is being publicly announced or explained, the impression is given that the decision was consensual, or that the organization had somehow 'arrived at' the most sensible course of action. But in reality we frequently suspect that the 'explanation' is at least partly justification—that a power-process was involved behind the scenes and that the 'decision' was in fact the outcome of a struggle. Decision-making is thus never purely rational or consensual; power is often the underlying reality.

The concept of power

The concept of power has always proved difficult to define, even though a common-sense grasp of the term seems easy enough. This is partly because the activity being described is itself dynamic and complex. For example, suppose someone has been influenced to follow a course of action against their original inclination. Has power been exercised over them? The answer might be yes, if their compliance was obtained with the use of threats, but no, if the advantages of a particular course of action of which they were unaware had simply been pointed out to them. However, if they were persuaded by force of argument, then it might be quite difficult to determine whether or not power had been used. It would depend upon exactly how aggressively the case was put: whether threats were implied or whether the case was merely stated enthusiastically.

The complex nature of these types of behaviour is reflected in the number of terms similar to power, such as authority, control, and influence, which are often used interchangeably in normal conversation. In social science analysis, however, one would want to know how precisely they differ from the notion of power. Do the different terms refer to types of power, or are they quite separate forms of behaviour?

The framework for the sociology of power, originally set out by Weber, stressed the ambiguous nature of the concept. For Weber power represented the *potential* to act in certain ways. Weber was interested in the way power could most often be effective when used as a threat rather than actually being exercised. Thus he spoke of the probability or chance of groups or individuals prevailing over others: 'We understand by "power" the chance of a man or a number of men to realize their own will in a communal action even against the resistance of others who are participating in the action' (Weber, 1970, p. 180). We can also see that Weber's definition stressed power as a *collective* phenomenon. This use of the term is certainly appropriate within organizations, where groups of one kind or another—teams, departments, divisions—typically exercise power as the product of collective and social relationships. Even where power appears to be exercised by an individual, its true basis often lies in some group or collectivity. The power of managers, for example, represents a mandate from the legal owners of the firm and is exercised on their behalf.

Lukes and the three faces of power

Since the pioneering work of Weber, a number of writers have developed different viewpoints on the operation of social power. One of the most widely influential models is that of Steven Lukes (1974). Lukes offers not so much a theory of power, or a distinctive approach in its own right, as a framework within which other major approaches can be located, and which makes sense of them in relation to each other. He builds a dimension of 'radicalness' into his account, arguing that three major perspectives—or, as he puts it, 'faces of power'—provide understandings that get increasingly closer to the real roots of power in society.

The first face of power, perhaps the simplest, rests on an account of actual power behaviour. In an early attempt the political scientist Robert Dahl (1957) argued that a common-sense definition along the following lines was a useful starting point: 'A has power over B to the extent that he can get B to do something that B would otherwise not do.' This raised the issue of *resistance* on the part of B, because his wishes are being overridden, and hence of *conflict* between A and B. Certainly for Dahl, and many others, the acid test of a power relationship was the existence of this observable, behavioural conflict as evidence of a clash of interests between persons or groups.

In addition, though, in order to arrive at the root causes of power we need to take account of behaviour that, in a sense, does not take place. According to Bachrach and Baratz (1962), this 'other face of power' reflects the ability of powerful groups to prevent various options or choices from even being considered. The original view expressed by Dahl—that power is reflected in the actions of the powerful—looked only at actual decisions and the groups which prevailed over them, so that even those who are overruled will still take part in the decision-making process. But what of the groups which are never admitted to the decision arena in the first place? Bachrach and Baratz argued that real power in this sense is exercised by suppressing their preferences. Thus, power in the form of 'non-decision-making' does not necessarily involve resistance or overt conflict at all. Indeed, the fact that those under power are never permitted to resist, or to engage in conflict, is a measure of the degree of power exercised over them.

Lukes then took the argument even further, saying that we need a fully radical view of power. This would include power that is exercised by preventing people from forming conscious preferences or choices. Such a type of power might apply, for example, to the way in which the social horizons of many working-class people are narrowed and constrained by education and upbringing. They perceive that certain ambitions and aspirations are simply 'not for them'—which means that they may never challenge the economic position of the middle and upper classes. This formed the basis of Lukes's 'three-dimensional view of power'. The first dimension was the most obvious one, power observable in the clash of interests between decision-makers (as stressed by Dahl). The second referred to the interests of certain groups being excluded from a particular bargaining arena (as in Bachrach and Baratz). The third, or radical, dimension referred to groups under power never being able to consciously formulate their real interests.

Organizational power

The view of power that results from an analysis like Lukes's is essentially structural. His 'radical face' of power reflects a dominant set of interests, a sovereign authority, that is somehow imposed on the majority. However, as Bacharach and Lawler (1980, p. 30) have argued, 'while authority may be a prime source of control, influence is the dynamic aspect of power and may be the ultimate source of change'. In this sense, an emphasis on power processes, such as influence and the strategies and tactics of political action, lead directly to accounts of organizational power, and have always been of more interest when explaining managerial interaction.

To begin with we need to understand the different terms related to power, and to focus on the types of power that are found in organizations. If we consider the amount of resistance offered by those under power, and also the strength of the sanctions brought to bear by those in power, then the different types of power can be seen to fall within a continuum. This represents the extent of conflict between the interests of the 'in-power' group and the 'under-power' group (Figure 16.1). As the figure shows, power covers a very broad range of behaviours, from almost pure agreement to the resort to violence. The topic of this chapter, organizational power, clearly applies to a much narrower band of activities. Forms of violent coercion would need to be left out when speaking of power in organizations—or at least power in the kinds of commercial and public sector organization we are most familiar with.

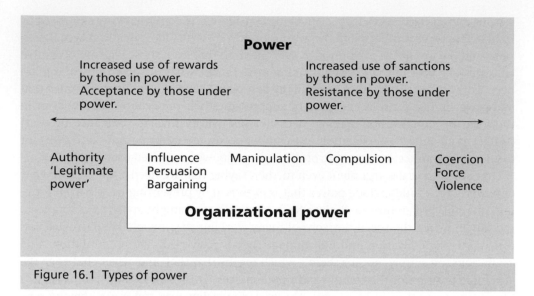

Figure 16.1 Types of power

In addition, the concept of authority overlaps with that of power, and the two terms can be quite ambiguously related. As we saw in Chapter 12, Weber regarded authority, in the sense of power accepted as legitimate by the under-group, as being of vital importance for maintaining social order; and within organizations authority remains the basis of formal control. Yet if authority were *purely* consensual, it is doubtful whether we would speak of power being exercised. However, authority is nearly always backed up by sanctions, so the resort to power remains a choice for the group in authority. Thus the other dimensions of power, discussed by Bachrach and Baratz and by Lukes, can be placed in the same category as authority—even though these authors make the point that the agreement of the under-group is hardly freely given.

Levels of power

It is also possible to suggest another way of looking at the kinds of power found in organizations, namely the different 'levels' on which power is constituted. Three main levels of analysis can be distinguished: processual, institutional, and organizational. The first, processual power, focuses on the 'micropolitics' of organizational life, and stresses power as negotiation and bargaining. The level of analysis is that of the 'lateral' relations between managerial interest groups, and the basis of explanation is *strategic*. Power is a dynamic phenomenon originating 'in the process' of daily interaction. The 'enactment' of rules is stressed. In other words, the emphasis is not on concrete power resources that people possess, but on how these resources are employed in the power game. It cannot be assumed, for instance, that people in power can simply 'give orders'; in reality they may use their position but only backed up by strategic action. A true processual analysis should also be longitudinal, studying power processes as they emerge over time. Research that does this (e.g. Pettigrew, 1973, 1985) is able to show how power positions reflect rich patterns of past alliances between groups.

At the other extreme, the institutional perspective sees managerial power resting on external social and economic structures, so that power is explained as being *mandated* to the organization. Here, for example, Willmott (1987) has stressed that wider economic structures—class, ownership, the state—create beliefs about the inevitability of managerial authority. In this sense, managers can draw on a set of institutionally produced rules when they seek to exercise power, such as cultural beliefs about the 'right to manage'. Another institutional factor that has attracted recent attention is that of *gender*. In the past a 'desexualized' model of the organization has often been assumed, because the rationalist view has tended to be accepted. Rational principles of control, even if oppressive, were regarded as being even-handed. However, many are now insisting that bureaucratic procedures are actually deeply imbued with sex-biased values, and that formal rationality itself is part of the ideological construct of 'maleness'. It is suggested that there are strong links between the formalist treatment of issues like promotion, and practices that favour the advancement of men (Hearn *et al.*, 1989). Similarly, the attitudes of organizational 'gatekeepers'—those who control access to training and entry into jobs, like personnel officers—have been identified as crucial factors in discrimination (Crompton and Jones, 1984).

These two levels of analysis—process and institution—have produced a dualist view of power. We saw a similar contrast in Foucault's link between disciplinary and traditional power. Others have linked action and structure, i.e. whether we take a view of social life constructed by individual agents, or one that depicts people as the objects of external constraints (Giddens, 1984). Reflected in these dichotomies is the deepest dilemma in social science, that of the relationship between the individual and the social; and corresponding problems are created for explaining power in these terms.

By themselves the processual and institutional views can appear unsatisfactory. The processual approach often seems to overstate the importance of power-play and to produce an exaggerated sense of choice. The institutional approach, on the other hand, can appear to be too fixed and deterministic; if power rests on structures external to the organization, deviance from those structures or forms of resistance become difficult to account for. What is obviously needed is a framework that brings the two together, and indeed this has been argued for in a number of debates (Reed, 1985). But attempts at a 'unified' account have also run into difficulties. The processual and institutional views tend to be incompatible: any stress on the spontaneous qualities of action finds it hard to take account of wider constraints, while the emphasis on structural factors has little sympathy for the detail of human strategies and motives. Various ways out of the 'structure and action' dilemma have been proposed. Hales (1988) argues that we need a level of analysis 'between something as specific as individual action and something as broad as capitalist production relations'.

This level of analysis stresses the organization's own power system, and the *hierarchy* as a means of reproducing power. A number of types of hierarchical relationship are pertinent here. For example, organizations are frequently observed to have *dominant beliefs*, the values and knowledge that set the 'rules of the game' and shape organizational priorities and solutions. These may reflect the interests of a ruling function (marketing or accounting, say) or dominant beliefs articulated around the interests of strategic groups, the senior managerial coalitions that hold real power. Furthermore, organizational *selection* is crucial as an instrument by which such strategic groups perpetuate themselves. Those in authority select others who will sustain the existing power structure. Some writers have doubted that selection can be effective as a power mechanism because of the impossibility of defining 'managerial qualities' (Armstrong, 1989). However, the lack of 'objective' criteria does not make selection ineffective. Selection rules are necessarily ambiguous and intangible; the point is that those with the power to choose know what *they mean*, even if the criteria are vague.

The organizational level, then, represents a kind of third way, between the strategic and the structural; and the three levels of analysis suggest how organizational hierarchies transmit power between institutional interests and the rules and resources governing action. In the final sections of the chapter, however, we need to return to one particular level: the processual. By far the strongest interest has been shown in this aspect, and in a sense 'organizational power' has come to mean the lateral relations within management and the specific power strategies that are used. Nor is the reason hard to find: the processual perspective has effectively opposed static systems models and emphasized power as a mobilizing force in organizational change.

The organization as a political system

The concern with power in organizations includes, first and foremost, an emphasis on *process* rather than structure. Although hierarchical position is one important power resource, it is not accepted that real power necessarily mirrors the formal hierarchy. Furthermore, managerial decision-making is seen as a *political* activity. People never suspend the pursuit of individual interests, nor cease to identify with the sectional loyalties which support them. So there are practical reasons for studying these political processes, since anyone who is to prosper, or even survive, in organizations must be able to bargain effectively for a share of resources. In short, they need to be equipped to play the game of organizational politics.

Thus, while power can be seen in terms of power *over* subordinates, the emphasis here is on the *use* of power and the range of tactics that people employ. This does not always mean the pursuit of career and self-interest. There is also a vitally important sense in which this power struggle and the broader attainment of organizational goals actually overlap and mutually support each other. It reflects management's responsibility for organizational development, and for designing an organization structure which is competent to meet a changing environment. Given the tendency of all institutions to resist change and settle into a routine, decision-makers in the real world often have their hands full merely getting organizations started towards change. Yet organizations must be made to adapt if they are to survive and prosper. It is only by deploying power that managers can intervene in the change process and guide their organizations along desired paths. First, though, we need to know something of the power resources that different groups are able to draw upon and about the organizational arena in which power is exercised.

Power resources

The social psychologists French and Raven, in a now-classic study (1959), developed a scheme of five categories of power, which reflected the different bases or resources that power holders rely upon. They identified reward, coercive, legitimate, referent and expert power.

Reward power depends upon the ability of the power-wielder to confer valued material rewards, such as promotions or increases in pay or responsibility. *Coercive power* is the reverse side of this coin, in the sense that those who have the power to reward usually also have the power to punish. Thus coercive power might refer to the ability to demote or to withhold other rewards. In both cases, it is the desire for valued rewards or the fear of having them withheld that ensures the obedience of those under power. *Legitimate power* is identical with authority, and depends upon the belief of individuals in the right of senior people to hold their positions, and their consequent willingness to accept the power-holder. *Referent power* is based on the 'charisma' of the power-holder. Here the person under power desires to identify with these personal qualities, and gains satisfaction from being an accepted follower. Lastly, *expert power* rests on the skills or expertise of the person holding power. Unlike the others, this type of power is usually highly specific and limited to the particular area in which the expert is trained and qualified.

There are, however, certain defects in the French and Raven scheme. Their reward and coercive forms of power are not in fact power resources in themselves—they merely describe the actions of people who have other power resources. So, for example, senior managers with formal positions in the organizational hierarchy (legitimate power) can confer or withhold promotions. In addition, their legitimate and referent forms of power are taken directly from Weber's typology of authority, although without the addition of his third type, namely traditional authority (see Chapter 12). Still, French and Raven's approach does serve to emphasize the fact that within organizations people can call upon a range of different bases of power and influence.

Although hierarchical rank—legitimate power—is obviously a crucial power resource, when we consider power as a political process the focus of interest shifts to the resources that people can mobilize irrespective of their official positions. Here expertise, or French and Raven's expert power, represents an important power resource. Professionals, technical experts and tradespeople, who are employed in organizations for their specific skills, derive power from the fact that the organization depends upon that skilled work being performed. The 'expert power' of the professional or the tradesperson very frequently comes into conflict with formal authority. In the long run this is a struggle for control in which experts are unlikely to prevail. The organization is still the employer and retains the ultimate power to hire and fire. Experts are also self-defeating in certain respects—it is often part of the expert's job to streamline and automate operations, and thereby to eliminate the need for his or her own skill. However, while there is innovation and growth in an organization expert power is enhanced, and in these kinds of circumstance experts can be highly influential, albeit in an informal way.

Power dependency

An attempt to explain power in more universal terms involves the twin concepts of *uncertainty* and *dependency*—ideas which have been developed most fully by Hickson *et al.* (1971) in their 'strategic contingencies' theory of power. Uncertainty for an organization stems from its system of operations (the technology and work organization) and from the environment. Reducing the uncertainty of operations is vital for management, and groups of employees who 'cope with uncertainty' gain influence and power. The more strategic the form of uncertainty for a particular organization, the more powerful will the group which controls it become. Therefore organizations become heavily dependent on the groups which cope with central areas of uncertainty. For example, Crozier (1964) has shown how skilled workers were able to exploit a source of residual uncertainty in an otherwise routine production system. Machine breakdowns were the only major contingency that disrupted operations. The organization was thus dependent on the maintenance crews which dealt with breakdowns, which enabled these workers to enhance their status and rewards.

Another important study using this approach is Pettigrew's *The Politics of Organizational Decision-Making* (1973). This was based on an expanding computer system in a retailing organization, and examined the impact of this huge new resource on organizational politics. The first computer was installed in the 1950s, when commercial data-processing was a very uncertain business. Skills of a high order were involved, and the company itself was anxious to get the system working due to a rapid expansion in their volume of business. All these factors made the organization heavily dependent on the group of programmers in charge of the installation, and this was reflected in the programmers' total control of computer operations—a clear example of expert power. However, the programmers simply did not fit into the organization. It was traditional and bureaucratic, while the programmers were university graduates who behaved and dressed casually, and who worked outside normal hours setting up the installation. They came to regard the firm's employees as dull and authoritarian, while the employees regarded the programmers as arrogant and immature. The very powerful antipathy between the two groups put paid to the programmers ever becoming an integral part of the organization; and senior management in particular greatly resented having to rely upon the programmers' skills. Pettigrew charts the struggle that ensued as management tried to undermine the programmers' control of technical information—by, for example, breaking up the programming function and hiving off parts of it to other staff. For their part, the programmers sought to protect their power base by mystifying their skills and withholding information. In this way, this professional group challenged formal authority essentially by seeking to retain the dependence of the organization upon their expertise.

Decision-making as a political process

Having examined the bases of power in organizations, we can now turn to the organizational setting in which the political process takes place. It is important to bear in mind here, as we stressed earlier, that management is not the harmonious group it is often made out to be. Persistent conflict exists within management which is manifest in a variety of ways: in the manipulation of information, in hostility and lack of trust in intergroup relations, and in unwillingness to co-operate with colleagues. While it is possible for conflict to escalate to the point where it becomes destructive of organizational effort, where groups isolate themselves and become suspicious and hostile, even in the normal process of reaching joint decisions conflict and co-operation occur together. If we regard organizational decision-making as a political process various elements of this model can be defined.

Organization as a bargaining arena If joint decisions are to be arrived at, and conflict continually resolved, a negotiation or bargaining model of organizational interaction is implied. Several studies have explored the notion of decision-making as a process of negotiation in this sense (Bacharach and Lawler, 1980; Pfeffer, 1981). The image emphasized is that of power play as a game, and the organization as a site where the ritual is played out. Conflict plays a central part in this because it is conflicts of interest that cause people to use their power resources to bargain for outcomes favourable to themselves. Yet conflict does not occur at random. It can also be a result of the formal structure of organizations.

Interest groups and stakeholders The familiar organizational model sees overall goals being broken down into sub-goals and allocated to specific units via the division of labour. The writers of the classical school thought that goals were formally integrated—which must to an extent be true otherwise little would ever get done in organizations—but we know the view of organizations as structures for the rational pursuit of goals to be much too simplistic. In reality the goals of sub-units form the basis of conflicting interest groups and stakeholders. An interest group can be any unit of people (or even an individual) that is identified with some shared goal (departments or divisions are common interest groups). Similarly, stakeholders are groups or individuals that have a legitimate concern within a particular enterprise or set of activities.

Differentiated value systems While specialization and departmentalization within management creates sub-units with discrete tasks and goals, there is more involved than simply a material interest. These groups also develop their own distinctive commitments and outlooks. We saw in Chapter 13 that on top of goal differences, organizational groups are differentiated by entire systems of values, attitudes, and beliefs; and while such values may seem somewhat vague they can be extremely potent forces in organization life. Managerial differentiation is necessary for organizational performance, nevertheless the conflict it gives rise to creates a motive force for power play.

Decisions as emergent phenomena A dynamic view of decision-making follows that stresses its open-ended and processual nature. Decisions are not simply 'made' or 'taken' but rather they *emerge* from interaction. Rules and relationships within organizations are outcomes of negotiation, constantly created and recreated; they are never merely part of an established structure.

Power strategies and tactics

Basing our analysis on the above model means taking a fully dynamic and strategic view of power. For example, if we look only at the *power resources* that actors possess, to some extent we receive a static picture of the negotiation process, as if actors merely commanded influence in some fixed proportion to their expert power or position power. In reality, organizational politics is more dynamic, and new sources of power can be generated in the process of negotiation itself. French and Raven were aware of this. They noted that there was also a 'subjective' side to power—people may not actually possess certain power resources, but as long as they can persuade others that they do, they can still gain the substance of power. Implied here is a *tactical* conception of decision-making, in which power-seekers can amplify (or reduce if they choose the wrong tactics) the power resources at their disposal.

For example, probably the most basic power tactic is the *control of information*. Information flows to high-ranking organizational members as part of the normal process of decision-making, and the possession of important information naturally reinforces their formal power. But lower-ranking members can also mobilize this particular resource to their advantage. They can exploit the fact that they are directly involved with the work process to gain control of strategic information. Withholding information, releasing information at the moment likely to cause maximum embarrassment to your opponent, and even distorting information are all very common tactics in the power game.

Morgan (1986, p. 159) provides an extensive account of the range of tactics that people employ in pursuit of individual and sectional interests. He identifies, for example, *persuasion* as a form of influence in which people try to amplify their power by convincing others that they possess power resources that they do not; a form of bluff, in other words. There is also *controlling the agenda*. This can be regarded as a version of Lukes's second face of power; it involves setting the terms of debate and preventing issues getting into the bargaining arena. Tactical power has also become the subject of a highly refined theory, which has been reviewed in detail by Bacharach and Lawler (1980). We have no space to go fully into their survey here, although we will indicate some of its main points.

Coalitions and interest groups

One common power tactic involves the formation of *sponsor–protégé relationships*. These are informal alliances between a senior and junior manager in which the protégé may assist the more senior person in some specialist area: he or she may perform various detailed work (e.g. write reports, speeches) and may provide the senior manager with intelligence reports. In return the sponsor will guide the career of the protégé. Sponsors often have clusters of protégés; and when the sponsor moves up or out, to a better job, he or she may move the whole team too. In this way corporate management is frequently made up of interlocking cliques of senior people and their followers.

*But perhaps the most important power tactic is *coalition formation* (indeed, sponsor–protégé relationships are a special kind of coalition). Coalition formation represents the essence of political action, since it holds out the possibility of groups actually creating power for themselves. When interest groups face powerful opposition, a viable course of action is for them to join forces with other similar groups. A coalition, then, is *an informal relationship between two or more interest groups for the purpose of increasing their joint power in relation to some other group or groups*.

The obvious reason why groups should form coalitions is the gains they expect to make. But this does not take us very far. The more important question concerns the conditions under which groups might expect to gain little or much from forming a coalition. At least three factors can be distinguished here.

1. The most important objective condition is usually the *relative power* of the interest groups involved, for this decides whether a winning coalition can be formed. Thus, if two weaker groups have sufficient power together to override a third group with which they are in conflict, then other things being equal it is likely they will form the coalition. On the other hand, if their joint power is still insufficient to prevail against the third group, they may well decide that the coalition is not worth forming.

2. Managerial *differentiation* also plays a part. Interest groups in which the members are very different from each other, and have conflicting priorities, are usually capable of forming only unstable coalitions. So even if an issue does arise over which such groups might usefully pool resources, they may find day-to-day co-operation so difficult that they have to pursue their interests separately.

3. In certain ways the *issue at stake* can itself become a condition of formation. First, if it is a specific issue, resolved once and for all at a given time, then the most unlikely groups may be tempted into a temporary coalition because they know there will be no lasting commitment. Secondly, a highly important issue—one in which the potential gains are large, or where the very survival of the groups is at stake—may also force into a coalition groups that would otherwise never contemplate joint action.

The circumstances in which groups might expect to gain more from going it alone are readily identified as the reverse of those that produce coalitions. Thus if an interest group is especially powerful, it will not need to engage in a coalition. Similarly, if it is highly differentiated from other organizational groups, its members may decide that they share no interest with other groups. In such circumstances the costs of coalition formation—the most obvious one being that any spoils have to be shared—are liable to outweigh the benefits. Moreover, benefits can be transformed into costs: interacting with colleagues, which is a rewarding experience among people of like mind, can itself become a burden if they share little in common.

Perhaps the most widespread example of organizational staff likely to rely upon interest-group tactics is *professionals*. Employed professionals (engineers, technical specialists, etc.) very often have a degree of expert power, perhaps conferred by control of strategic technology. They are likely to be differentiated from other organizational members in terms of occupational values, and their technical qualifications may also make them mobile and independent of the organization to a certain extent. Thus they are quite likely to pursue their interests via their profession rather than the organization.

The interest-group tactic represents true political behaviour only where it is actively chosen, or where it is used as an occupational strategy. However, in organizational terms it may often amount to opting out of the political game. The programmers in Pettigrew's (1973) case study, discussed above, seemed to present a good example of this. They clearly did see the organization in terms of the technical problems it provided rather than as secure employment. In the long term they seemed to be storing up trouble for themselves by choosing to defend an isolated position and not seeking wider organizational influence. On the other hand, of course, one might regard a defensive tactic as the only sensible course given their extreme social distance from other groups in the organization. In any case, the programmers managed to preserve some of their status, and their skills gave them the option of seeking other employment.

Human rationality in decision-making

While these structural factors influence coalition formation, they are not the whole story. In practice, losing coalitions form quite frequently, for, as we have stressed, decision-making is a human and political process, and factors other than the purely rational calculation of costs and benefits enter into it.

To begin with, coalition formation is an *indeterminate* process, one in which there is always uncertainty as to the outcome. This is so for several reasons. People's information is never perfect, nor their judgements completely objective. Thus when we speak of the gains and losses involved in a coalition, the unspoken qualifier is that these are always people's *expectations* of gains and losses. In addition, important elements in the political process are non-comparable. One can never say exactly how much power a potential ally or adversary has, and thus one can never be entirely sure in advance whether the combination of these powers would produce a winning coalition.

More important, though, is the *tactical* nature of the organizational power game. Leadership, the deployment of resources and the formation of intelligent alliances are all going to be decisive. These are open-ended factors, which involve initiative and which take shape only as part of the political process. It follows that it is possible only with hindsight to say that so-and-so would inevitably win, or could never have won. At the time of conflict, each participant had the opportunity of winning; otherwise, of course, no certain loser would ever enter the political arena. Indeed, the essence of political action lies in the ability to convert an apparently weak position into a winning one via the intelligent use of tactics.

Another reason why losing coalitions may be formed stems from the subtle and dynamic nature of political processes. Gains other than purely material ones may be had from coalition membership. Being part of such power cliques, playing the game of organizational politics, is far more rewarding than being left on the sidelines. Moreover, material gains may eventually be forthcoming, since a losing coalition today may be the basis of a winning coalition in the future. Thus, people often judge this kind of group experience as being useful as well as enjoyable. They are right to do so, because coalitions are an integral part of organizational life, and to be an active participant in these crucial processes is to be pursuing one's career in the long term.

Conclusion

The study of negotiation and power, then, has some very positive things to recommend it: the stress on 'real' organizational activity is refreshing when compared with the overly formal and prescriptive approach of the managerial theorists, while the ability to manipulate power is vital for organizational as well as managerial development. The mere fact that this side of the management role has been played down until quite recently encourages an interest in power—any new approach which promises to take our understanding forward is naturally welcome. Certainly the idea that power and negotiation are the 'name of the game' in organizations and remain the decisive factor in decision-making is very persuasive. However, in concluding we should consider the claims of a broader range of theories.

Perhaps the main weakness of the power in organizations approach lies in the 'bargaining' emphasis. This reflects Dahl's early behavioural view of power and tends to assume a real power arena and power interactions that are 'happening'. We saw that the thrust of Lukes's critique of this view was a concern with the 'hidden' dimensions of power. To really understand power, the groups that are excluded and the interests that never have the opportunity to form have to be taken into account. Of course, the radical view has its own problems in revealing that which is hidden. How do you know whether interest groups exist if they have been excluded, or worse not even constituted? You are on very shaky ground when telling people what their 'real interests' are. Yet the need for some notion of the concealed aspects of power comes through strongly from a number of quarters. Weber's view of power contained two such paradoxes—power as a potential for action rather than action itself; and the idea that power is strongest where it does not have to be wielded, or where the threat of power is the central resource. These more complex views have had an effect. We saw that a number of writers mentioned exclusionary tactics in their accounts of organizational power. The notion of management decision-making as a political process is broader than that of 'bargaining'.

Reviewing the different approaches to power reveals some strong lines of convergence. A common theme was the distinction between power generated in action and power devolved from wider structures. The 'two views' of power are long established. Thus Clegg (1989, p. 5) has indicated some much older lines of thinking on power: the Machiavellian and Hobbesian views. From the former we inherit a view of power as partial strategies appropriate in particular spheres. Machiavelli was preoccupied with tactical concerns and the attainment of power. Hobbes, by contrast, stressed the power of an established authority over a set of subjects.

This analysis allows us to pull together the diverse threads of the argument so far, as power is a concept that has cropped up in various guises in previous chapters. In particular we might refer back to Chapter 10 and the discussion of Foucault as the author of modern perspectives on power. His idea of sovereign power was more or less identical with the Hobbesian notion of an established authority. Then, for Foucault, sovereign power transforms into the concept of 'disciplinary power' as the central structuralist view of power in modern organizations. In addition, though, Foucault also had a notion of 'parallel power' much closer to the Machiavellian view of power as a fragmented and processual phenomenon.

These distinctions can be expressed more simply in the contrast between 'power for' and 'power over'—the former stressing the use of power to generate change and the latter emphasizing the established authority of sovereign or corporate groups. We can see this kind of power duality reflected in these processual and structural types. Thus the distinction in Lukes between the first and third 'faces' of power (the behavioural versus the radical) reflects the difference between power used in a process of interaction versus power imposed by an external social and class structure. Similarly, we noted that Foucault's disciplinary power echoed the structural emphasis on external control, while parallel forms of power are created in action on particular sites.

That said, we should not try to convince ourselves that all views can be completely reconciled. Clegg drew our attention to differences between the two fundamental perspectives on power, and indeed writers who have had a direct modern influence (Weber, Foucault) display these conflicts even within their theories. The more structured view of power relates to Weberian authority and Foucault's type of disciplinary power, and these share common ground in so far as both deal with the institutions of power that individuals find already established. But Weber's notion of authority was also built on the rational acceptance of legitimate position, while Foucault's disciplinary power contains much stronger elements of domination, and was heir to the kind of state-inspired terror behind his notion of sovereign power. On the other hand, as we saw in Chapter 12, Weber himself thought that legitimate authority might ultimately lead to the forms of insidious power and the bureaucratic nightmare (his 'iron cage' of bureaucracy) that in its own way was as dark a vision as Foucault's—while Foucault also had a more optimistic version of power in his concept of parallel power.

The search for a resolution between these different approaches is almost bound to be misleading. For as well as reality differing, our views of reality differ. The above are not competing theories that give either true or false explanations; they are perspectives, ways of seeing human activity and emphasizing some aspect of it. Ultimately the existence of different approaches reflects the complexity of behaviour and our own inability to ascribe a single 'reality' to it. To seek to encapsulate reality within one theory is asking a lot; different observers will have their preferred perspective, and the uses to which theory is put will differ across a wide spectrum. Still, the interest in organizational power tends to limit the options and simplify our task somewhat. Though different forms of power arising from different resources and bases co-exist in organizations, the competing views of wider social power do not intervene quite so much in this debate. Instead the focus is on interaction within managerial bodies and managers' power to direct and change organizations. The 'power for' perspective, as we saw, produced a strategic and processual emphasis on how managers use the power resources at their disposal, and how they actively construct the interests and groups that constitute power relationships.

Study questions for Chapter 16

1 Why should we be interested in organizational power, given the distaste most people have for 'politicking' and conflict?

2 Organizational decision-making is less likely to reflect an underlying rational process than the relative power of the groups involved. Discuss.

3 Power is often said to be at its most potent when absent. What is meant by this?

4 Outline Lukes's theory of power, and give examples of how power's 'three faces' are manifest in organizations.

5 Contrast power as structure with power as process. How are these two perspectives evident in organizations?

6 Distinguish the major organizational groupings by the different power resources they possess.

7 Outline three of the main organizational power tactics and give illustrations of their usage.

Further reading

Clegg, S. R. (1989) *Frameworks of Power*. London: Sage.

—— (1990) *Modern Organizations*. London: Sage.

Dawson, S. (1996) 'Power and conflict', chap. 7 in *Analysing Organisations*, 3rd edn. Basingstoke: Macmillan.

Lee, R. and Lawrence, P. (1986) *Organizational Behaviour: Politics at Work*. London: Hutchinson.

Lukes, S. (ed.) (1986) *Power*. Oxford: Blackwell.

Mintzberg, H. (1983) *Power in and around Organizations*. Englewood Cliffs, NJ: Prentice-Hall.

Morgan, G. (1997) 'Organizations as political systems', chap. 6 in *Images of Organization*. London: Sage.

Pfeffer, J. (1981) *Power in Organizations*. Marshfield, Mass.: Pitman.

Reed, M. and Hughes, J. (eds.) (1992) *Rethinking Organization*. London: Sage.

Section 6

Divisions of Labour

Divisions of Labour

The division of labour is perhaps the single most important theme that governs how industrial societies emerge and change, and helps to set out the topics discussed in this final section. This complex process reflects the many ways in which the productive work performed in society has become differentiated and apportioned. Within the work situation, the division between jobs is, as we have seen, the basis of control and efficiency in modern organizations. However, on another level, the division of labour has produced the occupational structure. The divide between different professions and crafts has always been characteristic, even in pre-industrial times. But in a modern economy we find an enormously complex system of occupations reflecting the vast numbers of different jobs available. Other aspects of the social division of labour also reflect the fact that certain groups of people (differentiated by factors like class, sex, and ethnic origins) are typically found in different types of work.

Following this general schema, in Chapter 17 we begin to explore some of this variation. A full account of the changing occupational structure is beyond our scope. What we do look at, though, are a number of groups selected for their prominence and visibility. We examine the labour market situation of manual workers, the nature of white-collar work, and the professions.

The employment situation created by the gendered nature of work is described in Chapter 18. The relationships between men and women in work go a long way towards explaining the great variations between men's and women's work. As well as looking at these forces that shape and structure jobs, we look at the groups filling jobs. Female employment has attracted great interest recently, and we focus on the patterns of discrimination against women at work, and the active ways in which women participate in employment.

In the final part of the book, Chapters 19 and 20 address some of the most recent and important changes in the character of work in our rapidly evolving industrial society. Chapter 19 discusses the new technology of microelectronics. The theme of technology was raised much earlier, in Chapter 9, and indeed has cropped up throughout previous sections, but the impact of computer-based systems represents a new wave of technological change. Many believe this is transforming the work process and merits study in its own right—though the themes and perspectives of much older debates are still relevant. Closely related are the new forms of work organization examined in Chapter 20. The search for 'flexibility' in production is a central response to recurring economic crisis that seems to be the common lot in today's global industrial economy. The appearance of new work systems has sparked off key debates about the era of 'post-Fordism'.

17 Markets and Occupations

Summary points and learning objectives

By the end of this chapter you will:

- have broadly reviewed *occupational themes* in the areas of manual labour markets, white-collar work, and the professions;
- understand the *labour-market situation* confronting the manual working class;
- have explored the debates around the *rationalization of white-collar work*;
- have examined the nature of the *new service work*;
- be able to distinguish the nature of *professional work* and the social influence of the professions;
- appreciate why the professions are best regarded as an *occupational strategy*;
- understand the problems of explaining *differences in professional status*;
- have examined the nature of new professionals such as the *knowledge worker*.

Introduction

While most people in a modern economy have to sell their labour, they do not all do so under the same conditions. Over and above common factors in organizations and the labour process (discussed in the previous two sections) there is also a wide variation in the kinds of jobs available and in the rewards attached to them. In order to examine this variety in work, and the range of available employment, we need to look at occupational themes. However, rather than survey the entire occupational structure, we will take a more selective approach and concentrate on particular occupational areas.

We look first at the labour market that confronts the manual working class. Some of the debates here relate to an earlier period when this type of work dominated the occupational structure, whereas more recent changes seem to be happening in areas of the service economy. Nevertheless, manual work is still done by a large section of the employed population, despite any decline in industrial jobs. More importantly, manual work itself is transforming in the new workplaces, and many of the issues of 'industrialized' work also apply increasingly in the new service work. Thus the nature of these job markets reflects the opportunities open to the bulk of the population and is important for an understanding of contemporary employment.

Secondly, we examine the nature of white-collar work. Here we are concerned mainly with routinized office work, or clerical labour, another of the largest job sectors. The debate we explore is one that has exercised the minds of academics for a great many years: what are the implications for white-collar workers of the declining status of office work? In addition, we look at the new kinds of service occupations and new workplaces that have emerged expanding the white-collar category.

In the third part we look at another occupational group that is the focus of much attention, namely professionals. The reasons for this interest are not hard to find. The professions are the most rapidly expanding group in the occupational structure, which itself has created uncertainty and ambiguity in their work situation. In examining the professions, the emphasis changes so that instead of looking at the structures of available jobs, we consider the strategies adopted by professionals to influence their occupational status. The professions also have a dynamic impact in that many of the skills crucial in an industrial economy are commanded by these occupations. New work categories around notions such as knowledge workers and information workers reflect the changing demand for skills.

As already suggested, this coverage does not by any means take in all the main occupational groupings. But the above are some of the most important ones, and they enable us to explore key debates in the current analysis of work.

The labour market

A key factor in labour-market behaviour is the notion of choice. If the market is to distribute labour rationally the employer must be able to match the requirements of the vacant job with the abilities of applicants. Workers must also be able to choose the kind of job they want if they are to obtain advantageous employment. Though labour markets are known to depart from conditions of free choice, they have been assumed to be essentially rational and to allow a reasonable amount of free movement of labour and efficient allocation. However, concepts of 'freedom' and 'choice' are highly problematic. How much choice is real choice? And what apparent choices really represent bowing to the inevitable? The concept of choice also obscures conflicting interests and power differences in society—choice for a powerful group may well appear as constraint to the less well placed. Thus any understanding of the way the labour market mediates the relationship between employers and employees must dig deeper than a face-value notion of individual choice. It has to take serious account of the *structural* forces (class, gender, race) that influence the opportunities open to people, and which shape the images of their own chances that they develop.

Job choice and work orientations

An early model of job choice was developed by Goldthorpe, Lockwood, *et al.* (1968) in their famous 'affluent worker' research. The car-assembly workers in the study experienced their work as it really was: routine and dead-end. But the research suggested they had, as it were, made a rational decision to enter a certain type of employment. This offered little intrinsic interest, but relatively high pay, and reflected their underlying 'orientations' to work—in this case an instrumental orientation. Workers were willing to tolerate work on the assembly line in return for levels of pay that enabled them to pursue other interests. The researchers therefore inferred a causal link between prior orientations to work and job choice: people with particular work orientations would seek employment which gave the balance of rewards they desired and the deprivations they were willing to put up with.

The affluent worker study focused on a certain type of worker—unskilled but in well-paid jobs—of which car assembly was a classic example. It was never meant to be representative of the manual working class but was intended to be *proto-typical*. In other words, though not necessarily typical at the time, Goldthorpe, Lockwood, *et al.* thought that this kind of work would become increasingly common.

For this and other reasons the study has long been criticized for implying a higher degree of job choice and a more rational labour market than exists in practice. The market experiences of these workers was a product of the 1960s, and does not accurately mirror the sorts of employment changes—the recurrent crises in demand for labour, the differentiation in work and new working patterns—that have occurred in more recent years. Also Goldthorpe, Lockwood, *et al.* ignored the possibility that it may be the labour-market experiences of workers that cause them to adopt instrumental orientations in the first place. The voluntary nature of the acceptance of unskilled work implied in the affluent worker model plays down the extent to which market choice for workers is limited by their educational attainment and the availability of opportunities.

Goldthorpe, Lockwood, *et al.* themselves were critical of so-called technologically determinist studies—the boredom and alienation of the assembly line had been commonly used to explain things like the hostile attitudes and industrial militancy of motor industry workers—and they wanted to avoid any narrow focus on production technology to explain workers' attitudes. But they may have overemphasized factors external to the workplace. Both sets of factors—structural conditions within work, as well as the perceptions that people bring to their employment—need to be taken into account. In particular, the happy coincidence between instrumental attitudes and the nature of car-assembly work may simply have reflected adjustments and responses to the work situation. Others have found that attitudes follow a career cycle. Young people enter work with a concern for intrinsic rewards (prospects, promotion) but with longer service they adjust to restricted opportunities, and their orientations shift to pay and security. For example, Beynon (1984) in his noted study of assembly workers at Ford's plant in Liverpool, emphasized a degree of realism. In a region of high unemployment and declining industries, Ford offered reasonably well-paid work. But workers' distaste for their jobs and powerful sense of alienation were not diminished.

Another account of the job choices open to workers has been provided by Blackburn and Mann (1979) in their intensive study of the labour market. They found that manual workers who possessed the skills or qualifications to enable them to exercise any real choice over their employment were in a small minority indeed. The jobs open to the vast majority of workers were mostly routine and poorly paid, with few difference between them. Very few jobs offered any real choice, and the only chance of gaining additional rewards came with simply getting a better job but this was both rare and outside workers' control.

... the *absolute* level of skill of all but the very highest jobs is—to say the least—minimal. Eighty-seven per cent of our workers exercise less skill at work than they would if they drove to work. Indeed, most of them expend more mental effort and resourcefulness in getting to work than in doing their jobs. From this remarkable result flow two important consequences. In the first place, nobody can choose a challengingly skilled job, no matter how much he is prepared to sacrifice in terms of wages and other work rewards. . . . Secondly, it follows that most workers are objectively capable of acquiring the skills necessary for most jobs; we estimate that 85 per cent of workers can do 95 per cent of jobs. (p. 280)

What workers look for in jobs reflected this restricted choice. Blackburn and Mann found little evidence in support of distinctive work orientations. Instead, they found 'weak orientations' in the form of complex patterns of preferences for certain types of work (a leaning towards outdoor work, elements of instrumentalism, a desire for jobs with some autonomy). They concluded that workers retain a sense of reality in their situation—'all orientations are confined within the limits of the labour market' (p. 282)—while at the same time making the best of things by valuing very highly the small differences between jobs that did exist.

Labour-market theory

The notion of workers competing equally in an open labour market is an ideal far removed from reality. In practice a great many 'substantive' factors—employers' preferences for certain kinds of worker, their desire not to disrupt established workforces, prejudice and discrimination of all kinds—tend to undermine the allocation of labour on a strictly rational basis. Indeed, as Blackburn and Mann (1979) discovered, in the majority of cases what employers look for in workers is co-operativeness, and this alone would restrict any attempt to select workers rationally on the basis of skills and abilities.

The dual labour market A major 'imperfection' in the market for labour to which certain economists and sociologists have drawn attention lies in the fact that it is not unified. In reality it is divided into distinct segments, and in particular into a primary and a secondary labour market. Jobs in the primary market are supplied by large firms that are technologically advanced and profitable. Wages and working conditions are relatively good, levels of unionization tend to be high, and employers are concerned with retaining stable workforces. However, this applies only to part of the economy. In addition, there are jobs in the secondary sector provided by small firms, usually in low technology industries and very competitive markets. Such firms normally experience great pressures to exploit their workers to the utmost, so wages tend to be low and conditions poor. In short, work in the primary sector provides what would usually be thought of as 'good jobs', found in the skilled trades and industries like engineering and advanced manufacturing. In the secondary sector are found the 'bad jobs'—or even 'sweated' labour—which tend to be concentrated in the services and in industries such as clothing and food processing.

Internal labour markets A further aspect of market irrationality is that much allocation of labour in fact occurs *inside* firms as a result of the selection of existing employees. To a large extent the division between internal and external labour markets overlaps that between primary and secondary markets. In other words, it tends to be large-scale organizations in the advanced sector of the economy that restrict opportunities for advancement and training to their own employees. An internal labour market is favoured in the primary sector because it helps firms to stabilize their labour forces. Production here tends to be technically complex, and firms will normally be locked into highly structured product markets, which leads to demands for stable output and quality. Furthermore, primary labour forces contain high proportions of skilled and experienced workers who are not easily replaceable. By restricting such a major reward as promotion to the established labour force, ties of loyalty can be strengthened. In contrast to this, secondary sector firms, which tend to be much less dependent on skilled workers, and are often too small to operate an internal market, rely much more on the wider labour market as a source of labour supply.

Market segregation The primary and secondary sectors form a stratified labour market mainly because the workers who fill those jobs are themselves segregated. Different groups of people are allocated to different work. Probably the most widespread form of segregation (one we pay particular attention to in Chapter 18) is based on discrimination between the sexes, and women workers rarely compete with men for the same jobs. But almost any kind of labour market disadvantage can drive workers into the secondary sector. As workers become older they may have to drop out of well-paid primary sector jobs and accept less advantageous work. Similarly, in areas containing large immigrant populations, sweated industries tend to flourish. Prejudice on the part of those placed to exert influence over selection, like personnel officers and senior management, helps to guarantee that factors like class, sex, race, and age are applied in practice.

It may be argued that this merely reflects workers' true value to employers. After all, the primary sector contains a high proportion of workers with marketable qualities, and these have to be rewarded if firms wish to retain such workers. However, this argument is unsatisfactory for at least two reasons. First, even if the purely rational reasons for allocating workers either to the low-wage or to the high-wage sector were removed, much residual prejudice and discrimination would remain. Secondly, the argument ignores the fact that changes to obtain skills are allocated in a discriminatory fashion in the first place. Women and ethnic minorities are often given very limited access to training; also youngsters from middle-class backgrounds have in-built advantages when it comes to obtaining further education and skills.

Constraints on job choice

All these distinctions are to an extent rather limited and static attempts to describe a complex reality. Labour-market theory is hotly disputed within the social sciences. To begin with, there is still disagreement about whether labour markets are truly segmented in the sense of particular sectors of jobs being entirely cut off from other sectors. While there are clearly major differences in the work open to different groups of people, this may not amount to fully developed segmentation. The need to refer in such cases to very detailed data on the distribution of rewards and choices between jobs has fuelled both sides of the debate.

Even assuming that labour markets are segmented (as opposed to being merely differentiated), the phenomenon has attracted major differences of interpretation and emphasis. Marxist writers, such as Edwards *et al.* (1975), have stressed that labour-market segmentation is the outcome of the control imperative at the heart of the labour process. Employers' need for control inside the firm, they argue, has to be supported by control in the wider labour market and by a 'divide and rule' strategy towards labour. In this sense, segmentation encourages rivalry between different groups of workers, preventing the labour force as a whole from attaining unity.

Criticism from other radical writers, most notably feminists, has stressed that the notion of some abstract form of 'capital' which exploits all workers equally is misleading. Pressures from wider society and from within labour itself, such as the forces of sexism, have an independent effect (Rubery, 1980). Sexism from men in general may be as important a factor in discrimination against women as that expressed by employers.

In more mainstream social science, the changing organization of work is seen as a varied process. The wide range of labour policies that employers adopt—not all of which can be reduced to a single-minded desire to control workers—challenges the notion of a fixed capitalist logic. This line of argument has strong ties with the critique of labour process theory (see Chapter 10), in which various factors, like 'responsible' patterns of job design, were put forward as alternatives to direct control by employers.

White-collar work

Turning to the other major area of employment, the non-manual or white-collar sector, we at once come up against problems of definition. Whereas manual jobs tend to be similar as regards the type of work performed and the rewards received, the non-manual sector is diverse and extensive. It ranges across managerial and administrative posts, employment in the professions, in scientific and technical activities, supervision, clerical and secretarial jobs, and jobs in sales and distribution. The differences between these types of work in pay, status and authority are often immense; and as a result, methods of classifying non-manual occupations are beset with ambiguities and inconsistencies.

The reasons for this diversity can be found in the changing occupational structure, itself a product of industrial and commercial development. Economic expansion in the major industrial nations during this century has been heavily concentrated in areas of non-manual employment. The fastest-growing industries have frequently been science-based ones which employ a high proportion of professional and technical staff; and added to this throughout industry managerial functions (e.g. work control, planning and product development) have expanded. The commercial and financial sector has also developed, enlarging the clerical workforce, while the growth of state provision in health and welfare has expanded the numbers of lower professionals. This trend may now be levelling off. Areas like clerical work are static or declining as the effects of new technology and productivity improvements begin to bite. However, as Table 17.1 indicates, the long-term expansion in white-collar work has persisted, with many groups of non-manual employees showing strong growth.

	1984 (000s)	1990 (000s)	1996 (000s)	1984–96 % increase
Managerial, administrative and related professional	3515	4589	4044	15.0
Professionals in education, welfare, and health	2053	2377	2727	3.3
Professionals in science, engineering, and technology	1047	1173	2455	134.5
Clerical	3546	4237	3788	0.7
Other non-manual	1779	1949	2127	19.6
Skilled manual	3993	4073	3147	−2.1
Other manual	6584	6797	7028	6.7
All non-manual occupations	12193	14703	15151	24.3
All manual occupations	10879	11018	10175	−0.6

Table 17.1 Occupational analysis of persons in employment

Source: Employment Gazette (London: HMSO), April 1991, p. 183 and Labour Force Survey Quarterly Bulletin (London: HMSO), No. 20, June 1997, p. 24.

The question of the nature of white-collar occupations is bound up with sociological analysis of class. Traditionally, the line dividing manual and white-collar jobs has demarcated the working class from the middle class. In the nineteenth century the middle classes shared in the ownership of *property* (small businesses, self-employment, and income from investment). However, the patterns of economic growth which brought about the expansion of white-collar occupations reversed this situation and the established property-owning middle class declined in numbers. The growing new white-collar groups derived their class position not from property but from *employment*. This created a problem for analysis since the factors describing occupations (such as pay, status, authority, and career expectations) are complex and not always consistent.

As Hyman (1983) points out, this adds to the 'structural ambiguity' of extended white-collar hierarchies.

Moreover, there has been no simple transfer from a class position based on economic ownership to one based securely on employment. Certainly there are higher professional and managerial groups which do enjoy superior occupational rewards. Equally clearly, however, groups like clerical and sales workers do not. The expansion in non-manual work has mostly taken place in these lower-ranked kinds of jobs. As Abercrombie and Urry point out: 'the numerical growth in salaried employees is especially traceable to a demand for subordinates rather than fully qualified responsible people' (1983, p. 53). Furthermore, a high proportion of white-collar jobs have been occupied by women, and the sexual divisions in society have been a major influence in reinforcing the downward pressure on employment conditions.

Some writers believe that the diversity and fragmentation of white-collar groups is such that they no longer constitute a single class. Hyman, for example, stresses: 'The range of internal differentiation in pay and conditions clearly casts doubt on the adequacy of the general category "white-collar employment" as a means of classifying occupations' (1983, p. 13). Thus the lower ranks of white-collar and service workers are to be distinguished from managerial and higher professional employees, who comprise the 'new' middle class. The latter have also been dubbed the 'service class', reflecting their responsibility for discharging functions, critical in a modern economy, of planning, administration and the control of labour.

In sketching out this analysis, however, we have disregarded some major problems. It is difficult imposing *a structure* (of class categories and boundaries) upon what are essentially dynamic *processes*. Moreover, the notion that some groups, like clerical employees, have actually changed their class membership is still hotly debated. While most writers would agree that their distinctive class position has been eroded, there is disagreement about how far this has gone.

The work process

In the nineteenth and early twentieth centuries, many white-collar employees were clearly differentiated from the manual working class. In the words of Lockwood:

> . . . the clerk generally enjoyed a natural status clearly removed from that of the manual worker. His salary, hours of work and holiday were decidedly more favourable; and to be added to these were security of tenure, a greater chance of promotion, and the probability of a pension of some kind . . . He was somehow a privileged type of proletarian. (1958, p. 41)

However, the occupational standing and class position of this largest section of the white-collar workforce have subsequently been threatened. In particular, it is trends towards deskilling and routinization, identified in Chapter 10 in relation to manual labour, that are also held responsible for alienation in the office.

The American C. Wright Mills was probably the first modern sociologist to write at length about the deterioration of office work. In his classic study *White Collar* (1951) Mills linked two basic processes: the introduction of machinery and the intensification of work.

As the army of clerks grew, they were divided into departments, specialized in function, and thus, before machines were introduced on any scale, socially rationalized. . . . It was this social reorganization, under the impetus of work load, higher cost, and the need for files and figures, that made possible the wide application of business machines. (p. 192)

Mills's concerns with the rationalization of office work invited the comparison between office and factory. Changes in work patterns, like open-plan layout and typing pools, led to a workflow that could be centrally planned and closely supervised. The application of 'scientific management' too, he notes, was common in larger American offices by the 1920s. Mills anticipated the full rationalization of office work; certain 'status complications' might delay it, but it was the 'model of the future'.

Another influential account is that of Braverman (1974, chaps. 15 and 16). We noted earlier the stimulus that he gave to the 'deskilling' debate, but Braverman extended these ideas into his account of white-collar work. He stressed the 'extraordinary enlargement' of these occupations—in the case of clerical workers rising from being less than 1 per cent of the employed population in the mid-nineteenth century, in both Britain and the United States, to developed labour forces respectively comprising 3 million and 14 million employees by the 1970s (p. 295). As these groups expanded, office work changes 'from something merely incidental to management into a labor process in its own right' (p. 304). And like Mills, Braverman emphasized the 'merging characteristics of clerical and production labor'. The need to 'systematize and control' white-collar work brought about mechanization (with the typewriter as early as the 1880s, then a range of office equipment, and most importantly the recent introduction of commercial computing), the growth of a separate hierarchy of office management, reorganization of work to give economies of scale, and the erosion of established white-collar skills (e.g. the replacement of shorthand by audio typing). The clerical occupations, Braverman stated emphatically, represented a major section of the working class, and any general white-collar category that included higher-level occupations was 'absolutely meaningless' (p. 295).

Occupational status

Unlike these accounts, which tend to be confined to the changing labour process, many social scientists have given prominence to subjective factors concerned with the *status* of white-collar occupations and the *class consciousness* of the incumbents of these jobs. David Lockwood's pioneering early study *The Blackcoated Worker* (1958) set out three separate dimensions of class position. (1) He referred to the basic economic factors related to occupation (pay, prospects, conditions) as 'market situation'; (2) 'work situation' stressed the nature of social relationships at work; and (3) 'status situation' was the prestige accorded to occupations in wider society (p. 15). Lockwood argued that, whereas the market situation of clerical employees differed little from that of manual workers, the modern office was still not rationalized to the extent that their respective work situations were identical (e.g. he insisted that office mechanization enhanced clerical work rather than reducing it to mere machine minding). Moreover, considerations of status revealed radical differences, a 'sheer social distance', between clerical and manual workers. Indeed, the very fact of clerical 'respectability' being insecure, and based on declining occupational advantages, provoked a powerful desire in clerks to remain aloof from the manual working class.

Two later surveys are those of Stewart *et al.* (1980) and Crompton and Jones (1984). Stewart *et al.* argued that if career expectations are significant in an occupation, any approach that focuses only on the job (whether in terms of its pay or social status, or the nature of the work involved) will convey a static and possibly misleading picture. Indeed, they discovered high rates of promotion out of clerical work: 'Clerk is not a well-paid position, or even a highly regarded position, but it is an early stage on relatively lucrative and highly regarded careers' (p. 172). However, their study was based on male clerks, which may have limited the relevance of their findings in an occupation three-quarters feminized.

Crompton and Jones's study did encompass both male and female clerical employees. While these researchers too discovered high rates of mobility for men, the vast majority of women were seen to occupy routine jobs with limited career chances. They particularly stressed the role of computers in deskilling clerical work. Crompton and Jones suggested that automated data processing so radically altered the clerical labour process as to be the decisive factor in creating a (female) proletariat. Hence they broadly agreed with writers like Mills and Braverman who argued that a white-collar working class had come into existence (though they implicitly disagreed on the timing, as these other writers believed that the routinization of clerical work was well advanced by the first half of the 20th century, and did not place such strong emphasis on the gender dimension).

That said, these arguments themselves can be challenged for suggesting that technical change is necessarily closed off. The centralized mainframe computer is not the end of the story, and a range of new service work is dependent on advances like integrated telephone and information systems. Much of this reflects the importance of customer liaison in the modern economy and may benefit clerical labour, giving clerks intimate knowledge of customer files and possession of key sources of management information (Fearfull, 1996).

The new service work

The reshaping of white-collar and office work over the past decade or so, and the emergence of a new kind of service sector, has been one of the most striking features of the current industrial landscape. The so-called 're-engineering' of office work has seen the downsizing of staffs and flattening of hierarchies. The radical redesign of many administrative functions has come about, it has been suggested, because office work became labour intensive and bureaucratic and lagged behind factory systems, which were being transformed to world-class standards during the 1980s. So the potential for cost-cutting and productivity growth is much greater within this type of work (Conti and Warner, 1994). In large part, too, the availability of new technology is the driver of these changes. The office is basically a place where information is processed, and the greatest advances in the recent past have been in information technologies. Computer-based systems like remote networking that enable organizations to divide their operations geographically, and changes to traditional technologies such as the telephone, have produced a revolution in service work and a range of new occupations.

Telework or telecommuting is one aspect. In the USA in 1993 there were 6.6 million telecommuters. People working from home via a computer link-up, and backed by fax, mobile phone, and other technologies, are one category. But various office–home combinations exist. Mobile workforces, such as a salesforce, are frequently reorganized using contact via mobile phones and perhaps access to satellite or local offices. There is also so-called hot-desking, where self-employed workers rent out office space in designated centres.

One of the most significant developments is the *call centre*. Customers phone a central point for information or services, and the centres deal with thousands of telephone calls per day. In Britain in 1997 fully 1.2 per cent of the workforce, or 250,000 people, were employed in call centres, and this is set to grow to 2.2 per cent or 1 million workers by 2001. Most of these jobs are located outside the metropolitan area where greenfield sites and regional development grants have been available. Call centres depend on highly sophisticated telephone systems for the automatic rerouting of calls, so that a customer's call may be answered at a centre hundreds of miles distant. Such systems enable companies to specialize in particular kinds of calls—technical support, customer service, telesales—and organizations can operate linked centres in different parts of the country. The work performed includes helpcentres, as part of strategies of enhanced customer service, which in cut-throat markets is one important area where added value can be provided. Financial services is another area in which telesales and call centres have mushroomed. Direct selling of mortgages, insurance policies, and other financial products is a growth industry and a type of business that no bank, insurance company, or building society can afford to ignore.

The kinds of new jobs created in this environment are sometimes termed 'emotional labour', as the emphasis is on customer-related skills: listening, counselling, giving advice, sorting out customers' problems. What is crucial is the employees' 'manner' and their capacity to project a desirable image of the company. Greenbaum (1995, p. 98) refers to these jobs as 'broadband' occupations, whereby the old bureaucratic hierarchies (which create specific job descriptions) are being replaced by jobs which assume a range of responsibilities and tasks. These are 'all-round occupations' in which the worker will be accepting a customer's call, dealing with requests and complaints, pulling customer records for screen display. In the case of direct-line selling, for example, employees are backed by automated systems for the likes of insurance underwriting and loan and mortgage applications, and can deal with requests and sales in a single customer transaction.

This type of work represents the industrialization of the office taken to a new level, and some of the main concerns have reflected the problems of Taylorization and work intensification. Teleworking is very closely monitored and controlled. Supervisors may listen in to samples of calls, and organizations set down targets for how long callers have to wait, how effectively the employee closes the episode, their accuracy and clarity in dealing with the call. Teleworking is high volume–low cost and with it go the pressures of this kind of business. The jobs reflect the quickening pace of office work and are often highly stressed. A range of health and safety issues crop up, including possible injuries from repetitive use of keyboards and monitors, and the so-called 'sick-building syndrome' which reflects the problems of working in these very large, enclosed, air-conditioned, artificially-lit spaces. The work environment thus raises the Orwellian spectre that emerged in previous discussion (see Chapter 10) as a key concern of modern organizations. The physical layout of call centres may be regimented and oppressive, and they suggest a form of industrial totalitarianism precisely because 'emotional labour' is exploited. What is being controlled is the interaction between worker and customer, so that human feelings of benevolence and helpfulness are being commodified and turned to commercial advantage.

Professions and professionalism

Changes in the nature of white-collar work are at the heart of the restructuring of the industrial economy. As we saw in Table 17.1, white-collar jobs in higher level categories also occupy a prominent place in the jobs structure. Indeed, these occupations are intimately tied in with the demands of a modern economy for skills and knowledge. This therefore raises as a separate issue the nature of higher-grade white-collar work, an important part of which consists of *professional* work. The term itself tends to be more meaningful than any general category of white-collar work since even low-ranking groups in the professions seem to enjoy prospects and conditions of employment that differentiate them from routine white-collar workers. Professional groups tend to have distinctive and integrated occupational cultures. Professionals have a common sense of identity and values, share a consensus as regards their social role, speak a common language, and tend to be lifetime members of their occupation.

Nevertheless, the occupational differences remain important as well. Differences among professional groups mean that established professions (such as law, medicine, or architecture) command superior status and earnings compared with lesser professions (like teaching and social work). There are also pronounced hierarchies within professions: the financial controller of a large corporation, for example, will receive far higher rewards than an auditor, yet both might be broadly described as accountants.

Characteristics of professions

The range of variation among and within professional groupings has meant that defining the essential features of professions has always proved difficult. What does seem to be of prime importance is the nature of professional work. Professions traditionally have enjoyed the high status and material rewards associated with positions of authority, yet they are also involved in the concrete process of work. Sometimes this may in fact be manual work (a surgeon, for example, carries out what is probably quite hard manual work, albeit delicate and skilled); and although most professions are white-collar in nature, there remains a belief that professionals should actually perform the work themselves and not merely delegate it to others. In trying to define professional work the following aspects may be singled out.

1. Professional work typically has a *service* element—either service to the common good, such as in health or education, or service to an individual client, or in an organization the provision of a staff service to line management.
2. The professionals are *ethical* occupations. Because they employ a complex technical language, and are often involved with matters of critical importance to society and to individuals, there is a need to regulate professional conduct by some code of ethics. The central relationship of trust between client and professional, upon which the legitimacy of professional advice is based, itself rests on the belief that professionals will act in the client's interest.
3. The professions tend to be *self-regulating* occupations. Their responsibilities usually involve extensive skills and technical knowledge, for which long periods of training are required; hence professionals themselves prefer to reserve the right to be sole judge of the competence of other colleagues. They determine training requirements, control entry to the profession, and in some cases grant the licence to practise.

The skills of professionals, and their concern with services of exceptional importance, have conventionally been used to explain the superior status and rewards these occupations attract. However, more critical writers have pointed out that to see professional status merely as a reflection of the intrinsic qualities of professional work is to paint a rather static picture. Johnson (1972) argued that accounts which focus on the supposed qualities of professions have never been able to agree a list of 'traits' that are typical of all professions in all circumstances. Similarly, the suggestion that professions serve fundamental social needs (for health, law and order, education, etc.) is also rather doubtful. The alleged 'altruism' of professionals has often been the basis of exaggerated claims about their ethical and progressive role. As Johnson indicates, this 'falls into the error of accepting professionals' own definitions of themselves' (1972, p. 25).

Instead of regarding professionalism as an inherent quality of select occupations, it is best regarded as an *occupational strategy*, whereby groups attempt to gain recognition as professions in order to reap the rewards of the established professions. This view was pioneered by the American sociologist Everett Hughes, who maintained that he 'passed from the false question "Is this occupation a profession?" to the more fundamental one, "What are the circumstances in which people in an occupation attempt to turn it into a profession and themselves into professional people?" ' (quoted in Johnson, 1972, p. 31). Here the emphasis shifts to the *dynamic* process of groups attempting collectively to upgrade their occupational standing.

Professionalism as occupational strategy

Although the older-established professions are often taken as the bench-mark by which the status of all professional groups is measured, the nature of professional work on the whole has undergone major changes. Indeed, professionalism as a strategy reflects both the opportunities that have arisen for groups to move up in status and the threats to the status of existing groups.

C. Wright Mills (1951) pointed out two main aspects of this dynamic situation. First, the established professions themselves have been transformed. The independent practitioner might once have represented the 'model' professional, but nowadays even high-status groups, like architects, accountants, and lawyers, are often employees rather than partners in independent practice. Secondly, technological changes and industrial development have meant that many entirely new engineering and scientific skills have appeared. Also, the growth of state provision has greatly expanded groups like teachers and social workers. Such a growth in numbers, as much as anything else, poses the problem for these groups of defining and protecting their occupational boundaries.

Several important tactics for securing occupational control can be singled out. One of the chief preconditions of wider occupational control is that the membership itself should be a united force. Thus *professional associations* are vitally important in representing and furthering the interests of the profession. In the more powerful professions, the association will regulate training and educational standards, in order to preserve the status of the occupation, by requiring a high level of technical knowledge and practical ability. Strict entry requirements also serve to limit numbers and to keep practitioners in short supply. Indeed, the main function of professional associations lies in keeping the profession an exclusive club.

The occupational strategy represented here differs from but also shares some common elements with the two other major strategies of advancement: the *trade union* strategy of workers and the *career* strategy of managers. A profession is a coalition of interests and acts collectively, rather like a trade union. Nor is it unknown for professional associations to resort to industrial action—though they are usually anxious not to be linked in the public eye with union militancy. Unlike the large general trade unions, however, which operate on the principle of including as many people as possible in the particular industry, the professions guard their exclusive nature jealously. Their purpose in controlling the supply of professional labour is to bump up the rewards going to the existing members of the profession. Yet it is a measure of the success of the professions that, while unions are often roundly condemned for using 'restrictive practices' in defence of jobs, the tactics of professions, which are aimed solely at exclusivity, are much more widely accepted. In contrast to this, the actual rewards being sought differ from those aimed at by workers. The professions provide a setting for members to pursue individualistic career paths and middle-class rewards, much as do managers and senior organizational members.

The historic success of many of these occupational strategies is reflected in the formidable social power of professions as a whole. Studies have shown how professional ethics, as well as ostensibly protecting clients, crucially serve the interests of professions. The issue here is the *ideological* character of the professional ethic, rather than the truth or otherwise of professional claims. Indeed, it may well be true that the wider public interest is served by having secure professions, yet it is certainly clear that these forms of control enhance the vested interests of the professions concerned. The professional ethic resembles a sort of occupational ideology uniting the members of the profession. For example, a practitioner threatened with legal action for alleged incompetence can normally expect his colleagues to close ranks behind him, providing he has not broken the code of ethics. Thus, members of the public often find it extremely difficult to bring a case against professionals unless some gross breach of conduct can clearly be proven. Internal discipline within professions tends to be overwhelmingly concerned with cases where the profession itself might have been brought into disrepute (mostly involving illegal or immoral behaviour) rather than with investigating cases of incompetence on behalf of clients or the public.

A major basis of professional privilege lies in the claim to superior knowledge. It is a mark of occupations struggling to gain exclusive rights to practise that they will make great efforts to have their claims on knowledge recognized; and it is characteristic of the established professions that they guard their monopoly of knowledge very closely. In daily contact with clients and the public, professionals seek to 'mystify' their knowledge, to make it appear that, while long training and experience are necessary, there are other indefinable skills that only members of the profession possess or even understand. Doctors, for example, are often extraordinarily reluctant to discuss patients' illnesses with them, the justification being that it would distress patients or that they would not understand anyway. While this may contain some truth, keeping patients in ignorance undeniably helps doctors to manipulate them. Thus the 'manner' that professionals adopt is an important tactic in maintaining their possession of vital knowledge.

The power of certain professions extends beyond control of their own occupation. Esland (1980) has stressed that the expertise which professions command confers on them a 'mandate to produce and generate certain kinds of knowledge for society as a whole'. While the public as clients may know broadly what service it requires, in important respects this is defined by the relevant profession, and it is this definition that will decide the actual service received.

Routine definitions of ill-health, social adequacy, school achievement, degrees of criminality, for example, can be seen as grounded in the specific forms of expertness which at any one time are dominant in society. . . . Many of the dominant categories of thought which permeate our commonsense attitudes—as well as the power to enforce them—are to some extent traceable to the political organization of particular occupations. (Esland, 1980)

Explaining occupational control

The question remains, however, how we explain the differences in the progress of different groups along the path of professionalism. Why are doctors, say, capable of sustaining their elite status, while teachers are not? It can be argued that the issue itself is unimportant: certain occupations have simply managed to acquire the totem of professional prestige while others have not. Some writers, however, seek more distinctive explanations. Any such answer clearly must take historical and institutional factors into account. Thus, for example, it has been pointed out that state intervention into an occupation seems to be a major factor explaining why such groups become only marginally professional (Johnson, 1972). In certain circumstances professions can flourish with the state as employer. But equally when control over the profession resides with the state this can detract from professional values. Particularly in recent years, the crisis in public spending has meant a dramatic decline in occupational standing in many public sector areas (universities, schools, local government).

On a more theoretical level, we can point to two related concepts that help to explain variations in professional autonomy. Carchedi (1977) has drawn attention to the contrasting forces, some of which degrade and constrain occupational control while others enhance an occupation's market position. The explanation Carchedi gives reflects the extent to which the 'functions of capital' are being served. If the occupation concerned plays an important role in administrative and control functions crucial to the production of surplus value, it will command the market power that will bring prestige and exceptional rewards. (A good example here would be that of accounting, the exclusive authority of which has grown because of its relation with corporate capital.) However, if a profession has only tenuous links with these fundamental capitalist processes, occupational prestige will be much more marginal.

Secondly, as well as the salience of the function performed, the rewards accruing to a profession are also determined by the nature of the work involved. Jamous and Peloille (1970) have argued that where a high degree of *indeterminacy* exists in the work of a profession—that is, where tasks are variable and non-rationalized—then people who control this uncertainty are likely to enjoy high status. Conversely, where such work has been systematized and subject to laid-down procedures, it becomes possible for forces outside the occupation to intervene and control the work process.

To a degree, both these types of explanation still seem circular. One still might want to know why a doctor's job should be indeterminate and salient for capital but a teacher's job not. However, salience and indeterminacy are objective features of the work process in only a partial sense—social and political factors also play a critical role in creating or failing to create these conditions. At crucial points in their development, elite professions are able to capitalize on the objective conditions of their work situation. In other cases, would-be professions have a self-defeating aspect. Their dilemma, as Jamous and Peloille (1970) point out, is that the pursuit of best practice may mean codifying and mechanizing their own work, thereby shifting control to outside managerial elements. In this sense, concepts of salience and indeterminacy link strategic factors with structural constraints. They point to the crucial act of groups seizing or failing to seize on the objective conditions which their work setting provides in their struggles to exert control over an occupational domain.

In recent years a number of models of professional development have combined these critical elements—seeing the professions as a device for the upward collective mobility of an occupation and using the strategy of investing areas of work with politically controlled knowledge. These attempt to explain comprehensively the varying fortunes of groups that seek professional standing.

The collective mobility project One of the most enduring images of the professions has been that of the 'collective mobility project' (Larson, 1977). This emphasizes the remaking of occupations in order to claim particular areas of work and expertise. Claims on professional status are 'projects' in which status is pursued by explicit means. So while the collective strategies of trade unions may seem defensive, collective professional mobility has often been highly successful. The classic corporate example is accountancy. As Armstrong (1985) has established, this profession has succeeded in imposing its own language of cost control and formal investment criteria at corporate level, particularly in British companies. This lies at the heart of accountancy's functional importance and the strong presence of accountants in board rooms.

Like any strategy, however, collective mobility is open-ended and can fail as well as succeed. There can be no guarantee that occupations will be successful in their demands for professional recognition—or if successful that they will retain their status over the long term. In the case of personnel managers, for example, members of this profession have made huge efforts in recent years to improve their standing. This has included redefining their expertise as 'human resource management', and even strategic HRM, as well as attempts to make the professional body (the Institute of Personnel and Development) into a stringent control over training and accreditation. Yet the evidence points to limited success in terms of actual mobility into the corporate sphere. As Armstrong (1995) once again has argued, the fate of personnel is partly linked to the success of financial and market criteria, and the decline of the importance of older patterns of industrial relations that once placed personnel at the heart of decisions. Thus there are few 'linking career paths' between routine personnel work and more strategic positions in organizations.

Similarly, many groups will enjoy a limited form of autonomy, though they themselves would not necessarily see it in that light. Occupations that hardly aspire to the status of the senior professions nevertheless can be jealous of the trappings of professional autonomy that they have acquired. Indeed, for groups that are not already influential, professionalism may not be their best strategy. Gall and Murphy's (1996) study of the regional press, for example, has shown the growing concentration of ownership in the industry, and with it journalists suffering reduced status and increased work intensification. Control has also shifted to editorial management and employers have mounted a concerted campaign against trade unions. The failure of the National Union of Journalists to resist these attacks on rights and conditions is attributed to contradictions in its own make-up. Despite the NUJ's trade-union identity it still harbours professional tendencies. Professionalism often means a commitment to the quality of the work and to the paper and its readership, and there have been circumstances in which journalists have acted in defence of professional standards, like the principle of press freedom. But on the whole the desire for professional status has reduced the likelihood of outright opposition.

This spectacle of some groups rising in influence and others failing has attracted much research interest. We now know about an array of winners and losers, and some for whom the jury is still out. Fincham (1996), for example, looks at factors shaping professional processes in the computing occupations. These occupations are changing in a range of not always consistent ways. On the one hand, the strategic role of information technology is opening up career paths at the highest levels. Also technical change is highly dynamic, and new computing specialisms have always kept the demand for skills buoyant. On the other hand, changes like the dispersal of centralized computing functions have been regarded as a threat to careers in computer-skilled work. So the question of whether the information technology function has made the journey from isolated technical service to full integration in corporate circles remains open.

Other complexities involve the issue of *hierarchies* within professions. For while mobility may be 'collective' in a general sense, the rise in importance of a particular occupation may not be good news for all its members. A successful profession may still not provide a career platform for all its specialist staff. There are several ways in which this might happen. Organizations may impose a 'trusted' managerial group on a rising specialism rather than draw senior management from within the specialist ranks. Another factor involves the possibility of divisions within a profession and deskilling within its lower ranks. Armstrong (1985) has suggested that in accountancy deskilling was a contributory factor in accountants' gaining a degree of managerial ascendancy. It enabled senior figures in the profession to demonstrate their possession of managerial skills.

The system of professions Armstrong has drawn attention to the importance of the rivalry between specific clusters of professions. He looks at groups that have sought access to corporate power in (mainly British) industrial organizations, and draws attention to the success of accounting and the relative failure of groups like engineers and personnel (Armstrong, 1985, 1995). However, perhaps the most influential and comprehensive of recent models that focuses on this idea of inter-professional relationships is that developed by Abbott (1988). The twin concepts Abbott uses are the idea of a *system of professions* and that of *jurisdiction*. He points out that most previous accounts have studied the professions 'one at a time' and have plotted a pathway of occupational development. We can see why this should be so. The variety and distinctiveness of the professions is what we first notice about them, while their acquiring the trappings of status and reward is the 'story' we expect to be told. Yet this particular narrative, Abbott points out, conceals what is actually the key element of professional life, namely inter-professional rivalry. We therefore need to move from 'an individualistic to a systemic view of professions' (p. 2) and look at interdependencies and the overall system of groups engaged in the fight for professional status.

We stressed above the necessity of understanding the professions in terms of the actual work they perform. Abbott further argues that competition over work is the basis of the dynamic relations between professions, and is best expressed using the idea of 'jurisdiction'. This refers to the control a profession exercises over a specific area of work—the right to perform the work, to exclude others, to define good practice. The appeal to various sources of authority—the law, public opinion, the state—represents the basis of jurisdictional claims. Jurisdictions can be newly created by forces like technological change; professions can vacate jurisdictions as they move to other areas; and they can lose their grip on an area of work to a more competent challenger. The jurisdiction therefore is an exclusive domain and the battle over jurisdictions is the medium through which the development of professions occurs.

Another factor Abbott builds into his model is that of professional knowledge. As well as the occupational control of work, it is also of paramount importance that the work itself is accorded a high status within society. Low-grade work is of little use to any aspiring profession, and enhancing the status of its work is a key aspect of a profession's political role. Here Abbott notes that a defining characteristic of professions is 'abstractions'—the possession of work-related knowledge that is formalized into an intellectual system. This represents the platform from which a profession can both defend itself from usurpers and strike out to new jurisdictions. If a profession has its own 'abstract knowledge system' (with a methodology, philosophy, ethics, and theory) it can lay claim to being the only legitimate occupant of a particular area, as well as able to define and solve new problems. In this sense professionals are a type of legitimate expert: they are able to seize on the human problems of societies and organizations, construct them into 'professional problems', and profess to solve them via their expertise.

the development of the formal attributes of a profession is bound up with the pursuit of jurisdiction and the besting of rival professions. The organizational formalities of professions are meaningless unless we understand their context. This context always relates back to the power of the professions' knowledge systems, their abstracting ability to define old problems in new ways. Abstraction enables survival. It is with abstraction that law and accounting fought frontally over tax advice, the one because it writes the law, the other because it defines what the prescribed numbers mean. It is with abstractions that psychiatry stole neurotics from neurology, the abstractions of its fancy new Freudianism. It is with abstraction that American medicine claims all of deviance, the abstraction of its all-powerful disease metaphor. (1988, p. 30)

In the development of professions and the battle over jurisdictions, then, there is an entire range of possibilities. Professions may attack one another if they perceive the other's hold is weak, external forces may open or close jurisdictions, or they may simply be vacated. Thus, for example, the creation of new knowledge within a profession can enable it to consolidate its grip. This happened with accountancy when it created techniques of auditing and investment appraisal in its original move out of providing simple bankruptcy services. Similarly, new knowledge enables groups to seek alternative jurisdictions, such as when accountancy more recently expanded into business services and management consultancy. On the other hand, new knowledge and the creation of new client groups may mean other patterns of the creation or destruction of organizational jurisdictions. A powerful profession may ignore a new clientele, which is then seized on by an aspiring group that gains a foothold, and later attacks the dominant group for the whole jurisdiction. Another possibility is shared jurisdictions. This is commonest between senior and junior professions, whereby the senior profession claims a 'supervisory' position but does not have the numbers to perform the work. The junior profession is content to accept its role so long as the senior profession does not attempt to take over the work itself. Various medical groupings fall into this type of relation, with junior groups (nurses, paramedics) conceding ultimate control over treatment decisions to doctors.

In this way inter-professional relations can be co-operative as well as competitive, and the 'system of professions' model provides a broad-based framework encompassing the range of professional development. It attempts to overcome any bias towards historically powerful groups like law and medicine as standard types, and embrace professions that have relied more heavily on the state, or an organizational base, or where development has not been unidirectional but may even have stalled or slipped back.

Knowledge and knowledge work

As we have seen, the key role of knowledge in professional strategies has increasingly been recognized, and among professional and managerial groupings has given rise to perhaps the most distinctive occupational identity of recent years, that of the *knowledge worker*. This category embodies the dominant role of science and technology and the science-based industries in most areas of modern life. It reflects the significance of the so-called information society and new technologies. In particular, it reflects a distinction between *data*, *information*, and *knowledge*. Whereas data are simply groups of related items, information is data that have been structured and processed to produce a higher level of usefulness. Knowledge goes one step further and represents solutions that society recognizes to be of key importance. We can see such an implicit hierarchy, for example, in the development of commercial computing. In the early days, 'data processing' referred to the manipulation of routine files and accounts; then came 'information systems', which reflected the growing application of computers to more complex organizational and managerial problems. Finally, knowledge workers supply the inputs that enterprises now need if they are to innovate at the highest level and compete as world-class organizations.

Reich (1991), for example, has highlighted knowledge work, though he uses his own category of 'symbolic analysts'. These are the new elite responsible for the wealth of nations and who spearhead an economy's success in global markets. Reich explicitly defines common attributes such as creativity, problem-solving, and powers of abstraction and collaboration which span the activities of groups like designers, researchers, marketers, media people, and financiers.

Clearly, this kind of argument casts a wide net, and it can be questioned whether such a range of occupations actually belongs in one category. Kumar (1979) has provided the classic critique of this type of knowledge work and the society based on it. The issue, he stresses, is not so much whether we live in a knowledge society, but whether any society was ever *not* a knowledge society. In other words, when did the central powers and influential groupings in society not control the key forms of knowledge and information? Kumar also queries the different forms of knowledge that these groups deploy. We have to question the use to which knowledge is put, and the fact that the success of many of the new occupations actually reflects the social and political power of groups to shape the demand for their skills (as we saw in the debate on professionalization above) rather than their possession of formal knowledge. In other words, not all 'knowledge' is of the same type. The assumption behind many of the claims is that new areas of knowledge are in essentials like scientific knowledge and share in its power and rigour. Yet in many respects this is patently not the case.

For example, consultants are for many the classic knowledge worker and the consulting agency the typical knowledge-intensive firm. Consultants are a kind of 'parallel management' supplying almost any type of managerial, technical, and financial skill deemed to be lacking internally in an organization. They create and sell knowledge in the shape of solutions to their clients' problems, yet their expertise is essentially about image manipulation and the power of persuasion. The knowledge they create is highly commodified—they have to differentiate their products, define their ownership of solutions, and target them at appropriate managerial clients. Consultants' strategies seek to build images of themselves as the possessors of unique skills that internal managers do not possess. This may sometimes involve the hard sell, and at other times an emphasis on solutions tailored to clients' needs (Bloomfield and Danieli, 1995; Fincham, 1995).

In spite of some doubts, however, what is clearly true is that 'higher-level' occupations are expanding and differentiating, and that within this structure opportunities can be exploited by the new professional groupings. Here, for example, Blackler *et al.* (1993) have argued that the capacity to cope with emerging areas of 'crucial uncertainty' explains the rise of the knowledge worker. Ironically, while the expansion of science and technology might be expected to bring control over our material lives, it has ushered in a profound insecurity. This is marked by the complexity of global relations, the compressing of cultures, and new choices over the environment. The demands that such forms of 'disorganization' place on expertise account for the new-found importance of knowledge workers. The power of these occupations rests on their knowledge and skills, even if the capacity to represent these skills to wider audiences is also crucial. Certainly this kind of power-base is less tangible than institutional bases, like independent practice and the secure bureaucracy, that have hitherto defined professional and managerial groups. Nor do knowledge workers have the broader cultural assets that the traditional professions have been able to draw on. Knowledge workers derive great kudos from being associated with modernizing trends and new technologies, but they are constantly being market-tested for the relevance of their skills and the organizational problems they claim to be able to solve (the distinctly marginal status of a group like consultants springs to mind here). In this sense, knowledge workers represent the culmination of a long haul, from the last century when the certainties of property secured your place in society, through the still relative security of employment and professional practice, to the post-modern world and reliance on the possession of market-relevant skills.

The 'free-floating' nature of knowledge work has been analysed across a range of impermanent structures. Typical strategies involve networks of communication and knowledge communities that may or may not coincide with traditional sites of knowledge creation, like the organization or occupation. Knowledge may also be patterned across groups of users who themselves may become sources of expertise in other networks, and who may have inputs into the generation of new systems rather than being passive recipients (Clark and Staunton, 1989; Friedman, 1989). Here, for instance, Newell, Swan, and Robertson (1996) echo the orthodox concern with the professional association as the basis of best practice, but describe a more complex model of knowledge. The different kinds of networks (formal and informal) that attach themselves to professional bodies reflect the importance of the contacts through which professionals learn about new ideas in the occupational domain. Thus professional associations are not just representative bodies: they are the focus of knowledge networks and a context for innovation.

Conclusion

In this chapter we have explored a number of well-established debates around the labour-market and work-process situation of occupations, focusing on broad areas of manual and non-manual work. We also sought to bring these arguments up to date with attention to the nature of the new service work and so-called knowledge work. What the different theories and frameworks show is a focus that shifts increasingly to 'subjective' factors the further up the occupational ladder one progresses. This reflects the shifting balance of choice versus constraint in the different occupational regions. With manual workers the debate concerns the nature of an albeit limited occupational choice; with white-collar jobs material conditions and perceptions of status have been intertwined; and with professions the strategic aspects of rivalry between groups becomes the main focus of interest. Change in these occupational sectors reflects some of the strongest forces shaping the industrial economy—such as the gender balance in work and the sexual division of labour, and the increasing importance of knowledge and technology in shaping the new workplaces. These are some of the factors considered in more depth in the remaining chapters of the book.

Study questions for Chapter 17

1 Why is the notion of 'choice' in labour markets so problematic?

2 Explain the concepts of the dual labour market and the internal labour market.

3 What are the factors that have shaped the emergence of the ranks of lower-grade white-collar work?

4 Many of the new service workplaces are referred as the 'white-collar factory'. What aspects of the new service work would warrant such a description?

5 Outline the main characteristics of professional occupations.

6 The professions are often jokingly called 'the best trade unions'. Why?

7 The professions are (less jokingly) referred to as a conspiracy against the public. Why?

8 Why is the world of the knowledge worker an uncertain one?

Further reading

Abercrombie, N. and Urry, J. (1983) *Capital, Labour and the Middle Classes*. London: Allen and Unwin.

Child, J. and Fulk, J. (1982) 'Maintenance of occupational control: the case of professions', *Work and Occupations*, 9: 155–92.

Fincham, R. (ed.) (1996) *New Relationships in the Organised Professions*. Aldershot: Avebury.

Freidson, E. (1994) *Professionalism Reborn: Theory, Prophecy and Policy*. Cambridge: Polity Press.

Huws, U. (1993) *Teleworking in Britain*. London: Employment Department.

Hyman, R. and Price, R. (eds.) (1983) *The New Working Class? White-Collar Workers and their Organizations*. London: Macmillan.

Kraut, R. E. (ed.) (1987) *Technology and the Transformation of White Collar Work*. New Jersey: Erbaum.

Sayer, A. and Walker, R. (1992) *The New Social Economy: Reworking the Division of Labour*. Oxford: Blackwell.

Smith, C. (1986) *Technical Workers: Class, Labour and Trade Unionism*. London: Macmillan.

——, Knights, D., and Willmott, H. (eds) (1991) *White-Collar Work: The Non-Manual Labour Process*. London: Macmillan.

Torstendahl, R. and Burrage, M. (eds.) (1990) *The Formation of the Professions*. London: Sage.

Zuboff, S. (1988) *In the Age of the Smart Machine: The Future of Work and Power*. Oxford: Heinemann.

18 Gender and Employment

Summary points and learning objectives

By the end of this chapter you will understand:

- the historic and current dimensions of male and female *labour-force participation*;
- the dimensions of vertical and horizontal *job segregation*;
- the issues around the *inequalities of pay* between men and women;
- the *social mechanisms* of workplace discrimination; particularly
- the links between *male power and technical skills*; and
- prejudicial attitudes based on *sexual stereotypes* in work;
- how the gendering process shapes the *career chances* of men and women; including
- the nature of the *selection process* that determines men's and women's potential as long-term employees.

Introduction

So far we have explored various kinds of structural constraints—occupational, labour-process, labour-market, organizational—that influence the nature of employment. But the constraints of social structure are evident in another way, in the sense that certain groups of people tend to occupy particular jobs. One aspect of this social division of labour, central to any discussion of work, involves the divisions between the sexes. It can readily be shown that all societies distinguish between the work that men do and the work that women do. But in modern industrial societies, with their enormously complex structure of occupations and authority levels, the sexual divisions superimposed on the jobs structure are likewise highly complex.

In past chapters, we have seen how gender formed a key aspect of recent debates around the labour process (Chapter 10). Indeed, there are many cogent reasons for wanting to understand the similarities and differences in the roles that women and men play in employment, and the role of employment in women's and men's lives. This whole subject is bound up with recent social and economic change, as well as the fact that women's experiences in the labour force have been ignored or labelled with simple stereotypes until comparatively recently.

An important point to make at the outset concerns the distinction between paid and unpaid work. In our society, unpaid work in the home in the form of child-rearing is sharply distinguished from employment, or work done outside the home for a wage or salary. This division between economic and domestic activities, between paid and unpaid work, marks a major division between the sexes. Indeed, the sexual division of labour reflects a fundamental element of social structure, and one which defines the relations between the sexes in wider society.

These structured inequalities originate in and are sustained by a range of factors. There are broad processes of socialization and the learning of gender roles. Child-rearing practices adopted by parent differ markedly for each sex. They reinforce an active role for boys, while for girls there is an emphasis on passivity and the importance of emotional rewards. Existing patterns of segregation are greatly reinforced by the education system. In spite of all trends towards equal treatment in schools—and the quite genuine desire of many teachers to liberalize curricula—a degree of restriction remains. Schools are also obviously places where socialization continues. Peer groups and friendship cliques are known to exercise a powerful influence on adolescent children, so that they internalize a highly specific image of what they believe is possible and proper for them to aspire to.

The division of labour that exists in the workplace is strongly related to these wider divisions between the sexes. When young women first enter the labour market, having been encouraged to take non-technical subjects at school and advised to seek these kind of jobs, their occupational placement then reinforces the traditional pattern of female employment. The types of work traditionally open to women frequently reflect their domestic role as wives and mothers. And domestic labour is seen as something that women perform 'naturally' rather than involving active choice, as in the pursuit of a career or occupation. Moreover, the domination of society by market relationships actually distorts our perceptions of the value of different forms of effort. Effort which commands a price, in terms of wages or a salary, alone enjoys status. But domestic labour, which has no exchange value, is hardly accepted as having any economic function, no matter how socially useful it might be. Thus the identification of women, and women's work, with domestic labour serves to undervalue their real contribution.

Each of the above factors—the self-images that men and women have, and the exclusion of domestic labour from the rest of the economy—reflect deeply rooted beliefs about women's place in a predominantly male-oriented society. They mean that even where women do work, there exists a sort of 'grand myth' that they are not naturally fitted for employment, or that it is not 'real work' they are doing. Many specific prejudices about women and employment can be understood only against the background of these very powerful beliefs.

Patterns of employment

The expansion of female employment in the post-war period has been one of the most significant of all social and economic trends. In Britain, between 1960 and 1980, the workforce increased by about 2 million due almost entirely to the entry of the group that traditionally did not work, namely married women. In Spring 1996, 44 per cent of the labour force were women, while 71 per cent of women of working age (16–59) were economically active compared with an equivalent activity rate for men of 85 per cent. Over the decade since 1986, this reflected a rise of 3 per cent for women and a fall of 3 per cent for men. Over that period too, the total number of male employees was almost static, increasing from 13.6 to 13.8 million, but total female employment rose by 1.3 million to 11.0 million. The employment scenario seems to have been stabilizing during the 1990s. Economic activity rates were constant for women between 1991 and 1996, and female employment increased only marginally. Nevertheless, this long period of growth has left women firmly entrenched in the economy.

Labour-force participation

Over the entire period of industrialization, however, the proportion of women in paid employment has varied considerably. Hakim (1980) compiled rates of female activity (i.e. the proportion of women who are eligible to work who are in employment) from the national census reports, and some of her data are set out in Table 18.1. The pattern is one of relatively high activity rates up to 1871, a sharp fall lasting until the period around the Second World War (during which no census was taken), then a steady rise back to the early levels. This, Hakim points out, gives us a longer perspective on the question of the economic role of women. The notion of women entering the labour market in recent years is seen as somewhat misleading; rather, women *returned* to employment after being excluded for the best part of a century.

	Women above minimum working age (%)	Married women aged 15–59 (%)	Women aged 15–59 (%)
1851	42		
1861	43		
1871	42		
1881	32		
1891	32		
1901	32	10	38
1911	32	10	38
1921	32	10	38
1931	34	11	38
1941	—	—	—
1951	35	26	43
1961	38	35	47
1971	43	49	55

Table 18.1 Rates of female economic activity 1851–1971
Source: Hakim (1980).

Explanations of this historical pattern need to take several factors into account. Family labour was frequently used in the early factories, but the rationalization of this system from the 1840s onwards gradually eliminated these forms of organized work, which had survived from the early domestic mode. From the middle of the nineteenth century a combination of factory legislation which banned women from certain types of work, the formation of male-dominated trade unions, and the onset of the first great depression in the 1870s did much to exclude women from paid work. The economic expansion that took place later, in the 1890s, came mostly in the new heavy industries—chemicals, steel, engineering—which provided work that women were unable to enter. In contrast, the return of full employment after the Second World War drew massive numbers of women into the economy. This period saw expansion in sectors which were labour-intensive and where women were already established: the welfare state, education, consumer manufacturing and, above all, clerical and secretarial work.

Even so, the variation in activity rates that the data show is perhaps not as great as one might have expected. Even at the height of the Victorian era, when there were powerful social pressures against women working, these were mostly confined to 'respectable' (that is to say, married and middle-class) women. But it has always been true that single women and working-class women have had to work. Thus, as the table shows, even at the point of their lowest economic activity about one-third of women were in paid work, while at the peaks of activity about half were and are working.

However, these changes are more sharply defined if we take into account factors which affect women's circumstances, such as marital status and age. As the data show, marital status once made a great difference to activity rates, while the tendency in recent years for married women to work has nearly eliminated differences between married women and women in general.

However, age and marital status only partially reflect the stages in the life cycle. Marriage by itself has no independent effect on rates of economic activity. By far the most significant factor causing women to leave employment is the need to care for a young child. A pronounced 'dip' in activity rates for the age-group around 25–35 years reflects women leaving work during the years when they are likely to be raising a family, and returning to work later. The age of the youngest child is the most significant factor, with the presence of pre-school children (0–4 years) causing a significant drop in economic activity rates. Older children cause relatively little change in activity rates, and secondary-school-age children none at all. Coupled with a trend for women to return to work sooner after the birth of their children, this seems to reflect life-cycle factors being pared down to the minimum, and women's attachment to work strengthening even further (Sly *et al.*, 1997).

Job segregation

The re-establishment of women in the economy has reflected their increased demands for economic independence, yet patterns of discrimination have also continued. Women are 'crowded' into a narrow band of occupations, whereas men tend to be more equally present in different kinds of work. Nor are there signs that occupational segregation is declining (Siltanen *et al.*, 1993). Female employment is concentrated in unskilled factory work and low-grade service work—in the minor professions (nursing, teaching), in the manual services (shop work, cleaning, canteen work, laundry work), and in the clerical and secretarial sector. In 1996 in Britain 85 per cent of women worked in the service industries compared with 59 per cent of men. Just over half of all working-age women worked in three major groups of the standard occupational classification—clerical/secretarial, personal and protective services, and sales—while only 18 per cent of employed men were in these occupations (Sly *et al.*, 1997). Conversely, women are poorly represented in occupational sectors such as skilled manual work and the senior professions.

The pattern of female employment is also vertically distorted. Only small proportions of women occupy top jobs in management and administration. Even in occupations where women are well represented, and which offer a career structure, they tend to be confined to junior levels. Thus, women teachers are concentrated in primary schools, while there are fewer in secondary schools and even smaller proportions in promoted posts. In industry, too, it is common to find entire departments of women workers, per-haps with a woman as immediate supervisor, but with higher levels occupied by men.

Another indicator of distorted employment patterns is the amount of part-time and temporary work filled by women. Part-time work in particular is almost a woman-only category, and Britain is highly unusual in the sheer amount of this work in the econ-omy. In 1996 women represented 82 per cent of those working part-time. Of all women in employment 44 per cent worked part-time compared with only 8 per cent for men. Moreover, much-vaunted growth in the economy and in total employment since the late 1980s was almost entirely accounted for by the growth in part-time work. Thus there has been a shift from full-time to part-time work coinciding with an increase in the numbers of women working.

In some ways, the availability of this kind of work has strengthened women's labour-market position and opened up job opportunities to women who are more accustomed than men to these work patterns. Yet jobs have only expanded as employers have sought more flexible work systems, and what counts as 'flexibility' to employers almost by definition means a second-class job as far as workers are concerned. Part-time workers especially are in every sense 'hired hands'. They have no real contract of employment, little job security or entitlement to benefits, and their rates of pay often fall well below those of full-time workers. Of course, this is not to say that women necessarily feel resentful at being forced into the part-time sector. As might be expected, women with young children take up a high proportion of part-time jobs, and most do not want to work full-time. But the fact remains that the allocation of women to this type of employ-ment represents a major element of discrimination.

International comparisons reveal some different patterns. Women in North America, for example, have gained markedly better access to management positions, and in Scandinavian countries women are better represented in the professions. Rubery and Fagan (1995) point to 'high and persistent levels of segregation' across the member countries of the European Union—with common patterns of a low female share of manual and production jobs, but the feminizing of clerical work and many of the professions. But closer inspection reveals important differences accounted for by differences in industrial cultures (catering work, for instance, is much less feminized in France than is usual in such service occupations). In this sense, they suggest that gender segregation needs to be understood within varying national patterns of industrial organization, labour markets, and social attitudes. However, across the industrialized countries the similarities outweigh the differences, and Rubery and Fagan stress converging trends across Europe. Indeed, the variations which suggest that women have 'done better' in some countries can be misleading. Women may be strongly represented in apparently high-status occupations, but because of historic traditions and priorities those particular jobs might in fact be quite low status. Thus different employment cultures from country to country may affect patterns of occupational segregation, but women still tend to be found in whatever are defined as the low-reward occupations (see also Bradley, 1989, p. 15).

	Men	Women
Canada	16.1	34.3
France	10.6	17.4
Germany	7.6	25.4
Italy	9.3	18.5
Japan	5.9	37.2
Sweden	3.0	8.4
United Kingdom	12.8	31.2
United States	19.6	32.5

Table 18.2 Incidence of male and female low paid employment: percentage of low-paid workers in different countries, 1996

Note: Data refer to full-time employees only. Low pay is defined as less than two-thirds of median earnings for all full-time workers.

Source: OECD, *Employment Outlook 1996*.

Pay inequalities and legislation

Gender segregation is closely tied to the wide differences between male and female earnings. Studies have shown that only about half of the variance in pay can be attributed to lesser skills and training of women; the remainder reflects discriminatory practices—the concentration of women in jobs that attract poor pay because they are defined as low-grade (Walby, 1988, p. 2).

Internationally, Britain has one of the poorest comparative pay distributions, with roughly three times more women than men in low-paid jobs (Table 18.2). This compares with a group of countries like France, Canada, and Italy, where the ratio is more like two to one. But Japan is a worse offender still, with more than five times as many women as men in lower-paid jobs. This would reflect in part at least the pronounced industrial dualism of Japan, where men almost exclusively fill the career posts in the large corporations, while the sweated jobs in the thousands of smaller firms are heavily feminized. The United States has high absolute levels of both men and women in low-paid jobs, reflecting an increase of low-grade service work in recent years.

Legal provision has gone some way towards closing these pay gaps. Britain has had nearly 30 years of legislation against pay and workplace discrimination. The Equal Pay Act 1970—aimed at the ideal of 'equal pay for equal work'—confers the right to the same treatment as an employee of the opposite sex who is doing identical or similar work, or work rated as equivalent under a job evaluation study. The other relevant piece of legislation is the Sex Discrimination Act 1975. This attempts to prevent discrimination on grounds of sex particularly at the stage of recruitment and over the distribution of promotion opportunities.

Before the legislation was introduced women received just under half the male wage, then the gap closed slightly and gradually improved. The earnings ratio stabilized during the 1980s, with women receiving about two-thirds of male earnings. This seemed to suggest that the legislation had an initial impact—probably by eliminating grossly unfair situations where men and women in the same jobs were paid at different rates— but the broader effect was more marginal. The improvement in women's pay took another step forward with the ratio edging up to around 80 per cent by 1997. Recent changes may reflect women's strength in the labour market and some employers' changing attitudes, rather than being the direct result of legislation. However, the trend is not all one way, and women's long battle to catch up has seen some reversals. Government policy to keep the lid on public sector pay has affected women disproportionately, as workers in occupations like teaching and nursing are predominantly women, whereas pay in some male-dominated occupations (like IT) has soared.

The most important piece of subsequent legislation was the 1984 amendment to the Equal Pay Act. The original act had long been criticized for having too narrow a definition of 'equal work'. It meant that employers could avoid paying equally as long as women were simply in different jobs. Thus the legislation was of no help to the majority of women concentrated in low-paid female-dominated occupations. The 1984 amendment brought Britain into line with European law, and required men and women to be paid equally for work of *equal value*. In other words, if it can be demonstrated that in a particular firm or industry a woman's job has a similar value to a man's—measured on criteria like skill content and responsibility—even if the two jobs are quite different they must be grouped in the same grading structure. This provides a legal foundation and possible forms of comparability on which to base claims.

As Jarman (1994) has argued, however, in reality the law has been 'complicated, expensive, slow, and largely ineffective'. The legislation does not work by outlawing job discrimination; cases in industrial tribunals have to be fought on an individual basis and are difficult and expensive. Employers contest claims tooth and nail, and hearings and appeals have proved lengthy and uncertain. There have been a number of breakthroughs in specific occupations and for individuals, but little success in getting precedents set or extending findings beyond single cases to classes of employees. Thus even now few firms assess their jobs on equal value criteria, and even when women are in the same grading structure firms can still contrive to pay them less. None the less, Jarman concludes, strengthening the Act is important as it challenges discrimination where it occurs, without necessarily forcing women to move into male occupations.

Experience in the workplace

It has proved difficult to legislate effectively in the broader area of job opportunities for women precisely because discrimination is so embedded in employment practices. Some of the main forms of pay discrimination occur in ways that legislation is powerless to change. Labour force segregation occurs at the occupational level, but more important is the much more detailed segregation that occurs at the level of firms. In their survey of a range of female occupations, Craig *et al.* (1983) observed that, though complex, segregation was always strictly observed, and invariably the feminization of jobs went with low pay and status. Women's employment was subject to a kind of ghettoized status: once an occupation or a job was defined as 'women's work' many social pressures came into play which then reinforced the distinction.

There was a time when women were considered unsuitable for jobs handling money, but building society customers are now said to expect attractive young female cashiers. Pharmaceutical dispensing has become so identified as a female job that the chemists had not received any applications from men, despite the general high level of unemployment. (p. 144)

Traditional custom and practice played a major part in sustaining this demarcation: 'women were allocated to particular jobs and excluded from others primarily because this had always been the case, at least as far as the current manager could remember'.

Male power and technology

Cynthia Cockburn's research (1983; 1985) has been very influential in focusing on the 'gendering process'. How do particular jobs acquire a gendered identity? Cockburn suggests that the active role that men play in differentiating their jobs from those of women is a key factor. (Other writers too have referred to male power as central in helping to structure segregation, e.g. Game and Pringle, 1983; Walby, 1988; West, 1990). Cockburn (1985) examined a number of occupations—clothing, mail order, and radiography—where new technologies had disturbed the traditional job segregation. In some cases these had been opened up to women, but the long-term tendency was for jobs to re-establish gender identity. Men often left certain types of work if it became feminized and joined new occupations. Men may also move out of women's work through vertical segregation.

However, the active role of male agents by itself is not enough; broader 'social gendering' acts independently of the workplace. As Cockburn points out, 'the gendering of men and women into "masculine" and "feminine" is a cultural process of immense power' (1985, p. 12). Indeed, gender segregation surrounds some of the strongest taboos and prohibitions in society. Given that our overall culture is gendered it would be surprising if the gendering of work were not equally persistent. Cockburn was particularly interested in the *subjectivity* of job segregation. Her research showed that male workers often felt alienated and resentful if required to do 'women's work'. While some men welcomed women as co-workers, the majority 'scorn and despise women as workers and feel their manliness degraded by the presence of women in "their" jobs' (1985, p. 129).

Perhaps the most important aspect of social gendering concerns *technology and skills*. Here Cockburn has emphasized the powerful affinity between men and machines, 'the identification of men with technology and of technology itself with masculinity' (1988, p. 38). Again this is partly a cultural process operating outside work. 'Technology enters our social identity: femininity is incompatible with technical competence; to feel technically competent is to feel manly' (1985, p. 12). Thus technology is a 'medium of power', and by colonizing technology men are claiming power for themselves and also power over women. But this process is greatly extended in the workplace where technologies are much more developed and potent. In operating the latest machines, men are working with equipment that massively increases the productive power of the human mind and body. Conversely, women's identities are constructed in non-technical ways. Supposedly lacking any natural mechanical know-how, women get excluded from a whole complex of skills and technologies and the power over work that this represents.

Women are to be found in greatest numbers operating machinery but . . . continue to be rarities in those occupations that involve knowing what goes on in inside the machine. . . . With few exceptions the design and development of the new systems, the people who market and sell, install, manage and service machinery are men. Women may push the buttons but they may not meddle with the works. (Cockburn, 1985, pp. 11–12)

Several of Cockburn's studies explored the theme of male-dominated occupations being displaced by technological change. For example, her 1983 account of printworkers was an extreme case of an occupation being entirely eliminated. The newspaper compositors were a classic labour aristocracy, contemptuous of other occupations in the industry and their masculine identity bound up with membership of an exclusive craft group. When methods of computerized typesetting came in their position was fatally weakened and women began to enter the work. Cockburn reports much stress and resentment of the new jobs as 'glorified typing'. Some men, however, managed to recolonize the technology—they 'found different and better work as the new corps of higher paid, technical and managerial workers who minister to the computerised system' (p. 10).

Interestingly, though, the hypothesis that links machinery to a masculine ideology of dominance and control may not be fixed or innate—it may be contingent on technology giving access to workplace power and advancement. Here, for example, Packer (1996) reports some fascinating research on laboratory technicians. Fully one-third of all women in SET (science, engineering, and technology) occupations are lab technicians, and this occupation is thus a strategic area of female employment. Packer found that the normal technophile–technophobe stereotypes of men and women were actually reversed in lab work. Women were much more at home with technology than men. They had the kind of interest in sophisticated equipment, and the status and control that went with this, that is normally associated with men. Women technicians were constantly discussing the equipment, manipulating and dismantling it. Men on the other hand had the kind of pragmatic engagement with technology usually associated with women. The male technicians spent more time on administrative tasks (dealing with customers and suppliers) which in this context prepared them for managerial responsibility. In this sense, the gendering of attitudes towards technology was not a 'stable psychological type', but rather there were some complex associations between technology and masculinity–femininity.

The sex-typing of work

The structure of workplace discrimination is sustained in important ways by stereo-typed attitudes towards women's abilities—and these are mirrored in the demarcation between male and female jobs to an often remarkable extent. Much of the work performed by women involves the servicing of needs, such as cleaning, the care of children or the sick, and the preparation of food—tasks which directly reflect the nature of women's unpaid domestic labour. Other feminized occupations exploit sexuality and glamour (the model, the air stewardess), while semi-skilled manufacturing jobs rely on women's manual dexterity and supposed ability to cope with monotony. Thus very clear ideas exist about what constitutes men's work and women's work, and in all occupational structures men's work is defined in terms of access to skills, authority and technology, while women's work is low-skilled and service-oriented (Bradley, 1989).

Once a particular job or occupation becomes established as either 'men's work' or 'women's work', the myths and prejudices about the relative abilities of the sexes become powerful justifications for retaining the status quo. Thus the supposed inferiority of women as regards physical strength and mechanical aptitude has long justified their exclusion from skilled manual work. Also, women's supposed lack of 'decisiveness' and willingness to take responsibility are often the justification for excluding them from managerial and supervisory positions. In a similar way, the supposed 'female virtues' such as patience and tenderness have all been given as reasons for allocating women to a whole range of subordinate jobs. The secretary who is supposed to minister to her (male) boss, the canteen assistant who prepares food, the caring professions of nursing and social work, all are heavily feminized and in all of them women supposedly exercise special female skills.

Nevertheless, the sex-typing of jobs perhaps more than anything else reveals that these are socially constructed images. Take the biscuit factory that one of the authors researched, where managers insisted on the production jobs being 'women's work'. Nimble fingers were needed in the main tasks of sorting and packing, the work was repetitive, and it involved food preparation. This last point itself was somewhat far-fetched as the processing of biscuits on a conveyor belt bears little resemblance to domestic food preparation. However, the other surprising thing was that the nightshift consisted entirely of men. Questions about whether the men had any problems coping with women's work—was the nightshift less efficient than the dayshift?—were denied by management and met with the simple answer that women would not work shifts. In the absence of women, the nightshift men were content that their jobs were not women's work. An example of this shows the persistence of sex-typing and how it can be maintained even without any real differences in the work. It shows these categories as artificially and self-consciously defined, rather than reflecting any 'natural' female or male attributes.

Women's work orientations

To emphasize the many ways in which workplace inequalities are imposed and maintained, in other words to focus on the *structure* of discrimination, inevitably paints a rather pessimistic picture of the role of work in women's lives, and some would say a static and one-sided picture. Feminist writers and researchers have tried to overcome this problem by concentrating instead on the actual experiences of women at work. Although this approach still reveals facets of discrimination, a more positive view has emerged of women's commitment to paid work. Women's attitudes and orientations to work, their ways of coping with the problems of the workplace, and their motives for wanting to work all reveal a stronger attachment to work than earlier preconceptions of female employment would have allowed.

Research of this kind has shown that women do have distinctive experiences of work, which challenge the simple stereotypes of their economic role as being unimportant to themselves and their families. It is now clear, for example, that women's earnings are not, nor do women see them, as a purely optional extra to the male wage; women's reasons for working are firmly based on financial need. It is also clear that work outside the confines of the home, in a collective environment, can be a liberating experience for women just as for men. On the other hand, women's attachment to work differs from that of men in significant ways. Women 'construct' their lives as wives, mothers, and employees in complex ways, balancing out domestic and employment responsibilities. The responsibilities for home and children are not left behind when women enter work but stay intimately with them; family matters are much discussed at work, for example, while tasks like shopping will be integrated in the working day.

However, it is important not to overstress the distinctiveness of women's orientations to work. As Dex (1985, p. 43) points out, 'men and women are more similar than was previously supposed' and what we increasingly see are converging attitudes and work experiences. Women's work orientations often tend to be explained by the importance of domestic responsibilities, while male attitudes assume work as the central life interest. Having different explanations of workplace behaviour, however, can be misleading. Women may reject promotion opportunities if these arise, and conventionally this is explained in terms of socialization, or the conflict with a woman's domestic role. However, gender-based accounts overlook the fact that 'promotion' may mean very different things for men and women. For men it is frequently the first rung on the ladder;

but for women the first promotion is often the only advancement they can expect, and many will see little attraction in the pressures of, say, a supervisor's job if there are no further career chances.

Sexual stereotyping at work can also be examined from the point of view of women's active participation in work. Stereotypes are not simply cultural beliefs about women as employees; they serve a crucial *ideological* function in assisting the control and oppression of women by employers and men in general. Ideological beliefs, however, are not simply imposed from the outside; they are partially accepted by those under control. Only this element of 'truth' makes them effective and plausible.

In this context, Anna Pollert's (1981) study of women's manual work in a cigarette factory—the experience of working-class women selling 'generalised unskilled labour power'—discovered powerful stereotyped attitudes held by managers and supervisors. She defined these as male-generated images of female experience, yet they were real for the women workers who had to 'live out' these stereotypes on a daily basis. Thus the supervisors firmly believed that women had an 'aptitude' for the repetitive, monotonous jobs that were typical in the factory. The women themselves rejected the crudest version of this stereotype, but they did accept their work as 'women's work' in the sense of knowing that no man could be persuaded to do it ('I'd like to see one of them do my job for a week!', p. 87). Although the women refused to believe in the fairness of low-grade jobs, they did accept the reality of themselves as cheap flexible labour, and of the necessity of this as probably the only way they could compete with men's labour. Pollert also analysed 'factory politics', or the relationship between male supervisors and female workers, and the complex ways in which 'sexual banter and pranks' served to bolster authority in the factory.

Supervision was sexually oppressive, the manner usually cajoling, laced with intimate innuendo, and provocative jokes, hands placed on girls' shoulders as they worked, imposition mixed with flattery. To survive with some pride, without melting into blushes or falling through the floor, the girls had to keep on their toes, have a ready answer, fight back. They were forced into a defensive–aggressive strategy—but always on the men's terms. They had to collude. And in this they also colluded with the language of control. (1981, p. 143)

Thus sexist attitudes were the conventional rules of interaction of the workplace, accepted at a certain level by most of the female workers. But while the women were able to manipulate the rules to their advantage, they had to do this by exploiting their own sex appeal; so these were only 'momentary victories of self-assertion', serving in the long run to confirm their subordinate status.

Collective consciousness

One very pervasive myth is that the 'proper sphere' of women is not in public activity but in private and domestic roles. In industrial relations this is reflected in beliefs about women lacking any real consciousness or militancy, that they are unresisting as employees and that they dilute male collective efforts to win better conditions. Considerable efforts at challenging this widely held view have been made by feminist writers. Purcell (1979), for example, attacks the 'myth of the passive woman worker' and explains women's lower rates of union activity by the *nature* of much women's work. Factors like the high proportion of part-time work done by woman, the breaks in their continuity of employment, and employment locations like offices, make the organization of women workers relatively difficult. However, in an industry or occupation with a tradition of independent action, women are likely to follow these traditions rather than any supposed orientations as female workers (see also Brown, 1984).

Hunt (1980) makes the interesting point that the 'isolation' of women in the domestic sphere may actually make them more militant. Women are less hidebound by tradition and bring to work expectations that serve to widen the struggle and include issues of control and working conditions—rather than just the narrowly conventional trade union objective of pay. And Beynon and Blackburn (1972) have criticized the attitudes of male trade unionists and their job protection strategies. They argue that we should not necessarily accept the popular image of trade union militancy; in fact many (male) unions are fairly docile, and in opposing them it may be women who are taking a radical stance. Thus Beynon and Blackburn found surprisingly positive attitudes towards unionism among women non-members. What the women objected to was the do-nothing attitudes of the male membership, their exclusion from the union, and the fact that it was perceived as 'a men's affair'.

The gendering of careers

The central aspect of the gendering process in employment is reflected in the career paths open to men and women. At its broadest, the issue of obtaining decent employment with an element of progression, and a return for an employee's own investment, has several distinct dimensions. A major issue is that of combining the long-term pursuit of a career with care of a family, given that the responsibility for childcare falls more or less exclusively on women. The difficulties of coming back to work after a break are a major cause of having to return to a worse job, and employment and family responsibilities become difficult for women to combine. For men not only are they compatible but family life is often taken as evidence of maturity and stability and is actually career-enhancing.

Organizational and occupational careers

The problem of skills, upon which so many career chances depend, reflects the containment of women in low-skill jobs. Skills clearly have a material reality but are not purely technical abilities: skills are socially created. It is not sufficient merely to possess a skill; practitioners have to be accorded a degree of prestige which is determined by their social power to protect skills. In this situation discrimination against women's occupational skills can occur at many levels. Where women do possess skills, they are often not recognized or accepted. Examples of women's jobs with as much skill or managerial content as comparable male jobs, yet with far less status or pay, demonstrate how women's tacit skills can be utilized by employers without women ever receiving the rewards commensurate with their effort. The formalization of training also plays a major part: formal training schemes with a recognized certificate at the end are frequently reserved for male workers, while women receive informal on-site training and are not then accepted as possessing equivalent skills.

Occupational group	Women £ per hr	Men £ per hr	Women's as a percentage of men's
Managers and administrators	10.28	14.49	71
Professional occupations	12.72	14.04	91
Associate professional/technical	9.31	11.79	79
Clerical and secretarial	6.33	6.73	94
Craft	4.95	7.29	68
Personal and protective services	5.22	7.39	71
Sales	5.42	7.99	68
Plant and machine operatives	4.96	6.45	77
Other occupations	4.31	5.51	78
All occupations	7.50	9.39	80

Table 18.3 Male and female earnings by occupation, 1996 in list of table
Source: New Earnings Survey 1996, Part A, Table 8 (London: HMSO).

Women seem to do better in jobs where other women form a high proportion of the workforce. Pay is probably a reasonable proxy for a range of material and symbolic rewards, and pay differentials broken down by occupation show some marked differences between job sectors (Table 18.3). The male–female differentials are much lower in sectors like professional and clerical, which are highly feminized, and higher in areas where relatively few women work, such as craft or skilled manual. The point remains, however, that these relative gains are made in specific areas at the expense of a wider occupational presence. Moreover, even within sectors where women have gained a significant presence, they may still be victims of micro-level job segregation and crowded into certain parts of the sector. Thus women now comprise about one-third of managers and administrators, yet as we see some of the largest differentials between male and female pay still occur in this sector. This partly reflects their concentration in areas like personnel and human resources, while significant numbers are also bunched in the lower strata, unable to break into higher-level jobs. Indeed, critics have suggested that the growth and apparent feminization of the managerial sector partly reflects organizations' massaging of the statistics, and reclassifying white-collar jobs with some element of supervision as 'management' in order to make their gender profile appear better.

The potential returns from qualifications for men and women also differ. For example, over many years there has been strong interest in giving women a better stake in the SET occupations. The 'women into engineering' movement, for example, has attempted to get more girls to take technical subjects at school, and to follow through at higher education level and subsequent employment. Yet far fewer women than men with SET degrees find employment in the science and technology sector, and women who are SET graduates are much more likely than men to be teaching. Science and technology remains one of the areas most hostile to women (as we saw above with Cockburn's account of male power and technology). As Devine (1992) has shown, the extreme patterns of gender segregation in the SET occupations persist. In Britain, women's representation in these professions grew slowly from 1 per cent in 1979 to only 7 per cent in 1994. There are some 'breakthroughs' in sub-sectors, notably biology and pharmacy, yet this is also evidence of micro-segregation. In 1994 nearly 40 per cent of women in SET occupations were concentrated in biology.

Social mechanisms of discrimination

The mechanisms of discrimination and factors that impede women's progress are deeply ingrained in the practices and cultures of work organizations—the rigid views that many employers hold about the unsuitability of women as long-term employees, the lack of practical support with childcare and flexible hours, and the macho culture and office politics that are exclusive to men. Women managers tend to be both more highly educated than their male counterparts and concentrated in the lower ranks of management. This reflects the barrier of the 'men's club' and the culture of long hours which is something women find difficult to compete with. More generally, career paths in large organizations are invariably acutely competitive. Career hierarchies rapidly narrow down, and with women competing for promotion alongside men the chances for men would become significantly reduced. So there is often a strong imperative for

---

Box 18.1 Progress in the skies

The job of airline stewardess presents a classic case of sex-typing according to sexuality and glamour. The key sector of the airlines' custom is business travellers, and the idea of the weary businessman being ministered to by an attractive female retains a strong marketing image. Traditionally the selection and training of stewardesses emphasized appearance and grooming, and the job itself was one that a 'girl' did for an exciting few years before 'settling down'. More recently, however, airlines have been making efforts to improve equal opportunities, which has meant creating real career prospects for stewardesses.

At British Airways in the early 1970s, when the equal opportunities legislation first came in, there were no promoted women in the entire cabin crew. Since then BA has enhanced career changes by creating new grades and, in the case of women, by encouraging them to stay on. The figures below review progress over the recent period.

Rank	Fleet	1984 Female	Male	1991 Female	Male	1997 Female	Male
Fleet director/	Longhaul			20	45	20	20
Performance	Shorthaul			11	21	16	14
manager	Mid Fleet			2	11	7	8
Cabin service	Longhaul	13	224	102	317	145	345
director	Shorthaul	2	75	104	197	139	187
	Mid Fleet	0	0	16	49	72	105
Purser	Longhaul	62	409	725	704	1079	854
	Shorthaul	121	268	421	224	538	195
	Mid Fleet	0	0	99	48	248	102
Steward/ess	Longhaul	1180	928	2664	788	4085	1341
	Shorthaul	865	250	1431	264	1682	376
	Mid Fleet	0	0	242	75	752	240
Support cabin crew	All	0	0	557	56	266	11
Total		2243	2154	6394	2799	9049	3798

Note: Longhaul is international flights and shorthaul is local or European. Mid Fleet operates a mix of long- and shorthaul routes. Support crew are employed on a permanent part-time basis.

Source: Reproduced with kind permission of British Airways.

We can see that women seem to have made steady progress: by 1991 they occupied almost one-third of top-level posts, and by 1997 there was parity in the top job of fleet director, and though the level under this (director) still had a higher representation of men, again women had made progress. In the first-line promotion of purser—this used to be the old job of senior steward and represents the bulk of promotion opportunities—women also have a higher representation than men, and their progress appears to be accelerating.

However, other trends are contained in the figures. For example, the long-haul division has traditionally higher prestige than local or European flights, and the promotion rates of men relative to women tend to be better in long-haul. Women tend to be concentrated in the shorthaul division, so that a high proportion of women on these flights must work only with other women and this is also where their promotion chances are best.

But the most marked change has been in the feminization of cabin crew. Women have moved into the expanding occupation at a much faster rate than men (perhaps ironically when the occupation did have a reputation as 'women's work' it was probably equally populated by men, whereas now that the image is more one of equality it is much more highly feminized). This means that though the raw figures for promoted women show an accelerating improvement, as a proportion of total women employed the changes may not be quite so favourable. As an exercise, try recalculating the table to show the changes in women's chances of promotion.

employers to exclude female employees from the promotion race, as well as an effective collusion between employers and the male employees underlining their common interest in excluding women.

Crompton and Jones (1984), in their study of clerical work, stressed that male clerical workers had good career prospects only because the vast majority of female clerks were denied promotion. They explained the very poor rates of female promotion in the banking, insurance, and local government settings they looked at by a combination of factors: (1) women tended to be less well-qualified on entry from school and university; (2) far fewer women obtained post-entry qualifications, due both to 'anticipation of their withdrawal from the workforce' and to being discouraged by management; (3) their actual withdrawal from the workforce to have children was of 'enormous significance' in denying them careers; and (4) lack of geographical mobility, due once again to family constraints, also restricted women's careers. The researchers found that men's and women's attitudes towards work were remarkably similar, with little to suggest that employment was of 'secondary' interest to women (p. 149). There were, however, marked differences in attitudes related to just one factor: promotion. Many more men were interested in and expected promotion, and were oriented towards aspects of their work associated with 'promotability' (e.g. seeking responsibility).

The picture that emerges . . . is that the majority of young women, especially if they are reasonably well qualified, initially approach employment with at least modest career expectations, comparable in many respects to those of men. (p. 159) . . . The really significant 'break' in the women's attitudes . . . occurs among the group having made the most emphatic commitment to the domestic role—leaving work to rear a family. Whereas 79 per cent of young, unmarried women express an interest in promotion, this proportion declines massively to 29 per cent, among older women in the second phase of their work cycle. (1984, p. 156)

Crompton and Jones (p. 141) also found an interrelation between the limits on women's careers and women's own aspirations. Rejection of responsibility at work and the chance of promotion, as these conflict with domestic responsibilities, sometimes come about because women anticipated the employer's prejudice. This then 'justified' their being overlooked for training and promotion. Employers' beliefs that young women will abandon work to raise a family may become a self-fulfilling prophecy, since, faced with few prospects of advancement, some women may indeed come to regard work as of secondary importance.

Within most organizations there are powerful pressures towards internal career paths and traditions of promotion from within. The existence of an internal labour market, when combined with male–female stereotyping and the prejudiced attitudes of managerial selectors, forms an almost insurmountable barrier to progress for women.

Here, for example, Collinson *et al.* (1990) were concerned with the gendering of organizational power, with the sheer strength of the male-as-breadwinner and female-as-homemaker stereotypes, and with managerial control as an expression of male power. They conducted a widely based set of case-studies in different industries in North-West England, and focused on how recruitment and promotion practices reinforce patterns of discrimination. Recruitment and promotion, they found, was gender-divided such that employers 'manage to discriminate' in a range of ways. One key mechanism was the high level of *informality* practised, especially via the internal labour market. Managerial selectors jealously guarded their rights to recruit and promote according to their own criteria; and where jobs were filled using informal contacts, and generalized notions of suitability instead of defined criteria, job segregation was invariably reproduced and a preference for men sustained. There were, for example, powerful prejudices around the male-as-breadwinner image and the importance assigned to domestic pressures (such as financing a mortgage) for motivation necessary in managerial jobs.

For men, real, imagined or potential domestic responsibilities were usually elevated as a positive indication of stability, flexibility, compatibility and motivation, while for women, they were often viewed negatively as confirmation of unreliability and a short-term investment in work. However, these selector assumptions could be reversed, where the jobs on offer were low-paying, low status and mundane with little career potential. For such jobs, it was often decided, on the basis of the stereotype of the dependent female homemaker that women would be more stable, flexible and able to 'fit in'. (pp. 193–4)

Collinson *et al.* found that managers regarded these stereotypes as entirely normal, and when challenged they rationalized decisions by reference to the overriding need not to disturb production. The researchers argue that these ruling prejudices and rationalizations were 'highly selective and exaggerated accounts of the formal and material realities of production' (p. 195)—justified by competitiveness and the high pressure of work, but reflecting a vested interest in the continuity of male or managerial power. They also emphasize the potency of this discriminatory culture. The appointment and promotion of women in jobs they did not normally hold was perceived as a challenge to the whole system. Managerial selectors and applicants alike reacted defensively, and saw such appointments as highly risky and a potential threat to their security.

Informal careers

Because gender divisions are structured in complex ways, the career chances of women can often only be understood in the context of specific work settings. Indeed, the very notion of 'career' for women can take on a subtly different meaning. Whereas for men careers consist of the climb up a defined hierarchy of positions, within an organization or a profession, the complex work histories that women have can effectively put an end to any hopes of this kind of structured progress. If women are to have careers, it quite often means that they have to create a niche in some alternative work situation. A good example of this comes from Attwood and Hatton's (1983) account of the gender, class, and age factors that shape the career patterns of women and men in the hairdressing industry. This is sharply divided into primary and secondary markets, ranging from the fashionable and lucrative end of the business, to the lower-status 'shampoo and set trade'. Attwood and Hatton distinguished two very different career paths. 'Getting on' in the industry meant becoming a salon-owner or manager in the fashionable sector, and this domain was dictated by the male stylists. Female apprentices usually lacked the confidence to advance, but some women did create longer-term careers in the secondary sector and some became salon-owners. The researchers stressed the sympathetic relationships that existed between these women and the mainly older working-class women who formed their clientele—a sharp contrast to the extremely competitive and exploitative world of 'fashion'.

Conclusion

The link between men's and women's abilities and men's and women's work, which seems natural to many, is quite arbitrary, and beliefs about the allegedly inherent capabilities of the sexes can rarely be substantiated. In different societies and at different times women have done the work that nowadays tends to be defined as exclusively male, and vice versa. However, the myths and prejudices about men and women in employment remain powerful constraints, so that the basis of sexual inequality and the allocation of women to inferior work, however that is defined, has hardly changed in recent years, in spite of the hugely increased economic contribution of women. Their domestic role and responsibility for the home and childcare has not been changed by their entry into work. As Wainright (1984) has pointed out, women's participation in the labour force constitutes an *accommodation* to the traditional division of labour rather than any erosion of basic inequalities.

As far as career progression is concerned, the male-dominated structure of professions and organizations remains. Surveys repeatedly show only a tiny percentage of firms with sponsored childcare or flexible work practices. Women make up a higher proportion of the workforce in Britain than in almost any other European Union country, yet the British male–female earnings gap is one of the widest in the EU. Similarly, the type of long-term commitment that the internal labour market requires means that careers are rigidly structured, making re-entry after an absence extremely difficult. So while there may be a considerable increase in the numbers of women entering promotion paths in junior grades, these changes do not work through to the top or even many middle managerial positions because of the mid-career barriers women face. Progress through the middle grades is unlikely in the face of employers who refuse to accept wider responsibilities for working times and reinstatement, and who simply define any conflict between career and family as the employee's problem.

But what are the agendas for change that have been suggested? One of the current trends favouring women is the changing composition of the labour force. The supply of school-leavers entering work is declining, which means employers have to target groups such as women with children (as well as the long-term unemployed, returners, and older workers). There is also the role that women are playing in the restructuring of work. To be sure, many of the new industries offer low-skill and low-pay jobs, and even some high-profile growth industries, such as electronics and financial services, are poorly paid. Yet employers require skilled, responsible workers as much as they need to cheapen labour, and not all female work is in marginal occupations. To the extent that change means moving towards 'high tech'—clean, quiet, physically less demanding—jobs, women's claim on work may be strengthened. If 'flexibility' is the future of the workplace, with people constructing their working and personal lives in complex ways, going back and forth between employment, education, and periods out of the labour market, women are already adapted to this.

Here Cockburn (1985, p. 106) has suggested that 'capitalism' is less to blame for the exclusion of women from skilled work than men. While there was prejudice amongst employers, those who had experienced skills shortages were more ready to take on qualified people of whatever sex. Interestingly, too, Cockburn notes that crossing the boundaries of sex-segregated work is easier for women than men. Women may suffer some initial embarrassment, but no complete denial of their sexual identity, and they also have strong incentives to enter previously male-dominated jobs. What is crucial is initiatives and schemes that help women to acquire professional and technical capabilities, to enable them to 'come forward' to meet the demand for skilled work. In this sense, Craig et al. (1983) were particularly interested in cases where women possessed equal value skills that were unrecognized and unrewarded. Such cases provided a potential for breaking into the vicious circle of workplace discrimination. Ellis (1988) has argued that within trade unions—a main institutional agent of male oppression in the workplace—a 'minor revolution has begun'. Change still largely occurs at the level of getting policies on women's issues into place, but unions are increasingly positive towards improving women's labour-market position. And Collinson et al. (1990) have drawn attention to the 'self-defeating and contradictory consequences of sex discrimination' (p. 198). Though discrimination appears to present a massive cultural barrier, paradoxically it may rest on a precarious foundation where men are 'trapped in the responsible role of provider' (p. 201) which they may be unable to sustain in these days of rapid work transition. Collinson et al. suggest various practical measures—an infusion of formalization into selection procedures, and childcare and flexible work patterns—that may form the basis from which equal opportunities can be fought for.

These then are areas where progress may be made. What is required to transform the prevailing division of labour and the domestic domination of women is change on a broader front. This must involve explicit challenges at all levels in employing organizations, trade unions and professional associations, and political institutions, and must be meaningfully applied not opportunistic or made to accommodate existing patterns of gender discrimination.

Study questions for Chapter 18

1 How active are women in the economy, and how has this changed over the years?

2 What do you understand by the terms *vertical* and *horizontal* job segregation? How have these practices distorted the distribution of work between men and women?

3 Can legislation put right discrimination over pay and other work opportunities?

4 Technology is a mechanism of male power. Discuss.

5 What part do sexual stereotypes play in gender discrimination?

6 What are the similarities and the differences in men's and women's work orientations?

7 What are the major career barriers that women face?

8 The same social mechanisms that constrain women's progress often enhance male careers. Discuss.

9 Discuss the factors—practical and theoretical—that have a potential for improving gender discrimination.

Further reading

Bradley, H. (1989) *Men's Work, Women's Work*. Cambridge: Polity Press.

Carter, S. and Cannon, T. (1992) *Women as Entrepreneurs*. London: Academic Press.

Crompton, R. (1997) *Women and Work in Modern Britain*. Oxford: Oxford University Press.

—— and Sanderson, K. (1990) *Gendered Jobs and Social Change*. London: Unwin Hyman.

Davidson, M. and Cooper, C. (1992) *Shattering the Glass Ceiling: The Woman Manager*. London: Paul Chapman.

Dex, S. (1985) *The Sexual Division of Work*. Brighton: Harvester Wheatsheaf.

Grint, K. and Gill, R. (eds.) (1995) *The Gender Technology Relation: Contemplating Theory and Research*. London: Taylor and Francis.

Hakim, C. (1996) *Key Issues in Women's Work*. London: Athlone Press.

Hatt, S. (1997) *Gender, Work and Labour Markets*. Basingstoke: Macmillan.

Hearn, J., Sheppard, D. L., Tancred-Sheriff, P., and Burrell, G. (1989) *The Sexuality of Organization*. London: Sage.

Knights, D. and Willmott, H. (eds.) (1986) *Gender and the Labour Process*. Aldershot: Gower.

Siltanen, J. (1994) *Locating Gender: Occupational Segregation, Wages and Domestic Responsibilities*. London: UCL Press.

Walby, S. (1986) *Patriarchy at Work*. Cambridge: Polity Press.

—— (ed.) (1988) *Gender Segregation at Work*. Milton Keynes: Open University Press.

Wilson, F. (1995) *Organizational Behaviour and Gender*. Maidenhead: McGraw-Hill.

19 Technology in the Workplace

Summary points and learning objectives

By the end of this chapter you will:

- understand the problems surrounding *technological determinism* as a form of explanation;
- appreciate the *positive and the critical perspectives* on technology;
- understand how technology affects *work orientations and behaviour*;
- have explored the development of *the new technology of microelectronics*, together with a range of applications of microelectronics;
- be able to distinguish the different *managerial motives* for introducing new technology;
- have reviewed the *employment effects* of new technology;
- have reviewed the effects of new technology on *skills and work organization*.

Introduction

Technology, as we have seen in previous chapters, is one of the great themes in social analysis. The initial reference in Chapter 9 was to the role of technology in the labour process, but the account of technology has been concerned with a wide range of ways in which workplace behaviour is influenced by advancing production systems. These debates have been extended in recent years by developments in the 'new technology' of microelectronics. The revolution based on computerized networks—information systems like email and the internet, service and financial sector applications, programmable industrial equipment—is transforming many areas of social and economic life.

New technology contains both threat and promise. The promise of a powerful and exciting new industrial society beckons. In this context to decide against adopting the new technologies is hardly a choice, since countries are using them as the basis of innovation and some are already far ahead in this race. Potential threats arise if, as many fear, the technology becomes a potent destroyer of jobs and skills. The new technologies are labour-saving, and they have arrived during an era defined by fluctuating levels of employment. The new technology debate therefore follows hard on the heels of public awareness about industrial decline and unemployment.

In this chapter we shall explore some of the main arguments around technology and work. Technology cannot be understood from a purely 'factual' point of view—indeed, it has always been the subject of conflicting social and political outlooks. We therefore look first at different *perspectives on technology* that developed around the more traditional areas of production, and how these influenced people's perceptions of work. This discussion of older technologies should help us understand positive and critical perspectives, as well as the problems with 'deterministic' views of technology. Turning to new technology, it will be helpful to explore some of the background with a brief account of *developments in microelectronics*, together with current applications and the motives for introducing the technologies. The effects of *microelectronics in the workplace* are then reviewed, particularly the influence on employment levels and skills. Empirical findings here confirm a non-deterministic approach to technology. The variety of contexts for implementing technology, and the role of human agency and choice, mean that the possibilities are open-ended and there is no fixed or one-dimensional 'impact' on work.

Perspectives on technology

Common-sense usage of the term, technology, usually conjures up the image of some complex machine or device. But social scientists do not restrict the meaning of technology to the hardware of production. Instead, they tend to refer to entire technical processes. We may speak of a mass-production technology like car assembly, for example, or a continuous-flow process technology, such as chemicals or oil refining. The hardware component (machinery, automation equipment) is included, but the skills and know-how involved are also important, as is the type of work organization and the social setting. By taking this broader context into account, we are recognizing that the application of technologies can have very different implications in different circumstances.

A related point concerns the notion of *technological determinism*. This refers to the suggestion that technology is the determining cause of particular conditions or behaviour at work. Such arguments are appealing because 'technology' provides a simple and dramatic explanation—the idea of certain industries being strike-prone because of the alienating conditions of the work, or particular technologies impacting on work (causing unemployment or deskilling). However, social scientists have always been sceptical of such arguments, their point being that technology by itself cannot be the independent cause of anything. It is the manner in which technologies are applied, and the motives and actions of groups which control technology, that is decisive. Thus, given the complexity of technological processes, and the active role of human agents, different and often contrasting viewpoints have come to define the study of technology.

Various critical perspectives have already been discussed in detail in previous chapters. These revolved around the labour process debate (Chapter 9 and 10) deriving from Marx's original view of 'the strife between workman and machine'. When the control and ownership of simple tools was alienated from workpeople, during the industrialization process, the technologies of the period became mechanisms that commodified labour, paying little heed to the physical and social needs of workers. These themes of labour displacement, deskilling, and work intensification were taken up by Braverman (1974) with his controversial thesis of the long-term 'degradation' of work. Braverman was particularly interested in the deskilling effects of technologies and techniques like Taylorism. The debate has since widened and taken in work systems like just-in-time and total quality, the role of new forces such as Japanese management, and the influence of modern information technologies, to see whether they are extensions of Taylorist principles. These newer critical perspectives are pursued later in this chapter and in the chapter following.

That said, it is also important to point out the more positive views of technology that exist. Given the 'drama' of technology, and the increasingly central role it plays in our lives, such perspectives should not be ignored; they often constitute the common-sense view, as well as being themes that recur in academic debate. Perhaps the classic version of positivism as regards technology was put forward by the American sociologist, Robert Blauner, in his *Alienation and Freedom* (1964).

Blauner and the positive view of technology

Blauner's actual research, which goes back to the 1960s, now seems long outdated. But his account of technology was an early example of a popular and influential position: the view of technology as a liberating and energizing force. It emphasized the potential of advanced forms of automation for upgrading the skills and occupational status of those who work with it.

Blauner contrasted the 'existence of critically different types of work environments in modern industry' with the Marxist notion that working conditions as a whole could become homogeneous and degraded. He chose four different types of technical system to illustrate this continuing diversity: craft technology, machine-minding, mass assembly, and continuous process technology. From his findings, worker alienation, first, seemed at a minimum in craft technology. Trade skills and powerful union organization gave these workers job security and control over their work; they were also able to see a job through from start to finish and so perceive meaning in their own contribution. In contrast, both machine-minding and mass-assembly technologies seemed to maximize alienation. Workers in these industries were powerless in the face of constant work pressure and lacked any choice over work methods. Jobs were repetitive and meaningless, people were isolated from co-workers, and the work itself provided no feelings of pride or self-esteem.

In process industry, however, alienation declined once more. Workers in these settings (Blauner picked the chemical industry as illustration) were often technically qualified and their jobs involved the monitoring of entire operations. Whilst routine for much of the time, their work carried responsibility and they tended to identify with the efficient running of the plant. As Blauner put it: 'the responsibility of automated production confers a new sense of dignity and worth on manual production—a possibility not foreseen by many students of alienation, who assess manual work by the yardstick of traditional craftsmanship' (p. 165).

Blauner also chose the four industries to reflect the historical development of technology. The craft occupations were intended to represent pre-industrial systems of production, while machine-minding and mass-assembly technologies represented mature industrialism. Most importantly, automated production technology was supposed to represent future trends. The long-term implications are that machine-dominated work will progressively give way to work typified by complex technology, and thus alienation will decline from a peak in the traditional industrial society. Hence, Blauner made his well-known assertion that the progress of alienation can be charted as an inverted U-curve.

. . . with automated industry there is a counter-trend, one that we can fortunately expect to become even more important in the future. The case of the continuous process industries shows that automation increases the worker's control over his work process and checks the further division of labour and growth of large factories. The result is meaningful work in a more cohesive, integrated industrial climate. The alienation curve begins to decline from its previous height as employees in automated industries gain a new dignity from responsibility and a sense of individual function—thus the inverted U-curve. (p. 182)

Technological development is therefore seen as a positive force. The progressive elimination of alienating working conditions, and their replacement by work which is socially integrating, is not only possible, it is happening more or less spontaneously under the normal course of industrial evolution. Alienation is regarded as an intermediate and passing phase of industrial society, rather than its culmination as in Marx's theory.

Technology, orientations, and attitudes

Blauner gave substance to the widely held belief that technological advances are somehow linked with positive progress. He dealt with the critique of technology not by rejecting Marx, but by defining the Marxist argument as a special case of his own broader theory. None the less, the positivist thesis itself became the subject of detailed criticism.

The break with classical tradition is clear enough. As we saw in Chapter 9, Marx and Weber both conceived of deep processes of change within capitalist economy and society. In contrast, for Blauner, alienation was a function of technology alone—confined to the work situation and not implicated in the structure of industrial authority or wider class relationships. This restricted meaning of alienation, it was argued, stripped the concept of much of its radical force (Hill, 1981, pp. 90–9; Salaman, 1981, pp. 89–98). Similarly, the conclusion that work within continuous process technologies was intrinsically rewarding was also challenged. The findings of several empirical studies cast doubt on any simple link between technology, work, and alienation. Studies revealed much low-grade, unskilled work, pressure on labour costs, and job insecurity in these industries. This was in sharp contrast to Blauner's claim that, because labour is both a small part of total costs and critical for production, workers in high-technology industries would be subject to few pressures. It was also discovered that attitudes to work in process industries were commonly those of indifference rather than commitment (Nichols and Beynon, 1977; Gallie, 1978).

Others concerned with the influence of technology on work looked at the relationships between technical systems and various behavioural factors: patterns of industrial conflict, workers' integration into firms, workers' attitudes. In this way, the use of technology as an explanatory variable accounting for work-related behaviours influenced a much wider debate. For example, in Woodward's (1965) study, the industrial relations climates in different firms were compared with the technologies in use, and improved relations in highly automated industries were noted. Wedderburn and Crompton (1972) also stressed that employees in continuous process plants had relatively favourable attitudes towards work, got on well with their supervisors, and enjoyed some autonomy. However, this was not extended to any broader 'moral' attachment to the firm. Process technology gave a more convivial work environment, but the harsh realities of employment were still present. These findings lent qualified support to the idea of automated technology providing better conditions—but no support to any sweeping notion of a new set of class relations emerging as the product of improving technical conditions. In the plant Wedderburn and Crompton studied, workers were militant and critical of the company, and the researchers took the view that technology was only one among many variables explaining attitudes and behaviour.

... there is no simple association to be postulated between expressed attitudes and behaviour ... The general norms of the community, the nature of the influence and leadership offered by the trade union, as well as the constraints of the immediate work situation, all contributed in the final event to a very complex interplay of forces. (p. 142)

It has also been argued that technology implies too narrow an explanation of attitudes and behaviour. This centres on the debate about technological determinism. Major critics were Goldthorpe, Lockwood *et al.* (1968) in their influential *Affluent Worker* study. These researchers argued that attitudes towards work were not shaped by factors (especially technology) internal to the work situation. The problem of understanding how people assign subjective meaning to work situations must be seen in the context of adjustments and responses to wider factors. They argued that attitudes were underpinned by 'orientations to work'—stable beliefs and values which originated in workers' past experience. As we saw in the previous chapter, their study of car assembly workers showed that, while being dissatisfied with the work itself, workers still wanted to retain their jobs and were uncritical of the company. Work had become a means to other ends—the enjoyment of family life, leisure pursuits and so forth. With low expectations of their jobs, and alternatives in their private lives to compensate, these workers were apparently satisfied with jobs that were objectively alienating. So the study of technology should not mean ignoring the interests of the groups involved or the social elements in the context of work.

That said, interest in the processes of technological renewal has not slackened. Technology is a powerful force for change, and the idea of automation placing people in control of the work process is both appealing and plausible. This type of positive explanation remains persuasive because it allows a measure of optimism about the future of work. On the other hand, researchers also recognize that working conditions, and people's responses to them, can vary independently of technology. Even when implemented, there remains a degree of flexibility over the use of technology. It is people who develop, select, and implement technologies, and they do so under the constraints of relations of production. Thus any impression of a closed debate would be misleading. In particular, in recent years, the new technology of microelectronics has created industries based on communications networks, as well as information technologies that pervade all areas of social and economic life. Many stress the pay-off from information technology in terms of expanding services and industrial applications. Equally, others express concern about the technological displacement of labour and the losses in traditionally high-skill industries. All this has opened up fresh discussion about the relationship between technology, work, and society.

Developments in microelectronics

The beginnings of these new industries can be traced to the development of the transistor in 1946. This was the first device to use the semiconducting material, silicon, as a basis for electrical circuits. It was the development of semiconductors that was the crucial step in the *miniaturization* of components. In the 1950s and 1960s the transistor market expanded enormously, based on consumer appliances, like television and radio, and on military uses and the early commercial computers. Then in the late 1950s came the 'planar' techniques which enabled large numbers of circuits to be packed into a chip of silicon. Since then the industry has evolved at astonishing speed, producing a stream of increasingly powerful devices.

In 1971 the general-purpose logic chip, or microprocessor, wasintroduced. This can be programmed to perform different tasks and hence used for thousands of different applications. It has become the fundamental building-block in the electronics business, and Intel, the company where the idea originated, is now the largest manufacturer of these basic devices. This has led to the boom in personal computers, which now sell at around 60 million a year, as well as a massive integrated industry in software, network systems, and online services.

Major users of microprocessors are the armaments, telecommunications, and computer industries. Programmable chips go into huge numbers of products including TV sets, video recorders and CD-players, mobile phones and fax machines; the driver's airbag in a car is controlled by a microprocessor, as is the supermarket checkout and the cash machine. In addition, there is a massive and growing range of industrial applications, and hardly an aspect of work that does not involve information processing in one form or another. The remarkable capacity of microprocessors to extend the range of automation has affected many industrial and commercial activities. An idea of the applications currently in use is given in the following paragraphs (see also Table 19.1).

COMPUTER-BASED SYSTEMS
Mainframe computers. Central servers. Personal computers (PCs). Local and wide area networks (LANs and WANs)

OFFICE INFORMATION SYSTEMS
Word processors. Electronic mail (email). Teleconferencing. Management information systems (MISs)

SERVICE SECTOR APPLICATIONS
Retail: electronic point of sales (EPOS) systems, computerized stock control
Airlines/travel: customer reservation systems (CRSs)
Financial services: electronic funds transfer, automated teller machines (ATMs), home/office banking, branch automation systems, cash management systems

INDUSTRIAL MACHINERY AND AUTOMATION
Industrial robots. Advanced manufacturing technology (AMT). Flexible manufacturing systems (FMSs). Computer numerically controlled (CNC) machine tools. Computer-aided manufacturing (CAM). Computer-aided design (CAD). Computer-aided engineering (CAE). Computer-aided production planning (CAPP). Continuous process monitoring and control

INDUSTRY-SPECIFIC APPLICATIONS
Telecommunications: computerized exchange equipment, fibre optics
Printing: photo-typesetting, computerized composition
Media: electronic news-gathering

Table 19.1 User applications of microtechnology

Computer-based systems The single most important piece of equipment is the computer. Mainframe computers are still important in large-scale administration for maintaining filing systems and for supporting access to centrally stored information. But the mainframe environment is giving way to distributed and open-system computing across a range of industrial, commercial, and administrative activities. Newer generations of smaller computers, as powerful as the older mainframes and far more adaptable, are coming into use as central processing units in integrated systems. The networking of computers, with central file-serving and database facilities, greatly increases range and power. Personal computers and workstations can be networked within a location, while telecomms nets provide long-distance data linkages.

Office information systems Within the white-collar sector new office technology is spreading rapidly. One of the best-known applications, the word processor, has replaced the typewriter. Also included are communications networks like electronic mail (email), the application of which is booming amongst many commercial, professional, and personal users, and electronic conferencing. In addition, systems that support decision-making within management are generally referred to management information systems (MISs) and divide into different levels—executive information systems (EISs) to strategic groups, decision support systems (DSSs) for managerial control, and so forth.

Service sector applications Outside the office, in the wider service sector, electronic point-of-sales (EPOS) equipment is used for check-out in retail stores and supermarkets, where the control of stock and shelving is now fully computerized using automated re-order systems. In the travel industry (airlines, travel agents) on-line customer reservation systems (CRSs) which provide automated ticketing are an absolute necessity for business survival. And financial services is perhaps one of the largest users of computer-based systems. These are information-intensive industries and among the earliest users of commercial computers; the basic clearing system and many new service delivery systems are heavily supported by information technology.

Industrial machinery and automation The range of applications in industry is also varied, and machinery that employs programmable controls is found in all areas of manufacturing. Advanced manufacturing technology (AMT) is a generic term used to refer to any kind of computer-controlled manufacturing system; it includes machine tools, design software, and industrial robotics. AMT implies design for production and is the key to the speedy introduction of new products and design modifications into the marketplace. Under this heading comes computer-aided design (CAD) which automates the work of manual drafting and enables engineering designs to be reproduced on computer. Also included are computer numerically controlled (CNC) machine tools, the operation of which is controlled by built-in minicomputers. The CNC lathe is the most familiar example, but again in the engineering industry the range is very wide. These machines are often stand-alones, but they can be integrated into different systems of factory automation. For example, computer-aided engineering (CAE) involves the use of design data (from CAD) to control manufacturing processes; this type of system is also called CAD/CAM. Similarly, design data can be used in production control, or systems of shopfloor data-gathering, as the basis of computer-aided production planning (CAPP). And the application that has most caught the public's imagination is the industrial robot. Microprocessors in the robot's control system enable it to 'learn' the series of movements involved in routine tasks like spot-welding and paint-spraying. In addition, in plants using continuous-process technology, which may include activities as diverse as beer-brewing, flour-milling, chemicals and petrochemicals, microelectronics can help to monitor and control plant automatically.

Industry-specific applications Lastly, there are industry-specific applications, particularly those in the 'information industries', such as telecommunications, the news media and printing. They are capital-intensive (especially telecommunications), but their product is information, and in these industries are found some of the most highly developed applications of microelectronics. In telecommunications, for instance, computerized telephone exchanges are replacing existing ones that use electromechanical switchgear, and optical fibres will eventually replace copper cable. In printing, perhaps the industry most affected, many traditional work practices have been completely transformed by computerized equipment for the direct input of copy.

This classification is not intended to be exhaustive, but merely to give some idea of the technologies being deployed. It illustrates the variable nature of technological change. Different technologies have very different implications for production and are themselves introduced unevenly. There are certain sectors where the effect will be dramatic, others where it will be attenuated, and others still where there are no immediately obvious uses. Thus the likely impact of the technology on work will need to be considered in some detail.

New technology and management

Before looking at these special problems, however, it will be useful to outline the managerial objectives and purposes behind the introduction of new technology, as the new systems also have a major impact on the management task and the structure of organizations. Returning to a theme we explored earlier, in Chapter 17, for a combination of reasons managers nowadays are compelled to act more *strategically* in relation to organizational resources and outputs than they have hitherto. Pressures of competition and receding markets have made it more or less a matter of survival that companies respond positively to these changes—and new technologies have emerged as both cause and effect in this process. On the one hand, they provide improved opportunities for strategic choice across the whole range of management tasks, while on the other, companies find themselves having to adopt new technology merely to keep up with competitors who threaten to move ahead in capital investment. The new microtechnologies contribute to key managerial objectives. Fundamental management problems, such as the control and integration of activities, the provision of fast accurate data and the improvement of performance, are potentially enhanced by computerized management information systems.

However, it is possible to become too preoccupied with the potential of these systems, and to ignore the practical aspects of their application. As a counter to this problem, Buchanan and Boddy (1983) developed case studies in several manufacturing industries which highlighted the realities of technological change. They showed, for example, that rather than change always being sweeping, most innovations were introduced on a piecemeal basis and integrated at each stage with existing equipment. Where electronic controls replaced manual or mechanical ones, intervention by operators was still often needed. And the impact of performance objectives (cost, quality, workflow improvements, reduction of scrap) was often ambiguous—that is, different performance measures varied inconsistently, or management sometimes used new technology to make changes that could not be measured in performance terms, and the technologies themselves sometimes introduced new functions which were not comparable with previous systems. Therefore, in some ways there is nothing 'new' about new technology.

The impact on work, as with all forms of technology, is complex and reliant on human judgment and decisions.

Other research has stressed the gap that frequently exists between strategy and its implementation. In the implementation of CAD in design offices, for example, Currie (1989) revealed a wide variation in management strategies, because technology was being initiated and carried through by middle managers and technical groups. Often this was in the absence of any close strategic control by senior levels who originally allocated the investment. Likewise, Senker and Simmonds's (1991) review of CAD applications points to fairly widespread strategic failures. Lack of technical know-how among senior people often resulted in a considerable problem of the management of technology and expertise. This could result in too little spending on training, and on other back-up activities necessary to obtain the full benefits from equipment. Senker and Simmonds also found a hit-or-miss side to technology strategy. Firms in industries like electronics, which have related technical skills, implemented CAD far more effectively than other industries, such as vehicles and engineering: 'failure to adopt appropriate strategies for innovation, lack of appropriate technical skills, reluctance to change work organization and failure to adopt appropriate organisational structures can all inhibit the use of technology' (1991, p. 98).

Perhaps the most familiar question about the effect of computers on managerial patterns has been whether they will cause firms to become more centralized in their power structures, or whether the new systems will encourage a more flexibly organized firm. Of course, these are not the only possibilities. There are also indications of organization structures becoming polarized, with junior managerial and senior clerical grades being eliminated. The work performed at these levels essentially involves the collation and processing of information for forward transmission, rather than actual decision-making which is a middle or senior management task. Flexible modern computing systems are able to produce information of this kind automatically, so the strong expectation is that considerable losses of employment in junior management will result.

In practice, the pattern of decision-making, while not constrained by any fixed technological choices, has favoured the tightening of organizational control. Various 'contextual' factors, like a complex market structure or primary task, may force firms to decentralize power to on-the-spot decision-makers. But new technologies enable managements to centralize power without losing the flexibility of operations that is vital for effectiveness, and thus tend to be treated as a window of opportunity to support the managerial instinct for centralized control.

Microelectronics, work, and skills

We saw above that fundamental questions about new technology centre on its effect on both the quantity and quality of work—and that in the debates around established technologies a number of theoretical issues (like technological determinism) and perspectives evolved. These different positive and critical perspectives have re-emerged in contemporary concerns. One viewpoint is that the dynamism of the new industries will stimulate the economy as a whole. While jobs and skills may be lost in traditional sectors, this is part of the normal process of industrial development, and these losses will be more than compensated for by new occupations and additional economic demand created by new technology. Set against this is a far more pessimistic argument. Even allowing for increased demand from improved products and equipment using microprocessors, there is an even larger potential for displacing labour across a range of industries and occupations. New technology, moreover, has the power to displace high-level skills, rather than simply automating away the lower-level jobs.

It is no simple matter to prove the truth or falsity of these views. As we have stressed, hardware is only one component of technology; just as important are the systems of work organization and the social contexts into which hardware is introduced. This leaves much room for human choice as a determining factor. None the less, some trends are beginning to emerge, and we can start to evaluate the effects of new technology on work and employment.

Employment effects

The general outcome of mechanization (and new technology is no exception) is to displace labour. In individual cases, new equipment need have no direct impact on jobs, but the aggregate effect of mechanization across an industry or occupation is to reduce the labour content. Taking the argument a step further, reduction of jobs need not then result in actual unemployment. If the economy is expanding, the labour displaced by capital investment will normally be absorbed elsewhere. Workers may be deployed within the same firm if their existing jobs are eliminated, or they may be able to move to other firms that are expanding. However, in times of economic recession, the chances of finding another job are drastically reduced. It is then that job creation slows down, while technological change is still being channelled into the elimination of jobs.

The case for new-technology-based firms (NTBFs) being responsible for significant employment *generation* has been examined by Shearman and Burrell (1988). They point out that while much research does stress the dynamism of new firms, it confuses industrial regeneration with 'reindustrialization', the development of declining industries. Particularly in Britain, NTBFs have tended to be confined to the latter. True industrial regeneration involves new industries, with innovative products and new markets; but this has been relatively rare. Shearman and Burrell argue that the belief that NTBFs create new jobs is largely a myth—part hype over the new industries, and part 'entrepreneurial rhetoric' about small firms dynamically expanding into large ones. In fact, many entrepreneurs wish to expand only to be bought out, or they simply want to stay small. Thus 'the quantity of employment opportunities generated by NTBFs is not high' and is probably less than 5 per cent of all new jobs.

Similarly, the automatic linking of new technology with job destruction is equally problematic. Because new technology has coincided with periods of economic recession, the two developments are often connected in people's minds. However, surveys have suggested that unemployment caused specifically by technology has in fact had a negligible impact. There are employment gains as well as losses, but estimates of technological unemployment suggest a residual figure of no more than 5 per cent of job losses in manufacturing associated with microelectronics. The net direct employment losses due to traditional causes and organizational change are much more significant. However, while new technology is not the destroyer of jobs that many once predicted, it does allow large-scale productivity and output gains to be made without any appreciable employment growth (Campbell, 1993).

None of this is to deny the scope of any eventual impact. Many authoritative studies are pessimistic about the long-term threat to jobs. Even the optimistic arguments are not always convincing, their optimism tends to stem from faith in unpredictable factors like prolonged economic upturn, or in standard remedies like increased training and education, while they concede the near certainty of reduced employment in specific occupations and industries. In the past a dynamic service sector provided a wellspring of new employment. But the level of service-sector employment is now declining, and the build-up of service jobs, evident over the past 40 years, seems to have come to a halt. If new technology does eliminate jobs on any significant scale, there are no obvious major sources of new employment to look to.

In examining specific areas of work, in the main white-collar sectors, for example, the mechanization of the sector is rapidly gathering pace. Powerful and highly integrated computer systems are rapidly automating the bulk of routine clerical work, and are also increasingly used in 'higher-level' tasks involving decision-making and the interface with customers. Storey (1986) has placed the growth of office automation in a longer perspective. He refers to the period up to the 1980s as a 'phoney war' when the threat of massive reductions in jobs always seemed to be around the corner, but never quite arrived. In fact, during this period productivity was rising, but it was being offset by growth in demand, especially in financial services. However, Storey argues, the real war has now begun: we see both a rapid spread of computer applications and a slow-down in service sector growth. By the early 1990s this was leading to some large-scale white-collar job reductions.

Gender implications A major concern about the impact of office technology is that women may bear the brunt of change. As we saw in Chapter 18, female employment is heavily concentrated in particular occupations and sectors, and while some of these do not seem directly at risk (particularly in social welfare, education and personal services), much female employment is focused in areas expected to suffer high technological unemployment. Office automation poses perhaps the major threat. About 2 million women in Britain work in clerical/secretarial jobs which are in direct line of fire of the new office technology. In addition, about three-quarters of a million women work in the distributional trades, and much of the work here (like stock control and retail sales) is being rapidly automated.

Despite such indications, the overall effect of new technology on female employment is likely to be quite complex. In clerical jobs, for example, gender issues and technology act on the work situation in complicated ways. Clerical work has always been extremely important for women. These highly feminized categories of employment may have suffered a process of decline over the past two or three decades, but (as we saw in Chapter 17) they are still favoured, even 'middle class' occupations. As Liff (1990) points out, clerk represents the highest job status that any significant proportion of women achieve. And while technical change is now widespread, and part and parcel of the transforming status of clerical work, it is not usually seen as gender-specific or targeted on women. Indeed gender has traditionally been a barrier to mechanization, with male managers reluctant to lose the prestige they gain from a secretary or clerical subordinate. In other ways, too, women's jobs may prove rather resilient to the impact of new technology. Female labour is generally cheaper than male labour and so is less likely to be mechanized. Certainly the prime candidates for mechanization—expensive organized labour like car assembly workers, engineers and printers—are rarely female. Given the high proportion of part-time work that women do, they are also more flexible and hence attractive to employers during a time of recession.

The very fact of employers treating women as a flexible labour force, however, means that the *quality* of their jobs may be undermined in other ways. In a wide range of women's occupations, health problems are being linked with new technology. Particularly in clerical and secretarial work, marked increases in stress and related hazards like eyestrain, headaches, and tiredness are being reported. Working at visual display units (VDUs) often means an increase in speed, concentration and monotony. Some workplaces increasingly resemble the white-collar factory with large female labour forces inputting data under highly intensive conditions. As well as stress-related problems, increasing numbers suffer from repetitive strain injury (RSI), a term which covers a range of injuries to the hands, wrists, arms, shoulders and back. RSI is a symptom common to specific and severely disabling industrial diseases like tendinitis and carpal tunnel syndrome (acute inflammation of the hand).

Much ambiguity surrounds this issue, however. The incorrect installation of equipment or inadequate training for workers—which results, for example, in screen-glare or poor posture—are often blamed rather than the technology itself. With correctly used equipment and work breaks, experts suggest that there is no danger to health. Nevertheless, the forms of work organization and level of capital investment in many installations create pressure for an intense pace of work. Thus, even where the numbers of women's jobs are maintained, the quality of work might be adversely affected and might increasingly fall into the category of cheap and degraded or even sweated labour.

Skills and work organization

Apart from labour displacement, new technology also has important repercussions on the labour process—on skills and on the ways in which work is organized. In Chapter 10 we reviewed the sociological debate in this area and compared models which stress the *deskilling* effect of technology and work organization with those which take a more positive approach and argue that there is no reason to suppose that the *regeneration* of skills is any less typical than their destruction. The parallel question arises here in relation to new technology: will the new applications on the whole degrade the skills of workers, or will they create new skills and enhanced opportunities for occupational development?

As before, a definitive answer lies beyond our scope, and in any case is probably not possible as the issue comes down to different viewpoints and schools of thought. However, one thing we have learned from the deskilling debate is that there is rarely a simple deskilling versus upskilling choice. Jobs may lose certain types of skill but retain others, or generate new ones; chances of promotion or other job boundaries may open up even if work is losing status, and there are crucial *subjective* factors that make people ambivalent even where a loss of skills seems obvious. The emphasis therefore must be on examining the detailed impact of applications and the choices that technology leaves open, rather than on seeking evidence for any generalized impact.

Studies in detail For example, the computer itself has created wholly new occupations and employment opportunities. Many thousands of jobs, ranging from unskilled assembly work to the highest level of engineering and system skills, have been created in the computer industry which simply were not in existence thirty years ago. Certainly this is skill (and job) creation on a grand scale. However, there are also indications of deskilling. If we take the occupation of programmer, in the early days of commercial computing the programmers controlled most aspects of machine operations. This was reflected in the level of skill required and in their status and pay. Since then, however, the job has been subject to rationalization. Higher-level work is now in the hands of an elite of systems analysts, while programmers mostly write routine specifications. This has caused Kraft (1979) to speak of the 'industrialization' of programming. On the other hand, the divisions of labour for producing software are changing fast and expertise is becoming distributed across complex organizational structures.

Friedman (1989) has argued that the deskilling thesis gives only half the picture. He proposes a three-stage model of computer systems development. In the early days of commercial computing, innovative programming was encouraged (or at least tolerated) in order to cope with poorly understood procedures and equipment; later a reaction occurred when much tighter work controls were imposed, which is the period that reflects deskilling. But more recently computing has increased greatly in its strategic importance, and the need now is to link it with wider organizational goals. This has meant more 'responsible' forms of work control and enhancement of the skills and autonomy of programmers.

To take a second example, that of the word processor, there were early concerns that the equipment was automating many of the skills of the secretary. But later research has painted a more complex picture. Thus Webster (1990) argues that there is 'no incipient tendency for word-processing to bring about a form of Taylorist control' (p. 117). Her case studies of white-collar work locations provide a detailed account of skills and tasks, stressing the *variability* of secretarial work. The context of the typing pool often did bring more repetitive work when converted to word-processing, but this was in contrast to employees with broader administrative control where the machines might enhance status and skills. Many of the women whom Webster interviewed found that

Box 19.1 Computer numerical control

Computer numerical control (CNC) at first sight appears to be a classic Taylorist/deskilling technology. Machinery is programmed away from the shopfloor by specialist technical staff, and workers are reduced to tasks like machine-minding and loading. The old craft skills of reading engineering drawings and operating machine tools are submerged in the computer program which controls machine operations. Several studies, particularly some early ones, confirmed the loss of skills and showed that workers in complex, CNC-driven systems little resemble the conventional skilled machinist (Noble, 1978; Shaiken *et al.*, 1986).

However, other research has found that deskilling 'impacts' are crucially mediated by the fact that there is scope for workers themselves to program machines. A number of contextual factors in the strategies and practices of organizations, rather than technology itself, determine job design (Campbell and Warner, 1987; Burnes, 1988). First, managerial objectives and values may stress either the remote control of machinery or the involvement of the workforce. For example, Hendry's (1990) survey of CNC found factories where the strategy was to retain apprenticeship schemes and to retrain workers out of loyalty to existing workforces. Hendry also showed that management strategy can vary on its own, independently of other factors. One operations manager expressed the following very positive view:

There are two ways you can do it. You can say to the operator, 'you just push the button, to start it and stop it; you don't put a finger on the programme'. And you'll have no development, neither in the person, nor in the component. But by having the man on the machine involved, he's found a better way round, and the company's gained the benefit of that, because he's applied his knowledge in paring down or improving the programme. (Quoted in Hendry, 1990, p. 33)

However, this policy was reversed by a later managing director who favoured the remote control of machine operations.

Secondly, the history of industrial relations and the nature of the trade union can influence skills changes and CNC automation. Shopfloor politics and workers' resistance can shape the work situation. The collective resistance of employees has often been important in protecting skills and, in the case of CNC, in claiming involvement in shopfloor programming.

Although sometimes acting independently, the above factors are more often merged into an overall work context. Thus in Hendry's (1990) study, covering seven factories, the impact on skills was 'affected by the existing skill base, the attitudes of employees and management and the strategic importance of particular groups'. He found in one case, where skilled male workers were concerned, CNC had enhanced skills and training and was 'eagerly embraced'; but in a shop containing women workers a major CNC investment had transformed their jobs into mere machine loading and visual inspection, while programming was done centrally by production engineers.

word-processing enhanced their jobs, despite the tendency among managers to look down on work like typing. As she points out, it is the complexity of office jobs that gives secretarial workers control; word processors are more complex than typewriters and, other things being equal, are associated with more job discretion.

Crompton and Jones's (1984) study of the impact of computerization on clerical work presents a more straightforward account of deskilling. Traditionally, clerical work resembled a craft in the sense of being based on the clerk's special knowledge of the firm's filing system. However, Crompton and Jones show how computerized batch systems for basic clerical tasks, like payroll and accounts, have eliminated this control of information, and now clerical work mainly consists of preparing information to be fed into the computer.

. . . the value of the clerk to the employer once resided both in a detailed knowledge of clerical work procedures (the clerical 'craft') and also in the fact that, to varying extents, clerical workers have exercised control on behalf of capital. . . . The clerk now typically performs the function of (deskilled) labour, being increasingly peripheral to the performance of the computer and having little or no responsibility for the coordination and completion of the many separate work tasks in the process as a whole. (1984, p. 76)

Other studies have confirmed this basic picture. For example, Knights and Sturdy's (1990) account of the insurance industry found an entrenched sexual division of labour. These researchers argued that office technology brought about large increases in routine clerical work, and that these jobs became feminized and separated out from managerial and career jobs.

Gender and skills A somewhat more positive view of such changes is apparent in research where workers' own perceptions are taken into account. Thus in Liff's (1990) survey of women office workers, the bulk of respondents reported that interest and skill had increased. On the whole they approved of the changes; they were pleased at being able to perform the work more efficiently and to give a better service to customers, and they found mastering the new equipment a challenge (although stress-related problems had increased and new skills were rarely recognized by regrading). Rolfe (1990) has taken this argument a step further and pointed out that earlier research on technology, by the likes of Woodward and Wedderburn (see above), did deal with workers' attitudes and reflected a broader concern with issues of class consciousness. Attitudes remain crucial to the experience of technical change. Rolfe's own study of non-manual workers found that, even where deskilling occurred, people's attitudes were never wholly negative—at worst they were ambivalent. Experiences of deskilling were offset by a 'prevailing ideology of progress'. Attitudes towards change were conditioned by the perceived inevitability of technical change, and by the common-sense logic of any situation in which the job could be performed better.

Similarly, Fearfull (1997) has stressed the importance of 'tacit skills' in women's employment, and found that new technologies like computer-supported telephone systems enhance workers' skilled and central role. She examined specialized clerical work in debt recovery. These were mainly female clerks taking on the cases of customers who fail to keep up with payments for goods bought on credit. Their job was 'to maximise debt recovery while maintaining customer goodwill'. Significant intellectual skills were involved—making sense of customers' problems, and negotiating arrangements for payment that satisfy the company and the customer. Clerks also exercised considerable discretion over their work, kept contact with field staff, were important in building an image of the company, and had a depth of knowledge of customer files and the computer systems. The downside was that (as with much of the new service work—see Chapter 17) their job descriptions and status did not reflect the real skills being exercised. The female clerks themselves tended to undervalue their skills—seeing them not as 'proper skills' but as 'just something I do'—whereas male clerks were much more positive about the skilled elements of their work. Fearfull thus showed that technology had if anything strengthened the traditional clerical craft, but she also stressed the kind of exploitation that is endemic in highly feminized work.

Examples such as these indicate the complexity of the skills issue and the importance of the work context. A great deal depends on the situations in which new technologies are introduced and the characteristics of the workers involved. The purely technical issue, whether or not it is feasible to mechanize a given work process, is by no means the only consideration.

The 'impact' of new technology?

A number of writers have been critical of what they call the 'impact' approach, in which attempts are made to survey or predict the overall effects of new technology. The counter-argument put forward is that the implementation of technology has to be seen as a much more complex process, involving social interaction. Any final 'impact' on work cannot be pre-defined; it can only be understood by focusing on the particular work context and the role of human agents. As Sorge *et al.* (1982) have argued: 'the constant reference to microelectronics as having "effects" is not often helpful; this glosses over the importance of industry-specific factors which become ever more important as microelectronics is used in an increasing range of industries, services and occupations'. In essence, therefore, this is an argument against technological determinism.

For example, Child *et al.* (1984) studied a range of different work settings in the service sector and argued that there is nothing inevitable about the way new technology is implemented. They found that, in cases of junior-level employees working with new technologies, elements of skill and control were lost and staff expressed dissatisfaction with the way the technologies impinged on their jobs. However, staff who had a developed professional ethic and a relatively strong organizational position remained in control of the new systems. Child *et al.* concluded that the effect of new technology upon work depends on the 'workplace power' of incumbents, and where key areas of organizational uncertainty are being controlled, technology can serve to enhance status and skills.

Another relevant case example is that of electronic mail. As a form of communication based on the personal computer email is rapidly spreading. It can link organizations internally, but also internationally, or it can provide an information network for a

Box 19.2 Computer-aided design

Computer-aided design (CAD) is a technology that has stimulated a large body of research. Studies have addressed the question of skills and the organizational implications of design automation.

CAD is a range of powerful graphics systems that enable drafting and design to be reproduced on the computer. Drawing is done on screen with an electronic stylus, and the design then forms a database which can be stored and retrieved from the computer library. Advantages over manual drafting include the enhancement of drawings—sections, elevations, enlargements and image rotations are produced automatically, and intermediate drawings can be merged on screen. These bring efficiency gains as well as improvements in drawing quality.

Attention was first focused on the potential of CAD for degrading draftsmen's jobs by Mike Cooley's research. The work of production design is increasingly fragmented and intensified by CAD, Cooley argued; manual drafting is marginalized, and only the elite few with design skills are able to use the system as a powerful tool. Also, the imposition of shift-working and bureaucratic hierarchies becomes necessary for this expensive equipment to be cost-effective (e.g. Cooley, 1987). Other research has likewise stressed the 'Taylorization of the drawing office'. CAD removes the craft element of drafting, and it contributes to routinization and managerial control because it enables drawings to be integrated centrally (Kaplinsky, 1982; Baldry and Connolly, 1986).

Nevertheless, as with some other technologies, more recent research has painted a more complex and optimistic picture. Researchers question whether managements actually pursue Taylorist strategies in relation to designers, or whether their objectives in adopting CAD are more varied and concerned with using their expensive labour more efficiently. The point has also been raised that earlier studies reflecting a Taylorist emphasis may have been based on anecdotal evidence, and may not support an overall trend towards deskilling (Jones, 1988). For example, McLoughlin's (1989) study of four drawing offices suggests that on balance the old manual drafting skills were being replaced by newer, conceptual skills. CAD did not diminish the need for engineering knowledge, instead its modelling systems enhanced the creative aspects of design. The survey that Senker and Simmonds (1991) conducted, which covered 32 establishments, also revealed mostly positive attitudes among designers; and they hint that the findings in early research may partly at least reflect a methods problem. Deskilling may in fact be relatively easy to identify, since it concerns the disappearance of familiar skills, whereas reskilling might be more difficult to spot as it involves new (and unfamiliar) skills—and, in the case of CAD, skills that are 'opaque' to the observer. Something of this problem comes through in this quotation from a designer.

My first impressions of CAD were unfavourable: I thought it took away a drafter's skills. But after learning to use CAD, I realised that the CAD 'only draws pictures'. It does not take skills of an engineer away—it enhances them. It does not take drafting skills away— you need drafting skills to produce good work on CAD. Advantages of CAD are that it is quick and you can do more complicated things. . . . CAD makes life easier. It would be a real pain to go back to the old ways of doing things. (Quoted in Senker and Simmonds, 1991, p. 97)

Furthermore, the impact of CAD on the social organization of work may have been overestimated. Senker and Simmonds found that the integration of CAD with manufacturing—to produce systems like CAD/CAM and CAPP—had hardly progressed at all. In most companies managerial objectives were confined to design automation, and electronic links to the shopfloor applied only to simple products. Studies in several European countries and North America have also challenged Taylorist predictions (Löwstedt, 1988). They find little evidence of any significant degree of organizational change, and indeed stress the determination of managements to introduce CAD without unduly affecting existing divisions of labour.

It would be misleading, however, to suppose that the earlier research stressing deskilling had been entirely supplanted. Somewhat paradoxically, the international studies lend some support to the view that in Britain at least CAD has had a relatively greater impact. Thus Lee's (1991) comparison of design engineers in Canada and Britain stressed the higher occupational status of the Canadian profession. In Britain CAD was seen more as an opportunity to rationalize the whole design process, and firms were under greater pressure to make productivity gains. A strong trade union presence in many British firms was at least as important in constraining attempts to impose flexible hours as was the goodwill of managers.

knowledge community like an occupation. As Brigham and Corbett (1997) argue, email is more than just a handy form of communication, it actually defines certain organizational realities. Their case-study of the introduction of email focused on an engineering firm that was undergoing major restructuring—away from traditional engineering excellence and towards a more commercial, cost-driven ethos. Email was part of the new culture that management was trying to impose, and represented a tool for monitoring work. Messages could be sent efficiently and management could be certain they were read, work schedules were distributed on the network, and its usage generally heightened pressure. Thus for Brigham and Corbett email was 'not simply a medium of communication, but, more fundamentally, an agent of organisational power'. A rather different emphasis comes from Pliskin *et al.* (1997), who studied the role of email in a strike situation. This was in the Israeli universities and email helped to maintain unity. Strikers boosted each other's morale by swapping stories and jokes over the network; it was a key communication mechanism enabling the stages in the dispute to be accurately debated, and it helped the strikers' representatives to keep in close touch with their members.

The different outcomes thus reflected different organizational contexts. In the former case the context was that of bureaucratic employment, whereas the latter involved a group of professionals (academics). In the former case the researchers found that email isolated people because they communicated via machine rather than face-to-face; in the latter this kind of communication reinforced their sense of community. Indeed, a group of strikers is itself a kind of 'virtual community' which email helped to consolidate. In this sense, it is meaningless to seek any one-dimensional 'impact' of technology. The technology was a tool of power in both cases—but with a centralizing outcome in one and benefits for organizational democracy in the other.

Conclusion

Whatever complexities exist in the relationship between technology and work, it would be wrong if we were to detract from the full scope and potential of advanced automation. For when one accumulates the evidence of areas likely to be affected—in office work, middle management, planning and mass production, as well as in specific industries like engineering and telecommunications—it is hard to avoid the conclusion that the medium- to long-term impact might be very dramatic indeed.

When new technology first began to attract attention it was often linked with extreme scenarios of future events. Optimistic scenarios looked to the benefits of a leisure society and an end to the alienating work of the industrial economy. The pessimistic scenario, in stark contrast, prophesied a future of mass unemployment and social decay. Depending on the route society took, each of these stemmed from the same belief that full automation in the long run would eliminate work in the traditional sense. The optimistic route meant expanding those areas which would creatively occupy people, involving kind of mass programme of social planning and intervention. Or it meant relying on science and technology spontaneously to produce the solutions to society's problems. Both approaches tended to be rather idealistic and utopian. They assumed that an aggressive capitalist system gives rise to the problems of automation (in the sense that competitiveness and the drive for profit makes automation an irreversible process), but they assumed away capitalism when it came to proposing solutions. Equally, the pessimistic predictions rest on a society incapable of any level of planned intervention and impervious to the needs of its members. Many of these visions of the 'future of work' now seem far-fetched. Along the way, too, various scenarios that were fashionable some years ago have dropped out of sight. Who remembers the paperless office or the automatic factory now?

One thing that the experience of high levels of unemployment has amply demonstrated is that we remain a society geared to employment. People identify in a fundamental way with work, just as their material well-being in a market economy depends on access to a wage or salary. This is the basic nature of the industrial society we live in, and whatever changes may bring us closer to the kind of 'post-industrial' or 'leisure' society that some envisage, they will have to start out from these existing realities. Indeed, we have witnessed what seems like the opposite of the 'end of work' scenario. Industrialization is actually extending its logic into areas like the white-collar sector, which were previously regulated by less formal rules and working arrangements. Recent debates have turned on these realities, and have taken a comparative look at work systems in different countries, as well as extending the focus on technology to broader organizational and industrial structures. It is to these aspect of work restructuring that we turn in the final chapter.

Study questions for Chapter 19

1 Why are 'technologically determinist' explanations so attractive, and what is wrong with them?
2 Give some examples and illustrations of the positivist view of technology.
3 Which are the main industrial sectors where computer-based technologies have taken hold, and what kinds of industrial and commercial processes are being automated?
4 Why do firms invest in new technology?
5 Does new technology cause unemployment?
6 Does new technology upskill or deskill workforces?

Further reading

Baldry, C. (1988) *Computers, Jobs and Skills: The Industrial Relations of Technological Change*. London: Plenum Press.

Buitelaar, W. (ed.) (1988) *Technology and Work*. London: Gower.

Burnes, B. (1989) *New Technology in Context*. Aldershot: Avebury.

Clark, J. (1995) *Managing Change and Innovation: People, Technology and Strategy*. London: Sage.

—— McLoughlin, I., Rose, H., and King, R. (1988) *The Process of Technological Change*. Cambridge: Cambridge University Press.

Cockburn, C. (1986) *Machinery of Dominance: Women, Men and Technological Know-how*. London: Pluto Press.

Davidson, M. J. and Cooper, C. L. (1987) *Women and Information Technology*. Chichester: Wiley.

Forester, T. (ed.) (1989) *Computers in the Human Context*. Oxford: Blackwell.

Grint, K. and Gill, R. (eds.) (1995) *The Gender Technology Relation: Contemplating Theory and Research*. London: Taylor and Francis.

Huws, U., Korte, W. B. and Robinson, S. (1990) *Telework: Towards the Elusive Office*. Chichester: Wiley.

Loveridge, R. and Pitt, M. (eds.) (1990) *The Strategic Management of Technological Innovation*. Chichester: Wiley.

Lyon, D. (1988) *The Information Society*. Cambridge: Polity Press.

McLoughlin, I. and Clark, J. (1994) *Technological Change at Work* (2nd edn.). Milton Keynes: Open University Press.

Scarborough, H. and Corbett, J. M. (1992) *Technology and Organization*. London: Routledge.

Wall, T., Clegg, C. W., and Kemp, N. J. (eds.) (1987) *The Human Side of Advanced Manufacturing Technology*. Chichester: Wiley.

Zuboff, S. (1988) *In the Age of the Smart Machine*. Oxford: Heinemann.

20 New Systems of Work Organization

Summary points and learning objectives

By the end of this chapter you will:

- understand the nature of *Fordism* and the debates around the so-called crisis of Fordism;
- have reviewed three *key production systems*: the flexible firm, flexible specialization, just-in-time/lean production;
- have explored the issue of whether the flexible firm describes *British industrial patterns*;
- have explored *the German model* of flexible specialization and the current pressures it is under;
- have explored the just-in-time/lean model at the heart of *Japanese production philosophy*;
- appreciate the *limits of Japanization*, i.e. the critique of Japanese production methods.

Introduction

In recent years changes have been taking place in the management and organization of production which suggest that industry worldwide is going through a period of transition. Many believe that the days of the traditional mass industries are numbered. Alternative approaches to manufacturing are taking over. The computerized technologies discussed in the previous chapter are important here, but the wider emphasis is on the market context and work organization in which technology is located. The keyword is *flexibility*: the use of labour and resources in a strategic fashion to enable production systems to be responsive to market changes. Flexibility means the removal of occupational barriers to the use of labour, and the creation of new skills that operate across a range of tasks. Such a level of responsiveness is regarded as vital in conditions of tough competition and market uncertainty.

Flexibility is not a totally new concern, of course. Lack of flexibility has been a constant drawback of factory production. In historic terms the highly centralized factory replaced the more loosely organized systems of out-working that dominated in the seventeenth and eighteenth centuries (see Chapter 9). However, this process was protracted, and factory production and out-working existed side by side well into the nineteenth century. Out-working may have put a definite ceiling on efficiency, but it was highly flexible, which made it the perfect form of production for a still-evolving industrial society. As we shall see, forms of out-working hold the key to several of the new manufacturing methods.

The enthusiasm for flexibility reflects a belief that it can resolve the most stubborn contradictions of existing industrial methods. With traditional production systems, for example, huge output could be produced but at some cost to quality; or it was felt that you could have customized goods or cheap goods but not both, or that specialization in skills has been achieved only at a cost to the efficient use of labour. However, the new flexible systems, it is claimed, can provide customized goods at low unit costs; they can produce quality *and* volume, and they are held to be both specialist and efficient. Most of the main quality systems were pioneered in manufacturing industry. But there have also been reverberations outside manufacturing. The service industries have been swept by changes that have much in common with the ethos of flexibility: new definitions of quality, customer orientations, and new market awareness.

The common interest in flexibility, however, exists alongside some important differences, which we follow through in this chapter. The British model that has achieved prominence in recent years is *the flexible firm*. Emphasis here has been on a set of employment and labour market practices that enable firms to respond quickly and cheaply to changing environments. However, the dominant economies of Japan and Germany are probably most directly linked to the new manufacturing. Some of these methods are well known. Japanese *just-in-time* production involves new systems of inventory and production control, and has attracted a massive amount of interest in Britain and America. Its impact is often seen as the 'Japanization' of our industries. Similarly, *lean production* is closely related to these production concepts, and reflects a stage in the western (particularly American) response to Japanese manufacturing practices. Another approach, called *flexible specialization*, has been used generally to describe the most progressive types of new production system, based on full-blown responsible autonomy for workers. This has not had the same impact on Anglo-American management thinking, but has been linked to the successful German economy with its distinctive emphasis on flexible skills.

Like the new technology debate, the flexibility debate has strong tendencies to adopt a positive and enthusiastic line. Many accounts seem to consist merely of a description of some idealized version of flexible automation on the basis of which companies, industries, or indeed nations are urged to adopt the new systems or get left behind. However, there have also been more critical evaluations which ask about the implications for labour, and whether the systems really can be seen as dramatic departures or whether they are developments of existing trends.

We will try to take account of both kinds of argument. In doing so we draw extensively on the account of industrial change developed in two books, Charles Sabel's

Politics and Work (1982), and *The Second Industrial Divide* (1984), which Sabel co-authored with Michael Piore. These studies in many ways have set the terms of the flexibility debate. In them the authors compare the different paths of industrial development in different countries. They avoid the modernizing tendency of seeing economic systems 'converging' on parallel paths of progress. They develop the broadest kind of framework, including cultural and historic factors, as well as interventions by the state and the strategies of labour and capital. But Piore and Sabel still see the roots of change in the changing nature of production systems. It is necessary to begin, however, by looking at existing forms of manufacture.

The Fordist system of production

'*A method for the efficient production of one thing.*' (Charles Sabel, 1982, p. 210)

In his 1982 book Sabel coined the term 'Fordism' to describe the method of production that has dominated western economies in the recent industrial period. Fordism reflects the rise of mass consumer markets and the standardization of products in the twentieth century. Fordism essentially means mass assembly carried out in the giant factory:

1. Work organization is based on large, mainly unskilled labour forces.
2. A standardized product is built in massive volumes.
3. Product design is extremely important; products are designed to be easily assembled.
4. Production uses 'dedicated' (i.e. specialized) machinery designed for a given product and production system.
5. Tight control of the labour process is provided by systems of work measurement.

Above all, Fordism is typified by the *assembly line*. This vitally important production technique was invented by Henry Ford in 1913. Ford was the pioneer of mass-produced motor vehicles and the car assembly plant is often taken as the prototype of Fordism—although the principles of line assembly are used in many industries. The first assembly lines were the culmination of that key period, between about 1880 and 1910, when modern markets and production systems were emerging, and Sabel is clear about the breakthrough in industrial methods that this represented.

. . . however they hit on the idea of moving the work to the men rather than the reverse, Ford's engineers knew at once that they had discovered a new secret of mass production. The first crude moving line cut the time needed for final assembly from just under 12.5 to about 5.8 man hours. It was as though the Ford engineers, putting in place the crucial pieces of a giant jigsaw puzzle, suddenly made intelligible the major themes of a century of industrialization. (Sabel, 1982, p. 33)

Fordism has strong connections with Taylor's work system, *scientific management*. Whereas the assembly line is a production technique, scientific management is a control of production: 'Fordism accomplished by technology what Taylor accomplished by administrative means' (Sabel, 1982, p. 236). But the broad attitudes towards work, the persistent downward pressure on labour content and skills, are common to both systems. Taylor's ideas on work study were well established by the time Ford developed the assembly line. Indeed, the assembly line proved to be the perfect means for translating Taylor's ideas into reality. The extreme division of labour and repetitive work cycle on the line can be achieved only by the setting of standard times and work methods. Nevertheless, Sabel identified the age of mass production with Ford, rather than with Taylor as many others had preferred to do.

Fordism is not, of course, a total system. Around every large factory small supplier firms will grow up where Fordist principles do not apply; and a large proportion of all value added originates from smaller enterprises. But this unevenness and variation, which occurs in all domestic economies, does not mean that an economy cannot be

---

Box 20.1 The assembly line

Line assembly is not a type of machinery or productive process. It is a *transfer technology*; it transports the product on a moving track or conveyor from one work station to another where components are assembled into it. Workers are stationed along the line under a strict division of labour with each job timed according to the line speed.

Like many great inventions, the assembly line is basically simple. If you think of the usual way of assembling anything—think of building a model aircraft—the article remains stationary and the workers move about, obtaining the necessary tools and materials to be assembled into the shell. This is known as 'dock assembly' since production takes place in a dock or bay. Most large scale products, like trucks, ships and aircraft, which tend to be produced in low volumes, are built by dock assembly. Ford's touch of genius was to reverse this natural method. The basic principle of high-volume line assembly is to move the work while the worker remains stationary.

The line has to be 'balanced' which means manning it for a specified range of tasks. Efficiency has to be paid for in terms of a high degree of rigidity in production. In a car plant, for example, the mix of models going down the line can vary only within strict limits—otherwise workers find themselves with either too little or too much time for performing the work cycle. In this environment variation in output creates high pressures of work, and ultimately quality and output deficiencies.

The assembly line is a *work-pacing technology*. It presents tasks to the worker on a regular cycle that allows little variation in the pace of work. For management this means very tight control over production. But for workers it means a major loss of control. Fragmented, deskilled jobs are bad enough, but having to keep up with the line can be extremely oppressive. It is the reason why this form of production has become a byword for monotony and alienation.

defined in a particular way. The basic industrial pattern can still be deemed Fordist in the sense that giant factories form the hub of the main networks of production and are crucial in the spread of new forms of work rationalization.

Fordism and post-Fordism

The Fordist system, however, has been challenged by new kinds of work organization. Fordist principles—fragmented work, dedicated machinery, serial rather than parallel task-sequencing—create enormous economies of scale but have one crucial weakness, namely *inflexibility*. The presence of a secondary market of small suppliers introduces important flexibilities, but line-based operations can cope only with a certain amount of fluctuation in output. Henry Ford's famous phrase, 'You can have any colour you like as long as it's black', goes right to the heart of the assembly line: it works best producing a uniform product. Fordism is thus dependent on stable mass markets that can absorb its huge volumes of standardized output.

And, indeed, the mass markets which stabilized the Fordist system are breaking up. Sabel argued that this has come about because of a number of global changes, but the chief factor is the changing nature of consumer tastes. The suggestion is that the latter part of the twentieth century witnessed a structural shift in the nature of markets; they are fragmenting and becoming increasingly specialized. This is partly due to the success of Fordism itself. Markets have become saturated with manufactured goods. The enormous impact on social tastes and expectations of placing motor vehicles and other products within the reach of the mass of people has meant that consumers have become much more sophisticated; they are no longer satisfied with standard products. Increasingly, the demand is for customized products that incorporate quality and design features. These social, technological, and market changes in the global environment of firms have left Fordism high and dry.

However, the thesis that Sabel (1982) initiated, and which was developed more fully in Piore and Sabel (1984), opposed any 'deterministic' outcome to the crisis. There are no laws of society or economy that automatically pick out the best kind of industrial system to succeed. Piore and Sabel hypothesized two main scenarios out of Fordism: an innovative and a reformist scenario, both of which have considerable uncertainties attached to them (Figure 20.1). Faced with crisis, firms could attempt to meet the demands to innovate, and shift to high-quality specialized products (which we shall explore more fully below). However, this innovative strategy means abandoning the production principles of Fordism, and it is uncertain whether firms could be so adaptive. Instead, firms might hedge their bets and develop types of 'neo-Fordism' which attempt to meet the demand for varied products while maintaining the basic Fordist principles of production. Piore and Sabel's thesis was that world economies are currently at a crossroads or, as they put it, a 'second industrial divide'. The innovative and the reformist paths both represent viable ways out of crisis, and embryonic forms of each can be detected in industrial systems in various countries.

If we consider the path of reform first, the neo-Fordist strategy involves piecemeal changes to improve efficiency by cutting costs, using labour more strategically, and new

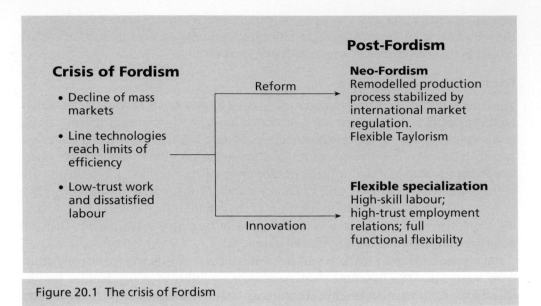

Figure 20.1 The crisis of Fordism

technologies which allow more flexibility. Sabel remains clear that these only reproduce Fordist forms of low-trust, intensified work.

When reorganization involves the introduction of new, computer-based technologies such as numerically controlled machine tools or computer-aided design of parts, managers perceive it as a bold step towards the Fordist ideal of the rationalized factory. . . . But if managers could step back from their work, as only a few of them can do, they would see that the present reorganization reinterprets Fordism as much as it perfects it and, depending on how workers respond to these changes, could perhaps undermine the existing factory hierarchies rather than reinforce them. (1982, p. 209)

It would be mistaken to dismiss such changes totally. Firms are extremely enthusiastic about these kinds of programme, which provide remodelled reproduction and a degree of flexible automation. Indeed, some neo-Fordist approaches are further along the spectrum towards innovative production than others. For example, Berggren (1989) examines the Swedish car maker Volvo and its programme of work design. He traces the progress made in each of Volvo's plants, some of which score quite highly on the extent of integration of work team and production tasks. However, the dominant trend is what Berggren calls 'flexible Taylorism', i.e. a certain level of group working and upskilling but still based on machine-paced assembly. Thus these are 'modified solutions rather than qualitative changes' (p. 193), or types of neo-Fordism. (For a more detailed account, see the Volvo case study in the Appendix to Chapter 11.)

The flexible firm

These kinds of flexible methods and technologies have come to be regarded by many firms as the only solution to market uncertainty and global competition. Particularly in

Britain—where the problems of recession never seem far away—emphasis was on the removal of occupational and skill barriers to the rational use of labour, and replacement of the old demarcated crafts by more integrated working arrangements. These changes highlight two distinct faces of flexibility: *functional* and *numerical*. Functional flexibility is a work process factor that refers to flexibility across different kinds of production technology and to workers' capacity to overlap technical, maintenance, and production work. Numerical flexibility is a labour market factor, and refers to employers' capacity to shed or take on the types of labour they require as market changes dictate.

Both forms of flexibility were combined in a new organizational model called *the flexible firm*. Originally developed by Atkinson (1984; 1985; 1988), the flexible firm is essentially an attempt to combine the control and efficiency of the factory with flexibility. A 'core' of workers, who are well rewarded and secure, possess the integrated skills that the firm needs to perform its central tasks; they provide functional flexibility. Numerical flexibility is provided by a 'periphery' of workers in less secure jobs who can be hired and fired easily. These workers perform less important tasks and comprise different types of labour—temporary, part-time, agency employees, subcontractors, self-employed, and so on. The flexible firm is therefore adaptable to market expansion and contraction (via numerical flexibility), and to qualitative changes in the demand for new types of product (via functional flexibility).

With its complex labour structure the flexible firm can pursue a strategic approach to labour utilization. Firms that want a stable workforce, with as little labour turnover as possible, can at the same time become less reliant on their workers—for example, by hiving off areas of production to subcontractors, or by mechanizing to eliminate skills. Headcount can be adapted to market changes, but key skills can be retained.

Evaluation of the flexible firm model Despite apparent benefits, though, many have cast doubt on this model of the firm. To begin with two types of 'flexibility' may be hard to contain in any one firm because of the different meanings they have for labour. Functional flexibility needs to be underpinned by extensive skills training and should result in upskilling. But British firms' record in this area is very poor. Britain is virtually alone among advanced nations in leaving training to voluntary forces. Most employers define training as an unwelcome cost, to be cut during recessionary times, rather than an investment. So while there is some evidence of a shift towards the enlargement of job responsibilities and creation of firm-specific skills, the kind of serious investment in training that would be needed to create true multi-skilled workers has been sadly lacking (Lee, 1989; Legge, 1995).

British firms have been much more interested in numerical flexibility. This broad trend results in a greater proportion of secondary-type jobs—which may be attractive for a minority of skilled workers, but the bulk of labour is increasingly being used as a mere commodity. In an authoritative survey of research evidence, Elger (1990) suggests that while recognizing the great variations in the impact on work, it is still possible to define a dominant pattern. He discounts the optimistic view that in Britain at least the quest for flexibility has brought change in the direction of high-trust teamworking. Rather 'the mix tends to remain that of increased flexibility at the margins through job enlargement and intensification, coupled with more concerted management efforts to enhance their control' (1990, p. 91).

While many firms pursue some version of flexibility, it appears that few adopt the full version of the flexible firm model. Indeed, it has been questioned whether firms can actually carry through this kind of systematic and coherent organizational design. Anna Pollert (1988) has confirmed the view that most of these claims are exaggerated. She surveyed a wide range of labour process and labour market practices and points out, for instance, that areas like out-working and temporary work show no signs of increasing; these traditional industrial sectors have always been with us. Part-time work has been a massive sector of employment in Britain, but it is stabilizing now, and in any case reflects the need for reserves of cheap labour rather than for flexibility. Pollert concludes that the flexible firm is something of a myth. The model is really a construct of trends that exist singly but are not actually present together in any one enterprise. The enthusiasm for the model in fact has come mostly from political quarters. During the 1980s the British government became strongly committed to the flexible firm as a new employment policy. It reflected broader interest in curbing trade union power and removing restrictions on the use of labour. From the employers' side, the concept of flexibility also tended to be expressed at the strategic level but, again, not necessarily followed through in practice. The reality, Pollert suggested, is mixed: certain kinds of flexibility have increased but the main feature of recent industrial relations has been the removal of employment rights (see also Hakim, 1990).

Flexible specialization

This brings us to the search for more meaningful examples of innovative work patterns. Is there any sign in the industrialized countries of production systems that make a decisive break with Fordism, and go beyond neo-Fordist solutions? Piore and Sabel, in the most influential part of their analysis, coined the term *flexible specialization* to refer to such systems. The flexibly specialized firm is diametrically opposed to Fordism with its intensive, fragmented work systems (Figure 20.1).

Defining this new production regime precisely is a little difficult. It is not a specific technique, such as the assembly line. Piore and Sabel (1984, p. 259) emphasized the link between computer technology and flexibility. They were enthusiastic about the use of programmable machines because such technologies permit customization at low unit cost; they can also be controlled by workers, thus enhancing skills. Production policies aimed at enhancing skills, and the demand for customized goods from changing consumer tastes, are also prerequisites. Additional features stand out in Piore and Sabel's model. The production process itself is reshaped and its components remodelled to provide adaptable responses. The flexibly specialized firm utilizes a high-skill labour force. Old craft demarcations have evolved into a multi-faceted skills that support integrated production systems. Worker–management relations are high-trust and the work itself conforms to meaningful job redesign. Others have also adopted this broad definition. Wood, for example, talks of

the new flexibly specialized firm which can quickly respond to sudden changes in costs, market opportunities and/or new technologies, through adapting flexible, multi-purpose equipment and creating a flexible reintegrated and cooperative workforce free of the shackles of rigid job specifications, narrow job-centred orientations and excessive regulation and control. (1989, p. 11)

How far the flexible specialization model has become a reality is unclear. Piore and Sabel surveyed some of the major industrial nations and concluded that the innovative path out of crisis was confined to some relatively small sectors within economies still dominated by mass production. But they drew a distinction between the group of countries (Italy, Japan, Germany) where the 'success stories' did at least extend to geographical regions or industrial sectors, and other countries (United States, France) where examples of flexible production were embryonic and 'founded often in opposition to the organizing principles of the national economy' (p. 222).

We can look at some of these countries separately. In Italy the example of the so-called 'Third Italy' was originally picked out by Sabel as a case of 'high technology cottage industry' (1982, p. 220). In this area in the Emilia-Romagna region in the north of the country, networks of small firms have developed a range of industries, such as ceramic tiles and textiles, producing high quality products with a high fashion/design content. The emphasis is on the use of sophisticated programmable equipment that can produce economically in small batches, adaptable highly skilled workers, and inter-firm co-operation. There was much enthusiasm for this as a model of skilled flexibility (e.g. Murray, 1985), though more recent counter-evidence suggests that earlier studies were somewhat anecdotal and that the industry is in fact rather more rationalized (Rowley, 1996). In Japan the application of numerical control machinery across small firms in the machine tools industry has also reflected flexible reorganization. By contrast, in the United States there have been only hesitant moves towards flexibility. America, of course, is the home of Fordism and Taylorism, and this legacy has meant that neo-Fordist solutions have dominated. The response of US corporations on the whole has been marked by protectionism and attempts to saturate existing mass markets. As Piore and Sabel argue, America is still trying to make the rest of the world play the game it knows best.

The German case is more important. Piore and Sabel acknowledge a much wider movement there toward flexible specialization across major industries like steel, chemicals, machine tools and cars. But they still classify Germany with countries (like Italy and Japan) where 'the success stories are not so exceptional'. However, other writers (notably Lane, 1988) claim that Germany is one country where innovative production has been established economy-wide. The German case is thus worth examining in more detail. First, however, we can put together a country-by-country analysis of flexibility trends. Three broad bands of countries can be detected (Figure 20.2):

1. A lowest band in which moves towards flexible specialization are restricted, and may sometimes merely be new forms of work intensification masquerading as 'flexibility'. Piore and Sabel describe France and the USA in these terms, but we could also

Exceptional success stories	USA	Saturation of mass-markets, protectionism
	France	Bureaucratic, state-supported growth in mass production
	Britain	Skills polarization, low-trust industrial relations/restrictive union practices
Success stories 'not so exceptional'	Italy	'Third Italy': high-technology cottage industries
	Japan	NC equipment in machine tools industry
	Sweden	Volvo, Saab: autonomous work groups
Relatively widespread flexibility	Germany	Steel, chemicals, machine tools, motor vehicles

Figure 20.2 The spread of flexible methods

nominate Britain for this category, where industries like engineering and motor vehicles have a long history of deskilling.

2. A middle band of countries where the success stories are more widespread. This includes Japan and Italy, and to these we might add Sweden. Sweden is interesting in so far as the 'Swedish model' is often put forward as the most advanced form of work organization, yet this is confined to relatively few examples (see Chapter 11).

3. In splendid isolation Germany represents the main example where the shift to greater flexibility has challenged the mass production paradigm.

Flexible specialization in Germany

The German industrial system, as we have said, may represent more than a short-lived or small-scale triumph over Fordism. Lane (1988) in particular has built on the work over the past two decades of a group of German researchers (notably Kern and Schumann, 1984) who have argued that Germany virtually alone among industrial nations has embraced a new strategy of production. This claim is based on research carried out in industries including chemicals, automobiles, machine tools, food-processing, and shipbuilding. These are all large-scale industries, neither 'cottage industries' nor regionally confined. German production patterns consistently reflect product quality and diversity and adaptive methods. Taylorism is replaced by new forms of labour deployment defined by the overlap between specialisms and the retention of skills. Lane points out a number of features of German industrial development that link it to flexible specialization.

Surviving craft traditions Germany has traditionally been a producer of customized goods for export. The craft skills on which this form of production is based represent an alternative to mass production and have resisted trends towards Taylorism/Fordism. Lane confirms this and argues that Taylorist methods never really took hold in Germany at any period. There has been some imitation of the Fordist model but far less than has happened in, for example, Britain. The craft model has not merely survived; it has adapted and been modified, with skills being constantly updated.

Polyvalent skills A resurgent craft tradition has meant that the manual working class as a whole in Germany still contains a predominance of skilled workers. Even in mass production the growth of these industries has drawn heavily on multi-skilled workers, with a resultant emphasis on group working and labour flexibility. Such 'polyvalent'

Box 20.2 Flexible skill strategies in Britain and Germany

This case example concerns the German and British subsidiaries of a multi-national car manufacturer. The company-wide job structure was based on a three-tier system of grades: A, B and C. A-graded jobs were purely for new entrants; B-grade jobs were for workers who had acquired the necessary speed and skills to perform a job on the line; and C-grade jobs were for multi-skilled workers who could perform several different types of assembly work, and tasks like basic maintenance and quality control.

Although this wage/skill structure was identical in both plants, the distribution of skills was very different. In the British plant the vast majority of manual employees were on the B grade and were regarded simply as normal line workers. Workers on the highest grade, the so-called C-men, were in a minority of around 10 per cent and were used as a labour pool. In cases of absenteeism, particularly on difficult or critical jobs, production foremen tended to request a C-man.

In the German plant, however, a far higher proportion of employees, between 60 and 70 per cent, were C-graded. The grading system was seen as kind of career structure for labour. Workers were encouraged to acquire skills and to move through the grades, and job rotation and training were provided to help them do this.

Significant points about this case include the difference in *managerial attitudes*. This was a company with a very strong corporate policy for uniform production operations across all plants, irrespective of national differences. Despite this the German management had secured the resources needed to maintain a high-skill workforce. The British attitude was to use skilled labour only selectively. Also important is the fact that the case is from *mass production*. This was a typical Fordist industry associated with deskilling. But the German management still succeeded in upskilling workers.

skills are based on a wide range of task experiences acquired by job rotation during training.

> Polyvalency of skill permits a broad and flexible utilisation of labour across boundaries between production work on the one side and technical and maintenance work on the other. Polyvalency has not, as in the case of British craftsmen, been undermined by the erection of highly formalised barriers between skills. Polyvalency of the German type also furthers co-operation within work-groups across hierarchical divisions and thus provides a natural foundation for the institution of semi-autonomous work groups. German semi-skilled workers' training, although less broad and deep, is nevertheless also systemically oriented towards polyvalency. (Lane, 1988, p. 144)

Product market strategy The German industrial strategy of producing high-quality goods for export has been based on technical and design excellence, rather than low price. In motor vehicles this is clearly demonstrated by firms like Mercedes Benz, BMW, Audi, and Volkswagen. German firms are also in the forefront of the machine-tool industry, and for many mass-produced consumer goods 'German made' is synonymous with quality. The success of this product market strategy, and the worldwide demand for German quality, is what has underwritten the other elements in the country's production matrix: the high social costs, the investment in skills, and so forth.

Thus in many large German industries work is characterized by upskilling, holistic tasks, and group working. How has Germany been able to achieve this? In large part it seems to reflect historic patterns. Germany seems to have got a number of key national policies right. State intervention in getting financial bodies to invest in industry is the opposite of British and American *laissez-faire*. At the same time Germany manages to avoid the pitfalls of the French type of bureaucratic interventionism. The role of the state in Germany has similarities to Japan. But compared with Japan, Germany seems to enjoy an even greater national consensus, particularly the deep-rooted belief in the skills of the ordinary workforce.

Lane (1988) has highlighted wider features of German industrial culture which may explain this approach to workplace regulation:

1. A harmonious, 'high-trust' form of industrial relations. The approach of German management of raising all labour to the highest standards assumes that an expensive labour force will pay for itself in terms of commitment and flexibility. There is also more confidence about the balance of control; German managements are not continually seeking tighter workplace regulation, but accept that effort and worker autonomy are compatible.
2. German employers have pursued functional rather than numerical flexibility. There has been little attempt to casualize employment or undermine job security.
3. German employers have managed to maintain a 'virtuous circle' of training and investment. High levels of expenditure on new technology have necessitated investment in training because only skilled and committed workforces are able fully to exploit the technology and justify capital investment.
4. German managers themselves are highly qualified, having a strong predominance of professional engineering skills. When managements are themselves skilled, they are

less interested in deskilling others. (This contrasts with a country like Britain, where poor levels of management education have often been suggested as a cause of shopfloor deskilling—in other words, because of insecurity about their own skills, managers seek to dilute and degrade workers' skills as a means of control.

The German model under pressure

Some researchers, as we have seen, accepted that flexible specialization was still not a consistent pattern even in German industries (Piore and Sabel, 1984; Kern and Schumann, 1984; Altmann *et al.*, 1982). It has also been pointed out that the research on which the flexibility claim is based is perhaps not all it should be, and used only simple observation and small-scale interviews (Wood, 1989, p. 34). Nevertheless, by 1988 Lane was arguing that the flexibility trend had emerged more strongly. She suggested that labour-market conditions (low unemployment plus large quantities of skilled labour) favoured flexible patterns, and that recent evidence points to a strengthening of flexibility trends.

However, more recent still are some less optimistic factors. Flecker and Schulten (1997), for example, refer to an emerging crisis of labour and production organization. They confirm the past success of the traditional German model—its stable industrial order and strong welfare systems being affordable given the success of the system's products—but they argue that the very high social settlement is now turning into a disadvantage. These traditional strengths are becoming liabilities in the face of global competition, and German industries are ceasing to be competitive with countries like Japan and the USA. Another factor is the impact of the unification of the two Germanies. The staggering cost of modernizing East German industry may prove unaffordable in the context of sustained flexible work organization. The availability of cheap labour from the east, and potential unemployment, may undermine these unique labour-market conditions and tip the balance in favour of mass production (Wiedermeyer, 1989).

The trends of the late 1990s and beyond will therefore need to be carefully watched. While the model appears to be approaching its limits, there is still a depth of resource in the industrial culture and the resilience of German labour to retain its skills base and status. Also, according to some accounts the situation is not without precedent. In the 1960s there were similar economic pressures, and the country flirted with 'Americanization' and mass production; but by the 1970s it had become clear that German industry was losing its distinctive edge, at which point the new forms of flexible production were developed. Thus there is a persuasive argument that the restructuring of work along non-Fordist (rather then neo-Fordist) lines constitutes a progressive production strategy.

Japan and Japanization

If we now turn to the other wonder economy of the past thirty years, the rise of Japan to the position of a major economic power has long attracted attention. Japanese industries seem to have developed as if the entire country has been on a learning curve.

Japan grew through stages, first copying western technology and being known for cheap consumer goods of doubtful quality, but gradually overhauling western industry and producing for the most sophisticated markets like consumer electronics, cars, and engineering machinery. The main motive behind western interest in Japan has undoubtedly been the head-on competition with our own industries. For two decades or more Japanese companies have been capturing markets in the United States and Europe—bringing out new products and models, design improvements and extra features at a cost and frequency that local manufacturers seem unable to match. How do they do it? and Can we learn it too? are questions that are asked repeatedly.

Japanese ascendancy has been attributed to many factors, among them cultural and historic influences. Japan was a feudal society until little more than a hundred years ago, and came very quickly into the industrial era. This was thought to provide tight vertically integrated industrial and financial structures. In particular, the broad cultural factors with which Japanese society seems imbued—the extreme diligence and self-sacrifice of workers (the supposed Japanese of ethic of 'living to work') and the capacity to identify with common goals at all levels of the organization—have been regarded as the bedrock of Japan's phenomenal industrial success.

More recently, though, another explanation has gained ground, namely that Japanese success is in large part due to Japanese management's organization of production. In reality this cannot be separated from social and cultural factors (especially the assumption that workers will actively co-operate). Nevertheless, distinctive new forms of work organization have been linked with Japan—both in terms of being identified with the country's practices, and in terms of emergent systems as other countries have interpreted and adapted these practices in their struggle to cope with Japanese competition.

One problem in identifying new work systems is that of fixing on the 'master' paradigm. There are many methods and much new jargon going the rounds—cellular production, teamworking, empowerment, total quality—and the new systems all employ an overlapping mix of these. Moreover, all have the same basic objective of post-Fordism: to achieve flexibility while retaining the economies of scale of mass production. So the choice as to which should be defined as a ruling production matrix, and which are subsidiary or contributing elements, is partly arbitrary. However, two have proved perhaps the most influential: the systems referred to as *just-in-time* and *lean production*.

Just-in-time production

JIT manages to combine flexibility and volume by ideally producing only the amount at each stage of production necessary to complete the next stage. A simple definition of JIT might be that it is a system for delivering the exact quantity and defect-free quality of parts just in time for each stage of production. The basic features of the system can be outlined as follows.

1. *A pull system.* The traditional assembly line has each work station on a fixed schedule, and if one stage of assembly fails or slows down, work piles up causing overproduction and storage problems. But JIT systems are more responsive because production is 'pulled' from the front end. Work at any given stage only goes ahead when some type

of signal is received from the stage in front. This is achieved via the so-called *kanban* system of parts control. *Kanban* principles can be observed in very simple systems of racks for components: when a *kanban* rack is emptied by the forward worker using the component, this activates production by the rear worker to replenish it.

2. *Total quality management.* A just-in-time system has to be operated with the reciprocal concept of total quality. This means using defect-free supplies of parts and materials—not 99 per cent or even 99.9 per cent but 100 per cent quality. The reason is that when exactly the right amount of parts is being supplied, just in time, any quality defects would immediately halt production. Of course, total quality management is itself a massive cost-saver and the basis of customer satisfaction.

3. *Stockless production.* In assembly-line production, traditional push systems need to be 'buffered' with internal stock zones. On lengthy assembly lines it is impossible to have every section working to the specified schedule. So assemblies are taken off in buffer zones (like being shunted on to a siding) and the stock is used to return the line to the correct schedule. But the buffer stock represents waste; capital is tied up and there are deterioration costs. Reducing buffer stocks ideally to zero is a key objective of JIT.

4. *JIT supply relationships.* Just-in-time principles should also extend upstream to a firm's suppliers. This means smaller, more frequent deliveries, synchronized with the main plant's production. The ideal is line-side deliveries that go straight into production. If JIT methods are used in the supplier plant as well, a complete production–supply chain can be achieved. Indeed, in practice when firms decide to adopt JIT methods one of the first things they look at is relationships with their suppliers. A central principle of JIT is the strong relations that develop between companies and their suppliers. When firms move towards JIT they shift to a smaller number of 'preferred suppliers' which enjoy long-term contracts and a more supportive relation with the main plant.

These production principles result in important advantages. Perhaps the central one is the removal of the safety-net that is normally provided by stocks of material and systems of inspection. If parts are introduced straight into production any quality faults have an immediate impact. The genuine threat that the process really would grind to a halt puts pressure on all groups (workers, supervisors, suppliers) to operate a zero defects regime.

Japanese production philosophy

In addition to specific techniques, however, Japanese management is credited with a deeper set of ideals. Its real basis lies in simplicity. JIT philosophy is suspicious of the complicated systems of production control often found in the west, and in some ways is even anti-technology. A main element is that of *kaizen* or continuous improvement, a multi-sided never-ending programme for cutting out all forms of waste. The ethos of production improvement means questioning every activity as parts move through a production sequence. The aim is to improve the throughput of work, focusing exclusively on operations that add value and eliminating forms of time-wasting that add cost but not value.

This is where worker involvement becomes critical. Under orthodox Taylorism, the streamlining of production was the task of specialist engineers. But the kind of methods improvement programmes envisaged by the new production philosophy depend on the broad mass of workers bringing forward problems for solution. This level of participation is supported by a range of methods embraced by the Japanese production style. Teamworking, for example, means a variety of tasks being assigned to workers, such as inspection, maintenance, and materials handling, so that they form self-supervised groups. Long, straight assembly lines undermine JIT principles, so flexible shorter units are used which encourage communication. Related to these methods, cellular manufacturing is a model that allows for worker autonomy and continuous improvement. Production cells encompass a whole production process, and so reduce classic forms of waste like work-in-progress, and allow for flexibility between products. Quality circles are typically employed as well. These involve periods of discussion amongst work-teams to review the day's problems and suggest remedial action.

The underlying factor is an attitudinal and cultural change within the whole enterprise workforce. Instilling the *kaizen* principle means encouraging all employees (production workers, supervisors, engineers, managers) to ask why production faults occur and to trace them to their root cause. Housekeeping and maintenance become important, not just as a way of keeping the workplace tidy and equipment up to scratch, but as a means of patrolling the work-space and revealing the symptoms of errors and faults. Thus, rather than ignore problems or feel that little will be done if they are highlighted, the Japanese production philosophy encourages workers to seek out and solve problems. In this sense, some observers have come to regard a system like JIT as a rather artificial attempt to place a simple label on the Japanese experience. They have stressed the pragmatism of the Japanese pioneers, and their emphasis on the accumulation of small gains and the long time-periods needed to get new production systems into place (Zipkin, 1990).

Lean production

While just-in-time is a type of production design technique, alternative interpretations of the Japanese influence have stressed a broader process of incremental improvement. In their book, *The Machine that Changed the World*, Womack, Jones, and Roos (1990) published the results of an influential study carried out at the Massachusetts Institute of Technology. In this they popularize the management system they call 'lean production'. This they assert is an unparalleled means of producing improved products at low cost and with fulfilling work, and is destined to become the new model for world-class manufacturing.

Womack *et al.* stress how the production systems developed by the US auto giants (Ford, General Motors) were copied in Britain and Europe, and by the 1950s and 1960s, with little international competition to spur innovation, had become the basis of a mature and indeed stagnating industry. Thus, in the early post-war years, when the

Japanese began to develop their own industry, they were struck by the inefficiencies that they saw in orthodox mass assembly—the heavy dependency on rework to keep lines running, the use of armies of expensive and inflexible specialists, the over-reliance on complicated automation. Their aim was therefore not to transfer technology whole-sale (as it had been in Europe) but to redesign and rethink western methods. As a result a new motor industry emerged in Japan: 'the true significance of this industry was that it was not simply another replication of the by now venerable American approach to mass production. The Japanese were developing an entirely new way of making things, which we call *lean production*' (Womack *et al.*, 1990, p. 47).

At the heart of the new system was the elimination of waste. We just saw that *kaizen* could be regarded as an element of Japanese production philosophy. But in lean production it becomes the driving principle. Womack *et al.* stress that the giant Toyota company was the birthplace of lean production and historically the most important agent for developing and disseminating the new style of management. In the early growth of Toyota an obsessive attention to shop-floor detail and worker responsibility for quality became the starting-point of the revolution (p. 56 ff.). Co-ordinating the supply chain was another key aspect of Toyota's success. In traditional mass assembly it is common to find widely different levels of integration, or for the main assembler to simply rely on market forces to organize the supply chain and require suppliers to compete against each other on price and delivery. This discourages quality and production innovation. But the methods pioneered at Toyota led to a much more systematic approach to components supply. Suppliers were organized into functional tiers, with first-tier suppliers working closely with the assembler on production improvements, and responsible for organizing a second tier of suppliers, and so forth.

Other elements of the lean production matrix emphasized progressively trying to eliminate or minimize buffers of stock, work-in-progress, and the rework of materials, in order to permit only activities that add value and not cost. Lean companies are also preoccupied with cutting out low-value-added activities, so techniques such as out-sourcing and the continuous redefining of what are the core competencies are practised. Space too is a resource that is often wasted in traditional assembly, but with lean production the emphasis is on getting maximum value-added from a given footprint of shopfloor space. This can be particularly important in modern sophisticated plants, where the factory shell itself is an important and often extremely expensive part of the production environment.

The account of Womack *et al.* is grounded in the development of the Japanese auto industry, especially that of Toyota. But the MIT researchers' main focus was on the success of the so-called Japanese 'transplants' in North America. This first wave of Japanese outward investment started with Honda and Nissan in the early 1980s but the major impact came in 1986 with the NUMMI plant, the Toyota–GM joint-venture. By 1990 there were ten Japanese-owned car plants in the United States and Canada, which were followed by hundreds of Japanese companies that set up whole supplier networks. The productivity and quality of the transplants on the whole matched Japanese levels and well exceeded the levels of US-owned and European plants. Nevertheless, Womack *et al.*

found that not all were particularly efficient, which led them to point out that 'lean does not necessarily equal Japanese' (p. 242). In other words, lean production is a model of manufacturing excellence that can be learned. Some American companies, like Ford, have successfully turned themselves into lean organizations.

The limits of Japanization

The desire to emulate the success of these methods strengthened with the overseas expansion of Japan's industries. The North American auto transplants gave direct experience of the new management techniques, as well as evidence that these production methods could be transferred and adapted outside the Japanese industrial culture. Japanese inward investment in Britain—essentially the bridgehead into the European Union—sparked a parallel debate about the 'Japanization' of British industry. The Japanization process meant British firms in increasing numbers adopting or adapting these methods, and attempts to get British workers to absorb the social attitudes of Japanese workers. Given this dissemination process, systems like JIT and lean production are now regarded as global best practice in production engineering terms. Of course, ideas like operating with minimum resources, or that quality should be built in rather than inspected out, are hardly new. The difference is that the Japanese appear to have done something about it. Rather than merely exhort workers to 'get it right first time', or run half-hearted 'suggestion schemes', Japanese firms have actually created systems of stockless production and responsible autonomy.

Or have they? While there is no doubting the success of Japan's production strategies, there have also been some highly critical evaluations of who has borne the cost. Questions have been asked about the limits to the application of these methods outside Japan, as well as inside the country, and the query has been raised about whether these are genuine innovations in the sense of a radical break with Fordism.

An intensified labour process? Advocates of just-in-time and lean systems see them as being based on forms of task variety and skills that enhance the work environment. Womack *et al.* (1990, p. 80) concede a harder pace of work under the lean regime, but stress that employers treat workers as partners in an enterprise, as a resource to be invested in rather than a mere cost of production, and that workers themselves have a greater sense of purposefulness and involvement. In this sense, JIT/lean regimes are seen as progressive new systems and placed within the broad movement towards worker autonomy and high-trust industrial relations.

On the other hand, there is also a mass of accumulated evidence about the potential of JIT/lean systems for intensifying work. Some accounts of conditions inside production plants describe an incredibly intense pace of work and long overtime hours (Klein, 1989; 1990). More specifically the idea that 'slack' (buffer stocks, work-in-progress) can be eliminated from the system and it still be human-centred is hotly disputed. In a JIT system work is initiated only when there is an immediate production need, so having to be responsive to *kanban* discipline means even less discretion than in conventional systems.

Oliver (1991), for example, points out that JIT environments are highly stressed. Stockless production may be objectively less intensive (because there tends to be increased idle time), but workers experience much more insecurity and pressure because they are 'hooked up' to the system; the removal of inventory means that work units become highly interdependent, so there is greater pressure from other work-groups and less scope for workgroup autonomy. Similarly, Delbridge *et al.* (1992) adopt a labour-process approach, and argue that in JIT factory regimes the 'frontier of control' between capital and labour is being pushed further back. In conventional large batch/line systems, important forms of worker autonomy depend on informal practices (see Chapter 10), but in a JIT system work is only initiated when there is an immediate production need. The elimination of 'slack' and 'waste' is thus aimed at eliminating forms of workers' counter-control and 'more completely subordinating labour to capital'. Delbridge *et al.* list a range of ways in which JIT systems are more controlled and intensified. The visibility of the work process means more detailed surveillance and monitoring of behaviour; more responsibility and accountability may appear to bring greater autonomy but in fact they tie workers closer to production goals; and the seemingly outward-looking emphasis on new entities like the 'team' and the 'customer' is really about introducing even greater pressures into the labour process.

Supplier and labour-market relationships The new supply-chain logistics also have implications for the nature of work. A 'close' relationship with a big manufacturer can be a double-edged sword for a supplier. The application of JIT methods upstream should in theory remove friction between companies and their suppliers—and for advocates of these regimes the image of the supply chain as one large co-operative machine has often been put across as reality (e.g. Womack *et al.*, 1990, p. 62)—but the supply-chain concept has often proved unrealistic. The preferred-status relationship, and becoming a cog in the just-in-time machine, may look very different from the supplier's viewpoint. The demand for zero defects and JIT deliveries may in reality mean the main assembler using its monopoly power to squeeze suppliers for additional burdens of delivery and quality. Supplier firms have had to expand their own stock levels and pressurize their workers in order to cope with JIT deliveries. Thus the overall production system may be no more efficient; the inefficiencies are merely being moved about and the costs borne by the weaker partner.

It is important to note here that Japan has one of the most strongly developed dual economies of all industrial nations. Industrial dualism (as we saw in Chapter 17) can mean savage downward pressures on labour in smaller companies. Unionization levels and working conditions in the secondary sector are relatively poor, so costs can be cut by shifting production there. Critics have argued that this is a central part of the JIT rationale—to offset tendencies to create expensive, centralized labour. In this sense, the popular image of Japanese lifetime employment is partly a myth; it applies to perhaps 20 per cent of Japan's workers employed by large companies. The other face of Japanese employment is a massive sector of 'sweated' industries that feed the major companies. For example, Sakai (1990) points out that in the consumer electronics industry the costs of constant redesign and product improvement that make Japanese firms so competitive are borne by anonymous suppliers.

How extensive is the sub-contracting pyramid? Would you guess a few dozen companies? A few hundred? Think again. One electronics company I know has well over 6,000 sub-contractors in its industrial group, most of them tiny shops that exist just to fill a few little orders for the companies above them. Welcome to the real world of Japanese manufacturing.

Sakai likens the relationship between the giant companies and their suppliers to almost a master–slave relation, with the big firms ruthlessly ordering price cuts from sub-contractors whenever their competitive position comes under threat. There is also a dynamic relation between primary and secondary sectors. Workers in the large companies tend to accept intensified labour because dismissal would mean moving down into secondary sector jobs.

This market structure has led to doubts about the *transferability* of Japanese methods. Outside Japan industrial dualism is not usually so pronounced. For example, Turnbull (1988) has examined the British West Midlands motor industry and found several cases where supplier firms resisted attempts by motor manufacturers to impose new demands. Workers have also been quick to realize that JIT systems are vulnerable to industrial action. Low stock levels and production integration mean that they can be operated only in the absence of disruption from labour, which gives workers considerable bargaining strength. Turnbull found that firms like Austin Rover were mostly interested in JIT delivery as a way of shifting costs on to suppliers. But he reports a number of cases where companies had to climb down in the face of threatened industrial action after trying to impose wage or price cuts.

Innovation or neo-Fordism?

In recent years, numerous writers and researchers have joined the debate about whether the new production systems coming out of Japan—just-in-time, lean production, Toyotaism—are truly innovative or not. Are they a radical break with the past, or merely a reformed Fordism and a refinement and continuity of orthodox mass production principles? The protagonists of Japanese methods are in no doubt that these are innovative systems. For Womack *et al.* we saw that lean production represented 'an entirely new way of making things' (1990, p. 47). The Japanese had led the way with this revolutionary manufacturing paradigm, and the rest of the world (the main concern of Womack *et al.*, of course, was with the United States) had better adapt and catch up.

The weight of critical academic opinion, it is probably true to say, disagrees and places Japan on the other, neo-Fordist side of Piore and Sabel's 'industrial divide'. The products on which Japan's industrial miracle has been based—cars, videos, TVs—are all mass produced, and the quality and specification that makes them so competitive come from refinements and extensions to the assembly line. As Wood notes, 'nothing in these innovations implies an end to mass production' (1989, p. 33); or, as Berggren more strongly argues, the Japanese are the 'modern masters' of standardization and Taylorism (1989, p. 172). Similarly, there is nothing in practices like teamworking and multi-skilling that necessarily enhances work; it depends entirely on how they are applied. Multi-skilling may simply be multi-tasking and mean an enlargement of responsibilities, while the work-group becomes the context for the removal of restrictions on the use of labour. Thus many researchers resist seeing the new systems as exciting and progressive, and instead view them as the next stage in the capital–labour relationship, one marked by a greater degree of exploitation and surveillance of labour (Oliver, 1991; Delbridge *et al.*, 1992).

Labour issues—reflected in worker autonomy and workers' attitudes—are pivotal as regards the 'innovativeness' of the new manufacturing. This is because the efficiency and productivity of these systems is not much in doubt. They do add flexibility and represent an advance on classic assembly-line methods. But if productive power is won mainly by tightening the grip on labour this would undermine claims about the innovative nature of production design. If, on the other hand, the systems can increase output and worker participation, they might truly be pronounced innovative. The real-ization of this point is behind claims by the protagonists of JIT/lean methods that they incorporate improved conditions for labour. Womack *et al.* argue that 'in the end, it is the dynamic work team that emerges as the heart of the lean factory' (1990, p. 99); and they suggest their research showed that self-regulating, problem-solving teams emerge where there is a 'reciprocal obligation' between management and workers—workers giving increased commitment, and firms showing they value that commitment by delegating real responsibility and providing job security (p. 99).

That said, it is clear that workers were not the main concern for Womack *et al.* Their evidence here is anecdotal and often just an assertion that lean production is 'humanly fulfilling'. Others have disputed their interpretation. For example, Stewart and Garrahan (1995) found that in four US and UK plants where lean regimes had been introduced there was no evidence of increased job satisfaction or interest in the work. Similarly, Conti and Warner (1993) point out that Taylorism had a much greater impact in Japan and was much more widely diffused than is usually acknowledged. It was well estab-lished in major industries as early as the 1920s. They argue that the culture of continu-ous improvement is what really distinguishes Japanese manufacturing; this substituted the specialization of Taylorism with a devoted and committed workforce. But the result was 'a mediated form of scientific management', or a 'Toyota version of Taylorism'.

Berggren (1993) in particular has engaged the MIT authors in debate and produced a detailed critique of *The Machine that Changed the World*. He points out that auto assembly is not typical of Japanese multinational investment, and that other industries (electron-ics, components supply) practise few advanced production and employee relations methods. The only thing they share with the auto transplants is an aversion to trade unions. Nevertheless, the auto transplants are still crucial as proof that 'lean production is possible to implement in a large-scale fashion outside Japan' (p. 170). Berggren con-cedes that work in these plants has certain 'attractive qualities'—employees often take a pride in the production operation and in being part of an elite workforce. However, the other side of the coin is the 'unlimited performance demands, long working hours and requirements to work overtime on short notice, recurrent health and safety complaints, and the rigorous factory regime' (p. 175). Berggren reports growing trade-union and labour disillusion in the transplants—a pattern of initially solid support and co-operation, gradually shifting to outright opposition to the relentless work pressures.

Indeed, the interesting suggestion is that the direct investments in the USA and Britain in part represent an international solution to a growing problem in Japan itself, where a strong cultural reaction against high pressure–long hours regimes is setting in. Labour-force surveys show increasing resistance and profound changes in workers' attitudes. This effectively reverses the assumptions of the transferability argument—which questioned whether the distinctive social conditions in Japan would prevent the successful transfer of industries overseas—and argues that Japan itself may not be able to keep recreating the conditions for the acceptance of these regimes. All the US and UK transplants employ the Toyota system of lean production, fast-paced assembly lines, and high demands on labour. The paradox is that these conditions could be imposed in precisely those countries (USA, UK) where traditional working cultures resisted them.

Conclusion

Interest in the new forms of work organization has revitalized debate about the nature of work. That debate was examined in previous chapters (mainly 9, 11, and 19). In particular the influential and long-running argument about the 'deskilling' of work, it will be recalled, put forth the controversial idea that under industrial capitalism work becomes progressively degraded and deskilled, especially as a result of Taylorist work practices. A tide of criticism suggested that this was a one-sided view, though there were also some notable defences of this basically Marxist position.

In this chapter we have seen many of these themes resurfacing. The flexibility thesis, originally formulated by Piore and Sabel, suggests a somewhat more positive view of industrial society. Flexible specialization was seen as a way out of the so-called crisis of Fordism, and a way of changing the alienating conditions of the assembly line. Piore and Sabel might therefore be classified alongside theorists who see in the future a progressive and harmonious economic culture and improved work-forms. Yet flexibility is nothing if not a complex concept, and Piore and Sabel did not directly challenge the idea of work degradation. Their 'industrial divide' presented two ways out of a stagnating Fordism. The breakthrough in flexible methods (which they saw occurring in embryonic form in countries like Italy, Germany, and Japan) was the preferred future, but neo-Fordism was no less likely an option.

The chapter continued by making distinctions between different models of flexibility. The flexible firm, flexible specialization, and just-in-time/lean production were each linked to a national culture. First the model of the flexible firm and its relevance to discussions about work restructuring in Britain. Debate here revolved around the degree of change, and whether flexible methods have actually spread beyond a few enclaves. The detailed evidence suggests that, while the elaborate flexible firm model may be something of a fiction, under the impact of new demands for flexibility there has indeed been a radical restructuring of work.

The main discussion then centred on production systems found in the leading economies of Germany, Japan, and the United States. In Germany *flexible specialization* rested on skilled traditions, stable industrial relations, and a high social settlement—all upheld as far as the present is concerned by a remarkably successful product market strategy (all the world wants a Mercedes). Japanese methods, which are much more famous and widely discussed, have led to a mass of new jargon, though the systems known as *just-in-time* and *lean production* are most widely applied. Both refer to the same mix of redesigned assembly methods, supply-chain management, and continuous improvement. The United States, still of course the world's largest economy, cannot claim a distinctive new system of its own, yet there is a strong sense that the popularization of Japanese methods has come about as a result of their impact in the USA—particularly lean production as the latest global paradigm.

The analysis we presented broadly corroborates the original flexibility thesis of Piore and Sabel—though in the period since they wrote (in 1984) the nature of the different national production systems has come into much sharper focus and we need to recast the theory somewhat. Champions of lean production like Womack *et al.* (1990) at a superficial level seem to be confirming the optimistic version of the flexibility thesis. They argue that lean methods are innovative and constitute the new form of best practice. However, as we have seen, the academic debate around 'Japanese' methods has been hotly contested, and many now argue that these methods represent a much more intensified use of labour. On this reading it is the pessimistic scenario of Piore and Sabel that has come about. The programmes of national renewal seem to have progressed along neo-Fordist lines. In this context, Berggren's (1993) critique was that Womack *et al.* were really attempting to shut down debate—to suppress alternatives, and put forward lean methods as the single 'best way' to organize production. Yet alternatives do exist. Flexible specialization in some German industries and enclaves of Scandinavian industry (like Volvo) seem to much better reflect the innovative work systems that Piore and Sabel had in mind—though their existence is under pressure.

Finally, our approach of linking production systems to national models has its drawbacks. By lumping together all 'Japanese methods' or all 'German methods', there are obvious dangers of understating the differences within countries. Also, such an approach might underestimate the potential of the flexibility movement. The alternative is simply to regard the label 'flexibility' as a standard model, and then study the new production systems industry by industry, or factory by factory, and so emphasize them as a force for change. On the other hand, there are certain advantages to be gained in making some attempt at comparative distinctions, and in clarifying the differences between the forms of work organization.

One important distinction lies in the varying impact that flexible systems have on management thought and practice. As we have noted Japanese systems have registered by far the largest impact. Talk of the 'Japanization' of Anglo-American management contrasts rather oddly with a far lower level of interest in alternative methods. The sense in which Japan has taken the west by surprise, and the new phase of Japanese multinational growth, may partly explain this. But the popularity of the Japanese model also seems to reflect the close match with the Taylorized industries of the United States and Britain. The weight of evidence we saw points to JIT/lean production being a revitalized Fordism, a system that makes more immediate sense to American and British managers given the production habits they are used to.

Study questions for Chapter 20

1 What is Fordism and why are Fordist production systems inflexible?

2 What has brought about the so-called crisis of Fordism?

3 Piore and Sabel's 'industrial divide' presented a set of stark choices as regards future industrial and social developments. What were they?

4 Describe the flexible firm model. Does it accurately describe British industrial patterns?

5 How is flexible specialization a superior model to its neo-Fordist alternatives?

6 What threatens the German version of flexible specialization?

7 Are there any differences between just-in-time and lean production?

8 What are the main criticisms of the Japanese production methods?

9 Why has the Japanese economic miracle attracted so much more attention than the German one?

Further reading

Altmann, N., Kohler, C., and Meil, P. (eds.) (1994) *Technology and Work in German Industry*. London: Routledge.

Berggren, C. (1995) 'Japan as Number Two: competitive problems and the future of alliance capitalism', *Work, Employment and Society*, 9/1: 53–95.

Kamata, S. (1983) *Japan in the Passing Lane*. London: Allen and Unwin.

Lane, C. (1995) *Industry and Society in Europe: Stability and Change in Britain, Germany and France*. Aldershot: Edward Elgar.

Lash, S. and Urry, J. (1987) *The End of Organized Capitalism*. Cambridge: Polity Press.

Ohno, T. (1988) *Toyota Production System*. Cambridge, Mass.: Productivity Press.

Oliver, N. and Wilkinson, B. (1988) *The Japanization of British Industry*. Oxford: Blackwell.

Pollert, A. (ed.) (1991) *Farewell to Flexibility?* Oxford: Blackwell.

Storey, J. (ed.) (1994) *New Wave Manufacturing: Organizational and Human Resource Dimensions*. London: Paul Chapman.

Womack, J. P. and Jones, D. T. (1994) 'From lean production to the lean enterprise', *Harvard Business Review*, 72, Mar/Apr, 93–103.

Wood, S. (ed.) (1989) *The Transformation of Work?* London: Unwin Hyman.

References

Abbott, A. (1988) *The System of Professions: An Essay on the Division of Expert Labor*. Chicago: University of Chicago Press.

Abercrombie, N. and Urry, J. (1983) *Capital, Labour and the Middle Classes*. London: Allen and Unwin.

Ackers, P. and Black, J. (1992) 'Watching the detectives: shop stewards' expectations of their managers in the age of human resource management', in A. Sturdy, D. Knights, and H. Willmott (eds.) *op. cit.*

——, Marchington, M., Wilkinson, A., and Goodman, J. (1992) 'The use of cycles: explaining employee involvement in the 1990s', *Industrial Relations Journal*, 23/4, 26–83.

——, Smith, C., and Smith, P. (eds) (1996) *The New Workplace and Trade Unionism*. London: Routledge.

——, ——, and—— (1996) 'Against the odds? British trade unions in the new work place', in P. Ackers, C. Smith, and P. Smith (eds.) *op. cit.*

Adams, J. S. (1965) 'Inequity in social exchange', in L. Berkowitz (ed.) *Advances in Experimental Social Psychology*, vol. 2. New York: Academic Press.

—— and Jacobsen, P. R. (1964) 'Effects of wage inequities on work quality', *Journal of Abnormal and Social Psychology*, 69, 19–25.

Alban-Metcalfe, B. (1984) 'Microskills of leadership: a detailed analysis of the behavior of managers in the appraisal interview', in J. G. Hunt, D. M. Hosking, C. A. Schriesheim, and R. Stewart (eds.) *Leaders and Managers*. New York: Pergamon.

Alderfer, C. P. (1972) *Existence, Relatedness and Growth*. New York: Free Press.

Allen, N. J. (1996) 'Affective reactions to the group and the organization', in M. A. West (ed.) *Handbook of Workgroup Psychology*. Chichester: Wiley.

Allen, V. L. (1975) *Social Analysis*. London: Longman.

Altmann, N., Binkelmann, P., Düll, K., and Stück, H. (1982) *Grenzen neuer Arbeitzformen*. Frankfurt: Campus.

Anderson, J. R. (1990) *Cognitive Psychology and its Implications*. New York: Freeman.

Anderson, N. (1997) 'The validity and adverse impact of selection interviews', *Selection and Development Review*, 13/5, 13–17.

—— and West, M. A. (1994) *The Team Climate Inventory: Manual and Users' Guide*. Windsor: ASE.

—— and —— (1996) 'The Team Climate Inventory: development of the TCI and its applications in teambuilding for innovativeness', *European Journal of Work and Organizational Psychology*, 5/1, 53–66.

Argyle, M. (1994) *The Psychology of Interpersonal Behaviour*, 5th edn. Harmondsworth: Penguin.

—— and Cook, H. (1976) *Gaze and Mutual Gaze*. Cambridge: Cambridge University Press.

Armstrong, P. (1985) 'Changing management control strategies: the role of competition between accountancy and other organisational professions', *Accounting, Organizations and Society*, 10, 124–8.

Armstrong, P. (1989) 'Management, labour process and agency', *Work, Employment and Society*, 3/3, 307–22.

—— (1995) 'Accountancy and HRM', in J. Storey (ed.) *Human Resource Management: A Critical Text*. London: Routledge.

Astley, W. G. and Van de Ven, A. (1983) 'Central perspectives and debates in organization theory', *Administrative Science Quarterly*, 28, 24–73.

Atkinson, J. (1984) 'Manpower strategies for flexible organizations', *Personnel Management*, August.

—— (1985) 'Flexibility: planning for an uncertain future', *Manpower Policy and Practice*, 1, Summer, 26–9.

—— (1988) 'Recent changes in the internal labour market structure in the UK', in W. Buitelaar (ed.) *Technology and Work*. Aldershot: Avebury.

Attwood, M. and Hatton, F. (1983) ' "Getting on": gender differences in career development: a case study in the hairdressing industry', in E. Gamarnikow, D. Morgan, J. Purvis, and D. Taylorson (eds.) *Gender, Class and Work*. London: Heinemann.

Axtell, C. M., Maitlis, S., and Yearta, S. K. (1997) 'Predicting immediate and longer-term transfer of training', *Personnel Review*, 26/3, 201–13.

Bacharach, S. B. and Lawler, E. J. (1980) *Power and Politics in Organizations*. London: Jossey-Bass.

Bachrach, P. and Baratz, M. S. (1962) 'The two faces of power', *American Political Science Review*, 56, 947–52.

Bacon, N. and Storey, J. (1996) 'Individualism and collectivism and the changing role of trade unions', in P. Ackers, C. Smith, and P. Smith (eds.) *op. cit.*

Baehr, M. (1987) *The Managerial Job Functions Inventory*. Chicago: NCS.

Bainbridge, L. (1978) 'The process controller', in W. T. Singleton (ed.) *The Analysis of Practical Skills*. Lancaster: MTP Press.

Baldamus, W. (1961) *Efficiency and Effort*. London: Tavistock.

Baldry, C. and Connolly, A. (1986) 'Drawing the line: computer-aided design and the organization of the drawing office', *New Technology, Work and Employment*, 1/1, 59–66.

Baron, A. (1992) 'Technology and the crisis of masculinity: the gendering of work and skill in the US Printing industry 1850–1920', in A. Sturdy, D. Knights and H. Willmott (eds.) *op. cit.*

Barrett, P. and Kline, P. (1980) 'Personality factors in the EPQ', *Personality and Individual Differences*, 1, 317–23.

Barrick, M. R. and Mount, M. K. (1991) 'The Big Five personality dimensions and job performance: a metaanalysis', *Personnel Psychology*, 44, 1–26.

Bass, B. M. and Avolio, B. J. (1993) 'Transformational leadership: a response to critiques', in M. M. Chemers (ed.) *Leadership Theory and Research: Perspectives and Directions*. New York: Academic Press.

—— and —— (1994) 'Shatter the glass ceiling: women may make better managers', *Human Resource Management*, 33/4, 549–60.

——, Burger, P. C., Doktor, R., and Barrett, G. V. (1979) *Assessment of Managers: An International Comparison*. New York: Free Press.

Beehr, T. A. (1995) *Psychological Stress in the Workplace*. London: Routledge.

Belbin, R. M. (1981) *Management Teams: Why they Succeed or Fail*. London: Heinemann.

—— (1993) *Team Roles at Work: A Strategy for Human Resource Management*. Oxford: Butterworth Heinemann.

—— (1996) *The Coming Shape of Organization*. Oxford: Butterworth Heinemann.

Bell, D. (1948) ' "Screening" leaders in a democracy', *Commentary*, 5, 368–75.

Bendix, R. (1956) *Work and Authority in Industry*. New York: Wiley.

Berggren, C. (1989) 'New production concepts in final assembly: the Swedish experience', in S. Wood (ed.) *op. cit.*

—— (1993) 'Lean production—the end of history?', *Work, Employment and Society*, 7/2, 163–88.

Beynon, H. (1984) *Working for Ford*, 2nd edn. Harmondsworth: Penguin.

—— and Blackburn, R. (1972) *Perceptions of Work*. Cambridge: Cambridge University Press.

Billings, A. G. and Moos, R. M. (1981) 'The role of coping responses in attenuating the impact of stressful life events', *Journal of Behavioural Medicine*, 4, 139–57.

Bion, W. R. (1959) *Experiences in Groups*. London: Tavistock.

Birdi, K., Pennington, J., and Zapf, D. (1997) 'Ageing and errors in computer-based work: an observational field study', *Journal of Occupational and Organizational Psychology*, 70, 35–47.

——, Warr, P., and Oswald, A. (1995) 'Age differences in three components of employee well-being', *Applied Psychology: An International Review*, 44/4, 345–73.

Blackburn, R. M. and Mann, M. (1979) *The Working Class in the Labour Market*. London: Macmillan.

Blackler, F. H. M. and Brown, C. A. (1980) 'Job redesign and social change: case studies at Volvo', in K. D. Duncan, M. M. Gruneberg, and D. Wallis (eds.) *op. cit.*

——, Reed, M., and Whitaker, A. (1993) 'Editorial introduction: knowledge workers and contemporary organizations', *Journal of Management Studies*, 30/6, 851–62.

Blau, P. M. (1955) *The Dynamics of Bureaucracy*. Chicago: University of Chicago Press.

—— and Schoenherr, R. A. (1971) *The Structure of Organizations*. New York: Basic Books.

Blauner, R. (1964) *Alienation and Freedom*. Chicago: University of Chicago Press.

Bloomfield, B. and Danieli, A. (1995) 'The role of management consultants in the development of information technology', *Journal of Management Studies*, 33/1, 27–46.

Boje, D. M. (1991) 'The story-telling organization: story performance in an office supply firm', *Administrative Science Quarterly*, 36/1, 106–26.

Boyatzis, R. E. (1982) *The Competent Manager: A Model for Effective Performance*. Chichester: Wiley.

Bradley, H. (1989) *Men's Work, Women's Work*. Cambridge: Polity Press.

Braverman, H. (1974) *Labor and Monopoly Capital: The Degradation of Work in the Twentieth Century*. New York: Monthly Review Press.

Bray, D. W., Campbell, R. J., and Grant, D. C. (1974) *Formative Years in Business: A Long-Term AT&T Study of Managerial Lives*. New York: Wiley.

Brett, J. M. (1980) 'The effect of job transfer in employees and their families', in C. L. Cooper and R. Payne (eds.) *op. cit.*

Brewer, M. B. and Miller, N. (1996) *Intergroup Relations*. Buckingham: Open University Press.

Brigham, M. and Martin Corbett, J. (1997) 'E-mail, power and the constitution of organisational reality', *New Technology, Work and Employment*, 12/1, 25–35.

Brown, G. W. and Harris, T. (1978) *Social Origins of Depression: A Study of Psychiatric Disorder in Women*. London: Tavistock.

Brown, R. (1984) 'Women as employees: social consciousness and collective action', in J. Siltanen and M. Stanworth (eds.) *op. cit.*

Brunsson, N. (1982) 'The irrationality of action and action rationality: decisions, ideologies and organizational actions', *Journal of Management Studies*, 21/1, 29–44.

Bryant, S. E. and Gurman, E. B. (1996) 'Contingent supervisory behaviour: a practical predictor of performance', *Group and Organizational Management*, 21/4, 404–13.

Bryman, A. (1984) 'Organizational studies and the concept of rationality', *Journal of Management Studies*, 21, 391–408.

Buchanan, D. A. (1992) 'High performance: new boundaries of acceptability in worker control', in G. Salaman (ed.) *Human Resource Strategies*. London: Sage.

—— and Boddy, D. (1983) *Organizations in the Computer Age*. Aldershot: Gower.

Bunce, D. (1997) 'What factors are associated with the outcome of individual-focused work-site stress management intervention?', Memo No. 50, Institute of Work Psychology, Sheffield.

—— and West, M. A. (1994) 'Changing work environments: innovation-requiring responses to occupational stress', *Work and Stress*, 8/4, 319–31.

—— and —— (1996) 'Stress management and innovation interventions at work', *Human Relations*, 49/2, 209–32.

Burawoy, M. (1979) *Manufacturing Consent*. Chicago: University of Chicago Press.

Burnes, B. (1988) 'New technology and job design: the case of CNC', *New Technology, Work and Employment*, 3/2, 100–11.

Burns, J. M. (1978) *Leadership*. New York: Harper and Row.

Burns, T. (1969) 'On the plurality of social systems', in T. Burns (ed.) *Industrial Man*. Harmondsworth: Penguin.

—— (1977) *The BBC: Public Institution and Private World*. London: Macmillan.

—— and Stalker, G. M. (1961) *The Management of Innovation*. London: Tavistock.

Burnstein, E. (1983) 'Persuasion as argument processing', in I. M. Brandstatter, J. H. Davis, and G. Stocker-Kreichgauer (eds.) *Group Decision Processes*. London: Academic Press.

Burrell, G. (1988) 'Modernism, post-modernism and organizational analysis 2: the contribution of Michel Foucault', *Organization Studies*, 9/2, 221–35.

—— and Morgan, G. (1979) *Sociological Paradigms and Organisational Analysis*. London: Heinemann.

Butler, G. and Hope, T. (1995) *Manage your Mind*. Oxford: Oxford University Press.

Butler, R. (1991) *Designing Organizations*. London: Routledge.

Byrne, D. G. and Rheinhart, M. I. (1989) 'Work characteristics, occupational achievement and the Type A behavior pattern', *Journal of Occupational Psychology*, 62, 123–34.

Cameron, R. and Meichenbaum, D. (1982) 'The nature of effective coping and the treatment of stress related problems: a cognitive-behavioural perspective', in L. Goldberger and S. Breznitz (eds.) *Handbook of Stress: Theoretical and Clinical Aspects*. London: Macmillan.

Campbell, A. and Warner, M. (1987) 'New technology, innovation and training', *New Technology, Work and Employment*, 2/2, 86–99.

Campbell, M. (1993) 'The employment effects of new technology and organizational change: an empirical study', *New Technology, Work and Employment*, 8/2, 134–40.

Cantor, N. and Kihlstrom, J. F. (1987) *Personality and Social Intelligence*. Englewood Cliffs, NJ: Prentice Hall.

Caplan, R. D., Cobb, S., French, J. R. P., van Harrison, R., and Pinneau, S. R. (1975) *Job Demands and Worker Health*, pp. 75–160. US Department of Health, Education and Welfare/NIOSH.

Carchedi, G. (1977) *On the Economic Identification of Social Classes*. London: Routledge.

Carey, A. (1967) 'The Hawthorne studies: a radical criticism', *American Sociological Review*, 32, 403–16.

Carnall, C. A. (1995) *Managing Change in Organizations*, 2nd edn. Hemel Hempstead: Prentice Hall.

Carrère, S., Evans, G. W. M., Palsane, N., and Rivas, M. (1991) 'Job strain and occupational stress among urban public transport operators', *Journal of Occupational Psychology*, 64, 305–16.

Carruthers, M. (1980) 'Hazardous occupations and the heart', in C. L. Cooper and R. Payne (eds.) *op. cit.*

Carver, C. S. and Glass, D. C. (1978) 'Coronary-prone behaviour patterns and interpersonal aggression', *Journal of Personality and Social Psychology*, 36, 361–6.

Cassidy, T. and Lynn, R. (1989) 'A multifactorial approach to achievement motivation: the development of a comprehensive measure', *Journal of Occupational Psychology*, 62, 301–12.

Cathcart, E. P. (1928) *The Human Factor in Industry*. Oxford: Oxford University Press.

Cattell, R. B. (1967) *The Scientific Analysis of Personality*. Harmondsworth: Penguin.

Cattell, H. (1989) *Deeper into Personality*. Windsor: ASE.

Chesney, M. A. and Rosenman, R. (1980) 'Type A behaviour in the work setting', in C. L. Cooper and R. Payne (eds.) *op. cit.*

Child, J. (1972) 'Organizational structure, environment and performance: the role of strategic choice', *Sociology*, 6/1, 1–22.

—— (1984) *Organization*, 2nd edn. London: Harper and Row.

—— and Fulk, J. (1982) 'Maintenance of occupational control: the case of professions', *Work and Occupations*, 9, 155–92.

—— and Smith, C. (1987) 'The context and process of organizational transformation—Cadbury Limited in its sector', *Journal of Management Studies*, 24/6, 565–93.

——, Loveridge, R., Harvey, J., and Spencer, A. (1984) 'Microelectronics and the quality of employment in services', in P. Marstrand (ed.) *New Technology and the Future of Work and Skills*. London: Frances Pinter.

Church, A. H. (1997) 'Managerial self-awareness in high performing individuals in organizations', *Journal of Applied Psychology*, 82/2, 281–92.

Cialdini, R. B. (1988) *Influence: Science and Practice*. Glenview, Ill.: Scott, Foresman, Little, Brown.

Claridge, G. S. (1970) *Drugs and Human Behaviour*. London: Allen Lane.

Clark, A. E. (1996) 'Job satisfaction in Britain', *British Journal of Industrial Relations*, 34, 189–217.

——, Oswald, A., and Warr, P. (1996) 'Is job satisfaction U-shaped in age?', *Journal of Occupational and Organizational Psychology*, 69, 57–81.

Clark, P. and Staunton, N. (1989) *Innovation in Technology and Organization*. London: Routledge.

Clarke, D. D. (1983) *Language and Action: A Structural Model of Behaviour*. Oxford: Pergamon Press.

Clegg, C. and Fitter, M. J. (1978) 'Management information systems: the Achilles Heel of job redesign', *Personnel Review*, 7, 5–11.

Clegg, S. (1989) *Frameworks of Power*. London: Sage.

—— and Dunkerley, D. (1980) *Organization, Class and Control*. London: Routledge and Kegan Paul.

Cockburn, C. (1983) *Brothers: Male Dominance and Technological Change*. London: Pluto Press.

—— (1985) *Machinery of Dominance: Women, Men and Technical Know-How*. London: Pluto Press.

—— (1988) 'The gendering of jobs: workplace relations and the reproduction of sex segregation', in S. Walby (ed.) *op. cit.*

Coe, T. (1997) *The Lean Organization*. Oxford: Butterworth Heinemann.

Cohen, M. D., March, J., and Olsen, P. (1972) 'A garbage can model of organizational choice', *Administrative Science Quarterly*, 17/1, 1–25.

Collinson, D. (1994) 'Strategies of resistance: power, knowledge and subjectivity in the workplace', in J. M. Jermier, D. Knights, and W. Nord (eds.) *Resistance and Power in Organizations*. London: Routledge.

——, Knights, D., and Collinson, M. (1990) *Managing to Discriminate*. London: Routledge.

Collis, J. M., Tapsfield, P. G. C., Irvine, S. H., Dunn, P. L., and Wright, D. (1995) 'The British Army Recruit Battery goes operational: from theory to practice in computer-based testing using item generation techniques', *International Journal of Selection and Assessment*, 3/2, 96–104.

Conger, J. A. (1991) *Inspiring Others: The Language of Leadership*. Academy of Management Executive, Vol. 5.

Conti, R. and Warner, M. (1993) 'Taylorism, new technology and JIT systems in Japan', *New Technology, Work and Employment*, 8/1, 31–42.

—— and —— (1994) 'Taylorism, teams and technology in "reengineering" work organization', *New Technology, Work and Employment*, 9/2, 93–102.

Cooley, M. (1987) 'Human centered systems: an urgent problem for systems designers', *AI and Society*, 1/1, 40.

Cooper, C. (1997) 'The implications of the new work millennium', *Selection and Development Review*, 13/6, 9–11.

Cooper, C. L. and Payne, R. (eds.) (1980) *Current Concerns in Occupational Stress*. Chichester: Wiley.

Costa, P. T. and McCrae, R. R. (1997) 'Longitudinal stability of adult personality', in R. Hogan, J. Johnson, and S. Briggs (eds.) *op. cit.*

Cowling, A. G., Stanworth, M. J. K., Bennet, R. D., Curran, J., and Lyons, P. (1988) *Behavioural Sciences for Managers*, 2nd edn. Oxford: Blackwell.

Cox, T. (1980) 'Repetitive work', in C. L. Cooper and R. Payne (eds.) *op. cit.*

Craig, C., Garnsey, E., and Rubery, J. (1983) 'Women's pay in informal payment systems', *Employment Gazette*, April. London: Department of Employment.

Crompton, R. and Jones, G. (1984) *White Collar Proletariat: Deskilling and Gender in Clerical Work*. London: Macmillan.

—— and Reid, S. (1982) 'The deskilling of clerical work', in S. Wood (ed.) *op. cit.*

Crossman, E. R. F. W. and Cooke, J. E. (1962) 'Manual control of slow response systems', in E. Edwards and F. P. Lees (eds.) *The Human Operator in Process Control*. London: Taylor and Francis.

Crozier, M. (1964) *The Bureaucratic Phenomenon*. London: Tavistock.

Currie, W. (1989) *Managerial Strategy for New Technology*. Aldershot: Avebury.

Cyert, R. and March, J. G. (1963) *The Behavioral Theory of the Firm*. Englewood Cliffs, NJ: Prentice Hall.

Dahl, R. A. (1957) 'The concept of power', *Behavioral Science*, 2, 201–5.

Daley, M. R. (1979) 'Burnout: smouldering problems in protective services', *Social Work*, 24, 375–9.

Daniels, K., Brough, P., Guppy, A., Peters-Bean, K. M., and Weathersone, L. (1997) 'A note on a modification to Warr's measures of affective well being at work', *Journal of Occupational and Organizational Psychology*, 70, 129–38.

Dawson, P. and Webb, J. (1989) 'New production arrangements: the totally flexible cage', *Work, Employment and Society*, 3, 221–38.

Dawson, S. (1997) *Analysing Organisations*, 3rd edn. Basingstoke: Macmillan.

Deal, T. and Kennedy, A. (1982) *Corporate Cultures*. Reading, Mass.: Addison Wesley.

de Jonge, J. and Schaufeli, W. B. (1998) 'Job characteristics and employee well-being: a test of Warr's vitamin model in health-care workers using structural equation modelling', *Journal of Organizational Behavior*, 19/4, 387–407.

Delbridge, R., Turnbull, P., and Wilkinson, B. (1992) 'Pushing back the frontiers: management control and work intensification under JIT/TQM regimes', *New Technology, Work and Employment*, 7/2, 97–106.

Devine, F. (1992) 'Gender segregation in the engineering and science professions: continuity and change', *Work, Employment and Society*, 6/4, 557–575.

de Waele, J. P. and Harré, R. (1976) *Personality*. Oxford: Blackwell.

Dex. S. (1985) *The Sexual Division of Work*. Brighton: Harvester Wheatsheaf.

Dipboye, R. L. (1997) 'Structured employment interviews: why do they work? why are they underutilised?', in N. R. Anderson and P. Herriot (eds.) *International Handbook of Selection and Assessment*. Chichester: Wiley.

Donaldson, L. (1985) *In Defence of Organization Theory*. Cambridge: Cambridge University Press.

Dopson, S. (1996) 'Why is it so hard to involve doctors in management? Seeking to understand the processes of managed social change', in R. Fincham (ed.) *op. cit.*

Dornstein, M. (1989) 'The fairness of judgements of received pay and their determinants', *Journal of Occupational Psychology*, 62, 287–99.

Downs, S. and Perry, P. (1982) 'How do I learn?', *Journal of European Industrial Training*, 6, 27–32.

Drazen, M., Nevid, J. S., Pace, N., and O'Brien, R. M. (1982) 'Worksite-based behavioural treatment of mild hypertension', *Journal of Occupational Medicine*, 24, 511–14.

Driver, R. W., Buckley, M. R., and Frink, D. D. (1996) 'Should we write off graphology?', *International Journal of Selection and Assessment*, 4/2, 78–86.

Duck, S. (1998) *Human Relationships*, 3rd edn. London: Sage.

Du Gay, P., Salaman, G., and Rees, B. (1996) 'The conduct of management and the management of conduct: contemporary managerial discourse and the constitution of the "competent" manager', *Journal of Management Studies*, 33/3, 263–82.

Duncan, K. D., Gruneberg, M. M., and Wallis, D. (eds.) (1980) *Changes in Working Life*. Chichester: Wiley.

Durbeck, D. C., Heinzelmann, F., Schacter, J., Haskell, W. I., Payne, G. H., Moxley, R. T., Nemeroff, M., Limoncelli, D. D., Arnoldi, L. B., and Fox, S. M. (1972) 'The National Aeronautics and Space Administration: US Public Health Service Evaluation and Enhancement Programme', *American Journal of Cardiology*, 30, 784–90.

Eder, R. A. and Mangelsdorf, S. C. (1997) 'The emotional basis of early personality development', in R. Hogan, J. Johnson, and S. Briggs (eds.) *The Handbook of Personality*. London: Academic Press.

Edwardes, M. (1984) *Back from the Brink*. London: Pan.

Edwards, P. (1995) 'Strikes and industrial conflict', in P. Edwards (ed.) *Industrial Relations: Theory and Practice in Britain*. Oxford: Blackwell.

Edwards, P. and Hyman, R. (1994) 'Strikes and industrial conflict: peace in Europe', in R. Hyman and A. Ferner (eds.) *New Frontiers in European Industrial Relations*. Oxford: Blackwell.

Edwards, P. K. (1979) ' "The awful truth about strikes in our factories": a case study in the production of news', *Industrial Relations Journal*, 10, 7–11.

—— (1990) 'Understanding conflict in the labour process: the logic and autonomy of struggle', in D. Knights and H. Willmott (eds.) *op. cit.*

—— (1992) 'Industrial conflict: themes and issues in recent research', *British Journal of Industrial Relations*, 30/3, 361–404.

Edwards, R., Reich, M., and Gordon, D. M. (eds.) (1975) *Labor Market Segmentation*. Lexington, Mass.: D. C. Heath.

Eerde, W. V. and Threry, M. (1996) 'Vroom's expectancy models and work-related criteria', *Journal of Applied Psychology*, 81/5, 575–86.

Elger, T. (1990) 'Technical innovation and work reorganization in British manufacturing in the 1980s: continuity, intensification or transformation?', *Work, Employment and Society*, May, 67–101.

Elliott, D. (1980) 'The organization as a system', in G. Salaman and K. Thompson (eds.) *op. cit.*

Ellis, V. (1988) 'Current trade union attempts to remove occupational segregation in the employment of women', in S. Walby (ed.) *op. cit.*

Equal Employment Opportunity Coordinating Council (EEOCC) (1978) *Uniform Guidelines on Employee Selection Procedures*. Federal Register, 38290–38315.

Esland, G. (1980) 'Professions and professionalism', in G. Esland and G. Salaman (eds.) *The Politics of Work and Occupations*. Milton Keynes: Open University Press.

Evans, P., Claw, A., and Hucklebridge, F. (1997) 'Stress and the immune system', *The Psychologist*, 10/7, 303–7.

Fairbrother, P. (1996) 'Workplace trade unionism in the state sector', in P. Ackers, C. Smith, and P. Smith (eds.) *op. cit.*

Fearfull, A. (1996) 'Clerical workers, clerical skills: case studies from credit management', *New Technology, Work and Employment*, 11/1, 55–65.

Fein, S. and Spencer, S. J. (1997) 'Prejudice as self-image maintenance: affirming the self through derogating others', *Journal of Personality and Social Psychology*, 73/1, 31–44.

Ferguson, D. A. (1973) 'Comparative study of occupational stress', *Ergonomics*, 16, 649–64.

Ferster, C. B. and Skinner, B. F. (1957) *Schedules of Reinforcement*. New York: Appleton.

Fiedler, F. E. (1967) *A Theory of Leadership Effectiveness*. New York: McGraw-Hill.

—— (1970) 'Leadership experience and leader performance—another hypothesis shot to hell', *Organizational Behavior and Human Performance*, 5, 1–14.

—— and Chemars, M. E. (1984) *Improving Leadership Effectiveness: The Leader Match Concept*. Chichester: Wiley.

—— and Garcia, J. E. (1987) *New Approaches to Effective Leadership*. Chichester: Wiley.

—— and Leister, A. F. (1977a) 'Intelligence and group performance: a multiple screen model', *Organizational Behavior and Human Performance*, 20, 1–11.

—— and Leister, A. F. (1977b) 'Leader intelligence and task performance: a test of a multiple screen model', *Organizational Behavior and Human Performance*, 20, 11–14.

—— and Mahar, L. (1979) 'The effectiveness of contingency model training: validation of leader match', *Personnel Psychology*, 32, 45–62.

——, Bons, P. M., and Hastings, L. (1975) 'The utilization of leadership resources', in W. T. Singleton and P. Spurgeon (eds.) *Measurement of Human Resources*. London: Taylor and Francis.

Fincham, R. (1995) 'Business process reengineering and the commodification of managerial knowledge', *Journal of Marketing Management*, 11, 707–19.

—— (ed.) (1996a) *New Relationships in the Organised Professions*. Aldershot: Avebury.

—— (1996b) 'Professionalisation and the computing occupations', in R. Fincham (ed.) *op. cit.*

Fisher, C. D. and Gitelson, R. (1983) 'A meta-analysis of the correlates of role conflict and ambiguity', *Journal of Applied Psychology*, 68, 320–33.

Fisher, S. G., Hunter, T. A., and Macrosson, W. D. K. (1998) 'The structure of Belbin's team roles', *Journal of Occupational and Organizational Psychology*, 71/3, 283–8.

Fisk, D. W. (1949) 'Consistency of the factoral structures of personality ratings from different sources', *Journal of Abnormal and Social Psychology*, 44, 329–4.

Fisk, J. E. and Warr, P. (1996) 'Age and working memory: the role of peripheral speed, the central execution and the phonological loop', *Psychology and Ageing*, 11/2, 316–23.

Flanagan, J. C. (1954) 'The critical incident technique', *Psychological Bulletin*, 51, 327–58.

Flecker, J. and Schulten, T. (1997) 'The end of institutional stability: what future for the German model?', 15th Labour Process Conference, Edinburgh, 26–28 March.

Fleishman, E. A. and Harris, E. F. (1962) 'Patterns of leadership behavior related to employee grievances and turnover', *Personnel Psychology*, 15, 43–56.

——, ——, and Burtt, H. E. (1955) *Leadership and Supervision in Industry*. Columbus: Ohio State University, Bureau of Educational Research.

Fletcher, C. (1991) 'Candidates' reactions to assessment centers and their outcomes', *Journal of Occupational Psychology*, 64, 117–27.

—— (1997) 'The impact of psychometric assessment: fostering positive candidate attitudes and reactions', *Selection and Development Review*, 13/4, 8–11.

Fodor, E. M. and Smith, T. (1982) 'The power motive as an influence on group decision making', *Journal of Personality and Social Psychology*, 42, 178–85.

Folkman, S. and Lazarus, R. S. (1980) 'An analysis of coping in a middle aged community sample', *Journal of Health and Social Behavior*, 21, 219–39.

Forester, T. (1987) *High-Tech Society: The Story of the Information Technology Revolution*. Oxford: Blackwell.

—— (ed.) (1985) *The Information Technology Revolution*. Oxford: Blackwell.

Fosh, P. (1993) 'Membership participation in workplace unionism: the possibility of union renewal', *British Journal of Industrial Relations*, 31/4, 577–92.

Foucault, M. (1979) *Discipline and Punish: The Birth of the Prison*. London: Penguin.

—— (1980) *Power/Knowledge: Selected Interviews and Other Writings 1972–1977*. Hemel Hempstead: Harvester Wheatsheaf.

French, J. R. P. and Raven, B. (1959) 'The bases of social power', in D. Cartwright (ed.) *Studies in Social Power*. Ann Arbor, Mich.: Institute for Social Research.

Frese, M. (1982) 'Occupational socialization and psychological development: an underemphasized research perspective in industrial psychology', *Journal of Occupational Psychology*, 55, 209–24.

Freud, S. (1939) *Moses and Monotheism*. Standard Edition, 23.

Friedman, A. L. (1984) 'Management strategies, market conditions and the labour process', in F. Stephen (ed.) *Firms, Organisation and Labour*. London: Macmillan.

—— with Cornford, D. S. (1989) *Computer Systems Development*. Chichester: Wiley.

—— (1990) 'Managerial strategies, activities techniques and technologies: towards a complex theory of the labour process', in D. Knights and H. Willmott (eds.) *op. cit.*

Friedman, M. and Rosenman, R. H. (1974) *Type A Behaviour and Your Heart*. New York: Knopf.

Furnham, A., Steele, H., and Pendleton, D. (1993) 'A psychometric assessment of the Belbin Team-Role Self Perception Inventory', *Journal of Occupational and Organizational Psychology*, 66, 245–57.

Galbraith, J. R. (1982) 'Designing the innovative organization', *Organizational Dynamics*, Winter, 5–25.

Gall, G. (1997) 'Research note: a review of a decade of industrial conflict in western Europe', University of Stirling (mimeo).

—— and Murphy, D. (1996) 'Journalism in changing times', in R. Fincham (ed.) *op. cit.*

Gallie, D. (1978) *In Search of the New Working Class*. London: Cambridge University Press.

Game, A. and Pringle, R. (1983) *Gender at Work*. Sydney: Allen and Unwin.

Gane, M. (ed.) (1986) *Towards a Critique of Foucault*. London: Routledge and Kegan Paul.

Gastil, J. (1997) 'A definition and illustration of democratic leadership', in K. Grint (ed.) *Leadership: Classical, Contemporary and Critical Approaches*. Oxford: Oxford University Press.

Geen, R. G. (1997) 'Psychophysiological approaches to personality', in R. Hogan, J. Johnson, and S. Briggs (eds.) *op. cit.*

Ghiselli, E. E. (1963) 'Intelligence and managerial success', *Psychological Reports*, 12, 898.

Gibson, J. J. (1968) *The Senses Considered as Perceptual Systems*. Boston: Houghton Mifflin.

Giddens, A. (1984) *The Constitution of Society*. Cambridge: Polity Press.

Glass, D. C. (1977) *Behavior Patterns, Stress and Coronary Disease*. Hillsdale, NJ: Lawrence Erlbaum.

Goethals, G. R. and Darley, J. M. (1977) 'Social comparison theory: an attributional approach', in J. M. Suls and R. L. Miller (eds.) *Social Comparison Perspectives*. Washington, DC: Hemisphere.

Goffman, E. (1968) *Asylums*. Harmondsworth: Penguin.

—— (1971) *The Presentation of Self in Everyday Life*. Harmondsworth: Penguin.

Goldthorpe, J. H., Lockwood, D., Bechofer, F., and Platt, J. (1968) *The Affluent Worker: Industrial Attitudes and Behaviour*. Cambridge: Cambridge University Press.

Goode, W. J. (1957) 'Community within a community: the professions', *American Sociological Review*, 22, 194–200.

Goodfellow, M. M. (1983) 'The schoolteacher' in W. T. Singleton (ed.) *Social Skills*. Lancaster: MTP Press.

Goodrich, C. L. (1975) *The Frontier of Control*. London: Pluto Press.

Gordon, L. V. (1993) *Survey of Interpersonal Values*. Chicago: Macmillan/McGraw-Hill.

Gottfried. H. (1994) 'Learning the score: the duality of control and everyday resistance in the temporary-help service industry', in J. M. Jermier, D. Knights and W. Nord (eds.) *op. cit.*

Gould, S. J. (1981) *The Mismeasure of Man*. Harmondsworth: Penguin.

Gouldner, A. W. (1954) *Patterns of Industrial Bureaucracy*. Glencoe, Ill.: Free Press.

—— (1955) *Wildcat Strike*. London: Routledge and Kegan Paul.

—— (1957) 'Cosmopolitans and locals', *Administrative Science Quarterly*, 2, 281–306.

Gowler, D. and Legge, K. (1982) 'The integration of disciplinary perspectives in problem-oriented organizational research', in N. Nicholson and T. D. Wall (eds.) *The Theory and Practice of Organizational Psychology*. London: Academic Press.

Graziano, W. G. and Eisenberg, N. H. (1997) 'Agreeableness: a dimension of personality', in R. Hogan, J. Johnson, and S. Briggs (eds.) *Handbook of Personality Psychology*. San Diego, Calif.: Academic Press.

Greenbaum, J. (1995) *Windows on the Workplace: Computers, Jobs and the Organization of Office Work in the Late Twentieth Century*. New York: Monthly Review Press.

Greene, C. N. (1975) 'The reciprocal nature of influence between leader and subordinate', *Journal of Applied Psychology*, 60, 187–93.

—— (1979) 'Questions of causation in the path goal theory of leadership', *Academic Management Journal*, 22, 22–1.

Guilford, J. P. (1967) *The Nature of Human Intelligence*. New York: McGraw-Hill.

—— (1982) 'Cognitive psychology's ambiguities: some suggested remedies', *Psychological Review*, 89, 48–59.

Guirdham, M. (1995) *Interpersonal Skills at Work*, 2nd edn. London: Prentice Hall.

Guzzo, R., Jette, R. D. and Katzell, R. A. (1985) 'The effects of psychologically based intervention programs on worker productivity: a meta analysis', *Personnel Psychology*, 38, 275–91.

Gyllenhammar, P. G. (1977) 'How Volvo adapts work to people', *Harvard Business Review*, 55, 102–13.

Hackman, J. R. and Oldham, G. R. (1975) 'Development of the job diagnostic survey', *Journal of Applied Psychology*, 60, 159–70.

Hakim, C. (1980) 'Census reports as documentary evidence: the Census Commentaries 1801–1951', *Sociological Review*, 28, 551–80.

—— (1990) 'Core and periphery in employers' workplace strategies', *Work, Employment and Society*, 4/2, 157–88.

Hales, C. (1988) 'Management processes, management divisions of labour and managerial work: towards a synthesis', 6th Labour Process Conference, Aston University, Birmingham.

Hall, J. (1971) 'Decisions decisions', *Psychology Today*, June.

Hallier, J. (1997) 'Middle managers and the employee psychological contract: agency, protection and advancement', *Journal of Management Studies*, 34/5, 703–28.

Halpin, A. W. and Winer, B. J. (1957) 'A factoral study of the leader and behavior descriptions', in R. M. Stogdill and A. E. Coons (eds.) *Leader Behavior: Its Description and Measurement*. Columbus: Ohio State University, Bureau of Business Research.

Halsey, A. H., Heath, A. F., and Ridge, J. M. (1980) *Origins and Destinations: Family, Class and Education in Modern Britain*. Oxford: Clarendon Press.

Hammer, M. (1990) 'Reengineering work: don't automate, obliterate', *Harvard Business Review*, 68, Jul/Aug, 104–12.

—— and Champy, J. (1993) *Reengineering the Corporation*. London: Nicholas Brealey.

Handley, P. (1988) *The Insight Inventory*. Worthing: OTL.

Handy, C. B. (1986) *Understanding Organizations*, 2nd edn. Harmondsworth: Penguin.

Hannan, M. T. and Freeman, J. H. (1977) 'The population ecology of organizations', *American Journal of Sociology*, 82/5, 929–64.

Harré, R. (1993) *Social Being*, 2nd edn. Oxford: Blackwell.

Harrell, T. W. and Harrell, M. S. (1945) 'Army classification test scores for civilian occupations', *Educational and Psychological Measurement*, 5, 229–39.

Harrison, R. V. (1976) 'Job stress as person–environment misfit', Annual Meeting of the American Psychological Association, Washington, DC.

Hartley, J. F. (1996) 'Intergroup relations in organizations', in M. A. West (ed.) *Handbook of Workgroup Psychology*. Chichester: Wiley.

Haworth, J. (1997) *Work, Leisure and Well Being*. London: Routledge.

Haynes, C. E., Wall, T. D., Bolden, R. I., and Rick, J. E. (1997) 'Measures of perceived work characteristics for health sciences research: test of measurement model and normative data', Memo No. 108, Institute of Work Psychology, Sheffield UK.

Hayward, M. L. A. and Hambrick, D. C. (1997) 'Explaining the premiums paid for large acquisitions: evidence of CEO hubris', *Administrative Science Quarterly*, 42/1, 103–27.

Hearn, J., Sheppard, D. L., Tancred-Sherriff, P., and Burrell, G. (eds.) (1989) *The Sexuality of Organization*. London: Sage.

Hemphill, J. K. (1950) 'Leader behavior description'. Columbus: Ohio State University, Personnel Research Board (mimeo).

Hendry, C. (1990) 'New technology, new careers: the impact of flexible specialisation on skills and jobs', *New Technology, Work and Employment*, 5/1, 31–3.

Hersey, P. and Blanchard, K. H. (1988) *Management of Organizational Behavior*, 5th edn. Englewood Cliffs, NJ: Prentice Hall.

Herzberg, F., Mausner, B., and Snydeman, B. B. (1959) *The Motivation to Work*. New York: Wiley.

Hickson, D. J., Hinings, C. R., Lee, C. A., Schneck, R. E., and Pennings, J. M. (1971) 'A strategic contingencies theory of intraorganizational power', *Administrative Science Quarterly*, 16, 216–29.

Hill, S. (1981) *Competition and Control at Work*, London: Heinemann.

Hodson, R. (1989) 'Good jobs and bad management: how new problems evoke old solutions in high-tech settings', in G. Farklas and P. England (eds.) *Industries, Firms and Jobs*. New York: Plenum.

Hofstede, G. (1978) 'Value systems in forty countries'. Proceedings of the 4th International Congress of the International Association for Cross Cultural Psychology.

Hofstede, G. (1991) *Culture and Organizations: Software of the Mind*. London: McGraw-Hill.

Hogan, J. and Ones, D. S. (1997) 'Conscientiousness and integrity at work', in R. Hogan, J. Johnson, and S. Briggs (eds.) *op. cit.*

Hogan, R., Johnson, J., and Briggs, S. (eds.) *Handbook of Personality Psychology*. San Diego, Calif.: Academic Press.

Hollander, E. P. (1958) 'Conformity, status and idiosyncrasy credit', *Psychological Review*, 65/11, 7–27.

—— (1961) 'Emergent leadership and social influence', in L. Petrullo and B. M. Bass (eds.) *Leadership and Interpersonal Behavior*. New York: Holt, Rinehart and Winston.

—— (1978) *Leadership Dynamics: A Practical Guide to Effective Relationships*. New York: Free Press.

Horner, M. (1972) 'Toward an understanding of achievement-related conflicts in women', *Journal of Social Issues*, 15, 157–75.

Howe, M. J. A. (1997) *IQ in Question: The Truth about Intelligence*. London: Sage.

Hoy, D. C. (1986) *Foucault: A Critical Reader*. Oxford: Blackwell.

Hrebiniak, L. G. and Joyce, W. F. (1985) 'Organizational adaptation: strategic choice and environmental determinism', *Administrative Science Quarterly*, 30/3, 36–49.

Huffcutt, A. I., Roth, P. L., and McDaniel, M. A. (1996) 'A meta-analytic investigation of cognitive ability in employment interview evaluation: moderating characteristics and implications for incremental validity', *Journal of Applied Psychology*, 81/5, 459–73.

Hughes, E. (1975) 'Professions', in G. Esland, G. Salaman, and M. Speakman (eds.) *People and Work*. Edinburgh: Holmes-McDougall/Open University Press.

Hunt, P. (1980) *Gender and Class Consciousness*. London: Macmillan.

Hyman, R. (1983) 'White-collar workers and theories of class', in R. Hyman and R. Price (eds.) *The New Working Class: White Collar Workers and their Organizations*. London: Macmillan.

—— (1989) *Strikes*, 4th edn. Basingstoke: Macmillan.

Irigaray, L. (1993) *An Ethics of Sexual Differences*, trans. C. Burke and G. Gell. London: Athlone Press.

Ivancevich, K. M. (1978) 'The performance to satisfaction relationship: a causal analysis of stimulating and non-stimulating jobs', *Organizational Behavior and Human Performance*, 22, 350–65.

Iverson, R. D. and Erwin, P. J. (1997) 'Predicting occupational injury: the role of affectivity', *Journal of Occupational and Organizational Psychology*, 70, 113–28.

Jackall, R. (1988) *Moral Mazes: The World of Corporate Managers*. New York: Oxford University Press.

Jackson, S. E. (1996) 'The consequences of diversity in multi-disciplinary work teams', in M. A. West (ed.) *Handbook of Work Group Psychology*. Chichester: Wiley.

—— and Schuler, R. S. (1985) 'A meta-analysis and conceptual critique of research on role ambiguity and role conflict in work settings', *Organizational Behavior and Human Decision Processes*, 36, 16–78.

James, W. (1907) *Pragmatism*. New York: Henry Holt.

Jamous, H. and Peloille, B. (1970) 'Professions or self-perpetuating systems?', in J. A. Jackson (ed.) *Professions and Professionalization*. London: Cambridge University Press.

Janis, I. L. (1972) *Victims of Groupthink*. Boston: Houghton Mifflin.

—— (1982) 'Decision making under stress', in L. Goldberger and S. Breznitz (eds.) *Handbook of Stress: Theoretical and Clinical Aspects*. London: Macmillan.

Jaques, E. (1989) *Requisite Organisation*. Arlington, Va.: Casson Hall.

Jarman, J. (1994) 'Which way forward? Assessing the current proposals to amend the British Equal Pay Act', *Work, Employment and Society*, 8/2, 243–54.

Jermier, J., Knights, D., and Nord, W. R. (eds.) (1994) *Resistance and Power in Organizations*. London: Routledge.

——, —— and —— (1994) 'Introduction', in J. Jermier, D. Knights, and W. R. Nord (eds.) *op. cit.*

Johnson, C. E., Woods, R., and Blinkhorn, S. F. (1988) 'Spuriouser and spuriouser: the use of ipsative personality tests', *Journal of Occupational Psychology*, 6, 153–62.

Johnson, T. (1972) *Professions and Power*. London: Macmillan.

Jones, E. E. and Gerard, H. B. (1967) *Foundations of Social Psychology*. New York: Wiley.

Jones, P. and Poppleton, S. (1998) 'Trends in personality assessment for the millennium', *Selection and Development Review*, 14/1, 16–18.

Jones, R. (1988) 'Work and flexible automation in Britain: a review of developments and possibilities', *New Technology, Work and Employment*, 2/4, 451–86.

Jung, C. A. (1927) *Psychological Types*. New York: Harcourt Brace.

Kanter, R. M. (1984) *The Change Masters*. London: Allen and Unwin.

—— (1989) *When Giants Learn to Dance: Mastering the Challenges of Strategy, Management and Careers in the 1990s*. London: Simon and Schuster.

—— (1991) 'Change: where to begin?', editorial, *Harvard Business Review*, 69, Jul/Aug, 8–9.

Kaplinsky, R. (1982) *Computer-aided Design: Electronics, Comparative Advantage and Development*. London: Frances Pinter.

Karasek, R. (1979) 'Job demands, job decision latitude and mental strain: implications for job redesign', *Administrative Science Quarterly*, 24, 285–306.

Karson, S. and O'Dell, J. W. (1976) *Clinical Use of the Z6PF*. Champaign, Ill.: Institute for Personality and Ability Testing.

Kasl, S. V. (1980) 'The impact of retirement', in C. L. Cooper and R. Payne (eds.) *op. cit.*

Katz, R. and Farris, G. (1976) 'Does performance affect LPC?', Boston: Massachusetts Institute of Technology (mimeo).

Kelly, G. A. (1955) *The Psychology of Personal Constructs*. New York: Norton.

Kelly, J. E. (1980) 'The costs of job design: a preliminary analysis', *Industrial Relations Journal*, 11/3, 22–34.

—— (1982) *Scientific Management, Job Redesign and Work Performance*. London: Academic Press.

—— (1985) 'Management redesign of work', in D. Knights, H. Willmott, and D. Collinson (eds.) *Job Redesign*. Aldershot: Gower.

—— (1996) 'Union militancy and social partnership', in P. Ackers, C. Smith, and P. Smith (eds.) *op. cit.*

—— and Clegg, C. W. (1982) *Autonomy and Control at the Workplace*. London: Croom Helm.

Kemp, N. J., Clegg, C. W., and Wall, T. D. (1980) 'Job redesign: content, process and outcomes', *Employee Relations*, 2, 5–14.

——, Wall, T. D. Clegg, C. W. and Cordery, J. L. (1983) 'Autonomous work groups in a greenfield site: a comparative study' *Journal of Occupational Psychology* 56, 271–88.

Kern, H. and Schumann, M. (1984) *Das Ende der Arbeitsteilung*. Munich: Verlag C. H. Beck.

Kets de Vries, M. F. R. (1989) *Prisoners of Leadership*. Chichester: Wiley.

—— (1993) *Leaders, Fools and Imposters: Essays on the Psychology of Leadership*. San Francisco: Jossey Bass.

—— (1995) *Organizational Paradoxes*, 2nd edn. London: Routledge.

—— (1997) 'The leadership mystique', in K. Grint (ed.) *Leadership: Classical, Contemporary and Critical Approaches*. Oxford: Oxford University Press.

—— and Miller, D. (1984) *The Neurotic Organization*. San Francisco: Jossey-Bass.

Kirkpatrick, S. A. and Locke, E. A. (1996) 'Direct and indirect effects of three core charismatic leadership components on performance and attitudes', *Journal of Applied Psychology*, 81/1, 36–51.

Klein, J. A. (1989) 'The human costs of manufacturing reform', *Harvard Business Review*, 67/2, 60–6.

—— (1990) 'A re-examination of autonomy in the light of new manufacturing practices', *Human Relations*, 43.

Klein, L. (1981) 'Trebor factory, Colchester, Essex: appraisal', *Architects' Journal*, June.

Kline, P. (1980) 'Burt's false results and modern psychometrics: a comparison', *Supplement to the Bulletin of the British Psychological Society*, 33, 2–3.

—— (1983) *Personality: Measurement and Theory*. London: Hutchinson.

Knights, D. and Sturdy, A. (1990) 'New technology and the intensification of production in insurance and clerical work', in S. Yearly (ed.) *Deciphering Science and Technology*. London: Macmillan.

—— and Vurdubakis, T. (1994) 'Foucault, power, resistance and all that', in J. Jermier, D. Knights, and W. R. Nord (eds.) *op. cit.*

—— and Willmott, H. (eds.) (1990) *Labour Process Theory*. Basingstoke: Macmillan.

——, Willmott, H., and Collinson, D. (eds.) (1985) *Job Redesign*. Aldershot: Gower.

Kobosa, S. C. (1979) 'Stressful life events, personality and health: an enquiry into hardiness', *Journal of Personality and Social Psychology*, 37, 1–11.

Kotter, J. P. (1982) *The General Managers*. New York: Free Press.

Kraft, P. (1979) 'The industrialization of computer programming: from programming to "software production" ', in A. Zimbalist (ed.) *op. cit.*

Kumar, K. (1978) *Prophecy and Progress*. Harmondsworth: Penguin.

Landy, F. (1982) 'Models of man: assumptions of theorists', in N. Nicholson and T. D. Wall (eds.) *The Theory and Practice of Organizational Psychology*. London: Academic Press.

Lane, C. (1988) 'Industrial change in Europe: the pursuit of flexible specialisation in Britain and West Germany', *Work, Employment and Society*, 2/2, 141–68.

Larson, E. W. and Gobeli, D. H. (1987) 'Matrix management: contradictions and insights', *California Management Review*, 14/4, 126–38.

Larson, M. S. (1977) *The Rise of Professionalism: A Sociological Analysis*. Berkeley: University of California Press.

Lawrence, P. R. and Lorsch, J. (1967) *Organization and Environment*. Cambridge, Mass.: Harvard University Press.

Lee, D. (1989) 'The transformation of training and the transformation of work in Britain', in S. Wood (ed.) *op. cit.*

—— and Newby, H. (1983) *The Problem of Sociology*. London: Hutchinson.

Lee, G. (1991) 'The challenge of CAD/CAM: some experiences of British and Canadian engineering companies', *New Technology, Work and Employment*, 6/2, 100–11.

Lee, R. T. and Ashforth, B. E. (1996) 'A meta-analytic examination of the correlates of the three dimensions of job burnout', *Journal of Applied Psychology*, 81/2, 123–33.

Legge, K. (1995) 'Rhetoric, reality and hidden agendas', in J. Storey (ed.) *Human Resource Management: A Critical Text*. London: Routledge.

Lewis, M. (1989) *Liar's Poker*. London: Hodder and Stoughton.

Liff, S. (1990) 'Clerical workers and information technology: gender relations and occupational change', *New Technology, Work and Employment*, 5/1, 44–55.

Likert, R. (1961) *New Patterns of Management*. New York: McGraw-Hill.

Lindblom, C. (1959) 'The science of muddling through', *Public Administration Review*, 19, 79–88.

Littler, C. R. (1982) 'Deskilling and changing structures of control', in S. Wood (ed.) *op. cit.*

—— (1990) 'The labour process debate: a theoretical review 1974–1988', in D. Knights and H. Willmott (eds.) *op. cit.*

—— and Salaman, G. (1982) 'Bravermania and beyond: recent theories of the labour process', *Sociology*, 16, 251–69.

Locke, E. A. (1968) 'Toward a theory of tasks motivation and incentives', *Organizational Behavior and Human Performance*, 3, 157–89.

—— (1976) 'The nature and causes of job satisfaction', in M. D. Dunnette (ed.) *Handbook of Industrial and Organizational Psychology*. Chicago: Rand McNally.

Lockwood, D. (1958) *The Blackcoated Worker*. London: Allen and Unwin.

Loher, B. T., Noe, R. A., Moeller, N. L., and Fitzgerald, M. P. (1985) 'A meta analysis of the relation of job characteristics to job satisfaction', *Journal of Applied Psychology*, 70, 280–9.

Lowstedt, J. (1988) 'Prejudices and wishful thinking about computer-aided design', *New Technology, Work and Employment*, 3/1, 30–7.

Ludwig, T. D. and Geller, E. S. (1997) 'Assigned versus participative goal-setting and response generalization: managing injury control among professional pizza deliverers', *Journal of Applied Psychology*, 82/2, 253–61.

Lukes, S. (1974) *Power: A Radical View*. London: Macmillan.

Lupton, T. (1963) *On the Shop Floor*. Oxford: Pergamon Press.

—— and Tanner, I. (1980) 'Work design in Europe', in K. D. Duncan, M. M. Gruneberg, and D. Wallis (eds.) *op. cit.*

MacInnes, J. (1983) 'The labour process debate and the commodity status of labour: some problems', 1st Aston/UMIST Labour Process Conference.

MacKay, C. and Cooper, C. L. (1987) 'Occupational stress and health: some current issues', in C. L. Cooper and I. T. Robertson (eds.) *International Review of Industrial and Organizational Psychology*. Chichester: Wiley.

Manwaring, T. and Wood, S. (1985) 'The ghost in the labour process', in D. Knights, H. Willmott, and D. Collinson (eds.) *op. cit.*

March, J. G. (1981) 'Footnotes to organizational change', *Administrative Science Quarterly*, 26/4, 563–77.

—— and Simon, H. A. (1958) *Organizations*. New York: Wiley.

Marchington, M. (1992) 'Managing labour relations in a competitive environment', in A. Sturdy, D. Knights, and H. Willmott (eds.) *op. cit.*

——, Goodman, J., Wilkinson, A., and Ackers, P. (1992) *New Developments in Employee Involvement*. Manchester School of Management UMIST/Employment Department.

Marglin, S. A. (1974) 'What do bosses do? The origins and functions of hierarchy in capitalist production', *Review of Radical Political Economics*, 6, 33–60. Reprinted in A. Groz (ed.) (1976) *The Division of Labour*. Hassocks, Sussex: Harvester Press.

Marlow, C. M., Schneider, S. L., and Nelson, C. E. (1996) 'Gender and attractiveness biases in hiring decisions: are non-experienced managers less biased?', *Journal of Applied Psychology*, 81/1, 11–21.

Marsh, P. (1982) 'Rules in the organization of action', in M. von Cranach and R. Harré (eds.) *The Analysis of Action*. Cambridge: Cambridge University Press.

Martin, J. (1985) 'Can organizational culture be managed?' in P. J. Frost, L. F. Moore, M. R. Louis, C. C. Lundbergand, and J. Martin (eds.) *Organizational Culture*. Beverley Hills, Calif.: Sage.

—— and Meyerson, D. (1988) 'Organizational cultures and the denial, channeling and acknowledgement of ambiguity', in L. R. Pondy, R. Boland, and H. Thomas (eds.) *Managing Ambiguity and Change*. New York: Wiley.

Martindale, D. (1977) 'Sweaty palms in the control tower', *Psychology Today*, October.

Marx, K. (1973) *Grundrisse*. Harmondsworth: Penguin.

—— (1974) *Capital*, i. London: Lawrence and Wishart.

—— (1975) *Early Writings*, trans. R. Livingstone and G. Benton. Harmondsworth: Penguin.

Maslow, A. H. (1954) *Motivation and Personality*. New York: Harper.

Masson, J. (1992) *The Assault on Truth: Freud and Child Sexual Abuse*. London: Harper Collins.

Mayo, E. (1943) 'Forward', in F. J. Roethlisberger and W. J. Dickson, *op. cit.*

McArdle, L., Rowlinson, M., Procter, S., Hassard, J., and Forrester, P. (1995) 'Total quality management and participation: employee empowerment or the enhancement of exploitation', in A. Wilkinson and H. Willmott (eds.) *Making Quality Critical: New Perspectives on Organizational Change*. London: Routledge.

McClelland, D. (1961) *The Achieving Society*. Princeton: Van Nostrand.

—— and Boyatzis, R. E. (1982) 'Leadership motive pattern and long-term success in management', *Journal of Applied Psychology*, 67, 737–43.

—— and Burnham, D. H. (1976) 'Power is the great motivator', *Harvard Business Review*, 54, 100–10.

McConkie, M. L. and Boss, W. R. (1986) 'Organizational stories: one means of moving the informal organization during change efforts', *Public Administration Quarterly*, 10/2, 189–205.

McCormick, E. J., Jeanneret, P. R., and Mecham, R. C. (1969) *The Development and Background of PAQ*. Report No. 5, Occupational Research Center, West Lafayette, Ind.: Purdue University.

McCrae, R. R. and Costa, P. T. (1997) 'Conceptions and correlates of openness in experience', in R. Hogan, J. Johnson, and S. Briggs (eds.) *op. cit.*

McGregor, D. (1960) *The Human Side of Enterprise*. New York: McGraw-Hill.

MCI (Management Charter Initiative) (1997) *Management Standards*. London: MCI.

McKinlay, A. and Taylor, P. (1996) 'Power, surveillance and resistance inside the "factory of the future" ', in P. Ackers, C. Smith, and P. Smith (eds.) *op. cit.*

McLoughlin, I. (1989) 'CAD—the Taylorisation of drawing office work', *New Technology, Work and Employment*, 4/1, 27–39.

McNulty, T. and Coalter, F. (1996) 'White-collar CCT and the politics of professionalism in local government', in R. Fincham (ed.) *op. cit.*

Meindl, J. R. (1990) 'On leadership: an alternative to conventional wisdom', in B. M. Staw and L. L. Cummings (eds.) *Research in Organizational Behavior*. Greenwich, Conn.: JAI Press.

Merton, R. K. (1940) 'Bureaucratic structure and personality', *Social Forces*, 18, 560–8.

Mettlin, C. (1976) 'Occupational careers and the prevention of coronary-prone behaviour', *Social Science and Medicine*, 10, 367–72.

Miller, E. J. (1975) 'Sociotechnical systems in weaving 1953–70: a follow-up study', *Human Relations*, 28, 349–86.

Miller, G. A. (1956) 'The magical number seven, plus or minus two: some limits on our capacity for processing information', *Psychological Review*, 63, 81–97.

Miller, H. (1996) 'Management of the key profession', in R. Fincham (ed.) *op. cit.*

Miller, P. and O'Leary, T. (1987) 'Accounting and the construction of the governable person', *Accounting, Organization and Society*, 12/3, 235–65.

Millon, T. (1990) *Towards a New Personology*. Chichester: Wiley.

Mills, C. W. (1951) *White Collar*. New York: Oxford University Press.

Minsky, R. (1996) *Psychoanalysis and Gender: An Introductory Reader*. London: Routledge.

Mintzberg, H. (1973) *The Nature of Managerial Work*. London: Harper and Row.

Mitroff, I. I. and Kilmann, R. H. (1975) 'Stories managers tell: a new tool for organizational problem-solving', *Management Review*, 64/7, 18–28.

Moos, R. H. and Billings, A. G. (1982) 'Conceptualizing and measuring coping resources and process', in L. Goldberger and S. Breznitz (eds.) *Handbook of Stress: Theoretical and Clinical Aspects*. London: Macmillan.

Morgan, G. (1997) *Images of Organization*, 2nd edn. Thousand Oaks, Calif.: Sage.

Mottaz, C. (1986) 'Gender differences in work satisfaction, work-related rewards and values, and the determinants of work satisfaction', *Human Relations*, 39, 359–76.

Mouzelis, N. (1975) *Organization and Bureaucracy*. London: Routledge and Kegan Paul.

Muchinsky, P. M. (1977) 'A comparison of within- and across-subjects analyses of the expectancy-valence model for predicting effort', *Academy of Management Journal*, 20, 154–8.

Mumford, E. (1976) 'A strategy for the redesign of work', *Personnel Review*, 5, 33–9.

Munz, D. C., Helsman, T. J., Konold, T. R., and McKinney, J. T. (1996) 'Are there methodological and substantive roles for affectivity in job diagnostic survey relationships', *Journal of Applied Psychology*, 81/6, 795–805.

Murphy, L. R. (1996) 'Stress management techniques: secondary prevention of stress', in M. J. Schabraig, J. A. M. Winnubst, and C. L. Cooper (eds.) *Handbook of Work and Health Psychology*. Chichester: Wiley.

Murray, R. (1985) 'Bennetton Britain: the new economic order', *Marxism Today*, November, 28–32.

Myers, C. S. (1924) *Industrial Psychology in Great Britain*. London: Cape.

National Institute for Occupational Safety and Health (1987) *Stress Management in Work Settings*. Cincinatti: NIOSH.

NCVQ (1990) *Core Skills in NVQs: Response to the Secretary of State*, July. London: NCVQ.

Neimeyer, G. J. and Hudson, J. E. (1985) 'Couples' constructs: personal systems in marital satisfaction', in D. Bannister (ed.) *Issues and Approaches in Personal Construct Theory*. London: Academic Press.

Nevin, J. A. (1996) 'The momentum of compliance', *Journal of Applied Behavior Analysis*, 29/4, 535–47.

Newell, S., Swan, J., and Robertson, M. (1996) 'The role of professional associations in operations management: a contested knowledge domain', in R. Fincham (ed.) *op. cit.*

Nichols, T. and Beynon, H. (1977) *Living with Capitalism*. London: Routledge and Kegan Paul.

Noble, D. (1978) 'Social choice in machine tool design', *Politics and Society*, 8, 313–47; also in A. Zimbalist (ed.) (1979) *Case Studies on the Labor Process*. London: Monthly Review Press.

O'Connell-Davidson, J. (1994) 'The sources and limits of resistance in a privatized utility', in J. M. Jermier, D. Knights, and W. R. Nord (eds.) *op. cit.*

Offe, C. (1976) *Industry and Inequality*. London: Edward Arnold.

Oliver, N. (1991) 'The dynamics of just-in-time', *New Technology, Work and Employment*, 6/1, 19–27.

Ones, D. S., Viswesvaran, C., and Reiss, A. (1996) 'Role of social desirability in personality testing for personnel selection: the red herring', *Journal of Applied Psychology*, 81/6, 660–97.

Packer, C. (1996) 'The context-dependent nature of the gendering of technical work: a case study in a scientific laboratory', *Work, Employment and Society*, 10/1, 125–49.

Parker, S. (1996) 'An investigation of attitudes amongst production employees', *International Journal of Human Factors in Manufacturing*, 6/3, 281–303.

Parker, S. K., Chimiel, N., and Wall, T. (1997) 'Work characteristics and employee well-being', Memo No. 92, Institute of Work Psychology, Sheffield.

Patterson, M. and West, M. (1998) 'People power: the link between job satisfaction and productivity', *Centrepiece*, 3/3, 2–5.

Paul, R. J. and Ebadi, Y. M. (1989) 'Leadership decision making in a service organization: a field test of the Vroom-Yetton model', *Journal of Occupational Psychology*, 62, 201–11.

Perrow, C. (1970) *Organizational Analysis: A Sociological View*. London: Tavistock.

Peters, T. (1987) *Thriving on Chaos*. London: Macmillan.

—— and Waterman, R. H. (1982) *In Search of Excellence*. New York: Harper and Row.

Pettigrew, A. (1973) *The Politics of Organizational Decision-Making*. London: Tavistock.

—— (1985) *The Awakening Giant*. Oxford: Blackwell.

Pfeffer, J. (1981) *Power in Organizations*. Marshfield, Mass.: Pitman.

—— and Salancik, G. (1978) *The External Control of Organizations*. New York: Harper and Row.

Piore, M. J. and Sabel, C. F. (1984) *The Second Industrial Divide*. New York: Basic Books.

Pliskin, N., Romm, C. T., and Markey, R. (1997) 'E-mail as a weapon in an industrial dispute', *New Technology, Work and Employment*, 12/1, 3–12.

Podsakoff, P. M., Ahearne, M., and MacKenzie, S. B. (1997) 'Organizational citizenship behavior and the quantity and quality of work group performance', *Journal of Applied Psychology*, 82/2, 262–70.

——, Mackenzie, S. B., and Bommer, W. H. (1996) 'Meta-analysis of the relationships between Kerr and Jermier's substitutes for leadership and employee job attitudes, role perceptions, and performance', *Journal of Applied Psychology*, 81, 380–99.

Pollert, A. (1981) *Girls, Wives, Factory Lives*. London: Macmillan.

—— (1988) 'The "flexible firm": fixation or fact?', *Work, Employment and Society*, 2/3, 281–316.

—— (1996) ' "Team work" on the assembly line: contradiction and the dynamics of union resistance', in P. Ackers, C. Smith, and S. Smith (eds.) *op. cit.*

Porter, L. W. and Lawler, E. E. (1968) *Managerial Attitudes and Performance*. Homewood, Ill.: Dorsey Press.

Presthus, R. (1979) *The Organizational Society*. London: Macmillan.

Price, K. H. and Garland, H. (1981) 'Compliance with a leader's suggestions as a function of perceived leader/member competence and potential reciprocity', *Journal of Applied Psychology*, 66, 329–36.

Psychological Corporation, The (1993) *The Millon Personality Style Inventory*. London: Harcourt Brace Jovanovich.

Pugh, D. S., Hickson, D. J., and Hinings, C. R. (1984) *Writers on Organizations*. Harmondsworth: Penguin.

Pugliesi, K. (1995) 'Work and well-being: gender influences on the psychological consequences of employment', *Journal of Health and Social Behaviour*, 36, 57–71.

Purcell, K. (1979) 'Militancy and acquiescence among women workers', in S. Burman (ed.) *Fit Work for Women*. London: Croom Helm. Reprinted in J. Siltanen and M. Stanworth (eds.) *op. cit.*

Quick, J. C., Nelson, D. L., and Quick, J. D. (1990) *Stress and Challenge at the Top: The Paradox of the Successful Executive*. Chichester: Wiley.

Ramsay, H. (1977) 'Cycles of control: workers' participation in sociological and historical perspective', *Sociology*, 11/3, 481–506.

—— (1985) 'What is participation for?: a critical evaluation of labour process analysis of job reform', in D. Knights, H. Willmott, and D. Collinson (eds.) *op. cit.*

—— (1991) 'Reinventing the wheel: a review of the development and performance of employee involvement', *Human Resource Management Journal*, 1/4, 1–21.

Ramsay, S., Gallois, C., and Callon, V. J. (1997) 'Social rules and attributes in the personnel selection interview', *Journal of Occupational and Organizational Psychology*, 70, 189–203.

Reason, J. (1987) 'The Chernobyl errors', *Bulletin of the Psychological Society*, 40, 201–6.

Reed, M. (1985) *Redirections in Organizational Analysis*. London: Tavistock.

Rees, C. (1997) 'Topical misunderstandings amongst test users', *International Journal of Selection and Assessment*, 4/1, 44–48.

Reich, R. (1991) *The Wealth of Nations: Preparing Ourselves for the 21st Century*. London: Simon and Schuster.

Rhodes, P. S. (1983) 'The prediction of success in business studies students', *Business Education*, 4, 31–5.

—— and Joseph, J. (1997) *Preventative Strategies for Coping with Highly Demanding Work Situations*. Worthing: OTL.

Rice, A. K. (1958) *Productivity and Social Organisation*. London: Tavistock.

Rice, B. (1982) 'The Hawthorne defect: persistence of a flawed theory', *Psychology Today*, February.

Ritzer, G. (1993) *The McDonaldization of Society*. Thousand Oaks, Calif.: Pine Forge Press.

Roethlisberger, F. J. and Dickson, W. J. (1943) *Management and the Worker*. Cambridge, Mass.: Harvard University Press.

Rogelberg, S. G., Barnes-Farrell, J. L., and Lowe, C. A. (1992) 'The stepladder technique: an alternative group structure facilitating effective group decision-making', *Journal of Applied Psychology*, 77, 730–37.

Rolfe, H. (1990) 'In the name of progress? skill and attitudes towards technological change', *New Technology, Work and Employment*, 5/2, 107–21.

Rose, M. (1975) *Industrial Behaviour: Theoretical Developments since Taylor*. London: Allen Lane.

Rose, R. M., Jenkins, C. D., and Hurst, M. W. (1978) 'Air traffic controller health change study: a prospective investigation of physical, psychological and work related changes', Galveston: University of Texas (mimeo).

Rosenman, R. H., Brand, R. J., Jenkins, D., Friedman, M., Straus, R., and Wurm, M. (1975) 'Coronary heart disease in the western collaborative group study', *Journal of the American Medical Association*, 233, 872–7.

Ross, L. and Nisbett, R. E. (eds.) (1991) *The Person and the Situation*. London: McGraw-Hill.

—— and Stillinger, C. (1991) 'Barriers to conflict resolution', in L. Ross, and R. E. Nisbett (eds.) *op. cit.*

Rotter, J. B. (1966) *Generalized Expectancies for Internal versus External Control of Reinforcement*. Psychological Monographs: 80.

Rowley, C. (1996) 'Flexible specialisation: some comparative dimensions and evidence from the ceramic tile industry', *New Technology, Work and Employment*, 11/2, 125–136.

Roy, D. (1952) 'Quota restrictions and goldbricking in a machine shop', *American Journal of Sociology*, 57, 427–42.

—— (1954) 'Efficiency and the "fix": informal inter-group relations in a piecework machine shop', *American Journal of Sociology*, 60, 255–66.

Rubery, J. (1980) 'Structured labour markets, worker organization and low pay', in A. Amsden (ed.) *The Economics of Women and Work*. Harmondsworth: Penguin.

—— and Fagan, C. (1995) 'Gender segregation in societal context', *Work, Employment and Society*, 9/2, 213–40.

Rushton, J. P. (1997) *Race, Evolution and Behavior*. New Brunswick: Transaction.

Rust, J. (1997) *The Giotto Manual*. London: The Psychological Corporation.

Sabel, C. F. (1982) *Work and Politics*. Cambridge: Cambridge University Press.

Sacks, H., Schegloff, E., and Jefferson, G. (1974) 'A simplest systematics for the organization of turn-taking for conversation', *Languages*, 50, 696–735.

Sakai, K. (1990) 'The feudal world of Japanese manufacturing', *Harvard Business Review*, Nov/Dec, 38–49.

Salaman, G. (1979) *Work Organisations: Resistance and Control*. London: Longman.

Salaman, G. (1981) *Class and the Corporation*. London: Fontana.

—— and Thompson, K. (1974) Media Booklets 1 and 2. *People and Organisations* DT352. Milton Keynes: Open University Press.

—— and —— (eds.) (1980) *Control and Ideology in Organizations*. Milton Keynes: Open University Press.

Schieffelin, B. B. (1983) 'Talking like birds: sound play in a cultural perspective', in E. Ochs and B. B. Schieffelin (eds.) *Acquiring Conversational Competence*. London: Routledge and Kegan Paul.

Schneider, J. and Locke, E. A. (1971) 'A critique of Herzberg's incident classification system and a suggestion revision', *Organizational Behavior and Human Performance*, 6, 441–57.

Schrears, P. J. G., Winnubst, J. A. M., and Cooper, C. C. (1996) 'Workplace health programmes', in M. J. Schabraig, J. A. M. Winnubst, and C. L. Cooper (eds.) *Handbook of Work and Health Psychology*. Chichester: Wiley.

Schriesheim, C. A. and Hosking, D. (1978) 'Review essay of F. E. Fiedler, M. M. Chemers, and L. Mahar: "Improving Leadership effectiveness: The Leader Match concept" ', *Administrative Science Quarterly*, 23, 496–505.

—— and Murphy, C. J. (1976) 'Relationships between leader behavior and subordinate satisfaction and performance: a test of some situational moderators', *Journal of Applied Psychology*, 61, 634–41.

Science Research Associates (1989) *Manual for the Leadership Questionnaire*. Henley: Science Research Associates.

Scott, M. J. and Stradling, S. G. (1992) *Counselling for Post-Traumatic Stress Disorder*. London: Sage.

Seligman, M. E. P. (1975) *Helplessness: On Depression, Development and Death*. San Francisco: Freeman.

Selye, H. (1936) 'A syndrome produced by diverse nocuous ages', *Nature*, 138, 32.

—— (1975) 'Stress', in *Employee Physical Fitness in Canada*. Ottawa: National Health and Welfare, Information Canada.

—— (1983) 'History and present status of the stress concept', in L. Goldberger and S. Breznitz (eds.) *Handbook of Stress: Theoretical and Clinical Aspects*. London: Macmillan.

Senior, B. (1997) 'Team roles and team performance: is there really a link?', *Journal of Occupational and Organizational Psychology*, 70/3, 241–58.

Senker, P. and Simmonds, P. (1991) 'Changing technology and design work in the British engineering industry 1981–88', *New Technology, Work and Employment*, 6/2, 91–9.

Sewell, G. and Wilkinson, B. (1992a) ' "Someone to watch over me": surveillance, discipline and the just-in-time labour process', *Sociology*, 26/2, 271–9.

—— and —— (1992b) 'Empowerment or emasculation? Shop floor surveillance in a total quality organization', in P. Blyton and P. Turnbull (eds.) *Reassessing Human Resource Management*. London: Sage.

Shaiken, H., Hertzenberg, S., and Kuhn, S. (1986) 'The work process under more flexible production', *Industrial Relations*, 25/2, 167–83.

Shamir, B., House, R. J., and Arthur, M. (1990) 'The transformational effects of charismatic leadership: a motivational theory', in J. G. Hunt (ed.) *Leadership*. London: Sage.

Shearman, C. and Burrell, G. (1988) 'New technology based firms and new industries: employment implications', *New Technology, Work and Employment*, 3/2, 87–99.

Sherif, M. and Sherif, C. W. (1982) 'Production of intergroup conflict and its resolution: robbers' cave experiment', in J. W. Reich (ed.) *Experimenting in Society: Issues and Examples in Applied Social Psychology*. Glenview, Ill.: Scott, Foresman.

——, Harvey, O. J., White, B., Hood, W. R., and Sherif, C. W. (1961) *Intergroup Conflict and Cooperation: The Robbers' Cave Experiment*. Norman: University of Oklahoma Press.

Siltanen, J., Jarman, J., and Blackburn, R. M. (1993) 'The analysis of occupational gender segrega-tion over time and place: considerations of measurement and new evidence', *Work, Employment and Society*, 7/3, 335–62.

—— and Stanworth, M. (eds.) (1984) *Women and the Public Sphere*. London: Hutchinson.

Silvester, J. and Chapman, A. J. (1996) 'Unfair discrimination in the selection interview: an attri-butional account', *International Journal of Selection and Assessment*, 4/2, 63–70.

Singleton, W. T. (1983) 'Final discussion', in W. T. Singleton (ed.) *Social Skills*. Lancaster: MIP Press.

Skinner, B. F. (1954) 'The science of learning and the art of teaching', *Harvard Educational Review*, 24, 86–97.

—— (1971) *Beyond Freedom and Dignity*. Harmondsworth: Penguin.

Slocum, J. W. and Sims, H. P. (1980) 'A typology for integrating technology, organisation and job redesign', *Human Relations*, 33, 193–212.

Sly, F., Price, A., and Risdon, A. (1997) 'Women in the labour force: results from the Spring 1996 Labour Force Survey', *Labour Market Trends*. London: HMSO.

Smircich, L. (1983) 'Concepts of culture and organizational analysis', *Administrative Science Quarterly*, 28/3, 339–58.

Smith, A. (1982) *The Wealth of Nations*. Harmondsworth: Penguin.

Smith. P. B. and Peterson, M. P. (1988) *Leadership, Organisations and Culture*. London: Sage.

Sorge A., Hartmann, M., Warner, M., and Nicholas, I. (1982) 'Technology, organization and man-power: applications of CNC manufacturing in Great Britain and West Germany', in N. Bjorn-Anderson, M. Earl, O. Holst, and E. Mumford (eds.) *Information Society: For Richer For Poorer*. Amsterdam: North Holland.

Spearman, C. (1904) 'General intelligence objectively determined and measured', *American Journal of Psychology*, 14, 201–93.

—— (1927) *The Abilities of Man*. New York: Macmillan.

Spector, P. (1986) 'Perceived control by employees: a meta-analysis of studies concerning auton-omy and participation at work', *Human Relations*, 11, 1005–16.

Spencer, L. M., McClelland, D. C., and Spencer, S. M. (1994) *Competency Assessment Methods: History and State of the Art*. London: Hay/McBer Research Press.

Staw, B. (1976) 'Knee deep in the big muddy: a study of escalating commitment to a chosen course of action', *Organizational Behaviour and Human Performance*, 16.

—— (1980) 'Rationality and justification in organizational life', *Research in Organizational Behavior*, 2.

Staw, B. M., Sandelands, L. E., and Dutton, J. E. (1981) 'Threat-rigidity effects in organizational behavior: a multilevel analysis', *Administrative Science Quarterly*, 26/4, 501–24.

Sternberg, R. J. (1985) *Beyond IQ: A Triarchic Theory of Human Intelligence*. Cambridge: Cambridge University Press.

Stewart, A., Prandy, K., and Blackburn, R. M. (1980) *Social Stratification and Occupations*. London: Macmillan.

Stewart, P. and Garrahan, P. (1995) 'Employee responses to new management techniques in the auto industry', *Work, Employment and Society*, 9/3, 517–36.

Stewart, V. and Stewart, A. S. (1981) *Business Applications of Repertory Grids*. Maidenhead: McGraw-Hill.

Stogdill, R. M. (1948) 'Personal factors associated with leadership: a survey of the literature', *Journal of Psychology*, 25, 35–71.

—— (1974) *Handbook of Leadership: A Survey of Theory and Research*. New York: Free Press.

Storey, J. (1983) *Managerial Prerogative and the Question of Control*. London: Routledge and Kegan Paul.

—— (1986) 'The phoney war? New office technology: organization and control', in D. Knights and H. Willmott (eds.) *Managing the Labour Process*. London: Gower.

Streslau, J. and Eysenck, H. J. (eds.) (1987) *Personality Dimensions and Arousal*. New York: Plenum.

Strube, M. J. and Garcia, J. E. (1981) 'A meta-analytic investigation of Fiedler's contingency model of leadership effectiveness', *Psychological Bulletin*, 90, 307–21.

Sturdy, A. (1992) 'Clerical consent: "shifting" work in the insurance office', in A. Sturdy, D. Knights, and H. Willmott (eds.) *op. cit.*

——, Knights, D., and Willmott, H. (1992) 'Introduction: skill and consent in the labour process', in A. Sturdy, D. Knights, and H. Willmott (eds.) *op. cit.*

——, ——, and —— (eds.) (1992) *Skill and Consent: Contemporary Studies in the Labour Process*. London: Routledge.

Summers, T. P. and Hendrix, W. H. (1991) 'Modelling the role of pay equity perceptions: a field study', *Journal of Occupational Psychology*, 64, 145–57.

Synder, M. (1979) 'Self-monitoring processes' in L. Berkowitz (ed.) *Advances in Experimental Social Psychology*. London: Academic Press.

Tait, M., Padgett, M. Y., and Baldwin, T. T. (1989) 'Job and life satisfaction: a re-evaluation of the strength of the relationship and gender effects as a function of the date of the study', *Journal of Applied Psychology*, 7, 502–7.

Tajfel, H. (1978) 'Social categorization, social identity and social comparison', in H. Tajfel (ed.) *Differentiation between Social Groups*. London: Academic Press.

—— (1981) 'Social stereotypes and social groups', in J. C. Turner and H. Giles (eds.) *Intergroup Behaviour*. Oxford: Blackwell.

Tapsell, J. and Cox, J. (1997) 'The writing on the wall: graphology and its validity in personnel assessment', *Selection and Development Review*, 13/3, 3–6.

Tausky, C. and Chelte, A. F. (1991) 'Employee involvement: a comment on Grenier and Hogler', *Work and Occupations*, 18, 334–42.

Teulings, A. (1986) 'Managerial labour processes in organized capitalism: the power of corporate management and the powerlessness of the manager', in D. Knights and H. Willmott (eds.) *Managing the Labour Process*. Aldershot: Gower.

Thompson, P. (1989) *The Nature of Work*, 2nd edn. London: Macmillan.

—— (1990) 'Crawling from the wreckage: the labour process and the politics of production', in D. Knights and H. Willmott (eds.) *op. cit.*

Thompson, V. (1961) *Modern Organization*. New York: Knopf.

Thurstone, L. L. (1938) *Primary Mental Abilities*. Chicago: University of Chicago Press.

Tomaka, J., Bascovich, J., Kibler, J., and Ernst, J. (1997) 'Cognition and physiological antecedents of threat and challenge appraisal', *Journal of Personality and Social Psychology*, 73/1, 63–72.

Trist, E. L. and Bamforth, K. W. (1951) 'Some social and psychological consequences of the longwall method of coal-getting', *Human Relations*, 1, 3–38.

Trompenaars, F. (1993) *Riding the Waves of Culture*. Avon: Economist Books/Bath Press.

Turnbull, P. (1988) 'The limits to Japanisation: "just-in-time" labour relations and the UK automotive industry', *New Technology, Work and Employment*, 3/1, 7–20.

—— (1989) 'Industrial restructuring and labour relations in the automobile components industry: "just-in-time" or "just-too-late"?' in S. Tailby and C. Whitson (eds.) *Manufacturing Change: Industrial Relations and Restructuring*. Oxford: Blackwell.

Turner, J. C. (1982) 'Towards a cognitive redefinition of the social group', in H. Tajfel (ed.) *Social Identity and Intergroup Relations*. Cambridge: Cambridge University Press.

—— (1991) *Social Influence*. Buckingham: Open University Press.

—— and Giles, H. (eds.) (1981) *Intergroup Behaviour*. Oxford: Blackwell.

Vernon, P. E. (1971) *The Structure of Human Abilities*. London: Methuen.

Waddington, J. and Whitston, C. (1996) 'Empowerment versus intensification: union perspectives of change at the workplace', in P. Ackers, C. Smith, and P. Smith (eds.) *op. cit.*

Wainright, H. (1984) 'Women and the division of labour', in P. Abrams and R. Brown (eds.) *UK Society*. London: Weidenfield and Nicolson.

Walby, S. (ed.) (1988) *Gender Segregation at Work*. Milton Keynes: Open University Press.

Wall, T. D., Bolden, R. I., Borrill, C. S., Carter, A. J., Goyia, D. A., Hardy, G. E., Haynes, C. E., Rick, J. E., Shapiro, D. A., and West, M. A. (1997) 'Minor psychiatric disorder in NHS trust staff: occupational and gender differences', Memo No. 106, Institute of Work Psychology, Sheffield.

—— and Cordery, J. L. (1982) *Work Design and Supervisory Practice*. Social and Applied Psychology Unit, Memo 470, University of Sheffield.

——, Jackson, P. R., Mullarkey, S., and Parker, S. K. (1996) 'The demands-control model of job strain: a non-specific test', *Journal of Occupational and Organizational Psychology*, 69, 153–66.

Wallis, D. and Cope, D. (1980) 'Pay-off conditions for organizational change in the hospital service', in K. D. Duncan, M. M. Gruneberg, and D. Wallis (eds.) *op. cit.*

Wanous, J. P., Reichers, A. E., and Hady, M. J. (1997) 'Overall job satisfaction: how good are single item measures?', *Journal of Applied Psychology*, 82/2, 247–52.

—— and Zwany, A. (1977) 'A cross-sectional test of need hierarchy theory', *Organizational Behavior and Human Performance*, 18, 78–97.

Warr, P. B. (1987) *Work, Unemployment and Mental Health*. Oxford: Oxford University Press.

—— (1996) 'Employee well-being', in P. B. Warr (ed.) *Psychology at Work*, 4th edn. Harmondsworth: Penguin.

—— (1997) 'The varying validity of personality scales', *Selection and Development Review*, 13/4, 3–7.

—— (1998) 'Well-being and the workplace', in D. Kahneman, E. Diener, and N. Schwarz (eds.) *Understanding Quality of Life: Scientific Perspectives on Enjoyment and Suffering*. New York: Russell Sage.

—— and Bunce, D. (1995) 'Trainee characteristics and the outcomes of open learning', *Personnel Psychology*, 48, 344–74.

Warr, P. and Gardner, C. (1998) 'Learning strategies and occupational training', in C. L. Cooper and I. T. Robinson (eds.) *International Review of Industrial and Organizational Psychology*. Chichester: Wiley.

Weaver, C. N. (1980) 'Job satisfaction in the United States in the 1970s', *Journal of Applied Psychology*, 65, 364–7.

Weber, M. (1964) *The Theory of Social and Economic Organization*. New York: Free Press.

—— (1970) *From Max Weber: Essays in Sociology*, trans. H. H. Gerth and C. W. Mills. London: Routledge and Kegan Paul.

Webster, J. (1990) *Office Automation: The Labour Process and Women's Work in Britain*. Hemel Hempstead: Harvester Wheatsheaf.

Webster, R. (1996) *Why Freud was Wrong*. London: Fontana.

Wedderburn, D. and Crompton, R. (1972) *Workers' Attitudes and Technology*. Cambridge: Cambridge University Press.

West, J. (1990) 'Gender in the labour process', in D. Knights and H. Willmott (eds.) *op. cit.*

West, M. A. (1996) 'Reflexivity and work group effectiveness: a conceptual integration', in M. A. West (ed.) *Handbook of Work and Group Psychology*. Chichester: Wiley.

—— and Altink, W. M. M. (1996) 'Innovation at work: individual, group, organizational and socio-historical perspectives', *European Journal of Work and Organizational Psychology*, 5/1, 3–11.

—— and Anderson, N. R. (1995) 'Innovation in top management teams', unpublished paper, Institute of Work Psychology, Sheffield.

—— and Farr, J. L. (1990) *Innovation and Creativity at Work*. Chichester: Wiley.

——, Nicholson, N., and Rees, A. (1987) 'Transitions into newly created jobs', *Journal of Occupational Psychology*, 60/9, 7–113.

Whalley, P. (1986) *The Social Production of Technical Work*. London: Macmillan.

White, L. and Doyle, C. (1997) 'Recruitment and selection in small professional firms and practices', *Selection and Development Review*, 13/6, 3–8.

Wiebe, D. J. and Williams, P. G. (1992) 'Hardiness and health: a social psychological perspective on stress and adaptation', *Journal of Social and Clinical Psychology*, 11, 238–62.

Wiedermeyer, M. (1989) 'New technology in West Germany: the employment debate', *New Technology, Work and Employment*, 4/1, 56–65.

Wigfield, D. (1997) 'Making good selection decisions with assessment centre data', *Selection and Development Review*, 13/5, 3–7.

Wiggins, J. S. and Trapnell, P. D. (1997) 'Personality structure: the return of the Big Five', in R. Hogan, J. Johnson, and S. Briggs (eds.) *op. cit.*

Wilkins, A. (1984) 'The creation of company cultures: the role of stories in human resource systems', *Human Resource Management*, 23/1, 41–60.

Willmott, H. (1987) 'Studying managerial work: a critique and a proposal', *Journal of Management Studies*, 24/3, 249–70.

—— (1993) 'Strength is ignorance; slavery is freedom: managing culture in modern organizations', *Journal of Management Studies*, 30/4, 515–32.

—— (1997) 'Rethinking management and managerial work: capitalism, control and subjectivity', 15th Labour Process Conference, Edinburgh University, 25–27 March.

Wilson, D. C. and Rosenfeld, R. H. (1990) *Managing Organizations*. Maidenhead: McGraw-Hill.

Womack, J. P., Jones, D. T., and Roos, D. (1990) *The Machine that Changed the World*. New York: Macmillan.

Wood, R. (1997) 'The interview: it's still not safe', *Selection and Development Review*, 3/6, 14–15.

Wood, S. (1979) 'A reappraisal of the contingency approach to organization', *Journal of Management Studies*, 16, 334–54.

—— (ed.) (1982) *The Degradation of Work?* London: Hutchinson.

—— (ed.) (1989) *The Transformation of Work*. London: Unwin Hyman.

—— (1989) 'The transformation of work?', introduction in S. Wood (ed.) *op. cit.*

Woodruffe, C. (1993) *Assessment Centres*, 2nd edn. Wimbledon: Institute of Personnel and Development.

Woodward, J. (1965) *Industrial Organization: Theory and Practice*. London: Oxford University Press.

Yearta, S. K., Maitlis, S., and Briner, R. B. (1995) 'An exploratory study of goal-setting in theory and practice: a motivational technique that works?', *Journal of Occupational and Organizational Psychology*, 68, 237–52.

Yukl, G. A. (1987) 'Development of new measures of managerial behaviour: preliminary report on validation of the MPS', Easter Academy of Management meeting, Boston.

—— (1989) *Leadership in Organisations*, 2nd edn. Englewood Cliffs, NJ: Prentice Hall.

Zaleznik, A. (1977) 'Managers and leaders: are they different?', *Harvard Business Review*, May/Jun.

Zimbalist, A. (ed.) (1979) *Case Studies on the Labor Process*. London: Monthly Review Press.

Zimbardo, P. G., Harey, C., Banks, W. C., and Jaffe, D. (1973) 'The mind is a formidable jailer: a Pirandellian prison', *New York Times Magazine*, 8 April, 38–60.

Zipkin, P. H. (1991) 'Does manufacturing need a JIT revolution?', *Harvard Business Review*, Jan/Feb, 40–50.

Author Index

Subject Index